Concurrent Prolog

Collected Papers

Volume 1

MIT Press Series in Logic Programming
Ehud Shapiro, editor
Koichi Furukawa, Fernando Pereira, David H. D. Warren, associate editors

The Art of Prolog: Advanced Programming Techniques, by Leon Sterling and Ehud Shapiro, 1986

Logic Programming: Proceedings of the Fourth International Conference, edited by Jean-Louis Lassez, 1987 (Vols. 1 and 2)

Concurrent Prolog: Collected Papers, edited by Ehud Shapiro, 1987 (Vols. 1 and 2)

Concurrent Prolog

Collected Papers

Volume 1

Edited by Ehud Shapiro
The Weizmann Institute of Science

with a foreword by Kazuhiro Fuchi
ICOT — Institute for New Generation Computer Technology

The MIT Press
Cambridge, Massachusetts
London, England

PUBLISHER'S NOTE

This format is intended to reduce the cost of publishing certain works in book form and to shorten the gap between editorial preparation and final publication. Detailed editing and composition have been avoided by photographing the text of this book directly from the authors' prepared copy.

This book was set in T$_E$X by Sarah Fliegelmann
at the Weizmann Institute of Science
and printed and bound in the United States of America.

Library of Congress Cataloging-in-Publication Data

Concurrent Prolog.

(MIT Press series in logic programming)
Bibliography: v. 1, p.
Includes index.
1. Prolog (Computer program language)
2. Parallel programming (Computer science)
I. Shapiro, Ehud Y.   II. Series.
QA76.73.P76C655   1987   005.13'3   87-3288
ISBN 0-262-19255-1 (set)
ISBN 0-262-19266-7 (v. 1)
ISBN 0-262-19267-5 (v. 2)

Contents

Volume 1

Part III: Streams and Channels

Volume 2

Part VI: Embedded Languages

Part VII: Implementations

The Authors

Curtis Abbott received his B.A. in Music and Mathematics at the University of California at San Diego in 1976 and pursued graduate studies in Computer Science at the University of California at Berkeley during 1983-1984. Currently, he works at Xerox PARC and is also affiliated with Stanford's Center for the Study of Language and Information. His address is Xerox PARC, 3333 Coyote Hill Rd., Palo Alto, CA 94304, USA.

Evyatar Av-Ron received his B.S. in Computer Science from SUNY at Stony Brook in 1980 and his M.Sc. in Computer Science from the Weizmann Institute of Science in 1984. He is presently a Ph.D. student at the Department of Computer Science, The Weizmann Institute of Science, Rehovot 76100, Israel.

Daniel G. Bobrow received his B.A. in Physics from Rensselaer Polytechnic Institute in 1957, his S.M. in Applied Mathematics from Harvard University in 1958, and his Ph.D. in Mathematics from MIT in 1964. After teaching for a year at MIT, he joined Bolt Beranek and Newman in Cambridge, Mass., where he started the Artificial Intelligence Department, and later became Vice President of the Computer Science Division. In 1972 he joined Xerox PARC where he is presently a research fellow in the Intelligent Systems Laboratory, Xerox PARC, Palo Alto, CA 94304, USA.

Takashi Chikayama received his B.E. degree in mathematical engineering in 1977 and his M.E. and D.Eng. degrees in information engineering in 1979 and 1982, respectively, all from the University of Tokyo. Since 1982, he has been a researcher at the Research Center of the Institute for New Generation Computer Technology (ICOT). His present address is Fourth Research Laboratory, Institute for New Generation Computer Technology, 4-28, Mita 1-chome, Minato-ku, Tokyo 108, Japan.

Keith L. Clark is a Reader in Computational Logic in the Department of Computing at Imperial College. He received his B.A. in Mathematics in 1964 from Durham University, his B.A. in Philosophy in 1966 from Cambridge University, and his Ph.D. in Computer Science in 1980 from London University. His present address is Imperial College of Science and Technology, Department of Computing, 180 Queen's Gate, London SW7 2BZ, England.

Michael Codish got his B.Sc. in Mathematics from the Ben Gurion University at Beer-Sheba in 1983 and his M.Sc. from the Weizmann Institute of Science in 1986. He is presently a Ph.D. student at the Department of Computer Science, The Weizmann Institute of Science, Rehovot 76100, Israel.

Shimon Cohen got his B.A. in Mathematics and Philosophy from Tel-Aviv University in 1977, his M.A. in Computer Science from the Weizmann Institute in 1979 and his Ph.D. in Computer Science from the Hebrew University in 1983. In 1983–84 he was a visiting professor in the Univeristy of California at Berkeley and then a research member of the Artificial Intelligence Laboratory of SPAR (Schlumberger Palo Alto Research Center). Since 1986 he is a faculty member at the Tel-Aviv University. His present address is the Department of Computer Science, Tel-Aviv University, Tel-Aviv 69978, Israel.

Shimon Edelman received his B.S. degree in Electrical Engineering from the Technion — Israel Institute of Technology, Haifa, in 1978 and his M.Sc. in Computer Science from the Weizmann Institute in 1985. He is currently working towards a Ph.D. degree at the Department of Computer Science, The Weizmann Institute of Science, Rehovot 76100, Israel. His main fields of interest are computational vision and motor control.

Koichi Furukawa received his B.E. degree in Instrumentation Physics, his M.E. degree in Mathematical Engineering, and his D.Eng. degree in Information Engineering from the University of Tokyo, in 1965, 1967, and 1980, respectively. He joined Electrotechnical Laboratory in 1967. He moved to the Institute for New Generation Computer Technology (ICOT) in 1982, and since then he has been working for the Fifth Generation Computer Project. He is currently a Deputy Director of ICOT. His present address is ICOT Research Center, Mita Kokusai Building 21F, 4-28, Mita 1-chome, Minato-ku, Tokyo 108, Japan.

Steve Gregory is an Advanced Research Fellow in the Department of Computing at Imperial College, London University. He received a B.Sc. (Eng.) in 1980 and a Ph.D. in 1985, both from London University. His present address is Imperial College of Science and Technology, Department of Computing, 180 Queen's Gate, London SW7 2BZ, England.

Lisa Hellerstein received her B.A. in Applied Mathematics/Computer Science in 1984 from Harvard University. She is currently enrolled in a Ph.D. program in Computer Science at the University of California at Berkeley. Her address is Computer Science Division, University of California, Berkeley, CA, 94720.

Michael Hirsch received his B.Sc. in Mathematics and Computer Science from the University of Cape Town in 1982, B.Sc. (Hons.) from the University of Cape

Town in 1983 and M.Sc. from the Weizmann Institute of Science in 1987. He is currently a staff member at the Weizmann Institute of Science, Rehovot 76100, Israel.

Avshalom Houri received his B.Sc. in Computer Science from Jerusalem College of Technology (JCT) in 1983, and his M.Sc. in Computer Science from the Weizmann Institute of Science in 1986. He is presently working at the Department of Computer Science, The Weizmann Institute of Science, Rehovot 76100, Israel.

Kenneth M. Kahn received his B.A. in Economics from the University of Pennsylvania in 1973. He received his M.S. in 1975 and Ph.D. in 1979 from MIT in Computer Science. After teaching for a year at MIT, he became a visiting professor at the University of Stockholm and a research scientist at Uppsala University. In 1984, he joined the Intelligent Systems Laboratory of Xerox PARC, Palo Alto, CA 94304, USA.

Dan Katzenenllenbogen received his B.Sc. in Mathematics and Computer Science from Tel-Aviv University in 1983, and his M.Sc. in Computer Science from The Weizmann Institute of Science in 1987. His present address is POB 173, Kohav Yair 44864, Israel.

Jacob Levy received his B.A. in Chemistry in 1979 and his M.Sc. in Organic Chemistry in 1982, both from the Hebrew University of Jerusalem. Since 1983 he has been studying towards his Ph.D. in Computer Science at the Department of Computer Science at the Weizmann Institute of Science. His present address is the Department of Computer Science, The Weizmann Institute of Science, Rehovot 76100, Israel.

Yossi Lichtenstein got his B.Sc. in Physics and Computer Science from Bar-Ilan University in 1982. He is presently a M.Sc. student at the Department of Computer Science, The Weizmann Institute of Science, Rehovot 76100, Israel.

Colin Mierowsky got his B.Sc. from the University of the Witwatersrand in Johannesburg, his B.Sc. (Hons) degree from the University of Cape Town in 1980, and his M.Sc. in Computer Science from the Weizmann Institute for Science in 1984.

Mark S. Miller got his B.S. in Computer Science from Yale University in 1980. He is an alumni of the Xanadu Hypertext Project and a former researcher at the Datapoint Technology Center. He is presently exploring marketplace mechanisms as a means for allocating resources and guiding evolution in open software systems. His present address is Xerox Palo Alto Research Center, 3333 Coyote Hill Rd., Palo Alto, California.

Toshihiko Miyazaki received his B.E. degree in Information Engineering from the University of Ohita in 1981. Since 1984, he has been a researcher at the Research Center of the Institute for New Generation Computer Technology (ICOT). His present address is Fourth Research Laboratory, Institute for New Generation Computer Technology, 4-28, Mita 1-chome, Minato-ku, Tokyo 108, Japan.

Shmuel Safra got his B.Sc. in Mathematics and Computer Science in 1984 from the Hebrew University and his M.Sc. in Computer Science in 1986 from the Weizmann Institute of Science. He is presently a Ph.D. student at the Department of Computer Science, The Weizmann Institute of Science, Rehovot 76100, Israel.

Vijay Saraswat got his B.Tech. in Electrical Engineering from Indian Institute of Technology, Kanpur, in 1982 and expects to obtain his Ph.D. in Computer Science from Carnegie-Mellon University in 1987. His present address is Department of Computer Science, Carnegie-Mellon University, Pittsburgh, PA 15216, USA.

Avner Shafrir got his B.Sc. in Mathematics from Tel-Aviv University in 1977 and his M.Sc. in Computer Science from the Weizmann Institute of Science in 1984. He is presently a Senior Analyst at Elron Electronics Industries, 24 Hacharoshet St., Or-Yehuda, Israel.

Ehud Shapiro received his B.A. in Mathematics and Philosophy from Tel-Aviv University in 1979 and his Ph.D. in Computer Science from Yale University in 1982. Since 1982 he has been a faculty member at the Weizmann Institute of Science. His address is Department of Computer Science, The Weizmann Institute of Science, Rehovot 76100, Israel.

William Silverman received his B.A. in Mathematics and Sociology from the University of Minnesota in 1960. Since 1971 he has been a member of the faculty of the Weizmann Institute of Science. His address is Department of Computer Science, The Weizmann Institute of Science, Rehovot 76100, Israel.

Leon Sterling received his B.Sc. (hons.) in Mathematics and Computer Science from Melbourne University in 1976 and his Ph.D. in Pure Mathematics from Australian National University in 1981. He spent three years at the University of Edinburgh and one year at the Weizmann Institute before joining the faculty at Case Western Reserve University in 1985. His address is Department of Computer Engineering and Science, Case Western Reserve University, Cleveland, Ohio, 44106, USA.

Akikazu Takeuchi received his B.E. and M.E. degrees in Mathematical Engineering from the University of Tokyo, in 1977 and 1979, respectively. In 1979, he joined Central Research Laboratory of Mitsubishi Electric Corporation. From 1982 to 1986 he stayed at the Research Center of the Institute for New Generation Computer Technology (ICOT). His present address is Central Research Laboratory, Mitsubishi Electric Corp., 8-1-1 Tsukaguchi-honmachi, Amagasaki, Hyogo 661 Japan.

Stephen Taylor completed an H.N.C. in Electrical and Electronic Engineering and an apprenticeship in Aeronautical Engineering with British Aircraft Corporation, Stevenage, England, in 1977. In 1982 he completed a B.Sc. in Computer Systems at Essex University, England, and in 1984 a M.Sc. in Computer Science at Columbia University in New York. He is currently a Ph.D. student at the Weizmann Institute of Science, Rehovot 76100, Israel. His research interests are primarily parallel architectures and languages.

Eric Dean Tribble is studying computer science at Stanford University and is a member of the Vulcan Project at Xerox PARC. His present address is Intelligent Systems Laboratory of Xerox PARC, Palo Alto, CA 94304, USA.

Kazunori Ueda received his B.E. degree in Instrumentation Physics in 1978 and his M.E. and D.Eng. degrees in Information Engineering in 1980 and 1986, respectively, all from the University of Tokyo. He joined NEC Corporation in 1983. Since 1985, he has been a researcher at the Research Center of the Institute for New Generation Computer Technology (ICOT) on leave from NEC. His present address is First Research Laboratory, Institute for New Generation Computer Technology, 4-28, Mita 1-chome, Minato-ku, Tokyo 108, Japan.

David Weinbaum got his B.Sc. in Engineering from Tel-Aviv University in 1981. Since 1984 he has been a M.Sc. student at the Electrical Engineering faculty of Tel-Aviv University. His present address is Department of Computer Science, The Weizmann Institute of Science, Rehovot 76100, Israel.

Eyal Yardeni got his B.Sc. in Computer Science and Mathematics from Ben-Gurion University in 1982 and his M.Sc. in Computer Science from the Weizmann Institute of Science in 1987. He is presently a Ph.D. student at the Department of Computer Science, The Weizmann Institute of Science, Rehovot 76100, Israel.

The Papers

A Relational Language for Parallel Programming, by Keith Clark and Steve Gregory, was published in the Proceedings of the ACM Conference on Functional Programming Languages and Computer Architecture, pp. 171–178, October 1981.

A Subset of Concurrent Prolog and Its Interpreter, by Ehud Shapiro, is a revised and shortened version of ICOT Technical Report TR-003, March 1983.

PARLOG: Parallel Programming in Logic, by Keith Clark and Steve Gregory, appeared as an Imperial College, Department of Computing, Technical Report DOC 84/4 in April 1984. A revision was published in ACM Transactions on Programming Languages and Systems 8(1), pp. 1–49, 1986. This volume includes a further revision of that paper.

Guarded Horn Clauses, by Kazunori Ueda, is a revision of a paper with the same title that appeared in Logic Programming '85 (edited by E. Wada), published as Volume 221 of Springer-Verlag's Lecture Notes in Computer Science, pp. 168–179, 1986. The original version of this paper appeared as ICOT Technical Report TR-103, June 1985.

Concurrent Prolog: A Progress Report, by Ehud Shapiro, appeared in IEEE Computer 19(8), pp. 44–58, August 1986.

Parallel Logic Programming Languages, by A. Takeuchi and K. Furukawa, was an invited contribution to the Proceedings of the Third International Conference on Logic Programming, published as Volume 225 of Springer-Verlag's Lecture Notes in Computer Science, pp. 242–255, July 1986.

Systolic Programming: A Paradigm of Parallel Processing, by Ehud Shapiro, appeared in the Proceedings of Fifth Generation Computer Systems, November

1984, pp. 458–471. This volume includes an extended and revised version of that paper, which also appeared as a Weizmann Institute Technical Report CS84-16.

Notes on the Complexity of Systolic Programs, by Stephen Taylor, Lisa Hellerstein, Shmuel Safra, and Ehud Shapiro, is in press in the Journal of Parallel and Distributed Computation, 1987.
Copyright © 1987, Academic Press, reprinted with permission.

Implementing Parallel Algorithms in Concurrent Prolog: The Maxflow Experience, by Lisa Hellerstein and Ehud Shapiro, was published in the Proceedings of the International Symposium on Logic Programming, IEEE, pp. 99–117, 1984, and in the Journal of Logic Programming 3(2), pp. 157–184, 1986.

A Concurrent Prolog Based Region Finding Algorithm, by Lisa Hellerstein, is a revision of part of an Honors Thesis submitted to the Department of Applied Mathematics, Harvard University, in 1984.

Distributed Programming in Concurrent Prolog, by Avner Shafrir and Ehud Shapiro, is a revision of Weizmann Institute of Science Technical Report CS83-12, 1983.

Image Processing with Concurrent Prolog, by Shimon Edelman and Ehud Shapiro, includes material from the first author's M.Sc. Thesis and from the paper "Quadtrees in Concurrent Prolog", by the same authors, that appeared in the Proceedings of the IEEE International Conference on Parallel Processing, pp. 544–551, 1985.

A Test for the Adequacy of a Language for an Architecture, by Ehud Shapiro, is a revision of Weizmann Institute of Science Technical Report CS86-01.

Fair, Biased, and Self-Balancing Merge Operators: Their Specification and Implementation in Concurrent Prolog, by Ehud Shapiro and Colin Mierowsky, is a revision of a paper with the same title that appeared in the Journal of New Generation Computing 2(3), pp. 221–240, 1984.

Multiway Merge with Constant Delay in Concurrent Prolog, by Ehud Shapiro and Shmuel Safra, was published in the Journal of New Generation Computing 4(3), pp. 211-216, 1986.

Merging Many Streams Efficiently: The Importance of Atomic Commitment, by Vijay A. Saraswat, appears in this volume for the first time.

Channels: A Generalization of Streams, by Eric Dean Tribble, Mark S. Miller, Kenneth Kahn, Daniel G. Bobrow, Curtis Abbott and Ehud Shapiro, was published in Logic Programming: Proceedings of the Fourth International Conference, edited by Jean-Louis Lassez, MIT Press, pp. 839–857, 1987.

Bounded Buffer Communication in Concurrent Prolog, by Akikazu Takeuchi and Koichi Furukawa, was published in the Journal of New Generation Computing 3(2), pp. 145–155, 1985.

Systems Programming in Concurrent Prolog, by Ehud Shapiro, appeared as an ICOT TR-034 in 1983, in the Conference Record of the 11th ACM Symposium on Principles of Programming Languages, pp. 93–105, 1984, and in Logic Programming and Its Applications, edited by M. van Caneghem and D.H.D. Warren, pp. 50–76, Ablex. It was revised and shortened for inclusion in this book.

Computation Control and Protection in the Logix System, by Michael Hirsch, William Silverman, and Ehud Shapiro, is a revision of Weizmann Institute of Science Technical Report CS86-19.

The Logix System User Manual, Version 1.22, by William Silverman, Michael Hirsch, Avshalom Houri, and Ehud Shapiro, is also available as Weizmann Institute of Science Technical Report CS86-21.

A Layered Method For Process and Code Mapping, by Stephen Taylor, Evyatar Av-Ron, and Ehud Shapiro, is in press in the Journal of New Generation Computing, 1987.

An Architecture of a Distributed Window System and Its FCP Implementation, by Dan Katzenellenbogen, Shimon Cohen, and Ehud Shapiro, is based on the first author's M.Sc. thesis. It appeared as a Weizmann Institute Technical Report CS87-09.

Logical Secrets, by Mark S. Miller, Daniel G. Bobrow, Eric Dean Tribble, and Jacob Levy, is a revision of a paper published in Logic Programming: Proceedings of the Fourth International Conference, edited by Jean-Louis Lassez, MIT Press, pp. 704–728, 1987.

Meta Interpreters for Real, by Shmuel Safra and Ehud Shapiro, appeared in Information Processing 86, Kugler, H.J. (ed.), pp. 271–278, 1986.
Copyright © 1986, IFIP, reprinted with permission.

Algorithmic Debugging of GHC Programs and its Implementation in GHC, by Akikazu Takeuchi, is a revision of ICOT Technical Report TR-185, 1986.

Representation and Enumeration of Flat Concurrent Prolog Computations, by Yossi Lichtenstein, Michael Codish, and Ehud Shapiro, appears in this volume for the first time.

A Type System for Logic Programs, by Eyal Yardeni and Ehud Shapiro, is based on the M.Sc. Thesis of the first author, and was published as a Weizmann Institute of Science Technical Report CS87-05.

Object Oriented Programming in Concurrent Prolog, by Ehud Shapiro and Akikazu Takeuchi, is a revision of a paper with the same title that appeared in the Journal of New Generation Computing 1(1), pp. 25–49, 1983.

Vulcan: Logical Concurrent Objects, by Kenneth Kahn, Eric Dean Tribble, Mark S. Miller, and Daniel G. Bobrow, appears also in Research Directions in Object-Oriented Programming, edited by P. Shriver and P. Wegner, MIT Press, 1987.

PRESSing for Parallelism: A Prolog Program Made Concurrent, by Leon Sterling and Michael Codish, appeared in the Journal of Logic Programming 3(1), pp. 75–92, 1986.

Compiling Or-Parellelim into And-Parallelism, by Michael Codish and Ehud Shapiro, is based on the first author's M.Sc. Thesis. A shortened version of this paper appeared in The Journal of New Generation Computing 5(1), pp. 45–61, 1987, and was presented at the Third International Conference on Logic Programming, 1986, London.

Translation of Safe GHC and Safe Concurrent Prolog to FCP, by Jacob Levy and Ehud Shapiro, appeared as a Weizmann Institute Technical Report CS87-08.

Or-Parallel Prolog in Flat Concurrent Prolog, by Ehud Shapiro, is a revision of a paper that appeared in Logic Programming: Proceedings of the Fourth International Conference, edited by Jean-Louis Lassez, MIT Press, pp. 311–337, 1987.

CFL — A Concurrent Functional Language Embedded in a Concurrent Logic Programming Environment, by Jacob Levy and Ehud Shapiro, is a revision and extension of Weizmann Institute of Science Technical Report CS86-28.

Hardware Description and Simulation Using Concurrent Prolog, by David Weinbaum and Ehud Shapiro, appeared in the Proceedings of CHDL '87, pp. 9–27, Elsevier Science Publishing, 1987.

A Sequential Implementation of Concurrent Prolog Based on the Shallow Binding Scheme, by Toshihiko Miyazaki, Akikazu Takeuchi, and Takashi Chikayama, was published in the Proceedings of the IEEE Symposium on Logic Programming, pp. 110–118, 1985.
Copyright © 1985, IEEE, reprinted with permission.

A Sequential Abstract Machine for Flat Concurrent Prolog, by Avshalom Houri and Ehud Shapiro, is based on the first author's M.Sc. Thesis. It is a revision of Weizmann Institute of Science Technical Report CS86-20.

A Parallel Implementation of Flat Concurrent Prolog, by Stephen Taylor, Shmuel Safra, and Ehud Shapiro, was published in the International Journal of Parallel Programming 15(3), pp. 245–275, 1987.
Copyright © 1987, Plenum Publishing Corp., reprinted with permission.

Foreword

by

Kazuhiro Fuchi

ICOT — Institute for New Generation Computer Technology

In the forty years since computers appeared, they have greatly influenced human society. Their capacity to improve information processing has had a particular impact in the business world. Another effect, which is harder to define, but no less important, is the influence of computers on human thinking and intelligence. Gerald Sussman of MIT said in this connection that the most important heritage that computers have brought to humans is a new expressive tool for thinking. It is through programming languages, the interface between machines and humans, that this new expressiveness came. The development of computer programming languages brought with it rapid growth in the field of algorithm design, and indeed it can be argued that the invention of algorithms is crucially dependent on the appropriate programming language structures.

Viewing programming language developments from the point of view of control structures, it can be seen that there has been a series of evolutions through iterative loops, recursion and co-routines. These evolutions made it possible to represent more and more complex problems more and more simply. However, almost all the programming languages developed so far are based on sequentiality; this has resulted in the development of a large number of sequential algorithms.

The central issue of this book is concurrent logic programming languages, which emerged about ten years after the invention of Prolog in 1972. The Relational Language was developed first, followed by Concurrent Prolog, PARLOG and Guarded Horn Clauses (GHC). It was found that concurrent logic programming languages are very suitable both for describing parallel objects and algorithms and for parallel execution. In other words, they seem to be capable of filling the gap which currently exists between application software and parallel computers. They offer the designer of parallel systems a far more powerful tool for thought.

History shows us that it takes more than ten years for a culture to grow up around a new computer programming language. This has been demonstrated in the case of both Prolog and Lisp, and is very likely to be the case with concurrent logic programming languages. In five or six years, there will be a well-developed culture around concurrent logic languages.

Concurrent logic programming plays a crucial role in the Fifth Generation Computer Project. A language called KL1 (Kernel Language 1) is being designed based on the concurrent logic programming language GHC. KL1 will be an interface between highly parallel computers and the software systems which operate on them. The main reason that GHC was chosen as the core of the interface language was its adequacy for both expressing and executing parallel objects and algorithms.

In the future of computer science, the importance of parallelism should not be underestimated. There are vast undeveloped areas in the field of parallel programming, which require a more and more mathematically formal treatment. This is another reason why concurrent logic languages are so important.

I hope that this book will contribute to the acceleration of the pace of research and development in parallel computing.

Tokyo, 1987

Preface

This book reports on a search for a general-purpose programming language for parallel computers, conducted within the logic programming framework. During the past six years several concurrent logic programming languages have been proposed, all capable of expressing concurrency and amenable to parallel execution. After surveying these languages in its first part, the book focuses on the concurrent logic programming language Flat Concurrent Prolog. It investigates how systems programming and the implementation of parallel algorithms can be carried out with this language; how advanced program development techniques can be applied; how to embed other high-level languages in it; and how to implement this language efficiently on sequential and parallel computers. The results of these investigations suggest that Flat Concurrent Prolog fulfills the requirements of a general-purpose high-level parallel machine language, a concept explained in the introduction.

Part I, Concurrent Logic Programming Languages, reports on a number of programming languages that are based on a parallel interpretation of logic programs — the Relational Language, Concurrent Prolog, PARLOG, Guarded Horn Clauses, and Flat Concurrent Prolog. Horn clauses, augmented with appropriate synchronization and control primitives, are found to be a convenient formalism for expressing concurrent systems; processes, communication, synchronization, indeterminacy, all seem to be expressible with as much ease as, and often with greater ease than, in other formalisms. Adhering to the philosophy of logic programming, the languages are pure Horn clause programs augmented with a few synchronization and control constructs. All are logic programming languages, in the sense that a successful computation of a program constitutes a constructive proof of the goal statement from the axioms in the program. Unlike sequential Prolog, these languages can go a very long way without using extra-logical constructs such as Prolog's input/output predicates or program modification predicates (assert and retract). These languages can express input/output in a purely logical way. They can implement a shared encapsulated data structure using a perpetual process with a modifiable internal state, where the specification of the behavior of such a process is a pure logic program.

There are differences between these languages in terms of their expressive power and implementability. The Introduction to Part I, the papers describing each language, as well as the comparative survey that ends this part address many of the differences and similarities.

Concurrent Prolog and its subset Flat Concurrent Prolog are both the vehicle and the target of most of the research reported in the rest of this book.

Part II, Programming Parallel Algorithms, investigates the use of concurrent logic programming languages for expressing parallel algorithms. Concurrent Prolog solutions to a wide range of algorithm implementation problems are presented, including techniques for the implementation of systolic algorithms, PRAM-based algorithms, distributed algorithms, and algorithms for image-processing. This part ends with a theoretical argument for the adequacy of Flat Concurrent Prolog as an algorithmic programming language for both sequential and parallel computers.

Part III, Streams and Channels, explores in depth the inter-process communication mechanisms available in Concurrent Prolog and Flat Concurrent Prolog. Methods are developed for the expression and efficient implementation of communication between dynamically changing sets of readers and writers.

Part IV, Systems Programming, investigates the use of Concurrent Prolog and Flat Concurrent Prolog as systems programming languages. It outlines a technique for a stream-based interface of I/O devices to a Concurrent Prolog system; a method for computation control and protection in a multi-tasking operating system; and a method for implementing process and code mapping in a parallel computer. These techniques were incorporated in the Logix system and in the parallel implementation of Flat Concurrent Prolog. Logix is a Flat Concurrent Prolog based operating system and programming environment, developed at the Weizmann Institute. Logix is described in this part; the parallel implementation of Flat Concurrent Prolog is described in Part VII. The control and mapping techniques draw heavily on the concepts of meta-interpretation and partial evaluation, described in Part V. The last paper in this part reports on a method for implementing secure communication in Flat Concurrent Prolog, which uses encapsulation rather than encription.

Part V, Program Analysis and Transformation, reports on research towards advanced techniques for program development. The first paper shows how meta-interpreters can be enhanced to express functions not directly available in Flat Concurrent Prolog, and how the technique of partial evaluation can eliminate the overhead of interpretation by program transformation. The second paper applies the concepts and techniques of algorithmic debugging to GHC. The third paper describes various methods for the representation of FCP computations, and a method for the exhaustive enumeration of all possible computations on a given initial goal, which is a precondition for the systematic testing of a concurrent program. The last paper describes a type system for logic programs.

Part VI, Embedded Languages, describes techniques for embedding the three major high-level programming paradigms — object-oriented, logic, and functional programming — in Flat Concurrent Prolog. It shows that from the point of view of both expressiveness and efficiency, Flat Concurrent Prolog is a feasible intermediate language for the implementation of higher-level languages. The last paper in this part reports on the use of Concurrent Prolog as a hardware description language.

Part VII, Implementations, describes a sequential implementation technique for Concurrent Prolog, and sequential and parallel implementation techniques for Flat Concurrent Prolog. The latter two form the basis of the current implementations of the language.

The book does not contain a section devoted to the semantics of concurrent logic programming languages. There is a lot of current research on this subject, as well as some preliminary results. The results of this research are essential for putting our intuitive understanding of concurrent logic programming on firmer grounds; they are also a precondition for more advanced research on program development, analysis and transformation. It is my hope that the results of the semantics research will ripen soon and will be put to use in advanced techniques for program analysis and transformation such as abstract interpretation, partial evaluation, and algorithmic debugging.

The book can be used for a comparative study of concurrent logic programming languages. Part I includes updated descriptions of the major languages proposed. The rest of the book falls into three broad categories: parallel algorithms (Part II), systems programming (Parts III, IV, and some of Part V), and high-level and low-level implementation techniques (Parts VI, VII, and some of Part V). Readers interested in a specific subject can study each category or part independently, following the necessary introductory material from Part I.

Although not ideal for this purpose, the book can be used for learning (Flat) Concurrent Prolog programming. The order of the material in the book, as well as the survey of programming techniques given in Chapter 5, reflects the structure of a course on Concurrent Prolog Programming Techniques that I taught several times. There are many programming examples in this book, and most of them are complete and executable. The Concurrent Prolog programs can be executed with the Prolog-based Concurrent Prolog interpreter, described in Chapter 2, and the Flat Concurrent Prolog programs with the Logix system (Chapter 21), available for educational and research purposes from the Weizmann Institute of Science. Implementations of PARLOG and GHC are available from Imperial College and ICOT, respectively.

The book attempts to distill results of about six years of research in a fast moving field. In order to provide an updated and consistent account, authors were given the opportunity to revise their papers in accordance with present knowledge, to correct errors, and to remove repetitions. Nevertheless, some of the papers provide a less mature perspective than others, and there are some inconsistencies, as well as overlap, between earlier and later papers. The section entitled 'The Papers' includes information on the origin of the papers, as well as an indication whether they have been revised for inclusion in this book. The introductions to the different parts of the book attempt to place the papers in perspective and to point out inconsistencies and changes in point of view between the different papers.

Much of the research discussed in this book was stimulated by the vision of the Fifth Generation project, and emerged as a result of interactions carried out at ICOT between ICOT members and visitors from throughout the world, including myself. I am grateful for the opportunity I have had to be exposed to and interact with this institute and its people.

This book was produced with the help and support of many. Sarah Fliegelmann assisted with the technical aspects of editing, and typeset the myriad of papers into an aesthetic collection. Without her I would have neither embarked on this project, nor completed it. The staff of MIT Press in general, and Terry Ehling in particular, have assisted and supported me throughout the editing task. I would like to thank the editors and publishers of the *Journal of Logic Programming* and *New Generation Computing* for permitting us to reprint so many papers, without which the book could not have appeared. I would like to thank the authors for revising, checking, and re-checking their papers. I would like to thank my colleagues and students at the Weizmann Institute, Michael Codish, Shimon Edelman, Yossi Feldman, John Gallagher, Michael Hirsch, Avshalom Houri, Dan Katzenellenbogen, Jacob Levy, Yossi Lichtenstein, Orna Meyers, William Silverman, Daniel Szoke, Steve Taylor, David Weinbaum, Bernie Weinberg, and Eyal Yardeni, who helped with the editing process.

Finally, I would like to thank my wife, Michal, with whom even proofreading is a joy.

Ehud Shapiro

July, 1987

Rehovot, Israel

Introduction

Since its early days, most research in computer science was concerned in one way or another with two problems:

1. Computers are too slow

2. Programmers are too slow.

Research on the computer performance problem, at the computer hardware level, attempted mainly to devise faster and faster components, and to optimize and fine-tune the well understood von Neumann architecture. At the algorithms level, research was concerned mainly with devising algorithms that exploit the structure of the problem in order to solve it in fewer computation steps. It was also concerned with devising algorithms that exploit the particular properties of the von Neumann architecture, by using data-structures and basic operations that are cheap to implement on this machine model. Often these two concerns were not separated, and the basic computation steps of an algorithm were assumed to be those operations that can be performed efficiently on a von Neumann machine.

There is increasing awareness, and perhaps almost a consensus, that this approach to the computer performance problem is close to reaching its limits; that von Neumann machines and algorithms have delivered almost all they could, and that to continue and progress, a new direction is necessary — parallelism.

Currently, hardware architects can build parallel computers, and they do. Algorithm designers understand how to construct and analyze parallel algorithms, and efficient parallel algorithms for many important problems are known. Nevertheless, parallel computers that solve real world problems using parallel algorithms are scarce.

Research on the second problem, the problem of programmer productivity, has progressed slowly but steadily. The main direction has been devising higher and higher level languages that allow programmers to express themselves more naturally and more abstractly, that support the construction of tools to reason about and manipulate programs, and that facilitate communication and cooperation among programmers, system designers, and system users.

Three main approaches to high-level languages that are problem and human oriented, rather than machine (von Neumann) oriented, have emerged: functional programming, object-oriented programming, and logic programming. By now, these three approaches have delivered a substantial number of language designs, language prototypes, and language implementations. Nevertheless, applications that use such high-level languages to solve real world problems are scarce.

We share the belief that these two directions — parallelism and high-level languages — are the right approaches to the computer performance and programmer productivity problems. However, we think that progress in these two research directions has been hampered since the two have been pursued mostly independently: parallel computers are not as usable as they should since they do not have appropriate high-level languages to program them with. High-level languages are not as usable as they should since they do not have appropriate parallel computer implementations to support them.

The gap between our knowledge in software and hardware on the one hand and the technology incorporated in actual computer systems we use on the other hand is embarrassingly large. On the software side, we have high-level languages with accompanying theories of program analysis, transformation, debugging, and verification; but the majority of real-life applications are being developed in low-level languages, with the most advanced software tool being a symbolic debugger. Switching in real-life applications to higher-level languages and employing the more advanced development tools they may offer is generally infeasible, given the inferior performance the resulting application system will exhibit on present computers. Even the development of advanced program development tools themselves is hampered by performance problems, which are partly responsible for the present gap between the promise of the theories related to program development and the usability of the tools that implement them.

On the hardware side, we can produce micro-processor chips almost as easily as we produce memory chips; but the majority of applications run on sequential computers and accept the limitations this imposes on system performance. Switching to present parallel computers is generally infeasible, given the additional development costs caused by the introduction of parallelism into existing programming languages and development environments.

We believe that the computer performance and programmer productivity problems are in an interlock — that they cannot be solved independently. To exploit parallel computers effectively, high-level languages that can express concurrency, as well as even higher level languages from which concurrency can be extracted automatically, must be devised and used. To support the increasingly higher-level programming languages we wish to program with, as well as the program development, analysis, transformation, and verification tools we wish to employ, the power of parallel computers is needed. Therefore, the next step should be to tackle these two problems simultaneously.

How can this be done? This book reports on one research direction that attempts this. This research is based on the conjecture, shared also by the Fifth Generation project (Fuchi, 1986; Fuchi and Furukawa, 1987) that there is a missing link — a layer of abstraction — that is required for parallel computers and high-level languages to be usable simultaneously, and that this link is a general-purpose high-level parallel machine language[1].

A machine language defines a computation model that can serve as an interface and meeting point for the hardware architect, the algorithm designer, the system architect, and the designer and the implementor of higher-level languages. It is a language that a hardware architect should look up to when designing a machine architecture. A language that an algorithm designer can use to think about algorithms, and should refer to when defining and counting the basic operations of an algorithm. It is a language that a system designer must find expressive enough to implement operating systems and programming environments with. A language that a higher-level language designer can use as the foundation for identifying useful abstractions, and that a higher-level language implementor should use as the target of his compilers.

We see that the machine language plays a central role in almost every aspect of computing. Indeed, the impact of the von Neumann machine language on all facets of computer science cannot be over-estimated.

When moving from sequential to parallel computers, the machine language should be changed appropriately. If the parallel computer is a conservative extension of the von Neumann machine model, e.g., a shared-memory computer, then a possible approach is to preserve the basic von Neumann instruction set, but extend the semantics of existing instructions (e.g., concurrent-read and concurrent-write), or add new basic instructions (e.g., fetch-and-add). Even when applicable, this approach leaves the question of programming the parallel computer open: the basic parallel constructs such as processes, communication, and synchronization are yet to be designed and implemented using this instruction set.

We believe that the complexity added by the introduction of parallelism is such that a complete parallel computer system constructed directly on a low-level foundation would collapse under its own weight. To master complexity, the tool offered by computer science is abstraction. Therefore we propose a more radical approach: to define a higher-level machine language, which supports directly a set of basic parallel constructs. Such a language can serve as the impenetrable layer of abstraction, separating the software from the hardware architecture and low-level implementation details.

---

[1] Following the terminological suggestion of Moto-Oka et al. (1981), we will use the terms 'high-level machine language' and 'kernel-language' interchangeably.

An example is the approach taken by INMOS, where Occam, a CSP-based concurrent programming language, serves as a high-level parallel machine language for the Transputer, a processor designed as a building block for parallel computers. The approach has many desirable properties. It provides the application designer as well as implementor with a simple concurrent computation model and programming language. Using Occam, the same application program can be executed sequentially or on various parallel architectures. The approach also gives conceptual guidance while leaving a large degree of freedom to the joint work of the Transputer architect and the Occam compiler designer. However, we find Occam not suitable as a general-purpose machine language. Its model of processes, communication, and synchronization is restrictive in a way that prevents it from being either an acceptable systems programming language or a useful intermediate language for the implementation of higher-level parallel languages.

The approach described in this book is similar to that of INMOS's in designing Occam and the Transputer, with two main differences. First, for parallel computers to become generally usable, they need operating systems. Hence we search for a kernel language which, unlike Occam, is suitable for systems programming. Second, for parallel computers to become and continue to be generally usable, they should support higher and higher level languages. Hence we search for a kernel language which, unlike Occam, has a good match with the computation models of high-level languages, and can be a convenient intermediate language for implementing them.

To succeed in the role of a general-purpose high-level parallel machine language, what properties should a language have?

First, a machine language is also a *programming language*, having its own syntax and semantics. Although not necessarily the main language used by the casual programmer, or even the systems programmer, the machine language should be graspable and usable by humans.

Second, it is a *parallel* programming language, in the sense that its parallel constructs are a natural and integral part of the language's syntax and semantics, and not a patch added as an afterthought to an existing sequential language or computation model. Furthermore, the language should be defined with parallel execution as the default, and sequencing, or any other form of synchronization, as the component that requires explicit programming, if needed.

Third, it is a parallel *machine* language, in the sense that it serves as an impenetrable layer of abstraction that stands between the higher-level software and the hardware architecture; a layer that is not crossed by the systems programmer or the high-level language compiler writer. To withstand such stringent demands, the language should be both *expressive* and *efficient*. To support systems programming it should be capable of expressing concurrency, communication, synchronization, dynamic process creation and termination, dynamic process network configuration and reconfiguration, nondeterministic process actions, state encapsulation, computation control, and resource control. To accommodate a wide range of higher-level languages it should support natural and efficient embeddings of the important high-level computation models, including the functional, object-oriented, and logic programming models. To be efficient, it should have a good fit with its target hardware architectures, so that its basic operations can be implemented efficiently, and that higher-level languages can be implemented via it on the target architectures with acceptable overhead.

Fourth, it is a *high-level* parallel machine language, in the sense that its basic operations are coarser and more abstract compared with today's machine languages. We do not insist, of course, that a high-level machine language be executed directly by the hardware. Depending on hardware and compilation technology considerations, it can either be compiled to a lower-level instruction set, or be interpreted directly. In other words, rather than defining a concrete architecture, the high-level machine language specifies a strict layer of abstraction — an abstract architecture. This abstract architecture leaves a large degree of freedom for the joint work of the hardware and compiler architects, and leaves all the systems programs and higher-level language compilers free from the low-level incidental details of the concrete architecture and low-level compilation technology.

This book reports on a search for such an abstraction — a general-purpose high-level parallel machine language — that has been carried out within the logic programming framework.

Part I

Concurrent Logic Programming
Languages

Introduction

In the broad sense, a logic programming language is a language in which a program can be interpreted as a collection of axioms in a certain logic, and a successful computation corresponds to a proof of a statement (called a goal statement) from these axioms. In practice, most research in logic programming has centered on a specific logic, called Horn clause logic, and on a specialized form of the resolution inference rule as the basic computation step.

We do not have, as yet, a satisfactory explanation why Horn clause logic is so successful as a programming formalism. Naturally, it forms a complete computation model in Turing's sense; but such models are abundant. Surprisingly, although the syntax of Horn clause logic is only a fragment of that of first-order logic, it is seldom the case that a full first-order logic specification of a program is more concise, readable, or elegant than the corresponding Horn clause program.

The initial motivation for logic programming was the belief that humans will find it easier to express themselves precisely, as required when programming, in a formalism that was invented in order to express precise thoughts, namely logic. Practice has shown that Horn clause logic was actually a convenient form of expression, and that with appropriate ingenuity it could be implemented efficiently on a von Neumann machine. The first and to date the major example of a practical logic programming language is Prolog.

Prolog is a sequential programming language, designed to run efficiently on a von Neumann machine by exploiting its ability to perform efficient stack management. Sequential Prolog can be parallelized, and much research is devoted to effective ways of doing so. Nevertheless, Prolog, whether executed sequentially or in parallel, cannot serve the role of the parallel machine language we are looking for, since it cannot express concurrency. For this purpose, languages of a new type have been defined — concurrent logic programming languages.

The first five chapters in Part I contain some of the major proposals for concurrent logic programming languages. The chapters are ordered chronologically. Chapter 1, "A Relational Language for Parallel Programming", by Clark and Gregory, 1981, contains the first concrete proposal for a concurrent logic programming language. It introduces the notion of nondeterministic committed-choice, implemented via the *commit* operator, into logic programming. It shows how one can specify nondeterministic concurrent systems of processes using logic programs augmented with the commit operator and an appropriate synchronization mechanism. Using guarded Horn clauses of the forms

$$A \leftarrow G \mid B$$

where "|" is the commit operator, an effect similar to Dijkstra's guarded-command is achieved. Under the procedural interpretation of the commit operator, each guarded clause in a procedure functions like an alternative in a guarded command, where the unification specified by the head A and the computation specified by the guard G serve as the "guard", and the computation specified by the body B serves as the "action".

The Relational Language uses a somewhat restricted form of mode declarations as its synchronization mechanism. A unique mode (input or output) for each argument in a process must be determined at compile time, in contrast to the general unification of the abstract model of logic programs used in Prolog. In contrast to some of the more recent concurrent logic programming languages, the Relational Languages allows only a limited set of simple test predicates in the guard, and requires that at the time they are called their arguments be ground, i.e., fully instantiated.

One implicit assumption made by the authors is that the language be used and implemented on highly distributed systems. As a result the language requires that the only data-type shared between processes be a stream of ground terms. The mode restrictions of the language implies that each stream must have at most one producer; however, it can be shared by several consumers. The Relational Language contains two types of conjunctive operators: sequential-And and parallel-And. It also includes a bounded-buffer output annotation, which can be used by a consumer to control the production rate of the stream by the producer.

Chapter 2, "A Subset of Concurrent Prolog and Its Interpreter", by Shapiro, 1983, reports on a richer language. Concurrent Prolog uses the read-only variable, rather than mode declarations, as its synchronization mechanism, and defines its synchronization effect by extending standard unification. While the standard unification of two terms can either succeed or fail, the read-only unification of two terms containing read-only variables can succeed, fail, or suspend. A read-only unification currently suspended may succeed or fail later, as new bindings for variables are produced by unifications performed by concurrently executing processes. Another major difference between Concurrent Prolog and the Relational Language is the type of guards that are allowed. In Concurrent Prolog, guards may contain calls to arbitrary user-defined processes, in addition to the system test-predicates allowed in the Relational Language.

This richer form of unification allows several powerful programming techniques. Most notable is that of incomplete messages. An incomplete message is a message containing a logical variable. It can be used for efficient back communication: the sender of a message with a variable keeps another occurrence of the variable; the receiver responds to the message by assigning a value to this variable; the sender can then observe the receiver's response by inspecting this variable. The execution model of Concurrent Prolog ensures that once a variable is assigned a value, this value is observable from all its occurrences. In addition, incomplete messages can be used to structure complex dynamic process networks: one process can send to a second process a message containing a communication channel with a third process. Arbitrarily complex communication networks can be formed this way; and networks can dynamically reconfigure if needed.

One of the strengths of Concurrent Prolog was having a working interpreter right from the start. The paper reports on a wealth of programming examples, which demonstrate the language's capabilities. They were developed using this interpreter, which is described in the paper as well.

Both sequential-And and the bounded-buffer annotation were abandoned in Concurrent Prolog for the sake of simplicity, without having alternatives at the time. However, subsequent research showed that they were dispensable, since they could be implemented in the language using, respectively, the short-circuit technique of Takeuchi (see Chapter 5) and the bounded-buffer technique of Takeuchi and Furukawa (Chapter 18).

This paper was critically examined by Ueda (1985) and Saraswat (1986). A severe error in the definition of atomic commitment, pointed out by these papers, has been corrected in the revision included in the book. The criticism of the operational nature, order-dependence, and vague points in the definition of read-only unification are answered by the improved definition, included in (Shapiro, Chapter 5). The arguments against the practicality of the full-blown multiple-environments mechanism of Concurrent Prolog were accepted, in a sense, as evident from the switch to Flat Concurrent Prolog as the primary focus of research, also described in Chapter 5.

Two languages have arisen, indirectly, out of these two critical analyses of Concurrent Prolog: Guarded Horn Clauses (Ueda, Chapter 4), and the CP family of languages (Saraswat, 1987).

Chapter 3, "PARLOG: Parallel Programming in Logic", by Clark and Gregory, reports on the most recent version of their second concurrent logic programming language. The original design of PARLOG was reported in 1984. Since then the language definition has undergone several modifications and refinements, with the most recent definition published in (Gregory, 1987) and in this book. PARLOG was developed as a sequel to the Relational Language, having several factors in mind: First, the inherent limitations of the strict mode declarations of the Relational Language. Second, the power of incomplete messages and recursive guards, as demonstrated by Concurrent Prolog. Third, a desire to keep the language efficiently implementable, avoiding the problems of implementing full unification and the multiple environments mechanism of Concurrent Prolog.

PARLOG incorporates a mode declaration mechanism, similar in spirit to that of the Relational Language, but relaxed so that a process can bind a variable in an input term, and can wait for input on a variable in a previously produced output term. This capability, although weaker than full unification, is rich enough to support incomplete messages. Guards in PARLOG can be general process calls, as in Concurrent Prolog. However, PARLOG avoids the multiple-environment mechanism implied by the recursive guard mechanism of Concurrent Prolog by requiring that a guard process write only on variables whose mode is declared to be output. A check verifying that in no execution of a program can a guard process write on non-output variables, called a *safety-check*, is reported by Clark and Gregory (1985). In general, this property is undecidable (see Chapter 32), and hence a safety checking algorithm can recognize only a subset of the safe programs.

PARLOG retains both the sequential-And and the parallel-And of the relational language, though it abandons its bounded-buffer annotation, since the bounded-buffer technique of Takeuchi and Furukawa (Chapter 18) is applicable to PARLOG as well. In addition, PARLOG includes two types of clause connectives: sequential-Or and parallel-Or. The former is not present in Concurrent Prolog, but it achieves an effect similar to Concurrent Prolog's *otherwise* construct.

The PARLOG paper describes the different components of the language and provides many examples of its use. It describes the single-solution subset of the language, and how incomplete messages and bounded buffers can be implemented in it; the all-solution subset with its associated set constructors; and the meta-call facility. Finally, a comparison with other languages is given.

Chapter 4, "Guarded Horn Clauses", by Ueda, 1985, reports on a language that attempts to integrate the best of Concurrent Prolog and PARLOG in a clean framework. GHC uses pure guarded Horn clauses as its syntax. Its semantics incorporates the committed-choice nondeterminism of the previous language, but combines it with a different synchronization rule: a computation invoked by the head or guard of a clause cannot bind variables in the process calling that clause. The only process that can bind variables is the special unification process "=", which, when called from the body of a clause, can bind variables allocated by the process calling that clause. Of the three languages Concurrent Prolog, PARLOG, and GHC, the latter is the simplest, both in terms of the number of constructs, and in its definition. GHC is also amenable to most of the important concurrent logic programming techniques explored for the other languages.

The language is similar to Concurrent Prolog in striving to employ a minimal number of constructs (in the case of GHC the commit operator and the special meaning assigned to "="), and the desire to keep general unification as the basic data manipulation mechanism. GHC is close to PARLOG in requiring that the major part of unification (input) be known at compile time, catering for more efficient implementation, and in avoiding the multiple-environment mechanism of Concurrent Prolog. It is also closer to PARLOG in terms of the type of atomic operations: unlike Concurrent Prolog, and like PARLOG, GHC can perform only input operations prior to commitment, while Concurrent Prolog performs a general unification, which includes both input matching and output assignment of values to variable prior to commitment. The implications of this difference on the expressive power of these languages are discussed further below.

In implementation terms, GHC stands between Concurrent Prolog and PARLOG. Since its suspension rules imply that a variable can be bound to at most one value, it does not need to implement the complex multiple-environments mechanism of Concurrent Prolog. However, unlike PARLOG, in order to decide whether a unification succeeds or suspends GHC needs to detect whether the variable to be bound belongs to the clause environment, to the parent environment or to some ancestor of the parent. Hence the identity of the layers of environments must be preserved. On the other hand PARLOG's safety check is expected to ensure at compile time that no attempt would be made to bind variables in the parent process's environment prior to commitment.

Another difference between GHC and the early designs of PARLOG was that the latter, like the Relational Language, required that the mode of unification of each argument be known at compile time, and be either input matching or output assignment. This implied that under certain circumstances the output assignment of PARLOG could be implemented more efficiently than the output unification of GHC, even if the safety of the GHC program could be determined. However, the more recent version of PARLOG allows output unification, not only output assignment, and hence the difference between PARLOG and GHC has diminished.

One natural restricted verison of GHC is Safe GHC, where safety is determinable at compile time. The resulting language becomes almost identical operationally to the single-solution subset of PARLOG. Indeed, the implementation technique of Safe GHC reported in Chapter 33 is applicable just as well to the single-solution subset of PARLOG. Another direction is restricting a language to its flat subset (explained below), as seems to be the preferred direction for implementation reasons. The difference between (the single-solution subset of) Flat PARLOG and Flat GHC is superficial, and they are essentially the same language.

Concerning the parallel execution of the three languages, GHC is again closer to PARLOG. One of the more complex aspects of a parallel implementation of Concurrent Prolog (discussed in Chapter 39), is the implementation of full unification as an atomic operation, or transaction, as required by the semantics of the language. Both PARLOG and GHC do not perform output operations prior to commitment and do not require unification to be executed atomically, hence can settle for a much simpler concurrency control mechanism, e.g., test-and-set.

The severe conceptual and implementation problems of the multiple-environments mechanism of Concurrent Prolog led to the definition of a subset of Concurrent Prolog, called Flat Concurrent Prolog (Mierowksy et al., 1984).

A definition of Flat Concurrent Prolog, as well as a survey of the developments that lead to its definition, are described in Chapter 5, "Concurrent Prolog: A Progress Report" by Shapiro, 1986. Flat Concurrent Prolog is Concurrent Prolog with simple guards. Flat Concurrent Prolog is the focus of the more recent research reported in the rest of this book. Presently, it is the concurrent logic programming language with the most advanced implementations, both sequential and parallel, and seems to have the largest number of applications.

Much of the complexity in the definition and implementation of Concurrent Prolog is a result of the interaction of the concepts of general unification and recursive guards. PARLOG, GHC, and Safe Concurrent Prolog (see Chapter 32) eschew the problem by restricting the type of unification employed and/or incorporating the notion of safety. Flat Concurrent Prolog, on the other hand, eliminates recursive guards. As reported in Chapter 5, we have found that recursive guards, although sometimes convenient, are hardly necessary, and that we were able to translate almost all our previously written Concurrent Prolog programs to Flat Concurrent Prolog without much difficulty. The one program that would not translate was Kahn's Or-parallel Prolog interpreter written in Concurrent Prolog. However, this interpreter relies in a crucial way on the multiple-environments mechanism of Concurrent Prolog, and can be implemented neither by a safe subset of Concurrent Prolog nor by any other safe language.

The integrity of the definition of Concurrent Prolog requires that read-only unification be an atomic operation. If it succeeds all variable bindings it has made are visible simultaneously. If it fails, it produces no bindings whatsoever. At the time, the importance of this requirement was not appreciated. It was felt to be an annoying requirement that complicated the parallel implementation of the language (see Chapter 39). However, as experience with concurrent programming in Concurrent Prolog accumulated, the power of this property became apparent. Indeed, the concept of atomic read-only unification is preserved in Flat Concurrent Prolog and is central to many of its programming techniques.

The paper describes Flat Concurrent Prolog and its programming techniques. It includes a more precise definition of read-only unification, which was lacking in the original definition of Concurrent Prolog. The new definition, besides being more precise, order independent, and given in terms of most-general unifiers, also reflects a change in perspective. In the original description (Chapter 2), read-only annotations were viewed as syntactic objects attached to occurrences of variables. Their semantics could be understood only operationally, by inspecting which occurrences of a variable were used in a unification. In the new definition, read-only variables are semantic objects, just like writable variables, and the semantics of the read-only annotation is given in terms of an operator mapping writable variables to their read-only counterparts. The effect of unification is appropriately extended to bind a read-only variable whenever its corresponding writable variable is bound. This change is expected to allow the use of the standard tools of logic programming, such as properties of most general unifiers, in the study of read-only unification and, more generally, in the investigation of the semantics of Flat Concurrent Prolog.

The paper can serve also as a more detailed introduction to the rest of the book, since it covers, albeit briefly, the conceptual foundations of concurrent logic programming, as well as the major Concurrent Prolog programming techniques. It contains also a historical account of the development of the language.

Chapter 6, "Parallel Logic Programming Languages" by Takeuchi and Furukawa, 1986, surveys and compares the concurrent logic programming languages along several dimensions: synchronization, safety, and flatness. They identify PARLOG and GHC as employing procedure-level synchronization, whereas Concurrent Prolog uses data-level synchronization. They claim that safety and flatness both contribute to reducing the complexity of the language. They classify PARLOG and GHC as safe languages, and Concurrent Prolog as unsafe, and suggest that unsafety is the source of difficulties in implementing full Concurrent Prolog. The paper ends by explaining why the standard semantics of logic programs is not adequate for concurrent logic programming languages and expressing the need for a denotational semantics for concurrent logic programming languages.

There are several dimensions not addressed by the review paper of Takeuchi and Furukawa, three of them being amenability to meta-programming, the granularity of the atomic operations, and the type of unification employed. The differences along these dimensions are not so significant for the implementation of parallel algorithms. However, they do seem to matter for systems programming and the implementation of higher-level languages, as explained in the introductions to the following parts.

The following parts provide evidence that Flat Concurrent Prolog can serve as a general-purpose high-level parallel machine language. Among the other concurrent logic programming languages reviewed, Concurrent Prolog is found to be impractical for this purpose in terms of its efficiency, whereas PARLOG and GHC are found to be less expressive than Flat Concurrent Prolog: On the one hand PARLOG and GHC are shown to have efficient translation schemes to Flat Concurrent Prolog. On the other hand no efficient translation scheme from Flat Concurrent Prolog to any of these languages is known. Furthermore, the book reports on various Flat Concurrent Prolog programming techniques that rely on read-only atomic unification, the fundamental operation of FCP, which have no known counterparts in the other languages. Because some of the key solutions described rely on these techniques in an essential way, the overall approach presented in this book seems to be implementable by Flat Concurrent Prolog, but not necessarily by other concurrent logic programming languages.

Chapter 1

A Relational Language
for Parallel Programming

Keith Clark and Steve Gregory

Imperial College of Science and Technology

Abstract

A parallel program often defines a relation not a function. The program constrains the output to lie in some relation R to the input, but the particular output produced during a computation can depend on the time behavior of component processes. The Horn clause subset of predicate logic is a relational language with an established procedural interpretation for non-deterministic sequential computations. In this paper we modify and extend that interpretation to define a special purpose parallel evaluator. We begin by incorporating committed (don't care) non-determinism, then generalize the interpreter to allow parallel evaluation of a set of component processes. Shared variables are the communication channels. Time-dependent behavior can result if a non-deterministic consumer process reads from more than one channel. Different communication rates of the different producers can then affect the consumer evaluation path. Then we allow bounded buffer or zero buffer communication constraints to be set for each channel. The inability of a producer to send a message down a channel can now affect the producer evaluation path.

1.1 Introduction

A parallel program often defines a relation not a function. The program constrains the output to lie in some relation R to the input, but the particular output produced during a computation can depend on the time behavior of component processes. This suggests the use of a relational language as an applicative language for parallel programming.

The Horn clause subset of predicate logic is a relational language with an established procedural interpretation for non-deterministic sequential computations (Kowalski, 1974). In this paper we modify and extend that interpretation to define a special purpose parallel evaluator.

We begin by restricting Kowalski's procedural interpretation to incorporate the committed (don't care) non-determinism of Dijkstra's (1976) guarded commands. We then generalize the interpreter to allow parallel and forking evaluation of a set of component processes. Shared variables become the communication channels between a single producer and several consumer processes. An annotation on each shared variable selects the producer. Time-dependent behavior can result if a non-deterministic consumer process reads from more than one channel. Different communication rates of the different producers can then affect the consumer evaluation path. This gives us a relational and non-deterministic variant of the Kahn and MacQueen (1977) model.

Using an additional annotation, we allow bounded buffer or zero buffer communication constraints to be set for each channel. The inability of a producer to send a message down a channel can now affect the producer evaluation path. With zero buffer communication on every channel, our model is an applicative analogue of Hoare's (1985) CSP.

1.2   The Sequential Interpreter

1.2.1   Notation and terminology

A *program* is a set of clauses.

A *clause* is a sentence of the form

$$P \leftarrow G_1 \& \ldots \& G_k | A_1 \& \ldots \& A_m. \qquad k \geq 0, \ m \geq 0 \qquad (1)$$

where P, each G_i and each A_j is an atom. P is the *consequent* or *head* of the clause while $G_1 \& \ldots \& G_k | A_1 \& \ldots \& A_m$ is the *Antecedent*. The antecedent consists of a *guard sequence* $G_1 \& \ldots \& G_k$ followed by a *goal sequence* $A_1 \& \ldots \& A_m$. These are separated by a *clause bar* '|'.

An *atom* is of the form $R(t_1, \ldots, t_n)$ where R is a relation name, and $t_1, \ldots, t_n$ are terms.

1.2.2 Data structures

The variable-free terms are the data structures of the language (we use identifiers beginning with upper-case letters for variables). Thus $\{0,1,2,\ldots\}$ are the numeral data objects, $\{nil,\ 2.nil,\ 2.3.nil,\ \ldots\}$ are lists of numerals and *salary(smith,10000)* is a record labelled *salary* containing a name and a numeral.

Note that this means that the function names are always the names of data constructors. More general functions on the data structures must be treated as relations. The relation names denote the relations over the data structures that we want to compute.

1.2.3 Declarative reading

Let $X_1,\ldots,X_n$ be the variables of the clause (1) above. The clause can be read

> For all data structures $X_1,\ldots,X_n$:
> P if G_1 and ... and G_k and A_1 and ... and A_m

Thus, each clause can be read as a statement about the computable relations to which it refers. The program is (partially) correct if each clause is a true statement.

Example. This defines the *min_of* relation on numerals in terms of the '$\leq$' relation.

> U min_of (U,V) ← U $\leq$ V | true.
> V min_of (U,V) ← V $\leq$ U | true.

Example. This defines the *merge_to* relation over lists. (X, Y) *merge_to* Z is the relation: Z is an arbitrary interleaving of the lists X and Y which preserves the order of their elements.

> (U.X,Y) merge_to U.Z ← (X,Y) merge_to Z.
> (X,V.Y) merge_to V.Z ← (X,Y) merge_to Z.
> (nil,Y) merge_to Y.
> (X,nil) merge_to X.

1.2.4 Procedural semantics

An *evaluable expression* is of the form

> t:B$_1$&...&B$_j$.

where t is a term and each B_i is an atom. The conjunction $B_1\&\ldots\&B_j$ is a sequence of *calls*. Each variable in t must appear in at least one of these calls.

A terminating evaluation of the expression returns a data structure $[t]s$, (t with its variables replaced by data structure bindings of variables given in s). s is a set $\{U_1/t_1,\ldots,U_n/t_n\}$ of data structure bindings for the variables $U_1,\ldots,U_n$ of $B_1\&\ldots\&B_j$. It is such that $[B_1\&\ldots\&B_j]s$ is a logical consequence of the statements of the program.

The following is a recursive description of the computation of the output substitution s.

Case 1: $j>1$

The computation of s for $B_1\&\ldots\&B_j$ is reduced to the computation of a substitution r of data structure bindings for the variables of B_1 followed by the computation of a substitution s' of data structure bindings for the variables of $[B_2\&\ldots\&B_j]r$. s is then the set of bindings $(r \cup s')$. Notice that this means that the output binding for a variable is always computed by the evaluation of the first call in which it appears. This output binding is then passed on to later calls.

Case 2: $j=1$

The computation of the substitution s of data structure bindings for the variables of a single call $R(t_1,\ldots,t_n)$ is non-deterministic. Let

$$R(t'_1,\ldots,t'_n)\leftarrow G_1\&\ldots\&G_k|A_1\&\ldots\&A_m.$$

be a program clause. This clause is a *candidate* clause for the computation of s if

(1) There is a (partial) *output substitution* r of bindings for some or all of the variables of $R(t_1,\ldots,t_n)$ and an *input substitution* r' of bindings for all the variables of $R(t'_1,\ldots,t_n')$ such that

$$[R(t_1,\ldots,t_n)]r = [R(t'_1,\ldots,t'_n)]r'$$

Here $(r \cup r')$ is a most general unifier of the two atoms; see Robinson (1965).

(2) The instance $[G_1\&\ldots\&G_k]r'$ of the guard sequence is a true conjunction of variable-free atoms. Notice that this means that all the variables in the guard sequence must be bound to data structures by the input substitution r'.

Using *any* candidate clause, the computation of the substitution s for the call $R(t_1,\ldots,t_n)$ is reduced to the computation of a substitution s' for variables of the input instance $[A_1\&\ldots\&A_m]r'$ of the goal conjunction of the clause. s is then the bindings of the output substitution r evaluated with respect to s'. (If r has the binding Y/t, s has the binding $Y/[t]s'$.) If $m=0$, i.e., the goal sequence of the candidate clause is empty, the evaluation of the call terminates with s equal to r.

If there are no candidate clauses for $R(t_1,\ldots,t_n)$, the computation *aborts*.

Example. Consider the single atom evaluable expression

    W: (2.3.nil,4.nil) merge_to W.

Each of the clauses

    (U.X,Y) merge_to U.Z ← (X,Y) merge_to Z.
    (X,V.Y) merge_to V.Z ← (X,Y) merge_to Z.

is a candidate clause.

For the first of these clauses the input substitution is $\{U/2,\ X/3.nil,\ Y/4.nil\}$ and the output substitution is $\{W/2.Z\}$.

For the second clause the input substitution is $\{V/4,\ X/2.3.nil,\ Y/nil\}$ and the output substitution is $\{W/4.Z\}$.

Neither clause has a guard sequence to check. In each case, the input substitution decomposes one of the data structure arguments of the call and the (partial) output substitution gives the first approximation to the data structure that will be the output binding for w if that clause is used.

Example.

    W: W min_of (2,3).

This time there is just one candidate clause:

    U min_of (U,V) ← U ≤ V | true.

The input bindings are $\{U/2,\ V/3\}$ and the output binding is $\{W/2\}$. The reason that the second *min_of* clause is not a candidate is that its guard $3 \leq 2$ is not true.

1.2.5 Concurrent search for a candidate clause

We assume that given the call $R(t_1,\ldots,t_n)$ all of the program clauses for R are tested in parallel for candidacy. The first clause to pass the test is the one that is used. There is no backtracking on this choice.

Notice that this is the committed choice non-determinism of Dijkstra's (1976) language of guarded commands. Indeed, our sequential language is the applicative analogue of his language.

What we have described is a special purpose resolution theorem prover featuring "don't care" non-determinism (Kowalski, 1979).

1.2.6 Example evaluation

The following sequence of calls represents one possible evaluation of the call *(2.3.nil,4.nil) merge_to W*

(2.3.nil,4.nil) merge_to W
$\qquad\downarrow$ partial output $\{W/2.Z\}$
(3.nil,4.nil) merge_to Z
$\qquad\downarrow$ partial output $\{Z/4.Z'\}$
(3.nil,nil) merge_to Z'
$\qquad\downarrow$ partial output $\{Z'/3.Z''\}$
(nil,nil) merge_to Z''
$\qquad\downarrow$ partial output $\{Z''/\text{nil}\}$
(empty)

As the evaluation proceeds the sequence of partial output bindings

$$W/2.Z,\ Z/4.Z',\ Z'/3.Z'',\ Z''/\text{nil}$$

gives us a sequence of partial approximations

$$2.Z,\ 2.4.Z',\ 2.4.3.Z'',\ 2.4.3.\text{nil}$$

to the final output data structure. Each new approximation gives a further element of the list. Lists approximated to in this way we shall call *streams*. This will be an important concept in our extension to parallel evaluations.

1.2.7 Modes

We have seen that the candidacy condition for a clause can only be satisfied if all the variables of a guard sequence are bound to data structures by the input substitution. In practice this means that a set of clauses for a relation are a usable program only for a restricted set of calls. Thus, the *min_of* program can only be used for calls of the form *U min_of (V,W)* where *V* and *W* are given.

Let us call each allowed pattern of call a *mode*. A declaration of the different modes in which the clauses for a relation will be used provides useful documentation. As with the Edinburgh Prolog compiler (Warren, 1977), it can also be used to optimize the compilation of the clauses.

A mode declaration for the *n*-ary relation *R* takes the form

$$\text{mode } R(m_1,\ldots,m_n).$$

where each m_i is either '?' or '↑'. '?' means that the corresponding argument in the call will be a data structure, while '↑' means that it will be a variable. There may be several mode declarations for a relation.

The following are two mode declarations for the *merge_to* program:

$$\text{mode } (?,?) \text{ merge\_to } \uparrow,\ (\uparrow,\uparrow) \text{ merge\_to } ?.$$

1.3   The Parallel Interpreter

We now extend the language to allow the goal sequence of a clause (and the initial evaluable expression) to be split into a number of sequential components, separated by the '// ' symbol:

P←G$_1$&...&G$_k$|S$_1$// ...// S$_p$.

A *sequential component* S$_i$ is a conjunction A$_1$&...&A$_m$ of atoms.

The declarative reading of the clause is unchanged by the splitting: '// ', like '&', is read as 'and'. Operationally, however, the sequential components are intended to be evaluated concurrently on independent processors. The evaluation of a sequential component is a *process*.

1.3.1   Shared variables

Provided the sequential components of a clause have no variables in common, there are no synchronization problems. However, if a number of components share a variable, the binding of this variable represents an inter-process communication. In the sequential language one call, the first in the sequence, generates the data structure binding for any shared variable. In the parallel language we shall similarly assume that there is exactly one *producer* of a shared variable x. Which one is the producer is signalled by annotating the producer occurrence of x with '↑'. All other sequential components in which x appears are now *consumers* of the data structure binding that will be generated by the producer.

1.3.2   Networks

We can think of a set of parallel processes with shared variables as a network of processes connected by one-way channels. For example:

a(X↑) // b(X) // c(X)

corresponds to the network

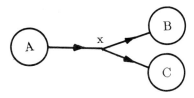

If, as here, there is more than one consumer, any values sent by the producer are replicated and conveyed to all consumers.

We shall use the term *channel variable* to refer to a variable shared between processes.

1.3.3 Procedural semantics of the parallel language

This is an elaboration of the sequential interpreter.
An evaluable expression is now of the form

$$t{:}S_1 // \ldots // S_q$$

where each variable in t has one of the sequential components S_i as its designated producer.

Each sequential component is evaluated in parallel. With each one, S_i, we associate a set I of *input channels* and a set O of *output channels*. The set I comprises those variables that the evaluation of S_i cannot bind because another sequential component is the producer for the variable. The set O comprises the variables for which S_i is the producer. I and O are the incoming and outgoing arcs, respectively, of the process node for S_i in the graph representation of the parallel evaluation.

Each process will generate a substitution s for its output channels. The answer computed by the evaluable expression is $[t]r$, where r is the union of the output substitutions of the component processes.

To generate an output substitution s for the output channels of a single process (S_i, I, O) (I the input channels of the process, O its output channels), we proceed as follows:

Case 1: $S_i = B_1 \& \ldots \& B_j, j > 1$

As in a strictly sequential evaluation, we first evaluate (B_1, I, O) to get a substitution r for the variables $Y_1 \ldots, Y_i$ of O that appear in B_1. s is then the union of r and s' where s' is the output substitution for $([B_2 \& \ldots \& B_j]r, I, O-\{Y_1, \ldots, Y_i\})$.

Case 2: $S_i = R(t_1, \ldots, t_n)$

Again, as in a sequential evaluation we can only use a candidate clause. However, there is an additional restriction on the use of a candidate clause to take account of the read-only constraints on the variables in the set I.

Suppose there is a program clause with head $R(t'_1, \ldots, t'_n)$ which satisfies the first condition of a candidate clause, i.e., there are substitutions r and r' such that

$$[R(t_1, \ldots, t_n)]r = [R(t'_1, \ldots, t'_n)]r'$$

To satisfy the read-only constraints, r must not bind any variable of input set I to a non-variable term. If it does, we shall say that the clause is *input suspended*.

The attempt to bind the input variable we shall call a *read match* on that input channel.

Given a call $R(t_1,\ldots,t_n)$ we now have three disjoint categories of program clauses:

(1) the non-candidate clauses (there is either a match failure or a false guard sequence),

(2) the input suspended clauses,

(3) the candidate clauses.

There are also three possibilities for the next step in the evaluation of $(R(t_1,\ldots,t_n), I, O)$:

(1) The evaluation is aborted if there are only non-candidate clauses.

(2) It is suspended if there are input suspended clauses but as yet no candidate clause.

(3) It is reduced to the computation of a substitution s' for

$$[S_1 /\!/ \ldots /\!/ S_p]r'$$

using any candidate clause

$$R(t'_1,\ldots,t'_n) \leftarrow G_1 \& \ldots \& G_k | S_1 /\!/ \ldots /\!/ S_p.$$

r' is the input substitution of the match between $R(t_1,\ldots,t_n)$ and $R(t_1',\ldots,t_n')$. The answer s is then the output substitution r of the match evaluated with respect to s'.

If there are parallel components in the new goal sequence, the evaluation of the current process forks. Each sequential component $[S_i]r'$ of the new goal sequence becomes a new process

$$([S_i]r', I', O')$$

Let I'' be the set of variables of $[S_i]r'$ that have a producer annotation in another component $[S_j]r'$, and let O'' be the set of variables having a producer annotation in $[S_i]r'$. Then I' is $(I \cup I'')$ and O' is $((O \cup O'') - I'')$.

Note that the rules for updating the I and O sets for offspring processes represent the reconfiguration of the corresponding network.

Example. Figure 1.1 shows the network corresponding to the evaluable expression

$$: p(Y\uparrow) /\!/ c(Y).$$

together with the reconfigured network which results from the $(p(Y),\{\},\{Y\})$ process using the candidate clause

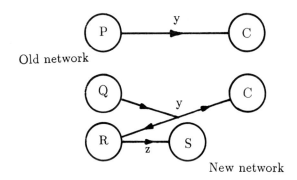

Figure 1.1: A producer-consumer network

$$p(X) \leftarrow q(X\uparrow) \;//\; r(X,Z\uparrow) \;//\; s(Z).$$

The use of the clause reduces the call $p(Y\uparrow)$ to $q(Y\uparrow) \;//\; r(Y,Z\uparrow) \;//\; s(Z)$ (the input substitution binds X to Y). This forks, with $(q(Y),\{\ \},\{Y\})$ taking on the role of the producer for Y. $(r(Y,Z),\{Y\},\{Z\})$ is an extra consumer of Y added to the network.

1.3.4 Inter-process communication

It remains to specify when data that is generated for an output channel Y of a process (P,I,O) is communicated to a process (P',I',O') which has Y as an input channel. There are two cases to consider: the first corresponding to the transmission of a single message, the second to the transmission of one of a stream of messages.

Case 1:

An evaluation step of process (P,I,O) binds a channel variable Y in O to a data structure s. The item s is communicated to each process (P',I',O') with Y in I' by binding Y to s in the input set I'. In a subsequent evaluation step of the consumer process a read match on Y accesses this binding and deletes it from the input set I'. As s is communicated, Y is deleted from the output set O of the producer process (P,I,O).

In terms of our network representation, the deletion of Y from the output set O closes down the Y channel. The binding Y/s held in each consumer process is a buffer holding s.

Case 2:

An evaluation step of process (P,I,O) binds Y in O to a first approximation $s \cdot Y'$ of a stream of messages that begins with the data structure s. This is communicated to each consumer (P', I', O') by binding the Y in I' to $s \cdot Y'$ and by adding Y' to the input set I'. Simultaneously Y is replaced by Y' in the output set O of the producer process.

In our network representation, this is the communication of s as a first message down the channel connecting the two processes. The channel remains and is logically identified with the stream of messages Y' that are yet to be generated. See Figure 1.2. The binding $Y/s \cdot Y'$ held in the consumer process is a buffer holding the first message. Again, when an evaluation step of the consumer has a read match on Y, the binding is accessed and then deleted from I'.

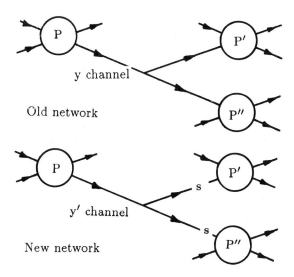

Figure 1.2: Network state

1.3.5 Unbounded buffers

It can happen that the producer process generates a new binding $s' \cdot Y''$ for Y' before the consumer has read and deleted the $Y/s \cdot Y'$ binding. This running ahead by the producer will build up a queue of messages at the consumer process. We impose no limit on the size of this stream build-up.

In allowing an unbounded build-up of messages in a channel, our language is similar to Kahn and MacQueen's (1977) applicative language for parallel programming. Ours differs in being relational rather than functional, and in allowing non-deterministic evaluations.

Example. This program is a solution to Hamming's problem (given by Dijkstra, 1976) of generating multiples of 2, 3 and 5 in ascending order:

>   mode multiples(↑).
>   multiples(X) ← times(2,1.X,R↑) //
>   times(3,1.X,S↑) // times(5,1.X,T↑) //
>   amerge(R,S,Y↑) // amerge(T,Y,X↑).
>
>   mode times(?,?,↑).
>   times(N,U.X,Y) ←
>   V is N * U & Y = V.Z & times(N,X,Z).
>
>   mode amerge(?,?,↑).
>   amerge(U.X,U.Y,U.Z) ← amerge(X,Y,Z).
>   amerge(U.X,V.Y,U.Z) ← U < V | amerge(X,V.Y,Z).
>   amerge(U.X,V.Y,V.Z) ← V < U | amerge(U.X,Y,Z).

amerge(X,Y,Z) names the relation: Z is an order-preserving merge of lists X and Y with duplicates deleted.

multiples(X) names the relation: X is the infinite list of numbers in the set $\{ 2^i\, 3^j\, 5^k \mid i,j,k \geq 0 \} - \{1\}$ in ascending order. The clause for this relation is a recursive description of such an X. It tells us that X is a fixed point of the operations

>   multiply the list 1.X by 2,
>   multiply the list 1.X by 3,
>   multiply the list 1.X by 5,
>   then merge the results, deleting duplicates.

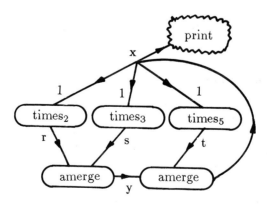

Figure 1.3: Hamming's problem

Figure 1.3 is a network representation of the evaluable expression

X: multiples(X).

The '1' placed on the input arcs to the three *times* processes comes from the *1.X* which they take as input. It is the seed for the entire computation.

1.4 Time-Dependent Programs

Consider the case when different clauses for a relation accept input from different arguments. (Our two recursive clauses for the *merge_to* relation in the mode $(?,?)$ *merge_to* $\uparrow$ are an example.) A situation can arise when one clause is input suspended while the other is a candidate clause. In this way, the availability of input to a process determines which clause is used, which in turn influences the evaluation path of the process. The relative timing of the parallel processes then determines which instance of the relation is computed. This time-dependence is essential for applications such as real-time systems.

Consider the following use of the *merge_to* program:

Z: proc1(X↑) // proc2(Y↑) // (X,Y) merge_to Z↑.

where *proc1* and *proc2* each generates a stream of messages.

If there is a message in the X channel from *proc1* but no message in the Y channel from *proc2*, we must use the clause

(U.X,Y) merge_to U.Z ← (X,Y) merge_to Z.

This passes on the message from *proc1*. Only if both channels have messages pending will the choice of which message is passed on be time-independent. Thus, the instance of the *merge_to* relation that is computed depends upon the time behavior of the generating processes.

The Friedman and Wise (1980) *frons* extension to Lisp similarly allows results to be time-dependent. However, their extension to this functional programming language destroys its referential transparency. We avoid that problem by explicitly referring to the input-output relation of the many-valued function.

Example. The following is an outline of a simple relational operating system with two user terminals. Each terminal is represented by a *keyboard* process and a *screen* process. Each command generated by a keyboard is tagged by the identifier of that terminal and the commands from both keyboards are merged into one stream. This stream is processed by a *monitor* which produces a stream of tagged responses. The responses are routed to the appropriate screen according to their tag. The system is depicted in Figure 1.4.

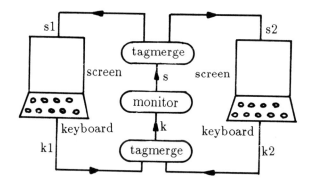

Figure 1.4: A simple operating system

mode keyboard(↑).
mode screen(?).
mode monitor(?,↑).

mode tagmerge(?,?,↑).
mode tagmerge(↑,↑,?).
tagmerge(U.X,Y,(1,U).Z) ← tagmerge(X,Y,Z).
tagmerge(X,V.Y,(2,V).Z) ← tagmerge(X,Y,Z).

: keyboard(K1↑) // keyboard(K2↑) //
  tagmerge(K1,K2,K↑) // monitor(K,S↑) //
  tagmerge(S1↑,S2↑,S) //
  screen(S1) // screen(S2).

keyboard(X) names the relation: X is a list of commands, in fact those which are typed at a particular keyboard.

screen(Y) names the relation: Y is a list of responses, which will be displayed on a particular screen.

monitor(X,Y) names the relation holding between a list of tagged commands X and a list of tagged responses Y. It is intended to provide all the required facilities of an operating system and give appropriate responses to commands from the users.

tagmerge(X,Y,Z) names the relation: Z is some order-preserving interleaving of the lists X' and Y', where X' is list X with each of its elements tagged by a *1* and Y' is list Y with each of its elements tagged by a *2*.

Notice that we have used the *tagmerge* relation in two modes. In the mode *tagmerge*(?,?,↑) the first two streams are tagged by *1* and *2* respectively and merged, in arrival order, to give the third argument. Using the same relation in reverse, i.e., in the mode $(\uparrow, \uparrow, ?)$, the tag is removed from each item in the incoming stream and used to route the item to either the first or second argument stream.

1.5 Bounded Buffers

In an implementation of stream communication between processes a set of bindings $Y/s \cdot Y'$, $Y'/s' \cdot Y''$, ..., $Y^{(n)}/s^{(n)} \cdot Y^{(n+1)}$ generated by a producer and not yet consumed by the consumer would be held in a buffer

$$\boxed{s} \; \boxed{s'} \; \boxed{\cdots} \; \boxed{s^{(n)}}$$

Y channel buffer

By default the buffer is unbounded. To specify a fixed sized buffer, we attach a positive integer to the '$\uparrow$' annotation on the channel variable. For example, writing $Y \uparrow 10$ puts a buffer size of 10 on the Y communication channel.

In the communication between processes there is now an extra case to consider. For an unbounded buffer channel a clause was either a candidate, input suspended or a non-candidate. Now a clause can also be output suspended. This occurs when the (partial) output substitution that would be generated by the use of the clause binds an output variable Y to a term $s \cdot Y'$ and some consumer for Y cannot take s without overflowing its buffer.

Just as the non-availability of input on a channel can affect the evaluation path, the inability to transmit output down a particular channel can now affect the evaluation path. In CSP terms (Hoare, 1985) we have both read guards and write guards on evaluation steps. A process can also become suspended because of its inability to write. The suspension occurs when there is at least one clause that is output suspended and there are no candidate clauses.

With an unbounded buffer the process that generates output for the channel simply transmits the data down the channel. The data is guaranteed to be accepted by each consumer. For a bounded buffer channel the use of a clause that generates output is conditional upon the output being accepted. To determine acceptability of the output, that is to determine whether the clause in question is a candidate, the producer must poll each consumer of the channel to see if it can accept a message. If all consumers can accept the message, the clause can be used and the message can be sent.

1.5.1 Synchronized communication

As a special case of a bounded buffer, we allow a zero size buffer. This gives us tight synchronization of processes. When two processes are connected by a zero-buffer channel, communication can occur only when the producer evaluation step that writes down the channel is synchronized with each consumer evaluation step that reads from the channel. The languages of both Hoare (1985) and Milne and Milner (1979) are designed specifically for this kind of communication.

Our next example illustrates both finite-buffer and zero-buffer communication. Suppose we have a computer system with two printers and a process *files* generating a stream of files to be printed. Our *merge_to* relation can be used in its splitting mode

$$\text{mode } (\uparrow,\uparrow) \text{ merge\_to ?.}$$

to distribute files between the two printers:

$$: \text{ files}(Z\uparrow 20) \text{ // } (X\uparrow 0, Y\uparrow 0) \text{ merge\_to } Z \text{ //}$$
$$\text{printer}(X) \text{ // } \text{printer}(Y).$$

printer(X) is the relation: X is a list of files. It has the side effect of printing these files on a particular printer. The logic of the program guarantees that each file in Z will be printed exactly once.

The buffer size of 20 on channel Z allows a queue of 20 files to accumulate before the *files* process suspends. Each file in Z is allocated to a printer only when one of the printers is ready to accept it, since until then both recursive *merge_to* clauses are output suspended. Thus, the goal sequence annotated as above gives a single queue, multiple server spooling system. A multiple queue system with the same capacity would result from

$$: \text{ files}(Z\uparrow 0) \text{ // } (X\uparrow 10, Y\uparrow 10) \text{ merge\_to } Z \text{ //}$$
$$\text{printer}(X) \text{ // } \text{printer}(Y).$$

in which each printer has its own input buffer of size 10.

1.5.2 Buffers as processes

Zero buffer communication is the primitive in terms of which both bounded and unbounded buffer communication can be implemented. If we have an unbounded buffer B then the relationship *buffer*(B,X,Y) between B, the list X of all the input messages to come and the list Y of all the subsequent output messages is satisfied when Y is $B()X$ (i.e., B appended to X). The following clauses describe this relation and in so doing implement an unbounded buffer between channels X and Y.

mode buffer(?,?,↑).
buffer(B,U.X,Y) ←
        B′ = B () U.nil & buffer(B′,X,Y).
buffer(U.B,X,U.Y) ← buffer(B,X,Y).

The goal sequence

     : prod(X↑0) // buffer(nil,X,Z↑0) // con(Z).

gives exactly the same behavior as

     : prod(X↑) // con(X).

By adding the guard $length(B) < k$ to the first clause of the program, we define a bounded buffer of size k. In a similar way, we can define a process that acts as a register.

1.6   Concluding Remarks

There are several extensions to the above model of parallel computation that we are investigating. One is the use of multiple producers. These multiple producers can either compete or co-operate. If they compete, the shared variable is a two-way channel. The first producer to generate the next message sends it down the channel. It must be accepted by the co-producers. If the producers co-operate, they share a communication channel to the consumer processes. Each message sent must be agreed by each producer, but a producer can generate a "don't care" message represented by an unbound variable.

We also need to address the issues of correctness and termination. Correctness is relatively straightforward. We can use the standard techniques for logic programs (see Clark, 1979). Termination is more of a problem. For sequential programs we need to show that for each allowed mode of call there is a terminating computation no matter what candidate clause is used. For parallel programs we are investigating conditions on the communication network that will guarantee termination of an unbounded buffer parallel evaluation if the sequential evaluation terminates. Loop network programs, such as that for the Hamming's problem, must be handled differently. One must reason about the flow of messages around the network. Thus, for the Hamming's program, one must show that the 'seed' of a single value on the incoming arcs of the three *times* processes is sufficient to ensure that a new seed is generated on each of these arcs. Finally, bounded buffers and synchronized communication introduce new complexities. But proofs of termination, or proofs of deadlock-free evaluation, should not be harder than such proofs for CSP programs.

1.6.1 Related work

MacQueen's (1979) paper is an excellent survey of various models of parallel computation. Many of these correspond to special cases of our model.

The use of Horn clause logic as a parallel programming notation has been investigated by van Emden and de Lucena (1982). However, they only treat the deterministic parallelism of Kahn and MacQueen's model. Dausmann et al. (1979) use an annotation '/B' on shared variables to synchronize processes: an occurrence of X/B delays the process until X is bound.

IC-PROLOG (Clark et al., 1982) is a Horn clause evaluator with a pseudo-parallel execution mode. It time-shares the evaluations of the different processes. Annotations on shared variables are also used to impose communication constraints, and a process is suspended if those constraints cannot be met.

Hogger (1982) discusses various aspects of concurrent logic programming. A backtracking parallel evaluator is assumed in which all shared variables represent two-way channels. He shows how disjunctive concurrency can be obtained by introducing extra shared variables between the parallel calls and using "head annotations" of IC-PROLOG.

Acknowledgements

The ideas presented in this paper germinated in discussions with Maurice Bruynooghe and developed in work with Frank McCabe. This work was supported by the Science and Engineering Research Council.

Chapter 2

A Subset of Concurrent Prolog
and Its Interpreter

Ehud Shapiro

The Weizmann Institute of Science

Abstract

Concurrent Prolog is a variant of the programming language Prolog, which is intended to support concurrent programming and parallel execution. The language incorporates guarded-command indeterminacy, dataflow-like synchronization, and a commitment mechanism similar to nested transactions.

This paper reports on a subset of Concurrent Prolog, for which we have developed a working interpreter. It demonstrates the expressive power of the language via Concurrent Prolog programs that solve benchmark concurrent programming problems. It describes in full detail an interpreter for the language, written in Prolog, which can execute these programs.

2.1 Introduction

Due to its expressive power, simple semantics, and amenability to efficient implementation, Prolog is a promising language for a large class of applications. Prolog also has another, as yet unexploited, aspect: it is a sequential simulation of an inherently parallel computation model.

There are two reasons for exploiting Prolog's underlying parallelism. One is to improve the performance of Prolog in some of its current applications, perhaps using novel computer architectures. The other is to incorporate, in the range of Prolog, applications that require concurrency. Concurrent Prolog is concerned with both.

Concurrent Prolog is currently under design by the author. This paper reports on a subset of the language for which we have developed a working interpreter. This subset is a variant of Sequential Prolog, but does not contain Sequential Prolog properly.

When Japan's Fifth Generation Computers Project chose logic programming as its basic framework, there was some concern it would have difficulties integrating ideas and techniques of object-oriented programming. Our example programs show that Concurrent Prolog is an object-oriented programming language *par excellence*.

The synchronization mechanism of Concurrent Prolog — read-only variables of dataflow synchronization — can be viewed as a generalization (Ackerman, 1982) from functional to relational languages. It is possible that Concurrent Prolog may be a suitable programming language for dataflow computers (Uchida, 1982; Wise, 1982a).

One need not wait, however, until dataflow computers become available. Our experience with implementing Concurrent Prolog, and the example programs below, suggest that this language may be a practical programming language for implementing operating system functions even on today's computers.

Two controversial features of Sequential Prolog, namely the *cut* and side-effects, are cleaned-up in Concurrent Prolog. Concurrent Prolog's *commit* operator (Clark and Gregory, Chapter 1) achieves an effect similar to *cut* in increasing the efficiency of the program, but has a cleaner semantics due to its symmetry, much the same way as Dijkstra's (1976) guarded-command has a cleaner semantics than the conventional if-then-else construct. Concurrent Prolog eschews the use of side-effects such as *assert* and *retract* to implement global data structures, since they can be implemented by perpetual processes, executing side-effect-free programs.

The paper is organized as follows. Section 2.2 introduces logic programs and Sequential Prolog. Section 2.3 defines the subset of Concurrent Prolog used in this paper, henceforth referred to as Concurrent Prolog, and sketches a distributed interpretation algorithm for it.

Since the programming style and concepts of Concurrent Prolog are rather different — both from Sequential Prolog and from other concurrent programming languages — we suspect that the only way to gain a true understanding of the language is to study, or to develop, Concurrent Prolog solutions to nontrivial concurrent programming problems. Section 2.4 includes in full detail Concurrent Prolog solutions to many such benchmark problems, including:

- a concurrent implementation of the quicksort algorithm,

- a recursive concurrent program for numbering the leaves of a tree,

- an airline reservation program,

- programs for merging streams using various scheduling strategies,

- a simple message-sending operating system,

- fragments of a Unix-like shell,

- shared FIFO and priority queues,

- a simulator of a multiprocessor Concurrent Prolog machine,

- a priority queue based multiple-printers spooler,

- an implementation of a concurrent algorithm for finding the connected components of a graph.

The programs are concise, elegant, and, once the Concurrent Prolog programming style is grasped, are also easy to understand.

Instead of studying someone else's programs, one is better off trying to develop some of his or her own. To facilitate such an endeavor, Section 2.5 describes a sequential Concurrent Prolog interpreter, and its implementation in Prolog-10. The implementation is 44 lines of code long and performs about 135 process reductions per CPU second (LIPS) on a DEC-2060. The initiated reader, who has an access to a Prolog implementation, is invited to type this interpreter in and gain some first-hand experience in programming in Concurrent Prolog.

Section 2.6 compares Concurrent Prolog with other concurrent programming languages, including the Relational Language of Clark and Gregory (Chapter 1), by which Concurrent Prolog was strongly influenced.

Section 2.7 compares Concurrent Prolog with Sequential Prolog, discusses deficiencies in the subset of Concurrent Prolog described in the paper, and explores possible extensions to it.

Section 2.8 explores future research directions relating to concurrent logic programming.

The listings of the full Concurrent Prolog interpreter, which contains a trace and statistics package together with some utility programs, are included as an appendix.

2.2 Logic Programs and Sequential Prolog

2.2.1 The logic programs computation model

Both Sequential and Concurrent Prolog are approximations to the logic program computation model. A *logic program* is a set of universally quantified first-order axioms of the form

$$A \leftarrow B_1, B_2, \ldots, B_n$$

where the A and the B's are atomic formulae, also called *atomic goals*. Such a clause reads "A if B_1 and B_2 and $\cdots$ and B_n". A is called the clause's *head* and the B's are called its *body*.

A computation of a logic program amounts to the construction of a proof of an existentially quantified conjunctive goal from the axioms. It can have two results: success or failure. If the computation succeeds, then the values found for the variables in the initial goal constitute the output of the computation. A goal can have several successful computations, each resulting in a different output.

The computation progresses via nondeterministic goal reduction: at each step it has a current goal $A_1, A_2, \ldots, A_n$; it arbitrarily chooses a goal A_i, for some $1 \leq i \leq n$; it then nondeterministically chooses a clause $A' \leftarrow B_1, B_2, \ldots, B_k$, $k \geq 0$ for which A and A' are unifiable via a substitution θ, and uses this clause to reduce the goal. The reduced goal is $(A_1, \ldots, A_{i-1}, \ldots, B_1, \ldots, B_k, A_{i+1}, \ldots, A_n)\theta$. The computation terminates when the current goal is empty.

This description readily suggests two forms of parallel execution: the reduction of several goals in parallel, also called *And-parallelism*, and a concurrent search of the computation paths resulting from different nondeterministic choices of the unifiable clause, also called *Or-parallelism* .

Different orderings of the goals to be reduced need not be investigated since they are immaterial to the result of the computation (Apt and van Emden, 1982). However, the chosen ordering can greatly affect the degree of nondeterminism in the computation. Hence the major concern of a practical logic programming language is to provide the programmer with control facilities with which he can reduce this degree of nondeterminism. Typically, such facilities enable the programmer to influence both the order in which goals are reduced and the clauses they are reduced with.

2.2.2 An example of a logic program

An example of a logic program that implements a variant of the quicksort algorithm is shown in Figure 2.1.

The program is adapted from the Prolog-10 manual (Bowen et al., 1981), and so are our notational conventions: Variables begin with an upper-case letter, all other symbols with lower-case letters. The binary term $[X \mid Y]$ (read "X *cons* Y") denotes the list whose head (*car*) is X and tail (*cdr*) is Y. The term $[X, Y \mid Z]$ is a shorthand for $[X \mid [Y \mid Z]]$ — the list whose *car* is X, *cadr* is Y, and *cddr* is Z. The constant $[\,]$ (read "nil") denotes the empty list. Underscore "_" stands for an anonymous variable that occurs only once, and hence does not deserve a name.

The best way to understand — and to document — a logic program is to state the relations it computes. The procedure *quicksort*(X, Y) computes the

quicksort(Unsorted, Sorted) ←
    qsort(Unsorted, Sorted\[ ]).

qsort([X | Unsorted], Sorted\Rest) ←
    partition(Unsorted, X, Smaller, Larger),
    qsort(Smaller, Sorted\[X | Sorted1]),
    qsort(Larger, Sorted1\Rest).
qsort([ ], Rest\Rest).

partition([X | Xs], A, Smaller, [X | Larger]) ←
    A < X, partition(Xs, A, Smaller, Larger).
partition([X | Xs], A, [X | Smaller], Larger) ←
    A ≥ X, partition(Xs, A, Smaller, Larger).
partition([ ], _, [ ], [ ]).

Figure 2.1: A logic program for quicksort

relation "sorting X gives Y" (or, "Y is an ordered permutation of X"). The procedure $qsort(X, Y)$ computes the relation "the difference-list Y is an ordered permutation of the list X". $partition(X, Y, Z, W)$ computes the relation "the list Z contains all elements of the list X less than or equal to Y, in the order they appear in Y, and W contains all elements of X greater than Y, in the order they appear in X".

The first clause of *partition* reads, "partitioning a list whose *head* is X and *tail* is Xs according to element A gives the lists *Smaller* and X followed by *Larger*, if A is less than X and partitioning Xs according to A gives the lists *Smaller* and *Larger*". Other clauses are read similarly.

2.2.3 Difference-lists: an example of a logic programming technique

The quicksort program illustrates an important logic programming technique, used throughout this paper, called *difference-lists* (Clark and Tärnlund , 1977). A difference-list represents a list L as the difference between two lists X and Y. As a notational convention, the term $X\backslash Y$ is used. But since logic programs do not evaluate logical terms, only unify them, the name of the binary functor representing a difference-list can be arbitrary, so long as it is used consistently.

Difference-lists increase both the efficiency and brevity of logic programs. They increase their efficiency since, in some cases, two difference-lists can be concatenated in constant time, and without copying data structures ("consing"). A difference-list *X1\X2* is *compatible* with *Y1\Y2* if *X2=Y1*. Compatible difference-lists can be concatenated using the following single-clause logic program:

concatenate(X\Y,Y\Z,X\Z).

concatenate(X,Y,Z) computes the relation "concatenating the difference-list X to the difference-list Y is the difference-list Z if X and Y are compatible".

One way to ensure that the two difference-lists $X1 \backslash X2$ and $Y1 \backslash Y2$ are compatible is to keep the value of $X2$ undetermined. In such a case the *concatenate* call is executed in constant time, independent of the length of the lists. For example, the result of the call *concatenate*$([a,b,c \mid X] \backslash X, [1,2] \backslash [\,], Y)$ is $X=[1,2]$ and $Y=[a,b,c,1,2] \backslash [\,]$.

Difference-lists increase the brevity of logic programs by eliminating the need to call *concatenate* explicitly, as in the quicksort example. The unification of the tail of the first list with the head of the second is done implicitly, by calling them with the same name, *Sorted1*, and the construction of the concatenated list is then immediate. Hence one would typically find neither the code for, nor a call to, the concatenate procedure in a logic program that uses difference-lists.

Difference-lists are the logic-programming counterpart of Lisp's *rplacd* (McCarthy et al., 1965), which is also used to concatenate lists in constant time and save "consing". There is a difference between the two: the former are side-effect free and can be discussed in terms of the abstract computation model, whereas *rplacd* is a destructive operation, which can be described only by reference to the machine representation of S-expressions.

2.2.4 An example of a computation

A successful computation of the *quicksort* program on the goal *quicksort*$([2,1,3],X)$ may proceed as follows. First the goal is reduced to *quicksort*$([2,1,3],X \backslash [\,])$ using the only clause of *quicksort*. Then the recursive clause of *qsort* is invoked; this is the only applicable clause, since the head of the second clause does not unify with the goal. The reduce goal is:

> partition([1, 3], 2, Smaller, Larger),
> quicksort(Smaller, Sorted\[2|Sorted1]),
> quicksort(Larger, Sorted1\[ ]).

To solve *partition*$([1,3],2,Smaller,Larger)$ we nondeterministically choose *partitions*'s second clause, and reduce it to $2 \geq 1$, *partition*$([3],2,Smaller1,Larger)$, while unifying *Smaller* with $[1 \mid Smaller1]$. The $\geq$ test is solved immediately, assuming that arithmetic is represented as a large table (simulated by the machine arithmetic operations, or by a suitable logic program). The recursive call to *partition* is solved by two more reductions, at the end of which *Smaller1* is unified with $[\,]$ and *Larger* with $[3]$. We next turn to the two recursive calls to *qsort1*, which are now instantiated to

> qsort([1], Sorted\[2 | Sorted1]), qsort([3], Sorted1\[ ]).

The correct nondeterministic choices result in unifying *Sorted* with $[1,2,3]$ and

Sorted1 with *[3]*, and the computation succeeds, with the variable *Sorted* in the
initial goal unified with *[1,2,3]*.

2.2.5 Controlling nondeterminism at the expense of completeness

In the computation of a logic program, the order in which subgoals are solved
is immaterial, so long as the correct nondeterministic choices are made. However,
a careless ordering in the example computation above may require choosing the
values of X and Y when solving $X \geq Y$, a choice that has a rather large degree
of nondeterminism.

To avoid making such hopeless choices, practical logic programming languages enable the programmer to control the computation, usually at the expense
of the completeness of the resulting proof procedure. This incompleteness is not
a "bug" in the design of a logic programming language, but a conscious design
decision, whose motivation follows.

A logic program can be executed in several ways, many of which are curious,
but of little practical value. For example, the *quicksort* logic program can be
run backwards to generate all permutations of a list; when invoked with its two
arguments undetermined, this program can be used to generate all pairs of lists
of integers such that one is an ordered permutation of the other.

For the sake of efficiency, practical logic programming languages give up the
ability to make such obscure uses of logic programs. Hence we refer to them
as approximations to the logic programming computation model. Unfortunately,
there are not yet any mathematically elegant characterizations of these approximations; all that can be said currently is that a logic program, using an incomplete
proof procedure, computes only a subset of its logical consequences. The precise
subset of computable consequences can be determined only by reference to the
operational semantics of the programming language.

This is in contrast to the abstract logic program computation model, which
has at least two other independent characterizations. Van Emden and Kowalski
(1976) show that the smallest interpretation in which a logic program is true equals
the subset of its Herbrand universe on which it succeeds. They also associate a
transformation with any logic program and show that its least fixpoint is equal
to its smallest interpretation. Hence we refer to the smallest interpretation in
which a logic program is true as *the interpretation* of the program. The price a
practical logic programming language pays for controlling non-determinism is that
its programs typically compute only a subset of their associated interpretations.

2.2.6 Sequential Prolog

Sequential Prolog is an example of an approximation of the logic program
computation model, especially designed for efficient execution on a von Neumann

machine. Sequential Prolog uses the order of goals in a clause and the order of clauses in the program to control the search for a proof. In Sequential Prolog the chosen goal is always the leftmost goal, and the nondeterministic choice of the unifiable clause is simulated by sequential search and backtracking. Given a goal $A_1,A_2,\ldots,A_n$ and a program $\boldsymbol{P}$, Prolog sequentially searches for the first clause in $\boldsymbol{P}$ whose head unifies with A_1, and reduces the goal using this clause. It then tries, in order from left to right, to solve the reduced goal, accumulating the bindings of variables as it goes along. If the Prolog interpreter ever fails to solve a goal, then it backtracks to the last choice of a clause made, resets the bindings made since that choice, and tries the next unifiable clause. If no choices remain the computation fails.

In addition to text order, Sequential Prolog uses the *cut* operator "!" to control its execution. A cut is inserted in a clause as a goal, and when used decently, can be ignored in the declarative reading of a clause. Operationally, a cut commits the interpreter to the current execution path and to all choices made since, and including, the choice of a clause in which the cut occurs.

Even though it originated in a rather abstract computation model, Sequential Prolog exhibits some resemblance to conventional sequential programming languages, as summarized in Figure 2.2. This resemblance is partially responsible for our understanding of how to implement Prolog efficiently on a von Neumann machine (Warren, 1977).

Procedure:	List of definite clauses with the same head predicate
Procedure call:	Goal
Binding mechanism data selection and construction:	Unification
Execution mechanism:	Nondeterministic goal reduction, simulated by sequential search and backtracking

Figure 2.2: Concepts of Sequential Prolog

2.3   Concurrent Prolog

2.3.1   Basic concepts and syntax

While comparing several concurrent programming languages, Bryant and Dennis (1982) wrote:

"Several issues must be considered when designing programming languages to support concurrent computation. Of primary importance is expressive power. The expressive power of a language, in the context of concurrent systems, means the form of concurrent operations, the type of communication, synchronization, and nondeterminacy which can be expressed in the language. A programming language which lacks expressive power will force the programmer to rely on a suitable set of operating system routines to implement desired behavior. A properly designed language, on the other hand, should have sufficient richness to express these functions directly".

We claim that the computational model of logic programs embodies all the mechanisms necessary for a concurrent programming language — *concurrency, communication, synchronization*, and *indeterminacy*. All one needs to do is uncover them.

A system of processes corresponds to a conjunctive goal, and a unit goal to a process. The state of a system is the union of the states of its processes, where the state of a process is the value of its arguments. *And*-parallelism — solving several goals simultaneously — provides the system with concurrency. *Or*-parallelism — attempting to solve a goal in several ways simultaneously — provides each process with the ability to perform indeterminate actions. Variables shared between goals serve as the process communication mechanism; and the synchronization of processes in a system is done by denoting which processes can "write" on a shared variable, i.e., unify it with a nonvariable term, and which processes can only "read" the content of a shared variable X, i.e., can unify X with a nonvariable term T only after X's principal functor is determined, possibly by another process. This analogy is incorporated in Concurrent Prolog, and is summarized in Figure 2.3.

System:	Conjunctive goal
Process:	Unit goal
Process state:	Values of goal arguments
Process computation:	Indeterminate process reduction
Process communication:	Unification of shared variables
Process synchronization:	Suspending instantiation of undetermined "read-only" variables
Process failure:	Goal finite-failure

Figure 2.3: Concepts of Concurrent Prolog

Concurrent Prolog adds two constructs to logic programs. *Read-only* annotation of variables, $X?$, and the *commit* operator "|". Both are used to control the computation, i.e., the construction of a proof, by restricting the order in which goals can be reduced, and restricting the choice of clauses that can be used to reduce them.

A *Concurrent Prolog program* is a finite set of guarded clauses. A *guarded clause* is a universally quantified axiom of the form

$$A \leftarrow G_1, G_2, \ldots, G_m \mid B_1, B_2, \ldots, B_m, \qquad m,n \geq 0$$

where the G's and the B's are atomic goals. The G's are called the *guard* of the clause and B's are called its *body*. When the guard is empty, the commit operator is omitted. The clause may contain variables marked "read-only".

The commit operator generalizes and cleans Sequential Prolog's cut. Declaratively, it reads like a conjunction: A is implied by the G's *and* the B's. Operationally, a guarded clause functions similarly to an alternative in a guarded-command (Dijkstra, 1976). It can be used to reduce process $A1$ to a system B if A is unifiable with $A1$ and, following the unification, the system G is invoked and terminates successfully.

Program 2.1 is a Concurrent Prolog implementation of quicksort. It differs from the logic program in Figure 2.1 in the read-only annotations that occur in the recursive calls to *qsort* and *partition*, and in the commit operator in the recursive clauses of *partition*.

```
(0)   quicksort(Unsorted, Sorted) ←
          qsort(Unsorted, Sorted\[ ]).

(1)   qsort([X | Unsorted], Sorted\Rest) ←
          partition(Unsorted?, X, Smaller, Larger),
          qsort(Smaller?, Sorted\[X | Sorted1]),
          qsort(Larger?, Sorted1\Rest).
(2)   qsort([ ], Rest\Rest).

(1)   partition([X | Xs], A, Smaller, [X | Larger]) ←
          A < X | partition(Xs?, A, Smaller, Larger).
(2)   partition([X | Xs], A, [X | Smaller], Larger) ←
          A ≥ X | partition(Xs?, A, Smaller, Larger).
(3)   partition([ ], _, [ ], [ ]).
```

Program 2.1: A Concurrent Prolog implementation of quicksort

The unification of terms containing read-only variables is an extension to normal unification (Robinson, 1965). The unification of a read-only term $X?$ with a term Y is defined as follows. If Y is non-variable then the unification succeeds only if X is non-variable, and X and Y are recursively unifiable. If Y is a variable then the unification of $X?$ and Y succeeds, and the result is the read-only variable $X?$. The symmetric algorithm applies to X and $Y?$. A unification that would have succeeded if only read-only annotations were removed is said to *suspend*. A unification that does not succeed even if read-only annotations are removed is said to *fail*[1].

In the Prolog implementation, we represent the read-only annotation as a unary functor written in postfix notation, and augment Prolog's unification algorithm to handle this term specially. The code that implements this extended unification algorithm is shown in Program 2.19, Section 2.5.

This definition of unification implies that being "read-only" is not an inherited property, i.e., variables that occur in a read-only term are not necessarily read-only. Stating it differently, the scope of a read-only annotation is only the principal functor of a term, but not its arguments. This design decision provides Concurrent Prolog with a unique and powerful object-oriented programming technique, called *incomplete messages*, used and explained in several of the example programs below.

The definition of unification also implies that the success of a unification may be time-dependent: a unification that suspends now, due to violation of a read-only constraint, may succeed later, after the principal functor of a shared read-only variable is determined by another process, in which this variable does not occur as read-only.

2.3.2 A sketch of a distributed Concurrent Prolog interpreter

The execution of a Concurrent Prolog system S, running a program P, can be described informally as follows. Each process A in S tries asynchronously to reduce itself to other processes, using the clauses in P. A process A can reduce itself by finding a clause $A1 \leftarrow G \mid B$ whose head $A1$ unifies with A and whose guard system G terminates following that unification. The system S terminates when it is empty. It may become empty only if some of the clauses in P have empty bodies.

The computation of a Concurrent Prolog program gives rise to a hierarchy of systems. Each process may invoke several guard systems, in an attempt to find a reducing clause, and the computation of these guard systems in turn may invoke other systems. The communication between these systems is governed by the commitment mechanism. Subsystems spawned by a process A have access only to variables that occur in A. Bindings computed by a subsystem to a variable in A are recorded on a privately stored copy of these variables, which is not accessible

---

[1] See Shapiro, Chapter 5, for an alternative, more rigorous, definition of read-only unification.

outside of that subsystem. Upon commitment to a clause $A1 \leftarrow G \mid B$, the private copies of variables associated with this clause are unified against their public counterparts, and if the unification succeeds, the body system B of the chosen clause replaces A.

A more detailed description of a distributed Concurrent Prolog interpreter uses three kinds of processes: an And-dispatcher, an Or-dispatcher, and a unifier; these processes should not be confused with the Concurrent Prolog processes themselves, which are unit goals.

The computation begins with a system S of Concurrent Prolog processes and progresses via indeterminate process reduction. After an And-dispatcher is invoked with S, the computation proceeds as follows:

- An *And-dispatcher*, invoked with a system S, spawns a child Or-dispatcher for every Concurrent Prolog process A in S, and waits for all its children to report. When a child reports commitment to a body B, it removes the child and spawns an Or-dispatcher for every goal A in B (if any). When no child Or-dispatchers left, it reports success and terminates. When one child reports failure, it reports failure and terminates.

- An *Or-dispatcher*, invoked with a Concurrent Prolog process A, operates as follows. For every clause $A1 \leftarrow G \mid B$, whose head is potentially unifiable with A, it invokes a unifier with A and the clause $A1 \leftarrow G \mid B$. Following that the Or-dispatcher waits for the unifiers to report. When one unifier reports success, the Or-dispatcher reports success to its parent And-dispatcher and terminates. When all report failure, it reports failure and terminates.

- A *unifier* , invoked with a Concurrent Prolog process A and a guarded-clause $A1 \leftarrow G \mid B$, operates as follows. It attempts to unify A with $A1$, storing bindings made to non read-only variables in A on private storage. If it fails, it reports failure and terminates. If and when successful, it invokes an And-dispatcher with G, and waits for it to report. When a success report arrives, the unifier attempts to commit, as explained below. If the commitment completes successfully it reports commitment to B. If it receives a failure report, or if commitment fails, it reports failure. In either case it terminates.

At most one unifier spawned by an Or-dispatcher may commit. This mutual-exclusion can be achieved by standard techniques, e.g., by using a test-and-set bit for each Or-dispatcher in a shared memory model.

To commit, a unifier first has to gain permission to do so. The mutual-exclusion algorithm must guarantee that at any point in time, at most one unifier will have permission to do so. After gaining permission, the unifier attempts to unify the local copies of its variables against their corresponding global copies. If successful, then the commitment completes successfully.

When committing, the unifier is required to perform the unification of the public and private copies of variable as an "atomic action".

The early detection and deletion of failing processes can be introduced as an optimization to the basic model, without affecting its semantics. Another useful optimization is the deletion of brother unifiers, once the first such process is successfully committed.

Since a unification that currently suspends may succeed later, the phrase "attempts to unify" in the description of a unifier should be interpreted as a continuous activity, which terminates only upon success or failure. This can be implemented using a busy-waiting strategy, but several optimizations can be incorporated, in the form of more sophisticated waiting techniques, for example the technique suggested by Alain Colmerauer, described in Section 2.5.

Our description of the distributed operational semantics of Concurrent Prolog is rather informal, and we are investigating ways to make it more precise. Two issues must be solved in developing a precise semantics to Concurrent Prolog. One is the meaning of infinite computations. Notions from infinitary logic, as proposed by van Emden and de Lucena (1982), and Smyth (1982), may be utilized. Another is capturing in the formalism the time dependent behavior of Concurrent Prolog. It is conceivable that one can time-stamp logical terms to achieve this.

2.3.3 An example of a computation

For example, we trace the execution of the process *quicksort([2,1,3],X)*. When invoked, this process can reduce itself with Clause (1) as follows:

quicksort([2,1,3],X) ← qsort([2,1,3],X\[ ])

qsort([2,1,3],X\[ ]) in turn has two clauses, but only Clause (1) unifies, resulting in the reduction:

qsort([2,1,3],X\[ ]) ←
    partition([1,3],2,Y,Z), qsort(Y?,X\[2 | W]), qsort(Z?,W\[ ])

The system now contains three processes. The two *qsort* processes are suspended, since they can proceed only by instantiating their first argument, which in both cases are read-only, either to [_|_] or to [ ]. The *partition* process, on the other hand, has two unifiable clauses — (1) and (2). It invokes two systems, for the two guards in these clauses, but only the first one, *1 < 3*, terminates successfully, and Clause (1) is used:

partition([1,3],2,[1 | X],Y) ← partition([3],2,X,Y)

During this reduction, the first argument of the first *qsort* process is instantiated to *[1 | X]*, so it can proceed:

qsort([1 | X], Y\[2 | Z])←

partition(X?, 1, V, W), qsort(V?, Y\[1 | Z1]), qsort(W?,Z1\[2 | Z])

However, all three new processes are suspended. The only process that can proceed is *partition([3],2,X,[3 | Y])*:

partition([3],2,X,[3 | Y]) ← partition([ ],2,X,Y)

This reduction instantiated the next element on *qsort*'s input stream, so it can proceed:

qsort([3 | X],Y\[ ])←
     partition(X?,3,U,V), qsort(U?,Y\[3 | Y1]), qsort(V?,Y1\[ ])

But, again, all new processes are suspended. All reductions left use unit clauses,

partition([ ], 2, [ ], [ ]) ← true
partition([ ], 1, [ ], [ ]) ← true
qsort([ ], [1 | X]\[1 | X]) ← true
qsort([ ], [2 | X]\[2 | X]) ← true
partition([ ], 3, [ ], [ ]) ← true
qsort([ ], [3 | X]\[3 | X]) ← true
qsort([ ], [ ]\[ ]) ← true

and the computation successfully terminates, with output substitution *X=[1,2,3]*.

The computation of the *quicksort* program resembles the computation of the corresponding Lisp program, provided that it uses *rplacd* and Lenient-*cons* (Friedman and Wise, 1976a).

2.4 Programming Examples

The power of Concurrent Prolog comes from the rich set of elegant programming techniques it supports. The example programs below intend to demonstrate some of them. The tool needed to understand and develop programs written in a high-level language is a mastery of the programming idioms and techniques the programming language lends itself to. Hence, when describing a program, we also attempt to identify the programming idioms and paradigms it exemplifies.

All programs numbered "Program 2.*n*:" have been debugged and tested using the interpreter described in Section 2.5, whose code is included in the appendix. Their code shown is readily executable without any modifications or additions, unless stated otherwise, with the mini-interpreter in Program 2.18, which lacks debugging and statistics functions. To run interactively, some of these programs need additional terminal interface programs, which are included in the appendix as well.

We tried to follow several notational conventions, demonstrated by the following Concurrent Prolog program for summing a stream of integers.

To denote a stream of elements, we use the variable name S or the suffix s. For example, a stream of X's is usually denoted by Xs, as in $[X \mid Xs]$. If a tail recursive (=iterative) program modifies some of its local arguments, then the variable denoting the modified value has the suffix 1, such as in $N1$ (a prime N' may be better, but is not supported by the current Prolog-10 syntax).

We use two procedures with the same name but different arities to initialize the local variables of a process and to hide their internal representation from the caller. Typically, the process with fewer arguments is invoked, and in turn invokes the other process with its local variables initialized, as in Program 2.2.

> sum(S, Total) ← sum(S?, 0, Total).
>
> sum([X | Xs], N, Total) ←
>   plus(X, N, N1), sum(Xs?, N1, Total).
> sum([ ], N, N).

Program 2.2: Summing the elements of a stream

The read-only annotation in the initialization call $sum(S?,0,N)$ is not strictly necessary, if $sum(S,N)$ is always called with S marked as read-only, but serves as an extra precaution, in case the caller forgets.

2.4.1 Divide and conquer with communication

The concurrent quicksort program combines divide-and-conquer with process communication. In quicksort, however, the "divider" process communicates with the two "conquering" processes, but the latter two do not communicate with each other.

Another algorithm that combines divide-and-conquer with process communication was suggested by Leslie Lamport (1982). In Lamport's algorithm the "conquering" processes do communicate. The problem is to number the leaves of a tree; its solution reads as follows: " The *count* algorithm is a recursive concurrent algorithm for numbering leaves from 'left to right'. When called on a node, it does the following:

> If the node is a leaf
>   then obtain the number of leaves to the left,
>   add one to obtain this leaf's number,
>   send this number to the leaf on the right,
>   else call *count* for each of the sons of this node.
> The obvious modifications are made when a node is at the
> left hand or the right hand edge of the tree..."

Program 2.3 implements the algorithm for binary trees with labeled leaves, constructed from the terms *leaf*(*X*) and *tree*(*L*,*R*). The procedure *count*(*T*) is invoked with the tree *T* whose leaves are to be numbered. It then calls an auxiliary procedure *count*(*T,N1,N2*), whose semantics is "*T* is a binary tree with leaves numbered sequentially from *N1* to *N2–1*".

count(T) ← count(T?, 0, N).

count(leaf(N), N, N1) ← plus(N, 1, N1).
count(tree(L, R), N, N2) ← count(L, N, N1), count(R, N1, N2).

Program 2.3: Numbering the leaves of a tree

The process *plus*(*X,Y,Z*) computes the relation "*X* plus *Y* is *Z*". It waits until at least two of its arguments are determined, then unifies the third with the appropriate number and terminates. Its implementation is shown in the appendix.

Note that no modifications are needed when the node is at the edge of a tree.

An implementation of Lamport's algorithm in Concurrent And/Or Programs is shown by Harel and Nehab (1982).

2.4.2 Perpetual processes with internal states

Traditionally, logic-programming researchers have emphasized the stateless, side-effect free, declarative style of programming in logic. This emphasis is justified when the problems to be solved can be described without reference to the state of the computation, and it helps to show the difference between logic programming and conventional programming. However, when discussing concurrent computations, sometimes the very nature of the problem contains reference to the state of the computation. Hence a slightly different "ideology" has to be adopted to understand the role of logic programming in concurrent computations.

In sequential logic programming, the axiom *A* ← *B* has, in addition to the declarative, model-theoretic reading: "*A* is true if *B* is true", also the operational, problem-reduction reading: "to solve *A*, solve *B*". In concurrent logic programming, a third kind of reading is necessary, the behavioral reading: "process *A* can reduce itself to system *B*". Under the behavioral reading, a concurrent logic program simultaneously provides an axiomatic definition of the possible behaviors of a process, and the "code" the process is executing.

As demonstrated below, a logic program that implements a concurrent system is stateless, side-effect free, and provides an axiomatic description of a set of legal behaviors of a system of processes, which have a state. Hence it is meaningful to talk about the implementation of processes with states by pure logic programs.

As mentioned earlier, the state of a process is the value of its arguments. According to the abstract computation model, a process cannot actively change its state, but only reduce itself to other processes. Hence, theoretically, Concurrent Prolog supports only ephemeral processes whose state is not self-modifiable. However, both from an intuitive and an implementation point of view, a process that calls itself recursively with different arguments can be viewed as a perpetual process that changes its state. If the implementation incorporates tail-recursion optimization, then the same process frame may actually be used for the different incarnations of such a process.

Under the behavioral interpretation, the arguments of the process not shared by other processes can be viewed as its internal state, since they can neither be accessed nor modified by other processes. The situation can be summarized with the following "equation":

tail recursion + local variables = perpetual process with internal state

The ability to implement multiple perpetual processes is one reason for the increased power of Concurrent Prolog over Sequential Prolog. Sequential Prolog can implement one perpetual process without side-effects, for example a text-editor (Warren, 1982b). However, when multiple independent global objects have to be manipulated, most programmers in Sequential Prolog resort to side-effects. In Concurrent Prolog, on the other hand, global data-structures are implemented by multiple perpetual processes in a side-effect free way. Instead of accessing global data using "read" and "write" operations, messages are sent to the process holding the data, which in turn informs the sender of the content of the data and/or modifies it, according to the message.

This approach is similar to the Actors (Hewitt, 1974) and Smalltalk approach in spirit (Ingalls,1978). However, in contrast with the pure operational character of other object-oriented formalisms, the logic programs that describe such processes enjoy the declarative/operational duality that singles out the logic programming solutions to other computing problems. In particular, the Concurrent Prolog implementation of a perpetual process with an internal state resembles the axiomatic definition of an abstract data type. For example, consider the implementation of a stack process in Program 2.4.

```
(0)   stack(S) ← stack(S?, [ ]).
(1)   stack([pop(X) | S], [X |X s]) ← stack(S?, Xs).
(2)   stack([push(X) | S], Xs) ← stack(S?, [X | Xs]).
(3)   stack([ ], [ ]).
```

Program 2.4: A stack process

A stack process has two arguments: the first is an input stream; the second stores the stack content, represented as a list of stack elements.

A stack process is invoked with the call *stack(S?)*, where *S* is the input stream. Using the first clause in Program 2.4, it initializes itself with an empty stack. It then iterates, processing the messages on its input stream. If no message is available, the process suspends, due to the read-only annotation S? in the recursive calls to *stack*. Otherwise, one of the following three cases, which correspond to the last three clauses in the program, must apply:

- Clause (1) applies if the next message on the input stream is $pop(X)$, and the stack is nonempty. It unifies X with the top of the stack and iterates with the rest of the input stream and the rest of the stack.

- Clause (2) applies if the next message is $push(X)$. It adds X to the top of the stack and iterates with the rest of the input stream and the new stack.

- Clause (3) applies if the end of the input stream is reached *and* the stack is empty. It simply terminates.

If none of these cases apply, the process fails. In particular, the process fails if the next message is $pop(X)$ and the stack is empty, or if the end of the input stream is reached and the stack is nonempty.

The model-theoretic semantics of the stack program is simple. The interpretation of the stack program contains all goals $stack(S,[\,])$ in which S is a balanced list over the alphabet $pop(X)$ and $push(X)$, where X ranges over the elements of the Herbrand universe of Program 2.4 and $pop(X)$ is considered to be the matching right parenthesis to $push(X)$, for any term X. The interpretation also contains all goals $stack(S,[X_1,X_2,\ldots,X_n])$, where S is a list that can be balanced by prefixing it with $push(X_n)$, $push(X_{n-1})$, $\ldots$, $push(X_2)$, $push(X_1)$.

It is easy to augment or modify the stack program. For example, if we want the stack process to terminate successfully even if the stack is not empty, then the third clause can be modified to be $stack([\,],\_)$. The interpretation of the program then grows to include all goals $stack(S,[\,])$ in which S is a prefix of some balanced list over $push(X)$ and $pop(X)$.

To make the stack process understand the message $is\_empty(X)$, by unifying X with *true* if the stack is currently empty and with *false* otherwise, we add the following two clauses to Program 2.4:

    stack([is_empty(true) | S], [ ]) ← stack(S?, [ ]).
    stack([is_empty(false) | S], [X | Xs]) ← stack(S?, [X | Xs]).

Typically, a process sends $pop(X)$ with X uninstantiated and waits for X to be instantiated when the message is processed by the stack. This habit can be made the rule: we can enforce the sender of a $pop(X)$ message to leave X uninstantiated, by replacing the first clause of Program 2.4 by the clause:

    stack([pop(X?) | S], [X | Xs]) ← stack(S?, Xs).

If $pop(X)$ is sent to a stack executing the modified program, with X instantiated, then the stack process fails.

It is not, however, always desirable to enforce this restriction. For example, Program 2.5, which tests whether a list (stream) is balanced over the alphabet '(', ')', '{', '}', would become more cumbersome if this restriction were in effect.

balanced(X) ← balanced(X, Y), stack(Y?).

balanced(['(' | X], [push('(') | Y]) ← balanced(X?, Y).
balanced(['{' | X], [push('{') | Y]) ← balanced(X?, Y).
balanced([')' | X], [pop(|(') | Y]) ← balanced(X?, Y).
balanced(['}' | X], [pop('{') | Y]) ← balanced(X?, Y).
balanced([ ], [ ]).

Program 2.5: Testing balanced lists

The *balanced* process is invoked with an input stream and then spawns two processes: one translates the input stream into a stream of stack messages; the other is a stack, which executes Program 2.4.

The *balanced* program can be explained using Actor's jargon (Hewitt, 1973). When the *balanced* process receives an '(' message, it sends a *push*('(') message to the stack; it operates similarly on an '{' message. When it receives an ')' message, it sends a *pop*(X) message to the stack and verifies that X='('; similarly with '}'. When the end of the message stream is reached, it terminates, and terminates its communication stream with the stack. If both processes terminate successfully, then the whole computation terminates, and the stream is balanced.

The *balanced* program fails if the list is not balanced or contains illegal elements. It is easy to modify *balanced* so it returns *true* if the list is balanced, *false* if it is imbalanced, and fails if it contains illegal elements. This can be done by adding another argument to the two *balanced* predicates, replacing the last clause with *balanced*([ ], [*is_empty*(*Response*)], *Response*), and adding to Program 2.4 the clauses for *is_empty*.

This example is a bit contrived, since *balanced* can be implemented with a local stack, rather than with a stack process. We leave this as an exercise to the reader.

2.4.3 The readers and writers problem

Many problems in which several processes share some resource can be modeled after the readers and writers problem (Hoare, 1974). A logic program solution for a specific readers and writers problem can be obtained by instantiating the following program scheme, based on an idea by Bowen and Kowalski (1982).

process([Transaction | S], Data) ←
    respond(Transaction, Data, NewData), process(S?, NewData?).
process([ ], _).

The process *process* has two arguments: one is a stream of transactions from several processes, serialized by *merge* processes (explained below); the other contains the data. On each transaction, the process *respond* is invoked with the transactions and the data. *respond* returns the modified data and possibly instantiates undetermined variables in the message.

The stack program is an instance of this scheme: *push* and *pop* messages "write" on the shared data, i.e., cause it to be modified, and the *is_empty* message only "reads" the data, without modifying it. The stack process responds to the "read" transaction $is\_empty(X)$ by instantiating X to *true* or *false*; it responds to the "write" transaction $push(X)$ by adding X to the top of the stack; and it responds to the "read/write" transaction $pop(X)$ by removing the top element from the stack and unifying it with X.

This scheme can be improved by distinguishing between "read" transactions that only query the data without modifying it and "write" transactions, which also modify the data. By doing so, a contiguous sequence of "reads" can be served in parallel, since the tail recursive call to *process* can be performed with *Data* rather than with *NewData*, and hence need not wait for the completion of *respond*. Once a "write" is received, however, this optimization cannot be done, since *process* must iterate with *NewData*.

process([read(Args) | S], Data) ←
    respond(read(Args), Data, _), process(S?, Data).
process([write(Args) | S], Data) ←
    respond(write(Args), Data, NewData), process(S?, NewData?).
process([ ], _).

Figure 2.4: A schematic solution to the readers and writers problem

Figure 2.4 contains a schematic implementation of this solution, assuming that transactions are either *read(Args)* or *write(Args)*.

2.4.4 An airline reservation system

A classical instance of the readers and writers problem is the airline reservation system problem. Bryant and Dennis (1982) used this system as a benchmark problem for comparing different approaches to concurrent programming. We contribute our own version to the contest.

Their description of the problem reads as follows:

"The process for the airline reservation system contains information about the flights of a single airline. Initially, each flight has 100 seats available. The system can accept two kinds of commands. To reserve seats on a flight an agent gives the command (*'reserve',f,n*). If at least *n* seats are available on flight *f*, seats will be reserved, and the system will respond with the message *true*. If that many seats are not available, the system will respond with the message *false*. To find out how many seats are available on flight *f*, a system user gives the command (*'info',f*). The system will respond with the number of seats which are available on the flight at the time the command is processed". (from Bryant and Dennis, 1982, p. 430)

Program 2.6 implements the system, using two primitive procedures: $value(A,N,V)$, which computes the relation: "the value of the Nth element of A is V", and $modify(A,N,V,A1)$, which computes the relation "changing the Nth element of A to V gives $A1$".

(1)   database([info(Flight, Seats) | S], DB) ←
        value(DB, Flight, Seats),
        database(S?, DB).

(2)   database([reserve(Flight, Seats, Response) | S], DB) ←
        reserve(Flight, Seats, DB, Response, DB1) |
        database(S?, DB1).

(3)   database([ ], _).

(1)   reserve(Flight, Seats, DB, Response, DB1) ←
        value(DB, Flight, FreeSeats),
        LeftSeats := FreeSeats – Seats,
        respond(DB, LeftSeats, Flight, Response, DB1).

(1)   respond(DB, Seats, Flight, true, DB1) ←
        0 ≤ Seats | modify(DB, Flight, Seats, DB1).

(2)   respond(DB, Seats, _, false, DB) ←
        Seats < 0 | true.

Program 2.6: An airline reservation system.

database is the main process. It has two arguments: an input stream of transactions and flight-availability data. Clause (1) handles requests for availability information. On a message *info(Flight, Seats)*, it unifies *Seats* with the number of free seats available on flight *Flight* and iterates with the rest of the input stream and the unmodified database. Clause (2) handles reservation requests. It uses a procedure *reserve(Flight,Seats,DB,Response,DB1)*, which unifies *Response* with *true* if the number of available seats in flight *Flight* is less than or equal to *Seats*, otherwise it unifies *Response* with *false*. It returns in *DB1* the resulting database. Clause (3) terminates the process when the end of the input stream is reached.

The *reserve* process invokes three concurrent processes. The first one finds the number of available seats, the second computes the number of free seats left if the request is granted, and the third responds to the request accordingly. The three processes are synchronized by the availability of input data. ':=' waits for *value* to determine the value of *FreeSeats*, and the guards of *respond* wait for ':=' to compute *LeftSeats*.

The *respond* procedure has two clauses. Clause (1) returns *true* and modifies the database if the number of seats left after granting the reservation is greater or equal to 0. Otherwise, Clause (2) returns *false*, without modifying the database.

The process $X \leq Y$ suspends until both of its arguments are determined and then succeeds or fails according to their values.

The airline reservation system is not very interesting unless it can serve many users concurrently. This is achieved by merging all streams of queries of the clients into one, as described in the following section.

2.4.5 Merging streams

Many concurrent programming languages use streams to support process communication. Streams are typically introduced as a new data-type, to which specialized "read" and "write" operations are defined (Ackerman, 1982; Kahn and MacQueen, 1977). The main difference between streams and lists is that the former are only partially determined at each point of the computation. Since partially determined (incomplete) data-structures are supported by Prolog — both sequential and concurrent — there is no need to introduce a new data-structure into Prolog in order to implement streams, and the usual list constructor will do. Unification is used to "read" or "write" the next stream element, and read-only annotations distinguish between the "readers" and the "writers" of a stream.

The use of streams was already demonstrated in the *quicksort* and *balanced* programs above.

A process can have several input and/or output streams, and use them to communicate with several other processes; but the number of these streams is fixed for any given process. It is sometimes convenient to determine or change at runtime the number of processes communicating with another process; this can be achieved by merging communication streams.

In some languages *merge* is a built-in primitive (Arvind and Brock, 1982). Logic programs, on the other hand, can express this relation directly, as shown by Clark (Chapter 1). Program 2.7 adapts and Gregory their implementation to Concurrent Prolog. It implements the process *merge(X,Y,Z)*, which computes the relation "Z contains the elements of X and Y, preserving the relative order of their elements".

> merge([X | Xs], Ys, [X | Zs]) ← merge(Xs?, Ys?, Zs).
> merge(Xs, [Y | Ys], [Y | Zs]) ← merge(Xs?, Ys?, Zs).
> merge(Xs, [ ], Xs).
> merge([ ], Ys, Ys).

Program 2.7: Merging two streams

The read-only annotation on *Ys* in the first clause and on *Xs* in the second clause are superfluous, provided that *merge* is initially invoked with its two input streams annotated read-only.

There is an ongoing discussion concerning the desired properties of a *merge* operator and how it can be specified (Park, 1980). Smyth (1982), apparently unaware of the work of Clark and Gregory, has suggested the axioms in Program 2.7 as a *specification* of a fair merge operator and has shown that this specification has desirable mathematical properties, such as commutativity and associativity.

We do not find the properties shown by Smyth sufficient, since they do not guarantee bounded-waiting. In other words, given the positions of two elements in an input stream, we cannot bound the difference between their positions in the output stream on the basis of this information alone. In implementation terms, if two elements are ready in both input streams, then, without any additional information on how the logic program is executed, we cannot bound the number of merge process reductions needed for the two elements to appear in the output stream.

However, since for us the logic program is also an implementation of the *merge* operator, not only a specification, we can employ information concerning the behavior of the abstract Concurrent Prolog machine (e.g., fairness of the scheduler) to determine whether the program achieves the desired effect or not.

Assume that the clauses in the program are ordered (say, by text order), and assume that a process A has several clauses $A_i \leftarrow B_i$, $1 \leq i \leq n$ with empty guards whose heads unify with a process A without instantiating read-only variables. We say that a Concurrent Prolog abstract machine is *stable* if it always chooses the first such clause $A_1 \leftarrow B_1$ to reduce the process A.

A Concurrent Prolog abstract machine for which this condition holds if the number of steps required to unify A with A_1 is less than or equal to those required to unify A with A_i, for $1 < i \leq n$, is called *weakly stable*. Note that a stable machine is also weakly stable.

Any reasonable sequential Concurrent Prolog interpreter should be stable, unless one makes a special effort to eliminate this property, as suggested by Dijkstra (1976). For example, the interpreter in Program 2.17 is stable. We suspect that any distributed Concurrent Prolog machine should be weakly stable, or at least weakly stable with high probability.

If the implementation is stable, then the *merge* program clearly does not achieve bounded waiting. If both streams have elements ready, then the first stream will always be chosen. When $merge(X,Y,Z)$ is invoked with X and Y finite and determined, Program 2.7 running on a stable machine simply concatenates X to Y. In extreme cases, when infinite computations are involved, this behavior can cause elements of the second stream to wait indefinitely before they appear in the output stream.

Nevertheless, this behavior is desirable in some cases. Since the first stream has "higher-priority" than the second, this program, or a similar one, can implement interrupts, where the second stream carries the normal communication, and the first one carries exceptional or urgent communication, which should interrupt the normal execution. Several such merge processes can be composed to implement interrupts with different relative priorities.

However, if a bounded-waiting merge is desirable, it can be implemented in at least two ways, provided the Concurrent Prolog machine is weakly stable. One is to alternate priorities between the two streams, an idea suggested by Johnson (1981) in the context of functional concurrent programming, and implemented by the following program:

merge([X | Xs], Ys, [X | Zs]) ← merge(Ys, Xs?, Zs).
merge(Xs, [Y | Ys], [Y | Zs]) ← merge(Ys?, Xs, Zs).

which has base clauses as before. In every reduction the first stream becomes the second, and vice versa. Note that the priority makes a difference only if both streams have elements ready; if only one stream is ready, then its elements are moved to the output stream regardless of priorities.

To fairly merge more than two streams, one can either compose this merge program, such as in the system

merge(X1?, X2?, X), merge(Y1?, Y2?, Y), merge(X?, Y?, Z)

or use an n-ary merge. The same priority-based technique generalizes to merging n streams, for any fixed n, and the resulting program is a kind of round-robin stream-scheduler. Its ith recursive clause is:

merge(X_1, X_2, ..., [X | X_i], ..., X_n, [X | Ys]) ←
    merge(X_2, X_3, ..., X_i?, ..., X_n, X_1, Ys).

This program rotates priorities between its streams. In each reduction the highest priority stream becomes the one with the least priority, and all other streams increase their relative priorities by one.

Another strategy to implement a fair merge is to decrease the priority of a stream that has been "read". The ith recursive clause in this type of n-ary merge is:

$$\text{merge}(X_1, \ldots, [X \mid X_i], \ldots, X_n, [X \mid Ys]) \leftarrow$$
$$\text{merge}(X_1, \ldots, X_{i-1}, X_{i+1}, \ldots, X_n, X_i?, Ys).$$

It is easy to show that if the Concurrent Prolog machine is weakly stable then both n-ary merge programs guarantee n-bounded waiting, which means that if the first element of an input stream is determined, then after at most n reductions of *merge* this element will appear in the output stream. The choice between the two strategies is application dependent, but we conjecture that in any reasonable Concurrent Prolog machine the round-robin scheduler would be more efficient, since the other strategy inspects most often the less busy streams before it finds a stream with an element ready.

We expect these scheduling strategies to be effective even in an implementation that is weakly stable with high probability only[2].

2.4.6 The MSG message-sending system

A simple application of the *merge* program is shown by Johnson (1981): "MSG is a full duplex message sending system for two computer terminals, *A* and *B*. Input from *A*'s (respectively *B*'s) keyboard, *K1* (*K2*) is echoed on *A*'s (*B*'s) screen, *S1* (*S2*). However, when *K1* (*K2*) issues a "send", the following form should be displayed *in a timely fashion* on *S2* (*S1*)". (From Johnson, 1981, p. 15)

$\text{msg}((K1, S1), (K2, S2)) \leftarrow$
    $\text{select}(K1?, K11, K12), \text{select}(K2?, K22, K21),$
    $\text{merge}(K21?, K11?, S1), \text{merge}(K12?, K22?, S2).$

$\text{select}([\text{send}(X) \mid Xs], [\text{send}(X) \mid Ys], [X \mid Zs]) \leftarrow$
    $\text{select}(Xs?, Ys, Zs).$
$\text{select}([X \mid Xs], [X \mid Ys], Zs) \leftarrow$
    $X \neq \text{send}(\_) \mid \text{select}(Xs?, Ys, Zs).$
$\text{select}([\,], [\,], [\,]).$

$\text{merge}(X,Y,Z) \leftarrow$
    See Program 2.7.

Program 2.8: The MSG system

---

[2] See Shapiro and Mierowsky , Chapter 14, Shapiro and Safra, Chapter 15, Saraswat, Chapter 16, and Tribble et al., Chapter 17 for further treatment of this subject.

The MSG system is invoked by the call *msg((K1?,S1),(K2?,S2))*, and is implemented by Program 2.8 which invokes a system whose configuration is shown in Figure 2.5.

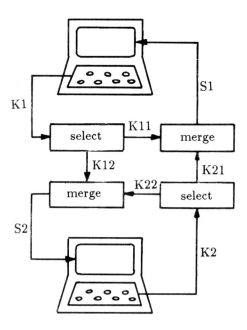

Figure 2.5: The MSG system

The *select* procedure selects the output streams on which the keyboard input is echoed. It uses a built-in Concurrent Prolog procedure, $X \neq Y$ (read "different"), which succeeds if and when it is established that X and Y are different, i.e. will not unify. Concurrent Prolog's $X \neq Y$ is a variant of a built-in procedur of Prolog-II (Colmerauer et al., 1981). A Prolog implementation of $X \neq Y$ is included in the appendix. The code needed to test the MSG system on a single terminal is included in the appendix as well.

2.4.7 A Unix-like shell

The following program fragments implement some of the functions of the Unix shell (Richie and Thompson, 1974).

The shell in Figure 2.6 receives a stream of commands and executes them. If the stream contains the abort command *control-C*, then it aborts the current

```
shell([X | Xs]) ← command(X) | shell(Xs?).
shell(Xs) ← control_c(Xs, Ys) | shell(Ys?).

control_c([X | Xs], Ys) ←
     X ≠ '↑C' | control_c(Xs?, Ys).
control_c(['↑C' |Xs], Xs).
```

Figure 2.6: A shell that handles an *abort* interrupt

execution, flushes the input stream until after the *control-C*, and resumes execution from there. The shell achieves this by racing the two guards. The first tried to solve the command X; the second to find a *control-C* in the input stream. The first to succeed commits the shell to the appropriate action.

Assuming that the input stream is generated by a user at a terminal, then such a user can delay typing *control-C* until he thinks that the process X may be looping, or discovers that X is not really the process he wanted to run, and types *control-C* then.

This program achieves the desired effect only if both guards are executed in parallel and hence does not run correctly on our interpreter, as explained in Section 2.5. Note that the program works correctly even if one types ahead of the execution speed of the shell.

Another convenient feature of the Unix shell is the ability of the user to specify that a process should run in the background. This increases the responsiveness of the system and enables the user to do other things while non-interactive programs such as a compiler are running. This behavior is easily achieved in Concurrent Prolog, as shown by the program fragment in Figure 2.7.

```
shell([fg(X) | Xs]) ← command(X) | shell(Xs?).
shell([bg(X) | Xs]) ← command(X), shell(Xs?).
shell([ ]).
```

Figure 2.7: A shell that handles background and foreground processes

The shell assumes that the user commands are tagged either *fg* or *bg*. If the command is intended to be executed in the "foreground", then the shell executes it as a guard, and only after it terminates it iterates, ready to receive the next command on the input stream. On the other hand, if the command is to be executed in the background, the shell spawns it as a sibling process and is immediately available to execute the next command.

Note that these code fragments do not handle terminal output. Presumably, if a process is spawned in the background, then a third *merge* process should be invoked to allow both the shell and the background process to communicate with the user[3].

2.4.8 Queues

Merged streams allow many client processes to share one resource; but when several client processes want to share several resources effectively, a more complex buffering strategy is needed. Such buffering can be obtained with a simple FIFO queue: a client who requires the service of a resource enqueues its request. When a resource becomes available it dequeues the next request from the queue and serves it.

Note that if there is only one resource but many clients, one can obtain the effect of a FIFO queue by fairly merging all the requests into one stream and letting the resource serve the requests in the order in which they arrive.

Program 2.9 is a Concurrent Prolog implementation of a FIFO queue. It handles two types of messages: *enqueue*(X), on which it adds X to the tail of the queue, and *dequeue*(X) on which it removes the first element from the head of the queue and unifies it with X. It represents the queue using two streams — the *Head* stream that contains the dequeued elements, and the *Tail* stream that contains the enqueued elements. The content of the queue is defined to be the difference between the *Head* stream and the *Tail* stream.

```
(1)  queue(S) ←
        queue(S, X, X).
(2)  queue([dequeue(X) | S], [X | NewHead], Tail) ←
        queue(S?, NewHead, Tail).
(3)  queue([enqueue(X) | S], Head, [X | NewTail]) ←
        queue(S?, Head, NewTail).
(4)  queue([ ], _, _).
```

Program 2.9: A queue

Clause (1) initializes the queue with the *Head* and *Tail* streams equal and undetermined. Clause (2) unifies dequeued elements with elements of the *Head* stream, and Clause (3) unifies enqueued elements with elements of the *Tail* stream. Clause (4) terminates the queue process when the end of the input stream is reached. The read-only annotation of the stream S in the recursive calls ensures that the queue process waits for the next message to be determined and does not decide to enqueue or dequeue an element on its own.

This program is very concise and has a simple model theoretic semantics. Its interpretation contains all goals *queue*(S,H,T) such that S is a list of terms

---

[3] See Shapiro, Chapter 19, and Hirsch et al., Chapter 20, for further treatment of the subject.

enqueue(X) and *dequeue*(X), T equals the list of X's for which *enqueue*(X) is in S, and H equals the list of X's for which *dequeue*(X) appears in S, where elements in both lists preserve the relative order of their corresponding terms in S. If we restrict the interpretation to goals in which $H=T$, as done by the Clause (1), which initializes the queue, then the list of enqueued elements in S is identical to the list of dequeued elements in S, as the intuitive definition of a queue requires.

Operationally, things are a bit more tricky. Under the expected use of a queue, *enqueue*(X) messages are sent with X determined, and *dequeue*(X) with X undetermined; typically, the sender of *dequeue*(X) waits for X to be determined. Since the *Head* and *Tail* streams are initially undetermined and equal, then so long as more elements are enqueued then dequeued, the *Tail* stream runs ahead of the *Head*, and the difference between the two are exactly the elements that were enqueued but not dequeued yet. However, if the number of *dequeue* messages received exceeds that of enqueue messages, then an interesting thing happens — the content of the queue becomes "negative". The *Head* runs ahead of the *Tail*, resulting in the queue containing a negative sequence of undetermined elements, one for each excessive *dequeue* message. Although the queue process serves each *dequeue*(X) message as it comes, if the queue is empty it does not unify X with a concrete element, but only generates another undetermined stream element. When enough *enqueue* messages are received, the *Tail* will reach this element, and unify it with the next enqueued element.

In Lisp implementation jargon, *Head* and *Tail* are pointers to *cons* cells of the same list. An *enqueue* message advances the *Tail* pointer by one, and a *dequeue* message advances the *Head* pointer by one. When the *Head* pointer overtakes the *Tail*, it starts allocating *cons* cells and unifies their *car* with the undetermined variables X in the messages *dequeue*(X). When the *Tail* pointer is advanced, it unifies the *car* fields of these cells with the enqueued elements.

It is interesting to observe that this behavior is compatible with common properties of queues, such as the associativity of queue concatenation. The concatenation of the two difference-lists $X\backslash Y$ and $Y\backslash Z$ is defined to be $X\backslash Z$. If we concatenate a queue $X\backslash[X1,X2,X3 \mid X]$ which contains minus three undetermined elements with a queue $[a,b,c,d,e\mid Y]\backslash Y$ which contains five elements, then the result will be the queue $[d,e\mid Y]\backslash Y$ with two elements, where the "negative" elements $[X1,X2,X3]$ are unified with $[a,b,c]$.

All this behavior is transparent to the user of a queue. A sender of a *dequeue*(X) message does not know whether X becomes determined when the queue process has actually received this message, or a bit later, when enough *enqueue* messages have arrived.

2.4.9 A simulator of a multiprocessor Concurrent Prolog machine

The simulator of a multiprocessor Concurrent Prolog machine in Program 2.10 is an exercise in utilizing the queue and merge programs. The simulator is invoked with a number N and a process X. It constructs a system of one queue, N processor-simulators, and a balanced-tree-shaped network of *2N–1* merge processes that support the communication between the processors and the queue.

```
processors(N, X) ←
    queue(S?, [X | Xs], Xs), processors(1, N, S).

processors(N, N, Q) ←
    processor(N, true, Q).
processors(N1, N4, Q) ←
    N2 is (N1+N4)/2, N3 is N2+1 |
    processors(N1, N2, Q1),
    processors(N3, N4, Q2),
    merge(Q1?, Q2?, Q).

processor(N, true, [dequeue(X) | Q]) ←
    processor(N, X?, Q).
processor(N, (A, B), [enqueue(A)|Q]) ←
    processor(N, B, Q).
processor(N, suspended(A), [dequeue(B), enqueue(A) | Q]) ←
    processor(N, B?, Q).
processor(N, A, Q) ←
    reduce(A, B) | processor(N, B, Q).
```

Program 2.10: A simulator of a multiprocessor Concurrent Prolog
machine

Each processor is invoked with an identifier N, a goal *true*, and communication stream Q to a queue. A processor implements the following algorithm:

- If its goal is *true*, it sends a *dequeue*(X) message to the queue and iterates with X.

- If its goal is (B,C), then it enqueues B and iterates with C.

- If its goal is *suspended*(A), it sends an *enqueue*(A) message and a *dequeue*(B) message to the queue and iterates with B.

- If its goal is reducible to B, then it iterates with B.

Program 2.10 abstracts away the management of the binding environment and deals only with the flow of control. The procedure *reduce* belongs to the underlying Concurrent Prolog interpreter, explained in Section 2.5.

A window-manager system, written in Concurrent Prolog, was used to animate the behavior of the simulator. We have implemented a program that runs each processor in a separate window and shows the progress of the computation. It creates a recursive structure of windows, depending on the number of processors in the network, as shown in Figure 2.8, and shows the progress of each processor and the content of the communication streams and the queue. The window system is described by Shapiro and Takeuchi (Chapter 29).

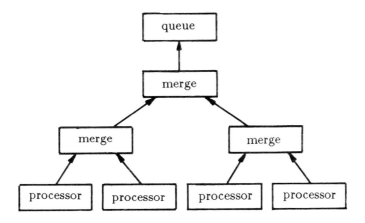

Figure 2.8: A multiprocessor Concurrent Prolog machine

In the trace below the messages from the Nth processor are:

dequeue(N): *A*   The processor requests a new process from the queue since its current process *A* cannot be reduced any further, either because *A* is *true* or because it is suspended.

enqueue(N): *A*   The processor enqueued process *A*, since it has more than one process.

reduction(N): *A←B* The processor reduced process *A* to system *B*.

We invoke the Concurrent Prolog interpreter of the appendix with the call to the simulator to solve the goal *qsort([2,1],X)* with four processors.

```
| ?- solve(processors(4, qsort([2, 1, 3], X))).

dequeue(1): true
dequeue(2): true
dequeue(3): true
dequeue(4): true
```

First the four processors complete the solution of the goal *true*, with which they were invoked, and send a *dequeue* message to the queue.

> reduce(1): qsort([2, 1, 3], X) ← qsort1([2, 1, 3], X\[ ])
> reduce(1): qsort1([2, 1, 3], X\[ ])←
>   partition([1, 3], 2, Y, Z), qsort1(Y?, X\[2 | W]), qsort1(Z?, W\[ ])

Processor 1 received the input goal, it reduced it twice, and now it enqueues two out of three new processes.

> enqueue(1): partition([1, 3], 2, X, Y)
> enqueue(1): qsort1(X?, Y\[2 | Z])

Processor 3 received the process enqueued by 1 and reduces it:

> reduce(3): (partition([1, 3], 2, [1 | X], Y) ← partition([3], 2, X, Y))

As a result the second process enqueued by Processor 1 and dequeued by Processor 2 becomes reducible:

> reduce(2): (qsort1([1 | X], Y\[2 | Z]) ←
>   partition(X?, 1, V, W), qsort1(V?, Y\[1 | Z1]), qsort1(W?, Z1\[2 | Z]))

Processor 3 completes the reduction, while 1 enqueues its suspended process and requests a new one and reduces it, and 2 enqueues two of the three processes in its system.

> reduce(3): (partition([3], 2, X, [3 | Y])←
>   partition([ ], 2, X, Y))
> dequeue(1): qsort1([3 | X], Y\[ ])
> enqueue(2): partition(X?, 1, Y, Z)
> reduce(3): (partition([ ], 2, [ ], [ ]) ← true)
> reduce(1): (qsort1([3], X\[ ]) ←
>   partition([ ], 3, Y, Z), qsort1(Y?, X\[3 | W]), qsort1(Z?, W\[ ]))
> enqueue(2): qsort1(X?, Y\[1 | Z])
> dequeue(3): true

following that all that remain are processes that reduce themselves to *true*:

> reduce(4): (partition([ ], 1, [ ], [ ]) ← true)
> enqueue(1): partition([ ], 3, X, Y)
> reduce(2): (qsort1([ ], [2 | X]\[2 | X]) ← true)
> reduce(3): (qsort1([ ], [1, 2 | X]\[1, 2 | X]) ← true)
> dequeue(4): true
> enqueue(1): qsort1(X?, Y\[3 | Z])
> dequeue(2): true
> dequeue(3): true

reduce(4): (partition([ ], 3, [ ], [ ]) ← true)
reduce(1): (qsort1([ ], [ ]\[ ])← true)
reduce(3): (qsort1([ ], [3]\[3]) ← true)
dequeue(4): true
dequeue(1): true
dequeue(3): true

Now all processors have sent a *dequeue* message to the queue and wait for its response, but the queue is empty. This deadlock is detected by the interpreter, which terminates and presents the locked processes and their interconnections. Note that the queue has minus four elements, one for every unsatisfied *dequeue* request from a processor.

∗ ∗ ∗ cycles: 17
∗ ∗ ∗ Deadlock detected. Locked processes:
processor(1, X?, Y)
processor(2, Z?, U)
merge(U?, Y?, X1)
processor(3, Y1?, Z1)
processor(4, U1?, V1)
merge(V1?, Z1?, Y2)
merge(X1?, Y2?, V2)
queue(V2?, X3, [Z, U1, X, Y1 | X3])

The interpreter also provides some statistics on the execution of each process:

enqueue(1): 4
enqueue(2): 2
dequeue(1): 3
dequeue(2): 2
dequeue(3): 4
dequeue(4): 3
reduce(1): 5
reduce(2): 2
reduce(3): 5
reduce(4): 2

which shows the load distribution between the processors. Statistics on the behavior of the interpreter — how many reductions and suspensions occured at each level of process invocation — are also provided:

reduction(1): 180
reduction(2): 37
suspension(1): 83

suspension(2): 20

The rate of suspensions to reductions measures the scheduling overhead. In this example it is close to 50%. Finally, we also get the output of the computation, which is $X = [1,2,3]^4$.

2.4.10 Priority queues

A priority queue requires a different representation from a FIFO queue since it needs to be manipulated explicitly. In the following example a priority queue is represented as a list of pairs (X,P), where X is the element and P is its associated priority. On *enqueue(X,P)* the queue process inserts X to the list according to its priority; on *dequeue(X)* it removes X from the head of the list. Program 2.11 was our first attempt at implementing a priority queue.

(1)   queue(S) ← queue(S?, [ ]).

(2)   queue([dequeue(X) | S], [(X, _) | Q]) ←
           queue(S?, Q).

(3)   queue([enqueue(X, P) | S], Q) ←
           insert((X, P), Q?, Q1), queue(S?, Q1?).

(4)   queue([ ], _).

(1)   insert((X, P), [(X1, P1) | Q], [(X, P), (X1, P1) | Q]) ←
           P ≤ P1 | true.

(2)   insert((X, P), [(X1, P1) | Q], [(X1, P1) | Q1]) ←
           P1 < P | insert((X, P), Q?, Q1).

(3)   insert((X, P), [ ], [(X, P)]).

Program 2.11: A priority queue (first trial)

Although this program looks benign, it has a serious bug. The reader may wish to meditate on the program, trying to find the bug (or, alternatively, prove the program correct) before proceeding.

The queue process will fail if its next message is *dequeue(X)* and the list representing the queue is empty: only Clause (2) handles a *dequeue* message, and it attempts to unify the second argument of *queue* with a nonempty list. One would like in this case to suspend processing the *dequeue* messages until an *enqueue* message arrives and process the *enqueue* message first. This can be attained by splitting the requests into two streams, one for *enqueue* and one for *dequeue* messages, as done in Program 2.12. The new implementation serves

---

[4] See Shapiro, Chapter 13, Weinbaum and Shapiro, Chapter 36, for further treatment of this subject.

> (1)   queue(Es. Ds) ← queue(Es?, Ds?, [ ]).
> (2)   queue(Es, [dequeue(X) | Ds], [(X, _) | Q]) ←
>   queue(Es, Ds?, Q).
> (3)   queue([enqueue(X, P) | Es], Ds, Q) ←
>   insert((X, P), Q?, Q1), queue(Es?, Ds, Q1?).
> (4)   queue([ ], [ ], _).
>
>   insert(X, Q, Q1) ← See Program 2.11.

Program 2.12: A priority queue (second trial)

dequeue messages only if its queue is nonempty; otherwise it waits for an *enqueue* message.

Clause (1) initializes the empty queue. Clause (2) handles the case in which the queue is nonempty and a *dequeue* message is ready. Clause (3) handles ready enqueue messages, and Clause (4) terminates the process if the end of the two streams is reached.

This type of priority queue is used in the implementation of the disk-arm scheduler described below. A more efficient priority queue can be obtained using balanced trees.

2.4.11 A spooler

Arvind and Brock (1982) describe an implementation of a priority printer manager. It manages one printer by maintaining two queues, a fast queue for small files, and a slow queue for large files. It prints the files on the printer, giving priority to the fast queue, and sends back a confirmation when the printing is completed.

Hewitt et al. (1979) describe an Actors implementation of a hard-copy server. It manages two printers, but does so with no priority considerations.

Program 2.13 combines the functionality of the two systems and does so in a more concise and elegant form. Instead of two queues it manages a priority queue, which provides a more refined response. It follows the approach of Arvind and Brock (1982) and treats system I/O in a side-effect free way, by identifying I/O devices with the streams they produce or consume. It is initialized with communication streams corresponding to its external I/O devices: in our example two printers and an interface to the users. The users can share the spooler by merging their streams.

The users of the system send messages *print(File,Response)* to the spooler. A simple filter wraps each message with *enqueue*, computes its priority, which is the size of the file, and sends it to a priority queue. Upon termination it puts two

spooler((ToPrinter1, ToPrinter2), FromUser) ←
    filter(FromUser?, FromUser1),
    printer(ToQueue1, ToPrinter1),
    printer(ToQueue2, ToPrinter2),
    merge(ToQueue1?, ToQueue2?, FromPrinters),
    queue(FromUser1?, FromPrinters?).

filter([print(F, R) | S], [enqueue(print(F, R), Size) | S1]) ←
    length(F, Size) | filter(S?, S1).
filter([ ], [enqueue(print(halt, _),0), enqueue(print(halt, _),0)]).

printer([dequeue(print(File, Response)) | S], P) ←
    printer1(File?, Response, S, P).

printer1(File, true, [dequeue(print(File1, R1)) | S], P) ←
    File ≠ halt | print(File, P, P1), printer1(File1?, R1, S, P1).
printer1(halt, true, [ ], [ ]).

print([ ], [end_of_file | P], P).
print([X | Xs], [X | P1], P) ←
    print(Xs?, P1, P).

queue(Es, Ds) ← See Program 2.12.

Program 2.13: A spooler

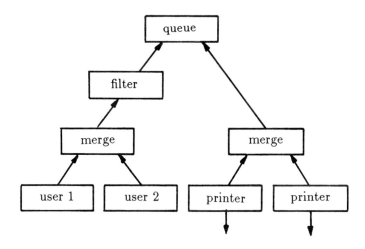

Figure 2.9: A spooler

halt messages in the queue, one for each printer.

A printer-controller process sends the queue a stream of *dequeue(print(File, Response))* messages, with *File* and *Response* undetermined. For each such message the printer waits for *File* to be determined, prints it, and unifies *Response* with *true*. The printer-controller terminates and closes its I/O streams when *File=halt*. In the above example the *halt* message is sent with priority 0, which means that the printers will halt immediately after finishing printing the current file, and that all files awaiting printing in the queue will be flushed. This behavior can be modified by changing the priority of the *halt* message; setting it to 1000 will cause the printers to halt only after all files in the queue of size < 1000 have been printed.

2.4.12 Dataflow computations and cyclic communication streams

Cyclic communication streams are commonly used in dataflow languages. A classical example is a dataflow program that computes the Fibonacci series by cycling the elements and adding each two consecutive elements to generate the following element (Wadge, 1979). A similar (nonterminating) Concurrent Prolog program is shown in Program 2.14.

> fib(S) ← fib1([0, 1 | S]).
>
> fib1([X1, X2, X3 | Xs]) ← plus(X1, X2, X3), fib1([X2, X3 | Xs]).

> **Program 2.14**: Generating the Fibonacci series

The Fibonacci program does not explicitly use a cyclic communication stream. A logic program that uses cyclic communication streams was developed by van Emden and de Lucena (1982), as a solution to Hamming's problem (Dijkstra, 1976) — generate all multiples of 2, 3, and 5 without repetition. Their solution, adapted to Concurrent Prolog, is shown as Program 2.15. Here we apply the same programming technique to another problem — finding the connected components of a graph. We associate with each node in the graph a distinct integer number. The name of a connected component is the smallest number of any node in the component. The algorithm, for a graph with vertices V is:

> For each node n in V do
> > Set Xn to n.
> > Repeat $|V|$ times:
> > > Send Xn to all nodes adjacent to n,
> > > Receive a number from every adjacent node,
> > > Let Xn' be the minimum of Xn and the numbers received.
> > > Set Xn to Xn'.
> > Set n's connected component number to Xn.

```
multiples(Xs) ←
    stream_multiply(2, [1 | X?], X2),
    stream_multiply(3, [1 | X?], X3),
    stream_multiply(5, [1 | X?], X5),
    opmerge(X2?, X3?, X23),
    opmerge(X5?, X23?, X).

stream_multiply(N, [U | X], [V | Z]) ←
    V := N*U, stream_multiply(N, X?, Z).

opmerge([U | X], [U | Y], [U | Z]) ← opmerge(X?, Y?, Z).
opmerge([U | X], [V | Y], [U | Z]) ← V ≤ U | opmerge(X?, [V | Y], Z).
opmerge([U | X], [V | Y], [V | Z]) ← U ≤ V | opmerge([U | X], Y?, Z).
```

Program 2.15: A solution to Hamming's problem

The algorithm is not very efficient. For an n-vertex graph its computation depth is in the order of n and its length is in the order of n^2 (Shapiro, 1984). This means, roughly, that given n processors, the algorithm runs in linear time. Better parallel algorithms are known (Shiloach and Vishkin , 1982a), but this algorithm — and its implementation — are certainly the simplest.

Program 2.16 assumes a specialized adjacency list representation of the graph. With each node N we associate a stream variable Xn. The graph is represented as a list of n triples (N,Xn,As), where N is the node number, Xn is its associated stream variable, and As is a list of the stream variables associated with the nodes adjacent to N. Given this graph, the program computes a list of pairs (N,C), where C is the name of the connected component of the node N.

Clauses (1)–(3) spawn a node process for each node in V; note that they generate the stream of pairs (N,C) before the component name C of each node is determined.

Each node process has four arguments. The first is the graph itself, which it uses to count $|V|$ iterations. Following are the Xn variables explained above, the list of streams of adjacent nodes, and the node's final component number. The node process iterates $|V|$ times, using Clause (1), and on each iteration performs the operations described above.

The *min* process extracts the smallest element among all the first elements of the adjacent streams and the current node number, and returns a list of the rest of the streams.

For example, if we invoke the program on the 7-vertex graph in which 1 is connected to 2 and 3, 2 is connected to 4, 5 is connected to no one, and 6 is

(1) cc(Graph, CList) ←
     cc(Graph, Graph, CList).

(2) cc(Graph, [(N, [N | Xn], As) | Gs], [(N, C) | Cs]) ←
     node(Graph, N, Xn, As, C),
     cc(Graph, Gs, Cs).

(3) cc(_, [ ], [ ]).

(1) node([_ | G], Xn, [Xn1 | Xns], As, C) ←
     min(Xn, As?, Xn1, As1), node(G?, Xn1, Xns, As1?, C).

(2) node([ ], C, [ ], _, C).

(1) min(Xn, [[B | Bs] | As], Xn1, [Bs | As1]) ←
     Xn < B | min(Xn, As?, Xn1, As1).

(2) min(Xn, [[B | Bs] | As], Xn1, [Bs | As1]) ←
     B ≤ Xn | min(B, As?, Xn1, As1).

(3) min(Xn, [ ], Xn, [ ]).

Program 2.16: Computing the connected components of a graph

connected to itself and to 7, we get the following result:

```
| ?– solve(cc([(1, X1, [X2, X3]), (2, X2, [X1, X4]), (3, X3, [X1]),
|     (4, X4, [X2]), (5, X5, [ ]), (6, X6, [X6, X7]), (7, X7, [X6])], Cs)).
|
Cs = [(1, 1), (2, 1), (3, 1), (4, 1), (5, 5), (6, 6), (7, 6)],
X1 = [1, 1, 1, 1, 1, 1, 1, 1],
X2 = [2, 1, 1, 1, 1, 1, 1, 1],
X3 = [3, 1, 1, 1, 1, 1, 1, 1],
X4 = [4, 2, 1, 1, 1, 1, 1, 1],
X5 = [5, 5, 5, 5, 5, 5, 5, 5],
X6 = [6, 6, 6, 6, 6, 6, 6, 6],
X7 = [7, 6, 6, 6, 6, 6, 6, 6]
```

which shows, in addition to the component numbers, at which cycle each node discovered its correct component name. We see that after three cycles every node knew its final component name.

A program for distributed array relaxation can be obtained following the same technique. Adjacent array cells are connected by communication streams, and a procedure that computes some average function replaces the *min* procedure. The termination condition of an array relaxation program is more difficult, but standard distributed termination detection algorithms can be applied, e.g., (Dijkstra et al., 1983).

2.5   A Sequential Concurrent Prolog Machine and Its Prolog Implementation

The sequential Concurrent Prolog interpreter in Program 2.17 is a simplification of the interpreter in the appendix, which we used to develop and debug the programs described in the paper. It is 44 lines of code long, and it performs about 135 process reductions per CPU second on a DEC 2060.

2.5.1   Control

The interpreter maintains two data structures: a queue of Concurrent Prolog processes, and a deadlock indicator. When invoked with a system of processes, the interpreter schedules the processes in the queue, sets the deadlock indicator on, and appends to the tail of the queue a cycle marker, used to detect deadlock. It then iterates, dequeueing a process, reducing it, and inserting the reduced system of processes into the queue, according to the scheduling policy. If a process cannot be reduced, then it is enqueued back. If no process in the queue can be reduced then the system is deadlocked, and the interpreter fails.

Each iteration proceeds as follows: If the queue contains only the cycle marker, then the interpreter terminates. Otherwise it dequeues an element from the queue. If that element is the cycle marker and the deadlock indicator is off, it enqueues the cycle marker back, sets the deadlock indicator on, and iterates. If the cycle marker is encountered when the deadlock indicator is on, the computation fails.

If the dequeued element is a process, then it attempts to reduce it, as explained below, and if the reduction is successful, it inserts the newly created processes into the queue, according to the scheduling policy, and iterates. If the reduction is not successful, then it enqueues the process and iterates.

To reduce a process A, the interpreter sequentially searches through the clauses $A1 \leftarrow G \mid B$ in the program, trying to unify A with $A1$ and, if successful, to solve the guard by calling itself recursively with G. If it finds such a clause, then the reduced system is B. Standard indexing mechanisms can be used to focus the search for a unifiable clause.

The overhead of a scheduling policy is measured by the ratio of unsuccessful vs. successful reductions. We have experimented with a variety of scheduling policies, including depth-first, breadth-first, and mixed. In depth-first scheduling, the reduced system is added to the head of the queue. This policy typically has less overhead, but it is not And-fair, since if the computation is nonterminating then some processes may never reach the head of the queue. In breadth-first scheduling, implemented in Program 2.17, the reduced system is added to the tail of the queue. This scheduling policy is fair, but may have a rather severe

```
solve(A) ←
    system(A), !, A.
solve(A) ←
    schedule(A, X, X, Head, [cycle | Tail]),
    solve(Head, Tail, deadlock).

solve([cycle], [ ], _) ← !.
solve([cycle | Head], Tail, deadlock) ← !, fail.
solve([cycle | Head], [cycle | Tail], nodeadlock) ← !,
    solve(Head, Tail, deadlock).
solve([A | Head], Tail, DL) ←
    system(A), !, A,
    solve(Head, Tail, nodeadlock).
solve([A | Head], Tail, DL) ←
    reduce(A, B, DL, DL1),
    schedule(B, Head, Tail, NewHead, NewTail),
    !, solve(NewHead, NewTail, DL1).

reduce(A, B, _, nodeadlock) ←
    guarded_clause(A, G, B),
    solve(G), !.
reduce(A, suspended(A), DL, DL).

guarded_clause(A, G, B) ←
    guarded_clause(A, B1), find_guard(B1, G, B).

find_guard((A|B), A, B) ← !.
find_guard(A, true, A).

schedule(true, Head, Tail, Head, Tail) ← !.
schedule(suspended(A), Head, [A | Tail], Head, Tail) ← !.
schedule((A, B), Head, Tail, Head2, Tail2) ← !,
    schedule(A, Head, Tail, Head1, Tail1),
    schedule(B, Head1, Tail1, Head2, Tail2).
schedule(A, Head, [A | Tail], Head, Tail)
```

Program 2.17: A sequential Concurrent Prolog interpreter

overhead. The scheduling overhead in the examples we tried ranged from 0 to 100 percent. For example, in the simulator of the multiprocessor reduction machine in Program 2.10 we used a breadth-first scheduler for the processors, but a depth-first scheduler for the communication processes — the merge processes and the queue. With this policy we obtained a scheduling overhead of 30 percent.

One drawback of this interpretation algorithm is that it does not discriminate between suspension and failure. Another is that it does not incorporate true Or-parallelism, or, in other words, that it is not Or-fair. If there are both non-terminating and terminating guard systems, the interpreter may fail to solve any of the guards. This interpreter, therefore, does not execute correctly the program in Figure 2.6, which implements a shell program that handles an *abort* interrupt.

Program 2.17, together with the implementation of unification in Program 2.18 and the *guarded_clause* procedure described below, should execute all Concurrent Prolog programs shown in the paper. The few additions necessary are incorporated in the full Concurrent Prolog interpreter shown in the appendix, which includes trace and statistics packages. When compiled, that interpreter performs around 100 reductions per CPU second on a DECsystem 2060.

2.5.2 Unification

The interpreter is so simple partly because it uses Prolog's unification to implement the extended unification algorithm, shown in Program 2.18. To understand this program, note that semi-colon is Prolog's Or; the predicate = is defined by the unit clause $X=X$; $nonvar(X)$ and $var(X)$ are built-in Prolog meta-logical predicates, which succeed if X is instantiated or not instantiated to a non-variable term, respectively; $X=..Y$ explodes the term X into a list Y whose head is the main functor of X and tail is the list of arguments of X.

(1) unify(X, Y) ←
        (var(X) ; var(Y)), !, X=Y.
(2) unify(X?, Y) ← !,
        nonvar(X), unify(X, Y).
(3) unify(X, Y?) ← !,
        nonvar(Y), unify(X, Y).
(4) unify([X | Xs], [Y | Ys]) ← !,
        unify(X, Y), unify(Xs, Ys).
(5) unify([ ], [ ]) ← !.
(6) unify(X, Y) ←
        X=..[F | Xs], Y=..[F | Ys], unify(Xs, Ys).

Program 2.18: Read-only unification

Clause (1) deals with the case where one of the terms is a variable and defaults to Prolog to do the unification; Clauses (2) and (3) deal with unification of read-only terms; Clauses (4), (5), and (6) recur on the structure of the term, if previous clauses do not apply.

Using this unification procedure and Prolog's built-in predicates *clause* and *functor*, we can invoke clauses without instantiating read-only variables, with the procedure *guarded_clause*:

```
guarded_clause(A, B) ←
    functor(A, F, N), functor(A1, F, N),
    clause(A1, B),
    unify(A, A1).
```

functor(A,F,N) names the relation "A is a term whose principal functor has name F and arity N". When invoked with its first argument A instantiated to a term, it unifies F and N with the name and functor of A. When invoked with F and N instantiated, it unifies A with a most general term whose principal functor has name F and arity N. *clause*(A,B) unifies B with a clause whose head unifies with A; it requires A to be instantiated to a nonvariable term.

2.5.3 Optimizations

Several optimizations are essential to make this interpreter a more practical tool. The first is to incorporate the unification of read-only terms in the underlying unification algorithm of Prolog.

Another essential optimization is the reduction of scheduling overhead by elimination of busy waiting. This can be done using a technique suggested by Alain Colmerauer, and incorporated in Prolog-II to implement the "freeze" predicate (Colmerauer et al., 1981).

The technique is extremely simple and elegant and eschews the need for elaborate hardware mechanisms such as associative memory to implement the dataflow-based synchronization mechanisms of Concurrent Prolog. If one or more processes are waiting for some variable's principal functor to be determined, then the memory cell representing this variable is temporarily assigned to a pointer to the list of these processes. When another process unifies this variable with a non-variable term, it first removes this pointer, instantiates the variable, and activates all the processes on the waiting list.

A third important improvement is saving the state of locked subsystems. Currently, if a subsystem is locked, then the interpreter executing it fails, its state is lost, and its execution starts from scratch the next time the process that invoked this subsystem is scheduled. It would be better to save the state of such a system; but this requires some additional bookkeeping to garbage-collect irrelevant subsystems.

2.6   Comparison With Other Concurrent Programming Languages

"*Occam's Razor* [William of *Ockham*]: A scientific and philosophical rule
that entities should not be multiplied unnecessarily which is interpreted
as requiring that the simplest of competing theories be preferred to the
more complex or that explanations of unknown phenomenon be sought
in terms of known quantities".

— Webster's New Collegiate Dictionary.

2.6.1   The Relational Language of Clark and Gregory

The roots of Concurrent Prolog can probably be traced back to the work of
Kahn and MacQueen (1977). They have shown that concurrent programming can
be modeled naturally by processes computing relations over streams. Van Emden
and de Lucena (1982) provided a translation of the model of Kahn and MacQueen
into the formalism of logic programming. However, both the language of Kahn
and MacQueen and its logical counterpart are deterministic.

Clark and Gregory extended the approach of van Emden and de Lucena to
indeterminate computations with the concept of a guarded-clause. Their Relational Language can implement indeterminate stream merge, for example. The
subset of Concurrent Prolog described in this paper is a result of an attempt to
generalize and clean up the Relational Language of Clark and Gregory. Several
differences can be found between the two.

The Relational Language requires that a guard be ground before an attempt
is made to solve it; hence it is immaterial whether it is solved sequentially or in
parallel. Our guards may contain general systems; there is no restriction that a
guard system be ground before it is invoked. This enables Concurrent Prolog to
support a hierarchy of concurrent systems, which is essential for implementing
operating systems. See for example the shell problem, Program 2.6.

The Relational Language restricts the variables shared between processes to
be of type "stream", and requires that each such variable will have at most one
producer; this has to be verified at compile time, based on mode declarations
and variable annotations. The producer and consumer annotations are inherited,
so, for example, a receiver of a message cannot respond to it by instantiating an
undetermined variable in it. Hence this language does not support programming
with incomplete messages, a key concept in Concurrent Prolog.

Concurrent Prolog alleviates all these restrictions since it incorporates a simpler and more basic synchronization mechanism. Instead of mode declarations and
consumer and producer annotations, Concurrent Prolog has one synchronization
primitive: the read-only annotation. This mechanism is expressive enough to

achieve behaviors induced by the mechanisms of the Relational Language, and more. The generality of this mechanism enables us to share variables of any type between processes, not only streams. It also enables the use of incomplete messages. In addition, our synchronization mechanism can be implemented very efficiently, in contrast to the requirement that an invoked clause should have a ground guard.

We view the read-only annotation as the major contribution of Concurrent Prolog over the Relational Language.

The requirement that a shared variable has only one producer is not incorporated in Concurrent Prolog. This allows sophisticated systems programming techniques, such as blackboards[5].

It should be mentioned that read-only mode declarations, such as

mode merge(?, ?, _)

can be used as shorthand for annotating the first two arguments of *merge* as read-only in every call to *merge* in the program. A preprocessor can use such declarations to install the appropriate annotations in the Concurrent Prolog code prior to its compilation.

Another extension of Prolog to a parallel programming language, called Epilog, was proposed by Wise (1982a). Apparently, Epilog is not concerned with solving concurrent programming problems, but only with the parallel execution of logic programs. Nevertheless, it has some, constructs in common with the Relational Language and Concurrent Prolog. The most apparent difference between Concurrent Prolog and Epilog is in the design methodology: we strive to find the minimal set of basic control constructs necessary to express concurrent computations, while Epilog enjoys a proliferation of these.

2.6.2 Concurrent functional programming languages

There is a natural mapping from any (first order) functional program to a logic program: replace every n-ary function symbol by an $n+1$-ary predicate symbol, annotate the output variable of the predicate as read-only in its occurrence as an input, and replace function composition by process conjunction. As discussed earlier, this translation achieves the effect of programming with Lenient-*cons* (Friedman and Wise, 1976a). The effect of *frons* (Friedman and Wise, 1979) can also be achieved in Concurrent Prolog, using stream merge.

In comparison, the translation from logic to functional programs is not so straightforward. Since the output of a process can be named explicitly, complex communication patterns between processes can be specified, including cyclic ones. The basic computational model of functional languages supports only hierarchical

---

[5] See Tribble et al., Chapter 17.

communication — between child and parent processes. Functional programming languages must add extraneous features to their basic computational model to achieve flexibility in communication.

One approach to the problem was taken by Harel and Nehab (1982) in Concurrent And/Or programs, which extended the functional And/Or programming language with a CSP-like communication mechanism.

Another approach was taken by Johnson (1981), who describes a system of processes as a system of functions computing a solution to a set of simultaneous equations. The result is quite similar to Concurrent Prolog each equation corresponds to a goal with one output variable, and a set of simultaneous equations corresponds to a conjunctive goal. However, lacking logical variables, the language does not support incomplete messages.

It may be the case that by adding additional features to functional languages, such as Lenient-*cons* and simultaneous equations, one can get closer and closer to the expressiveness of a logic language; but I do not see a reason not to work directly with the more expressive formalism.

The preference of relations over functions in concurrent programming is evident also in the theoretical treatments of this issue (for example, Brock and Ackerman, 1981; Park, 1980; Pratt, 1982; Smyth, 1982).

2.6.3 Dataflow languages

The synchronization mechanism of Concurrent Prolog is very similar to that of dataflow languages (Ackerman, 1982): a process suspended on undetermined read-only variables is analogous to an operator waiting for its arguments to arrive. Concurrent Prolog, however, lends itself to more concise and elegant programming. For example, dataflow languages extensively use the "let" construct, which achieves only a subset of the effects of unification, and does so in a cruder and more verbose way.

Another difference is that dataflow languages are deterministic, and hence must introduce *merge* as a built-in operator. According to Bryant and Dennis' (1982) version of Occam's Razor mentioned earlier in Section 2.3, this constitutes evidence in favor of Concurrent Prolog. One immediate implication of the determinacy of dataflow languages is that they must introduce a new *merge* operator for every scheduling policy described in Section 2.4; on the other hand all of these are user programmable in Concurrent Prolog.

Another important difference between Concurrent Prolog and dataflow languages is related to monitors and is discussed in the next section.

2.6.4 Monitors

Dataflow languages are a cleaner computational model than conventional concurrent programming languages such as Concurrent Pascal (Hansen, 1975) and CSP/k (Holt et al., 1979), which use monitors (Hoare, 1974). In spite of that, programs that implement shared resources are simpler and more readable when monitors are used.

To share a resource, dataflow languages use tagged-merge operators, that tagged merge requests from several processes to the shared resource and tag them with the origin of the request. After the resource receives the request, it replies back to the sender using the tags on the message. Such a communication network includes both tagged-merge and tagged-split operators and cannot be modified easily at runtime. A solution to this problem, termed *managers*, is admitted by its inventors to obstruct the initial simplicity and clarity of the dataflow model (Arvind and Brock, 1982).

The crux of the problem is that the resource has to know who issued the request in order to respond to it. A monitor can execute a monitor call without knowing the identity of the caller explicitly, since the caller can find the response to its monitor call by inspecting the appropriate arguments in the call. In implementation terms, a monitor call contains the identity of the caller in the memory address of its result arguments. The monitor can respond to the call by placing the desired values in those memory addresses, thus avoiding the communication protocol overhead a dataflow language requires in order to ship the response back to the sender.

One may argue that the difference between the two approaches is only in the level at which the problem is solved. Monitors solve the problem of responding to requests at the implementation level, whereas dataflow languages solve it at the programming level. We agree, but find this difference crucial for the convenience and flexibility of the language.

The Concurrent Prolog solution to implementing shared resources enjoys the benefits of both worlds, due to the concept of incomplete messages. An incomplete message is sent to a shared resource via merged streams, just as in a dataflow language; but the shared resource responds to it by placing values in undetermined variables in the message, just as in a monitor call. Hence our examples use only merge, not tagged-merge, and consequently do not use tagged-split either.

In implementation terms, the recipient of an incomplete message can respond to it without knowing the explicit identity of the sender, since its identity is hidden in the address of the undetermined variables in the message.

This analogy provides an interesting distinction between procedure calls and monitor calls in Concurrent Prolog. In monitor-based programming languages a procedure call and a monitor call are two basic, mutually irreducible operations. On the other hand in Concurrent Prolog a procedure call, i.e., a process invocation, is a basic operation, executed directly by the Concurrent Prolog machine, whereas a monitor call is a data-structure, which is sent, received and processed by the Concurrent Prolog processes. This may be another instance in which Bryant, Dennis, and Occam's razor applies.

2.6.5 Actors

The Actors model (Hewitt, 1973; Lieberman, 1981) is also closely related to Concurrent Prolog, as our use of Actors jargon to explain Concurrent Prolog programs suggests. One similarity is the "light-weight" and dynamic nature of Concurrent Prolog processes and the actors of an Actor system. Another is the use of pattern-matching to select and construct the response to a message.

One difference between the two is the simplicity and clarity of the computational model. The Actor model is centered around an operational semantics, which freely mixes object-level and meta-level operations.

Another is the difference in the mechanism for accessing objects. Actor objects have direct pointers to other objects. Concurrent Prolog processes have logical variables, which may be shared by other processes and used indirectly to communicate with them[6].

2.7 Relation to Sequential Prolog

Initially, our goal was to extend Prolog to a concurrent programming language, and one of our design criteria was to properly contain Sequential Prolog. However, as our research progressed, we have realized that this heads-on approach is not appropriate, since Prolog looks the way it does precisely because it was designed to run efficiently on a sequential von Neumann machine. As a result, it suffers from many of the illnesses that make conventional programming languages not suitable for new architectures.

For example, the state of the computation of Sequential Prolog is very complex. In addition to the binding environment and the stack, also maintained by other programming languages, Prolog maintains the backtrack point for each goal on the stack and a trail-stack that says which variable bindings should be reset upon backtracking. In addition, Prolog variables are not single-assignment, which is one property advocated as essential for advanced architectures: the value of a variable can be set and reset many times upon backtracking.

Hence we currently believe that properly containing Prolog may not be a desirable goal. However, since in the meantime we would like to see Concurrent

---

[6] The subject is discussed further by Shapiro and Takeuchi (Chapter 29) and Kahn et al. (Chapter 30).

Prolog as the systems programming language of a von Neumann Prolog machine, there is a need to find some way to integrate the two. One possibility is already available in our Concurrent Prolog interpreter: to call Prolog from Concurrent Prolog we use the predicate *call(X)*, which defaults to Prolog to solve X. Since both Sequential and Concurrent Prolog maintain the same binding environment, there are no interface problems[7].

Ultimately, there should be a more direct way to incorporate in Concurrent Prolog some of the powerful properties of Sequential Prolog it currently lacks. Kowalski (1979) drew a distinction between two types of nondeterminism: *don't-care nondeterminism* and *don't-know nondeterminism*. In other circles the first is referred to as indeterminacy, while the second simply as nondeterminism. Concurrent Prolog incorporates don't-care nondeterminism, but not don't-know nondeterminism. The latter is simulated in Sequential Prolog by sequential search and backtracking.

For example, the following Sequential Prolog program for finding an element in the intersection of two lists

intersect(X, L1, L2) ← member(X, L1), member(X, L2)

would not work correctly in Concurrent Prolog, since the first process to find a value for X will commit to it and not backtrack, even if its choice does not suit the other process. This, of course, does not mean that Concurrent Prolog cannot implement list intersection; but to do so it needs to iterate explicitly on at least one of the two lists:

intersect(X, [X | L1], L2) ← member(X, L2) | true.
intersect(X, [_ | L1], L2) ← intersect(X, L1, L2) | true.

The ability to talk about process failure is another important extension, essential to make Concurrent Prolog a practical systems programming language. For example, we would like the shell process to report to the user when the execution of his command has failed and would like the operating system to reboot itself upon a software crash.

Adding the ability to talk about process failure is similar to extending Sequential Prolog with negation-as-failure (Clark, 1978), but not quite the same. Earlier we claimed that *commit* is a cleaned-up *cut*. This is due to its symmetry: since all guards are assumed to be executing in parallel, the first to reach the *commit* kills alternative computation paths both above and below it. In contrast, *cut* kills only alternatives left below it.

The relation of Sequential Prolog's cut to Concurrent Prolog's commit is similar to the relation of conventional if-then-else to Dijkstra's guarded-command.

---

[7] See Codish and Shapiro, Chapter 32, and Shapiro, Chapter 34, for further work on this subject.

The same argument Dijkstra uses against if-then-else and in favor of the guarded-command is applicable to cut and commit: the lack of symmetry and the reliance on default in the former, versus symmetry and explicit conditions in the latter.

One consequence of this difference is the inability to implement negation-as-failure using commit. The standard implementation of negation-as-failure in Sequential Prolog

$$not(X) \leftarrow X, !, fail.$$
$$not(X).$$

is essentially an if-then-else. It reads: "if X succeeds then fail, else succeed". The corresponding Concurrent Prolog program would not have the desired effect, since the second clause may succeed even when X is solvable.

Cut is a controversial component in Prolog, and for good reasons. We believe that commit captures the essence of cut, which is the ability commit the execution to the current computation path, without introducing its less desirable features, i.e., the ability to implement if-then-else and implicit negation.

In spite of what has been said, Concurrent Prolog is not immune to awkward programming practices. For example, if the Concurrent Prolog machine is stable (cf. Section 2.4.5), then a weak form of implicit negation can be expressed, a possibility that led Dijkstra (1976) to recommend non-stable implementations.

We believe that having process failure as a primitive concept and the hierarchical structure of systems created during computation, make Concurrent Prolog a robust systems programming language. Consider the following implications of these properties:

- If a process fails, then its system fails; but this does not mean that the whole computation fails, unless the failing process is in the top-level system.

- If all processes in a system are suspended, then the system is said to be locked; but this is not necessarily a deadlock. A subsystem *S1* may be locked at some point in time, and unlocked later, because a sister subsystem *S2* instantiated some variable, which appears as read-only in *S1*. Only if the top-level system is locked, then the situation cannot be cured, and deadlock can be established.

- The scope of interference between processes is restricted to subsystems. If two brother processes commit to unify a shared variable with non-unifiable terms, they fail, and their subsystem fails, but other subsystems are not affected. This scope restriction follows from the requirement that bindings computed by a guard system are made public only after the guard system terminates successfully[8].

---

[8] A similar approach to the problem, which uses layers interpretation, rather than hierarchies

2.8   Future Research

Throughout the paper we have mentioned several outstanding theoretical problems. We expect the solution to one of them — the definition of a binding environment that supports simultaneous unification — to be of practical application to the design of a multi-processor Concurrent Prolog machine.

In some sense, both Sequential and Concurrent Prolog resemble an assembly language more than a high-level language. We refer to the flat name space of procedures and to the lack of any type or other declarations whose consistency with the program is checked statically. The roots of this deficiency, however, are sociological, not conceptual. To the contrary, we believe that logic programs lend themselves to modular programming and static analysis at least as well as other types of programs, perhaps even more. The same costumes suggested to cover Prolog's naked body can equally well fit Concurrent Prolog (Bruynooghe, 1982; Furukawa et al., 1983; Futo and Szeredi, 1981)[9].

In addition to extending the language, we consider several other research directions as worth pursuing. First is implementing in Concurrent Prolog a multi-tasking operating system for a single-user computer. We hope that the efficiency of Concurrent Prolog will be sufficient for such a machine, and that any lack thereof will be compensated by the ease in which sophisticated software can be developed in it, as our experience suggests. Considering multi-user operating systems, it seems that the ability to pass streams as arguments in a message may be a sound and simple basis for a capabilities system[10].

Yet another research direction is related to work on systolic algorithms (Kung, 1982). We find in several Concurrent Prolog programs that once the network of processes is spawned, it starts behaving like a systolic array. This is manifested most clearly in the array relaxation program (a variant of Program 2.16, not shown in the paper). This suggests the use of Concurrent Prolog as a specification language for systolic algorithms[11].

---

of guard systems, is described by Hirsch et al., Chapter 20.

[9] See also Yardeni and Shapiro, Chapter 28.

[10] See Miller et al., Chapter 24.

[11] See Shapiro, Chapter 7, and Taylor et al., Chapter 8.

Acknowledgements

The author acknowledges Lawrence Byrd, Shimon Cohen, David Harel, Michael Fischer, Steven Gregory, Toni Kusalik, Frank McCabe, Bob Nix, Fernando Pereira, Stan Rosenschein, Akikazu Takeuchi, and David Warren for helpful discussions.

This research began while the author was at Yale University, supported by NSF grant no. MCS80002447, and continued under the support of the DAI project at SRI International, ONR contract no. N000014-80-C-0296.

The experimental part of the research, including the definition of the subset of Concurrent Prolog described in the paper, was carried out while the author was a visiting scientist at ICOT — the Institute for New Generation Computer Technology.

Orna Meyers assisted in editing this paper.

Appendix 2.1: Concurrent Prolog Interpreter

```
%% Interpreter for a subset of concurrent Prolog.
← public solve/1,
      reduce/2,
      display_counters/0,
      trace/2,
      wait/2,
      wait/1,
      dif/2.

← op(450, xf, '?').

← call((value(initialized, true);
      compile([dsutil, 'system.def']),
      % dsutil contains some utilities.
      % system.def contains the definition of the predicate system1(_).
      set(smode, depth_first),
      set(smode(read(_)), breadth_first),
      set(countingset, [reduction(_), suspension(_), system(_)]),
      set(traceset, [reduction(_), suspension(_)]),
      set(initialized, true))).

solve(A) ←
      clear_counters,
      solve(A, 0),
      display_counters.
```

```
solve(true, _) ← !.
solve(A, D) ←
    system(A), !, trace(system(D), A), A;
    trace(solve(D), A),
    schedule(A, X, X, Head, [cycle(1) | Tail]),
    solve(Head, Tail, deadlock, D),
    trace(solved(D), A).
solve([cycle(N)], _, _, D) ← !,
    (D=0, writel(['*** cycles: ', N]), nl; true).
solve([cycle(N) | Head], [ ], deadlock, D) ← !,
    D=0, writel(['*** cycles: ', N]), nl,
    writelnl(['*** Deadlock detected. Locked processes:'| Head]) ;
    fail.
solve([cycle(N) | Head], [cycle(N1) |Tail], nodeadlock, D) ← !,
    N1 is N+1,
    solve(Head, Tail, deadlock, D).
solve([A | Head], Tail, DL, D) ←
    system(A), !, trace(system(D), A), A,
    solve(Head, Tail, nodeadlock, D).
solve([A | Head], Tail, DL, D) ←
    D1 is D+1,
    trace(call(D1), A),
    reduce(A, B, DL, DL1, D1),
    trace(reduction(D1), (A←B)),
    schedule(B, Head, Tail, NewHead, NewTail),
    !, solve(NewHead, NewTail, DL1, D).

reduce(A, B, _, nodeadlock, D) ←
    guarded_clause(A, G, B, D),
    trace(try_clause(D), (A←(G | B))),
    solve(G, D), !.
reduce(A, suspended(A), DL, DL, D) ←
    trace(suspension(D), A).

reduce(A, B) ←
    guarded_clause(A, G, B, 1),
    solve(G, 1), !.
reduce(A, suspended(A)) ←
    trace(suspension, A).

schedule(true, Head, Tail, Head, Tail) ← !.
schedule(suspended(A), Head, [A | Tail], Head, Tail) ← !.
```

schedule((A, B), Head, Tail, Head2, Tail2) ←
    value(smode, breadth_first), !,
    schedule(A, Head, Tail, Head1, Tail1),
    schedule(B, Head1, Tail1, Head2, Tail2).
schedule((A, B), Head, Tail, Head2, Tail2) ←
    value(smode, depth_first), !,
    schedule(B, Head, Tail, Head1, Tail1),
    schedule(A, Head1, Tail1, Head2, Tail2).
schedule(A, Head, Tail, [A | Head], Tail) ←
    value(smode(A), depth_first), !.
schedule(A, Head, [A | Tail], Head, Tail) ←
    value(smode(A), breadth_first), !.
schedule(A, Head, Tail, [A | Head], Tail) ←
    value(smode, depth_first), !.
schedule(A, Head, [A | Tail], Head, Tail) ←
    value(smode, breadth_first), !.

guarded_clause(A, G, B, D) ←
    ready_clause(A, B1, D), find_guard(B1, G, B).

find_guard((A | B), A, B) ← !.
find_guard(A, true, A).

ready_clause(A, B, D) ←
    functor(A, F, N), functor(A1, F, N),
    clause(A1, B),
    trace(unify(D), (A, A1)),
    unify(A, A1).

unify(X, Y) ← (var(X) ; var(Y)), !, X=Y.
unify(X?, Y) ← !,
    nonvar(X), unify(X, Y).
unify(X, Y?) ← !,
    nonvar(Y), unify(X, Y).
unify([X | Xs], [Y | Ys]) ← !,
    unify(X, Y), unify(Xs, Ys).
unify([ ], [ ]) ← !.
unify(X, Y) ←
    X=..[F | Xs], Y=..[F | Ys], unify(Xs, Ys).

trace(_, _) ←
    value(trace, off), !.
trace(A, B) ←
    add_counter(A),

```
    % break(A, B), % add a break package
    value(traceset, S),
    ( member(A, S) ; S=all ),
    writel([A, ': ', B]), nl, !.
trace(_, _).

clear_counters ←
    value(counter(X), Y), Y > 0, set(counter(X), 0), fail ; true.

add_counter(A) ←
    value(countingset, S), member(A, S), add1(counter(A), _) ; true.

display_counters ←
    value(countingset, S), member(X, S),
    value(counter(X), Y), Y > 0, writel(['# ', X, ': ', Y]), nl, fail ;
    sum_counters.

sum_counters ←
    value(countingset, S),
    setof(Y, (X, S) | (member(X, S), value(counter(X), Y)), S1),
    sum(S1, 0, Total),
    writel(['Total: ', Total]), nl.
```

Appendix 2.2: Some Utilities

```
% "Built-in" predicates.

%wait(X, Y) ←
    % wait until X is instantiated, "peel-off" extraneous '?'
    % annotations, and return the result in Y. Useful for interfacing
    % to regular Prolog.
wait(X) ←
    wait(X, _).

wait(X, _) ← var(X), !, fail.
wait(X?, Y) ← !, wait(X, Y).
wait(X, X).

%dif(X, Y) ← X and Y are not unifiable.
dif(X, Y) ←
    (var(X) ; var(Y)), !, fail.
dif(X?, Y) ← !,
    dif(X, Y).
dif(X, Y?) ← !,
```

```
        dif(X, Y).
dif([ ], [ ]) ← !,
        fail.
dif([X | Xs], [Y | Ys]) ← !,
        dif(X, Y) ; dif(Xs, Ys). dif(X, Y) ←
        X=..[Fx | Xs], Y=..[Fy | Ys],
        ( Fx\=Fy ; dif(Xs, Ys) ).
dif(X, Y) ←
        (var(X) ; var(Y)), !, fail.

system(wait(_, _)).
system(wait(_)).
system(dif(_, _)).
system(X) ← system1(X).
```

% Interface to tty
```
instream(Xs) ← % Xs is the current input stream
        read(X) | instream(X, Xs).

instream(end_of_file, [ ]).
instream([ ], Xs) ←
        instream(Y?, Xs), read(Y).
instream([X | Xs], [X | Ys]) ←
        instream(Xs, Ys).
instream(X, [X | Xs]) ←
        wait(X) | instream(Y?, Xs), read(Y).

outstream([X| Xs]) ← % Xs is the current output stream
        writel(['*** outstream: ', X]), nl | outstream(Xs?).
outstream([ ]).

wait_write(X, Y) ← % wait for X and output Y to current output stream
        wait(X) | call((write(Y), nl)).
```

% wrap stream elements with an identifying tag
```
wrap([ ], _, [ ]).
wrap([X | Xs], W, [WrappedX | Ys]) ←
        WrappedX=..[W, X] | wrap(Xs?, W, Ys).

lt(X, Y) ← wait(X, X1), wait(Y, Y1) | X1 < Y1.
le(X, Y) ← wait(X, X1), wait(Y, Y1) | X1 ≤ Y1.
```

% lazy evaluator of arithmetic expressions

```
':='(X, Y) ← wait(X, Y), integer(Y) | true.
':='(X+Y, Z) ← ':='(X?, X1), ':='(Y?, Y1), plus(X1, Y1, Z).
```

':='(X–Y, Z) ← ':='(X?, X1), '='(Y?, Y1), plus(Z, Y1, X1).
':='(X∗Y, Z) ← ':='(X?, X1), ':='(Y?, Y1), times(X1, Y1, Z).

plus(X, Y, Z) ← wait(X, X1), wait(Y, Y1) | Z is X1+Y1.
plus(X, Y, Z) ← wait(X, X1), wait(Z, Z1) | Y is Z1\X1.
plus(X, Y, Z) ← wait(Y, Y1), wait(Z, Z1) | X is Z1\Y1.

times(X, Y, Z) ← wait(X, X1), wait(Y, Y1) | Z is X1∗Y1.
times(X, Y, Z) ← wait(X, X1), wait(Z, Z1) | Y is Z1/X1.
times(X, Y, Z) ← wait(Y, Y1), wait(Z, Z1) | X is Z1/Y1.

Chapter 3

PARLOG: Parallel Programming in Logic

Keith Clark and Steve Gregory

Imperial College of Science and Technology

Abstract

PARLOG is a logic programming language in the sense that nearly every definition and query can be read as a sentence of predicate logic. It differs from Prolog in incorporating parallel modes of evaluation. For reasons of efficient implementation, it distinguishes and separates And-parallel and Or-parallel evaluation.

PARLOG relations are divided into two types: single-solution relations and all-solutions relations. A conjunction of single-solution relation calls can be evaluated in parallel with shared variables acting as communication channels for the passing of partial bindings. Only one solution to each call is computed, using committed choice non-determinism. A conjunction of all-solutions relation calls is evaluated without communication of partial bindings, but all the solutions may be found by an Or-parallel exploration of the different evaluation paths. A set constructor provides the main interface between single-solution relations and all-solutions relations.

This paper is a tutorial introduction to PARLOG. It assumes familiarity with logic programming.

3.1 Introduction

PARLOG is a logic programming language in the sense that nearly every procedure can be read as a definition of a relation in first order predicate logic. PARLOG differs from Prolog in incorporating parallel evaluation. It incorporates both And-parallelism and Or-parallelism.

The paper assumes some familiarity with the general concepts of logic programming and with Prolog. For introductory reading we suggest the papers by Kowalski (1974, 1983) or the books by Clark and McCabe (1984), Clocksin and Mellish (1984), and Hogger (1984). A further account of PARLOG can be found in (Gregory, 1987).

3.1.1 PARLOG And-parallelism

The And-parallelism of PARLOG is a generalization of that of our earlier Relational Language described in (Clark and Gregory, Chapter 1), which was itself a derivative of IC-PROLOG (Clark et al., 1982). PARLOG also has many features in common with the languages Concurrent Prolog (Shapiro, Chapter 2) and Guarded Horn Clauses (GHC) (Ueda, Chapter 4), which are both derivatives of the Relational Language. There are, however, significant differences between these three languages which we detail in the final section of this paper.

In PARLOG, the attempt to find a solution to each condition of a parallel conjunction becomes a separate concurrent process. The shared variables of the conditions (the calls) are the communication channels between the processes. Because of mode declarations, which restrict the unification between a call and an invoked clause to "input matching" on certain arguments, usually only one process will be able to bind each shared variable. This process is called the *producer* process for the variable. Any other (consumer) process needing the value of the shared variable suspends until the variable is bound by the producer of the variable. Suspension waiting for a value of a shared variable is the means of process synchronization in PARLOG.

Example parallel conjunction with shared variables

We introduce the special characteristics of PARLOG And-parallel evaluation through a simple example.

Suppose we have the parallel conjunction

prod1(X), prod2(Y), merge_consumer(X,Y,Z).

with *merge_consumer* defined by the program

mode merge_consumer(List1?,List2?,Merged_list↑).

merge_consumer([U|X],Y,[U|Z]) ← merge_consumer(X,Y,Z).
merge_consumer(X,[V|Y],[V|Z]) ← merge_consumer(X,Y,Z).
merge_consumer([ ],Y,Y).
merge_consumer(X,[ ],X).

The *merge_consumer* program is a complete definition of the relation *merge_consumer*(*List1,List2,Merged_list*):   *Merged_list* is an arbitrary interleaving of *List1* and *List2*.

Each clause is implicitly universally quantified with respect to each variable. The first clause covers the case when *Merged_list* begins with the item at the head of *List1*. Its logical reading is:

> For all U, X, Y, and Z, a list of the form $[U|Z]$ is an arbitrary interleaving of a list of the form $[U|X]$ and a list Y if Z is an arbitrary interleaving of X and Y.

We leave the reader to check the correctness of the other clauses.

Mode declarations

The mode declaration for the program constrains the unification between any *merge_consumer* call and the clauses of the program.

An argument annotated with a '?' in the mode declaration for a relation signifies that a non-variable term appearing in that argument position in the head of a clause can only be used for input matching. Thus, in a call to *merge_consumer*, the first clause can only be used if the first argument of the call is a substitution instance of the pattern $[U|X]$, and the third clause can only be used if the first argument of the call is the empty list [ ]. The second and fourth clauses have similar constraints with respect to the second argument of the call.

A '↑' annotation in the mode declaration means that a non-variable term appearing in that argument position in the head of a clause can be used for output unification against the corresponding argument in the call. So, a call to *merge_consumer* can have any term as its third argument.

The PARLOG mode declarations express constraints on the unification between call and clause head similar to the mode constraints of DEC-10 Prolog (Bowen et al., 1981). The difference is that, in DEC-10 Prolog, the attempt to use a clause when a mode constraint is not satisfied is always considered an error. In PARLOG, if an input mode is not satisfied, the attempt to use the clause is suspended.

An input mode is not satisfied if an argument A of the call is not yet a substitution instance of the corresponding term T in the head of the clause but A *would* unify with T with a substitution that binds one or more variables of A to non-variable terms. These variables in A must be given non-variable bindings by *other* processes, that is, via the unification with other calls. When this occurs, the attempt to use the clause is resumed. Of course, if one of the variables in A is given a non-variable value that does not unify with T the attempt to use the clause fails.

Returning to the example, in the parallel conjunction

: prod1(X), prod2(Y), merge_consumer(X,Y,Z).

the mode declaration for *merge_consumer* means that this call cannot bind either of the shared variables X and Y. Therefore, *prod1* and *prod2* should have modes

mode prod1(List1↑), prod2(List2↑).

and be defined such that their evaluation will eventually generate non-variable bindings for their variable output arguments, X and Y respectively. Until one of these producer processes generates a non-variable binding for its output argument, the *merge_consumer* process is suspended because each of its clauses will be suspended on an input match.

Non-deterministic evaluation

The four *merge_consumer* clauses represent alternative evaluation paths for the *merge_consumer* process.

Initially, the evaluation of the *merge_consumer* call is a concurrent attempt to apply each clause to the call. Each clause is then suspended waiting for one of the two producer processes to generate a non-variable binding for either X or Y. Let us suppose that the *prod1* process binds X to the term $[2|X1]$. The input match constraint on the first *merge_consumer* clause is now satisfied because $[2|X1]$ is a substitution instance of the term $[U|X]$. The clause can therefore be used to reduce the call

merge_consumer([2|X1],Y,Z)

to the recursive call

merge_consumer(X1,Y,Z1)

and at the same time the output variable Z of the top-level call is bound to $[2|Z1]$. The *merge_consumer* process must now again suspend because it has been reduced to another *merge_consumer* call that cannot proceed until there is a non-variable binding for either $X1$ or Y. It must wait until either the *prod1* process generates a binding for $X1$ or the *prod2* process binds Y.

Stream communication

We can think of the number 2 as the first message of the list or stream of messages that will be sent by the *prod1* process to the *merge_consumer* process. $[2|X1]$ is the first approximation to this stream of messages where $X1$ represents the rest of the message stream. The second message will be given when *prod1* generates another partial list binding for the variable $X1$, say the binding $[3|X2]$. A subsequent empty list binding $[\,]$ for the variable $X2$ would signal the end of the message stream. By binding its output variable Z to the partial list $[2|Z1]$, the *merge_consumer* process is passing the first received message through to its output stream.

Time-dependent computation

For each *merge_consumer* call of the recursive *merge_consumer* process there
is a concurrent attempt to use each of the clauses. As soon as the input match
constraint for a clause is satisfied, that clause can be used. The merging of the
message streams sent by the two producer processes will partly depend upon the
rate at which the two processes send messages. If *prod1* sends three messages
before *prod2* sends its first message, these three messages will usually be the
first three on the *merge_consumer* output stream. If the two producers both
send messages while the *merge_consumer* process is being reduced to its recursive
call, then either message may be passed through to the output stream. This is
because the input match constraints of both recursive clauses will be satisfied.
(The program as written does not guarantee that the merging of the message
streams will be fair. A fair merge program is given in Section 3.3.3.)

Committed choice non-determinism and guards

When a clause is used to reduce a call, there is no backtracking on the
choice of the clause. As a logic programming language the distinguishing feature
of PARLOG is that its operational semantics incorporates the *committed choice*
non-determinism of Dijkstra's (1976) guarded commands and Hoare's (1985) CSP.
Indeed, it was the elegant use of this concept in CSP that inspired us to incorporate it into the Relational Language (Clark and Gregory, Chapter 1), and hence
into PARLOG.

In general, the attempt to find a solution to some call $R(\ldots)$ invokes an Or-
parallel search for a clause that can be used to evaluate the call, from among all of
the program clauses for R. (We shall see later that we can constrain this parallel
search and even force a Prolog-style sequential search for the clause to be used,
but the default is a parallel search.) A *candidate* clause for the reduction is one
which "read-only matches" with the call on all its input arguments *and* which has
a successfully terminating guard. The *guard* is an optional initial conjunction of
conditions in the body of the clause, separated from the rest of the conditions by
a '|'.

Example guarded clauses

Suppose we replace the first clause for *merge_consumer* by the pair of clauses

    merge_consumer([U|X],Y,[U|Z]) ← accept(U) |
        merge_consumer(X,Y,Z).
    merge_consumer([U|X],Y,Z) ← reject(U) |
        merge_consumer(X,Y,Z).

The conditions *accept(U)* and *reject(U)* which precede the '|' in the clauses are
guards. Now the first clause can only be used to pass a message through to

the *merge_consumer* output stream if a message U has been sent by the *prod1* producer *and* the condition *accept*(U) is true for the transmitted message. The second clause is used if the message is to be rejected. This clause causes the process to recurse without passing the message through. (The output is just Z, the output stream of the recursive call.) With this modification the program now describes the relation

> *merge_consumer*(*List1*,*List2*,*Merged_list*): *Merged_list* is an arbitrary interleaving of *List2* with the sublist of *List1* which are the "accept" elements; all other elements of *List1* are "reject" elements.

Test role of guards

A guard can only *test* values of variables obtained by input matching. It cannot generate a binding for any variable in an input argument of the call. However, the evaluation of a guard may generate bindings for local variables of the clause (i.e., variables not appearing in the head) and for variables that appear in output arguments of the head of the clause.

Any candidate clause for a call can be used to reduce the call to the conjunction of conditions constituting the body of the clause. If this is a parallel conjunction, the process forks into several component processes which may communicate via bindings for a new set of shared variables in the body of the clause. The evaluation *commits* to the use of one of the candidate clauses. Usually this will be the first clause to become a candidate clause.

Bindings to call variables made only on commitment

At the point of commitment the output unification for the output arguments of the call is performed. (Thus, for the *merge_consumer* call of our example query, the output $[U|Z]$ of the first of the above guarded clauses will only be transmitted to the call if and when the input match with $[U|X]$ succeeds and the *accept* guard succeeds.) Since the evaluation of a guard is not allowed to generate bindings for any variables in the input arguments of the call, no variables in a call will be bound until there is a commitment to use some candidate clause. As there is no backtracking on the choice of the candidate clause, bindings made to variables in the call are never retracted. This property considerably simplifies the implementation of PARLOG and is the main reason why PARLOG has this "commit then bind" style of non-determinism rather than the Prolog "bind, fail and rescind bindings" style of non-determinism.

Minimal guards for maximum parallelism

Since the evaluation of a call may commit to the use of any candidate clause, we must use the guard and the matching terms for the input arguments of a clause to ensure that if the input matches succeed and the guard is true, then either

(1) a solution to the matched call can be found using that clause, or

(2) no solution can be found using any other clause.

We cannot rely on the failure to find a solution to the call using the chosen clause to automatically invoke a backtracking attempt to use an alternative clause as we can in Prolog.

We can trivially ensure that each candidate clause has the required property by making the guard of each clause contain its entire conjunction of conditions. However, since output bindings are not made until the guard computation terminates, and other processes may be suspended waiting for the output bindings, this tactic will considerably reduce the amount of overlapped computation. To achieve the greatest degree of parallelism, we must keep the guards as simple as possible.

Logical reading of programs

In PARLOG we can write logic programs that behave as a set of communicating, forking, non-deterministic processes. The programs define a set of relations over message streams (or any other incrementally constructed data structure) and each process computes some instance of the relation its program defines. Which instance is computed will generally depend upon the rate of progress of the processes with which it communicates.

This is exactly the logical property of many concurrent communicating systems. The program for each process in the system constrains the process so that its observed history of communications with other processes satisfies some relation. For example, the history of file retrievals of a filestore manager must correspond to some interleaving of the sequence of requests sent by each user. This guarantees that a later file retrieval request from a user will not be answered before an earlier request from that user.

In imperative programming languages, the relation that the communications of a process must satisfy is often heavily disguised by the highly procedural nature of the code. In PARLOG, the relation that must be satisfied by the process can nearly always be determined by a straightforward logical reading of its program. This is because each program has a dual interpretation: a logical interpretation as a set of statements about a relation, and an imperative interpretation as a description of a communicating forking process. Both interpretations are important and should be kept in mind. The former enables us to write correct programs, the latter efficient programs.

Co-operating construction of binding terms

One of the elegant features of Prolog is the "logical variable". This is the ability to have the evaluation of some condition c bind a variable X to a term T which contains variables that are bound by the evaluation of some other condition

c'. c and c' have, in effect, co-operated in the construction of T', the final value of X. The style of programming that this allows is one of the most important features of Prolog and the logic programming approach to computation (see, for example, Warren , 1980).

A co-operating construction of the final term binding for a shared variable can also be programmed in PARLOG. Indeed, it is a much more powerful device in PARLOG and related parallel logic languages than it is in Prolog. In Prolog, the communication is in one direction only, from c to c'. In PARLOG, because the calls can be evaluated concurrently, the process c which binds X to T can suspend, waiting for a "back communication" from the consumer of the binding, c'. The back communication occurs when c' binds some variable in T.

Example back communication

Suppose that our original *merge_consumer* program is modified so that the two recursive clauses become:

merge_consumer([(K,V)|X],Y,[(K,V)|Z]) ←
    check(K,V), merge_consumer(X,Y,Z).
merge_consumer(X,[(K,V)|Y],[(K,V)|Z]) ←
    check(K,V), merge_consumer(X,Y,Z).

The program now only accepts messages which are pairs of the form (K, V) and there is an extra call $check(K, V)$ in each clause. Our modified program now defines the relation

merge_consumer(List1,List2,Merged_list): *Merged_list* is an arbitrary interleaving of *List1* and *List2* which are lists of pairs of elements of the form (K, V) such that $check(K, V)$ is true.

Let us also suppose that *check* has the mode declaration

mode check(Key?,Value↑).

accepting a given *Key* argument and returning a *Value* associated with that key.

The behavior of the *merge_consumer* process is now subtly different. It still accepts a message on either input stream and passes it through to its output stream, but it also further instantiates the message as it passes through. The producer processes of the streams feeding into *merge_consumer* generate messages comprising a key K paired with a variable V. When a producer has generated such a message pair, it may suspend waiting for the variable of the pair to be given a value. If it does, we not only have co-operating construction; we also have back communication.

The limit case of back communication is the sending of messages that are unbound variables. As we shall see in Section 3.3, we can use message streams of variables to implement bounded buffer communication and to emulate lazy evaluation.

3.1.2 Single-solution and all-solutions relations

Because of the use of committed choice non-determinism, the evaluation of a parallel conjunction can only ever return one solution to the conjunction. However, there are·applications of logic programming, such as deductive databases, where all solutions to a conjunction of conditions are required.

To allow for this type of application, PARLOG relations are divided into two disjoint types. There are *single-solution* relations and *all-solutions* relations. Single-solution relations have mode declarations and are defined by guarded clause programs, as described above. In contrast, programs for all-solutions relations are normal Prolog-style sequences of clauses. There are no mode declarations and no guards.

Set constructor interface

The interface between the single-solution and the all-solutions subsets of PARLOG is via set constructors that return a single list comprising all or some of the solutions to a conjunction.

PARLOG has two set constructor primitives, one eager and one lazy. The one which corresponds to the normal Prolog set constructors is the eager constructor

set(Solutions↑,Term?,Conjunction?)

This incrementally binds the *Solutions* variable given as the first argument to the stream of the different instantiations of *Term* given by all of the successfully terminating evaluations of *Conjunction*. The conjunction comprises calls to all-solutions relations.

The stream of solution terms generated by the evaluation of a *set* condition can be concurrently consumed by an And-parallel consumer condition.

Example use of set

The evaluation of the parallel conjunction

set(Y,U,takes(U,c101)&takes(U,c102)), sort(Y,Z).

will result in Z being bound to a sorted list of the names of all the students taking *c101* and *c102*. As the stream of names of the students is being generated by the evaluation of the set call

set(Y,U,takes(U,c101)&takes(U,c102))

it is concurrently consumed by the *sort* process defined by a single-solution PARLOG program.

We deliberately leave unspecified the operational semantics of the set constructor. This allows different implementations of PARLOG to implement it with different degrees of parallelism. A possible Or-parallel operational semantics is defined by Clark and Gregory (1985) by an And-parallel interpreter written in PARLOG. The PARLOG programmer should make no assumptions about the order in which the solutions are generated. This allows a parallel search for the different solutions. If *set* is implemented by an Or-parallel rather than a backtracking evaluation, the use of the Prolog backtracking control primitive, the cut, must not be allowed in all-solutions relation definitions.

Note that the set constructor provides an appropriate interface to relational databases as well as to all-solutions logic programs.

3.1.3 Structure of the paper

The rest of the paper is divided into five sections. In Section 3.2 we examine more closely the single-solution, And-parallel component of PARLOG through a series of example programs. Various unification primitives of PARLOG are introduced and used to give a more precise account of the operational semantics.

In Section 3.3 the use of variables in messages is more fully explored. Following the method of Takuechi and Furukawa (Chapter 18), it is shown how lazy and bounded buffer evaluation can be implemented in PARLOG using message streams of request variables.

In Section 3.4 the use of the *set* primitive is more fully described and illustrated. The lazy *subset* primitive is also introduced. This accepts and instantiates a stream of request variables, like the lazy processes described in Section 3.3. The *subset* primitive is then used to define a Prolog-like query evaluator which obtains and displays the different solutions to a query one at a time. The set primitives enable PARLOG to be viewed as a parallel extension to Prolog.

In Section 3.5 the metacall feature of PARLOG is described and its use illustrated. In keeping with the communicating process operational semantics of PARLOG, it is more general than the metacall feature of Prolog. It reports the succeed/fail result of the call, and it allows the evaluation of the call to be suspended or prematurely terminated.

The final section examines the relationship of PARLOG with other work on parallel logic programming.

3.2   Single-Solution Relations

3.2.1   Syntax and semantics of single-solution relation definitions

A single-solution relation is one that can be used in And-parallel evaluations. A program for such a relation comprises a single mode declaration and a sequence of guarded clauses.

The *mode declaration* takes the form

$$\text{mode } R(m_1,\ldots,m_k).$$

Each m_i of the mode declaration is '?' or '↑', optionally preceded by an argument identifier which has no semantic significance.

A '?' in a mode declaration specifies that a non-variable term T in that argument position in the head of a clause for R can only be used for input matching against the corresponding argument A of the call. The match succeeds only if there is a substitution s such that Ts is identical to A.

A '↑' signifies that a non-variable term T in that argument position in the head of a clause can be used for output unification. This succeeds only if the call argument unifies with T.

A *guarded clause* is a clause of the form

$$R(T_1,\ldots,T_k) \leftarrow \langle \text{guard conditions} \rangle \mid \langle \text{body conditions} \rangle.$$

where the '|' signals the end of the guard and $T_1,\ldots,T_k$ are argument terms.

Logical reading

> The logical reading of a guarded clause is:
>
> For all term values of the variables of the clause, $R(T_1,\ldots,T_k)$ is true if all of the guard conditions and the body conditions are true.

A relation definition is read as the conjunction of all of its clauses.

Search for a candidate clause

> A clause c is a *candidate* for a call G if the head of c input matches with G on all input arguments and c has a successfully terminating guard.
>
> The clauses for a relation are separated from one another by either a '.' or a ';' operator. These define the order in which the clauses are tried in order to find a candidate clause for some call to the relation.
>
> All clauses in a '.'-separated group are to be tried in parallel.
>
> A ';' indicates that the clauses following the ';' should be tried only if all of the preceding clauses are found to be non-candidate clauses.
>
> A clause is a *non-candidate* if it fails to match the call on one of its input arguments or it has a terminating and failing guard.

If a clause is suspended in its input matching or in its guard evaluation, because it is waiting for some other process to bind a variable in the call, it is not classed as a non-candidate clause. Thus, if one of the clauses preceding a ';' is suspended, the search for a candidate clause does not move past the ';'.

In testing a clause for candidate status, the input matching and the guard evaluation proceed in parallel, but all of the output unification is deferred. In general, the first candidate clause to be found is the one that is used to solve the call. The evaluation *commits* to that clause. There is no backtracking on the choice of clause. At commitment all of the output unification is done: the terms in the output argument positions in the head of the chosen clause are unified with the corresponding arguments in the call. It is an error if the guard evaluation of a clause attempts to bind a variable of the call made accessible via an input match.

Example search control

A definition of the form

        Clause1;
        Clause2.
        Clause3;
        Clause4.

specifies that *Clause1* should be tried first. If it fails to input match the call or has a failing guard, then *Clause2* and *Clause3* are to be tried in parallel. Finally, if both of these clauses fail to input match or have failing guards, then *Clause4* should be tried. The later clauses are not tried if *Clause1* suspends during the test for candidate status. They are tried only when it is known that *Clause1* definitely is not a candidate clause. The final '.' has no control significance. We shall use '.' as a terminator of definitions, queries and mode declarations.

The guard and body conditions are conjunctions of calls to single-solution relations, including primitive relations of PARLOG such as the set constructors. The conjunctions are built up using either ',' or '&' as conjunction operators. The ',' is the parallel conjunction and the '&' is the sequential conjunction.

        (C1 , C2)

signals that the combined conjuncts *C1* and *C2* are to be evaluated in parallel.

        (C1 & C2)

indicates that *C2* is to be evaluated only when the evaluation of *C1* successfully terminates.

Example Program 1: list partition

The following program is a recursive definition of the relation

partition(*Pivot*,*List*,*Less_list*,*Greater_list*): *Less_list* is the subsequence of elements on *List* less than *Pivot* and *Greater_list* is the subsequence of *List* greater than or equal to *Pivot*.

mode partition(Pivot?,List?,Less_list↑,Greater_list↑).

partition(U,[V|X1],[V|Y1],Z) ← V < U | partition(U,X1,Y1,Z).
partition(U,[V|X1],Y,[V|Z1]) ← U ≤ V | partition(U,X1,Y,Z1).
partition(U,[ ],[ ],[ ]).

We leave the reader to check that the program is a correct and complete description of the relation under its logical reading.

Imperative interpretation

The '.' operators mean that in trying to solve a *partition* call all clauses will be tried in parallel to find a candidate clause. The $V < U$ and $U ≤ V$ conditions are guards. The mode declaration means that the third clause is a candidate only if the second argument of the call is given and is the empty list [ ]. The first clause is a candidate only if the second argument of the call is a partial list structure (it input matches [V|X1]) and U and V are sufficiently determined so that the guard can be evaluated and found to be true. Similar conditions apply to the second clause.

For this program there is never more than one candidate clause. If the second argument of the call is not yet sufficiently determined to enable the input matches with [ ] or [V|X1] to succeed, each clause is suspended waiting for some other process to supply the requisite data. Even if the second argument is given as a partial list structure of the form [V|X1], the first and second clauses will suspend until both U and V are sufficiently determined so that the guards can be evaluated.

When the candidate clause is found, the output unification for its third and fourth arguments is performed. If it is one of the recursive clauses the *partition* call is reduced to a new *partition* call to which the same mode constraints apply. The call will therefore suspend until some other process binds the tail X1 of the input list to the empty list [ ] or to a term of the form [V1|X2] that gives the head of this tail list.

Because only one clause can be a candidate, using the ';' operator between clauses will not affect which clause is selected. It will just limit the number of Or-processes generated during the evaluation of the program in exchange for a slightly slower selection of the candidate clause (on a parallel architecture). The ';' operator allows the PARLOG programmer to make these trade-offs.

3.2.2 Standard form

Example Program 1 is equivalent to the "standard form" program

partition(U,X,Y,Z) ←
    [V|X1] ⇐ X, V < U |
    Y = [V|Y1], partition(U,X1,Y1,Z).
partition(U,X,Y,Z) ←
    [V|X1] ⇐ X, U ≤ V |
    Z = [V|Z1], partition(U,X1,Y,Z1).
partition(U,X,Y,Z) ←
    [ ] ⇐ X |
    Y = [ ], Z = [ ].

where '⇐' and '=' are special unification primitives of PARLOG. In a standard form program all arguments in the head of each clause are variables; all input matching and output unification is done by explicit unification conditions in the guard or body of the clause. The input matching is done in the guard and the output unification in the body. *The mode declaration of a normal PARLOG program determines its standard form.*

The standard form of our *partition* program makes explicit the constraints on unification that are implicit in the head argument terms and the mode declaration of the original program. The mapping into standard form is the first stage of a compilation of the program.

The '⇐' is the *one-way unification* primitive of PARLOG. It can only bind variables in its left argument. It suspends if it could only proceed by binding a variable in its right argument. The '=' is the *full unification* primitive. It unifies its two arguments, possibly binding variables in both. In the logical reading of the program both '⇐' and '=' should be read as the equality relation.

Let us consider the first clause. The term $[V|X1]$ that was in the second (input) argument position of the clause now appears as the left argument of a condition

[V|X1] ⇐ X

in the guard of the clause, where the variable X replaces the term as the second argument in the head of the clause. This tells us explicitly that this term can only be used for input matching against the given argument X of the call. The term $[V|Y1]$ that appeared as the third (output) argument of the call now appears as the right argument of the unification

Y = [V|Y1]

in the body of the clause. Y is the variable that now appears as the third argument of the head of the clause, and it will be unified with the actual argument when the clause is invoked. The use of the full unification primitive rather than '⇐', and the placing of it in the clause body rather than in the guard, reflects the output mode constraint on the third argument term. $[V|Y1]$ is unified with the given third argument of the call. The output unification can be performed immediately after the commitment, when the clause becomes the selected candidate clause.

By first mapping into standard form, and then further compiling the '⇐' calls, we can completely compile most of the unification of a PARLOG single-solution relation definition. The only other residue of run-time unification is a test that two terms are syntactically identical. This test does *not* bind variables in either term; this is a very significant property of the language. The compilation of PARLOG programs is more fully treated by Clark and Gregory (1985) and Gregory (1987).

Example Program 2: quicksort

The following is a recursive definition of the relation

sort(List,Sorted_list): *Sorted_list* is an ordered permutation of *List*,

which behaves as a parallel quicksort algorithm. The program uses the above *partition* relation and an auxiliary relation

append(List1,List2,Appended_list): *Appended_list* comprises the sequence of elements on *List1* followed by those on *List2*.

```
mode sort(List?,Sorted_list↑), append(List1?,List2?,Appended_list↑).

sort([Hd|Tail],Sorted_list) ←
    partition(Hd,Tail,List1,List2),
    sort(List1,Sorted_list1),
    sort(List2,Sorted_list2),
    append(Sorted_list1,[Hd|Sorted_list2],Sorted_list).
sort([ ],[ ]).

append([Hd|Tail],List2,[Hd|Atail]) ←
    append(Tail,List2,Atail).
append([ ],List2,List2).
```

These definitions have the following standard forms:

```
sort(List,Sorted_list) ← [Hd|Tail] ⇐ List |
    partition(Hd,Tail,List1,List2),
    sort(List1,Sorted_list1),
    sort(List2,Sorted_list2),
    append(Sorted_list1,[Hd|Sorted_list2],Sorted_list).
sort(List,Sorted_list) ← [ ] ⇐ List |
    Sorted_list = [ ].
```

append(List1,List2,List) ← [Hd|Tail] ⇐ List1 |
 List = [Hd|Atail],
 append(Tail,List2,Atail).
append(List1,List2,List) ← [ ] ⇐ List1 |
 List = List2.

Note that all the conditions in the body of the recursive clause for *sort* are joined by the parallel conjunction operator ','. This means that as soon as this clause is used to reduce some *sort* call with input argument a non-empty list (or non-empty partial list), the process evaluating the call forks into four concurrent processes. Because of the mode declarations, the variables *List1* and *List2* become one-way communication channels between the *partition* process and the two recursive *sort* processes and the variables *Sorted_list1* and *Sorted_list2* become one-way communication channels between the two *sort* processes and the *append* process. The first *sort* process will suspend (because of the read-only constraint on its first argument) until the *partition* process finds an element E on its *Tail* argument less than the pivot element *Hd*. At that point, this recursive *sort* process itself forks into four processes with their own local communication channels and E as its pivot element. Similarly, the second *sort* process forks into four processes as soon as the *partition* process has found an element on *Tail* greater than or equal to *Hd*.

The *append* process is constrained by the supply of the stream of elements on the channel *Sorted_list1*. And when they are sent from the first *sort* process, it passes them through to the output stream *Sorted_list*. When the *append* process terminates on reaching the end of the *Sorted_list1* input stream, its output stream *Sorted_list* is identified with *append*'s second input argument [*Hd*|*Sorted_list2*] via the output unification of the second *append* clause. This has the effect of immediately placing all elements that have already been generated by the second *sort* process onto *Sorted_list*. Any further elements put onto *Sorted_list2* by this process are then put directly onto *Sorted_list*.

3.2.3 Constraining the parallelism

As with the *partition* program, the Or-parallel search for a candidate clause for each *sort* and *append* call can be replaced by a sequential search by using ';' operators between the clauses. Again, this will not affect the choice of the candidate clause since there is always only one candidate for any *sort* or *append* call in the declared modes.

The degree of forking of each *sort* process can usefully be constrained by using '&' operators. If we write the recursive clause as

 sort([Hd|Tail],Sorted_list) ←
  partition(Hd,Tail,List1,List2) &

> (sort(List1,Sorted_list1), sort(List2,Sorted_list2)) &
> append(Sorted_list1,[Hd|Sorted_list2],Sorted_list).

the *sort* process does not immediately fork. The '&' following the *partition* call means that this process must terminate before there is a fork into two concurrent recursive *sort* processes. Finally, the '&' after the parallel conjunction means that the *append* process will only start when the recursive *sort* processes have both terminated. This yields a "fork and join" control. The join before the *append* means that elements on the *Sorted_list* output are not passed through as soon as they are produced by the recursive processes. They are only piped through to *Sorted_list* when both processes have terminated.

All parallelism can be removed by using ';' operators between clauses and only the '&' operator between the calls of the recursive clause. The evaluation of a *sort* call will then be the same as in Prolog.

3.2.4 Use of difference lists

The following program is an alternative definition of the *sort* relation over lists in terms of an auxiliary *sort_d* relation between a list and a sorted version of the list, represented as the difference between a pair of lists. The representation of a list as the difference between two lists Y and Z (i.e., as all the elements on Y up to the start of the sublist Z of Y) is an extremely useful logic programming device first formalized by Clark and Tärnlund (1977). In general, it allows lists to be concatenated without an explicit *append*.

Example Program 3: quicksort using difference lists

> mode sort(List?,Sorted_list↑),
>   sort_d(List?,Front_sorted_list↑,Remainder?).
>
> sort(List,Sorted_list) ←
>   sort_d(List,Sorted_list,[ ]).
>
> sort_d([Hd|Tail],Front_sorted_list,Remainder) ←
>   partition(Hd,Tail,List1,List2),
>   sort_d(List1,Front_sorted_list,[Hd|Remainder_plus]),
>   sort_d(List2,Remainder_plus,Remainder).
> sort_d([ ],List,List).

In the logical reading *sort_d* is the relation

> *sort_d(List,Front_sorted_list,Remainder)*: the difference between *Front_sorted_list* and *Remainder* is the sorted version of *List*.

We leave the reader to check that, relative to that reading, the definition of *sort* in terms of *sort_d* is correct and that the two clauses for *sort_d* are both true statements about the relation. The insertion of the pivot element *Hd* into the sorted output is achieved by the requirement that the sorted version of the left partition *List1* is the difference between *Front_sorted_list* and the list [*Hd|Remainder_plus*], where *Remainder_plus* minus *Remainder* is the sorted version of the left partition *List2*.

Because there is no explicit *append* process, this is a much more efficient parallel *quicksort* algorithm than Example Program 2. We use difference lists again when considering bounded buffers in Section 3.3.

3.2.5 Negation as failure

As in Prolog, negation in PARLOG is implemented as failure. The '¬' symbol is the negation-as-failure operator. A condition ¬ *c* succeeds (is considered true) if the condition *c* terminates with failure. As in Prolog, '¬' can be defined in PARLOG by a metalogical program. We give the definition in Section 3.5.

The logical justification of the PARLOG implementation of negation is an elaboration of the justification of negation as failure given by Clark (1978). Essentially, each program is assumed to be a complete definition of its relation. In addition, the second desired property of guards and input terms noted in the introduction must be satisfied in each definition of a relation which will be called in a negation-as-failure proof. That is, the input matches and guard conditions of each clause must be such that, if they are satisfied (the clause is a candidate), the body conditions of the clause are false if and only if the body conditions of every other candidate clause are false. Without this condition being satisfied, failure of the computation of a selected candidate clause could not be interpreted as falsity of the condition being evaluated; we need to know that every other candidate clause would fail.

Example Program 4: parallel search of two lists

Hogger (1982) developed an IC-PROLOG program that would check if a given element was on either one of a pair of lists by searching down the lists in parallel. The following program treats the same example in PARLOG:

```
mode on(Element?,List?), on_either(Element?,List1?,List2?).

on(Element,[Element|Tail]).
on(Element,[Element1|Tail]) ← ¬ Element == Element1 |
    on(Element,Tail).

on_either(Element,List1,List2) ← on(Element,List1) | true.
on_either(Element,List1,List2) ← on(Element,List2) | true.
```

In the definition of *on_either*, the '.' operator between the two clauses tells us that they are to be tried in parallel for candidate status. Both clauses will match any call, so there will be a race between their guard evaluations, which means that the element is being tested for membership of both lists in parallel. As soon as one guard succeeds by finding the element on its list, the call will succeed.

The test unification primitive '=='

In the definition of *on*, a '==' test has been used. This is the third PARLOG unification primitive. It tests that two given terms can be unified but *it does not bind variables in either term*. It suspends if it can only continue the test by binding a variable. It waits for some other process to give the variable a value. It fails if the two terms cannot be unified. If it succeeds, the two argument terms are syntactically identical. Like the other two unification primitives '⇐' and '=', a '==' call should be interpreted as a normal equality condition in the logical reading of programs.

The standard form of the *on* program is

> on(Element,List) ←
>   [Element1|Tail] ⇐ List, Element == Element1 | true.
> on(Element,List) ←
>   [Element1|Tail] ⇐ List, ¬ Element == Element1 |
>   on(Element,Tail).

Notice that the repeated use of *Element* in the arguments of the first clause of the original program has now become an explicit test unification *Element == Element1* in the guard. The variable *Element1* now replaces the second use of *Element* in the second argument term *[Element1 | Tail]*. This is because both occurrences of *Element* in the original program are in input arguments. A repeated use of a variable within the input argument terms of a clause is understood by PARLOG as an implicit test that the values passed to the clause in these argument positions are identical. The use of the clause is not allowed to make them identical by binding variables. Hence the translation into the '==' test.

3.2.6 Back communication

Example Program 5: find and retrieve

The following program defines the relation

> *find_retrieve(Pair,List_of_pairs)*: *Pair* is of the form *(Key, Value)* and it is a member of *find_retrieve((Key, Value),Rem_list)*.

We leave the reader to check that the clauses are true statements about the intended meaning of *find_retrieve*. Remember that '=' is read as normal equality.

Although the program defines a list membership relation, its use is to retrieve a value for a given key. It will co-operate with some other process to construct a (*Key, Value*) pair that is on the list. The other process must generate the pair structure because the *find_retrieve* program performs an input match on its first argument, so the first argument must be a term of the form (*Key, Value*). That process must also generate a non-variable value for the *Key* variable of this pair because this must be compared, in the input matching of the first clause and in the guard of the second clause, with the key of the first pair on the second argument, *List_of_pairs*. Notice that neither the input matching nor the guard requires the *Value* variable of the input term (*Key, Value*) to be instantiated.

In fact, in normal use, the *Value* variable of the input pair will not be given a value by the other process: it will be bound by the *find_retrieve* process when it finds the given key on its list of pairs. When it finds the key, the first clause becomes a candidate clause. The single body call of this clause is a unification *Value = Value1* that binds the variable *Value* (if unbound) to the *Value1* associated with the given key.

The explicit use of the unification '=' is essential. If we were to replace the first clause by

> find_retrieve((Key,Value),[(Key,Value)|Rem_list]).

then both the search *Key* and its associated *Value* would have to be given in any call to the program. Like the *on* program of Example Program 4, it could only be used for testing. This is because the standard form of the above alternative is

> find_retrieve(Pair,List_of_pairs) ←
>   (Key,Value) ⇐ Pair,
>   [(Key1,Value1)|Rem_list] ⇐ List_of_pairs,
>   Key == Key1,
>   Value == Value1 | true.

whereas the standard form of the original (correct) clause is

> find_retrieve(Pair,List_of_pairs) ←
>   (Key,Value) ⇐ Pair,
>   [(Key1,Value1)|Rem_list] ⇐ List_of_pairs,
>   Key == Key1 |
>   Value = Value1.

The important difference is that in the standard form of the original clause the unification of *Value* and *Value1* is done by the unifier '=' in the body, whereas in the alternative clause the unification is performed by a test unification in the guard. Recall that the repeated use of a variable in the input argument terms of a clause is always understood as a test that the values given in the respective positions in the arguments of the call are identical.

3.2.7 The PARLOG unification related primitives

We have now introduced three of the unification related primitives of PAR-LOG. In addition, there are two others: *var* and *data*. All of them can be used in source PARLOG programs. To summarize, the unification primitives are as follows:

$T \Leftarrow T'$ *One-way unification.* No variable in T' will be bound. It suspends if it can proceed only by binding a variable in T'. Variables in T must be unbound at the time of the call. The call generates bindings for variables in T in order to make T and T' syntactically identical.

$T = T'$ *Full unification.* T and T' are unified, with the possibility of variables in both T and T' being bound.

$T == T'$ *Test unification.* No variable in either T or T' will be bound. It suspends if it can proceed only by binding a variable. It succeeds if T and T' are syntactically identical. It fails if they cannot be unified because of a mismatch of constants or functors.

$var(X)$ The *var* primitive is the usual Prolog metalogical primitive for testing if a variable is unbound. Succeeds if X is an unbound variable; fails otherwise.

$data(X)$ Suspends if X is an unbound variable; succeeds otherwise. The condition $data(X)$ is *not* equivalent to $\neg var(X)$. A $\neg var(X)$ condition will succeed if X is instantiated at the time that the condition is evaluated but will fail if X is an unbound variable when the condition is evaluated. A $data(X)$ condition will similarly succeed if X is non-variable, but it will *suspend* if it does not have a value, waiting for some other process to supply the value.

The first three are read as normal equality conditions. The *var* and *data* tests in a clause should be ignored in the logical reading of a program. They have no logical weight; they are used purely for the control effect.

3.2.8 Converting Or-parallel search to And-parallel evaluation

Example Program 6: generalized list membership test

mode member(Element?,List?,Stop_message?,Answer↑).

member(Element,[ ],Stop_message,no).	(1)
member(Element,[Element|List],Stop_message,yes);	(2)
member(Element,[Element1|List],yes,dont_know).	(3)
member(Element,[Element1|List],Stop_message,Answer) ←	
member(Element,List,Stop_message,Answer).	(4)

This program is a generalization of the *on* relation of Example Program 4. It is a program for the relation

member(Element,List,Stop_message,Answer): *Answer=yes* and *Element* is on *List*; or *Answer=no* and *Element* is not on *List*; or *Answer=dont_know* and *Stop_message=yes* and *Element* may or may not be on *List*.

The program for *member* always succeeds with an explicit answer to a list membership question even if this is a *dont_know*. The role of the *Stop_message* argument is interesting. This input argument is only tested by clause (3). Clause (4) just passes the argument through to its recursive call unchanged. Let us suppose that the *Stop_message* argument is initially an unbound variable. Clause (3) will suspend, but this will not prevent one of the other clauses being used. So the search down the list can proceed as normal and eventually terminate with a *yes* or *no* answer. However, if this *stop-message* variable is given the value *yes* by some other process during the search down the list, clause (3) becomes a candidate. If it is selected, its use will prematurely terminate the search with the *dont_know* answer. This is the role of the *Stop_message* argument.

Notice that the use of ';' after the second clause means that our premature termination clause (3) only competes for candidate status with the recursive clause (4). Clause (2), which terminates the search with a *yes* answer, will be selected in preference to the third clause if they are both candidate clauses. However, clause (4) is as likely to be selected as clause (3). To make sure that the search is terminated as soon as possible, we must add a guard to clause (4) which fails if the *Stop_message* has been set.

Simply adding the test

$\neg$ Stop_message == yes

to the guard of clause (4) is not sufficient, because this will suspend the clause until *Stop_message* has some value. We want the clause to be a candidate if *Stop_message* has a value that is not equal to *yes* or it has not yet been given a value. We must therefore use the test

not_stopped_by(Stop_message)

where *not_stopped_by* is defined by the program

mode not-stopped-by(?).

not_stopped_by(Stop_message) $\leftarrow$ var(Stop_message) | true.
not_stopped_by(Stop_message) $\leftarrow$ $\neg$ Stop_message == yes | true.

Like the *var* test used in its definition, *not_stopped_by* has no logical interpretation. If used in the guard of the fourth *member* clause, it is to be ignored in the declarative reading of the *member* program.

Example Program 7: And-parallel communicating search

Using the modified program for *member*, we can give an alternative single-clause definition of *on_either* which achieves the effect of the Or-parallel race between the two guard evaluations of Example Program 4 by an And-parallel evaluation of communicating calls.

> mode on_either(Element?,List1?,List2?), compose(Answer1?,Answer2?).

> on_either(E,List1,List2) ←
>   member(E,List1,Answer2,Answer1),
>   member(E,List2,Answer1,Answer2),
>   compose(Answer1,Answer2).

> compose(yes,X).
> compose(X,yes).

Because the answer produced by each *member* process is used as the *stop_message* argument of the other process, the behavior of this program is very similar to the behavior of the two clause definition of Example Program 4. The other *member* process will be terminated if one of them produces a *yes* answer. This is the PARLOG version of the IC-PROLOG program that Hogger (1982) gave. There is no IC-PROLOG analogue of the two clause PARLOG program because IC-PROLOG does not have parallel search for a candidate clause.

3.2.9 Safety check on guards

The *find_retrieve* program of Example Program 5 is an example of a process whose evaluation binds a variable to which access was gained by an input match. This form of back communication can only be effected by calls in the body of the clause. In the case of the *find_retrieve* program it was effected by the unification in the body. No guard condition is allowed to side-effect an input argument by binding one of its variables, because this would be a communication of a binding to the call prior to commitment to use the clause. The following program, which makes use of *find_retrieve*, illustrates the potential pitfall.

Example Program 8: a file store manager

> mode filestore(Commands?),
>   fs(Commands?,In_fs?,Out_fs↑),
>   trans(Command?,In_fs?,Out_fs↑).

> filestore(Commands) ←
>   fs(Commands,[ ],Out_fs).

> fs([Command|Commands],In_fs,Out_fs) ←
>   trans(Command,In_fs,Fs),

> fs(Commands,Fs,Out_fs).
> fs([ ],Fs,Fs).

The relations should be read:

filestore(Commands): *Commands* is a legal history of commands which update and check for membership of a filestore that is initially empty,

fs(Commands,In_fs,Out_fs): *Commands* is a legal history of commands that update and check for membership of a filestore *In_fs*, leaving the filestore in state *Out_fs*,

trans(Command,In_fs,Out_fs): *Out_fs* is the state of the *In_fs* filestore after execution of the command *Command*.

We assume that the command stream is a list of the form

> [add(fred,"..contents1...",ok),
> in(fred,"..contents1..."),
> add(fred,"..contents2...",already_exists),
> delete(fred,ok),...]

That is, a command is a term the functor of which is the command name and the arguments are the arguments of the command, sometimes accompanied by an appropriate response message (e.g., *ok* and *already_exists*). A legal history is one satisfying requirements such as: an *in* command must have the same contents associated with a file name F as the immediately preceding *add* command for F, and an *add* command must have the response *already_exists* if there is a preceding *add* for the same file name with no intervening *delete* for that file. We leave the reader to check that, given the intended meaning of the *trans* relation, the above program is a correct definition of *filestore*. The legality of the history is guaranteed by the inclusion of the state of the filestore as an argument of the auxiliary relation *fs*.

The way in which *trans* is defined is crucial to the way we can use this program. The best use is not to simply check some completely specified history of commands but to co-operate with some other process in the construction of the history.

Let us assume that the other process generates a sequence of partial commands such as

> [add(fred,"..contents1...",Response1),
> in(fred,Response2),
> add(fred,"..contents2...",Response3),
> delete(fred,Response4),...]

where *Response1*, *Response2*, *Response3* and *Response4* are unbound variables. Like the *find_retrieve* program, we need to define *trans* so that it accepts such partial messages, finds the new state of the filestore, and binds the variable of the message to make it a valid command in the history.

If we represent the filestore database as a list of (*Filename,File*) pairs ordered by a '<' relation on filenames, we can use the *find_retrieve* program to retrieve a file associated with a given filename. The key will be the file name.

find_retrieve will be the program called by *trans* when it accepts an *in* message. We need analogous programs to handle *add* and *delete* commands. We shall therefore need to define the auxiliary relations:

add((*Key,Value*),*List,Newlist*): *Newlist* is the ordered *List* with (*Key,Value*) inserted,

delete(*Key,List,Newlist*): *Newlist* is the ordered *List* with a pair (*Key,Value*) deleted.

They are defined by:

    mode add(?,?,↑), delete(?,?,↑).

    add((Key,Value),[ ],[(Key,Value)]).
    add((Key,Value),[(Key1,Value1)|List],[(Key,Value),(Key1,Value1)|List]) ←
        Key < Key1 | true.
    add((Key,Value),[(Key1,Value1)|List],[(Key1,Value1)|New_list]) ←
        Key1 < Key |
        add((Key,Value),List,New_list).

    delete(Key,[(Key,Value)|List],List).
    delete(Key,[(Key1,Value1)|List],[(Key1,Value1)|New_list]) ←
        Key1 < Key |
        delete(Key,List,New_list).

We can now write the *trans* program. It must have clauses for the three types of command, and for each command it must bind the response variable to the correct response by a call in the body of the clause. For the command *in*(*Filename,Reply*), *Reply* will be the contents of the named file if it is in the database; otherwise the message *not_found*. For the command *add*(*Filename,Newfile,Reply*), the given file *Newfile*, named *Filename*, will be added to the database if it is not there and the *Reply* bound to *ok*; otherwise the *Reply* will be *already_exists*. For *delete*(*Filename,Reply*), the named file will be deleted and an *ok* reply given if it is in the database; otherwise the *Reply* will be *not_found*.

    trans(in(Filename,Reply),Fs,Fs) ←
        find_retrieve((Filename,File),Fs) | Reply = File.
    trans(add(Filename,Newfile,Reply),In_fs,Out_fs) ←
        add((Filename,Newfile),In_fs,Out_fs) | Reply = ok.

trans(delete(Filename,Reply),In_fs,Out_fs) ←
    delete(Filename,In_fs,Out_fs) | Reply = ok;
trans(in(Filename,Reply),Fs,Fs) ←
    Reply = not_found.
trans(add(Filename,Newfile,Reply),Fs,Fs) ←
    Reply = already_exists.
trans(delete(Filename,Reply),Fs,Fs) ←
    Reply = not_found.

Notice the use of the ';' to separate the first three clauses from the last three which report the unsuccessful attempt to apply a command. This is the first use of the sequential search operator that affects the logical reading of the program. For a correct logical reading, each of the last three clauses should be read as though they had an extra guard condition which is the negation of the guard in the corresponding clause before the ';'. For example, the second clause for an *add* command must be read as though it were the clause

trans(add(Filename,Newfile,Reply),Fs,Fs) ←
    ¬ add((Filename,Newfile),Fs,Out_fs) :
    Reply = already_exists.

The assignment to the response variable *Reply* is achieved in each of the program clauses by a unification in the body of the clause. Since the guard condition of the first clause does generate a binding for the *File* variable of the call, it would have been more natural to write it as

trans(in(Filename,Reply),Fs,Fs) ←
    find_retrieve((Filename,Reply),Fs) | true.

But this would result in a guard evaluation that tries to bind a variable *Reply* in an input term and, hence, in the call. In this case, it is very easy for a compiler to discover that a variable in an input term may be bound by a call in the guard. This is because the variable appears in the output argument position of the guard call. More generally, we can use the mode declarations of the program coupled with a data flow analysis to check that each guard of a clause is *safe*, i.e., is such that its evaluation will not attempt to bind a variable in an input argument term of the clause. The details are given by Clark and Gregory (1985).

    The fact that it is possible to check at compile-time for the safety of guards means that no complex mechanism is needed to protect call variables from being bound by a guard evaluation. The compile-time safety check, and the compilation of all output unification into '=' calls in the body of the clause, guarantee that no bindings can be made to variables in the call until the evaluation commits to the use of some candidate clause. It is a significant bonus that results from using modes to specify the communication constraints on processes.

3.2.10 Back communication versus tagged merging

The ability to communicate directly back to a process by binding a variable transmitted in a message sent by it means that message streams do not need to be tagged. Consider the conjunction

user1(Requests1), user2(Requests2),
merge(Requests1,Requests2,Requests), filestore(Requests)

where *filestore* and *merge* are as already defined. When the filestore process receives a message of the form *in(Filename,Reply)*, it simply binds the *Reply* variable to the contents of the named file. The contents value is then immediately communicated back to the user process that sent the request message, despite the fact that this request has been merged with those from the other user. This is because *Reply* is a variable that is shared with a particular user process.

In our earlier Relational Language (Clark and Gregory, Chapter 1), and in most functional languages, e.g., Henderson (1982), the *merge* process would have to tag the messages so that the responses can be routed back to the appropriate user. The communication would also require an extra channel for responses. It could be expressed as

user1(Requests1,Replies1), user2(Requests2,Replies2),
tagged_merge(Requests1,Requests2,Requests),
filestore(Requests,Replies),
tagged_split(Replies1,Replies2,Replies)

There is a potential penalty associated with messages containing variables. It calls for an implementation in which there is a global address space for variables that will be passed between processes.

3.3 Lazy Evaluation and Bounded Buffer Processes

Every parallel process in PARLOG is eager. The only constraint on evaluation is the non-availability of data that must be supplied by some other process because of a mode constraint. This means that a producer process can run ahead of its consumers to an arbitrary extent. If we wish to constrain a producer, we must invert the normal consumer-producer relationship, making the consumer a producer of a request list of variables that are given values by the producer.

As a simple example, consider the eager program

mode integers_from(Int?,Int_list↑).

integers_from(Int,[Int|Int_list]) ←
    Intplus is Int+1,

integers_from(Intplus,Int_list).

which describes the relation

integers_from(Int,Int_list): *Int_list* is the infinite list of successive integers beginning at *Int*.

Once supplied with the initial value of *Int* in a call such as

integers_from(2,Stream)

the process will continue to autonomously generate successive integers, each of which is placed on the output *Stream*.

To transform this into a lazy program, we must change the mode so that the second argument is input, not output. Like the *filestore* program of the last section, we can initially think of the required lazy program as a program for checking that some given integer seed and some given list of integers satisfies the relation. The checking version of *integers_from* would be defined by

mode integers_from(Int?,Int_list?).

integers_from(Int,[Int|Int_list]) ←
    Intplus is Int+1,
    integers_from(Intplus,Int_list).

This checking program is constrained by the supply of integers on its second argument *Int_list*. It cannot run ahead of the rate at which this list is generated by some other process because of the input match constraint on the second argument. The check of the incoming integer values results from the repeated use of *Int* in the two input arguments of the head of the clause. Remember that this repetition is equivalent to the inclusion of a '==' test in the guard.

The final transformation is to make this a program that will accept a list of variables (rather than a list of integers) as its second argument, which it instantiates to produce the list of successive integers. We can do this by using an explicit unification in the body of the clause. This makes the first element of the incoming stream of variables the same as the seed integer by binding the request variable at the head of the stream to the seed value. The program becomes

mode integers_from(Int?,Int_list?).

integers_from(Int,[Int1|Int_list]) ←
    Int1 = Int,
    Intplus is Int+1,
    integers_from(Intplus,Int_list).

This program again generates successive integers but is constrained by the rate at which the list of variables to be instantiated is supplied by some other process. The instantiation of each supplied variable is a back communication of the next integer to the process that placed the variable on the list.

Finally, to allow for termination of the *integers_from* program when the generator of the request list requires no more successive integers, we simply add the termination clause

integers_from(Int,[ ]).

This generalizes the described relation so that it holds for any list of successive integers. The *integers_from* process terminates when the request generator terminates the request stream.

3.3.1 An eager primes program and its lazy variant

Let us now treat a more elaborate example. The following program implements the "sieve of Eratosthenes" algorithm for generating the infinite list of primes. It is an eager generator of the infinite list of successive primes starting at 2. It makes use of the above eager *integers_from* program.

```
mode integers_from(Int?,Int_list↑),
     primes(Prime_list↑),
     sift(List?,Sifted_list↑),
     filter(Filter_num?,List?,Filtered_list↑),
     divides(Int1?,Int2?).

integers_from(Int,[Int|Int_list]) ←
     Intplus is Int+1,
     integers_from(Intplus,Int_list).

primes(Prime_list) ←
     integers_from(2,Int_list),
     sift(Int_list,Prime_list).

sift([Num|List],[Num|Sifted_list]) ←
     filter(Num,List,Filtered_list),
     sift(Filtered_list,Sifted_list).

filter(Filter_num,[Num|List],[Num|F_list]) ←
     ¬ divides(Filter_num,Num) |
     filter(Filter_num,List,F_list).
filter(Filter_num,[Num|List],F_list) ←
     divides(Filter_num,Num) |
     filter(Filter_num,List,F_list).
```

The relations should be read:

primes(Prime_list): *Prime_list* is the infinite list of prime numbers beginning at 2.

sift(List,Sifted_list): *Sifted_list* is the infinite *List* except that each number on *List* which is a multiple of a preceding number has been removed.

filter(Filter_num,List,Filtered_list): *Filtered_list* is the infinite *List* except that all numbers that are multiples of *Filter_num* have been removed.

integers_from(Int,Int_list): *Int_list* is the infinite list of successive integers beginning at *Int*.

divides(Int1,Int2): *Int2* is an integer multiple of *Int1*.

Behavior of the program

An evaluation of the call

primes(Prime_list)

will cause two top-level processes to be spawned: an *integers_from* process generating the infinite list of integers beginning at 2, and a *sift* process sifting this list of integers by removing from the list any integer which is an exact multiple of an integer earlier in the list. The *sift* process recursively spawns new processes. A new *filter* process is set up for each integer that passes through all preceding *filter* processes. The process picture after two *filter* processes have been set up is

integers_from(4,Int_list)
↓
filter(2,Int_list,F_list1)
↓
filter(3,F_list1,F_list2)
↓
sift(F_list2,Rem_primes)
↓
[2,3|Rem_primes]

The *integers_from* process is not constrained in any way once it has started. It can therefore run ahead of the other processes to an arbitrary extent. This is related to another problem: we cannot terminate the *primes* process after some initial sequence of primes has been generated. To do this, we must reverse the top-level data flow of the program and generalize the program so that the relations it describes also hold for finite lists of integers.

As with the above transformation of *integers_from*, we must transform each producer process into a consumer of a list of variables that are requests for the output values it would generate in the normal producer mode. Correspondingly, we must also transform each consumer into a generator of the list of request variables. Because each transformed producer cannot run ahead of its request stream of variables, it will then be constrained by the needs of its former consumer.

The following is a rewrite of the above program to produce a "lazy" primes program. It is essentially a program to check that some given list of integers is a sequence of successive primes, modified so that it accepts a list of variables which it instantiates to a list of primes.

```
mode integers_from(Int?,Int_list?),
    primes(Prime_List?),
    sift(List↑,Sifted_list?),
    filter(Filter_num?,List↑,Filtered_list?),
    divides(Int1?,Int2?),
    test(Filter_int?,Int?,In_list?,Out_list↑).

integers_from(Int,[Int1|Int_list]) ←
    Int1 = Int,
    Intplus is Int+1,
    integers_from(Intplus,Int_list).
integers_from(Int,[ ]).

primes(Prime_list) ←
    integers_from(2,Int_list),
    sift(Int_list,Prime_list).

sift([Num|List],[Num|Sifted_list]) ←
    filter(Num,List,Filtered_list),
    sift(Filtered_list,Sifted_list).
sift([ ],[ ]).

filter(Filter_num,[Num|List],[F_num|F_list]) ←
    test(Filter_num,Num,[F_num|F_list],R_list).
    filter(Filter_num,List,R_list).
filter(Filter_num,[ ],[ ]).

test(Filter_num,Num,[F_num|F_list],F_list) ←
    ¬ divides(Filter_num,Num) |
    F_num = Num.
test(Filter_num,Num,R_list,R_list) ←
    divides(Filter_num,Num) | true.
```

Notice that *integers_from*, *filter* and *sift* have each been generalized so that they are not restricted to infinite list arguments. For each relation there is now an explicit base case clause. The new *test* relation should be read

test(Filter_num,Num,In_list,Out_list): either *In_list* is *Out_list* and *Filter_num* divides *Num* or *In_list* is *[Num|Out_list]* and *Filter_num* does not divide *Num*.

Behavior of the program

The program is invoked with a call such as

primes([U,V,W,X,Y,Z]).

in which a list of variables specifying the number of primes required is given as input or is supplied incrementally by some other process.

The call is immediately reduced to

integers_from(2,Int_list), sift(Int_list,[U,V,W,X,Y,Z])   (A)

The *sift* process has the mode ($\uparrow$,?). It accepts the list of variables representing the request for a list of six primes. It generates on its *Int_list* argument a request list of variables to the *integers_from* process. As we shall see, *sift* generates a request list of exactly the right length. It requests from *integers_from* the exact number of consecutive integers that will *sift* into a list of six primes.

We have already described the behavior of the lazy *integers_from* program, so we shall just examine the *sift* process. This passes on the request for an integer passed to it from the parent *primes* call to the *integers_from* process. It does this by binding the output variable *Int_list* of the *sift* call in (A) to the term [*Num*|*List*]. *Num* will now be the variable *U* at the head of the request list sent to *primes*. *sift* then reduces to a *filter* process and a recursive *sift* process:

filter(U,List,Filtered_list), sift(Filtered_list,[V,W,X,Y,Z])

The *filter* process must immediately suspend until it gets a request on its *Filtered_list* input argument sent by the recursive *sift* call. Neither *filter* clause can yet be used because of the read-only constraint on the match with the third argument. The recursive *sift* process can generate the required request by consuming the next variable *V* on its input request list and passing it through to the suspended *filter* process by binding *Filtered_list* to [*V*|*List1*]. Indeed, it can consume all of the variables that are on its input request stream before terminating when it reaches the end of the list. If this happens before any other call has been reduced, the result will be six suspended *filter* calls and an *integers_from* call:

integers_from(2,[U|List]),
filter(U,List,[V|List1]),
filter(V,List1,[W|List2]),
filter(W,List2,[X|List3]),
filter(X,List3,[Y|List4]),
filter(Y,List4,[Z|List5]),
filter(Z,List5,[ ])

As soon as *filtered_list* is bound to [*V*|*List1*], the first *filter* clause becomes a candidate clause for the first *filter* call:

> filter(Filter_num,[Num|List],[F_num|F_list]) ←
>   test(Filter_num,Num,[F_num|F_list],R_list),
>   filter(Filter_num,List,R_list).

By the output unification on the second argument, the *List* variable in the call will be bound to [*Num*|*List1*] and a second request will be sent to *integers_from*, for the next integer to compare with the value of *Filter_num*, which as a result of the input match will be the variable *U*. *U* will be bound to 2 by the first reduction of *integers_from*.

The test call in this selected *filter* clause will suspend until both *Filter_num* and *Num* have been returned from *integers_from*. The *test* process compares the numbers. If *Filter_num* does not divide *Num* it passes *Num* back to *sift* by binding the request variable *F_num* to *Num* by the unification

> F_num = Num

Again, notice the essential use of the explicit unification. Writing the first clause of *test* as

> test(Filter_num,Num,[Num|F_list],F_list) ←
>   ¬ divides(Filter_num,Num) | true.

would cause a suspension of the clause waiting for the *sift* process to give a value to the request variable it has sent, so that *filter* can compare this with the *Num* value returned from *integers_from*.

The use of the *test* condition, and the collapse of the two recursive clauses for *filter* of the original eager program into one clause in the lazy program, is needed to avoid a deadlock. Let us see why. Suppose that we had minimally rewritten the original eager *filter* definition, merely inverting the modes of the stream arguments and using an explicit unification for the repeated variables in input arguments.

> filter(Filter_num,[Num|List],[F_num|F_list]) ←
>   ¬ divides(Filter_num,Num) |
>   F_num = Num,
>   filter(Filter_num,List,F_list).
> filter(Filter_num,[Num|List],F_list) ←
>   divides(Filter_num,Num) |
>   filter(Filter_num,List,F_list).
> filter(Filter_num,[ ],[ ]).

Because the *divides* tests are in the guards of the two recursive clauses, and necessarily so, the output unification using the second argument of either clause cannot be made until the guard succeeds. But in each case the guard needs the value of *Num* which can only be returned after the request has been sent to *integers_from* by the output unification on the second argument. There would be deadlock. This is a trap to watch for when writing programs that transmit request streams of variables.

It is actually straightforward for a PARLOG compiler to check for this likely error. It can issue a warning message whenever a variable in an output argument of the clause appears in a guard condition. It must only be a warning because, quite validly, the guard condition may be being used to generate a value for the variable, not to test a value returned by some other process.

3.3.2 Converting a producer-driven interaction into a consumer-controlled interaction

Generalizing from the above example, we can formulate a strategy for transforming a producer-driven interaction into a consumer-controlled interaction. Suppose *producer* is a process generating a stream of values on its last argument that is being consumed by a *consumer* process on its first argument. The programs for the two relations will have mode declarations of the form

mode producer(...,↑), consumer(?,...).

Assuming there is no other communication path between *consumer* and *producer*, the producer will control the rate at which messages are sent to *consumer* and so can exceed the rate at which the messages are used by *consumer*. To transform the program so that the producer cannot run ahead of the consumer's use of the values communicated, we do the following.

First, we change the mode declarations to:

mode producer(...,?), consumer(↑,...).

The producer is probably now a program that can only be used to check that some given stream of messages are messages that it would have sent, and *consumer* will have become a generator of a request stream of variables. To harmonize the communication, we must ensure that the *producer* is a *constructive* checking program. If necessary, we must introduce unifications or other calls capable of binding the variables of the request stream sent by *consumer*. (The introduction of the unification into the body of the *integers_from* clause is an example of this.)

We must also check the *consumer* program for possible deadlock. We must check that no tests are made in a guard on a request variable that will be sent to *producer* only if the clause is selected. If this is the case, we transform the program so that such a test does not need to be made in the guard. This may require the merging of two or more clauses into one clause with a single selecting call outside the guard. (This is exemplified by the rewrite of *filter*, with *test* being used as the selecting call.)

Finally, it may be necessary to amend the producer so that it can respond to a request list of any length (as we had to amend the *integers_from* program). If the *producer* can only generate some finite but unknown number of values, we should generalize it so that when it has returned all the values that it can generate, it signals that there are no more *real* values by binding any further request variables to some special value such as the constant *end*. We then further modify the consumer so that it looks for this value and stops sending requests when it is received.

If *producer* is itself a consumer of a stream of values sent by an auxiliary producer, the same rewrite will need to be applied to this pair if we want to transmit the consumer-controlled interaction through the program.

The above transformation method applies provided there was no non-deterministic merging of messages from a pair of eager producers in the original program. This will need special treatment, as exemplified by the transformation of an eager *merge* into a lazy demand-driven *merge* given below.

The fact that we can achieve the behavior of lazy or demand-driven evaluation in a language with only an eager evaluation operational semantics is a significant bonus. The programming technique, which requires the ability to send messages which are variables, was first illustrated by Takeuchi and Furukawa (Chapter 18) using Concurrent Prolog.

3.3.3 Eager and lazy merging

Consider the program:

mode merge(List1?,List2?,Merged_list↑).

merge([U|X],Y,[U|Z]) ← merge(X,Y,Z).
merge(X,[V|Y],[V|Z]) ← merge(X,Y,Z).
merge([ ],Y,Y).
merge(X,[ ],X).

This can be used as an eager *merge* process in the manner described in Section 3.1. If we change the mode declaration to

mode merge(List1↑,List2↑,Request_list?).

we get a program that will accept a stream of variables on its third argument. Unfortunately, the program does not behave very well as a lazy merge.

A major problem is that when a request is sent (i.e., when the last argument of the call is a partial list of the form $[U1|Z1]$), all four clauses are candidate clauses. If either of the last two clauses are used, a decision is made to prematurely terminate the requests to one or the other of the lazy producers feeding the *merge*.

To avoid premature closure of either the *List1* or the *List2* request streams, before the incoming request stream is itself terminated, we need to replace the last two clauses by the single clause

     merge([ ],[ ],[ ]).

Now, only when the request stream coming in to the lazy *merge* is terminated will the lazy producers feeding the *merge* process have their request streams terminated. Notice that the program is still a complete definition of the merge/split relation.

Fair splitting

    There remains a problem. If the first clause is used, the incoming request is transmitted to the *List1* lazy producer. For fairness, the next request should be sent to the *List2* producer. However, the first clause may again be used when the next request comes. The program does not guarantee the fair distribution of requests down the two channels. Similarly, our original eager *merge* program did not ensure fair merging, a deficiency that we noted in Section 3.1.

A fair demand-driven merge program

    A fair demand-driven merge can be defined by the program:

mode lazy_merge1($\uparrow,\uparrow$,?), lazy_merge2($\uparrow,\uparrow$,?).

lazy_merge1([U|X],Y,[U|Z]) ← lazy_merge2(X,Y,Z).
lazy_merge1([ ],[ ],[ ]).

lazy_merge2(X,[V|Y],[V|Z]) ← lazy_merge1(X,Y,Z).
lazy_merge2([ ],[ ],[ ]).

The alternating recursion ensures the alternation of the onward transmissions of request variables. Either *lazy_merge1* or *lazy_merge2* can be used to initiate the lazy merge; both provide a complete definition of the merge/split relation.

A fair eager merge program

    A fair eager merge can be defined by the program:

    mode eager_merge(?,?,$\uparrow$).

    eager_merge([U|X],[V|Y],[U,V|Z]) ← eager_merge(X,Y,Z).
    eager_merge([U|X],Y,[U|Z]) ← var(Y) | eager_merge(X,Y,Z).
    eager_merge(X,[V|Y],[V|Z]) ← var(X) | eager_merge(X,Y,Z).
    eager_merge([ ],Y,Y).
    eager_merge(X,[ ],X).

The *var* guards in the second and third clauses ensure that they are only used when there are no messages on the other input stream. The *var* tests only affect which clause is selected; they can be ignored in the declarative reading of the program. The first clause must be used when a pair of messages are waiting and both are passed on. Fair and biased merge processes are more fully discussed by Gregory (1987) and Shapiro and Mierowsky (Chapter 14).

3.3.4 Bounded buffer processes

As a relaxation of lazy evaluation, we might allow the producer to run ahead by some fixed number K of transmitted values. When it has generated K values that have not yet been consumed by the consumer, it must suspend. Only when the consumer has picked up the first value in the "buffer" of K pending values should the producer resume in order to transfer another value to the buffer.

To write such a program, we first write the demand-driven program. Then we interpose a bounded buffer process between the consumer and producer. That is, where the consumer and producer are communicating via the request list *Channel* between the two calls

> producer(...,Channel), consumer(Channel,...)

we introduce a new linking call

> producer(...,Channel),
> buffer(K,Channel,Channel1),
> consumer(Channel1,...)

buffer(K,Channel,Channel1) has the logical reading: *Channel1* is *Channel* or some initial sublist of *Channel*. It can be ignored in the declarative reading of the program.

> mode buffer(Size?,Out_requests↑,In_requests?),
>   aux_buffer(Out_requests?,Rem_out_requests↑,In_requests?),
>   diff_list(Size?,Var_list↑,Remainder?).

> buffer(K,Out_requests,In_requests) ←
>   diff_list(K,Out_requests,Remainder),
>   aux_buffer(Out_requests,Remainder,In_requests).

> diff_list(0,List,List).
> diff_list(K,[X|List],Remainder) ← 0 < K |
>   K1 is K–1,
>   diff_list(K1,List,Remainder).

> aux_buffer(Out_requests,[ ],[ ]).
> aux_buffer([Prod_request|Out_requests],[New_request|New_remainder],
>   [Consumer_request|In_requests]) ←
>   Consumer_request = Prod_request,

aux_buffer(Out_requests,New_remainder,In_requests).

The auxiliary relations should be read:

> *diff_list(Size, Var_list,Remainder)*: *Remainder* is *Var_list* minus the first size elements.

> *aux_buffer(Out_req,Rem_req,In_req)*: *In_req* is some initial sublist of the list *Out_req*, and the difference in length between *Rem_req* and *Out_req* is constant.

A declarative reading will not convince us that we have defined a K-element buffer. It can only convince us that *buffer(K,Channel,Channel1)* has the logical reading given above, and hence the introduction of buffer calls will not affect the declarative semantics of a program. To check that we have implemented a buffer, we need to examine the operational semantics.

Let us follow through the behavior of the *buffer* process when $K=3$. The *diff_list* process will generate a difference list of three variables represented by the pair (*Out_requests,Remainder*). The effect will be to bind *Out_requests* to the partial list $[X,Y,Z|Remainder]$.

In the context

```
producer(...,Channel),
buffer(3,Channel,Channel1),
consumer(Channel1,...)
```

the effect will be to immediately send three request variables to producer because the *Channel* variable will be bound to $[X,Y,Z|remainder]$. This allows *producer* to start running and to continue until it fills up the three variables with values. The difference between *Out_requests* and *Remainder*, the list $[X,Y,Z]$, is the buffer between *producer* and *consumer*.

The *aux_buffer* process to which the *buffer* process is reduced accepts requests from *consumer* on its third argument stream; it transfers the value at the head of the buffer to the consumer and it sends a new request to the producer.

For a buffer of size 3, the call to *aux_buffer*, when *consumer* has generated a request, will have the form

aux_buffer([X,Y,Z|Remainder],Remainder,[C_req|C_reqs])

and the variables X, Y, Z already sent to the *producer* may or may not yet have values assigned by the *producer*. The second clause for *aux_buffer* is now a candidate clause:

```
aux_buffer([Prod_request|Out_requests],[New_request|New_remainder],
           [Consumer_request|In_requests]) ←
    Consumer_request = Prod_request,
```

aux_buffer(Out_requests,New_remainder,In_requests).

The output unification between the variable *Remainder* and the [*New_request*|*New_remainder*] second argument in the head of the clause will have the effect of transforming the request list [*X,Y,Z|Remainder*] previously sent to *producer* into the extended request list

[X,Y,Z,New_request|New_remainder]

The request from *consumer* represented by the *C_req* variable is then satisfied by the unification

Consumer_request = Prod_request

which, due to bindings made during the input matching, will be the unification

C_req = X

The *aux_buffer* process then recurses with the call

aux_buffer([Y,Z,New_request|New_remainder],New_remainder,C_reqs)

where the difference between [*Y,Z,New_request|New_remainder*] and *New_remainder* is the new run-ahead buffer for *producer* of size 3.

If we want to ensure that the variable *X* at the head of the buffer has been given a value by *producer* before the consumer request is answered with the unification, we can insert the guard

data(Prod_request)

in the second *aux_buffer* clause. Now the *buffer* process only accepts a request from the consumer if the producer has had time to fill the head of the buffer.

Notice that the buffer process should not be used for the case *K=0*. For this case *aux_buffer* will be invoked with the call

aux_buffer(Remainder,Remainder,[C_req|C_reqs])

and the evaluation will deadlock. This is because the input match constraint on the first argument of the *aux_buffer* second clause can only be satisfied when *Remainder* has been bound to [*New_request|New_remainder*] by the output unification on the second argument. But the output unification can be effected only after the input match constraint is satisfied. The case of *K=0* is the lazy evaluation interaction which does not need an intervening buffer process.

The above implementation of a bounded buffer process is based on the method described by Takeuchi and Furukawa (Chapter 18).

3.4 All-Solutions Relations

An all-solutions relation is one that can appear in the query condition of the two PARLOG set constructor primitives: the eager constructor *set* and the lazy constructor *subset*. The definition of an all-solutions relation comprises a sequence of clauses with no associated mode declaration and no guards. Each clause is terminated by a '.', and the '&' operator is used to "and" together preconditions of the clauses.

The absence of a mode declaration for an all-solutions relation definition suggests that it can be used to find a solution to any pattern of call. This is indeed the case. The match between an all-solutions relation call and one of its clauses is full and unrestricted unification, which can be implemented as an algorithm in the single-solution subset of PARLOG; see Clark and Gregory (1985).

The use of the sequential '&' suggests that the preconditions of the clauses will be evaluated sequentially in the left-to-right order in which they appear in the program. We assume that this is the case, or at least that whenever a clause body is evaluated and there is an unbound shared variable, then the leftmost condition in which it appears will be evaluated sequentially before any other condition in which the variable appears. This means that there is no communication of partial bindings between the conditions of the conjunction, and that the "flow" of bindings is left-to-right as in Prolog. However, it does allow a possible parallel evaluation of conditions with no shared unbound variables.

Finally, the use of the '.' to separate clauses suggests that the clauses may be tried as Or-parallel alternatives when trying to find all of the solutions to a call. This is the case when the program is invoked to find the solutions to a call as part of an eager *set* evaluation. When it is being used to find the *next* solution to a call as part of a lazy *subset* evaluation, the order of the clauses is significant, as in Prolog.

3.4.1 The eager set constructor

The eager set constructor has the mode

$$\text{set(Solutions}\uparrow,\text{Term?},\text{Conjunction?)}$$

and its evaluation will incrementally bind the *Solutions* argument to a list of instantiations of *Term*, one for each successfully terminating evaluation of the *Conjunction*. Thus, the *Solutions* list it generates can be concurrently consumed by an And-parallel process. No assumptions should be made about the order in which the solutions are placed on the output list. All that is guaranteed is that a value of *Term* for every successful evaluation will appear somewhere on the *Solutions* list and that only these values will appear. Duplicate values will occur if two different evaluations of the conjunction produce identical values of *Term*.

The only output from a *set* evaluation that is communicated to other processes is the value produced for the *solutions* argument of the condition. All *global* variables of the defining conjunction (variables that also appear outside the *set* call in calls to other processes) must be given completely constructed values *before* the evaluation of the *set* call is started. This constraint on the global variables of a set constructor is quite common in logic programming languages that have such constructors. As we show (Clark and Gregory, 1985), the restrictions we impose regarding communication between a *set* call and other processes allow a straightforward implementation of an Or-parallel set constructor as an And-parallel PARLOG program.

Logical reading

In a logical reading of a program, the call

set(Solutions,Term,Conjunction)

can be read as the equivalence

For all $X_1,\ldots,X_n,$
    For some $U_1,\ldots,U_k,$
        Conjunction iff *on(Term,Solutions)*

Here, $U_1,\ldots.U_k$ are the *local* variables of *Conjunction*, i.e., the variables that only appear inside *Conjunction*, and $X_1,\ldots,X_n$ are the variables occurring only in *Conjunction* and *Term*. *on* is the list membership relation. The evaluation of the *set* call generates a *Solutions* list that makes this equivalence true.

Example 1

Suppose that

append([ ],Y,Y).
append([U|X],Y,[U|Z]) ←
    append(X,Y,Z).

is given as a definition of an all-solutions relation. The evaluation of the call

set(Segments,X,append(X,Y,[1,2,3]))

will bind *Segments* to some permutation of the list of lists

[[ ], [1], [1,2], [1,2,3]]

The variable Y is local to the defining conjunction and so is implicitly existentially quantified. The *set* call can therefore be read as

For all $X,$

For some Y,
$$append(X, Y, [1, 2, 3]) \text{ iff } on(X, Segments)$$

set calls can be used freely inside single-solution relation definitions:

mode front_segments(List?,List_of_lists↑).

front_segments(List,List_of_lists) ←
  set(List_of_lists,X,append(X,Y,List)).

When *front_segments* is invoked, the *List* input argument must have been completely constructed because the variable *List* is global to the set constructor in the clause. We can check for this by placing an *is_list* condition sequentially before the *set* call. *is_list* is defined by the program

mode is_list(?).

is_list([U|X]) ← is_list(X).
is_list([ ]).

Example 2

Consider the small all-solutions logic database:

monthly_salary(smith,1000).
monthly_salary(jones,1500).

annual-salary(Person,Amount) ←
  monthly_salary(Person,Monthly_amount) &
  Amount is Monthly_amount*12.
annual_salary(brown,12000).

The call

set(Salaries,Amount,annual_salary(Anyone,Amount))

will produce a list of the annual salaries of *jones*, *smith* and *brown* in *some* order. In the evaluation of the rule defining annual salary the rule defining annual salary in terms of monthly salary, the condition *monthly_salary* will be evaluated before the *is* condition in order to generate a binding for their shared variable *monthly_amount*.

In the all-solutions definition

people_with salary(People_list,Salary) ←
  ¬ var(Salary) &
  set(People_list,Person,annual_salary(Person,Salary)).

the variable *Salary* is global and must be given a value before any *people_with_salary* condition is evaluated. The negated *var* test prevents misuse of the clause. In the call

set(Answers,(Salary,People_list),
    of_interest(Salary) & people_with_salary(People_list,Salary)).

this constraint is satisfied, since *Salary* will be given a value by the *of_interest* condition before the *people_with_salary* condition is evaluated. It would be invalid if the conditions were reversed. Because of the check ¬ *var(Salary)* in the *people_with_salary* clause, the incorrect ordering would result in an empty list of answers.

3.4.2 The lazy subset constructor

The lazy subset constructor has the mode

subset(List_of_vars?,Term?,Conjunction?)

The *List_of_vars* that it accepts as its first argument must be given in the call or be generated by some other process. The variables in this list are bound to different instantiations of *Term* given by different successful evaluations of the *Conjunction*. The evaluation of *subset* cannot run ahead of the generator of its input list of variables. In finding the different successful evaluations of its conjunction of conditions, the clauses for each all-solutions relation are tried sequentially, in the order in which they appear in the program.

The evaluation is a Prolog-style backtracking search which may suspend after it has found an answer because it is waiting for another variable on its request *List_of_vars*. If the backtracking search terminates before the end of the request list is reached, all excess request variables are bound to the constant *end*. Only the variables in its *List_of_vars* argument are given values by the evaluation of the lazy subset constructor. As with the eager set constructor, this means that all global variables must have completely constructed values before the evaluation of a *subset* call is begun.

Logical reading

In a logical reading of a program, the call

subset(Solutions,Term,Conjunction)

can be read as the implication

For all $X_1,\ldots,X_n$,
    For some $U_1,\ldots,U_k$,
        [*Conjunction* or *Term=end* if *on(Term,Solutions)*] and
        [*on(Term,Solutions)* if *Conjunction* and *on(end,Solutions)*]

Again, $U_1,\ldots,U_k$ are all the *local* variables of *Conjunction* and $X_1,\ldots,X_n$ are the variables occurring only in *Conjunction* and *Term*. The evaluation of the *subset* call instantiates a given list of variables *Solutions* so that it makes this conditional true.

Example 3

The call

subset([X1,X2],X,append(X,Y,[1,2,3]))

will generate the bindings

X1 = [ ], X2 = [1]

The bindings are *these* two sublists of *[1,2,3]* because the *append* clauses will be used in the order given in Example 1 in the search for the first two solutions of the *append* condition.

Example 4

The sequential conjunction

Z = [X1,X2,X3,X4,X5] &
subset(Z,Salary,annual_salary(Person,Salary))

will produce the answer

Z = [12000,18000,12000,end,end]

Again, the salaries appear in this order because of the ordering of the clauses given in Example 2.

Example 5

The following program could be used as an alternative definition of the lazy *integers_from* program given in Section 3.3. Here, *less_or_eq* is an all-solutions relation and the ordering of the clauses means that a call *integers_from(Int,Int_list)* will generate on *Int_list* a sequence of successive integers starting at *Int*.

```
mode integers_from(?,?).

integers_from(Int,Int_list) ←
    data(Int) &
    subset(Int_list,Num,less_or_eq(Int,Num)).

less_or_eq(Int,Int).
less_or_eq(Int,Num) ← N is Int+1 & less_or_eq(N,Num).
```

3.4.3 A Prolog front-end

Since the *subset* primitive gives a backtracking Prolog-style evaluation, we can use it as the basis of a complete Prolog system embedded in PARLOG. The program below is written in the single-solution relation subset of PARLOG and provides the user interface to the Prolog system.

The interface accepts commands of the form *end*, *add(Clause)*, *delete(Clause)* and *which(Term,Conj)*. *add(Clause)* causes the *Clause* to be added to the database of all-solutions relations, *delete(Clause)* causes it to be deleted. *which(Term,Conj)* invokes the backtracking evaluation of conjunction *Conj* and reports each *Term* solution, one at a time, to the user. After each solution the user can either request the next solution or terminate the search.

At the top level the interface comprises a parallel conjunction

front_end(Commands), user_control(Commands)

of calls which co-operatively construct a history of the interaction represented as a list of *reply(Prompt,Response)* and *display(Message)* terms. The top-level data flow is from *front_end* to *user_control* with back communication via the *Response* variables in messages.

front_end will begin by sending a partial message of the form

reply('Command?',Response_var)

to *user_control*. The 'Command?' is a prompt string that will be displayed on the screen by the *user_control* process. *front_end* will now suspend waiting for a *Response_var* to be given a value which will be a command term that is read in by the *user_control* process. It is the user's response to the prompt. If the command term is *add(Clause)*, the reactivated *front_end* process uses an *assert* primitive to add *Clause* to the database, and a message *display(yes)* is sent to the *user_control* process to report the successful completion of the command.

For a *which(Term,Conj)* command, *front_end* uses the *subset* primitive to evaluate the query, and a request variable is sent to the *subset* process as a request for the first solution. The subsequent entries on the command sequence will then be a sequence of *reply* terms comprising a prompt which is a found answer to the query and a user response which determines whether more solutions are to be found. A user response *c* indicates that the next solution is to be found, while a user response *s* causes the evaluation of the *subset* call to be terminated.

After the successful processing of a command, the *front_end* process recurses to send a new message

reply('Command?',Response_var1)

to the *user_control* process. The interaction terminates when the user enters the command *end*.

The modes of the main relations are

mode front_end(Cmds↑),
    command_response(Cmd?,More_cmds↑),

which_dialogue(F_soln?,More_solns↑,More_cmds↑,Rest_cmds?),
user_control(Cmds?).

and they should be read

front_end(Cmds): *Cmds* is a history list of *reply* terms of the form *reply(Prompt_message,User_response)* and *display* terms of the form *display(Message)* which correspond to a valid query and update interaction with a Prolog database.

command_response(Cmd,More_cmds): *More_cmds* is a history of *reply* and *display* terms which begins with the sequence of terms recording the interaction history for *Cmd*.

which_dialogue(F_soln,More_solns,More_cmds,Rest_cmds): the difference between lists *More_cmds* and *Rest_cmds* is a history of *reply* and *display* terms, beginning with a sequence of *reply* terms which have as their prompt messages the term *F_soln* and then the terms on the list *More_solns*. The last two commands in this history are *reply(Term,s)* and *display(yes)* where *Term* is the last element of *More_solns*, or the last command is *display('no more solutions')* and *end* is the last element of *More_solns*. The preceding commands are all of the form *reply(Term,c)*.

user_control(Cmds): same reading as *front_end(Cmds)*.

They are defined by the program

front_end([reply('Command?',Command)|More_commands]) ←
command_response(Command,More_commands).

command_response(add(Clause),[display(yes)|More_cmds]) ←
assert(Clause) &
front_end(More_cmds).
command_response(delete(Clause),[display(yes)|More_cmds]) ←
retract(Clause) &
front_end(More_cmds).
command_response(which(Term,Conj),More_cmds) ←
subset([Soln|More_solns],Term,Conj),
which_dialogue(Soln,More_solns,More_cmds,Rest_cmds),
front_end(Rest_cmds).
command_response(end,[ ]).

which_dialogue(end,[ ],
[display('no more solutions')|More_cmds],More_cmds);
which_dialogue(F_soln,Solns,
[reply(F_soln,Response)|More_cmds],Rest_cmds) ←

handle_response(Response,Solns,More_cmds,Rest_cmds).

handle_response(c,[Soln|Solns],More_cmds,Rest_cmds) ←
    which_dialogue(Soln,Solns,More_cmds,Rest_cmds).
handle_response(s,[ ],[display(yes)|More_cmds],More_cmds).

handle_response(Response?,Solns↑,More_cmds↑,Rest_cmds?) is an auxiliary
relation needed to test the *c* or *s* value returned in the request variable *Response*
sent by the *which_dialogue* process with the solution *F_soln* to be displayed as
a prompt. If the value is *c*, another request variable *Soln* is sent to the *subset*
process and a recursive call to *which_dialogue* handles this next solution. If the
value is *s*, the output [ ] terminates the request stream to *subset* and the rest of
the command history for this dialogue comprises only the term *display(yes)*.

user_control just writes out messages and reads in response values for request
variables using I/O primitives.

user_control([reply(Message,Reply)|More_cmds]) ←
    write(Message) &
    read(Reply) &
    user_control(More_cmds).
user_control([display(Message)|More_cmds]) ←
    write(Message) & nl &
    user_control(More_cmds).
user_control([ ]).

3.5   Metalevel Programming in PARLOG

3.5.1   The three-argument metacall primitive

The metacall primitive of PARLOG is a three-argument relation: *call(Goal?,
Status↑,Control?)*.

The first argument, *Goal*, is a term denoting a call to a single-solution relation to be evaluated by the metacall. If this evaluation succeeds, the metacall
will succeed with *Status* bound to the constant *succeeded*. Output bindings to
variables of *Goal* are made in the same way as they would be if *Goal* were being evaluated as a normal call. So they may be incrementally constructed, with
the partially constructed terms communicated to other And-parallel calls in the
normal way.

The difference between the metacall and an ordinary call is the handling of
the failure of *Goal*. If the evaluation of *Goal* fails, the metacall will still *succeed*,
but with *Status* bound to the constant *failed*. Any partially constructed output
bindings for variables of *Goal* generated by the evaluation up to the point of
failure remain as bindings for these variables. This contrasts with the failure of

an ordinary call, which causes failure of the guard from which the call was invoked, or the failure of the entire top-level process if it was part of that evaluation. The metacall is used precisely to avoid such a global failure of the computation.

The third argument will normally be an uninstantiated variable at the time of the call. If it is bound to the term *stop* by another process, the evaluation of *Goal* will be terminated with *Status* bound to *stopped*. More generally, the *Control* variable can be incrementally bound to a stream of control messages of the form

[suspend,continue,suspend,continue,. . .|stop]

When the first *suspend* message is sent, the evaluation of the metacall is suspended and the *Status* output variable is bound to

[suspend|Status1]

and when the *continue* is sent, *Status1* is bound to

[continue|Status2]

and so on. Thus, when the *Control* is a stream of messages, the *Status* report is also a stream of messages of the form

[suspend,continue,suspend,continue,. . .|Result]

where the final *Result* is *succeeded*, *failed* or *stopped*.

Logical reading

Because the metacall always succeeds, the condition

call(Goal,Status,Control)

is not logically equivalent to the condition

Goal

Instead, it has the metalogical reading

> *call(Goal,Status,Control):*
> either *Status* is a message stream of the form
>> [*suspend,continue,. . .|succeeded*]
>> and *Control* is a message stream of the form
>> [*suspend,continue,. . .*]
>> and *Goal* is true
> or *Status* is a message stream of the form
>> [*suspend,continue,. . .|failed*]
>> and *Control* is a message stream of the form
>> [*suspend,continue,. . .*]

and *Goal* is false
or *Status* is a message stream of the form
[*suspend,continue*,...|*stopped*]
and *Control* is a message stream of the form
[*suspend,continue*,...|*stop*]
and *Goal* is true or false

The evaluation of *call*(*Goal,Status,Control*) generates bindings for *Status* and the variables of *Goal* for which this metastatement holds.

The simple metacall

The general metacall primitive subsumes the simple single-argument form familiar to Prolog programmers. This evaluates its single argument goal and succeeds or fails depending on the evaluation of *Goal*. It can be defined by the program

mode call(Goal?).

call(Goal) ←
    call(Goal,Status,Control) & Status == succeeded.

During the evaluation of *call*(*Goal*), bindings to variables in *Goal* are made public immediately. However, because of the added test *Status == succeeded*, the call will succeed only if the evaluation of *Goal* succeeds.

call(Goal)

is logically and behaviorally equivalent to

Goal

We can define a two-argument metacall that has the *Status* output argument but lacks the *Control* input. Like the three-argument form, it always succeeds, and bindings to variables in *Goal* are made public as soon as they are made public by the program for *Goal*.

mode call(?,↑).

call(Goal,Status) ←
    call(Goal,Status,Control).

3.5.2 Defining negation as failure

As in Prolog, negation as failure can be defined in PARLOG by a metalogical program. The definition that is analogous to the Prolog definition is

mode ¬ goal?.

> ¬ goal ←
>   call(Goal) | fail;
> ¬ goal.

fail is a PARLOG primitive that always fails. This form of negation as failure is given a logical justification by Clark (1978). The justification requires that a successful evaluation of *Goal* does not generate any bindings for its variables. This condition cannot be guaranteed in Prolog, but in PARLOG we can use mode declarations to ensure that *Goal* is a test-only evaluation. Then, as sketched in Section 3.2.5, the argument of Clark (1978) can be modified to justify the use of this negation as failure operator in PARLOG.

3.5.3 Defining sequential "and"

The sequential "and" ('&') can also be defined by a metalogical program. The conjunction *A* & *B* is evaluated by executing a call to *A* in parallel with a process which is input-suspended awaiting the result of *A*. If the result of *A* is *succeeded*, the second call *B* is called; otherwise the conjunction fails.

> mode Cond1? & Cond2?, nextcall(Status?,Call?).

> A & B ←
>   call(A,Status), nextcall(Status,B).

> nextcall(succeeded,B) ←
>   call(B).

This means that sequential evaluation of calls need not be a primitive control facility of a PARLOG implementation.

We can similarly dispense with sequential search for a candidate clause and implement this using the metacall primitive. The details are given by Clark and Gregory (1984).

3.5.4 Implementing a Unix-like shell

The powerful metacall primitive is an ideal tool for implementing a Unix-style operating system for a PARLOG system in PARLOG. We can define a shell program that accepts a stream of commands to initiate the evaluation of PAR-LOG programs as foreground or background processes and to suspend, resume or prematurely terminate background processes. The methods of programming such a shell are presented by Clark and Gregory (1984), where the PARLOG programs are also compared with similar Concurrent Prolog programs presented by Shapiro (Chapter 19). Here, we give one simple example to illustrate the approach.

The example is a very elementary shell program that handles a stream of commands to run foreground and background processes. The following program for *shell(Cmds?)* behaves as a process which consumes the stream of user commands *Cmds* and invokes each as an auxiliary process using the *call* metacall. The commands are denoted by terms of the form *fg(Proc)* (foreground) or *bg(Proc)* (background), where *Proc* is the PARLOG call to be evaluated as the user process.

> mode shell(cmds?).

> shell([bg(Proc)|Cmds]) ←
>   call(Proc,Status), shell(Cmds).
> shell([fg(Proc)|Cmds]) ←
>   call(Proc,Status) & shell(Cmds).
> shell([ ]).

The first clause terminates the shell evaluation when the command stream is terminated. The second deals with a background command *bg(Proc)* by invoking *Proc* concurrently with the recursive *shell* invocation to process the next command. The third clause is similar but handles foreground commands. It waits for the command process to terminate successfully before recursing to accept the next command. This is due to the use of the sequential "and" ('&') in place of the parallel "and" (',').

Notice that, because of the use of the two-argument form of the metacall, the shell is protected from failure of a user process. If we had used the single-argument metacall, the shell would fail on failure of a user process.

3.6   Concluding Remarks

3.6.1   A brief history of PARLOG

As mentioned in the introduction, PARLOG is a development of earlier work on IC-PROLOG (Clark et al., 1982) and the Relational Language (Clark and Gregory, Chapter 1).

IC-PROLOG began as an attempt to emulate in logic programming the coroutining ideas of lazy LISP (Friedman and Wise, 1976b; Henderson and Morris, 1976) and Kahn and MacQueen's (1977) extension to parallel evaluation. In IC-PROLOG, the equivalent of *data* and *var* tests were expressed by annotations on terms in clause heads, while producer-consumer communication was specified by annotations on variables in clause bodies. The use of annotations was inspired largely by the work of Schwarz (1977).

IC-PROLOG also featured guards, but their role was simply to delay communication; they did not have the effect of commitment. This meant that the implementation of pseudo-parallel evaluation of calls had to provide for backtracking and undoing variable bindings on failure. The implementation of this was crude: on the failure of a process, all evaluation steps that took place after the choice point of the failed process were undone, even evaluation steps of other processes. It proved impossible to efficiently implement a more selective backtracking scheme.

IC-PROLOG was quite well suited to problem solving applications of logic programming (Kowalski , 1979), as was the similar experimental logic programming language of Hansson et al. (1982). In both of these, one could implement such algorithms as the sieve of Eratosthenes primes generator that require some form of non-sequential evaluation. However, we were dissatisfied with the overhead associated with process failure. Moreover, the global backtracking scheme appeared to be viable only in a single-processor implementation. For an efficient parallel implementation, the failure independence of processes seemed to be essential.

The desired property was attained by strengthening the role of guards so that they also had the effect of commitment, as of Dijkstra's (1976) guarded commands and Hoare's (1985) CSP. Our Relational Language incorporated this idea and also introduced mode declarations as the means of imposing communication constraints on processes.

The communication constraints of the Relational Language were actually very strong. The language was designed to allow efficient implementation on a loosely coupled distributed architecture, so messages passing between processes were restricted to variable-free terms. The communication was unidirectional.

The major difference between PARLOG and the Relational Language is the relaxation of the communication constraints to allow the co-operating construction of bindings of shared variables. We made this change when we started to explore the implementation of the Relational Language on the tightly coupled ALICE architecture (Darlington and Reeve, 1981), in which processes share a global memory of packets.

This change was also prompted by a programming need, when we attempted to write a compiler for the Relational Language in itself. As shown by Warren (1980), the use of the logical variable makes Prolog an elegant language for compiler writing; we wanted to use the same techniques in a parallel context. We were further convinced of the need to relax the communication constraints when the elegant use of two-way communication was demonstrated by Concurrent Prolog (Shapiro, Chapter 2). The language resulting from this change was named PARLOG.

3.6.2 Implementations of PARLOG

The first implementation of the language described in this paper was one that runs on top of a Prolog system (Gregory, 1984b). This compiles PARLOG programs to Prolog clauses and simulates And-parallel evaluation by a breadth-first or depth-first scheduling strategy. Sequential PARLOG programs can be run at a speed of up to 20 percent of that of the host Prolog implementation.

We have investigated the implementation of PARLOG on abstract instruction sets designed for Prolog. Gregory (1984a) considers the suitability of McCabe's (1984) Abstract Prolog Machine for this purpose. The same techniques have since been adapted to Warren's (1983) abstract Prolog instruction set by Moens and Yu (1985).

Current implementation efforts are directed toward both parallel and conventional sequential machines. A fast portable implementation of PARLOG (in C) has been constructed and is currently being further enhanced. This is centered on an abstract instruction set, the Sequential PARLOG Machine (Gregory et al., 1987), which is loosely based on Warren's (1983) Prolog machine, but was designed especially for the sequential implementation of PARLOG. Work has begun to extend this instruction set to multiprocessor operation.

Following a pilot implementation of PARLOG on the parallel machine ALICE (Darlington and Reeve, 1981) in 1982, both PARLOG and ALICE have developed substantially. Work has begun on a new compiler from PARLOG to ALICE CTL (Compiler Target Language) (Reeve, 1985), in association with the Alvey "Flagship" project. The principles of this compilation are explained by Lam and Gregory (1987).

3.6.3 Applications of PARLOG

The use of PARLOG as a systems programming language was investigated by Clark and Gregory (1984).

PARLOG is an ideal language for programming runnable specifications of parallel systems. A specification written in PARLOG can be evaluated in several different ways. By running it in the normal manner, the specified system is *simulated* and so exhibits a single evaluation history. The simulation can be controlled by discrete event-driven time, as considered by Broda and Gregory (1984). Alternatively, by combining PARLOG with a backtracking facility, more than one of the possible non-deterministic evaluation histories can be obtained. This allows a user to *browse* through several possible evaluations to explore the behavior, or to obtain all possible histories in order to *verify* that the specification satisfies certain properties. These topics are treated by Gregory et al. (1985).

Natural language processing is another application area for PARLOG. Matsumoto (1986) has rewritten a bottom-up parser, originally written in Prolog, as a PARLOG program. His original logic program is evaluated with a form of Or-parallelism, to explore alternative candidate parsings of a natural language sentence. This is achieved by a transformation into an And-parallel PARLOG program.

3.6.4 Related work

Concurrent Prolog

Although Concurrent Prolog (Shapiro, Chapter 2) and the single-solution component of PARLOG have a great deal in common — both use guarded clauses, committed choice non-determinism and the ability to have variables in messages — there remain significant differences. The major difference is in the way the inter-process communication constraints are expressed. Mode declarations determine the communication constraints on PARLOG processes. A clause invoked by a process can only perform read-only matches with terms in the input argument positions for its declared mode of use and it is suspended if this constraint is not satisfied.

In Concurrent Prolog, programs do not have fixed modes of use. Read-only annotations on variables provide the communication constraint. For example, a read-only constraint on the use of some non-variable term T in the head of a clause is usually specified by a read-only annotation which is placed on the corresponding variable in the call to the relation. A read-only annotated variable cannot be bound to a non-variable. A different call to the relation might not have a read-only annotated variable in that argument position so the term T can then be used for output. That is, the mode of use is determined by the call.

Certain uses of the read-only annotation correspond exactly to PARLOG modes. Indeed, PARLOG programs can be rewritten as Concurrent Prolog programs. However, the use of modes does have significant advantages with respect to efficient implementation. First, as mentioned in Section 3.2, most of the unification in PARLOG is input matching, a simpler operation which can be compiled to simple instructions. These issues are further discussed by Clark and Gregory (1985). Concurrent Prolog must support an elaboration of unification that knows about read-only variables.

Second, the declared modes enable a PARLOG compiler to check that no clause guard binds variables in the call (this was also illustrated in Section 3.2). In Concurrent Prolog this cannot be guaranteed, so that environments must be copied for each clause that is being tried to solve the call (Levy, 1984; Miyazaki et al., Chapter 37). In general, the copying of environments can be very complex and expensive and is one reason why implementation of Concurrent Prolog is limited to the simpler variant, Flat Concurrent Prolog (Mierowsky et al., 1985).

Modes and read-only annotations constitute distinct methods for controlling communication in a parallel logic program. We believe that they have equivalent expressive power. Using the *var* primitive, we believe that we can rewrite Concurrent Prolog programs as PARLOG programs. However, we contend that the mode concept is more natural and easier to use correctly.

Guarded Horn clauses

Another parallel logic programming language, Guarded Horn Clauses, has been described by Ueda (Chapter 4). This is rather similar to PARLOG in which clauses are in standard form (Section 3.2.2) and, as in PARLOG, there is no need to copy environments. The language uses a different communication constraint: a guard must not bind variables belonging to the environment of the invoking call; if it tries to make such a binding, the clause suspends. This constraint is essentially the same as the "safe guards" property of PARLOG. A difference is that, in PARLOG, an error occurs if it is not satisfied (rather than a suspension).

In general, Guarded Horn Clauses require, each time a variable is to be bound, a run-time suspension test that determines whether a variable is global or local to a guard evaluation. This might prove to present a considerable constraint on the target architecture. This is not required in PARLOG because of the insistence that a program pass a *compile-time* safety check. The *run-time* suspension test in PARLOG is much simpler: it simply tests whether a variable is bound. For this reason, current implementation efforts at ICOT are limited to a simpler subset of GHC: Flat GHC.

Or-parallelism

There have been many variants of Prolog proposed that incorporate full Or-parallel evaluation for finding *all* solutions to a conjunction of conditions. For reasons of efficient implementation, none of these proposals combine an Or-parallel search for all solutions of a conjunction with an And-parallel evaluation of the conjunction which has inter-process communication via partial bindings for shared variables. To our knowledge there is only one detailed study, by Pollard (1981), of the problem of integrating And-parallelism — with communication of partial bindings — with the Or-parallel search for all solutions. However, Pollard's underlying abstract machine is highly complex.

Most proposals combine Or-parallel search for all solutions of a conjunction with a *sequential* evaluation of the conjunction, e.g., Ciepielewski (1984), Moto-Oka et al. (1984). The proposals that do allow some And-parallelism usually restrict the parallel evaluation to groups of conditions with no shared variables, e.g., Conery (1983), Conery and Kibler (1981), DeGroot (1984), Kasif et al. (1983).

Other work

The use of lazy set constructors in PARLOG was inspired by the set expressions in the lazy functional language KRC (Turner, 1981). There have been other proposals to incorporate lazy set constructors into logic programming languages, including Kahn (1984b) and Moss (1983).

Acknowledgements

This research was supported by the Science and Engineering Research Council under grant GR/B/97473.

We are grateful to all the people who have read and commented on earlier versions of this paper.

Chapter 4

Guarded Horn Clauses

Kazunori Ueda

NEC Corporation

Abstract

A set of Horn clauses augmented with a *guard* mechanism is shown to be a simple and yet powerful parallel logic programming language.

4.1 Introduction

Kowalski (1974) showed that a Horn clause is amenable to procedural interpretation. Prolog was developed as a sequential programming language based on the procedural interpretation of Horn clauses (Roussel, 1975), and it has proved to be a simple, powerful, and efficient sequential programming language (Warren et al., 1977).

As Kowalski (1974) points out, a Horn clause program allows parallel or concurrent execution as well as sequential execution. However, although a set of Horn clauses may be useful for uncontrolled search as it is, it is inadequate for a parallel programming language capable of describing important concepts such as communication and synchronization. We need some additional mechanism to express these concepts, and this paper shows that this can be effected with only one construct, the *guard*.

We introduce guarded Horn clauses in the following sections. Guarded Horn Clauses (GHC) will be used as the name of our language. We compare GHC with other logic/parallel programming languages. GHC is intended to be the machine-independent core of the Kernel Language for ICOT's Parallel Inference Machine.

4.2 Design Goals and Overview

Our goal is to obtain a logic programming language that allows parallel execution. It is expected to fulfill the following requirements:

(1) It must be a parallel programming language 'by nature'. It must not be a sequential language augmented with primitives for parallelism. That is, the language must assume as little sequentiality among primitive operations as possible in order to preserve parallelism inherent in a Horn-clause program. This would lead to a clearer formal semantics, as well as to an efficient implementation on a novel architecture in the future.

(2) It must be an expressive, general-purpose parallel programming language. In particular, it must be able to express important concepts in parallel programming — processes, communication, and synchronization.

(3) It must be a simple parallel programming language. We do not have much experience with either theoretical or pragmatic aspects of parallel programming. Therefore, we must first establish the foundations of parallel programming with a simple language.

(4) It must be an efficient parallel programming language. We have a lot of simple, typical problems to be described in the language as well as complex ones. It is very important that such programs run as efficiently as comparable programs written in existing parallel programming languages.

Concurrent Prolog (Shapiro, Chapter 2) and PARLOG (Clark and Gregory, Chapter 3) seem to lie near the solution. Both realize processes by goals and communication by streams implemented as lists. Synchronization is realized by read-only variables in Concurrent Prolog and by one-way unification in PARLOG.

GHC inherits the *guard* construct and the programming paradigm established by these languages. The most characteristic feature of GHC is that the guard is the only syntactic construct added to Horn clauses. Synchronization in GHC is realized by the semantic rules of guards.

GHC is expected to fulfill all the above requirements. We have succeeded in rewriting most of our Concurrent Prolog programs. Miyazaki and Ueda have independently written GHC-to-Prolog compilers in Prolog by modifying different versions of Concurrent Prolog compilers on top of Prolog (Ueda and Chikayama, 1985).

4.3 Syntax and Semantics

4.3.1 Syntax

A GHC program is a finite set of guarded Horn clauses of the following form:

$$H \leftarrow G_1, \ldots, G_m \mid B_1, \ldots, B_n. \quad m \geq 0, n \geq 0.$$

where H, G_i's, and B_i's are atomic formulas that are defined as usual. H is called a clause head, G_i's are called guard goals , and B_i's are called body goals. The operator '|' is called a commitment operator. The part of a clause before '|' is called the guard, and the part after '|' is called the body. Note that *the clause head is included in the guard*. The set of all clauses whose heads have the same predicate symbol with the same arity is called a procedure. Declaratively, the above guarded Horn clause is read as "H is implied by G_1, ... , and G_m and B_1, ... , and B_n".

A goal clause has the following form:

$$\leftarrow B_1, \ldots, B_n. \quad n \geq 0.$$

This can be regarded as a guarded Horn clause with an empty guard. A goal clause is called an empty clause when n is equal to 0. The nullary predicate *true* is used for denoting an empty set of guard or body goals.

4.3.2 Semantics

The semantics of GHC is quite simple. Informally, to execute a program is to reduce a given goal clause to an empty clause by means of input resolution using the clauses constituting the program. This can be done in a fully parallel manner under the following rules of suspension:

Rules of Suspension:

(a) Any piece of unification invoked directly or indirectly in the guard of a clause cannot bind a variable appearing in the caller of that clause with

   (i)   a non-variable term or

   (ii) another variable appearing in the caller.

(b) Any piece of unification invoked directly or indirectly in the body of a clause cannot bind a variable appearing in the guard of that clause with

   (i)   a non-variable term or

   (ii) another variable appearing in the guard

   until that clause is selected for commitment (see below).

A piece of unification which can succeed only by making such bindings is suspended until it can succeed without making such bindings. ∎

Note that a set of variables whose instantiation is inhibited by the above rules can vary as computation proceeds. When a variable X in the set S is bound to a non-variable term T (in a way not disallowed above), we include all the variables in T in S and remove X itself from S.

Another rule we have to add is the *commitment* rule. When some clause succeeds in solving (see below) its guard for a given goal, that clause tries to be selected exclusively for subsequent execution of the goal. To be selected, it must first confirm that no other clauses belonging to the same procedure have been selected for the same goal. If confirmed, that clause is selected indivisibly; we say that the goal is committed to that clause and also that that clause is selected for commitment.

We say that a set of goals *succeeds* (or is *solved*) if it is reduced to an empty set of goals by using a selected clause for each initial or intermediate goal: We are interested in a reduction path in which only selected clauses are involved. The notion of failure is not introduced here, but it will be discussed in Section 4.6.1.

It must be stressed that under the rules stated above, anything can be done in parallel: Conjunctive goals can be executed in parallel; candidate clauses for a goal can be tested in parallel; head unification involved in resolution can be done in parallel; head unification and the execution of guard goals can be done in parallel. However, what is even more important is that we can also execute a set of tasks in a predetermined order as long as this does not change the meaning of the program.

The rules of suspension could be more informally restated as follows:

(a) The guard of a clause cannot export any bindings to (or, make any bindings observable from) the caller of that clause, and

(b) the body of a clause cannot export any bindings to (or, make any bindings observable from) the guard of that clause before commitment.

Rule (a) is used for synchronization, so it could be called the rule of synchronization. Rule (b) is rather tricky; it states that we can solve the body of a clause not yet selected for commitment. However, the above restrictions guarantee that this never affects the selection of candidate clauses nor the other goals running in parallel with the caller of the clause. So Rule (b) is effectively the rule of sequencing.

In Concurrent Prolog, the result of unification performed in a guard (including a head) and which would export bindings is recorded locally. In GHC, such unification simply suspends. Suspension of unification due to some guard may be released when some goal running in parallel with the goal for which the guard is being executed has instantiated the variable that caused suspension.

An example may be helpful in understanding the rules of suspension. Let us consider the following program:

> Goal: ← p(X), q(X).   (i)
> Clauses: p(ok) ← true | ....   (ii)
>   q(Z) ← true | Z=ok. (iii)

The predicate '=' is a predefined predicate which unifies its two arguments. This predicate must be considered as predefined, because it cannot be defined in the language.

Clause (ii) cannot instantiate the argument X of its caller to the constant *ok*, since this unification is executed in the guard. This clause has to wait until X is instantiated to *ok* by some other goal. On the other hand, Clause (iii) can instantiate X to *ok* after it is selected for commitment, and this clause can be selected almost immediately. Therefore, no matter which of the two goals of Clause (i) starts first, the head unification of Clause (ii) can succeed only after the $Z=ok$ goal in Clause (iii) is executed.

The semantics of the following program should be more carefully understood:

> Goal: ← p(X), q(X).   (i)
> Clauses: p(Y) ← q(Y) | ....   (ii′)
>   q(Z) ← true | Z=ok. (iii)

To solve the guard of Clause (ii′), we have to do two things in parallel: unify X and Y (i.e., parameter passing), and solve $q(Y)$. Let us assume that parameter passing occurs first. Then the goal $q(Y)$ tries to unify Y (now identical to X) with *ok*. However, this unification cannot instantiate X because it is indirectly invoked by the guard of Clause (ii′). Let us then consider the other case where the goal $q(Y)$ is executed prior to parameter passing. The variable Y is bound to *ok* because this itself does not export a binding to the caller of Clause (ii′), namely $p(X)$. However, this binding causes the subsequent parameter passing to suspend because it would export a binding. Hence, no matter which case actually arises, Clause (ii′) behaves exactly like Clause (ii) with respect to bindings given to the variable X.

Some important consequences of the above rules follow:

(1) Any unification intended to export bindings to the caller of a clause through its head arguments must be specified in the body. Such unification must be specified using the predefined predicate '='.

(2) The unification of the head arguments of a clause may, but need not, be executed in parallel. It can be executed sequentially in any predetermined order.

(3) The unification of head arguments and the execution of guard goals can be executed in parallel. That is, the execution of guard goals can start before the unification of head arguments has completed. However, the usual execution method that solves guard goals only after head unification is also allowed; it does not change the meaning of a program.

(4) The execution of the body of a clause may, but need not, start before that clause is selected. Bindings made by the body are unobservable from the guard before commitment, so the meaning of the program is independent of whether the body starts before or only after commitment.

(5) We need not implement a multiple environment mechanism, i.e., a mechanism for binding a variable with more than one value. This mechanism is in general necessary when more than one candidate clause for a goal is tried in parallel. In GHC, however, at most one clause, a selected clause, can export bindings, thus eliminating the need of a multiple environment mechanism.

Unfortunately, properties (2) and (3) do not hold if we introduce the concept of failure. For example, the following goal

> Goal: ← and(X, false).
> Clause: and(true, true) ← true | true.

fails if the arguments are unified in parallel, but suspends if they are unified from left to right (Gregory, private communication).

4.4 Program Examples

4.4.1 Binary merge

> merge([A|Xs], Ys, Zs) ← true | Zs=[A|Zs1], merge(Xs, Ys, Zs1).
> merge(Xs, [A|Ys], Zs) ← true | Zs=[A|Zs1], merge(Xs, Ys, Zs1).
> merge([ ], Ys, Zs)   ← true | Zs=Ys.
> merge(Xs, [ ], Zs)   ← true | Zs=Xs.

The goal *merge(Xs, Ys, Zs)* merges two streams *Xs* and *Ys* (implemented as lists) into one stream *Zs*. This is an example of a nondeterministic program. The language rules of GHC do not state that the selection of clauses should be fair. In a good implementation, however, the elements of *Xs* and *Ys* are expected to appear on *Zs* almost in the order of arrival.

Note that no bindings can be exported from the guards; bindings to *Zs* must be made within the bodies. This programming style, however, serves to clarify causality. In most cases, bi- (or multi-) directionality of a logic program is only an illusion; it seems far better to specify the data flow which we have in mind and to enable us to read it from a given program.

Note that the declarative reading of the above program gives the usual, logical specification of the nondeterministic merge: arbitrary interleaving of the two input streams makes the output stream.

4.4.2 Generating primes

primes(Max, Ps) ← true | gen(2, Max, Ns), sift(Ns, Ps).

gen(N, Max, Ns) ←
    N ≤ Max | Ns=[N|Ns1], N1 := N+1, gen(N1, Max, Ns1).
gen(N, Max, Ns) ←
    N > Max | Ns=[ ].

sift([P|Xs], Zs) ← true | Zs=[P|Zs1], filter(P, Xs, Ys), sift(Ys, Zs1).
sift([ ],   Zs) ← true | Zs=[ ].

filter(P, [X|Xs], Ys) ← X mod P=:=0 | filter(P, Xs, Ys).
filter(P, [X|Xs], Ys) ← X mod P≠0 | Ys=[X|Ys1], filter(P, Xs, Ys1).
filter(P, [ ],   Ys) ← true | Ys=[ ].

The call *primes(Max, Ps)* returns through *Ps* a stream of primes up to *Max*. The stream of primes is generated from the stream of integers by filtering out the multiples of primes. For each prime *P*, a filter goal *filter(P, Xs, Ys)* is generated which filters out the multiples of *P* from the stream *Xs*, yielding *Ys*.

The binary predicate ':=' evaluates its right-hand side operand as an integer expression and unifies the result with the left-hand side operand. The binary predicate '=:=' evaluates its two operands as integer expressions and succeeds iff the results are the same. These predicates cannot be replaced by the '=' predicate because '=' never evaluates its arguments. The predicate '≠' is the negation of '=:=.'

Readers may wish to improve the above program by eliminating unnecessary filtering.

4.4.3 Bounded buffer stream communication

test(N) ← true | buffer(N, Hs, Ts), ints(0, 100, Hs), consume(Hs, Ts).

buffer(N, Hs, Ts) ← N > 0 | Hs=[_|Hs1], N1:=N–1, buffer(N1, Hs1, Ts).
buffer(N, Hs, Ts) ← N=:=0 | Ts=Hs.

ints(M, Max, [H|Hs]) ←
    M < Max | H=M, M1:=M+1, ints(M1, Max, Hs).
ints(M, Max, [H|_]) ←
    M ≥ Max | H='EOS'.

consume([H|Hs], Ts) ← H\='EOS' | Ts=[_|Ts1], consume(Hs, Ts1).
consume([H|Hs], Ts) ← H ='EOS' | Ts=[ ].

This program illustrates the general statement that demand-driven computation can be implemented by means of data-driven computation. It uses the bounded-buffer concept first introduced by Takeuchi and Furukawa (Chapter 18) in a logic programming framework. The predicate *ints* returns a stream of integers through the third argument in a lazy manner. It never generates a new box by itself; it only fills a given box created elsewhere with a new value. In the above program, the goal *consume* creates a new box by the goal $Ts=[_|Ts1]$ every time it has confirmed the top element H of the stream. The top and the tail of the stream are initially related by the goal *buffer(N, Hs, Ts)*.

The binary predicate '\=' is the negation of the predicate '='. It succeeds when its two arguments are proved to be ununifiable; it suspends until then.

4.4.4 Meta-interpreter of GHC

call(true)   ← true | true.
call((A, B)) ← true | call(A), call(B).
call(A = B) ← true | A = B.
call(A)   ← A \= true, A \= (_, _), A \= (_ = _) |
    clauses(A, Clauses), resolve(A, Clauses, Body), call(Body).

resolve(A, [C|Cs], B) ← melt_new(C, (A ← G|B2)), call(G) | B = B2.
resolve(A, [C|Cs], B) ← resolve(A, Cs, B2) | B = B2.

This program is basically a GHC version of the Concurrent Prolog meta-interpreter by Shapiro (Chapter 19). The predicate *clauses* is a system predicate which returns in a *frozen* form (Nakashima et al., 1984) a list of all clauses whose heads are potentially unifiable with the given goal. Each frozen clause is a ground term in which original variables are indicated by special constant symbols, and it is *melted* in the guard of the first clause of *resolve* by *melt_new*. The goal *melt_new(C, (A ← G|B2))* creates a new term (say T) from a frozen term C by giving a new variable for each frozen variable in C and tries to unify T with $(A ← G|B2)$.

The predicate *resolve* tests the candidate clauses and returns the body of an arbitrary clause whose guard has been successfully solved. This many-to-one arbitration is realized by the combination of binary clause selection performed in the predicate *resolve*.

It is essential that each candidate clause is melted after it has been brought into the guard of the first clause of *resolve*. If it were melted before passed into the guard, all variables in it would be protected against instantiation from the guard.

4.5 Important Features of GHC

4.5.1 Simplicity

GHC has only a small number of primitive operations all of which are considered small:

(1) calling a predicate leaving all its arguments unspecified, i.e., after making sure only that they are new distinct variables,

(2) unifying a variable with another variable or with a non-variable term whose arguments are all new distinct variables, and

(3) commitment.

Operation (1) is effectively resolution without unification. From the viewpoint of parallel execution, resolution in the original sense (Robinson, 1965) need not be considered as an indivisible operation. Resolution can be decomposed into goal rewriting and unification, and the latter can be executed in parallel with the newly created goals, as stated in Section 4.3.2.

Operation (2) shows that the unification of a variable and a non-variable term is not necessarily a primitive operation. For example, the unification $X=f(a)$ can be decomposed into the two operations $X=f(Y)$ and $Y=a$, where Y is a new variable. This was also suggested by Hagiya (1983).

Furthermore, the semantics of guard and commitment is powerful enough to express the following notions:

(1) conditional branching,

(2) nondeterministic choice, and

(3) synchronization.

This feature is much like CSP (Hoare, 1978), but CSP provides additional constructs '?' (input command) and '!' (output command) for synchronization. The Relational Language (Clark and Gregory, Chapter 1) was the first to introduce the guard concept to logic programming for reasons similar to ours[*]. However, GHC has removed the restrictions on the guard of the Relational Language together with mode declarations and annotations.

4.5.2 Descriptive power

We have succeeded in rewriting most of the Concurrent Prolog programs we have. In particular, we have written a GHC program which performs bounded

---

[*] IC-Prolog (Clark et al., 1982) was the first to introduce the guard concept to logic programming, but for rather different purposes.

buffer communication (Section 4.4.3), and a meta-interpreter of GHC itself (Section 4.4.4).

4.5.3 Efficiency

It cannot be immediately concluded that GHC can be efficiently implemented on parallel computers. The efficiency of GHC will depend very much on future research on the language itself and its implementation. However, GHC is more amenable than Concurrent Prolog to efficient implementation: It needs no mechanism for multiple environments; and it provides more information on synchronization statically. We made a compiler of a subset of GHC which compiles a GHC program into Prolog (Ueda and Chikayama , 1985), and an *append* program ran at more than 12KLIPS on DEC2065. The current restriction is that user-defined goals are not allowed in guards. Another GHC-to-Prolog compiler was made by Miyazaki (unpublished). Although less efficient than ours, his compiler is capable of handling nested guards.

For applications in which efficiency is the primary issue but little flexibility is needed, we could design a restricted version of GHC which allows only a subclass of GHC and/or introduces declarations which help optimization. Such a variant should have the properties that additional constructs such as declarations are used only for efficiency purposes and that a program in that variant is readable as a GHC program once the additional constructs are removed from the source text.

4.6   Possible Extensions

This section suggests some possible extensions, which are currently not part of GHC. Issues such as their necessity, implementability, and compatibility with other language features should be examined carefully before they are actually introduced.

4.6.1 Finite failure and the predicate *otherwise*

The semantics of GHC as described in Section 4.3.2 does not include the concept of failure. However, failure of unification can be readily introduced into the language. We can say that a set of goals fails if it contains or derives some unification goal and its two arguments are instantiated to different principal functors. Then, in general, a suspended unification may turn out later either to fail or to succeed.

Another kind of failure is caused by a goal for which there proves to be no selectable clauses. Calling a non-existent predicate also falls under this category.

This kind of failure must be detected as failure only under the *closed world assumption*; otherwise, that goal would have to suspend until somebody adds a selectable clause to the program.

The predicate *otherwise* proposed by Shapiro and Takeuchi (1983) can be introduced to express 'negation as failure'. The predicate *otherwise* can appear only as a guard goal. A goal *otherwise* succeeds when the guards of all the other candidate clauses for a given goal have failed; until then it suspends. This predicate could be conveniently used for describing a *default* clause.

4.6.2 Metacall facilities

We sometimes want to see whether a given goal succeeds or fails without making the test itself fail. Consider, for example, a monitor program. A monitor program may create several processes, some of which are user programs and others service programs. In this case, the user programs must be executed in a fail-safe manner, because if one of them should fail, so does the whole system. Furthermore, a monitor program must have some means to abort its subordinate user programs.

Let us consider a program tracer next. A program tracer must execute a given program, generating trace information every moment. Even if the program fails, the tracer should generate appropriate diagnostic information without failing. The tracer may even have to trace the execution of guards, which is really an impure feature since information should be extracted from the place from where no bindings must otherwise be exported.

A partial evaluator is another example. A partial evaluator rewrites a program clause by executing the goals in the clause. For example, the first clause in the program

$$p(Y) \leftarrow q(Y) \mid \ldots .$$
$$q(Z) \leftarrow \text{true} \mid Z = ok.$$

in Section 4.3.2 can be partially evaluated to the following clause:

$$p(ok) \leftarrow \text{true} \mid \ldots .$$

To do such rewriting, it must be possible to execute a given goal to obtain a finite set of substitutions and, in the case of suspension, a finite set of remaining (suspended) goals. In this case, the initial goal and the result must be represented in a frozen form. For if ordinary variables were used, the solver of the initial goal could not know when that goal had been fully instantiated, nor could we know when all bindings had been made. The binding delay is not guaranteed to be bounded.

We are considering language facilities which support all of these applications.

However, we have not reached a satisfactory solution yet. The metacall facility proposed by Clark and Gregory (1984) was a candidate solution, but it proved to have some semantical problems. Their two-argument metacall *call(Goal, Result)* tries to solve *Goal* possibly generating output bindings, and it unifies *Result* with *succeeded* upon success and with *failed* upon failure. However, consider the following example (Sato and Sakurai, 1984):

$$\leftarrow \text{call}(X=0, \_), X=1.$$

If the first goal is executed first, X becomes 0. Then the unification $X=1$ fails and so does the whole clause. If the second goal is executed first, X becomes 1. But since the first goal never fails, the whole clause succeeds. This is a new kind of nondeterminism resulting from the order of unification; without this facility, all nondeterminism would result from the arbitrary choice of selectable clauses.

Let us consider another example:

$$\leftarrow \text{call}(X=0, \_), \text{call}(X=1, \_).$$

The semantics of a GHC variable is intended to allow the above goal to be rewritten as follows (Ueda, 1985),

$$\leftarrow \text{call}(X=0, \_), X = Y, \text{call}(Y=1, \_).$$

because they are logically equivalent. However, this rewriting shows that the failure of unification cannot be confined in either *call*. The failure can creep out and topple the whole goal. This means that the metacall facilities as proposed by Clark and Gregory cannot protect a system program from unpredictable behavior by a user program. Further investigation is necessary to find a better solution.

4.7 Implementation Outline

The purpose of this section is to demonstrate that the suspension mechanism of GHC can be implemented. We will first show an easy-to-understand but possibly inefficient method: pointer coloring. Here we do not consider the suspension of bodies. The body of a clause is assumed to start after the clause has been selected.

When a term in a goal and a variable in the guard of a clause are unified, we color the pointer which indicates the binding. A term dereferenced using one or more colored pointers cannot be instantiated. When the clause is selected, colored pointers created in its guard are uncolored. For this purpose, the guard of a clause must record all pointers colored for that guard. Uncoloring can be done in parallel with the other operations in the body.

Care must be taken when the term in a goal to be unified with the variable in the guard is itself dereferenced using colored pointers. Consider the following example:

$$\leftarrow \text{p}(\text{f}(A)). \qquad \text{(i)}$$
$$\text{p}(X) \leftarrow \text{q}(X) \mid \dots . \qquad \text{(ii)}$$
$$\text{q}(Y) \leftarrow \text{true} \mid Y{=}\text{f}(\text{b}). \qquad \text{(iii)}$$

If the variable Y should directly point to the term $f(A)$ by a colored pointer and uncolor it upon selection of Clause (iii), the variable A would be erroneously instantiated to the constant b. There are a couple of possible remedies:

(1) Disallow a pointer which goes directly out of nested guards and use a chain of pointers instead.

(2) Let each pointer know how many levels of guards it goes through.

(3) Allow a pointer to go directly through nested guards. However, let each colored pointer know for what guard it is colored. When directly pointing a term dereferenced using colored pointers, that new pointer must be recorded in the guard which records the last colored pointer in the dereferencing chain (Miyazaki, unpublished).

The pointer-coloring method explained above is general. In many cases, however, we can analyze suspension statically. The simplest case is the following clause:

$$\text{p}(\text{true}) \leftarrow \dots \mid \dots .$$

The head argument claims that the corresponding goal argument must have been instantiated to *true* for this clause to be selected. We can statically generate the code for this check and need not use colored pointers in this case.

In general, if a guard calls only system predicates for simple checking (e.g., integer comparison), compile-time analysis is easy because no consideration is needed on other clauses. On the other hand, if it calls a user-defined predicate, global analysis is necessary to determine which unification may suspend and which unification cannot. There will be no general method for static analysis, but in many useful cases, static analysis like PARLOG's compile-time mode analysis (Clark and Gregory, 1985) will be effective.

4.8 Comparison with Other Languages

4.8.1 Comparison with Concurrent Prolog and PARLOG

GHC is like Concurrent Prolog and PARLOG in that it is a parallel logic programming language which supports committed-choice nondeterminism and stream communication. However, GHC is simpler than both Concurrent Prolog and PARLOG.

Firstly, unlike Concurrent Prolog, GHC has no read-only annotations. In GHC, the semantics of guards enables process synchronization.

Secondly, Concurrent Prolog needs a multiple environment mechanism while GHC and PARLOG do not. In Concurrent Prolog, bindings generated in each guard are recorded locally until commitment and are exported into the global environment upon commitment. However, this mechanism contains semantical problems whose solution would require an additional set of language rules, as Ueda (1985) pointed out. More importantly, we have not obtained any evidence that we need multiple environments in stream-And-parallel programming.

Thirdly, unlike PARLOG, we require no mode declaration for each predicate. PARLOG's mode declaration is nothing but a guide for translating PARLOG program into Kernel PARLOG (Clark and Gregory, 1984), so we can do without modes. In fact, GHC is closer to Kernel PARLOG than to PARLOG. However, unlike Kernel PARLOG, we have only one kind of unification. Although each unification operation occurring in a GHC program might be compiled into one of several specialized unification procedures, GHC itself needs (and has) only one.

Another difference from (Kernel) PARLOG is that a (Kernel) PARLOG program requires compile-time analysis in order to guarantee that it is legal, i.e., it contains no unsafe guard which may bind variables in the caller of the guard (Clark and Gregory, 1984). On the other hand, a GHC program is legal if and only if it is syntactically legal; it can be executed without any semantic analysis.

4.8.2 Comparison with Qute

Qute (Sato and Sakurai, 1984) is a functional language based on unification. Qute allows parallel evaluation which corresponds to And-parallelism in logic programming languages, but the result of evaluation is guaranteed to be the same irrespective of the particular order of evaluation. That is, there is no observable nondeterminism.

Although Qute and GHC were developed independently and may look different, their suspension mechanisms are essentially the same. The Qute counterpart of GHC's guard is the condition part of the *if-then-else* construct, from which no bindings can be exported.

The major difference between Qute and GHC is that Qute has no committed-choice nondeterminism while GHC has one. Qute does not have committed-choice nondeterminism (though Sato and Sakurai, 1984, suggest it could), because it pursues the Church-Rosser property of the evaluation algorithm. GHC has one because our applications include a system which interfaces with the real world (e.g., peripheral devices).

Another difference is that Qute has sequential And while GHC does not. We deliberately excluded sequential And, because our programming experience with

Concurrent Prolog has never called for this construct. One may think that sequential And could be used for the specification of scheduling and for synchronization. However, the primitives for scheduling should be introduced at a different level from that of GHC, and sequential And as a synchronization primitive is of no use in the intended computation model of GHC which allows delay for communication by shared variables.

4.8.3 Comparison with CSP

GHC is similar to CSP (Communicating Sequential Processes) (Hoare, 1978) in the following points:

(1) Both encourage programming based on the concept of communicating processes.

(2) The guard mechanism plays an important role for conditional branching, nondeterminism and synchronization.

(3) Both pursue simplicity.

The major difference is that CSP tries to rule out any dynamic constructs — dynamic process creation, dynamic memory allocation, recursive call, etc. — while GHC does not. Another major difference is that CSP has a concept of sequential processes while GHC does not. CSP is at a level nearer to the current computer architecture. GHC is more abstract and has a smaller set of primitives: it uses unification instead of input, output, and assignment commands, and it uses a recursive call instead of a repetitive command.

4.8.4 Comparison with (sequential) Prolog

Comparison with sequential Prolog must be made from the viewpoint of logic programming languages, not of parallel programming languages.

First of all, GHC has no concepts of the order of clauses or the order of goals in a clause. GHC is undoubtedly nearer Horn clause logic on this point. The semantics of Prolog must explain its sequentiality; without it, we cannot discuss some properties of a program such as termination.

GHC deviates from first-order logic in that it introduces the guard construct. It will be hard to give a semantics to the guard within the framework of first-order logic. However, Prolog also suffers from the same problem because of the notorious, but useful, cut operator. The commitment operator corresponds to the cut operator. However, since the commitment operator of GHC has been introduced in a more controlled way, it should be easier to give a formal semantics to it.

One problem with Prolog is that the use of *read* and *write* predicates prevents declarative reading of a program. In GHC, we no longer need imperative predicates because the concept of streams can well well be adapted to input and output. Large data structures such as mutable arrays and databases can also be logically and efficiently handled using transaction streams as the interface (Ueda and Chikayama, 1984).

4.8.5 Comparison with Delta Prolog

Delta-Prolog (Pereira and Nasr, 1984) is an extension of Prolog which allows multiple processes. Communication and synchronization are realized using the notion of an *event*. The underlying logic which explains the meaning of events is called Distributed Logic.

One of the differences between Delta-Prolog and GHC is that Delta-Prolog retains the sequentiality concept and the cut operator of Prolog. Both seem to be peculiarities of Prolog, so GHC avoided them. A parallel program in Delta-Prolog may look quite different from comparable sequential programs in Delta-Prolog itself and in Prolog. On the other hand, a class of GHC programs which have only unidirectional information flow (like pipelining) is easily rewritable to Prolog by replacing commitment operators by cuts, and a class of Prolog programs which use no deep backtracking and each of whose predicates has only one intended input/output mode is also easily rewritable to GHC.

4.9 Conclusions

We have described the parallel logic programming language Guarded Horn Clauses. Its syntax, informal semantics, programming examples, important features, possible extensions, implementation technique of synchronization mechanism, and comparison with other languages were outlined and discussed.

We hope the simplicity of GHC will make it suitable for a parallel computation model as well as a programming language. The flexibility of GHC makes its efficient implementation difficult compared with CSP-like languages. However, a flexible language could be appropriately restricted in order to make simple programs run efficiently. On the other hand, it would be very difficult to extend a fast but inflexible language naturally.

Acknowledgments

The author would like to thank Akikazu Takeuchi, Toshihiko Miyazaki, Jiro Tanaka, Koichi Furukawa, Rikio Onai and other ICOT members, as well as the ICOT Working Groups, for useful discussions on GHC and its implementation.

Thanks are also due to Ehud Shapiro, Steve Gregory, Anthony Kusalik and Vijay Saraswat for their comments on the earlier versions of this paper. Katsuya Hakozaki, Masahiro Yamamoto, and Kazuhiro Fuchi provided very stimulating research environments.

This research was done as part of the R&D activities of the Fifth Generation Computer Systems Project of Japan.

Yosee Feldman assisted in editing this paper.

Chapter 5

Concurrent Prolog: A Progress Report

Ehud Shapiro

The Weizmann Institute of Science

Abstract

Concurrent Prolog is a logic programming language designed for concurrent programming and parallel execution. It is a process oriented language, which embodies dataflow synchronization and guarded-command indeterminacy as its basic control mechanisms.

The paper outlines the basic concepts and definition of the language, and surveys the major programming techniques that emerged out of three years of its use. The history of the language development, implementation, and applications to date is reviewed. Details of the performance of its compiler and the functionality of Logix, its programming environment and operating system, are provided.

5.1 Orientation

Logic programming is based on an abstract computation model, derived by Kowalski (1979) from Robinson's (1965) resolution principle. A logic program is a set of axioms defining relationships between objects. A computation of a logic program is a proof of a goal statement from the axioms. As the proof is constructive, it provides values for goal variables, which constitute the output of the computation.

Figure 5.1 shows the relationships between the abstract computation model of logic programming and two concrete programming languages based on it: Prolog, designed by A. Colmerauer (Roussel, 1975) and Concurrent Prolog. It shows that

	Logic Program	
Abstract model:	Nondeterministic goal reduction	
	Unification	
Language:	Prolog	Concurrent Prolog
Control:	Goal and clause order define sequential search and backtracking	Commit and read-only operators define guarded-command indeterminacy and dataflow synchronization
Implementation:	stack of goals + trail for backtracking	queue of goals + suspension mechanism

Figure 5.1: Logic programs, Prolog, and Concurrent Prolog

Prolog programs are logic programs augmented with a control mechanism based on sequential search with backtracking; Concurrent Prolog's control is based on guarded-command indeterminacy and dataflow synchronization. The execution model of Prolog is implemented using a stack of goals, which behave like procedure calls. Concurrent Prolog's computation model is implemented using a queue of goals, which behave like processes.

Figure 5.2 argues that there is a homomorphism between von Neumann and logic, sequential and concurrent languages. That is, it claims that the relationship between Occam and Concurrent Prolog is similar to the relationship between Pascal and Prolog, and that the relationship between Pascal and Occam is similar to the relationship between Prolog and Concurrent Prolog[1].

---

[1] Some of the attributes in the figure are rather schematic, and shouldn't be taken literally, e.g., Pascal has recursion, but its basic repetitive construct, as in Occam, is iteration, whereas in Prolog and Concurrent Prolog it is recursion. Similarly Occam has if-then-else, but its basic conditional statement, as in Concurrent Prolog, is the guarded-command.

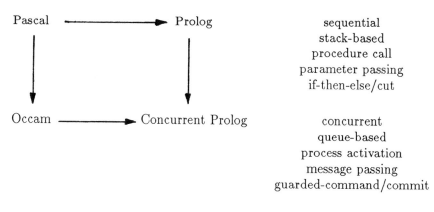

Figure 5.2: A homomorphism between von Neumann and logic, sequential and concurrent languages

5.2 Logic Programs

A logic program is a set of axioms, or rules, defining relationships between objects. A computation of a logic program is a deduction of consequences of the axioms.

The concepts of logic programming and the definition and implementation of the programming language Prolog date back to the early seventies. Earlier attempts were made to use Robinson's (1965) resolution principle and unification algorithm as the engine of a logic based computation model (Green, 1969). These attempts were frustrated by the inherent inefficiency of general resolution and by the lack of a natural control mechanism which could be applied to it. Kowalski

(1979) has found that such a control mechanism can be applied to a restricted class of logical theories, namely Horn clause theories. His major insight was that universally quantified axioms of the form

$$A \leftarrow B_1, B_2, \ldots, B_n \qquad n \geq 0$$

can be read both declaratively, saying that A is true if B_1 and B_2 and ... and B_n are true, and procedurally, saying that to prove the goal A (execute procedure A, solve problem A), one can prove subgoals (execute subprocedures, solve subproblems) B_1 and B_2 and ... and B_n. Such axioms are called *definite-clauses*. A *logic program* is a finite set of definite clauses.

Program 5.1 is an example of a logic program for defining list intersection. It assumes that lists such as $[1,2,3]$ are represented by recursive terms such as $list(1,list(2,list(3,nil)))$.

> intersect(X,L1,L2) $\leftarrow$ member(X,L1), member(X,L2).
>
> member(X,list(X,Xs)).
> member(X,list(Y,Ys)) $\leftarrow$ member(X,Ys).

Program 5.1: A logic program for List intersection

Declaratively, its first axiom reads: X is in the intersection of lists $L1$ and $L2$ if X is a member of $L1$ and X is a member of $L2$. Procedurally, it reads: to find an X in the intersection of $L1$ and $L2$ find an X which is a member of $L1$ and is also a member of $L2$.

The axioms defining *member* read declaratively: X is a member of the list whose first element is X. X is a member of the list $list(Y,Ys)$ if X is a member of Ys.

The difference between the various logic programming languages, such as sequential Prolog (Roussel, 1975), PARLOG (Clark and Gregory, Chapter 3), Guarded Horn Clauses (Ueda, Chapter 4), and Concurrent Prolog (Shapiro, Chapter 2), lie in the way they deduce consequences from such axioms. However, the deduction mechanism used by all these languages is based on the abstract interpreter for logic programs, shown in Figure 5.3. The notions it uses are explained below.

On the face of it, the abstract interpreter seems nothing but a simple nondeterministic reduction engine: it has a resolvent, which is a set of goals to reduce; it selects a goal from the resolvent, a unifiable clause from the program, and reduces the goal using the clause. What distinguishes this computation model from others is the logical variable, and the unification procedure associated with it.

The basic computation step of the interpreter, as well as that of Prolog and Concurrent Prolog, is the unification of a goal with the head of a clause (Robinson, 1965).

Input: A logic program P and a goal G

Output: $G\theta$, which is an instance of G proved from P,
or *failure*.

Interpreter:

Initialize the resolvent to be G, the input goal.

While the resolvent is not empty, do
choose a goal A in the resolvent
and a fresh copy of a clause
$A' \leftarrow B_1, B_2, \ldots, B_k,\ k \geq 0$, in P,
such that A and A' are unifiable with a substitution θ
(exit if such a goal and clause do not exist).
Remove A from, and add $B_1, B_2, \ldots, B_n$ to, the resolvent
Apply θ to the resolvent and to G.

If the resolvent is empty, then output G, else output *failure*.

Figure 5.3: An abstract interpreter for logic programs

The unification of two terms involves finding a substitution of values for variables in the terms that make the two terms identical. Thus unification is a simple and powerful form of pattern matching.

Unification is the basic, and only, data manipulation primitive in logic programming. Understanding logic programming is understanding the power of unification. As the example programs below show, unification subsumes the following data-manipulation primitives, used in conventional programming languages:

- Single-assignment (assigning a value to a single-assignment variable).

- Parameter passing (binding actual parameters to formal parameters in a procedure or function call).

- Simple testing (testing whether a variable equals some value, or if the values of two variables are the same).

- Data access (field selectors in Pascal, *car* and *cdr* in Lisp).

- Data construction (*new* in Pascal, *cons* in Lisp).

- Communication (as elaborated below).

The efficient implementation of a logic programming language involves the compilation of the known part of unification, as specified by the program's clause heads, to the above mentioned set of more primitive operations (Warren, 1983).

A *term* is either a variable, e.g., X, a constant, e.g., a and *13*, or a compound term $f(T_1, T_2, \ldots, T_n)$, whose main functor has name f, arity n, and whose arguments $T_1, T_2, \ldots, T_n$, are terms.

A *substitution element* is a pair of the form *Variable=Term*. An (idempotent) *substitution* is a finite set of substitution elements $\{V_1=T_1, V_2=T_2, \ldots, V_n=T_n\}$ such that $V_i \neq V_j$ if $i \neq j$, and V_i does not occur in T_j for any i and j.

The application of a substitution θ to a term S, denoted $S\theta$, is the term obtained by replacing every occurrence of a variable V by the term T, for every substitution element $V=T$ in θ. Such a term is called an *instance* of S.

For example, applying the substitution $\{X=3,\ Xs=list(1,list(3,nil))\}$ to the term $member(X, list(X, Xs))$ is the term $member(3, list(3, list(1, list(3, nil))))$.

A substitution θ *unifies* terms T_1 and T_2 if $T_1\theta = T_2\theta$. Two terms are *unifiable* if they have a unifying substitution. If two terms T_1 and T_2 are unifiable then there exists a unique substitution θ (up to renaming of variables), called *the most general unifier* of T_1 and T_2, with the following property: for any other unifying substitution σ of T_1 and T_2, $T_1\sigma$ is an instance of $T_1\theta$. In the following we use 'unifier' as a shorthand for 'most general unifier.'

For example, the unifier of X and a is $\{X=a\}$. The unifier of X and Y is $\{X=Y\}$ (or $\{Y=X\}$). The unifier of $f(X,X)$ and $f(A,b)$ is $\{X=b,\ A=b\}$, and the unifier of $g(X,X)$ and $g(a,b)$ does not exist. Considering the example logic program above, the unifier of $member(A, list(1, list(2, nil)))$ and $member(X, list(X, Xs))$ is $\{X=1, A=1, Xs=list(2, nil)\}$.

5.3   Concurrent Prolog

We first survey some common concepts of concurrent programming, tie them to logic programming, and then introduce Concurrent Prolog.

5.3.1 Concurrent programming: processes, communication, and synchronization

A concurrent programming language can express concurrent activities, or processes, and communication among them. Processes are abstract entities; they are the generalization of the execution thread of sequential programs. The actions a process can take include inter-process communication, change of state, creation of new processes, and termination.

It might seem that a declarative language, based on the logic programming computation model, will not be unsuitable for expressing the wide spectrum of actions of concurrent programs. This is not the case. Sequential Prolog shows that, in addition to its declarative reading, a logic program can be read procedurally. Concurrent Prolog shows yet another possible reading of logic programs, namely the *process behavior reading*, or *process reading* for short. The insight we would like to convey is that the essential components of concurrent computations — concurrent actions, indeterminate actions, communication, and process creation and termination — are already embodied in the abstract computation model of logic programming, and that they can be uncovered using the process reading.

Before introducing the computation model of Concurrent Prolog that embodies these notions, we would like to dwell on the intuitions and metaphors that link the formal, symbolic, computational model with the familiar concepts of concurrent programming, via a sequence of analogies, shown in Figure 5.4.

a1) Goal = Process

a2) Conjunctive goal = Network of processes

a3) Shared logical variable = Communication channel =
        Shared single-assignment variable

a4) Clauses of a logic program =
        Rules, or instructions, for process behavior

Figure 5.4: Concepts of logic programming and concurrency

We exemplify them using the Concurrent Prolog program for quicksort, Program 5.2. In the meantime the read-only operator '?' can be ignored, and the commit operator '|' can be read as a conjunction ','.

The clauses for *quicksort* read: Sorting the list $[X|Xs]$ gives Ys if partitioning Xs with respect to X gives *Smaller* and *Larger*, sorting *Larger* gives Ls, sorting *Smaller* gives Ss, and appending $[X|Ss]$ to Ls gives Ys. Sorting the empty list gives the empty list.

The first clause of *partition* reads: partitioning a list $[X|In]$ with respect to X gives $[Y|Smaller]$ and *Larger* if $X \geq Y$ and partitioning In with respect to X gives *Smaller* and *Larger*.

(a1) *Goal = Process*

A goal $p(T_1, T_2, \ldots, T_n)$ can be viewed as a process. The arguments of the goal $(T_1, T_2, \ldots, T_n)$ constitute the data state of the process. The predicate, p/n (name p, arity n), is the program state, which determines the procedure (set of clauses with same predicate name and arity) executed by the process. A typical state of a *quicksort* process might be $qsort([5,38,4,7,19|Xs], Ys)$.

(a2) *Conjunctive goal = Network of processes*

```
quicksort([X|Xs],Ys) ←
    partition(Xs?,X,Smaller,Larger),
    quicksort(Smaller?,Ss),
    quicksort(Larger?,Ls),
    append(Ss?,[X|Ls?],Ys).
quicksort([ ],[ ]).

partition([Y|In],X,[Y|Smaller],Larger) ←
    X ≥ Y | partition(In?,X,Smaller,Larger).
partition([Y|In],X,Smaller,[Y|Larger]) ←
    X < Y | partition(In?,X,Smaller,Larger).
partition([ ],X,[ ],[ ]).

append([X|Xs],Ys,[X|Zs]) ←
    append(Xs?,Ys,Zs).
append([ ],Xs,Xs).
```

Program 5.2: A Concurrent Prolog Quicksort program

A network of processes is defined by its constituent processes and by the way they are interconnected. A conjunctive goal is a set of processes. For example, the body of the recursive clause of *quicksort* defines a network of four processes, one *partition* process, two *quicksort* processes, and one *append* process. The variables shared between the goals in the conjunction determine an interconnection scheme. This leads to a third analogy.

(a3) *Shared logical variable = Communication channel = Shared single-assignment variable*

A communication channel provides a means by which two or more processes may communicate information. A shared variable is another means for several processes to share or communicate information. A logical variable, shared between two or more goals (processes), can serve both these functions. For example, the variables *Smaller* and *Larger* serve as communication channels between *partition* and the two recursive *quicksort* processes.

Logical variables are single-assignment, as a logical variable can be assigned only once during a computation. Hence, a logical variable is analogous to a communication channel capable of transmitting only one message, or to a shared variable that can receive only one value.

The single-assignment restriction has been proposed as suitable for parallel programming languages independently of logic-programming (Ackerman, 1982). At first sight it would seem a hindrance to the expressiveness of Concurrent Prolog, but it is not. Multiple communications and cooperative construction of a complex data structure are possible by starting with a single shared logical variable, as explained below.

Note that under this single-assignment restriction the distinction between a communication channel and a shared-memory variable vanishes. It is convenient to view shared logical variables sometimes as analogous to communication channels and sometimes as analogous to shared-memory variables.

(a4) *Clauses of a logic program = Rules, or instructions, for process behavior*

The actions of a process can be separated into control actions and data actions. Control actions include termination, iteration, branching, and creation of new processes. These are specified explicitly by logic program clauses. Data actions include communication and various operations on data structures, e.g., single-assignment, inspection, testing, and construction. As in sequential Prolog, data actions are specified implicitly by the arguments of the head and body goals of a clause, and are realized via unification.

5.3.2 The process reading of logic programs

We show how termination, iteration, branching, state-change, and creation of new processes can be specified by clauses, using the process reading of logic programs.

(1) *Terminate*

A unit clause, i.e., a definite clause with an empty body:

$$p(T_1, T_2, \ldots, T_n).$$

specifies that a process in a state unifiable with $p(T_1, T_2, \ldots, T_n)$ can reduce itself to the empty set of processes, and thus terminate. For example the clause $quicksort([\ ],[\ ])$ says that any process which unifies with it, e.g., $quicksort([\ ], Ys)$, may terminate. While doing so, this process unifies Ys with $[\ ]$, effectively closing its output stream.

(2) *Change of data and/or program state*

An iterative clause, i.e., a clause with one goal in the body:

$$p(T_1, T_2, \ldots, T_n) \leftarrow q(S_1, S_2, \ldots, S_m).$$

specifies that a process in a state unifiable with $p(T_1, T_2, \ldots, T_n)$ can change its state to $q(S_1, S_2, \ldots, S_m)$. The program state is changed to q/m (i.e., branch), and the data state to $(S_1, S_2, \ldots, S_m)$.

For example, the recursive clause of *append* specifies that the process $append([1,3,4,7,12\,|\,L1],[21,22,25\,|\,L2],L3)$ can change its state to $append([3,4,7,12\,|\,L1],[21,22,25\,|\,L2],Zs)$. While doing so, it unifies $L3$ with

$[1\,|\,Zs]$, effectively sending an element down its output stream. Since *append* branches back to itself, it is actually an iterative process.

(3) *Create new processes*

A general clause, of the form:

$$p(T_1, T_2, \ldots, T_n) \leftarrow Q_1, Q_2, \ldots, Q_m.$$

specifies that a process in a state unifiable with $p(T_1, T_2, \ldots, T_n)$ can replace itself with m new processes as specified by $Q_1, Q_2, \ldots, Q_m$.

For example, the recursive clause of *quicksort* says that a *quicksort* process whose first argument is a list can replace itself with a network of four processes: one *partition* process, two *quicksort* processes, and one *append* process. It further specifies their interconnection and initializes the first element in the list forming the second argument of *append* to be X, the partitioning element.

Note that under this reading an iterative clause can be viewed as specifying that a process can be replaced by another process, rather then change its own state. These two views are equivalent.

Recall the abstract interpreter in Figure 5.4. Under the process reading the resolvent, i.e., the current set of goals of the interpreter, is viewed as a network of concurrent processes, where each goal is a process. The basic action a process can take is *process reduction*: the unification of the process with the head of a clause, and its reduction to (or replacement by) the processes specified by the body of the clause. The actions a process can take depend on its state — on whether its arguments unify with the arguments of the head of a given clause.

Concurrency can be achieved by reducing several processes in parallel. This form of parallelism is called *And-parallelism*. Communication is achieved by the assignment of values to shared variables, caused by the unification that occurs during process reduction. Given a process to reduce, all clauses applicable for its reduction may be tried in parallel. This form of parallelism is called *Or-parallelism*, and is the source of a process's ability to take indeterminate actions.

5.3.3 Synchronization using the read-only and commit operators

In contrast to sequential Prolog, in Concurrent Prolog *an action taken by a process cannot be undone*: once a process has reduced itself using some clause, it is committed to it. The resulting computational behavior is called *committed-choice nondeterminism*, *don't-care nondeterminism*, and sometimes also *indeterminacy*, to distinguish it from the "don't-know" nondeterminism of the abstract interpreter.

This design decision is common to other concurrent logic programming languages, including the original Relational Language (Clark and Gregory, Chapter 1), PARLOG (Clark and Gregory, Chapter 3), and GHC (Ueda, Chapter 4). It implies that a process faced with a choice should better make a correct one, lest it might doom the entire computation to failure.

The basic strategy taken by Concurrent Prolog to ensure that processes make correct choices of actions is to provide the programmer with a mechanism to delay process reductions until enough information is available so that a correct choice can be made.

The two synchronization and control constructs of Concurrent Prolog are the read-only and the commit operators. The *read-only operator* (indicated by a question-mark suffix '?'), can be applied to logical variables, e.g., $X?$, thus designating them as read-only. The read-only operator is ignored in the declarative reading of a clause, and can be understood only operationally.

Intuitively, a read-only variable $X?$ cannot be written upon, i.e., be instantiated. It can receive a value only through the instantiation of its corresponding writable variable X. A unification that attempts to instantiate a read-only variable suspends until that variable becomes instantiated.

For example, the unification of $X?$ with a suspends; of $f(X, Y?)$ with $f(a, Z)$ succeeds, with unifier $\{X=a,\ Z=Y?\}$. Considering Program 5.2, the unification of $quicksort(In?, Out)$ with both $quicksort([\,],[\,])$ and $quicksort([X|Xs], Ys)$ suspends, as does the unification of $append(L1?, [3,4,5|L2], L3)$ with the heads of its two clauses. However, as soon as $In?$ gets instantiated to $[3|In1]$, for example, by another *partition* process who can access the writable variable In, the unification of the *quicksort* goal with the head of the first clause fails, and with the second clause succeeds. The notion of read-only unification is defined more rigorously below.

Definition. We assume two distinct sets of variables, writable variables and read-only variables. The *read-only* operator, ?, is a one-to-one mapping from writable to read-only variables. It is written in postfix notation. For every writable variable X, the variable $X?$ is the *read-only variable corresponding to* X. The extension of the read-only operator to terms which are not writable variables is the identity function. ∎

Definition. A substitution θ *affects* a variable X if it contains a substitution element $X=T$. A substitution θ is *admissible* if it does not affect any read-only variable. ∎

Definition. The *read-only extension* of a substitution θ, denoted $\theta?$, is the result of adding to θ the substitution element $X?=T?$ for every $X=T$ in θ. ∎

Definition. The *read-only unification* of two terms T_1 and T_2 *succeeds*, with *read-only mgu* $\theta?$, if T_1 and T_2 have an admissible mgu θ. It *suspends* if T_1 and T_2 unify, but every mgu of T_1 and T_2 is not admissible. It *fails* if T_1 and T_2 do not unify. ∎

Note that the definition of unifiability prevents the unification attempt to instantiate read-only variables. However, once the unification is successful, the read-only unifier instantiates read-only variables in accordance with their corresponding writable variables.

This definition of read-only unification resolves several ill-defined points in the original description of Concurrent Prolog (Shapiro, Chapter 2), discussed by Saraswat (1986) and Ueda (1985), such as order-dependency. It implicitly embodies the suggestion of Ramakrishnan and Silberschatz (1986), that a single unification should not be able to "feed itself", that is simultaneously write on a writable variable and read from its corresponding read-only variable. In particular, it implies that the unification of both $f(X,X?)$ and $f(X?,X)$ with $f(a,a)$ suspends.

The second synchronization and control construct of Concurrent Prolog is the commit operator. A guarded clause is a clause of the form:

$$A \leftarrow G_1,G_2,\ldots,G_m \mid B_1,B_2,\ldots,B_n \qquad m,n \geq 0.$$

The *commit operator* '|' separates the right hand side of a rule into a *guard* and a *body*. Declaratively, the commit operator is read just like a conjunction: A is true if the G's and the B's are true. Procedurally, the reduction of a process A_1 using such a clause suspends until A_1 is unifiable with A, and the guard is determined to be true. Thus the guard is another mechanism for preventing or postponing erroneous process actions.

As a syntactic convention, if the guard is empty, i.e., $m=0$, the commit operator is omitted.

The read-only variables in the recursive invocations of *quicksort*, *partition*, and *append* cause them to suspend until it is known whether the input is a list or nil. The non-empty guard in the recursive clauses for *partition* allows the process to choose correctly on which output stream to place its next input element. It is placed on the first stream if it is smaller or equal to the partitioning element. It is placed on the second stream if it is larger then the partitioning element.

Concurrent Prolog allows G's, the goals in the guard, to be calls to general Concurrent Prolog programs. Hence guards can be nested recursively, and testing the applicability of a clause for reduction can be arbitrarily complex. In the following discussion we will restrict our attention to a subset of Concurrent Prolog called Flat Concurrent Prolog (Mierowsky et al., 1985). In Flat Concurrent Prolog the goals in the guards can contain calls to a fixed set of simple test-predicates only. For example, Program 5.2 is a Flat Concurrent Prolog program.

In Flat Concurrent Prolog, the reduction of a goal using a guarded clause succeeds if the goal unifies with the clauses' head, and its guard test predicates succeed. Flat Concurrent Prolog is both the target language and the implementation language for the Logix system, to be discussed in Section 5.5. It is a rich

Input: A Flat Concurrent Prolog program P and a goal G

Output: $G\theta$, if $G\theta$ was an instance of G proved from P
or *deadlock* otherwise.

Interpreter:

Initialize the resolvent to be G, the input goal.

While the resolvent is not empty do
    choose a goal A in the resolvent
    and a fresh copy of a clause
    $A' \leftarrow G_1, G_2, \ldots, G_m \mid B_1, B_2, \ldots, B_n$ in P
    such that A and A' have a read-only unifier θ
    and the tests $(G_1, G_2, \ldots, G_m)\theta$ succeed
    (exit if such a goal and clause do not exist).
    Remove A from and add $B_1, B_2, \ldots, B_n$ to the resolvent
    Apply θ to the resolvent and to G.

If the resolvent is empty then output G,
    else output *deadlock*.

Figure 5.5: An abstract interpreter for Flat Concurrent Prolog

enough subset of Concurrent Prolog to be sufficient for most practical purposes. It is simple enough to be amenable to an efficient implementation, resulting in a high-level concurrent programming language which is practical even on conventional uniprocessors.

5.3.4 An abstract interpreter for Flat Concurrent Prolog

Flat Concurrent Prolog is provided with a fixed set T of guard predicates. Typical guard predicates include $string(X)$ (which suspends until X is a non-variable, then succeeds if it is a string; fails otherwise), and $X \leq Y$ (which suspends until X and Y are non-variables, then succeeds if they are integers such that $X \leq Y$, else fails). The list of guard predicates of Flat Concurrent Prolog is given in the Logix System User Manual (Silverman et al., Chapter 21).

Definition. A *flat guarded clause* is a guarded clause of the form

$$A \leftarrow G_1, G_2, \ldots, G_m \mid B_1, B_2, \ldots, B_n \qquad m, n \geq 0.$$

such that the predicate of G_i is in T, for all i, $0 \leq i \leq m$.

A *Flat Concurrent Prolog program* is a finite set of flat guarded clauses. ∎

An abstract interpreter of Flat Concurrent Prolog is defined in Figure 5.5. The interpreter again leaves the nondeterministic choices for a goal and a clause unspecified: the scheduling policy, by which goals are added to and removed from the resolvent, and the clause selection policy, which indicates which clause to choose for reduction, when several clauses are applicable.

Fairness in the scheduling and clause selection policies are further discussed by Taylor et al. (Chapter 39). For concreteness, we will explain the choices made in Logix. Logix implements *bounded depth-first* scheduling. In bounded depth-first scheduling the resolvent is maintained as a queue, and each dequeued goal is allocated a *time-slice t*. A dequeued goal can be reduced t times before it is returned back to the queue. If a goal is reduced using an iterative clause $A \leftarrow B$, then B inherits the remaining time-slice. If it is reduced using a general clause $A \leftarrow B_1, B_2, \ldots, B_n$, then, by convention, B_1 inherits the remaining time-slice, and B_2 to B_n are enqueued to the back of the queue. Bounded depth-first scheduling reduces the overhead of process switching, and allows more effective caching of process arguments in registers. Logix also implements *stable clause selection*, which means that if a process has several applicable clauses for reduction, the first one (textually) will be chosen. Stability is a property that can be abused by programmers. It is hard to preserve in a distributed implementation (Taylor et al., Chapter 39), and makes the life of optimizing compilers harder. It is not part of the language definition.

In addition Logix implements a non-busy waiting mechanism, in which a suspended process is associated with the set of read-only variables which caused the suspension of its clause reduction attempts. If any of the variables in that suspension set gets instantiated, the process is activated, and enqueued to the back of the queue.

The abstract interpreter does not distinguish between failure and suspension. A failure transition can be incorporated in it to do so.

The abstract interpreter models concurrency by interleaving. The truly parallel implementation of the language requires that each process reduction be viewed as an atomic transaction, which may read from and write to several logical variables. A parallel interpreter must ensure that its resulting behavior is serializable, i.e., can be ordered to correspond to some possible behavior of the sequential interpreter. Such an algorithm has been designed and implemented on Intel's iPSC Hypercube at the Weizmann Institute (Taylor et al., Chapter 39).

5.4   Concurrent Prolog Programming Techniques

In the past three years of its use, Concurrent Prolog has developed a wide range of programming techniques. Some are simply known concurrent programming techniques restated in the formalism of logic programming, e.g., divide-and-conquer, monitors, stream-processing, and bounded buffers. Others are novel techniques, which exploit the unique aspects of logic programs, notably the logical variable. Examples include difference-streams, incomplete-messages, and the short-circuit technique. Some techniques exploit properties of the read-only variable, e.g., blackboards, constraint-systems, and protected data-structures.

Perhaps the most important in the long-run are the meta-programming techniques. Using enhanced meta-interpreters, one can implement a wide spectrum of programming environment and operating system functions, such as inspecting and affecting the state of the computation, and detecting distributed termination and deadlock, in a simple and uniform way (Safra and Shapiro, Chapter 25; Hirsch et al., Chapter 20).

In the following account of these techniques breadth was preferred over depth. References to deeper treatment of various subjects are provided.

5.4.1 Divide-and-conquer: recursion and communication

Divide and conquer is a method for solving a problem by dividing it into subproblems, solving them, possibly in parallel, and combining the results. If the subproblems are small enough they are solved directly, otherwise they are solved by applying the divide-and-conquer method recursively. Parallel divide-and-conquer algorithms can be specified easily in both functional and logic languages. Divide-and-conquer becomes more interesting when it involves cooperation, and hence direct communication, among the processes solving the subproblems. Chapter 2 by Shapiro provides examples of Concurrent Prolog programs for divide-and-conquer, with and without communication between processes solving subproblems.

5.4.2 Stream processing

Concurrent Prolog is a single-assignment programming language, in that a logical variable can be assigned to a non-variable term only once during a computation. Hence it seems that, as a communication channel, a shared logical variable can transmit at most one message between two processes. This is not quite true. A variable can be assigned to a term that contains a message and another variable. This new variable is shared by the processes that shared the original variable. Hence it can serve as a new communication channel, which can be assigned to a term that contains an additional message and an additional variable, and so on *ad infinitum*.

This idea is the basis of stream communication in Concurrent Prolog. In stream communication, the communicating processes, typically one sender and one receiver (also called the stream's producer and consumer) share a variable, say Xs. The sender, who wants to send a sequence of messages $m_1, m_2, m_3, \ldots$

assigns Xs to $[m_1|Xs1]$ in order to send m_1, then instantiates $Xs1$ to $[m_2|Xs2]$ to send m_2, then assigns $Xs2$ to $[m_3|Xs3]$, and so on.

The receiver inspects the read-only variable $Xs?$ attempting to unify it with $[M_1|Xs1]$. When successful, it can process the first message M_1, and iterate with $Xs1?$, waiting for the next message.

Exactly the same technique would work for one sender and multiple receivers, provided that all receivers have read-only access to the original shared variable. A receiver that spawns a new process can include it in the group of receivers by providing it with a read-only reference to the current stream variable.

Program 5.2 for Quicksort demonstrates stream processing. Each *partition* process has one input stream and two output streams. On each iteration it consumes one element from its input stream, and places it on one of its output streams. When it reaches the end of its input stream it closes its two output streams and terminates. The *append* process from the same program is a simpler example of a stream processor. It copies its first input stream into its output stream, and when it reaches the end of the first input stream it binds the second input stream to its output stream, and terminates.

5.4.3 Stream merging

Streams are the basic communication means between processes in Concurrent Prolog. It is sometimes necessary, or convenient, to allow several processes to communicate with one other process. This is achieved in Concurrent Prolog using a stream merger.

A stream merger is not a function, since its output — the merged stream — can be any one of the possible interleavings of its input streams. Hence stream-based functional programming languages incorporate stream mergers as a language primitive. In logic programming, however, a stream merger can be defined directly, as was shown by Clark and Gregory (Chapter 1); their definition, adapted to Concurrent Prolog, is shown in Program 5.3.

```
merge([X|Xs],Ys,[X|Zs]) ← merge(Xs?,Ys?,Zs).
merge(Xs,[Y|Ys],[Y|Zs]) ← merge(Xs?,Ys?,Zs).
merge([ ],[ ],[ ]).
```

Program 5.3: A binary stream merger

As a logic program, Program 5.3 defines the relation containing all facts $merge(Xs,Ys,Zs)$, in which the list Zs is an order preserving interleaving of the elements of the lists Xs and Ys. As a process, $merge(Xs?,Ys?,Zs)$ behaves as follows: If neither Xs nor Ys are instantiated, it suspends, since unification with all three clauses suspends. If Xs is a list then it can reduce using the first clause, which copies the list element to *Zs*, its output stream, and iterates with the updated streams. Similarly with *Ys* and the second clause. If it has reached the end of its input streams it closes its output stream and terminates, as specified by the third clause.

In case both *Xs* and *Ys* have elements ready, either the first or the second clause can be used for reduction. The abstract interpreter of Flat Concurrent Prolog, defined in Figure 5.3, does not dictate which one to use. This may lead to an unfortunate situation, in which one clause (say the first) is always chosen, and elements from the second stream never appear in the output stream. A stream merger that allows this is called unfair.

There are several techniques to implement fair mergers in Concurrent Prolog. They are discussed by Shapiro and Mierowsky (Chapter 14), Shapiro and Safra (Chapter 15), Saraswat (Chapter 16) and Ueda and Chikayama (1984).

5.4.4 Recursive process networks

The recursive structure of Concurrent Prolog, together with the logical variable, makes it a convenient language for specifying recursive process networks.

An example is the Quicksort program. Although hard to visualize, the program forms two tree-like networks: a tree of *partition* processes, which partitions the input list into smaller lists, and a tree of *append* processes, which concatenates these lists together.

Process trees are useful for divide-and-conquer algorithms, and for searching, among other things. Here we show an application to stream merging. An *n*-ary stream merger can be obtained by composing *n-1* binary stream mergers in a process tree. A program for creating a balanced tree of binary merge operators is shown as Program 5.4.

> merge_tree(Bottom,Top) ←
>   Bottom≠[_] |
>   merge_layer(Bottom,Bottom1),
>   merge_tree(Bottom1?,Top).
> merge_tree([Xs],Xs).
>
> merge_layer([Xs,Ys|Bottom],[Zs|Bottom1?]) ←
>   merge(Xs?,Ys?,Zs),
>   merge_layer(Bottom?,Bottom1).
> merge_layer([Xs],[Xs]).
> merge_layer([ ],[ ]).
>
> merge(Xs,Ys,Zs) ← See Program 5.3.

Program 5.4: A balanced binary merge tree

Program 5.4 creates a merge tree layer by layer, using an auxiliary procedure *merge_layer*. The merge trees defined are static, i.e., the number of streams to be merged should be defined in advance, and cannot be changed easily. Shapiro and Mierowsky (Chapter 14) showed how to implement multiway dynamic merge trees in Concurrent Prolog, using the concept of 2-3-trees. Ueda and Chikayama (1984) and Shapiro and Safra (Chapter 15) improve this scheme further.

More complex process structures, including rectangular and hexagonal process arrays (Shapiro, Chapter 7), quad-trees and pyramids (Edelman and Shapiro, Chapter 12), can easily be constructed in Concurrent Prolog. These process structures are found useful in programming systolic algorithms, and spawning virtual parallel machines (Taylor et al., Chapter 22).

5.4.5 Systolic programming: parallelism with locality and pipelining

Systolic algorithms were designed originally by Kung (1982) and his colleagues for implementation via special purpose hardware. However, they are based on two rather general principles:

(1) Localize communication

(2) Overlap and balance computation with communication.

The advantages of implementing systolic algorithms on general purpose parallel computers using a high-level language, compared to implementation in special purpose hardware, are obvious. The systolic programming approach (Shapiro, Chapter 7) was conceived in an attempt to apply the systolic approach to general purpose parallel computers.

The specification of systolic algorithms in Concurrent Prolog is rather straightforward. However, to ensure that performance is preserved in the implementation, two aspects of the execution of the program need explicit attention. One is the mapping of processes to processors, which should preserve the locality of the algorithm, using the locality of the architecture. Another is the communication pattern employed by the processes.

In the systolic programming approach, the mapping is done using a special notation, LOGO-like Turtle programs (Papert, 1980). With each process, like a turtle in LOGO, we associate a position and a heading. A goal in the body of a clause may have a Turtle program associated with it. When activated, this Turtle program, applied to the position and heading of the parent process, determines the position and heading of the new process. Using this notation, complex process structures can be mapped in the desired way. Programming in Concurrent Prolog augmented with Turtle programs as a mapping notation is as easy as mastering a herd of turtles.

Pipelining is the other aspect that requires explicit attention. The performance of many systolic algorithms depends on routing communication in specific patterns. The abstract specification of a systolic algorithm in Concurrent Prolog often does not enforce a communication pattern. However, the necessary tools are in the language. By appropriate transformations, broadcasting can be replaced by pipelining, and specific communication patterns can be enforced (Taylor et al., Chapter 8).

```
mm([ ],_,[ ]).
mm([X|Xs],Ys,[Z|Zs]) ←
    vm(X,Ys?,Z)@right,
    mm(Xs?,Ys,Zs)@forward.

vm(_,[ ],[ ]).
vm(Xs,[Y|Ys],[Z|Zs]) ←
    ip(Xs?,Y?,Z), vm(Xs,Ys?,Zs)@forward.

ip([X|Xs],[Y|Ys],Z) ←
    Z:=(X*Y)+Z1, ip(Xs?,Ys?,Z1).
ip([ ],[ ],0).
```

Program 5.5: Matrix multiplication

For example, Program 5.5 is a Turtle-annotated Concurrent Prolog program for multiplying two matrices, based on the classic systolic algorithm which pipelines two matrices orthogonally on the rows and columns of a processor array (Kung, 1982). It assumes that the two input matrices are represented by a stream of streams of their columns and rows respectively. It produces a stream of streams of the rows of the output matrix. The program operates by spawning a rectangular grid of *ip* processes for computing the inner-products of each row and column. Unlike the original systolic algorithm, this program does not pipeline the streams between *ip* processes but rather broadcasts them. However, pipelining can be easily achieved by adding two additional streams to each process (Shapiro, Chapter 7).

5.4.6 The logical variable

All the programming techniques shown before can be realized in other computation models, with various degrees of success. For example, stream processing can be specified with functional notation (Kahn and MacQueen, 1977). By adding to functional languages a non-deterministic constructor, they can even specify stream mergers (Friedman and Wise, 1979). Using simultaneous recursion equations, one can specify recursive process networks.

In this section we show Concurrent Prolog programming techniques which are unique to logic programming, as they rely on properties of the logical variable. Of course, one can take a functional programming language, extend it with stream constructors, non-deterministic constructors, simultaneous recursion equations, and logical variables, and perhaps achieve these techniques as well. But why approximate logic programming from below, instead of just using it?

Incomplete messages

An incomplete message is a message that contains one or more uninstantiated variables. An incomplete message can be viewed in various ways, including:

- A message that is being sent incrementally.

- A message containing a communication channel as an argument.

- A message containing implicitly the identity of the sender.

- A data structure that is being constructed cooperatively.

The first and second views are taken by stream processing programs. A stream is just a message being sent incrementally, and each list-cell in the stream is a message containing the stream variable to be used in the subsequent communication. Similarly, the processes for constructing the merge trees communicated via incomplete messages, each containing a stream of streams.

However, it is not necessary that the sender of an incomplete message would be the one to complete it. It could also be the receiver. Two Concurrent Prolog programming techniques — monitors and bounded-buffers (Takeuchi and Furukawa, Chapter 18) — operate this way. Monitors also take the third view, that an incomplete message holds implicitly the identity of its sender. This view enables rich communication patterns to be specified without the need for an extra layer of naming conventions and communication protocols, by providing a simple mechanism for replying to a message.

Monitors in Concurrent Prolog are discussed further by Shapiro (Chapters 2 and 19).

Detecting distributed termination: the short-circuit technique

Concurrent Prolog does not contain a sequential-And construct. Suggestions to include one were resisted for two reasons. First, a desire to keep the number of language constructs down to a minimum. Second, the belief that even if eventually such a construct would be needed, introducing it at an early stage would encourage awkward and lazy thinking. Instead of using Concurrent Prolog's dataflow synchronization mechanism, programmers would resort to the familiar sequential construct[2].

In retrospect, this decision proved to be very important, both from an educational and an implementation point of view. Concurrent Prolog still does not have sequential-And and Logix does not have the necessary underlying machinery to implement it, even if it were desired. The reason is that implementing sequential-And in Concurrent Prolog on a parallel machine requires solving the problem of distributed termination detection. To run $P \& Q$ (assuming that & is the sequential-And construct), one has to detect that P has terminated in order to proceed to Q. If P spawned many parallel processes that run on different processors, it requires detecting when all of them have terminated, which is a rather difficult problem for an implementation to solve.

On the other hand, there is sometimes a need to detect when a computation terminates. First of all, as a service to the programmer or user who wishes to know whether his program worked properly and terminated, or if it has some useful or useless processes still running there in the background. Second, when interfacing with the external environment there is a need to know whether a certain set of operations, e.g., a transaction, has completed in order to proceed.

This problem can be solved using a very elegant Concurrent Prolog programming technique, called the short-circuit technique, which is due to Takeuchi (1983). The idea is simple: chain the processes in a certain computation using a circuit, where each active process is an open switch on the circuit. When a process terminates, it closes the switch and shortens the circuit. When the entire circuit is shortened, global termination is detected.

The technique is implemented using logical variables, as follows: each process is invoked with two variables, *Left* and *Right*, where the *Left* of one process is unified with the *Right* of another. The leftmost and rightmost processes each have one end of the chain connected to the manager. The manager instantiates one end of the chain to some constant and waits till the variable at the other end is instantiated to that constant as well. Each process that terminates unifies its *Left* and *Right* variables. When all terminate, the entire chain becomes one variable and the manager sees the constant it sent on one end appearing on the other.

An example of using the short-circuit technique is shown in Program 5.9.7.

---

2   Early Prolog-in-Lisp implementations, which provided an easy cop-out to Lisp, had a similar fate. Users of these systems — typically experienced Lisp hackers — would resort to Lisp whenever they were confronted with a difficult programming problem, instead of thinking it through in Prolog. This led some to conclude that Prolog "wasn't for real".

5.4.7 Meta-programming and partial evaluation

Meta-programs are programs that treat other programs as data. Examples of meta-programs include compilers, assemblers, and debuggers. One of the most important and useful type of meta-programs is the meta-interpreter, sometimes called a meta-circular interpreter, which is an interpreter for a language written in that language.

A meta-interpreter is important from a theoretical point of view, as a measure for the quality of the language design. Designing a language with a simple meta-interpreter is like solving a fixpoint equation: if the language is too complex, its meta-interpreter would be large. If it is too weak, it won't have the necessary data-structures to represent its programs and the control structures to simulate them.

A language may have several meta-interpreters of different granularities. In logic programs, the most useful meta-interpreter is the one that simulates goal reduction, but relies on the underlying implementation to perform unification. An example of a Flat Concurrent Prolog meta-interpreter at this granularity is shown as Program 5.6. The meta-interpreter assumes that a guardless clause $A \leftarrow B$ in the interpreted program is represented using the unit clause $clause(A,B)$. If the body of the clause is empty, then $B=true$. A guarded clause $A \leftarrow G|B$ is represented by $clause(A,B) \leftarrow G|true$. A similar interpreter for full Concurrent Prolog is shown by Shapiro (Chapter 19).

```
reduce(true).                    % halt
reduce((A,B)) ←                  % fork
    reduce(A?), reduce(B?).
reduce(A) ←                      % reduce
    A≠true, A≠(_,_) |
    clause(A?,B), reduce(B?).
```

Program 5.6: A plain meta-interpreter for Flat Concurrent Prolog

The plain meta-interpreter is interesting mostly for a theoretical reason, as it does nothing except simulate the program being executed. However, slight variations on it result in meta-interpreters with very useful functionalities.

For example, by extending it with a short circuit, as in Program 5.7, a termination-detecting meta-interpreter is obtained.

Many other important functions can be implemented via enhanced meta-interpreters (Safra and Shapiro, Chapter 25). In Prolog, they have been used to implement explanation facilities for expert systems (Sterling and Shapiro, 1986). In compiler-based Prolog systems, as well as in Logix, the debugger is based on an enhanced meta-interpreter, and layers of protection and control are defined via

```
reduce(A,Done) ←
    reduce1(A,done–Done).

reduce1(true,Done–Done).                                    % halt
reduce1((A,B),Left–Right) ←                                 % fork
    reduce1(A?,Left–Middle), reduce1(B?,Middle-Right).
reduce1(A,Left–Right) ←                                     % reduce
    A≠true, A≠(_,_) |
    clause(A?,B), reduce1(B?,Left–Right).
```

Program 5.7: A termination detecting meta-interpreter

meta-interpreters (Hirsch et al., Chapter 20).

Such meta-interpreters, including failsafe, interruptible, and controlled meta-interpreters, are shown and explained by Hirsch et al. (Chapter 20). One problem with using such meta-interpreters directly is the execution overhead of the added layer of interpretation, which is unacceptable in many applications.

Safra and Shapiro (Chapter 25) showed how partial evaluation, a program-transformation technique, can eliminate the overhead of meta-interpreters. In effect, partial evaluation can turn enhanced meta-interpreters into compilers, which produce as output the input program enhanced with the functionality of the meta-interpreter.

5.4.8 Modular programming and programming-in-the-large

The techniques shown above refer mostly to programming in the small. This does not mean that Concurrent Prolog is not suitable for programming in the large. To the contrary, we found that even using the simple module system developed for bootstrapping Logix many people could cooperate in its development. We expect the situation to improve further using the hierarchical module system, currently under development (Silverman et al., Chapter 21).

The key idea in these module systems, which are implemented entirely in Concurrent Prolog, is to use Concurrent Prolog message-passing to implement inter-module calls. This means that no additional communication mechanism is needed to support remote procedure calls between modules which reside on different processors.

5.5   The Development of Concurrent Prolog

Concurrent Prolog was conceived and first implemented in November 1982, in an attempt to extend Prolog to a concurrent programming language, and to clean-up and generalize the Relational Language of Clark and Gregory (Chapter 1). Although one of the goals of the language was to be a superset of sequential Prolog, the proposed design did not seem, on the face of it, to achieve this goal, and hence was termed "A Subset of Concurrent Prolog" (Shapiro, Chapter 2).

A major strength of that language, which later became known simply as Concurrent Prolog, was that it had a working, usable, implementation: an interpreter written in Prolog. Since the concepts of the language were quite radical at the time, it seemed fruitful to try and explore them experimentally, by writing programs in the language, rather than to get involved in premature arguments on language constructs, or to implement the language "for real" before its concepts were explored and understood, or to extend this "language subset" prematurely, before its true limitations were encountered.

In this respect the development of Concurrent Prolog deviated from the common practice of research on a new programming language. This typically concentrates on theoretical aspects of the language definition (e.g., CCS, Milner, 1980), or attempts to construct an efficient implementation of it (e.g., Pascal), but rarely focuses on actual usage of the language through a prototype implementation.

This exploratory activity proved tremendously useful. Novel ways of using logic as a programming language were unveiled (Shapiro, Chapter 2; Shapiro and Takeuchi, Chapter 29; Takeuchi, 1983), and techniques for incorporating conventional concepts of concurrent programming in logic were developed (Shapiro, Chapter 19; Shapiro and Mierowsky, Chapter 14). Most importantly, a large body of working Concurrent Prolog programs that solve a wide range of problems and implement many types of algorithms were gathered. This activity, which continued for a period of about two years mostly at ICOT and at the Weizmann Institute, resulted in papers on "How to do X in Concurrent Prolog" for numerous X's (Edelman and Shapiro, Chapter 12; Furukawa et al., 1984b; Hellerstein, Chapter 10; Hellerstein and Shapiro, Chapter 9; Hirakawa, 1983; Shafrir and Shapiro, Chapter 11; Shapiro, Chapter 19, Chapter 7; Shapiro and Mierowsky, Chapter 14; Shapiro and Safra, Chapter 15; Shapiro and Takeuchi, Chapter 29; Suzuki, 1986).

A programming language cannot be general purpose if only a handful of experts can grasp it and use it effectively. To investigate how easy it is to learn Concurrent Prolog, I have taught Concurrent Prolog programming courses at the Weizmann Institute, at the Hebrew University at Jerusalem and at Stanford University. Altogether about 120 graduate and 100 undergraduate students in Computer Science have attended these courses. Based on performance in programming assignments and on the quality of the course's final programming projects, it seems that more then three-quarters of the students became effective Concurrent Prolog programmers.

The accumulated experience suggested that Concurrent Prolog would be

an expressive and productive general-purpose programming language, *if* implemented efficiently. The strength of the language was perceived mostly in systems
programming (Hirsch et al., Chapter 20; Safra and Shapiro, Chapter 25; Shapiro,
Chapter 19; Takeuchi and Furukawa, Chapter 18) and in the implementation
of parallel and distributed algorithms (Hellerstein, Chapter 10; Hellerstein and
Shapiro, Chapter 9; Shafrir and Shapiro, Chapter 11; Shapiro, Chapter 7); it also
seemed suitable for the implementation of knowledge-programming tools for AI
applications (Furukawa et al., 1984b; Hirakawa, 1983), and as a system-description
and simulation language (Broda, 1984; Suzuki, 1986).

The next step was to try and develop an efficient implementation of the language on a uniprocessor, to serve as a building-block for a parallel implementation
and as a tool for exploring and testing the applicability of the language further.
This proved to be surprisingly difficult. Interpreters for the language developed
at the Weizmann Institute exhibited miserable performance (Levy, 1984). A compiler of Concurrent Prolog on top of Prolog was developed at ICOT (Ueda and
Chikayama, 1985) Although the latest version of the compiler reached a speed
of more then 10K reductions per second, which is more then a quarter of the
speed of the underlying Prolog system on that machine, it did not scale to large
applications since it employed busy waiting.

In addition to the implementation difficulties, subtle problems and opacities
in the definition of the Or-parallel aspect of Concurrent Prolog were uncovered
(Saraswat, 1986; Ueda, 1985).

As a result of these difficulties we decided to switch research direction and
concentrate our implementation effort on Flat Concurrent Prolog, the And-
parallel subset of Concurrent Prolog. Flat Concurrent Prolog was a "legiti-
mate" subset of Concurrent Prolog for two reasons. First, it has a simple meta-
interpreter, shown as Program 5.6. Second, we have discovered that almost all the
applications that have been written in Concurrent Prolog previously are either
in its Flat subset already, or can be easily hand-converted into it. This demonstrated the utility of having a large body of Concurrent Prolog code. Without it
we would not have had the courage to make what seemed to be such a drastic cut
in the language.

There was one Concurrent Prolog program that would not translate into Flat
Concurrent Prolog easily: an Or-parallel Prolog interpreter. This four-clause program, written by Ken Kahn, and shown as Program 5.8, was simultaneously
the final victory of Concurrent Prolog, and its death-blow. It was a victory to
the pragmatic expressiveness of Concurrent Prolog, since it showed that without
extending the original "Subset of Concurrent Prolog", the language was as expressive as Prolog: any pure Prolog program can run on a Concurrent Prolog
machine (with Or-parallelism for free!), by adding to it the four clauses of Kahn's
interpreter. Thus the original design goal of Concurrent Prolog — to have a

concurrent programming language that includes Prolog — was actually achieved, though it took more then a year to realize that.

```
solve([ ]).
solve([A|As]) ←
    clauses(A,Cs),
    resolve(A?,Cs?,As?).

resolve(A,[(A←Bs)|Cs],As) ←
    append(Bs?,As?,ABs),
    solve(ABs?) | true.
resolve(A,[C|Cs],As) ←
    resolve(A?,Cs?,As?) | true.

append(Xs,Ys,Zs) ← See Program 5.2

clauses(A,Cs) ← Cs is the list of clauses in A's procedure.
```

Program 5.8: Kahn's Or-parallel Prolog interpreter

It was a death-blow to the implementability of Concurrent Prolog, at least for the time being, since it showed that implementing Concurrent Prolog efficiently is as hard as, and probably harder than, implementing Or-parallel Prolog, and an efficient Or-parallel Prolog implementation is yet to be demonstrated.

Once the switch to Flat Concurrent Prolog was made, in June 1984, implementation work began to progress rapidly. A simple interpreter for the language was implemented in Pascal (Mierowsky et al., 1985). An abstract instruction set for Flat Concurrent Prolog, based on the Warren (1983) Instruction set for unification and the abstract machine embodied in the FCP interpreter, was designed (Houri and Shapiro, Chapter 38), and an initial version of the compiler was written in Flat Concurrent Prolog.

In July 1985, the bootstrapping of this compiler-based system was completed. The system, called Logix (Silverman et al., Chapter 21) is a single-user multitasking program development environment. It consists of: a five-pass compiler, including a tokenizer, parser, preprocessor, encoder, and an assembler. An interactive shell, which includes a command-line editor, and supports management and inspection of multiple parallel computations. A source level debugger, based on a meta-interpreter; a module system that supports separate compilation, runtime linking, and a free mixing of interpreted (debuggable) and compiled modules. A tty-controller, which allows multiple parallel processes, including the interactive shell, to interact with the user in a consistent way. A simple file-server, which interfaces to the Unix file system; and some input, output, profiling, style-checking, and other utilities. The system is written in Flat Concurrent Prolog. Its source is about 10,000 lines of code long, divided between 45 modules. About half of it is the compiler.

The system uses no side-effects or other extra-logical constructs, except in a few well-defined places. In the interface to the physical devices, low-level kernels make the keyboard and screen look like Concurrent Prolog input and output streams of bytes, and the Unix file system looks like a Concurrent Prolog monitor that maintains an association table of ⟨FileName,FileContents⟩. In the multi-way stream merger and distributer, which are used heavily by the rest of the system, destructive-assignment to mutual-references is used to achieve constant delay (Shapiro and Safra, Chapter 15), compared with the logarithmic delay that can be achieved in pure Concurrent Prolog (Shapiro and Mierowsky, Chapter 14).

The other part of the system, written in C, includes an emulator of the abstract machine, an implementation of the kernels, and a stop-and-copy garbage collector (Houri and Shapiro, Chapter 38). It is about 6000 lines of code long. When compiled on the VAX, the emulator occupies about 60K bytes, and Logix another 300K bytes. When idle, Logix consists of about 750 Concurrent Prolog processes. Logix itself is running as one Unix process.

The compiler compiles about 100 source lines per cpu minute on a VAX/11-750. A run of the compiler on the encoder, which is about 400 lines long, creates about 31,000 temporary Concurrent Prolog processes, and generates about 1.5M bytes of temporary data structures (garbage). During this computation about 90,000 process reductions occur and 10,000 process suspensions/activations.

Overall, the system achieves at present about a fifth to a quarter of the speed of Quintus Prolog (1985), which is one of the fastest commercially available Prolog on the VAX. The number is obtained by comparing Concurrent Prolog process reductions to Prolog procedure calls for the same logic programs. This indicates that the efficiency of Warren's (1983) abstract Prolog machine, which is at the basis of Quintus Prolog, and our Flat Concurrent Prolog machine is about the same. The gap can be closed by rewriting our emulator in assembly language, as Quintus does. To explain this similarity in performance, recall that although Flat Concurrent Prolog needs to create and maintain processes, which is a bit more expensive then creating stack frames for Prolog procedure calls, it does not support deep backtracking, where Prolog does and pays dearly for it.

5.6 Efforts at ICOT and Imperial College: GHC and PARLOG

In the meantime ICOT did not stand still. Given their decision to use Concurrent Prolog as the basis for Kernel Language 1 (Furukawa et al., 1984a), the core programming language of their planned Parallel Inference Machine, they have also attempted to implement its Or-parallel aspect. Prototype implementations of three different schemes were constructed, namely shallow-binding (Miyazaki et al., Chapter 37), deep-binding , and lazy-copying (the scheme we tried at Weizmann) (Tanaka et al., 1984). Shallow binding proved to be the fastest, but did not seem to scale to multiprocessors. Lazy copying was the slowest, so the choice seemed to fall on deep-binding. Unfortunately the implementation scheme was rather complex, and the subtle problems with Concurrent Prolog's Or-parallelism were still unsolved. On the other hand, ICOT did not want to follow the Flat Concurrent Prolog path since it seemed to take them even further away from Prolog and from the AI applications envisioned for the Parallel Inference Machine.

An elegant solution to these problems was found in Guarded Horn Clauses (Ueda, Chapter 4), a novel concurrent logic programming language. The main design choice of GHC was to eliminate multiple Or-parallel environments from Concurrent Prolog. Besides avoiding a major implementation problem, this decision also provided a synchronization rule: if you try to write on the parent environment, then suspend (in Concurrent Prolog a process would allocate a local copy of the variable and continue instead). This rule made the read-only annotation somewhat superfluous. The resulting language exhibits elegance and conciseness, and seems to capture most of Concurrent Prolog's applications and programming techniques, excluding, of course, Kahn's Or-parallel Prolog interpreter. GHC is the current choice of ICOT for Kernel Language 1. Besides solving some of the difficulties in the definition and implementation of Concurrent Prolog, GHC is "Made in Japan", which certainly is not a disadvantage from ICOT's point of view. Recent implementation efforts at ICOT concentrate on Flat GHC, which is the GHC analogue to Flat Concurrent Prolog.

So why didn't we switch to GHC? Long discussions were carried out in our group about this option. Our general conclusion was that even though GHC is a simpler formalism, it is also more fragile, less expressive, and more difficult to extend. We felt it would either break or lose much of its elegance when faced with the problems of implementing a real operating system, which includes a secure kernel, error-handling for user programs, and distributed termination and deadlock detection. Furthermore, it would be less adequate for AI applications, since it has a weaker notion of unification.

Another related research effort is the development of the PARLOG programming language by Clark and Gregory (Chapter 3) at Imperial College. PARLOG is compiler-oriented, even more than GHC, in a way that seems to render it unsuitable for meta-programming. Given our commitment to implement the entire programming environment and operating system around the concepts of meta-interpretation and partial-evaluation, we cannot use PARLOG. On the performance side, PARLOG and GHC seem quite similar, except that GHC has to make a runtime check that guards do not write on the parent's environment, whereas PARLOG ensures this at compile-time, using what is called a *safety-check* (Clark and Gregory, 1985). On the expressiveness side, there does not seem to be a great difference between PARLOG and GHC, except for meta-programming.

Alternative synchronization constructs to the read-only variable were proposed by Saraswat (1985) and by Ramakrishnan and Silberschatz (1986).

5.7 Current Research Directions

The main focus of our current research at the Weizmann Institute is the implementation of a Flat Concurrent Prolog based general-purpose parallel computer system. Our present implementation vehicle is Intel's iPSC d4/me, a memory-enhanced four-dimensional hypercube, which, incidentally, is isomorphic to a 4×4 mesh-connected torus. As a first step, a distributed FCP interpreter was implemented in C, based on a distributed unification algorithm which guarantees the atomicity of goal reductions (Taylor et al., Chapter 39). Also a technique for implementing Concurrent Prolog virtual machines that manage code and process mapping on top of the physical machine has been developed (Taylor et al., Chapter 22).

Since Logix is self-contained, once the abstract FCP machine runs on a parallel computer, an entire program development environment and operating system will also become available on it. For example, the Logix source-level debugger, as well as other meta-interpreter-based tools such as a profiler, would preserve the parallelism of the interpreted program while executing on a parallel computer. So with this system a parallel computer could be used both as the development machine and as the target machine, which is clearly advantageous over the sequential front-end/parallel back-end machine approach. Since both source text, parsed code, and compiled code are first-class objects in Logix, routines that implement code-management algorithms on the parallel computer could be written in Concurrent Prolog itself (Taylor et al., Chapter 22).

A technique for compiling Concurrent Prolog into Flat Concurrent Prolog was developed (Codish and Shapiro, Chapter 32). It involves writing a Concurrent Prolog interpreter in Flat Concurrent Prolog, and then partially evaluating it (Futamura, 1971) with respect to the program to be compiled. It avoids the dynamic multiple-environment problem by requiring static output annotations on variables to be written upon. An attempt to provide Concurrent Prolog with a precise semantics is also being made, following initial work by Levi and Palamidessi (1985) and Saraswat (1985).

Another research direction pursued is partial evaluation (Safra and Shapiro, Chapter 25), a technique of program transformation and optimization which proves to be very versatile when combined with heavy usage of interpreters and meta-interpreters (Hirsch et al., Chapter 20; Silverman et al.,Chapter 21), as in Logix.

We believe that parallel execution is not a substitute for, but rather is dependent upon, efficient uniprocessor implementation. To that effect a high-performance FCP compiler is being developed (Kliger, 1987). Initial timings of a prototype implementation show performance of about 65K LIPS for a 15MHz 68020.

Lastly, Logix itself is still under development. Short term extensions include a hierarchical module system, type system (Yardeni and Shapiro, Chapter 28) and a window system (Katzenellenbogen et al., Chapter 23). Longer term research includes extending it to a multiprocessor/multiuser operating system.

5.8   Conclusion

Our research on Concurrent Prolog has demonstrated that a high-level logic programming language can express conveniently a wide range of parallel algorithms.

The performance of the Logix system demonstrates that a side-effect-free language based on light-weight processes can be practical even on conventional uniprocessors. It thus "debunks the expensive process spawn myth". Its functionality and pace of development testifies that Concurrent Prolog is a usable and productive systems programming language.

We have yet to demonstrate the practicality of Concurrent Prolog for programming parallel computers. Our prototyping engine is Intel's iPSC.

We find the ultimate and most important question to be: which of the currently proposed approaches will result in a scalable parallel computer system, whose generality of applications, ease of use, and cost/performance ratio in terms of both hardware and software would compete favorably with existing sequential computers.

Until such a system is demonstrated, the question of parallel processing could not be considered as solved.

Acknowledgements

The research reported on in this survey has been conducted in cooperation with many people at ICOT, The Weizmann Institute, and other places; perhaps too many to recall by name. I am particularly indebted to the hospitality and stimulating research environment provided by ICOT and its people. The early development of Logix was supported by IBM Poughkeepsie, Data Systems Division.

Contributors to its development include Avshalom Houri, William Silverman, Jim Crammond, Michael Hirsch, Colin Mierowsky, Shmuel Safra, Steve Taylor, and Marc Rosen. I am grateful to Vijay Saraswat for discussions on read-only unification, and to Orna Meyers, Steve Taylor and William Silverman for comments on earlier drafts of the paper.

Chapter 6

Parallel Logic Programming Languages

Akikazu Takeuchi and Koichi Furukawa

Institute for New Generation Computer Technology

Abstract

This paper surveys and compares parallel logic programming languages along several dimensions: whether the access restriction mechanism employed is at the level of procedure or data; whether the language requires multiple environments or guard safety; and whether its computation structure is hierarchical or flat. Finally, the paper explains why the standard semantics of logic programs is not adequate for parallel logic programming language, and why a different semantics is needed.

6.1 Introduction

Any programming language which can be treated mathematically has its own logic in its semantic model. Logic programming languages are an example. They are based on predicate logic and characterized by the fact that logical inference corresponds to computation. Owing to this, a program can be written declaratively and can be executed procedurally by a computer. Many logic programming languages can be imagined. Those based on Horn logic are the most successful and have been extensively studied.

A logic program is represented by a finite set of universally quantified Horn clauses. A program can be read procedurally and declaratively (Kowalski, 1974). A goal statement is used to invoke a computation that can be regarded as a proof of the goal statement from the given set of clauses. Prolog is the first language which realized this idea (Roussel, 1975). Its computation rule corresponds to left-to-right and depth-first traversal of an And-Or tree.

Given a set of Horn clauses, there are many proof strategies other than the one adopted in Prolog. Among these, parallel strategies are of great interest. These correspond to the parallel interpretation of logic programs. Conery and Kibler (1981) classified them into four models — Or-parallelism, And-parallelism, Stream-parallelism and Search-parallelism. Stream-parallelism has received much attention recently, because its expressive power is suitable for systems programming and other applications. Several parallel logic programming languages based on stream-parallelism have been proposed. These include the Relational Language (Clark and Gregory, Chapter 1), Concurrent Prolog (Shapiro, Chapter 2), PAR-LOG (Clark and Gregory, Chapter 3), Guarded Horn Clauses (Ueda, Chapter 4), and Oc (Hirata, 1985).

The following ideas and requirements seem to have motivated these languages. The first was to create a parallel execution model for logic programs that fully utilizes new parallel computer architectures. As hardware technology evolves, highly parallel computers become realizable using VLSI technology. However, to write a program for a parallel computer is a complicated task and involves new problems quite different from those encountered in programming on a sequential computer. The gap between hardware and software seems to grow. It is believed that the success of parallel computers depends on software technology. Choosing which language to use for parallel programming is the most important decision in parallel software technology. In order for a programmer to avoid various problems and extract parallelism easily, languages should have clear semantics and be inherently parallel themselves. Because of their semantic clarity and high level constructs useful for programming and debugging, logic programming languages are regarded as candidates for fully utilizing the power of parallel architectures.

The second issue is the extension of control of logic programming languages. The control facilities of Prolog are similar to those of conventional procedural languages, although the logic programming model includes no specific control mechanism. There have been several proposals for more flexible control mechanisms. These augment Prolog by introducing new control primitives such as coroutines (Clark et al., 1982; Colmerauer et al., 1982; Naish, 1984). Languages based on stream-parallelism can be regarded as an alternative attempt to extend control. These languages abandon the rules of sequential execution, and introduce parallelism. A great deal of effort was devoted to finding a reasonable set of control primitives for managing the parallelism obtained as a result.

The third point is how to exploit new programming styles in logic programming and thus to explore new application areas of logic programming. Logic programming languages such as Prolog are suitable for database applications and natural language processing, but are thought to be inadequate for applications such as operating systems. Parallel logic programming languages with control primitives for managing parallelism aim at covering such applications as systems programming, object oriented programming and simulation and thus widen the applicability of logic programming.

Parallel logic programming languages have a relatively short history, just six years or so. In this short time intensive research has taken place around the world and many fruitful results have been obtained. A general view of these languages is presented in this paper. The purpose of this paper is to present common features of the languages, to delineate the differences between them at the abstract level and to address the problems they present.

The paper is organized as follows. The stream-parallel computation model is informally introduced in Section 6.2. Section 6.3 provides definitions of several parallel logic programming languages. Common features among them and their differences are discussed. In the final section, unsolved problems of the semantics of parallel logic programming languages are discussed briefly.

6.2   Stream-Parallel Computation Model

Stream-parallel computation models were studied by Clark et al. (1982) and by van Emden and de Lucena (1982) independently as extended interpretation models of logic programs. Without introducing specific languages, we review the stream-parallel computation models informally. Consider the following logic program (syntax similar to Edinburgh Prolog (Bowen et al., 1981) is used throughout).

$$\text{quicksort(List,Sorted)} \leftarrow \text{qsort(List,Sorted,[ ]).} \tag{1}$$

$$\text{qsort([ ],H,H).} \tag{2}$$
$$\text{qsort([A|B],H,T)} \leftarrow$$
$$\quad \text{partition(B,A,S,L),}$$
$$\quad \text{qsort(S,H,[A|T1]),}$$
$$\quad \text{qsort(L,T1,T).} \tag{3}$$

$$\text{partition([ ],X,[ ],[ ]).} \tag{4}$$
$$\text{partition([A|B],X,[A|S],L)} \leftarrow \text{A} < \text{X, partition(B,X,S,L).} \tag{5}$$
$$\text{partition([A|B],X,S,[A|L])} \leftarrow \text{A} \geq \text{X, partition(B,X,S,L).} \tag{6}$$

The predicate *quicksort(List,Sorted)* expresses the relation that *Sorted* is the sorted list of elements in the list *List*. *qsort(List,H,T)* represents the fact that the difference list $H \backslash T$ is the sorted list of elements in the list *List*. *partition(List,E,S,L)* says that S is a sublist of *List* each element of which is less than E, and L is a sublist each element of which is greater than or equal to E. Given the above program and the following goal statement,

?– quicksort([2,1,3],X),

the Prolog interpreter will return the following answer substitution,

X = [1,2,3].

The algorithm used in the above logic program is "divide and conquer". Given a list, the tail is divided into two lists, one consisting of elements less than head, and the other of elements greater than or equal to head. Both lists are sorted independently and they are combined to construct the sorted list of the original list. The algorithm is typically embodied in clause (3). This clause can be read procedurally in the following way: to sort a list $[A|B]$, partition B into S and L with respect to A, and sort S and L. According to the sequential computation rule of Prolog, these subgoals are executed from left to right, that is, first the list B is partitioned, then S is sorted and finally L is sorted.

There are two possibilities for exploiting parallelism in the above program, especially in clause (3). One is cooperative parallelism. Since the lists S and L can be sorted independently, execution of the two *qsort* goals can be done in parallel. Although they share a variable, $T1$, they can cooperate in the construction of a list $H \backslash T$ by constructing non-overlapping sublists, $H \backslash T1$ and $T1 \backslash T$, of $H \backslash T$ in parallel. Another is pipelining parallelism. Note that both lists, S and L, are constructed incrementally from the heads by *partition* and that these two lists are consumed from their heads by two separate *qsort* goals. Therefore, it is possible to start execution of the two *qsort* goals with the available parts of the lists before *partition* completes the construction of the lists. The parallelism of the calls to *partition* and the two separate *qsort* goals is an example of pipelining parallelism. Both forms of parallelism, processed by a parallel computer, are expected to be effective in reducing computation time.

Cooperative parallelism and pipelining parallelism are typical kinds of parallelism which stream-parallel interpretation can extract from logic programs. Generally speaking, there are two kinds of parallelism in stream-parallel interpretation, one for parallel interpretation of conjunctive goals and the other for parallel search for clauses. Cooperative and pipelining parallelism are special cases of the former kind of parallelism. The latter is not discussed in this section; it is introduced in the next section.

In the former kind of parallelism, goals sharing variables are not independent and can interact with each other. Stream-parallelism involves cooperation of goals executed in parallel through shared variables. This is in clear contrast with And-parallelism, where no collaboration among goals is considered. Under And-parallel interpretation, conjunctive goals are solved independently and consistent solutions are extracted from their solutions. And-parallel interpretation is in danger of generating a lot of irrelevant computation, since unnecessary computation is only discovered to be irrelevant when it terminates.

Stream-parallel interpretation avoids this problem in the following way. First, bindings created in the course of computation are propagated to other computations as soon as possible. This helps parallel computations to exchange bindings of shared variables in order to maintain consistency. Secondly, it provides new control primitives which restrict access modes to shared variables. There can be two modes of access to a variable, although the mode is implicit and multiple in logic programming. These modes are "input (read)" and "output (write)". New primitives can be used to restrict the access mode to a shared variable to either input or output. Appropriate restriction of access modes to a shared variable allows the variable to be used as an asynchronous communication channel between parallel computations. Using such asynchronous communication channels, programmers can coordinate parallel goals and suppress irrelevant computation. In summary, the parallelism explored in stream-parallelism is controlled parallelism and languages based on stream-parallelism can extract maximum parallelism while reducing irrelevant parallel computation.

6.3 Languages

Several parallel logic programming languages have been proposed. These are the Relational Language, Concurrent Prolog, PARLOG, Guarded Horn Clauses (hereafter called GHC) and Oc. We start by defining the common features of these languages. These common features were first proposed in the Relational Language.

6.3.1 Common features

Syntax

For notational convenience, we define the common syntax. A program is a finite set of guarded clauses. A guarded clause is a universally quantified Horn clause of the form:

$$H \leftarrow G_1, \ldots, G_n \mid B_1, \ldots, B_m. \qquad n, m \geq 0.$$

"$\mid$" is called a *commitment* operator or *commit*. $G_1, \ldots, G_n$ are the guard part and $B_1, \ldots, B_m$ the body part. H is called the head of the clause. A set of clauses sharing the same predicate symbol with the same arity is called the definition of that predicate. A goal statement is a conjunction of goals of the form:

$$\leftarrow P_1, \ldots, P_n. \qquad n > 0.$$

Declarative semantics

The declarative meaning of "," is *and* ("∧"). The clause can be read declaratively as follows:

> For all term values of the variables in the clause,
> H is true if both $G_1,...,G_n$ and $B_1,...,B_m$ are true.

Sketch of operational semantics

Roughly speaking, "," procedurally means fork. Namely a conjunction, p,q, indicates that goals p and q are to be solved by different processes. The procedural meaning of a commitment operator is to cut off alternative clauses. We give a sketch of operational semantics using two kinds of processes, an And-process and an Or-process (Miyazaki et al., Chapter 37).

The goal statement is fed to a root-process, a special case of an Or-process. Given a conjunction of goals, a root-process creates one And-process for each goal. When all these And-processes succeed, the root-process succeeds. When one of these fails, it fails.

Given a goal G with the predicate symbol P, an And-process creates one Or-process for each clause defining the predicate P and passes the goal to each process. When at least one of these Or-processes succeeds, the And-process commits itself to the clause sent to that Or-process, and aborts all the other Or-processes. Then it creates an And-process for each goal in the body part of the clause and replaces itself by these And-processes. It fails when all these Or-processes fail.

Given a goal and a clause, an Or-process unifies the goal with the head of the clause and solves the guard part of the clause by creating an And-process for each goal in the guard. When all these And-processes succeed, it succeeds. If one of these fails, it fails.

Remarks

Conjunctive goals are solved in parallel by And-processes. A clause such that the head can be unified with the goal and the guard can successfully terminate is searched for in parallel by Or-processes, but only one is selected by commitment. Parallel search is similar to Or-parallelism, but is not the same since it is bounded in the evaluation of guard parts. A commitment operator selects one clause, cuts off the rest and terminates Or-parallelism.

Computation is organized hierarchically as an And- and Or-process tree. Each Or-process may be associated with a local environment storing bindings that would influence other competing Or-processes if they were revealed to them. This will be discussed later.

In general, if access to a variable is restricted to input mode, then no unification which instantiates the variable to a non-variable term is allowed and such unification is forced to suspend until the variable is instantiated. This kind of synchronization mechanism is useful for delaying commitment until enough information is obtained. The languages proposed so far have different syntactic primitives for specification of restriction of access mode. We review them in the next section.

6.3.2 Restriction of access mode

Mode declaration

PARLOG and its predecessor, the Relational Language, take this approach. Restriction of access mode is specified by mode declaration. In PARLOG, each predicate definition must be associated with one mode declaration. It has the form

$$\text{mode } R(m_1, \ldots, m_k).$$

where R is a predicate symbol with arity k. Each m_i is "?" or "↑". "?" indicates that access to this position in a goal is restricted to "input" mode. "↑" indicates "output" mode. Note that there is no neutral (multiple) mode. During head unification, any attempt to instantiate a variable appearing in an argument specified as input in a goal to a non-variable term is forced to suspend. Output mode indicates that a term at the corresponding argument position in the head will be issued from the clause. Unification between such output terms and corresponding variables in the goal can be performed after the clause is selected. An implementation of PARLOG is presented by Clark and Gregory (1985). The approach there is to translate a general PARLOG program to a program (called standard form) in a simple subset of the language, called Kernel PARLOG. Kernel PARLOG has only And-parallelism and has no mode declaration. Input-mode unification and output-mode unification are achieved by special one-way unification primitives. For example, if the relation p has a mode declaration stating that the first argument is input and the second is output, the clause

$$p(\text{question}(P), \text{answer}(A)) \leftarrow \text{good\_question}(P) \mid \text{solve}(P,A).$$

has the standard form

$$p(X,Y) \leftarrow \text{question}(P) <= X, \text{good\_question}(P) \mid$$
$$Y := \text{answer}(A), \text{solve}(P,A).$$

$T <= X$ is one-way unification which can bind variables in T, but suspends on an attempt to bind variables in X. $Y := T$ is assignment unification. A precondition for its successful execution is that Y is a variable. Note that mode declaration only restricts head unification. In general, there may be a case in which a variable appearing in an input argument in a goal is instantiated to a non-variable term during computation of a guard part. In PARLOG, a program in which this possibility can occur is regarded as an incorrect program and excluded at compile-time by mode analysis.

A merge operator merging two lists into one in arbitrary order can be defined in PARLOG as follows:

> mode merge(?,?,↑).
>
> merge([A|X],Y,[A|Z]) ← true | merge(X,Y,Z).
> merge(X,[A|Y],[A|Z]) ← true | merge(X,Y,Z).
> merge([ ],Y,Y) ← true | true.
> merge(X,[ ],X) ← true | true.

Read-only annotation

Concurrent Prolog adopts this primitive. Read-only annotation is denoted by "?". It can be attached to any variable. A variable with a read-only annotation is called a read-only variable. Read-only annotation restricts access to the variable to read mode only. Any attempt to instantiate an unbound variable with a read-only annotation to a non-variable term is forced to suspend until the variable is instantiated. The general unification procedure must handle the read-only annotation, since read-only variables can appear anywhere in a term. Using this annotation, the merge operator can be defined as follows:

> merge([A|X],Y,[A|Z]) ← true | merge(X?,Y,Z).
> merge(X,[A|Y],[A|Z]) ← true | merge(X,Y?,Z).
> merge([ ],Y,Y) ← true | true.
> merge(X,[ ],X) ← true | true.

Invocation of the goal takes the form:

> merge(X?,Y?,Z).

Input guard

This is adopted in GHC and Oc. Restriction of access mode to variables in a goal is implicit in the definition of a guard part. In GHC, given a goal G and a clause C, during head unification and computation of the guard part of C, any attempt to instantiate a variable appearing in the goal to a non-variable term is forced to suspend. Oc has no guard condition, in other words, a guard part is always "true". Hence, specification of synchronization in Oc is simpler than in GHC. In Oc, any attempt to instantiate a variable in the goal to a non-variable term in head unification is forced to suspend. Intuitively, head and guard parts of clauses in GHC and Oc specify conditions to be satisfied by input data received from a goal. The definition of merge is:

```
merge([A|X],Y,Oz) ← true | Oz=[A|Z], merge(X,Y,Z).
merge(X,[A|Y],Oz) ← true | Oz=[A|Z], merge(X,Y,Z).
merge([ ],Y,Oz) ← true | Oz=Y.
merge(X,[ ],Oz) ← true | Oz=X.
```

Note that output unification must be put in the body part of each clause; otherwise it will cause suspension, since the output pattern will be regarded as an input pattern.

Comparison

Different primitives for restricting access mode are adopted by the different languages. In fact, the way to represent this restriction characterizes each language. They are basically separated into two classes. One is *procedure level* representation and the other is *data level*. The Relational language, PARLOG, GHC and Oc belong to the first class. Concurrent Prolog belongs to the second class. The fact that procedures and data are complementary objects in a programming language indicates the clear contrast between these two approaches.

Procedure level representation of input and output: The Relational language and PARLOG adopt mode declarations for specification of input and output. One mode is given for each predicate definition. An input guard specifies input behavior for a single clause. GHC and Oc utilize a guard part for the specification of input. Although they put input specifications at different levels, a predicate definition and a clause, both approaches associate input specification with a procedure.

Data level representation of input and output: Concurrent Prolog adopts the read-only annotation to restrict access mode. A variable with a read-only annotation cannot be instantiated (written), but can be read. In general, a variable with a read-only annotation can be regarded as a "protected term" (Hellerstein and Shapiro, Chapter 9; Takeuchi and Furukawa, Chapter 18) since it is protected from instantiation. Only a process which has access to the variable without a read-only annotation can instantiate it. Since input synchronization is embedded in a data object, it becomes difficult to predict where and when synchronization will occur. This may impair transparency of control flow of the program. On the other hand, embedding control in a data object will enable novel control abstraction. This was investigated in the implementation of bounded buffer communication using protected terms (Takeuchi and Furukawa, Chapter 18).

6.3.3 Or-parallel multiple environments and guard safety

Given a goal and a clause, an Or-process evaluates head unification and the guard part. Since there are competing Or-processes, bindings made for variables in the goal must be hidden from processes other than descendants of the Or-process. Therefore, conceptually, each Or-process has a local environment where these bindings are stored. Local environments associated with Or-processes form a tree, since And-processes and Or-processes are hierarchically organized. The tree can dynamically expand and contract as the computation proceeds. There is no need to manage this dynamic tree if no local bindings are made, but otherwise it is an unavoidable task.

A clause in a program is defined to be safe if and only if, for any goal, evaluation of head unification and the guard part never instantiates a variable appearing in the goal to a non-variable term. The definition is due to Clark and Gregory (1985). We add a few definitions. A program is defined to be safe if and only if each clause in the program is safe. A language is defined to be safe if and only if any program written in it is safe. If a language is safe, then it does not need to manage local environments. The concept of safety clarifies the difference between the languages.

PARLOG, GHC and Oc are safe languages. The design philosophy of PAR-LOG excludes any program which requires multiple environments. In PARLOG, a program which may be unsafe is considered incorrect and excluded at compile-time mode analysis. GHC and Oc also do not need multiple environments. In fact, the rule of suspension in GHC and Oc can be paraphrased so that any attempt to make bindings which should be stored in a local environment is forced to suspend. Thus, safety is guaranteed at run-time by the suspension mechanism.

Concurrent Prolog is not safe. Thus, the tree of local environments has to be managed. Several attempts to implement Concurrent Prolog have been reported (Levy, 1984; Miyazaki et al., Chapter 37). Levy proposed a lazy copying scheme for implementation of multiple environments. Miyazaki et al. proposed a shallow binding scheme for this purpose. Implementations of Concurrent Prolog must solve two complicated problems associated with multiple environments. One is value access control. The other is detection of inconsistency between local and global environments.

Local environments are organized as a tree structure. An environment in a node must be accessible from nodes under the node, but must be hidden from others until the Or-process associated with the environment succeeds in being selected. Once the Or-process successfully terminates and is selected, its local environment is merged with the local environment of the parent And-process (the local environment associated with the parent Or-process of the And-process). Controlling the scope of variable access in this way is called value access control. On commitment, however, it may happen that these two environments contain inconsistent bindings. When should the inconsistency be detected? This is called the problem of detection of inconsistency of local bindings. Ueda (1985) presents two possible solutions. One is called *early detection*, which seeks to detect inconsistency as soon as possible. If an inconsistency exists, the clause fails before commitment and is never selected. The other solution is called *late detection* and seeks to detect inconsistency immediately after commitment. In this case, the clause succeeds in being selected, but immediately fails after commitment. Programmers may prefer early detection, but it requires a complicated locking mechanism for variables when implemented on a distributed memory machine. Ueda (1985) examines the semantics of Concurrent Prolog from the point of view of parallel execution and highlights several subtle issues which become crucial problems in a distributed implementation of the language.

Codish and Shapiro (Chapter 32) define a concept of safety in Concurrent Prolog which is different from the one stated here. An output annotation is introduced into Concurrent Prolog. Output annotation is used to declare which terms will be issued to a goal in head unification. In this model, a clause is defined to be safe if, for any goal, no binding for variables in the goal is made except those declared by output annotation during head unification and guard computation. Management of local bindings becomes simple in execution of a program ensured to be safe, since such bindings are syntactically predictable. Codish and Shapiro define a subset of Concurrent Prolog with output annotation such that the safety of any program written in it can be verified syntactically.

6.3.4 Hierarchical computation structure and flatness

As already mentioned, a computation is organized as an And- and Or-process tree. The depth of the tree corresponds to the depth of nesting of guard computations. Some parallel logic programming languages have a flat computation structure.

Flat Concurrent Prolog

Flat Concurrent Prolog is a subset of Concurrent Prolog in which guard parts are restricted to contain only system predicates (Mierowsky et al., 1985). Since no general computation is allowed in a guard, the computation structure is always flat. No tree-structured multiple local environments exist. This greatly reduces the complexity of implementation of the language, but it does not eliminate the problem of detecting inconsistency. Flat Concurrent Prolog seems to adopt late detection, but it is not clear how it is realized in a distributed memory environment.

PARLOG

Owing to the safe property of a clause, Or-parallel search for a clause can be translated into And-parallel goals. In the course of translation from a legal PARLOG program to a Kernel PARLOG program, clauses defining a predicate are collected into one clause. In this clause, Or-parallel evaluation of guards is expressed by And-parallel evaluation of a conjunction of meta-calls, each of which calls the guard of an original clause. The commitment operator is also expressed by a goal, which receives results from meta-calls, selects one and aborts the other meta-calls. Thus, there is a simple hierarchy of And-processes in PARLOG.

GHC

And- and Or-process tree is essential. In GHC, unification suspends if and only if binding made by the unification has to be stored in a local environment. In order to know whether a binding of a variable has to be stored in a local environment or not, the "birth place" of the variable in the hierarchy has to be identified. If it is the location where the binding is about to be made, then the binding can be made. Otherwise the attempt to bind is forced to suspend. This is why the hierarchical computation structure has to be managed with appropriate information on variables.

Oc and Flat GHC

Flat GHC is a subset of GHC. In Flat GHC, as well as in Flat Concurrent Prolog, a guard part is restricted to being a set of system predicates. Both Oc and Flat GHC have no computation hierarchy, since no general computation is allowed in a guard and this makes implementation of suspension simpler than in GHC. In fact, it can be implemented by one-way unification primitives similar to those of PARLOG.

6.3.5 Summary of comparison

We have reviewed parallel logic programming languages from the following three viewpoints –

(1) Suspension mechanism.

(2) Multiple Or-parallel environments.

(3) Hierarchically organized computation.

Safety and flatness contribute to reducing the complexity of the implementation. Safety makes the management of multiple local environments quite simple. Flatness excludes the hierarchical structure of the computation.

The suspension mechanism is independent of the other mechanisms in Concurrent Prolog. However, management of the hierarchy of computation and multiple environments is complicated. Safe Concurrent Prolog is an attempt to revise the language to reduce the complexity of managing multiple environments. Flat Concurrent Prolog has neither a hierarchy of computation nor multiple environments.

Owing to compile-time mode analysis, at run-time a PARLOG program has a simple computation model, where suspension is realized by one-way unification primitives, computation hierarchy management is simple and no multiple environments exist. What the PARLOG compiler does at compile-time can be regarded as detection of requirements for multiple environments over the hierarchical structure inferred from a program with mode declarations. One flaw of PARLOG is that one cannot write a meta-interpreter for the language in itself, while in other languages this is possible. The ability to write a meta-interpreter for the language in itself is an important property of a language for the self-contained development of its programming system.

In GHC, the suspension mechanism and computation hierarchy are closely coupled, though GHC needs no multiple environments. Oc and Flat GHC are similar to Kernel PARLOG. In fact, any program written in Oc and Flat GHC can be translated into a Kernel PARLOG program. If we can imagine Flat Kernel PARLOG which prohibits general goals and meta-calls in a guard, then Oc, Flat GHC and Flat Kernel PARLOG are equivalent to each other and constitute the simplest parallel logic programming language.

6.4   Semantics of Parallel Logic Programming Languages

In this final section, we present an open problem in the semantics of parallel logic programs.

The semantics of logic programs has been extensively investigated (van Emden and Kowalski, 1976; Apt and van Emden, 1982; Lloyd, 1984). These provide a rigorous basis for various mathematical manipulations of logic programs such as program verification, equivalence-preserving program transformation and declarative debugging. Logical foundations for parallel logic programming languages are also indispensable for the development of the theory of parallel logic programming including verification, transformation and debugging. However, the results for pure logic programs are not directly applicable to parallel logic programming languages because of the new control primitives.

Given a program P (a set of Horn clause), the success set of the program is defined to be the set of all A in the Herbrand base of P such that $P \cup \{\leftarrow A\}$ has an SLD-refutation. The finite-failure set is defined to be the set of all A in the Herbrand base of P such that there exists a finitely-failed SLD-tree with $\leftarrow A$ as its root. It is well known that the success set, the least model and the least fixpoint of the function associated with the program are equivalent. The finite-failure set is characterized by the greatest fixpoint under a certain condition. If a goal succeeds under sound computation rules, the result is assumed to be included in the success set. If a goal finitely fails, then that goal is in the finite-failure set.

The declarative semantics of parallel logic programming languages recommends reading a guarded clause as just a Horn clause. This is sufficient as long as a goal succeeds, but this does not happen in many cases. Suppose that a goal failed. This implies neither that the result is not in the success set, nor that the result is in the finite-failure set, since the goal may fail even if there is a possibility of success because of commitment to an incorrect clause. The declarative semantics becomes insufficient also if two programs with different input/output behavior need to be distinguished.

Parallel logic programming languages have two control primitives that do not appear in pure logic programs. These are a commitment operator and a synchronization primitive. Parallel logic programming relies heavily on these control primitives. However, a commitment operator changes the semantics of failure and a synchronization primitive introduces some procedural flavor. It is now obvious that the declarative semantics of pure logic programs cannot characterize such aspects of parallel logic programs as failure and input/output behavior.

Let us consider algorithmic debugging for parallel logic programming languages, where the intended interpretation of a program plays an important role in guiding debugging. Declarative semantics such as success set is no longer sufficient. Intended interpretations should be abstract semantics characterizing all aspects that programmers intend to express. One of the authors developed an algorithmic debugger for GHC, where the intended interpretation with procedural flavor of a GHC program was defined (Takeuchi, Chapter 26). Lloyd and Takeuchi (1986) refined the framework for the above algorithmic debugger and discussed some cases that proved difficult to handle. These are just starting points.

The semantics of the parallel logic programming languages discussed in this paper have been defined only operationally. None of them provides a method for modelling the abstract meaning of a program. What is required is semantics of parallel logic programs that can characterize what a programmer intends to express in a program. Meanings of programs should be abstract and independent of concrete implementations since the details of the implementation are of no interest. Furthermore, semantics should be mathematically manipulatable so that important properties of programs can be derived from their meanings. Such a semantics is strongly desired for the theory of parallel logic programming.

Acknowledgements

Jacob Levy assisted in editing this paper.

Part II

Programming Parallel Algorithms

Introduction

Historically, pure logic and functional programming languages in general, and Prolog in particular, were not considered good algorithmic languages. The lack of mutable arrays and destructive pointer manipulation prevented the efficient implementation of many common sequential algorithms in these languages. Adding such constructs to these languages interferes with their semantic elegance, and results in awkward programming styles and practices.

The situation with respect to parallel algorithms and concurrent logic programming languages is quite different. We find that in parallel algorithms process structures can play a role similar to that of data-structures in sequential algorithms. As shown by the following papers, concurrent logic programming languages are powerful formalisms for expressing process structures. Algorithms expressed in terms of dynamic networks of communicating processes can be implemented in concurrent logic programming languages quite directly and efficiently. As shown in Chapter 13, any algorithm for a Random Access Machine (RAM) or a network of RAMs can be implemented in such a language with a constant overhead in time and space, if the language is augmented with a constant-time stream merger and distributor. Unlike mutable arrays and destructive manipulation of pointers in sequential logic and functional languages, stream mergers and distributors are naturally expressed in concurrent logic languages, and the incorporation of efficient versions of these constructs does not interfere with their semantics or programming practices.

This part reports on the use of concurrent logic programming for the implementation of parallel and distributed algorithms. Although the specific languages used are Concurrent Prolog and Flat Concurrent Prolog, the concepts and techniques developed are quite general, and apply to other concurrent logic programming languages as well.

Chapter 7, "Systolic Programming — a Paradigm of Parallel Processing", by Shapiro, proposes a framework for programming parallel computers. It argues that for reasons of scalability, future parallel computers must be based on local interconnections, and that efficient parallel algorithms must exploit such locality. It claims that to be able to specify such locality, the kernel-language of a parallel computer must include a process-to-processor mapping notation, and proposes LOGO-like Turtle programs as a mapping notation extension to Concurrent Prolog. The systolic approach is a major example of algorithms based on locality of communication and the overlapping and balancing of computation with communication. The paper shows how systolic algorithms can be specified and implemented in Concurrent Prolog, augmented with a mapping notation.

Chapter 8, "Notes on the Complexity of Systolic Programs", by Taylor, Hellerstein, Safra, and Shapiro, explores two techniques for improving the communication complexity of systolic programs, namely pipelining and input spreading, and proves some upper bounds on the parallel speedup of systolic programs.

Chapter 9, "Implementing Parallel Algorithms in Concurrent Prolog: The Maxflow experience", by Hellerstein and Shapiro, reports on an implementation of the parallel Maxflow algorithm of Shiloach and Vishkin. Although the algorithm was designed for the PRAM model of computation, it was possible to convert it to the single-assignment computation model of Concurrent Prolog without loss of efficiency, by translating the original PRAM data-structures into Concurrent Prolog process structures.

Chapter 10, "A Concurrent Prolog Based Region Finding Algorithm", by Hellerstein, reports on a parallel region finding algorithm and its Concurrent Prolog implementation. This algorithm was devised with Concurrent Prolog as the target implementation language; as a result some of its basic operations are somewhat unusual, compared to conventional algorithms. Nevertheless, it is shown that under reasonable assumptions the algorithm, executed on a conventional parallel machine model, will attain the desired complexity, which is better than that of known sequential algorithms for this problem.

Chapter 11, "Distributed Programming in Concurrent Prolog", by Shafrir and Shapiro, describes the implementation of two distributed algorithms — one simple, the other rather complex — in Concurrent Prolog, and uses the implementation to illustrate the formation of process networks and process communication and synchronization in the language.

Chapter 12, "Image Processing with Concurrent Prolog", by Edelman and Shapiro, describes parallel image processing algorithms and their implementation in Concurrent Prolog. Like the Region Finding algorithm of Hellerstein, some of the quad-tree and pyramid based algorithms in this paper are novel, and their development was inspired and motivated by the capabilities of the implementation language, Concurrent Prolog.

These six papers provide scattered evidence that many types of algorithms can be implemented effectively in Concurrent Prolog, and show that under reasonable assumptions on the machine model and the language implementation technology, the implementation of an algorithm in Concurrent Prolog incurs no more than a constant overhead, compared to an implementation in a low-level language.

The last paper in this part, Chapter 13, "A Test for the Adequacy of a Language for an Architecture", by Shapiro, suggests that the phenomenon reported in the previous papers is not incidental. Under reasonable assumptions, Flat Concurrent Prolog can implement any algorithm on a RAM or a network of RAMs with only a constant overhead. This is shown by constructing simulators for a RAM and a network of RAMs, and arguing that the language can be implemented on these respective machine models so that each simulator can simulate the machine with only a constant overhead. This ability is proposed as a general test for determining the adequacy of a programming language for a machine model. Clearly, any language claiming to be a practical kernel language for a certain machine model must possess this ability.

Chapter 7

Systolic Programming:
A Paradigm of Parallel Processing

Ehud Shapiro

The Weizmann Institute of Science

Abstract

Even though the systolic approach shows great promise for realizing massive parallelism, it has been viewed so far only as a method for designing special-purpose attached processors for conventional computers. We claim that the systolic approach has a much greater potential. That it can lead to an algorithm design and programming methodology for general purpose, self-contained, high-level language parallel computers.

This paper proposes a framework for realizing this potential, termed systolic programming. The framework comprises an abstract machine, a programming language, a process-to-processor mapping notation, and an algorithm development and programming methodology.

7.1   Prologue: A Tribute to Our Forefathers' Wisdom

Socrates: I understand from your note that you came to tell me about a parallel computer architecture you are thinking of ...

Gera: Yes, it is a rectangular grid of ...

Socrates: ... but before that, since I know so little about this topic, could you tell me how to evaluate your new idea?

Gera: Well, an important criterion for evaluating parallel architectures is scalability. It says that for twice the money you should get twice the computer. Or that the architecture should remain feasible as the number of processors goes to infinity.

Socrates: Why is this criterion important?

Gera: First, from an aesthetic point of view, a scalable architecture is more elegant and robust. From a practical point of view, we would not want to resolve the parallel processing problem every two years afresh, when the number of processing elements per wafer doubles.

Socrates: Are there any implications you can draw from this criterion? Properties that hold for any scalable parallel architecture?

Gera: Yes. Non-uniform costs of communication and memory reference. An architecture in which every processor is "close", in some natural sense, to all other processors, is not scalable. For example, cross-bar switches and their approximations are not scalable. So in a scalable architecture a processor would have "neighbors", and "non-neighbors".

Socrates: So it seems that some pairs of processors will have a hard time talking to each other?

Gera: Yes. So I think that ensuring the locality of communication is the critical problem of parallel processing.

Socrates: Why? Are you sure that all these processors will have so much to talk about? Won't they work most of the time on their own and only occasionally communicate?

Gera: I don't think so. If you have a scalable architecture and try to exploit parallel processing to its fullest, you end up breaking your problem into smaller and smaller subproblems. The resulting algorithms involve a lot of communication.

Socrates: And I thought that the real CPU-killers are number crunching programs, that, presumably, involve a lot of computation and very little communication.

Gera: My statement is true even of number-crunching problems. Consider for example systolic algorithms. They seem to be the most promising approach to highly-parallel numeric algorithms. They show that, even for a compute-bound problem, a highly parallel algorithm involves an awful lot of communication. If this is true of compute-bound problems, it is even more so of communication-bound problems. In other words, it seems that a highly parallel solution to any problem is communication-bound.

Socrates: You probably wouldn't make these statements without thinking you have some method for localizing communication. But I heard that the major problem of parallel processing is load-balancing. And it seems that dynamic load-balancing and maintaining the locality of communication don't mesh very well, do they? I mean, if you start moving processes around, it becomes difficult to make sure that processes that talk to each other stay near each other, right? So your load-balancing algorithm must be pretty smart, is it?

Gera: No.

Socrates: No? Oh, I see ... You probably don't want to do the analysis of who talks to whom every time you spawn a process; you'd rather do it once and for all at compile time. Make the compiler map processes to processors so that they are both evenly spread and perform only local communications. So, a smart compiler, is that what you've got?

Gera: No.

Socrates: Good. I see you've learned something from me. It raises my blood-pressure when someone tells me he has a "smart gadget" for solving a problem that smells NP-hard miles away. Theory aside, it seems that designing efficient process-structures for a parallel program is as difficult as designing efficient data-structures for a sequential program. And we don't have any "smart gadgets" for the latter problem. Do we?

Gera: No, I don't know of any widely used ones.

Socrates: I am getting curious. What's the pigeon in your hat?

Gera: I don't have any, except for good old programmers and algorithm designers.

Socrates: ???

Gera: I mean that if designing efficient process structures for parallel programs and mapping them effectively on the target architecture are important and diffi-cult problems, then we have to solve them. And we should have a way to tell the computer what our solution is. So we must have a language for describing process structures and for describing how to map these structures on our computer. I guess that's the idea I wanted to tell you about.

Socrates: Hmmm ...

Gera: Consider this: you know the systolic band-matrix multiplication algorithm of Kung and Leiserson Leiserson, do you?

Socrates: Yes. I think it's ingenious, even though moving transparencies around to define it involves too much hand-waving for my age.

Gera: You would like to implement this algorithm, or this kind of algorithm, on a parallel general purpose computer, would you?

Socrates: Probably.

Gera: This algorithm wouldn't make sense if the systolic system is spread all over the place, would it?

Socrates: Probably not.

Gera: And we both agree that a general-purpose method that can automatically identify the hexagonal process structure of that algorithm from its formal definition and finds a way to map it onto the plane is, today, out of the question.

Socrates: Well, I would not propose to halt research on automatic programming. Besides, mapping process structures seems slightly easier then designing them.

Gera: But even if we discover a mapping method 2 or 20 years hence, it would need to specify the mapping of process structures somehow, right? So we're back to square one. Whether we specify the mapping of process structures manually, or let a "smart compiler" do the job, the kernel programming language of a scalable parallel computer needs a notation for mapping processes to processors. Quod erat demonstrandum.

Socrates: Hold it, we're not over yet. Ignoring the futuristic "smart compiler", isn't your proposal a major setback for programming, in some programming, insense? Isn't programming difficult as is? Won't it become horrendous if the programmer will have to control explicitly a new dimension, the definition of process structures and the mapping of processes to processors?

Gera: That's precisely the point. Parallel processing introduces a new dimension to programming. In addition to time and space usage, we must also control communication costs. And the thrust of my argument is that if we want to break the sequentiality barrier, we must bite the bullet. We must solve the communication problem at the algorithm design and programming level and not rely on the hardware architect to solve it for us, because he can't.

Socrates: I like your enthusiastic style of arguing, but you didn't answer my question.

Gera: Well, there are several answers, which are substantiated by my experience with programming using a mapping notation.

Socrates: Experience? Don't tell me you've already built your computer?

Gera: No, not yet. But I have implemented a software simulator which I have been programming extensively. It's just as good.

Socrates: Good for writing a paper.

Gera: No, just as good for my argument. My answers are as follows. One is that programming in higher-level languages is easier. When switching from sequential to parallel processing, the 2-fold or 10-fold speed difference between conventional languages and very high-level language programs is shadowed by the difference in the ease of programming. If the choice is between programming a von Neumann machine using a conventional language, and programming a parallel machine using a very high-level language, augmented with a mapping notation, then I choose the latter.

The second answer is that I have noticed a correspondence between the complexity of data-structures in sequential programs and communication structures in parallel programs (this is *not* a theorem). When converting sequential programs into parallel ones, an array of data of a sequential program is translated into an array of processes in the corresponding parallel program, where each process has only simple data-structures (scalars and I/O streams). A tree data-structure of a sequential program is translated into a process-tree of the parallel program, where nodes are processes and edges are communication channels. And, in general, the difficulty of defining the data-structures of a sequential program is translated into the difficulty of defining the process structures of a parallel program and their mapping, so it seems that overall programming difficulty is preserved.

The third answer is that the mapping component of a program can be developed independently, typically after, the development of the main program, and is relatively easy to specify (some say it is kids' stuff).

The fourth answer is that I don't see any other viable alternative.

Socrates: I am still uncomfortable with your solution. Actually, I am a bit surprised to hear it from you: haven't you learned anything from Lisp and Prolog? Isn't explicit allocation of storage an anachronism? Why is allocation of processes to processors different?

Gera: You certainly have a point. However, process-to-processor mapping has much more profound effects on the performance of a parallel program than memory-allocation strategy on a sequential program. And it is a much more difficult problem to solve automatically. Even in dynamic storage allocation, the programmer is the one who determines the data-structures used, although he does not control their location in memory. However, as you have pointed out, mapping is the simpler part. It is conceivable that common process structures could be mapped automatically, and mapping them manually in the meantime is not such a big burden.

Socrates: Maybe. But it seems to me that some load-balancing is still necessary, at least in a multi-user environment.

Gera: I agree. Such a load-balancing algorithm, however, should specify the origin, orientation, and perhaps also the density (number of processes per processor) of a systolic system. But I don't think it should fiddle with the internal mapping of the process structure. Besides, the person to implement this load-balancing algorithm should be the systems hacker, not the hardware architect, so the kernel programming language should have a mapping notation. Quod erat demonstrandum ...

Socrates: This argument is getting boring. I resign.

Gera: So my architecture is ...

Socrates: Before diving into the details, are there any general implications that hold for any scalable architecture programmed with a mapping notation?

Gera: Let me see. I think that the interconnection pattern of such a machine should be simple and regular. If it is not simple and intuitive, programmers will have a hard time utilizing it. I also think it should be of general-purpose and match the structure of many types of problems. Otherwise algorithm designers will have difficulties in mapping problems into algorithms with efficient communication patterns.

Socrates: Simple, regular, intuitive, huh? I like such conclusions. Motherhood and apple-pie. And what about the programming language?

Gera: Clearly it should be a high-level, expressive concurrent programming language. It should be self-contained, simple, and amenable to efficient implementation. It should be easy to debug. It should have clear semantics. It ...

Socrates: If you emit another buzz-word, I quit.

Gera: Sorry. I apologize.

Socrates: What makes a concurrent programming language expressive? What makes it high-level?

Gera: A concurrent programming language should be able to specify process creation, communication, synchronization, and indeterminacy. It is expressive if it can implement easily a broad range of algorithms, and if it lends itself to a rich set of programming techniques. I don't think the expressiveness of the language depends so much on its vocabulary, as on the richness of its programming idioms.

Socrates: Programming idioms? Do you want to get your computer to do something useful or to become another Shakespeare?

Gera: A language is high-level if... Well, high-level is sort of a buzz-word. I guess it means that it supports convenient ways for structuring data and methods for treating data abstractly. It has control structures such as recursive process and function invocation. Dynamic storage allocation and reclamation. These sorts of things.

Socrates: What makes it self-contained?

Gera: This is another loaded term. A language is self-contained if it can implement its own programming environment, the tools that are necessary to use the language conveniently. If you can easily implement an interpreter for the language in the language, then many software tools, particularly debugging tools, are also easy to implement. If you can implement a complete operating system in that language, all the better.

Socrates: I think the remaining properties are rather straightforward. So let's enumerate what we have concluded to be essential properties of a framework for general-purpose parallel programming:

(1) The computer architecture should be scalable and have a simple and regular interconnection pattern.

(2) Programming should be carried out in a high-level concurrent programming language, augmented with a mapping notation.

(3) It is the responsibility of the application programs, not the architecture or the operating system, to ensure locality of interprocess communication.

I guess the rest is just incidental details, and I am a bit tired now, so let's hear them tomorrow.

7.2 Introduction

Systolic algorithms were developed by Kung (1979, 1982) and Leiserson (1983) in order to exploit the parallelism inherent in computational problems. The systolic approach is one of the few that shows how to put into effective use the capabilities of VLSI technology. Since systolic algorithms were designed for direct implementation in hardware, they assumed rigid constraints: a synchronous array of microprocessors of a fixed size and interconnection pattern, where each processor has limited processing and communication capability and a local memory that can accommodate a small program and a few registers.

As a result of these constraints, an implementation of a systolic algorithm via a systolic array can solve problems of up to a fixed size only. Complex interfaces to a conventional von Neumann machine have to be developed, and methods for breaking problems into subproblems of a size that fits the systolic processor array and for combining the partial results to form the solution are also necessary. Modifying the function of a systolic array is either not possible, or can be done only by halting its execution and downloading a different microprogram (Fisher et al., 1983). In addition, programming systolic arrays to execute a desired algorithm turned out in practice to be more difficult than expected, despite the relative simplicity of the inner loop of the algorithm each systolic processor implements.

The systolic approach was introduced as a hardware-oriented methodology for constructing special-purpose attached processors to conventional von Neumann machines. We believe that this view unnecessarily limits its inherent potential.

We find the essence of the systolic approach to be the construction of algorithms that:

(1) Require only local communication.

(2) Overlap and balance communication with computation.

Such algorithms can be conceived, designed, and implemented ignoring constraints required by direct implementation in hardware.

In this paper we propose a framework for constructing general-purpose parallel computers, which incorporates the essence of the systolic approach in a software-oriented methodology of algorithm design and implementation.

The proposed framework, termed *systolic programming*, comprises an abstract machine, a programming language, a process-to-processor mapping notation, and an algorithm development and programming methodology. The abstract machine is an infinite processing surface (Martin, 1979). The programming language is Concurrent Prolog, augmented with LOGO-like Turtle programs (Papert, 1980) as a process-to-processor mapping notation. The algorithm development and programming methodology identifies two separate, though interrelated activities: the design and implementation of process structures and process behaviors (Kung, 1979), and the design and implementation of the mapping of these structures into the processing surface (Bokhari, 1981; Snyder, 1984).

Algorithms suitable for this methodology are best defined in terms of a dynamically changing collection of software processes, synchronized by dataflow. They might be called *soft-systolic* algorithms (Vijay Saraswat, personal communication), in contrast to the classical *hard-systolic* algorithms, which are typically defined in terms of a static collection of synchronous hardware processors.

Some key aspects of the systolic programming approach are:

(1) It is potentially applicable to general-purpose, multi-tasking, multi-user computers.

(2) Arbitrarily large computers which approximate the infinite abstract machine, are realizable using current technology. These computers are scalable with respect to the programming methodology, since the performance of most systolic algorithms improves linearly with the machine's size.

(3) Many important computational problems admit efficient hard-systolic solutions. It is conceivable that even more have soft-systolic solutions. Also, parallel solutions to problems which, historically, are not associated with the systolic approach, such as Monte-Carlo simulations and array relaxation on

mesh-connected computers, are also easily implementable within this framework.

(4) Programming a processing surface using Concurrent Prolog and Turtle programs is comparable to (and perhaps even easier than) programming a von Neumann machine using a conventional language.

The rest of the paper explains in more detail the components of the systolic programming approach — the abstract machine, programming language, mapping notation, and algorithm design and programming methodology — and illustrates it with several programming examples.

7.3 The Abstract Machine

The abstract machine we propose is an infinite *processing surface* (Martin, 1979): A regular arrangement of processors, each of which has some local memory, can timeshare between several software processes, and can communicate with the neighbors connected to it. For concreteness we assume that the processing surface is an infinite two-dimensional grid of processors, each connected to four neighbors, but other arrangements with higher-connectivity, topology, and dimension are also possible.

Various torus-based architectures that can approximate an infinite two-dimensional processing surface have been proposed in the literature (Martin, 1979; Hewitt, 1980; Sequin, 1981; Shamir and Fiat, 1986). They differ in the ease in which process arrays of various dimensions can be mapped into them with even load and with no communication penalty.

A naive implementation of a virtual infinite processing surface is obtained by folding a finite rectangular array of processors into a torus. A torus can be mapped onto the plane using constant length wires and a small number of crossovers, as shown by Zippel and Halstead (Hewitt, 1980). The twisted-torus, and then the doubly-twisted torus, were suggested as improvements to the simple torus by Martin (1979) and Sequin (1981). A further improvement, termed Polymorphic Arrays, was proposed by Shamir and Fiat (1986). A detailed comparison of these architectures is carried out by Fiat et al. (1984).

A process structure larger than the actual processing surface can be mapped on it using two complementary techniques: folding and condensation. Folding treats the processing surface as infinite and, in case it is approximated by a torus-like structure, effectively folds the process structure several times around it. Since each processor can timeshare between several processes, this folding will affect only the level of multi-tasking on each processor. Using folding, the program can view the machine as a virtual infinite processing surface, maintaining ignorance of the particular way in which it is being approximated.

However, simple folding will not always give optimal performance, in case the program is communication-bound. If the communication-to-computation ratio required by the software processes is larger than the one provided by the hardware processors, then it is better to increase the density of the mapping, by grouping adjacent processes into one processor, thus increasing the ratio of intra-processor to inter-processor communication.

It turns out that for some soft-systolic algorithms an optimal mapping density, in which computation and communication are balanced, can be computed analytically (Kung, 1985). This optimal density has the property that the performance of the algorithm on a very large (even infinite) processing surface will not improve even if the process structure is mapped with lower density (thus reducing the computation load per processor); neither will it improve on a very small processing surface even if mapped with higher density (thus reducing the communication load per channel). In other words, in some cases process structures can be mapped on a virtual infinite processing surface in an optimal way, regardless of the actual dimensions of the finite processing surface that emulates it.

Current technology is sufficient for building a processing surface. One of the more difficult questions the architecture of a general purpose processing surface must address is the interface to and usage of external I/O devices. One feasible approach is to connect devices such as a disk drive and a local-area network interface to the processing surface at regular intervals.

7.4   The Programming Language

In principle, the systolic programming approach is insensitive to the particular programming language chosen, as long as it is expressive enough and is amenable to efficient implementation. A programming language for a processing surface should be able to specify the dynamic creation of processes, the formation of inter-process communication structures, and process behaviors. Process behaviors include process communication, synchronization and indeterminate actions, as well as conventional control and manipulation of data.

It seems that at least five major types of candidates may claim to have this ability, namely CSP-based languages (Hoare, 1985; Milner, 1980; INMOS, 1984b), dataflow languages (Dennis, 1974; Ackerman, 1982), functional languages (McCarthy, 1963; Friedman and Wise, 1980; Henderson, 1982; Halstead, 1985), Actor languages (Hewitt, 1980), and logic languages (Kowalski, 1974; Clark and Gregory, Chapter 1, Chapter 3; Shapiro, Chapter 2; Ueda, Chapter 4).

A detailed comparison of the expressiveness of these languages and their amenability to efficient implementation is outside the scope of this paper. However, two points will be made.

On the efficiency side, Occam (INMOS , 1974b), a CSP-based language developed at INMOS, seems to have the most efficient implementation on uniprocessors to date among concurrent programming languages, and will probably be the first to have a high-performance multi-processor implementation. Concurrent Prolog, as well as the other languages mentioned, have yet to manifest their amenability to efficient parallel implementation.

On the expressiveness side, the example Concurrent Prolog programs in the rest of this book, as well as those in this paper, form an outstanding challenge for any concurrent programming language. These programs demonstrate several powerful programming techniques, including the recursive formation of complex communication structures; the use of incomplete messages; the design of fail-safe system hierarchies and meta-programming, and also several more conventional ones, such as side-effect free treatment of I/O, monitors, interrupts and priorities, bounded-buffer and unbounded-buffer communication.

Instead of trying further to justify our choice of Concurrent Prolog as the language for systolic programming, it may be more honest to admit that the course of development was the other way round. The systolic programming approach was conceived as a consequence of the experience accumulated in programming in Concurrent Prolog and as a result of attempts to devise a suitable parallel architecture for it. The systolic programming style was not invented in the abstract, searching for a programming language to be imposed upon, but rather was a natural outcome of attempts to solve difficult problems in Concurrent Prolog.

After implementing Concurrent Prolog (Shapiro, Chapter 2), I started playing with the language. I could not help but notice that many straightforward, innocent-looking logic programs exhibit systolic-like behavior once viewed through the execution model of Concurrent Prolog. Two phases were identified in the behavior of these programs: a "spawning"-phase, in which the program spawns a set of communicating processes, and a "systolic"-phase, in which these processes behave as a systolic system, overlapping computation and communication. The programs that exhibited this behavior were not composed in an attempt to implement systolic algorithms. Rather, they were the most naive and natural way to express a solution to a problem in Concurrent Prolog. Some of them were not even original Concurrent Prolog programs, but common Prolog programs that were converted to Concurrent Prolog by adding read-only annotations and the commit operator at the appropriate places. Examples are the insertion-sort and matrix-multiplication programs shown below.

Following these experiences, I have attempted to implement systolic algorithms explicitly. One of the more challenging systolic algorithms is the band-matrix multiplication algorithm of Kung and Leiserson (1980). To implement it in Concurrent Prolog, this time-synchronous algorithm had to be converted into a data-flow synchronized one. The resulting Program 7.10 is, as far as I know, one of the few working implementations of this algorithm.

These experiences suggest that there is some natural relationship between concurrent logic programming and systolic systems; that systolic systems provide a natural, behavioral reading to many logic programs, in addition to the familiar declarative and procedural (or problem-reduction) readings (Kowalski, 1974).

Beyond these programming experiences, the main insight that led to the proposed framework was that the inherent locality of these systolic-like Concurrent Prolog programs must be exploited to execute them efficiently. Even though systolic-like architectures provide such locality, only a sophisticated process-to-processor mapping mechanism can ensure that the locality of both the program and the architecture will match. Since devising such a general-purpose mapping mechanism is difficult, we were led to the conclusion that mapping deserves a programming language of its own.

7.5   The Mapping Notation

Languages, like Occam, which specify static process arrays, may benefit from a mapping notation that assigns processes to processors based on horizontal and vertical coordinates. We have found, after trial and error, that a recursive language such as Concurrent Prolog can make better use of a different mapping notation, namely LOGO-like Turtle programs (Papert, 1980).

Each process, like a Turtle, has a position on the processing surface and a heading. A fixed-instruction Turtle program T is associated with every process P, as in $P@T$ (read 'execute P at T'). Initially, the position and heading of a process P is inherited from the process that invoked it. Its final position and heading are determined by 'executing' its associated turtle program T. The process then runs on the processor at its final position.

A fixed-instruction Turtle program is a finite sequence of Turtle commands. An example of such a program is

$$(forward(1), right(90), forward(1), left(90))$$

which is used by Programs 7.8 and 7.9 to walk along a grid's diagonal. The *forward* and *back* Turtle commands take a distance as an argument and change the position of a process accordingly. The *left* and *right* commands take angles as arguments and change the process's heading. In the following, *forward* and *fd* are a shorthand for *forward(1)*, and *right* and *rt* are for *right(90)*.

Arguments of Turtle commands are not necessary integers, which may be useful, for example, for mapping process structures with density higher than one. In case the coordinates of the final position of a process are not integers, the processor to run on can be determined by some form of rounding.

Although the mapping notation can be added and debugged independently of the main program, we have found that a graphical simulator of a processing surface, which shows the actions of the processes in each processor, is one of the better debugging tools for the program itself. Such a simulator, written in Prolog, was used to debug all programs in this paper.

Our experience using Turtle programs so far is that mapping simple structures — vectors, arrays, and H-trees — is rather straightforward. However, once the tool is there, the temptation to implement more and more sophisticated process structures and mappings is present. Debugging the Turtle programs that mapped the ℵ-trees (Program 7.6) and the Dynamic H-trees (Program 7.7) shown below was not a trivial task.

Since the architecture is completely distributed, when a process is to be executed on a remote processor it must be sent there together with its associated program. This is not a major source of inefficiency as it first seems. A heavily used program that dynamically spawns a process structure of a certain size for every input can be converted into a program that spawns a similar process structure once, and then processes an entire stream of inputs.

7.6   Algorithm Design and Programming Methodology

Given our aforementioned observations, the following approach to algorithm design may be concluded:

(1) Compose a pure logic program that defines the desired input/output relation.

(2) Convert it into Concurrent Prolog by adding the appropriate read-only annotations and commit operators.

(3) Observe the program's behavior: you've just discovered a new systolic algorithm!

Even though this methodology is not proposed quite seriously, it is not completely a joke either, as the novel systolic readings of the familiar logic programs below demonstrate.

On a more serious note, even for sequential, von Neumann computers, algorithm design is more of an art than a science. Nevertheless, the basic tools for designing sequential algorithms, namely data-structures, are well understood. We have found that process-structures serve a similar role for soft-systolic algorithms. Many algorithms share the same process structures, and vice versa: when attempting the design of a new algorithm, a rich arsenal of process structures is an asset.

The relationship between sequential data-structures and parallel process-structures is even deeper. We have found that a sequential algorithm that operates on a certain data-structure, more often then not, has a counterpart: a parallel algorithm that uses a similar process structure: a list of data is converted into a list of processes (Programs 7.1 and 7.2); a tree of data is converted into a process tree (Program 7.4); and an array of data is converted into a process array (Programs 7.3, 7.7, 7.8 and 7.9).

The algorithm development strategy implied by the systolic programming approach is similar to that of designing conventional systolic algorithms. A solution to a problem is defined in terms of a collection of processes that overlap computation with communication, where the difficult design task is to ensure that computation and communication are balanced. If they are, then most processes will have data ready for continued processing most of the time. The communication structure should be designed so that, in addition to not introducing bottlenecks, it can be mapped into the plane without much penalty. In contrast to hard-systolic algorithms, a detailed design and analysis of the timing of communication is unnecessary for obtaining a correct algorithm and can be deferred until fine-tuning for performance is necessary, since operations are synchronized via dataflow (Snyder, 1984).

The claim for the greater freedom of soft-systolic over hard-systolic algorithms can be substantiated by two types of evidence. One is showing that known hard-systolic algorithms are easier to specify and implement when viewed as soft-systolic ones. This should be expected, since it is easier to simulate a synchronous system with a dataflow synchronized system than vice versa. Examples include the Concurrent Prolog implementation of a systolic algorithm for Gaussian elimination (Program 7.7) and band-matrix multiplication (Program 7.8) shown below, and the algorithms implemented in (Shapiro, 1983b; Shafrir and Shapiro, Chapter 11; Hellerstein and Shapiro, Chapter 9).

Another type of evidence is novel algorithms which seem to be easier to conceive or implement under the soft-systolic approach. Some first examples are (Edelman and Shapiro, Chapter 12; Hellerstein, Chapter 10; Shapiro and Mierowsky, Chapter 14).

7.7 Systolic Programming Examples

The example programs below demonstrate the specification and mapping of various process structures using Concurrent Prolog as the programming language and Turtle programs as the mapping notation.

7.7.1 Linear pipes

Sieve of Eratosthenes

> primes(Ps) ←
>   integers(2,Is), sift(Is?,Ps)@forward.
>
> integers(N,[N|Is?]) ←
>   N1:=N+1, integers(N1?,Is).
>
> sift([Prime|In],[Prime|Out1?]) ←
>   filter(In?,Prime,Out),
>   sift(Out?,Out1)@forward.
>
> filter([N|In],Prime,Out) ←
>   0=:=N mod Prime | filter(In?,Prime,Out).
> filter([N|In],Prime,[N|Out?]) ←
>   0=\=N mod Prime | filter(In?,Prime,Out).

Program 7.1: Sieve of Eratosthenes

Variants of this program are abundant in the logic-programming folklore. Logically, it defines the relation {*primes(Ps)*: *Ps* is the (infinite) list of primes}. Behaviorally, it defines a soft-systolic algorithm. Using an auxiliary *sift* process, it spawns a dynamically growing set of linearly-connected *filter* processes, one for each prime number found. In Figure 7.1, as well as in the following figures, we use graphical recursion equations to illustrate the spawning process. Boxes represent processes, and lines communication channels. The direction of an arrow represents the direction of communication. At the moment this notation is used informally, as a convenient way to document and explain the spawning component of Concurrent Prolog programs. It is conceivable, however, that this notation can be extended to an interface language for Concurrent Prolog.

A *filter* process copies its input stream to its output stream, filtering out multiples of its local prime number. The *sift* process creates a *filter* process for every prime number found and also collects the prime numbers in its output stream.

The mapping strategy of Program 7.1 is not optimal, in the sense discussed in Section 7.3. Given the distribution of primes among the integers, it seems that in an optimal mapping the density of the *filter* processes should increase exponentially, or, in other words, that the argument of the *forward* command of the *sift* process should be a function which decreases in N, for example

> sift([Prime|In],[Prime|Out1?]) ←
>   filter(In?,Prime,Out),
>   sift(Out?,Out1)@forward(2/Prime).

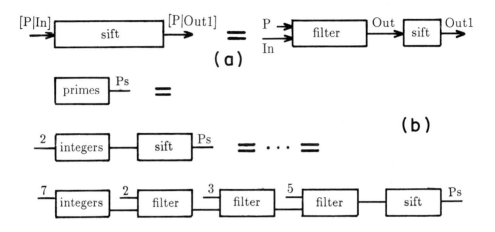

Figure 7.1: Recursive construction of a pipe of *filter* processes

rather then the constant 1. This mapping will cause *integers* and the *filter* process for 2 to have one processor each. The filters for 3 and 5 will share the third processor, the filters for 7, 11, 13, 17, 19, 23, 29 will share the fourth processor, and so on. Although the use of Concurrent Prolog program variables as arguments in the mapping Turtle program violates modularity somewhat, it proves to be a powerful technique.

Insertion sort

Another example in which a sequential list-processing algorithm has a parallel counterpart with a linear-pipe process structure is insertion sort. When the logic program definition of sorting, shown in Program 7.2, is read as a Prolog program, it defines the standard recursive insertion-sort algorithm. When read as a Concurrent Prolog program, it defines a linear-pipe parallel sorting algorithm.

Under the execution model of Concurrent Prolog, Program 7.2 behaves as follows: it first spawns a linearly connected sequence of *insert* processes, one for every element in its input stream, as shown in Figure 7.2. The last *insert* process is spawned with the empty input stream, due to the clause *sort*([ ],[ ]). At this time the pipe begins propagating data backwards: starting from the last process, each process copies its ordered (or empty, in case of the last process) input stream to its output stream, inserting its local number in the output stream so that the latter remains ordered.

As is, this program runs in quadratic time using a linear number of processors. By adding pipelines, as described by Taylor et al. (Chapter 8), the running

sort([X|Xs],Ys) ←
    insert(X,Zs?,Ys), sort(Xs?,Zs)@forward.
sort([ ],[ ]).

insert(X,[Y|Ys],[Y|Zs?]) ←
    X>Y | insert(X,Ys?,Zs).
insert(X,[Y|Ys],[X,Y|Ys]) ←
    X≤Y | true.
insert(X,[ ],[X]).

Program 7.2: Insertion sort

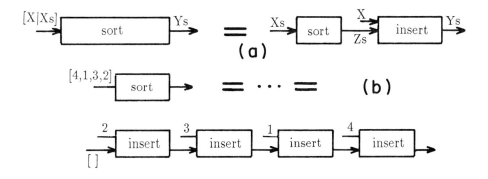

Figure 7.2: Recursive construction of a pipe of *insert* processes

time can become linear. The Concurrent Prolog implementation of merge-sort (Shapiro, 1983b), whose code is about twice as long, runs in linear time using only a logarithmic number of processors.

7.7.2 Process arrays

Matrix multiplication

A simple systolic algorithm for matrix multiplication is shown in Figure 7.3. Two matrices are fed into an array of processors. Each processor in the array computes the internal product of the two vectors that pass through it. At the end of the computation each processor contains one element of the resulting matrix.

An almost identical behavior is achieved by Program 7.3, which defines the relation $\{mm(X,Y,Z) : Z$ is the result of multiplying the matrix X with the

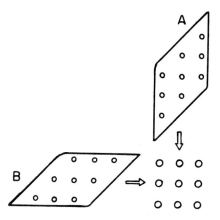

Figure 7.3: A systolic algorithm for matrix multiplication

mm([ ],_,[ ]).
mm([X|Xs],Ys,[Z|Zs]) ←
    vm(X,Ys?,Z)@right,
    mm(Xs?,Ys,Zs)@forward.

vm(_,[ ],[ ]).
vm(Xs,[Y|Ys],[Z|Zs]) ←
    ip(Xs?,Y?,Z), vm(Xs,Ys?,Zs)@forward.

ip([X|Xs],[Y|Ys],Z) ←
    Z:=(X * Y)+Z1, ip(Xs?,Ys?,Z1).
ip([ ],[ ],0).

Program 7.3: Matrix multiplication

transposed matrix Y}. When called with two matrices, *mm* spawns an array of *ip* processes, each computing the internal-product of two vectors (represented as lists or streams).

The Turtle programs of *mm* spawn a vector of *vm* processes, whose heading is orthogonal to the spawning direction. Each *vm* process, in turn, spawns a vector of *ip* processes. A snapshot of the spawning phase is shown in Figure 7.4. The final result is a rectangular array of *ip* processes, one for each inner-product that needs to be computed.

The behavior of this program is different from the systolic algorithm in Figure

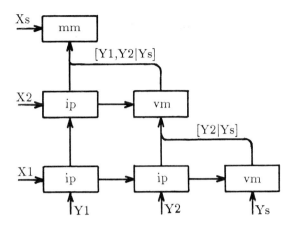

Figure 7.4: A snapshot of spawning a process array

mm([ ],−,[ ]).
mm([X|Xs],Ys,[Z|Zs]) ←
    vm(X,Ys?,Ys1,Z)@right, mm(Xs?,Ys1?,Zs)@forward.

vm(−,[ ],[ ],[ ]).
vm(Xs,[Y|Ys],[Y1|Ys1],[Z|Zs]) ←
    ip(Xs?,Xs1,Y?,Y1,0,Z), vm(Xs1?,Ys?,Ys1,Zs)@forward.

ip([X|Xs],[X|Xs1],[Y|Ys],[Y|Ys1],Z0,Z) ←
    Z1:=(X * Y)+Z0, ip(Xs?,Xs1,Ys?,Ys1,Z1,Z).
ip([ ],[ ],[ ],[ ],Z,Z).

Program 7.4: Matrix multiplication with vector pipelining

7.5, in that the vectors are not pipelined between *ip* processes, but are shipped independently to each *ip* process. However, Program 7.3 can be transformed to do the pipelining. This is achieved by adding two output streams to each *ip* process, one for copying each input stream, and one for connecting the *ip* processes accordingly. The result is Program 7.4.

The recursive construction of the communication structure of Program 7.4 is explained in Figure 7.5. Figure 7.5a is a pictorial description of the first clause of *mm*, and Figure 7.5b of the first clause of *vm*. The superior readability of the figures over the clauses may suggest that a graphical front-end, similar to the one of the Poker programming environment (Snyder, 1984), would be a useful tool.

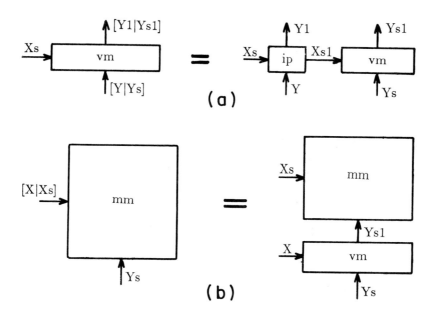

Figure 7.5: Recursive construction of the *mm* process array

Program 7.4 can multiply two $n \times n$ matrices in time linear in n, using n^2 processors, provided the input is spread appropriately. A technique for doing so is described by Taylor et al. (Chapter 8).

7.7.3 Process trees

<u>Towers of Hanoi and ℵ-trees</u>

The next example shows how to spawn the process structure of a divide-and-conquer program using H-trees (Leiserson, 1983). It computes the relation {$hanoi(N,A,B,X)$: the sequence of moves X can be used to move N disks from peg A to peg B, such that no disk is ever placed on a smaller one}. It is adapted from a similar Prolog program by H. Yasukawa. The notation $p(N{+}{+},\ldots) \leftarrow \ldots$ is a shorthand for $p(N1,\ldots) \leftarrow N1{>}0 \mid N{:=}N1{-}1,\ldots$.

Program 7.5 spawns a tree of *free* processes, one for each step in the solution. The computation of these processes is trivial: given two pegs, they compute the remaining peg. If the overhead associated with spawning a remote process is very high, then spawning only a partial H-tree may be a better solution. Spawning a static H-tree to solve several problems, a possibility mentioned earlier, is not applicable in this case: who would want to solve the same Towers of Hanoi problem more than once?

hanoi(0,A,B,(A,B)).
hanoi(N++,A,B,(Before?,(A,B),After?)) ←
    free(A,B,C),
    hanoi(N,A,C?,Before)@(left,forward($2^{(N/2)}$)),
    hanoi(N,C?,B,After)@(right,forward($2^{(N/2)}$)).

free(a,b,c). free(a,c,b). free(b,a,c).
free(b,c,a). free(c,a,b). free(c,b,a).

Program 7.5: The towers of Hanoi

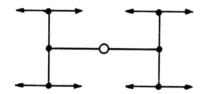

Figure 7.6: Spawning an H-tree

One problem with H-trees is that they are not evenly spread on the processing surface, therefore may utilize it ineffectively. In the portion of the processing surface covered by an H-tree, roughly one third of the processors contain leaf processes, one third contain non-leaf processes, and one third are either idle or serve only as communication-relays. This may cause load-imbalance if the tree is fairly static and performs heavy computations, e.g., a parallel search tree.

To solve this load-imbalance, we have developed an alternative to *H*-trees named ℵ-*trees* (read 'Aleph-trees'). ℵ-trees, called this way since their structure resembles the Hebrew letter ℵ (Aleph), are a method for evenly mapping complete binary trees of depth $2k$ on a processing surface of size $2^k \times 2^k$, by allocating one leaf process and one internal-node process to each processor (except one). The simplest ℵ-tree is a mapping of a complete binary tree of depth 2 into a square of size 2×2, shown in Figure 7.7a. In this figure, and in the discussion below, each grid square represents a processor. A general ℵ-tree, shown in Figure 7.7b, has the property that one internal node and one leaf node are mapped into every grid square, except the (*1,1*) grid square, the leftmost lowest one, to which only a leaf node is mapped. That grid square is called the *half-empty* square of the ℵ-tree. Another property of an ℵ-tree is that its root is mapped into the ($2^{k-1},2^{k-1}$) grid square, the one immediately above and to the right of the center.

ℵ-trees larger then 2×2 are defined inductively, as shown in Figure 7.8. To build an ℵ-tree of size $2^{k+1} \times 2^{k+1}$, four ℵ-trees of size $2^k \times 2^k$ are placed as

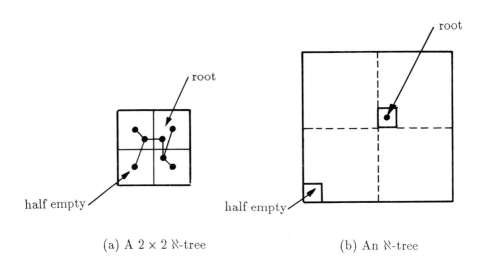

(a) A 2×2 ℵ-tree   (b) An ℵ-tree

Figure 7.7: ℵ-trees

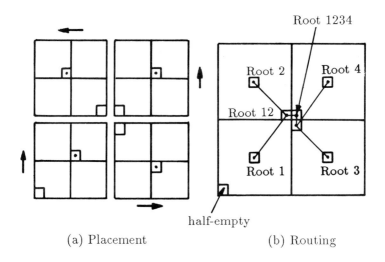

(a) Placement   (b) Routing

Figure 7.8: Constructing an ℵ-tree

shown in Figure 7.8a. The bottom-left and top-right trees are oriented north, the top-left tree oriented west, and the bottom-right tree oriented east.

The four trees are then connected as shown in Figure 7.8b, to form an ℵ-tree four times as big. The roots of the two left trees are connected to a new sub-root, which is placed in the half-empty grid square of the top-left tree. The roots of the two right trees are connected into another sub-root, which is placed in the half-empty grid square of the bottom-right tree. The two sub-roots are connected into the root of the new tree, which is placed in the half-empty grid square of the top-left tree. The result is an $\aleph$-tree whose $(1,1)$ grid square is empty and whose root is in the $(2^k,2^k)$ grid square.

Program 7.6 shows how to map a process tree of depth N, composed of *leaf(Root)* and *internal(Root,LeftSon,RightSon)* processes, using $\aleph$-trees. The program uses an auxiliary *arm* process to spawn the top-left and bottom-right $\aleph$-trees and their associated sub-roots.

> aleph(0,Root) ←
>   leaf(Root).
> aleph(N++,Root1234) ←
>   aleph(N,Root1),
>   arm(N,Root1,Root12)@(rt,fd(2^{N-1}),lt,fd(2^N),lt),
>   aleph(N,Root3)@(fd(2^N),rt,fd(2^N),lt),
>   arm(N,Root3,Root34)@(fd(2^{N-1}),rt,fd(2^N)),
>   internal(Root12,Root34,Root1234)@(fd(2^N),rt,fd(2^N),lt).
>
> arm(N,Root1,Root12) ←
>   aleph(N,Root2),
>   internal(Root1,Root2,Root12).
>
> leaf(Root) ← code for leaf.
>
> internal(LeftSon,RightSon,Root) ← code for internal node.

Program 7.6: Spawning an $\aleph$-tree

$\aleph$-trees take only a quarter of the processing surface taken by H-trees, and their communication links are half as long (or even shorter, if communication along the diagonals is allowed). On the other hand they are not planar, hence they may not be as useful for VLSI layout. Another disadvantage of $\aleph$-trees is that their naive routing would cause logarithmic congestion of communication lines along the main diagonals. A routing scheme that eliminates this logarithmic congestion is yet to be designed.

Dynamic H-trees

The mapping strategies used by Programs 7.5 and 7.6 are required to know the depth of the computation tree in advance, which may be a limitation for some applications. A method for spawning computation trees on a processing surface which does not suffer from this problem is described by Martin (1979) and Sequin

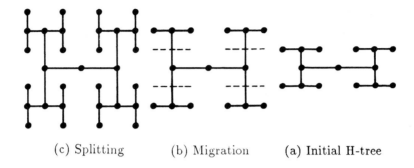

(c) Splitting   (b) Migration   (a) Initial H-tree

Figure 7.9: Growing an H-tree

(1981). However, that mapping strategy may cause an exponential imbalance in processor load. We have developed another approach to this problem, which does not suffer from exponential load imbalance, namely to grow H-trees dynamically.

Here we explain how this method, called *Dynamic H-trees*, can be applied to the implementation of a parallel relational database. The processes that maintain a given relation in a relational database can be arranged in a tree structure, where queries are addressed to the root process; the leaf processes store the different parts of the relation, probably on the disk associated with the processor they are mapped to, and internal node processes implement query routing, using hashing or other indexing techniques and do the merging of the response streams. A desired size of such a tree may be determined according to various parameters such as the performance of the processor and the disk, and the types of queries that are expected. Assume that some upper limit on the number of tuple entries per leaf process is decided upon. Then as the relation grows in size, as a result of updates, the H-tree should grow accordingly.

Growing the H-tree is done by splitting each leaf node into two, dividing the relation tuples between the two new leaves, and creating an internal node whose routing function knows how its part of the relation was divided. A simple splitting is shown in Figure 7.9. When splitting occurs, pieces of the tree need to relocate, to make room for the newly created leaves. During the relocation process each node preserves its relative position to its parent. However, alternating levels in the tree also relocate an additional distance, which is an exponential function of the height of their subtree. The splitting algorithm, including the formula for the relocation distance, is implemented in Program 7.7.

Program 7.7 dynamically grows an H-trees. It uses the abstract stream operation *send* defined by the clause *send(Message,[Message|Out],Out)*.

```
dhtree(In) ←
    root(0,In?,Out),
    leaf(Out?).

root(D– –,[ split|In],[split(D,stay)|Out]) ←
    root(D,In?,Out).
root(D,[ ],[ ]).

leaf([split(1,TP)|In]) ←
    tree(In?,OutLeft,OutRight)@TP,
    leaf(OutLeft?)@(TP,left,forward),
    leaf(OutRight?)@(TP,right,forward).
leaf([ ]).

tree([split(Height++,TP)|In],OutL,OutR) ←
    relocation(Height?,Distance),
    send(split(Height,(right,TP,left,fd(Distance))),OutL,OutL1),
    send(split(Height,(left,TP,right,fd(Distance))),OutR,OutR1),
    tree(In?,OutL1,OutR1)@TP.
tree([ ],[ ],[ ]).

relocation(Height,Distance) ←
    even(Height) | Distance:=(2^{⌊Height/2-1⌋})
relocation(Height,0) ←
    odd(Height) | true.
```

Program 7.7: Dynamic H-trees

The program operates as follows. When an external agent decides to split the H-tree, it sends a *split* message to the *root* process, which converts it to a *split(Height,stay)* message to the *tree* process which is the actual root of the H-tree. *Height* is the current height of the H-tree, and *stay* is the null Turtle program. A *leaf* process receiving a *split(1,TurtleProgram)* message splits into three processes, a *tree* process and two *leaf* processes, and relocates all of them by the *TurtleProgram*. The two new leaves are further separated from the parent using the *(left,forward)* and *(right,forward)* commands.

A *tree* process receiving a message *split(Height,TurtleProgram)* computes the relative relocation for its two child processes, using the auxiliary *relocation* procedure, and sends them the updated *split* messages. The updated message *split(Height,(left,TP,right,fd(Distance)))* incorporates the Turtle program *TP* with which the parent relocates, wrapped with *left* and *right* commands to compensate for the fact that the orientation of the child process is orthogonal to that of the parent, followed by the computed relative relocation distance *Distance*.

The formula computed by the *relocation* procedure was found experimentally.

The Dynamic H-tree program illustrates meta-Turtle-programming, where processes construct Turtle programs, send them to other processes, and relocate using Turtle programs received from others.

7.7.4 Forming complex communication structures

Gaussian elimination

Program 7.8 is a Concurrent Prolog implementation of a systolic algorithm for Gaussian elimination. It demonstrates the ability of Concurrent Prolog to form complex communication structures (and also the need for a graphical notation to support the construction and understanding of systolic algorithms).

```
gauss([[A0|As]|Columns],[B0|Bs],[X|Xs]) ←
    pivot(A0,B0,Bs?,Bs1,As?,Factors),
    X:=(B0–Sum)/A0,
    row(Factors?,Columns?,Columns1,Xs,Sum)@(right,forward),
    gauss(Columns1?,Bs1?,Xs)@(fd,rt,fd,lt).
gauss([ ],[ ],[ ]).

pivot(A0,B0,[B|Bs],[B1|Bs1],[A|As],[Factor|Fs]) ←
    Factor:=A/A0,
    B1:=B–(B0*Factor),
    pivot(A0,B0,Bs?,Bs1,As?,Fs).
pivot(A0,B0,[ ],[ ],[ ],[ ]).

row(Factors,[[A|As]|Columns],[As1|Columns1],[X|Xs],Sum1) :
    cell(Factors,A,As?,As1),
    Sum1:=Sum+(A*X),
    row(Factors,Columns?,Columns1,Xs,Sum?)@forward.
row(Factors,[ ],[ ],[ ],0).

cell([Factor|Fs],A0,[A|As],[A1|As1]) ←
    A1:=A–(A0*Factor),
    cell(Fs?,A0,As?,As1).
cell([ ],A,[ ],[ ]).
```

Program 7.8: Gaussian elimination

Program 7.8 defines the relation $\{gauss(A,B,X) : X$ is the solution vector to the linear equation defined by the coefficient matrix A and vector of values $B\}$. It spawns a lower-triangular array of processes that has *pivot* processes on the diagonal and *cell* processes below it. The computation has two phases: a spawning and elimination phase, and a back-substitution phase. In the spawn-

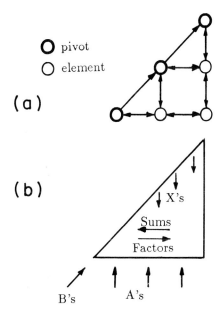

Figure 7.10: Information flow in Gaussian elimination

ing and elimination phase, factors are computed and broadcasted east, and the updated coefficients are forwarded north. The updated *Bs* are forwarded north-east, along with their pivot processes. In the back-substitution phase, the values of the variables are computed and broadcasted south, and partial sums are being accumulated for each equation from east to west. The general information flow in the two phases is shown in Figure 7.10.

The recursive construction of the process array is shown in Figure 7.11. This figure is a graphical representation of the first clause of Program 7.8.

The program spawns the nth row with the coefficients of the nth equation, in which the first n–1 variables have been eliminated. The nth row eliminates the coefficients of the nth variable from all subsequent equations in the elimination phase and computes the value of that variable in the back-substitution phase.

A row is composed of a *pivot* process and a *cell* process. The behavior of the *pivot* process is shown in Figure 7.12.

To eliminate the coefficient *A* of the first remaining variable in an equation, the pivot computes the factor $F:=A/A0$, where $A0$ is the coefficient of the pivot variable. The factor *F* is broadcasted to the rest of the row, which subtracts itself,

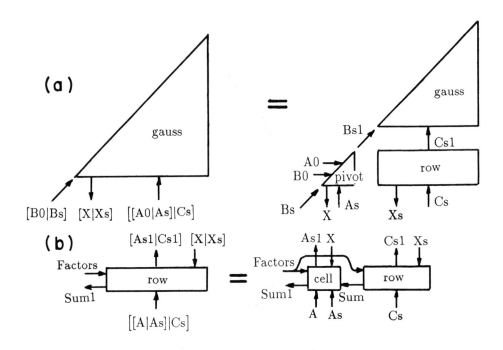

Figure 7.11: Recursive construction of the Gauss process array

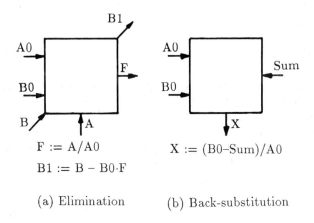

$$F := A/A0$$
$$B1 := B - B0 \cdot F$$

$$X := (B0 - Sum)/A0$$

(a) Elimination   (b) Back-substitution

Figure 7.12: Behavior of a *pivot* process

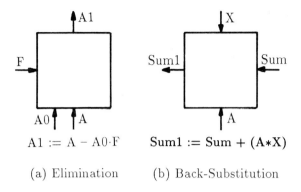

Figure 7.13: Behavior of a *cell* process

multiplied by the factor, from the equation, and forwards the modified equation to the next row. The pivot also modifies the B value of the equation accordingly. During back-substitution, the pivot receives Sum from the row and computes the value of X.

The behavior of a *cell* process is shown in Figure 7.13.

When receiving a factor F, each cell process computes $A1:=A-(F*A0)$, where A is the coefficient received from the south and $A0$ is the local coefficient, and sends the result north. Note that the processes that compute the back-substitution, $X:=(B-Sum)/A$, and $Sum1:=Sum+(A*X)$, are created during the spawning phase, and are suspended on their Sum variables until the elimination phase is complete.

Program 7.8 can solve n equations in n variables in time linear in n on a processing surface whose size is linear in n^2 provided the input is spread appropriately, and pipelines for factors and solutions are added (see Taylor et al., Chapter 8). It can be extended to handle zero-pivots.

Band-matrix multiplication

Program 7.9 implements a soft-systolic variant of the band-matrix multiplication algorithm of Kung and Leiserson, shown in Figure 7.14. In this algorithm the diagonals of two band-matrices and the resulting matrix (which is initially zero) are fed into a rectangular hex-connected process array, as shown in Figure 7.14. Each process in the array implements a simple inner-product step: multiply A and B, and add them to C. It also forwards the A, B, and the updated C to its appropriate neighbors.

The algorithm has three phases: spawning, copying, and computation. The

band_mm(D,As,Bs,Cs) ←
   % *D* is the index of the main diagonals of *As* and *Bs*
   mm(D,As?,Bs,Ca,C,Cb),
   reverse(Ca?,[C|Cb?],Cs)@back.

mm(D,[A|As],[B|Bs],Ca1,C1,Cb1) ←
   copy_and_ip(D,0,C?,C1,A?,A1,B?,B1),
   arm(D,0,As?,As1,Ca,Ca1,B1)@forward,
   arm(D,0,Bs?,Bs1,Cb,Cb1,A1)@(right,forward),
   D1:=D−1,
   mm(D1,As1?,Bs1?,Ca,C,Cb)@(forward,right,forward,left).
mm(D,[ ],[ ],[ ],[ ],[ ]).

arm(D,V,[ ],[ ],[ ],[[ ]],−).
arm(D,V− −,[A|As],[A1|As1],[C|Cs],[C1|Cs1],B) ←
   copy_and_ip(D,V,C?,C1,A?,A1,B?,B1),
   arm(D,V,As?,As1,Cs,Cs1,B1)@forward.

copy_and_ip(0,V,C,C1,A,A1,B,B1) ← % we are in the *0*'s area ...
   ip(C,C1,A,A1,B,B1).
copy_and_ip(D,V,C,C1,A,A1,B,B1) ← % we are in the *A* (or *B*) area ...
   D>0 | copy(min(D,V),A,Af,A1,A1f), ip(C,C1,Af?,A1f,B,B1).
copy_and_ip(D,V,C,C1,A,A1,B,B1) ← % we are in the *C* area ...
   D<0 | copy(−D,C?,Cf,C1,C1f), ip(Cf?,C1f,A,A1,B,B1).
copy(0,In,In,Out,Out).
copy(N++,In0,In1,[C|Out],Out1) ←
   get_c(C,In0,In) | copy(N,In?,In1,Out,Out1).

ip(Cs0,[Cab|Cs1],[A|As],[A|As1],[B|Bs],[B|Bs1]) ←
   get_c(C,Cs0,Cs) |
   Cab:=C+(A ∗ B),
   ip(Cs?,Cs1,As?,As1,Bs?,Bs1).
ip(Cs,Cs,As,As,[ ],[ ]).
ip(Cs,Cs,[ ],[ ],Bs,Bs).

get_c(0,[ ],[ ]).
get_c(C,[C|Cs],Cs?).

Program 7.9: Band-matrix multiplication

recursive spawning of the process array, which corresponds to the first clause of
mm, is shown in Figure 7.15.

   The difficult part in implementing the hard-systolic algorithm, besides con-

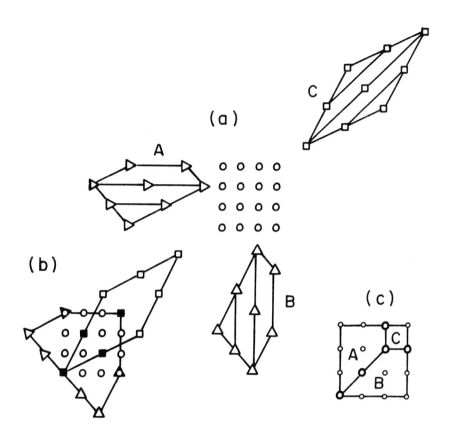

Figure 7.14: A systolic algorithm for band-matrix multiplication

structing the hardware, is the synchronization: ensuring that the first elements of the main diagonals of the three matrices meet at the central processor at the same time, that the other diagonals are behind the main diagonals by a certain delay, and that there is a certain constant delay between any two consecutive diagonal elements. Formal tools for defining these delays were proposed by Weiser and Davis (1981).

The purpose of the copying phase of the corresponding soft-systolic algorithm is to achieve this synchronization effect in a time-independent fashion. In the copying phase, each process in the array copies a certain number of elements of one of the diagonals from its input to its output stream. The direction and amount of copying of each *ip* process guarantees that an *A*, *B*, and *C* elements

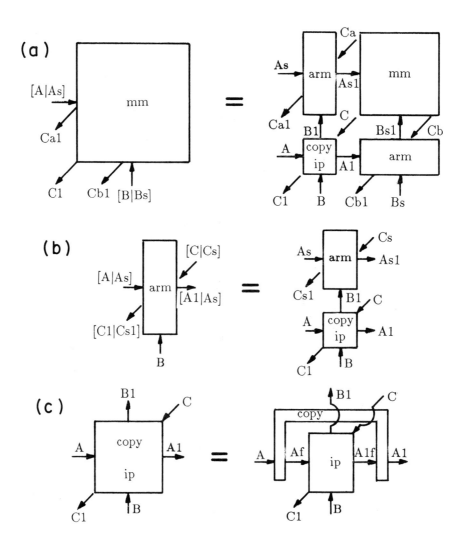

Figure 7.15(a–c): Recursive construction of a hex-connected process array

would be ready for it when it enters the computation phase.

The direction and amount of copying for each process is determined by its location in the process array, as shown in Figure 7.14c. Processes in the A (B or C) area copy elements of the A (B or C, respectively) matrices. Processes in

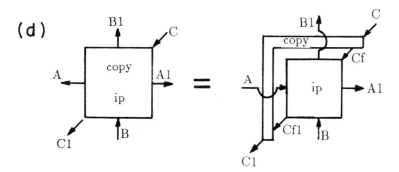

Figure 7.15(d): Recursive construction of a hex-connected process array

the *0*-area do not do any copying. The number of elements each process copies is determined by its distance from the process-array's main diagonal (V), and its distance from the meeting point of the three diagonals (D). The exact formula (which was found experimentally) is embedded in Program 7.9.

Program 7.9 has three major parts, corresponding to the three phases of the algorithm: spawning (*mm* and *arm*), copying (*copy_and_ip* and *copy*), and computing (*ip*). It is interesting to note that the spawning and copying parts constitute about 40 percent of the code each, and that the actual computation is specified by the remaining 20 percent.

Note also that since the program is dataflow synchronized, its correctness (though not its performance) is not affected by the existence of diagonal communication links in the processing surface, or lack thereof. If diagonal links are missing, a diagonal message can be routed by the processing surface through two other links to its destination.

Another interesting aspect of the program is the behavior of the north and east boundary processes. Since the initially zero C matrix is not actually fed into the array, they must "invent" it. Also, they have no-one to copy the A's (or B's) matrices to. These problems are not solved by introducing special boundary processes. Instead, the first problem is solved by introducing a special routine *get_c*, to get elements of C's diagonals. If the C's stream is closed, as is the case with the north and east boundary processes, *get_c* generates a 0 upon request, instead of delivering the next stream element. The second problem, of having no-one to copy the A's and B's matrices to, is solved by ignoring it: the matrices are copied nevertheless, with no one on the receiving end. This uniformity makes the program more concise, but less efficient. Defining specialized *boundary_ip* processes, and eliminating the *get_c* routine from the normal *ip* ones is not difficult.

7.8   Systolic Programming, Concurrent Prolog, and the Fifth Generation of Computers

We find it intriguing that even though logic-programming and Prolog were conceived in the context of Artificial Intelligence research, the most natural and immediate applications of Concurrent Prolog are the hard-core computer science algorithms, shown in this paper, and systems programming. In this context one may wonder whether the systolic programming approach in general, and Concurrent Prolog in particular, are suitable for the AI applications envisioned by the Japanese Fifth Generation Project (Moto-Oka et al., 1981). It would be ironic if a language whose conception was motivated mainly by the Fifth Generation project would find its ecological niche to be systems hacking and number-crunching, rather then Artificial Intelligence.

I do not feel this is the case. Rather, I find this course of development encouraging. If logic programming is to form the foundation for a new generation of computers, as envisioned by Kowalski, Fuchi (1984), and others, then it must address the full spectrum of applications of computers. It is a sign of health and continuity that problems which, historically and conceptually, were easier to tackle under the von Neumann framework, are also those which one encounters first when attempting to devise an alternative framework.

In this context, Concurrent Prolog perhaps is best viewed as a machine language for a new type of computer, rather then as the result of a sequence of abstractions and refinements of a well understood model. Higher level languages and new programming methods suitable for the more sophisticated applications of computers, namely Artificial Intelligence, may be built on top of Concurrent Prolog and systolic programming.

7.9   Comparison With Other Work

Systolic programming shares the belief that architectures based on global communication, such as NYU's Ultracomputer (Gottlieb et al., 1983), TRAC (Sejnowiski et al., 1980), Alice (Darlington and Reeve, 1981), and others, are not the ultimate approach to parallel processing. Such architectures are reactionary, since they capitalize on our ignorance of parallel computations. Their attractiveness will decrease steadily as our understanding of parallelism increases and as we know more about designing and programming systolic and other local-communication based algorithms.

Several similar architectures based on local interconnections have been proposed, including the Apiary (Hewitt, 1973), the CHiP computer (Snyder, 1984), FAIM (Anderson et al., 1987), Rediflow (Keller et al., 1983), and Martin's (1979) original Processing Surface.

They differ mainly in their programming methods. The CHiP Computer provides a graphical programming environment, called Poker. Poker seems to be convenient for specifying finite process structures and their mappings. However, it is not clear how well it supports the construction and mapping of general, recursive, size-independent, process structures. It is interesting to compare the Poker programming environment and the systolic programming debugger/graphical simulator. Both are interactive program development environments that support symbolic debugging and graphical animation of the target parallel computer. Both simulate the underlying machine in a detailed enough level to allow the development of complex programs. Given the complexity of the examples shown in this paper and those by Snyder (1984), it seems that our simulator is a software-development environment at least as productive as Poker. However, the Poker programming environment, which was written in C, is 40,000 lines of code long, whereas our simulator which includes a Concurrent Prolog interpreter, debugger, and a graphics animation package, is 900 lines of Prolog code.

Another direction pursued in cunjunction with the CHiP computer is the development of a mapping-compiler (Bokhari, 1981). The goal of the compiler is to allocate statically processes to processors, and to compile the amalgamated programs of processes mapped to the same processor into code that timeshares between them (Berman and Snyder, 1984). This approach is feasible for programming an attached processor, but not for a general-purpose computer. A similar direction was pursued with the Cm* (Schwans, 1982).

On the other extreme, the Apiary allows for the dynamic creation of processes ("objects"), and relies on algorithms (or heuristics?) for runtime migration of processes to ensure load-balancing and locality of communication (Hewitt and Lieberman, 1984). The Rediflow, like the global-communication approach and the Apiary, accepts ignorance of the behavior of computations as a basic assumption.

We feel that the ignorance assumption is overly pessimistic and is counterproductive as a working hypothesis. To date, progress in science resulted from assuming, in spite of superficial evidence to the contrary, that there is some order in the world, and that science's goal is to uncover it. Declaring the world to be unpredictable would be a self-fulfilling prophecy, but would not further our understanding.

The systolic programming approach advocated in this paper is in some sense a mixture of the two approaches and in another sense more conservative then both. It allows the dynamic creation of processes, but relies on the programmer, rather than on the compiler, to map process structures on the processing surface.

Although it is conservative it is also future-proof. Should a successful mapping-compiler be developed, it can be incorporated as a preprocessor to mapping-less programs. Should some techniques for runtime load-balancing be found useful for certain applications, they can be implemented by adding a layer of interpretation, which may be compiled away for specific programs using techniques of partial evaluation. Needless to say, a statically-allocated distributed meta-interpreter is one of the best tools for experimenting with load-balancing algorithms (see Shapiro, Chapter 34).

7.10   Conclusions

Many discussions on parallel processing go in circles: "to exploit parallelism fully we must spread the computation as much as possible", "but if we spread it too much we will generate an unmanageable amount of communication". The systolic approach seems to be the only one to date that shows how to cut this Gordian knot — to allow massive parallelism without communication bottlenecks.

So far the systolic approach was viewed as having only limited applications. Systolic programming may carry the insights of the systolic approach into the realm of general purpose parallel computing.

Acknowledgements

Part of this research was carried out while visiting ICOT, and I am grateful for this stimulating research environment.

The ideas in this paper were developed in collaboration with many. Walter Wilson suggested that one should not worry about small multiprocessors, but rather design an infinite multiprocessor first. Marc Snir pointed out the importance of a mapping notation. Ken Kahn suggested the use of fixed-instruction Turtle programs, instead of a weaker mapping notation I have been using. Amos Fiat and Leon Sterling helped with the design of the Gaussian elimination algorithm. Leon Sterling and David Harel provided useful comments on the paper. Yosee Feldman assisted in editing this chapter.

Chapter 8

Notes on the Complexity of Systolic Programs

Stephen Taylor[1], Lisa Hellerstein[2], Shmuel Safra[1]
and Ehud Shapiro[1]

[1] *The Weizmann Institute of Science*
[2] *University of California at Berkeley*

Abstract

This paper presents two notes which discuss basic theoretical issues concerning the systolic programming methodology and demonstrates simple techniques which can be used to structure communication. The first note shows how the complexity of two simple algorithms is adversely affected by the cost of data movement in a parallel system. Programming techniques, which introduce pipelining, are used to overcome the problem and improve the complexity. The second note shows an upper bound on the speed-up which can be obtained using the methodology on a mesh connected architecture. This bound is stated in terms of the sequential lower bound for the algorithm concerned.

8.1 Why Systolic Programming?

The systolic programming methodology (Shapiro, Chapter 7) is an approach to parallel processing which attempts to capture the essential notions of systolic algorithm design (Kung, 1982). It permits the balancing and overlapping of computation with local communication but allows algorithm development to be carried out largely independent of hardware design. The essential characteristics of the execution model are:

- Processors are connected via a regular interconnection topology, e.g., a mesh and a ring.

- There is no global storage, each processor has access to local storage.

- Processors may communicate with some small number of neighboring processors via message passing.

- Computations are described as a set of communicating processes in some convenient programming language.

- Dynamic process mapping allows processes to be assigned to neighboring processors.

An important aspect of the above characteristics is that they preserve *scalability*; this quality is of increasing importance as the cost of hardware continues to diminish. Algorithm development using this methodology involves a number of interrelated activities: the design of process structures (Kung, 1982), structuring communication, and mapping process structures to processors (Bokhari, 1981).

A simple, process oriented, concurrent programming language called Flat Concurrent Prolog (FCP) (Mierowsky et al., 1985; Shapiro, Chapter 5) is used. FCP provides an interesting framework to investigate parallel processing problems for a variety of reasons:

- The parallel execution algorithm involved in its implementation is simple and, we believe, amenable to efficient compilation. An initial, interpreter based, parallel implementation is operational on an Intel iPSC Hypercube using the above execution model (Taylor et al., Chapter 39).

- FCP supports meta-programming allowing many non-trivial system functions to be supported without complicating the language semantics (Safra and Shapiro, Chapter 25). These include methods for process and code mapping (Taylor et al., Chapter 22).

- Due to its simplicity and uniformity, the language can be used to investigate a number of program transformation techniques aimed at improving efficiency. These include partial evaluation (Safra, 1986) and abstract interpretation.

- An efficient uni-processor implementation exists which is comparable in speed to commercially available Prolog compilers (Houri and Shapiro, Chapter 38).

- FCP is a practical language which has been used for a number of non-trivial programming problems. These include a bootstrapping compiler, a programming environment, sections of an operating system, and various parallel algorithms.

The systolic programming methodology can express a variety of systolic algorithms (Shapiro, Chapter 7); this represents an interesting but secondary use of the methodology. Systolic algorithms are by definition (Kung, 1982) a class of simple, regular computations. Many algorithms in this class are well understood, are reasonably easy to implement in hardware or a convenient programming formalism and various testbeds are available. In general, like all pipelines, the performance of systolic architectures is limited by the speed of the slowest element. Since each cell in a systolic system performs the same algorithm, there is unlikely to be significant speed variation. This produces little opportunity for the overlapping of computation which generally makes asynchronous systems attractive. Systolic programming does not circumvent these fundamental limitations and is unlikely to provide a significant speed-up on systolic applications. In addition, systolic programming is unlikely to compete in cost-effectiveness with special purpose devices (Kung, 1984) when executing specific sets of algorithms.

The primary use of systolic programming is as a basic research tool to investigate problems associated with general purpose parallel programming. As the complexity of tasks increase, algorithm design becomes a recurring cost while the cost of a homogeneous architecture is non-recurring. The need to minimize design costs becomes acute as the range of applications increases. This requires efficient, simple and versatile programming tools which provide the programmer with insight into the nature of parallel execution. Given simple tools, programmers must learn how to design process structures, map processes to processors, and localize communication. The systolic programming approach promises cost-effective design through simplicity and flexibility.

This paper presents some basic theoretical results concerning the formalism and two initial techniques for structuring communication.

8.2 Structuring Communication

The complexity analysis that follows will use two methods for structuring communication. The first, *pipelining*, uses software processes to mimic a conventional pipeline; it provides a mechanism to move values between processors to ensure locality of communication. Consider the linear array of processors shown in Figure 8.1 in which processes A, B, C, and D all perform operations on the data in processor 1.

It is obvious that communication is not balanced since processor 1 receives all the messages and intermediate processors must route communication. It is also true that the delay for processor N to obtain its values depends upon the routing scheme and interconnection topology. If communication is constrained to occur along the linear array it may require time $O(N)$ to access data; if a binary N-cube connection were used data might be accessible in time $O(\log N)$. An alternative

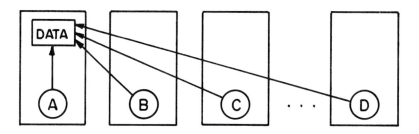

Figure 8.1: Linear array of processors

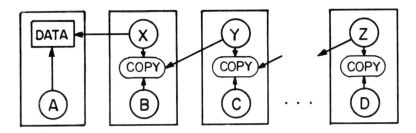

Figure 8.2: Software pipelining

scheme, *pipelining*, is shown in Figure 8.2.

In this scheme, processes X, Y, and Z copy values only between adjacent machines. The resulting communication structure is more balanced and can be organized to ensure that data is available when requested or will become available within some constant time. Note that like all pipelines the data must arrive at processor i before processor $i + 1$ may begin computation. Pipelining is in essence a producer-consumer relation; we believe that this specific programming idiom can be compiled more efficiently than arbitrary communication structures.

The second technique that will be used is termed *spreading* and is more a conceptual tool than a programming technique. The essential idea is to separate the operations of data distribution and algorithm execution. This allows the algorithm and data distribution to be reasoned about and optimized individually.

8.3 Note 1: Communication Complexity

The cost of data movement can significantly impact the performance of parallel algorithms (Gentleman, 1978; Thompson and Kung, 1977; Lint and Agerwala, 1981); moreover, in any practical system it is necessary to consider the initial and final configurations of the data.

The complexity analysis which follows assumes that if communication occurs only between adjacent PE's, and the size of messages is constant, each message takes constant time to travel. In addition, the relative processor speed is independent of the input size n.

Consider the problem of sorting using an insertion sort algorithm. The algorithm may be visualized as spawning a linearly connected set of processes; each process holds a number from the unsorted data. When the process network has been spawned, an initially empty, sorted list of data is propagated back through the process array. Each process reads the sorted data as it passes and inserts its own number into the appropriate place. The sorted result eventually appears at the origin of the process network.

Program 8.1 implements insertion sort using the systolic programming approach on a ring architecture. We assume for the purposes of complexity analysis that the unsorted input resides at the processor where computation originates. The sort program spawns a linearly connected sequence of *insert* processes, one for each element in its input stream. The last insert process is spawned with the empty input stream due to the last sort rule. At this time, processes begin propagating data backwards starting from the last process. Each process copies its ordered (or empty in the case of the last process) input stream, inserting its local number in the output stream so that the latter remains ordered.

```
sort([X| Xs],Ys) ←              % sort list into sorted list
    insert(X?,Zs?,Ys),
    sort(Xs?,Zs)@fwd.           % sort rest at forward
sort([ ],[ ]).                  % input end, spawning complete

insert(X,[Y| Ys],[Y| Zs?]) ←    % keep searching
        X > Y | insert(X?,Ys?,Zs).
insert(X,[Y| Ys],[X,Y| Ys]) ←   % place found
        X ≤ Y | true.
insert(X,[ ],[X]).              % insert at end
```

Program 8.1: Insertion sort

Assume that when a process is spawned it can access its data in constant time. Since there is one sort process for each element of the list, it takes time $O(n)$ to spawn all the sort processes. Each parallel insert process takes time $O(n)$

to execute; it is possible to conclude that the total running time is $O(n)$ (Shapiro, Chapter 7).

Unfortunately the above assumption does not always hold. Consider a scheme where communication occurs along the path of spawning and processes request data only when needed. Under this scheme the ith process spawned in insertion sort reads only the ith element of the list and is not provided with any other elements. When the $i+1^{st}$ process is spawned, the $i+1^{st}$ element of the list is therefore only available in the input list at the initial processor. Since the process structure is a linear pipe, it takes approximately $2(i+1)$ communication steps for the $i+1^{st}$ process to access its data after it is spawned.

The fact that the process is not able to access its data in constant time significantly degrades the performance of insertion sort. The $i+1^{st}$ process cannot be spawned until the ith list structure arrives. Hence the elements of the list are requested sequentially with approximately $2i$ communication steps required to access the ith element for every i. Thus the total time to spawn the network of insert processes is $O(n^2)$.

Program 8.1 may be modified to obtain the desired time complexity of $O(n)$ using the *pipelining* technique. The inclusion of pipes in a program does not change the result of the computation. Pipes are used in order to allow copying of data to be overlapped with program execution; thus the time that processors would normally stand idle is used for copying. A one level pipe is written in FCP as:

```
pipe([X| Xs],[X| Ys]) ←      % pipe Xs to Ys
    known(X) |               % wait for head
    pipe(Xs?,Ys).            % copy the rest
pipe([ ],[ ]).               % all copied
```

It is invoked with a process of the form:

```
pipe(Xs?,Ys)
```

Assume the stream Xs in the process is located on another processor. The effect of $known(X)$ is to wait until the value of X is known locally. The effect of the program is to copy the input stream locally. Program 8.1 can now be re-written to execute in time $O(n)$.

In Program 8.1 each processor carries out one sort reduction and then waits for Zs to be given a value. Program 8.2 copies Xs locally so that when the neighboring sort process attempts to read Xs the values are only a single communication step away. A similar idea, denoted by the second pipe process in Program 8.2, allows the sorted list to be pipelined backwards when the insert process terminates; the necessity for this pipe can be seen by considering a sorted input.

```
sort([X| Xs],Ys) ←
    pipe(Xs?,Xs1),                    % pipe values forward
    sort(Xs1?,Zs)@fwd,
    pipe(Zs?,Zs1),                    % pipe values backward
    insert(X?,Zs1?,Ys).
sort([ ],[ ]).
```

Program 8.2: Pipelined insertion sort

Since processes are never required to read values which are more than one communication step away it is possible to show a linear upper bound on the complexity of Program 8.2.

Lemma. If a data element resides in an adjacent processor, then the time required to bring it locally is constant.
Proof. Since all communication is executed locally and constant sized messages take constant time to travel between adjacent processors, it takes constant time to bring the data. We show by induction that there is linear delay for propagating the list *Xs* through the process structure. ∎

Claim. After the kth step, for each $0 \leq i < k$ the first $k-i$ elements are in the $i+1^{st}$ processor.

Basis. $k = 1$. All elements initially reside at the 0th processor, and thus by the above lemma the first element may be transferred to the first processor.

Induction. After k steps, for each $0 \leq i < k$.

(1) The first $k-i$ elements are in the ith processor (IH).

(2) The first $k-i+1$ elements are in the $i-1^{th}$ processor (IH).

Thus the $k-i+1$ element can be transferred to the $k-i^{st}$ processor by the lemma.
Similarly, a linear delay exists for propagating the resulting lists in the reverse direction except that the data elements are produced by the *insert* process.

8.3.1 Matrix multiplication

Program 8.3 performs matrix multiplication on a mesh connected architecture. The matrices are input as a list of rows, each row is a list of matrix elements; the second matrix is input in transposed form. The initial process begins execution in the bottom corner of the mesh, facing right. Under the assumption that the input matrices are located at the initial processor, the lower bound on the program $O(n^2)$. This bound arises because n^2 elements must be read from the initial processor. Delays in reading data similar to those demonstrated in Pro-

mm([Xv| Xm],Ym,[Zv| Zm]) ←   % $X \times Y = Z$
    vm(Xv?,Ym?,Ym1,Zv)@left,   % spawn vector multiply
    mm(Xm?,Ym1?,Zm)@fwd.   % spawn the rest
mm([ ],Ym,[ ]).   % matrix end, terminate

vm(Xv,[Yv| Ym],[Yv1| Ym1],[Z| Zv]) ←   % vector multiply
    ip(Xv?,Xv1,Yv?,Yv1,Z),   % inner product
    vm(Xv1?,Ym?,Ym1,Zv)@fwd.   % spawn the rest
vm(Xv,[ ],[ ],[ ]).   % vector end, terminate

ip(Xv,Xv1,Yv,Yv1,Z) ←   % initialize to 0
    ip1(Xv?,Xv1,Yv?,Yv1,0,Z).

ip1([X| Xv],[X| Xv1],[Y| Yv],[Y| Yv1],Z0,Z) ←   % multiply an element
    Z1 := (X * Y) + Z0,
    ip1(Xv?,Xv1,Yv?,Yv1,Z1?,Z).   % multiply rest
ip1([ ],[ ],[ ],[ ],Z,Z).   % terminate

Program 8.3: Matrix multiplication

gram 8.1 can cause the complexity of the program to increase to $O(n^3)$; there are n lists each of which may take $O(n^2)$ to access.

The high complexity of the above program results from the necessity to distribute the data during algorithm execution. It can be improved by first distributing or *spreading* the data and then executing the algorithm. In Program 8.3 the data needs to be *spread* over the axes of the processor array since this is the time critical operation. It can be achieved in time $O(n^2)$ using a two level pipe. Figure 8.3 illustrates the data configuration after the X matrix has been spread over the horizontal axis.

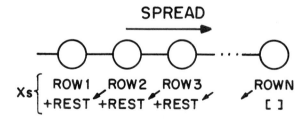

Figure 8.3: Data distribution after spreading

After spreading, Program 8.4 computes matrix multiplication in time $O(n)$ using the data already in place.

```
new_mm(X,Y,Z) ←                          % new matrix multiply
    spread(X?,X1),                       % spread X on X-axis
    spread(Y?,Y1)@left,                  % spread Y on Y-axis
    mm(X1?,Y1?,Z).                       % do old mm algorithm

spread([Xv| Xm],[Xv1?| Xm2?]) ←
    pipe(Xv?,Xv1),                       % copy one row
    pipe1(Xm?,Xm1),                      % copy the rest
    spread(Xm1?,Xm2)@fwd.                % spread rest at forward
spread([ ],[ ]).                         % spread complete

pipe1([Xv| Xm],[Xv1?| Xm1?]) ←           % copy list of lists
    pipe(Xv?,Xv1),                       % copy one list
    pipe1(Xm?,Xm1).                      % copy rest
pipe1([ ],[ ]).                          % copying complete
```

Program 8.4: Matrix distribution

Program 8.3 performs some copying in the head of the first *ip1* rule. This rule copies both Xs and Ys synchronously with the calculation of an inner product. Copying in matrix multiplication serves two different purposes. The first is to pipeline the data (c.f. the *ip* process). The second purpose is to provide references which do not follow the path of process spawning; observe that while the *vm* processes are spawned vertically in the array they access elements from the Y matrix horizontally.

The synchronous copying described is not always a good technique. In Program 8.3, it delays the execution of *ip* processes (*ip1*) unnecessarily. As Figure 8.4 demonstrates, the *ip* processes need both the X and Y inputs to reduce. A given *ip* process thus requires the *ip* processes to the left and below to have received both their inputs before it can begin operation. For example, process A must wait for both inputs to B (i.e., 1 and 2) and also both inputs to C (i.e., 3 and 4). This causes A to wait unnecessarily for inputs 2 and 3. In Figure 8.4, the path taken by the data which process A needs is indicated by routes X and Y. If piping is carried out asynchronously with *ip* processes, then *ip* processes can begin as soon as the one input they require from each of the neighboring *ip* processes is available.

When the program does not require synchronization and data is not used locally but generated purely for the benefit of communication, the asynchronous pipe process is more appropriate since it makes the operation autonomous and explicit. The program can be re-formulated as shown in Program 8.5 and executes in time $O(n^2)$. If the matrix has already been spread, then the *mm* process can be

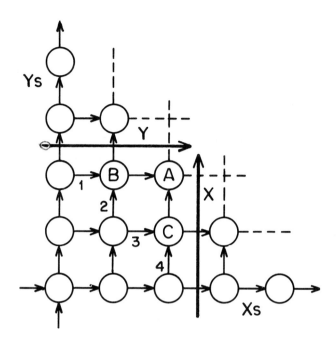

Figure 8.4: Process structure for matrix multiply

mm([Xv| Xm],Ym,[Zv| Zm]) ←
    vm(Xv?,Ym?,Ym1,Zv)@left,
    mm(Xm?,Ym1?,Zm)@fwd.
mm([ ],Ym,[ ]).

vm(Xv,[Yv| Ym],[Yv1| Ym1],[Z| Zv]) ←
    ip(Xv?,Yv?,Z),
    pipe(Xv?,Xv1),   % asynchronous pipe for X
    pipe(Yv?,Yv1),   % asynchronous pipe for Y
    vm(Xv1?,Ym?,Ym1,Zv)@fwd.
vm(Xv,[·],[ ],[ ]).

ip(Xv,Yv,Z) ← ip1(Xv?,Yv?,0,Z).

ip1([X| Xv],[Y| Yv],Z0,Z) ←   % ip does no copying
    Z1 := (X * Y) + Z0,
    ip1(Xv?,Yv?,Z1?,Z).
ip1([ ],[ ],Z,Z).

Program 8.5: Matrix multiplication with an asynchronous pipe executed in time $O(n)$. If matrix multiply is used as part of some more complex matrix calculation (e.g., multiplication by a scalar, addition or subtraction etc.) it is possible that the matrix would already have been spread.

The *vm* process specified passes *Ym* and *Ym1* recursively without any pipelining. This is an example where pipelining should not be incorporated into the algorithm as it will produce less efficient code. If a pipeline were added to the *vm* process to create local copies of *Ym*, then communication would be forced to follow the path of process spawning. This path is substantially (i.e., $O(n)$) longer than the path which can be utilized to a horizontally neighboring processor (i.e., constant path length). Thus it is not always beneficial to add pipes since a direct route through the network may be shorter.

In summary, the two programs described have illustrated how data movement and configuration can adversely effect algorithm performance. Simple programming techniques have been used to improve the algorithm complexity.

8.3.2 Observations and heuristics

At present the insertion of pipes into FCP programs must be carried out manually by the programmer. The previous programs provide some heuristics for detecting where and where not to add pipes.

- Only procedures which involve remote spawning require consideration.

- In general, an indication of which values to pipeline can be obtained by inspecting the arguments of the process spawning call. The most frequent case to consider occurs when a call in the body of a rule involves a variable argument which is provided directly from the procedure head. If this occurs the argument should be considered for piping (e.g., *Xs* in insertion sort).

- The initial input configuration and the required output configuration must be considered since data movement may provide a lower bound on the complexity (e.g., *spread* in matrix multiply).

- When the spawning path is substantially longer than a direct route between processors, piping should not necessarily be used (e.g., *Ym* of matrix multiply).

8.4 Note 2: Spawning Complexity

This note provides a general result for the speed-up of algorithms which can be obtained using the systolic programming methodology. The result is valid when the methodology is used on a mesh connected architecture under the following constraints:

- Computation originates at a single processor.

- A processor P can only begin execution if another, already active, processor P' explicitly maps a process onto P.

8.4.1 Result 1

Consider any problem with a sequential lower bound $Q(n)$. Any algorithm which solves the problem on a mesh has a speed-up bounded from above by:

$$8Q(n)^{2/3}$$

To show that the above result holds observe that an algorithm which uses $P(n)$ processors on a mesh is subject to the following lower bounds:

    a. $Q(n)/P(n)$

    b. $(\sqrt{P(n)}/2) - 1/2$

Lower bound a is well known and applies to parallel architectures in general (Hwang and Briggs, 1984).

Lower bound b is a direct result of the complexity of activating $P(n)$ processors on a mesh. The proof technique we use is similar to that used by Gentleman (1978) to achieve analogous results. If, during the execution of an algorithm on the mesh, a processor is activated a distance D away from the starting processor then the algorithm has a lower bound of time D. We show that a mesh algorithm which requires the use of P processors causes at least one processor to be activated at a distance: $(\sqrt{2P(n) - 1} - 1)/2$ away from the starting processor. This term is bounded below by $(\sqrt{P(n)}/2 - 1/2)$, which constitutes the lower bound.

In order to bound the maximum distance of any processor from the starting processor we consider the best possible arrangement of the *P–1* processors around the original processor. This arrangement is a *circle* with the original processor at its center. Since we are constrained to a mesh, the *circle* is realized as a diamond like configuration. A *circle* of processors of radius R contains $2R^2 + 2R + 1$ processors (Lint and Agerwala, 1981). The *circle* produced by P processors has a radius of $(\sqrt{2P(n) - 1} - 1)/2$. Therefore, an algorithm on the systolic mesh, using P processors, activates processors a distance at least $(\sqrt{2P(n) - 1} - 1)/2$ away from the initial processor.

Using lower bounds a and b, Result 1 follows by manipulation. The lower bounds imply that the algorithm is bounded below by the term:

$$\max(Q(n)/P(n), (\sqrt{P(n)}/2) - 1/2)$$

or:

$$\max(Q(n)/P(n) - 1/2, (\sqrt{P(n)}/2) - 1/2) \qquad \text{(Expression 1)}$$

For a fixed $Q(n)$, the value of this term is minimized when $P(n)$ causes the components of the term to be equal, i.e., when:

$$P(n) = (2Q(n))^{2/3}$$

Thus the minimum value of Expression 1 for fixed $Q(n)$ is:

$$(Q(n)/(2Q(n))^{2/3}) - 1/2 = ((1/2^{2/3})\ Q(n)^{1/3}) - 1/2$$

The maximum speed-up that can be obtained is bounded from above by:

$$Q(n)/((1/(2^{2/3})\ Q(n)^{1/3}) - 1/2)$$

which is bounded from above by:

$$Q(n)/((Q(n)^{1/3}/4) - 1/2) = 8Q(n)^{2/3}$$

for all but small values of $Q(n)$. ∎

It clearly follows that problems with exponential sequential lower bounds cannot be solved in sub-exponential time on a mesh even with an exponential number of processors.

A similar argument can be used to prove the following results which apply when the input is not taken from a single processor. The limiting factor in this case is data movement rather than processor activation.

8.4.2 Result 2

Consider an algorithm executed on a mesh in which there are $P(n)$ processors whose execution depends on input located at $K(n)$ processors. The running time of the algorithm is bounded from below by: $\sqrt{P(n)/K(n)}/2 - 1/2$.

It is easy to prove the above result in the case where $K(n)=1$, that is, in the case where input is located at a single processor. The proof involves calculating the radius of a *circle* of $P(n)$ processors.

A small extension of the proof makes it apply to arbitrary values of $K(n)$, as desired. We say that a processor p is associated with a processor k if the execution of p is dependent upon the input located at k. Since there are $P(n)$ processors whose execution is input dependent, there exists a processor k which has at least $P(n)/K(n)$ processors dependent on input from it. The minimum communication distance from k to any of the $P(n)/K(n)$ processors assigned to it provides a lower bound. This is similar to the case where an algorithm uses $P(n)/K(n)$ processors whose execution is input dependent on a single processor. The *circle* used in the proof in this case thus contains $P(n)/K(n)$ processors, and the bound immediately follows. The lower bound for the algorithm as a whole is the communication lower bound for any group of processors associated with an input processor.

The next result is analogous to Result 2 and can be proved in the same way.

8.4.3 Result 3

Consider an algorithm executed on an unconstrained mesh in which there are $P(n)$ processors whose actions affect the output, and the output is placed in $K(n)$ processors. The running time of the algorithm is bounded below by: $(\sqrt{P(n)/K(n)}/2)-1/2$.

8.5 Related Work

Tamaki (1985) has investigated a parallel language similar to FCP. A constrained version of the pipe process, called *vmcopy*, is used in a matrix multiplication program. The essential difference between the techniques is that Tamaki's underlying model requires the copying operation in order for programs to work; local communication is enforced. The model does not treat variable to variable bindings and thus does not allow control of the direction of communication. In addition, it does not specify how non-local communication is to be effected.

Under Tamaki's scheme slight variations to a program may cause it not to work. Consider spawning matrix multiply in a skewed fashion; this change results in non-local communication along diagonal elements of the matrix. A complete restructuring of the algorithm is necessary to achieve this simple new configuration. In contrast, the approach advocated in this paper allows values and variables to be referenced from processes spawned in any part of the processor network. Simple programming techniques may be used to constrain communication to be in some particular fashion. Programs work according to their specification in both shared memory and non-shared memory parallel systems; their asymptotic complexity in a non-shared memory parallel system may not be as expected without careful analysis. Pipes are more flexible than the form suggested by Tamaki since they allow pipelining of data to be in arbitrary directions and pipes need not be placed at every adjacent processor.

8.6 Conclusion

This paper attests to the importance of localizing and correctly structuring communication in parallel systems (Lint and Agerwala, 1981; Kung and Leiserson, 1980; Gentleman, 1978). The techniques we describe allow the programmer to structure communication but do not change the meaning of the program. These techniques have been demonstrated in the context of program examples and can be used to improve the complexity of algorithms. A general speed-up result has been given expressed in terms of the sequential lower bound of an algorithm. This result arises directly from dynamic process mapping in a mesh since this constrains data movement.

It is not yet clear under what circumstances the pipelining techniques can be used in practice and what overheads they introduce. Experiments are yet to be conducted to evaluate these concerns.

Acknowledgements

Lisa Hellerstein was supported by an NSF Graduate Fellowship, and by a grant from the AT&T Bell Laboratories Graduate Research Program for Women.

Chapter 9

Implementing Parallel Algorithms in Concurrent Prolog: The Maxflow Experience

Lisa Hellerstein

University of California at Berkeley

Ehud Shapiro

The Weizmann Institute of Science

Abstract

This paper reports on the experience of implementing Shiloach and Vishkin's (1982b) parallel MAXFLOW algorithm in Concurrent Prolog. We have adapted the algorithm to the computational model of Concurrent Prolog and produced a Concurrent Prolog program that implements the algorithm and achieves the expected complexity bounds. The lack of destructive assignment in the logic programs computation model prevents Prolog from being an efficient implementation language for many sequential algorithms. Our main conclusion is that, in concurrent algorithms, message passing is a powerful substitute for destructive assignment. It is therefore possible to write efficient Concurrent Prolog implementations of concurrent algorithms.

9.1 Introduction

This paper is a part of a research program to explore the expressiveness and applicability of the programming language Concurrent Prolog. The goal of this program is to evaluate whether a high-performance parallel computer whose "machine language" is Concurrent Prolog would be usable and useful. In (Shapiro, Chapter 2, Chapter 19) evidence was given that a virtual Concurrent Prolog machine provides the functionality required to implement a multiuser multitasking operating system. Hence we believe that such a machine would be usable.

To determine its usefulness, various applications have been implemented in Concurrent Prolog. The solution of classical concurrent programming problems in Concurrent Prolog was explored by Takeuchi and Furukawa (Chapter 18), and by Shapiro (Chapter 2). Shapiro and Takeuchi (Chapter 29) showed that the main concepts and techniques of object-oriented programming can be realized naturally in this language. This was demonstrated via a working prototype of a multiple-window system. We have also investigated the applicability of Concurrent Prolog as a specification and implementation language for systolic algorithms, and several such algorithms have been implemented and tested (Shapiro, Chapter 7).

In this paper we set out to investigate the applicability of Concurrent Prolog to the implementation of well-known parallel algorithms.

Traditionally, logic was considered suitable only as a specification language, but not as a programming language. Even though the goal of logic programming was to dispense with this myth, the applications of Prolog, the first practical logic programming language, were remote from the "hard-core" algorithms studied in computer science. The main reason was that these algorithms were designed for a von Neumann machine model. These algorithms were implementable in Prolog, but usually the implementation did not achieve the algorithm's expected complexity bound. This was due to the lack of destructive assignment, or, more specifically, the lack of mutable arrays and destructive pointer manipulation.

The experience reported in this paper suggests that these limitations do not hold when parallel algorithms are considered. We have investigated a complex parallel algorithm, which is described in terms of destructive operations on a shared memory. We were able to transform it into the computational model of Concurrent Prolog, by replacing destructive memory manipulation with data-structure copying and message passing. Moreover, we were able to implement it without loss of efficiency, under reasonable assumptions about the machine model.

We think that this is an example of a general phenomenon, not just a coincidence. We believe that the added expressiveness gained by having many processes communicating with each other can compensate for the lack of destructive assignment in the efficient implementation of parallel algorithms. Another explanation of the same phenomenon is that in parallel algorithms the importance of destructive assignment is diminished and that its main use is for communication.

The problem we investigate in this paper is determining the maximum flow through a network. Maximum flow is one of the more difficult problems that admit polynomial-time solutions. Hence we thought it would be a good benchmark problem.

The parallel MAXFLOW algorithm of Shiloach and Vishkin (1982b) is one of the more complicated parallel algorithms we have encountered. It solves the maximum-flow problem by solving $O(n)$ *maximal* flow problems (described in Section 9.2). Appalled by the intricacy of this maximal-flow algorithm, we set out to explore simpler algorithms, which are more suitable for the computational model of Concurrent Prolog and have good complexity bounds. Alas, the algorithms we came up with did not admit the complexity bounds of the Shiloach-Vishkin algorithm, which has a depth complexity (a term described in Section 9.6) of $O(n \log n)$. After a series of complications, we ended up with an algorithm which is almost isomorphic to the Shiloach-Vishkin algorithm. The paper describes three algorithms which are milestones in this development. The first algorithm, the simplest one, with 17 types of processes and 33 clauses, has a depth complexity of $O(n^3)$. It is 93 lines of uncommented Concurrent Prolog code. The second algorithm, by using more sophisticated data structures, achieves a depth complexity of $O(n^2 \log n)$. Its implementation is composed of 18 types of processes and 42 clauses, and is 107 lines long. The third algorithm complicates further both the data structures and the control structure, and achieves the same depth complexity as the Shiloach-Vishkin algorithm, namely $O(n \log n)$. Its implementation is composed of 18 processes and 42 clauses, and is 218 lines long. The main problem in achieving this complexity bound was implementing the key data structure of this algorithm, partial sum trees, in Concurrent Prolog. We have done so successfully, without destructive operations.

We present our three algorithms below, in order of decreasing computational complexity and increasing programming difficulty. Our documentation is designed to help the reader understand the algorithms and to address some of the programming and complexity issues which arose in implementing them. Complete listings of the three Concurrent Prolog programs appear in Appendices 9.2, 9.3, and 9.4.

9.2   Preliminaries

For completeness, we include a standard definition of the MAXFLOW problem, taken from Shiloach and Vishkin (1982b). The interested reader is referred to Even (1979) for further details.

A *directed flow network* $N = (G,s,t,c)$ is a quadruple where

(1) $G = (V,E)$ is a directed graph;

(2) s and t are distinct vertices, the source and the target respectively;

(3) $c:E \to \mathbb{R}^+$ assigns a nonnegative capacity $c(e)$ to each e in E.

Let $u \to v$ denote a direct edge from u to v. A function $f:E \to \mathbb{R}^+$ is a *flow* if it satisfies

(a) The capacity rule:

$$f(e) \leq c(e) \qquad \text{for all } e \text{ in } E.$$

(b) The conservation rule:

$$in(f,v) = out(f,v) \qquad \text{for all } v \text{ in } V - \{s,t\}.$$

Here

$$in(f,v) = \sum_u f(u \to v)$$

is the total flow entering v, and

$$out(f,v) = \sum_u f(v \to u)$$

is the total flow emanating from v.

The flow value f is $out(f,t) - in(f,s)$.

The flow value f is a maximum flow if

$$f \geq f' \qquad \text{for any other flow } f'.$$

A flow f *saturates* an edge e if $f(e) = c(e)$.

A flow f is *maximal* if every direct path from s to t contains at least one saturated edge.

A directed network $N = (G,s,t,c)$ is called a layered network if G has the following properties:

Each vertex v has a layer number $l(v)$, such that $l(s) = 0$ and $0 \leq l(v) \leq l(t)$ for all v in V. If $u \to v$ is in E, then $l(v) - l(u) = 1$.

E.A. Dinic (1970) showed that it is possible to transform a maximum-flow problem into $O(n)$ maximal-flow problems in layered networks. Our algorithms solve the main problem of finding maximal flow in a layered network.

9.3 The General Algorithm

The three algorithms are all variations of a general algorithm, which has the following features.

A process is associated with each node in the graph. Two communication channels are associated with each edge, one in each direction. During execution of the algorithm, the node processes send integer messages to each other. The passage of messages from node to node corresponds to the transfer of flow from node to node.

The algorithm begins by sending an initial amount of flow into the graph via the source. This flow travels through the graph until it is expelled from the graph at either the source or the target. The algorithm finds maximal flow by controlling and tracing the passage of this flow through the graph.

Assume that the flow moves vertically, that the source is at the top of the graph, and that the target is at the bottom. An edge connected to a vertex in the previous (following) layer is called an in-edge (out-edge). With every in-edge we associate a flow, which is initially 0. The flow value of an in-edge e upon termination of the algorithm is $f(e)$, where f is a maximal flow. With every out-edge we associate a (residual) capacity, which is initially the capacity of the corresponding edge in the network.

When a node receives a quantum of flow, it tries to push that flow downward through its out-edges. The amount of flow it pushes down an edge may not exceed the capacity of that edge. So, a node may not be able to send downward all the flow it receives. Any flow which the node cannot send downward, it returns upward through its in-edges. When flow reaches the source or the target, it is considered to have left the graph. The algorithm terminates when all flow has left the graph.

A *blocked* vertex is a vertex which has returned a nonzero quantum of flow. If a vertex is blocked, then all its out-edges have a residual capacity of zero. It is useless to send flow downward to a blocked vertex, because the blocked vertex will send it right back up. The algorithm uses the following method to prevent the wasted effort. When a vertex first becomes blocked, it sends some sort of block message up all its in-edges. The vertices receiving the block messages set the residual capacity of their out-edges to zero. This prevents new downward flow from reaching the blocked vertex.

The algorithm is physically intuitive. Imagine a vertical network of pipes, where each pipe has a volume capacity. Push a steady volume of liquid into the network by way of the source. The liquid will flow downward through the pipes as long as the pipes have enough capacity to accommodate it. At some point, though, a quantum of flow may reach a junction of pipes and not be able to continue downward. The liquid will then be returned upward until it finds another route down, or is expelled from the network at the source. If we assume that the liquid travels downward whenever possible, and the volume of flow entering the graph at the source is relatively large, it seems intuitively that we will have maximal flow through the network.

9.4 Pulse Operations

The algorithm is divided into "pulses". During each pulse the vertex processes all perform an identical series of operations.

In the first pulse, the source sends a message C on all its out-channels, where C is the capacity of the channel. The target sends a zero message on all its in-channels, and the other vertices send zeros on their in and out channels.

Subsequently, a pulse consists of the following four operations.

pushed: Take one message (flow quantum) from each of the vertex's in-channels. Increase the flow associated with the channel by the amount of the quantum. Add together the total amount of flow received on the in-channels.

returned: Take one message from each of the vertex's out-channels. If the message is not zero, then it has been returned from a blocked vertex. Prevent further flow from being pushed to the blocked vertex by setting the residual capacity of the edge to zero. Add together the total amount of flow received on the out-channels.

Note. The flow (integer messages) received by the vertex on its in and out channels is considered to be "excess" flow stuck at the vertex. The excess flow is expelled from the vertex in the push and return operations.

push: Send as much excess flow as possible along the out-channels. Flow pushed down a channel cannot exceed the capacity of that channel. Decrease the capacity of each channel by the amount of flow sent along it.

return: Send upwards along the in-channels any excess flow that could not be pushed from the vertex. Flow returned up a channel cannot exceed the amount of flow associated with that channel. Decrease the flow associated with each channel by the amount of flow sent along it. If a nonzero amount of flow is returned from the vertex, send messages along all the vertex's in-channels to signal that it is blocked.

The algorithms include a monitor process which halts execution of the vertex processes when a maximal flow is found. The algorithms are initiated by starting all the vertex processes associated with a given graph. In our implementations, this means that each initial vertex process is given two lists: one of the channels associated with incoming edges, and one of the channels associated with outgoing edges. The outgoing channels have associated capacity values. The incoming channels have initial flow values of 0.

9.5   The Three Algorithms

The general algorithm is underspecified in two major areas. First, it does not specify the data structure used by each vertex process to manage its edges. Second, it does not specify push and return policies. Suppose a vertex has a quantum of flow which it wants to return along its in-edges. Suppose also that any of several of the in-edges is able to accommodate the flow. The algorithm must have some policy which determines which of the in-edges is to be used.

Our three algorithms differ in their data structures and in their return policies. The differences significantly affect the complexity bounds of the algorithms.

Algorithm 1 is the simplest of the algorithms. Each vertex process in the algorithm stores its edges in list form. Edge operations accordingly take linear time. The return policy of Algorithm 1 is to proceed linearly down the list of in-edges. When a vertex process reaches an edge, it sends as much of the remaining flow down the edge as possible.

Algorithm 2 has the same return policy as Algorithm 1, but stores its edges at the leaves of a binary tree. The tree structure allows $O(\log n)$ edge manipulation.

Algorithm 3 also uses binary trees for edge manipulation. It has a more sophisticated return strategy: vertices return flow in LIFO order. Each vertex keeps a stack which, conceptually, puts an element (Q,e) on the stack for each message received on an in-edge. Q is the value of the message, and e identifies the in-edge. If a vertex has to return a quantum Q of flow, it pops a total Q of flow off the stack and returns the flow along the edges indicated by the popped elements.

We now describe characteristic elements of each of the three algorithms. The characteristics of each algorithm and their complexity bounds appear in Table 9.1.

9.5.1   Algorithm 1

Two separate lists of edges are kept for each vertex v, one for the in-edges, and one for the out-edges. Each element in the in-list is associated with an in-edge e, and has the form $c(Flow\ value,Down\_channel,Up\_channel)$. The flow value is the value $f(e)$ of the edge.

The down-channel is a read-only channel which transmits messages from a vertex $v1$ in the previous layer. All flow quanta pushed to vertex v through edge e are received by v on this down channel. The up-channel leads to vertex $v1$. Vertex v returns flow and sends block messages (described below) on this up-channel.

Each element in the out-list is similarly associated with an out-edge $e1$, and

Table 9.1

	Algorithm 1	Algorithm 2	Algorithm 3
Data structure for edge management	List	Binary tree	Binary tree
Return policy	Return in order edges appear in list	Return in order edges appear in leaves of tree	Return flow in LIFO order along edges which have transmitted flow
Maximum number of pulses	$O(n^2)$	$O(n^2)$	$2n$
Complexity of a pulse	$O(n)$	$O(\log n)$	$O(\log n)$
Overall	$O(n^3)$	$O(n^2\log n)$	$O(n\log n)$

has the form $c(Flow\ capacity, Down\_channel, Up\_channel)$. Vertex v pushes flow down through edge $e1$ using this down-channel. The up-channel is read only, and receives returned quantities and block messages from a vertex in the following layer.

We begin by presenting an explanation of the push and return routines, the Concurrent Prolog code, and relevant comments. Note that Algorithm 1 has identical linear push and return policies.

The programs were developed under a Concurrent Prolog interpreter written in Waterloo Prolog (Roberts, 1979). Hence we follow its syntactic conventions, especially the use of $X.Y$ as the list constructor and *nil* as the list terminator.

push(Q,Outlist,NewOutlist)

Q is the amount of flow to be pushed from the vertex.

Proceed down the list of out-edges (*Outlist*). If an out-edge has a residual capacity C, then send $min(Q,C)$ through the down-channel of the edge. Decrease both Q and C by the amount sent and proceed to the next edge with the new value of Q. If $Q1$ is the total amount of flow to be pushed from our vertex, then *Excess* is the amount of flow remaining after we send as much of $Q1$ as possible down the out-edges:

    push(N,Qin,c(Cap,Qout?.Down,Up).List,
        c(Cap1?,Down,Up).List1,Excess) ←
    Qout := min(Qin,Cap),
    Cap1 := Cap–Qout,
    Qin1 := Qin–Qout,
    push(N,Qin1?,List?,List1,Excess).

    push(N,Excess,nil,nil,Excess).

The process $X := T$ performs a lazy evaluation of the arithmetic expression T and, if and when successful, unifies the result with X.

The first clause of *push* demonstrates the use of read-only occurrences of variables in the head of a clause. This novel use for the read-only variable is discussed in detail in Appendix 9.1.

return(Q,Outlist,Newoutlist)

The *return* routine, like the *push* routine, sends flow quanta to other vertices and alters values associated with edges. However, if a vertex returns a nonzero quantity of flow, the vertex becomes blocked, and the *return* routine must notify all adjacent vertices on the previous layer of the fact. Consider a node which returns a nonzero quantity of flow and which has more than one in-edge. It is possible that after sending the return flow down the first few in-edges, the node will have no more flow to send along the other in-edges. Nodes on the previous layer, when receiving the positive quantities of returned flow, will know that the channels used lead to blocked vertices. Therefore, it is not necessary to send a specific block message along these channels in addition to the returned flow. To notify the vertices not receiving part of the returned flow, the return process sends the constant "block".

    return(Qout,List,List1) ←
        Qout ≠ ∅ |
        return1(Qout,List?,List1).

    return(∅,List,List1) ←
        send(∅,up,List,List1).

    return1(∅,c(Flow,Down,block.Up).List,c(Flow,Down,Up).List1) ←
        return1(∅.List?,List1).

    return1(Amt,c(Flow,Down,Backflow?.Up).List,
        c(Flow1?,Down,Up).List1) ←
        Amt ≠ ∅ |
        Backflow := min(Flow,Amt),

Flow1 := Flow − Backflow,
Amt1 := Amt − Backflow,
return1(Amt1?,List?,List1).

return1(∅,nil,nil).

send(X,up,c(Amt,Down,X.Up).List,c(Amt,Down,Up).List1) ←
    send(X,up,List?,List1).

send(X,Dir,nil,nil).

pushed(Q,Inlist,NewInlist) and returned(Q,Outlist,NewOutlist)

The *pushed* and *returned* routines of Algorithm 1, like the *push* and *return* routines, are fairly symmetrical. Both linearly traverse edge lists and collect flow messages. They total the amount of flow received. The *returned* routine has the added task of receiving and interpreting block messages. Either the constant "block" or a nonzero message, when received on an out-channel, indicates that the channel leads to a blocked vertex. The *returned* routine handles such block messages by setting the capacity of the transmitting edge to 0 in *NewOutlist*. In summing flow messages, *returned* understands the constant "block" to signify a zero quantity of flow:

pushed(Amt,c(Flow,X.Down,Up).List,c(Newflow?,Down?,Up).List1) ←
    pushed(Amt1,List?,List1),
    Newflow := Flow + X,
    Amt := X + Amt1.

pushed(∅,nil,nil).

returned(Amt,c(Cap,Down,X.Up).List,c(∅,Down,Up?).List1) ←
    X ≠ ∅ |
    returned(Amt1,List?,List1),
    add_returned(X,Amt1?,Amt).

returned(Amt,c(Cap,Down,∅.Up).List,c(Cap,Down,Up?).List1) ←
    returned(Amt,List?,List1).

returned(∅,nil,nil).

add_returned(X,Amt,Total) ←
    X ≠ block|
    Total := X + Amt.

add_returned(block,Amt,Amt).

For completeness, we also include here the code for a vertex, and the monitor's code:

vertex(N,Inlist,Outlist,Control) ←
    send(∅,down,Outlist,Outlist1),
    send(∅,up,Inlist,Inlist1),
    vertex1(N,Inlist1?,Outlist1?,Control).

vertex1(N,Inlist,Outlist,halt) ←
    infowrite(vertex(N),inlist,Inlist),
    infowrite(vertex(N),outlist,Outlist).

vertex1(N,Inlist,Outlist,Control) ←
    pushed(Amt,Inlist,Inlist1),
    returned(Amt1,Outlist,Outlist1) |
    Excess := Amt1 + Amt,
    push(N,Excess?,Outlist1?.Outlist2,Excess1),
    return(Excess1?,Inlist1?,Inlist2),
    vertex1(N,Inlist2?,Outlist2?,Control).

monitor(∅,_,_,halt).

monitor(Goal,X.Xs,Y.Ys,Control) ←
    Goal > ∅ |
    Goal1 := Goal − X − Y,
    monitor(Goal1?,Xs?,Ys?,Control).

9.5.2 Algorithm 2

Algorithm 2 makes use of partial sum trees. A partial sum tree is a complete binary tree with numerical values at its leaves. Each node of the tree is assigned a value. If N is a node in tree T, and S is the largest subtree having N as its root, then the value assigned to node N is the sum of all the leaves of S.

Algorithm 2 builds two partial sum trees for each vertex, one for the in-edges (the intree), and one for the out-edges (the outree). Each leaf of the intree has the form $c(Flow\_value, Down\_channel, Up\_channel)$, exactly like the elements of the in-list in Algorithm 1. Each leaf of the outree has the form $c(Capacity, Down\_channel, Up\_channel)$, exactly like the elements of the out-list in Algorithm 1.

The trees are built at the start of the algorithm. The value at the root of each intree is the total amount of flow which has been sent to the associated vertex. The value at the root of each outree is the total residual capacity of edges emanating from the vertex.

The *pushed* and *returned* operations use the partial sum tree to recursively sum the flow sent along the channels at the leaves.

pushed(Q,Intree,NewIntree)

For every node N in the tree, simultaneously and independently find the sums of the leaves of its left tree and the sums of the leaves of its right tree.

Add the two values together to find the flow pushed to the leaves of the tree having N as its root.

> pushed(Amt,c(Flow,c(A,B,C),Y),c(Newflow?,W?,Z?)) ←
>   pushed(Amt1,c(A,B,C),W), pushed (Amt2,Y?,Z),
>   Amt := Amt1 + Amt2,
>   Newflow := Flow + Amt.
> pushed(X,c(Flow,strm(X.Xs),Y),c(Newflow?,strm(Xs?),Y)) ←
>   Newflow := Flow + X.

Returned is basically an identical procedure, except that it handles block messages also.

Push and *return* use the values stored at the nodes of the partial sum trees.

push(Q,Outree,NewOutree,Excess)

Check the value V at the root of *Outree*. Then $min(Q,V)$ will be sent down the partial sum tree to the channels at the leaves. Any flow $Q - min(Q,V)$ that can not be sent to the leaves is considered to be excess flow. It is sent upward the vertex in the subsequent return operation.

Send the flow down to the leaves as follows. Given an amount of $Q1$ at a node N of the tree, find the values QL and QR at the roots of the left and right subtrees. Send $min(Q1,QL)$ down the left subtree and any excess to the right subtree. When a flow quantum reaches a leaf of the tree, place that quantum on the down-channel stored at the leaf to send the quantum to another vertex:

> push(Qin,c(Cap,X,Y),Newtree,Excess) ←
>   Qout := min(Qin,Cap),
>   Excess := Qin – Qout,
>   push1(Qout?,c(Cap,X,Y),Newtree).

> push1(Q,c(Cap,c(Cap1,W,X),c(Cap2,Y,Z)),c(Newcap?,M?,N?)) ←
>   Newcap := Cap – Q,
>   Q1 := min(Q,Cap1),
>   push1(Q1?,c(Cap1,W,X),M),
>   Q2 := Q – Q1,
>   push1(Q2?,c(Cap2,Y,Z),N).

> push1(Q,c(Cap,strm(Q.Out),strm(In)),
>   c(Newcap?,strm(Out),strm(In))) ←
>   Newcap := Cap – Q.

Return is similar to *push*.

9.5.3 Algorithm 3

Algorithm 3 is a Concurrent Prolog implementation of the Shiloach-Vishkin algorithm. Changes in the data structures were necessary to adapt the algorithm to the capabilities of Concurrent Prolog. Shiloach and Vishkin's implementation utilizes destructive assignment. Multiple processes are allowed to simultaneously access and update an entire single data structure. This is not possible in Concurrent Prolog, but the use of communication channels and structure copying proved an effective substitute. The algorithm is inherently difficult because of the extensive use of trees and tree manipulation.

Remember that in Algorithm 3 a stack is associated with every vertex v to record incoming flow. The implementation of Algorithm 3 attaches a partial sum tree to the stack to allow pushing and popping of the stack in $O(\log n)$ time. This tree is called the stacktree. Another partial sum tree, called the intree, is also associated with every vertex. It is used during every pulse to sum in $O(\log n)$ time, for every in-edge of v, the total amount of flow popped off the stack belonging to that edge.

9.6   The Stacktree and the Intree

The stacktree is a two-tiered tree. The top tier S' is a complete binary tree. Each leaf is associated with a pulse. At pulse p, the tree S' has $2^{\lceil \log p \rceil}$ leaves.

Attached to each leaf of S' is a subtree S''. Each leaf of S'' is associated with an edge e. At each leaf (p,e) of S'' (where p is the pulse number associated with S'', and e is the edge associated with the leaf), is a value indicating the amount of flow pushed through e to v during pulse p. Each leaf of the stacktree also contains a communication channel to an associated leaf in the intree.

The leaves of the stacktree, read from left to right, compose a stack.

Figure 9.1 shows the stacktree for a vertex v, at the end of four pulses. Vertex v has incoming edges a, b, c, and d. Edge a has brought flow quanta of 3 and 2 to vertex v during pulses 2 and 4 respectively. Edge c has brought a flow quantum of 3 during pulse 4. All other elements of the stack record the receipt of 0 flow messages.

The intree also has two tiers. The top tier I' is essentially the intree of Algorithm 2. At its leaves it has up and down communication channels and a flow value.

The leaves of I' also contain a subtree I''. Each leaf of I'', like each leaf of S', is associated with a pulse. I'' is used during each pulse to sum the values popped off the stack belonging to that edge. Each leaf (e,p) of the intree holds a communication channel to the leaf (p,e) of the stacktree.

Conceptually, we speak of popping an element (q,e) off of the stack. Let

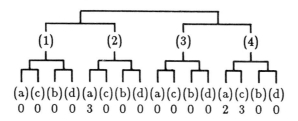

Figure 9.1: A stacktree

us assume that an element (q,e) was "placed" on the stack during pulse p, and that we now want to pop that element from the stack. This "pop" is actually performed by having the stacktree send a message to the intree. The message q is sent along the channel at leaf (e,p) of the stacktree. This message is received at leaf (p,e) of the intree. Leaf (p,e) of the intree is part of the subtree I'' associated with edge e. Each leaf of I'' will receive a similar, possibly zero, message. These messages will be summed in $O(\log n)$ time by utilizing the tree structure of I''. The sum will equal the total amount of flow to be returned along edge e during pulse p. (See Figure 9.2.)

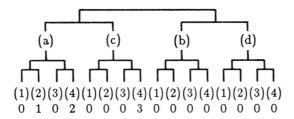

Figure 9.2: Values received at leaves of intree during pulse 4, after
the stacktree in Figure 9.1 has "popped" quantity 6 of flow.

pushed(Q,CurrentPulse,PulsesInTree,NumberOfOutedges,Stacktree,
    Intree,NewPulsesInTree,NewStree,NewIntree)

The *pushed* routine puts received values onto the stack by changing values
at the leaves of the stacktree[1].

On pulse p, find the subtree S'' of the stacktree which is associated with pulse
p. If pulse p doesn't exist on the tree, then double the size of the tree. Then,
travel down S'' and I' in parallel. To find Q, the total quantity pushed into the
vertex, sum the values at the leaves of I' using the tree structure. Upon reaching
the leaves of I' and S'', travel down subtree I'' to find the leaf associated with
pulse p. Establish a communication channel between each leaf (p,e) in S'' and
each leaf (e,p) in I''. If flow quantum Q was received at leaf e of I'', push Q onto
the stack by giving leaf (e,p) of S'' the value Q. Change the node values of the
stacktree, which is a partial sum tree, to take account of the added quantities at
the leaves:

    pushed(Amt,Pulse,Pulses,Edges,Stacktree,Intree,Pulses1,Stacktree1,
        Intree1) ←
    findpulse(stacktree,Stacktree, Pulse,Pulses,Edges,Edgetree,
        Stacktree1,Pulses1,Amt?,Edgetree1?),
    pushed1(Amt,Pulse,Pulses,Edgetree?,Intree,Edgetree1,Intree1).

    pushed1(Amt,Pulse,Pulses,c(∅,Edgeleft,Edgeright),c(Inval,Inleft,Inright),
        c(Amt?,Edgeleft1?,Edgeright1?),c(Inval,Inleft1?,Inright1?)) ←
    pushed1 (Amt1,Pulse,Pulses,Edgeleft,Inleft,Edgeleft1,Inleft1),
    pushed1(Amt2,Pulse,Pulses,Edgeright,Inright,Edgeright1,Inright1),
    Amt := Amt1 + Amt2.

    pushed1(X,Pulse,Pulses,c(∅,nil),c(Inval,strm(X.Xs),strm(Ys),Subtree),
        c(X,strm1(Z)),c(Inval1?,strm(Xs?),strm(Ys),Subtree1?)) ←
    Inval1 := Inval + X,
    findpulse(intree,Subtree,Pulse,Pulses,_,Leaf,Subtree1,_,∅,strm1(Z?)).

    pushed1(∅,Pulse,Pulses,c(∅,nil),c(Inval,strm(nil),strm(nil),Subtree),
        c(∅,nil),c(Inval,strm(nil),strm(nil),Subtree)).

    findpulse(Type,Tree,Pulse,Pulses,Edges,Leaf,Tree1,Pulses,Val,Leaf1) ←
    Pulse ≤ Pulses |
    P1 := Pulses /2,
    findpulse(Tree,Pulse,P1?,P1?,Leaf,Tree1,Val,Leaf1).

    findpulse(Type,Tree,Pulse,Pulses,Edges,Leaf,Tree2,Pulses1,Val,Leaf1) ←

---

[1]   In our implementation, the values at the internal nodes of I' and I'', and at the leaves of
   I'', are not significant and are used to simplify the code for the algorithm.

Pulses < Pulse |
Pulses1 := Pulses * 2,
build_pulses(Type,Pulses,Edges,New_halftree),
join(Tree,New_halftree?,Tree1),
findpulse(Tree1?,Pulse,Pulses,Pulses,Leaf,Tree2,Val,Leaf1).

findpulse(c(V,Left,Right),Pulse,Midpt,Partsize,Leaf,
       c(V1?,Left,Right1?),Val,Leaf1) ←
Midpt < Pulse |
V1 := V + Val,
Partsize1 := Partsize /2,
Midpt1 := Midpt + Partsize1,
findpulse(Right,Pulse,Midpt1?,Partsize1?,Leaf,Right1,Val,Leaf1).

findpulse(c(V,Left,Right),Pulse,Midpt,Partsize,Leaf,
       c(V1?,Left1?,Right),Val,Leaf1) ←
Pulse ≤ Midpt, Partsize ≠ ∅ |
V1 := V + Val,
Partsize1 := Partsize /2,
Midpt1 := Midpt − Partsize1,
findpulse(Left,Pulse,Midpt1?,Partsize1?,Leaf,Left1,Val,Leaf1).

findpulse(c(X,Y),Pulse,Midpt,∅,Y,c(X1?,New),Val,New) ←
       X1 := X + Val.

We are aware that this code does not please the eye. This may reflect in part the intricacy of the algorithm, and in part the lack of an established Concurrent Prolog programming culture and indentation style. It is also possible that, by its very nature, Concurrent Prolog cannot be used to express this algorithm elegantly.

return(Q,Stacktree,Intree,NewStree,Newintree)

Q is the value to be returned. A total Q of flow will be sent from the leaves of the stacktree to the leaves of the intree.

Start out with amount Q of flow. At each node of the stacktree, find the values VR and VL which appear at the roots of the left and right subtrees. Because the stacktree is a partial sum tree, VR and VL are the sums of the values at the leaves of the respective subtrees. Recurse on the right subtree with $Q = \min(Q, VR)$. Recurse on the left subtree with the excess, $Q - \min(Q, VR)$. This guarantees a LIFO popping of the stack.

When the recursion reaches a leaf of the stacktree with flow quantity Q, send the message Q along the communication channel to the intree. Decrease the value at the leaf by Q to indicate that the amount Q has been removed from the stack. Adjust the values at the nodes of the stacktree so that it will retain the properties of a partial sum tree.

For every subtree I'' of the intree, sum the total amount of flow T sent to its leaves from the stacktree. If I'' is associated with edge e, then T is the amount of flow to return along edge e. Place T in the appropriate up-channel in the leaves of I:

```
return(∅,Stacktree,Intree,Stacktree,Intree1) ←
    send(∅,up,Intree,Intree1).

return(Q,Stacktree,Intree,Stacktree1,Intree1) ←
    Q ≠ ∅ |
    write(return(Q)),
    pop_stack(Q,Stacktree,Stacktree1),
    collect_return(Amt,Intree,Intree1).

pop_stack(Q,c(Val,Left,Right),c(Val1?,Left1?,Right1?)) ←
    Val1 := Val − Q,
    val(Right,V2),
    Q1 := min(Q,V2),
    pop_stack(Q1?,Right,Right1),
    Q2 := Q − Q1,
    pop_stack(Q2?,Left,Left1).

pop_stack(Q,c(Val,Subtree),c(Val1?,X1?)) ←
    subtree(Subtree) |
    Val1 := Val − Q,
    pop_stack(Q,Subtree,X1).

pop_stack(Q,c(Val,strm1(Q.Xs)),c(Val1?,strm1(Xs))) ←
    Val1 := Val − Q.

pop_stack(∅,c(∅,nil),c(∅,nil)).

collect_return(Amt,c(Val,Left,Right),c(Val,Left1?,Right1?)) ←
    collect_return(Amt1,Left,Left1),
    collect_return(Amt2,Right,Right1),
    Amt := Amt1 + Amt2.
collect_return(Q,c(Val,strm(Xs),strm(Q1?.Ys),Subtree),
    c(Val1?,strm(Xs),strm(Ys),Subtree1)) ←
    collect(Q,Subtree,Subtree1),
    what_to_send(Q?,Q1),
    Val1 := Val − Q.

collect(Q,c(V,Left,Right),c(V,Left1?,Right1?)) ←
    collect(Q1,Left,Left1),
    collect(Q2,Right,Right1),
    Q := Q1 + Q2.
```

collect(Q,c(V,strm1(Q.Zs)),c(V,strm1(Zs?))).

collect(∅,c(V,nil),c(V,nil)).

push and *returned* use an Outree like the one in Algorithm 2, and are similar to the related operations in Algorithm 2.

9.7 Correctness and Complexity

All three algorithms are correct, by the correctness proof of Shiloach and Vishkin (1982b). We differ slightly from Shiloach and Vishkin's implementation in our definition of a blocked vertex. This does not, however, affect the proof of correctness, since their theoretical definition of blocked is the same as ours.

When we speak of complexity, we refer to the depth complexity of an algorithm. The depth complexity is the time from the execution of the first operation of the algorithm to the time the last processor stops working.

Complexity calculations are based on a definition of basic operations, which are considered to take unit time. The complexity of a Concurrent Prolog program is dependent on the amount of time that is spent in unifying goals with the heads of clauses. The unification of a variable with a variable, or of a variable with a constant, is equivalent to a conventional assignment. An attempt to unify two simple constants is equivalent to the comparison of two simple constants. The unification of a term with a term is simply the unification of the functor names (a constant with a constant), and the recursive unification of the arguments. We define as basic operations all elementary arithmetic operations and all variable-variable, variable-constant, and constant-constant unifications. In our three programs, because of the nature of the clauses and goals in the programs, it takes constant time to unify a goal with the head of a clause.

Our complexity bounds are based on a shared-memory machine model with an unlimited number of processors. There is no charge for access of the processors to memory or for the allocation of tasks to the processors.

This model is identical to the model of Shiloach and Vishkin.

Definition 1. A Concurrent Prolog machine is *stable* if, given a process that can unify with one clause that has an empty guard, it reduces the process using the first unifiable clause with an empty guard.

Definition 2. In the case that there are not enough processors for each Concurrent Prolog process, some processor will have to handle more than one process at a time. If processor P is given two processes $P1$ and $P2$, and it does not divide its processing time equitably between the two processes, the processor is deemed to have an *unfair scheduler*. In the worst case, $P1$ is an infinite process, and processor P devotes all its time to $P1$.

If the implementations are run on a stable machine, then they will find maximal flow and terminate within the expected time bounds. On an unstable machine, maximal flow will be found within the expected time, that is, the proper flow values will be assigned to the edges within the expected time. However, the program may not terminate within a constant time after this flow is found. This is due to the fact that a vertex process does not halt until it unifies with the first *vertex1* clause which appears in the text of the program. If neither the source process, nor the target process, nor any vertex process halts, the vertices can send 0 messages to each other forever.

Our implementations will run correctly on a machine with an unfair scheduler, because each vertex process must receive messages from other processes in order to run. Therefore, no vertex process can run indefinitely at the expense of the other vertex processes.

In calculating the complexity of each of our three algorithms, we find an upper bound on the complexity of a single pulse and an upper bound on the total number of pulses. The upper bound on the complexity of each algorithm is thus the product of these two bounds.

Shiloach and Vishkin (1982b) proved that maximal flow is found in all the algorithms in at most $2l(n+1)$ pulses, where l is the number of layers in the graph. This is an $O(n^2)$ bound. In Algorithm 1, all edge operations are performed on lists of edges. The number of edges in a list is bounded by $n - 1$, and therefore each pulse operation can take $O(n)$ operations. This implies an $O(n^2)$ bound on Algorithm 1.

In Algorithm 2, all edge operations are performed on binary trees. These trees have at most $2^{\log(n-1)}$ leaves, so the depth of the tallest tree is $\log(n-1)$. Each pulse operation can thus take time $O(\log n)$, and the algorithm has an $O(n \log n)$ upper bound.

Because of the use of the stack, Algorithm 3 finds maximal flow in at most $2n$ pulses (Shiloach and Vishkin, 1982b). Each stacktree has at most $(n-1)2n$ leaves, because each leaf of the stacktree is associated with a pair (p,e). The depth of the stacktree is therefore bounded by $\log((n-1)2n)$, which is $O(\log n)$. The intree is the same size as the stacktree. Operations on the intree and the stacktree therefore take at most time $O(\log n)$. The *push* and *returned* operations take time $O(\log n)$ also, as in Algorithm 2. Algorithm 3 therefore has complexity $O(n \log n)$.

9.8 Characteristics of the Concurrent Prolog Implementation

The Shiloach-Vishkin algorithm is written for a shared-memory model. One vertex process is allowed to change the values associated with another vertex process (e.g., the set of available edges). Our implementations, in contrast, view processes as being independent. There are well-defined communication channels between processes, and explicit messages are sent. No process has write access to data belonging to another process, such as another vertex's out-edges.

A nice result of the independence of the processes is that we can break up the processes in the following natural way and, under reasonable assumptions, still preserve the depth complexity of our algorithms. Suppose we give the monitor, source, target, and vertex processes their own pool of processors and their own local memory. Suppose further that the processes are linked only by communication channels, and that it takes constant time for a "message" (constant or variable) to travel from one process to another once it is placed in a communication channel. Under those assumptions, it is easy to see that the passing of messages does not add to the complexity of the algorithms. The monitor process sends n messages once at the end of the algorithm. The source and target send one or two messages each pulse to the monitor, in addition to the messages they send to the vertices. In Algorithm 1, each vertex process sends its messages in $O(n)$ time during each pulse. In Algorithms 2 and 3, the vertices place their messages into the communication channels in parallel, and so constant time is spent in sending messages during each pulse.

The implementation of Algorithm 3 was affected by our desire to maintain the independence of processes. Rather than build a large stacktree at the beginning of the algorithm, we grow the stacktree dynamically. This way, no vertex has to know the total number of vertices in the graph.

In some sense the independence of processes is induced or encouraged by the language itself. If one process is allowed to access data associated with another process, then those data must be explicitly shared between the two processes. The shared data must appear as shared variables in the heads of the process clauses.

Shiloach and Vishkin's implementation involves a good deal of explicit processor management. Similar processors are indexed. Often, the program specifies which processors will run by computing a range of indices. Only those processors whose index falls within that range are allowed to execute. In contrast, our vertex processes run as soon as they receive messages from adjacent vertices. The only central process management comes from the monitor process.

9.9   Future Research

The MAXFLOW experience shows that the message passing and structure copying capabilities of Concurrent Prolog make it a powerful concurrent programming language. Using Concurrent Prolog, it is possible to implement even an algorithm which, conceived in a traditional manner, seems to require destructive assignment. Substituting message passing and structure copying for destructive assignment, however, can cause a fundamental change in the nature of an algorithm.

Viewing message passing, rather than variable assignment, as the basic computation step of parallel processing may result in parallel algorithms whose implementation in Concurrent Prolog is more efficient, easier, and more elegant. Systolic algorithms are an example (Kung, 1979; Shapiro, Chapter 7).

Our belief in the central role of message passing in parallel processing is shared by other "radical" approaches to parallel computation, including Actor systems (Hewitt, 1973), dataflow languages (Ackerman, 1982), and systolic algorithms (Kung, 1979).

Acknowledgement

Research of the first author was carried out while a participant in the Karen Kupcinet International Science School at the Weizmann Institute of Science.

We thank Amos Fiat for many useful discussions, Henryk Jan Komorowski for his suggestions and advice, and John Reif for his comments. Eyal Yardeni assisted in editing the paper.

Appendix 9.1:   Read-Only Variables in the Head of a Clause

The first clause of *push* in Algorithm 1 demonstrates a new use for read-only variables. It is potentially dangerous for the *push* process to send an uninstantiated, unprotected variable $Qout$ on the down-channel, because some other process may unintentionally instantiate it. Several solutions to the problem were available. One solution was to have *push* instantiate $Qout$ in the guard of the clause, e.g.,

```
push(N,Qin,c(Cap,Qout?.Down,Up).List,
        c(Cap1?,Down,Up).List1,Excess) ←
    Qout := min(Qin,Cap) |
    Cap1 := Cap – Qout,
    Qin1 := Qin – Qout,
    push(N,Qin1?,List?,List1,Excess).
```

This way, no other process can access *Qout* until *Qout* is instantiated. This solution was rejected, however, because it results in an overuse and a misuse of the guard. The proper use of a guard is to distinguish between candidate clauses for process reduction. A simple arithmetic calculation, which is expected to always succeed, does not fall in this category.

Another solution was to require other processes to access the downstream in read-only mode. This is, in fact, the standard method of access by one process to a variable instantiated by another process. This solution, however, introduced programming problems. Suppose a process wanted to access the out-list instantiated by *push*. It is reasonable that the process use a variable *Outlist?* which waits for *push* to instantiate it. However, the *Outlist?* variable unifies with *c(Q,Down,Up).List* as soon as its head has the form *c(A,B,C)*. The internal values *A*, *B*, and *C* are not protected by making *Outlist* read-only, and thus the down-channel is not protected. To protect the down-channel it would have been necessary to use a variable *c(A,B?,C).Outlist* instead of *Outlist?*. This is not a feasible solution when the down-channel has the value *nil*. The best solution was therefore to explicitly protect the down-channel in the head of the clause. The variable *Cap1* was protected in the head for the same reason.

Read-only variables in the head of a clause are thus used by a process to export a protected data structure. This proved to be a simple and useful technique in our implementations.

Appendix 9.2: The Implementation of Algorithm 1

```
pushed(Amt,c(Flow,X.Down,Up).List,c(Newflow?,Down?,Up).List1) ←
    pushed(Amt1,List?,List1),
    Newflow := Flow + X,
    Amt := X + Amt1?.
pushed(∅,nil,nil).

returned(Amt,c(Cap,Down,X.Up).List,c(∅,Down,Up?).List1) ←
    X ≠ ∅ |
    returned(Amt1,List?,List1),
    add_returned(X,Amt1?,Amt).
returned(Amt,c(Cap,Down,∅.Up).List,c(Cap,Down,Up?).List1) ←
    returned(Amt,List?,List1).
returned(∅,nil,nil).

add_returned(X,Amt,Total) ←
    X ≠ block |
    Total := X + Amt.
```

add_returned(block,Amt,Amt).

push(N,Qin,c(Cap,Qout?.Down,Up).List,c(Cap1?,Down,Up).List1,Excess) ←
  Qout := min(Qin,Cap),
  Cap1 := Cap – Qout,
  Qin1 := Qin – Qout,
  push(N,Qin1?,List?,List1,Excess).
push(N,Excess,nil,nil,Excess).

return(Qout,List,List1) ←
  Qout ≠ ∅ |
  return1(Qout,List?,List1).
return(∅,List,List1) ←
  send(∅,up,List,List1).
return1(∅,c(Flow,Down,block.Up).List,c(Flow,Down,Up).List1) ←
  return1(∅,List?,List1).
return1(Amt,c(Flow,Down,Backflow?.Up).List,c(Flow1,Down,Up).List1) ←
  Amt ≠ ∅ |
  Backflow := min(Flow,Amt),
  Flow1 := Flow – Backflow?,
  Amt1 := Amt – Backflow?,
  return1(Amt1?,List?,List1).
return1(∅,nil,nil).

send(X,up,c(Amt,Down,X.Up).List,c(Amt,Down,Up).List1) ←
  send(X,up,List?,List1).
send(X,down,c(Amt,X.Down,Up).List,c(Amt,Down,Up).List1) ←
  send(X,down,List?,List1).
send(X,Dir,nil,nil).

vertex(N,Inlist,Outlist,Control) ←
  send(∅,down,Outlist,Outlist1),
  send(∅,up,Inlist,Inlist1),
  vertex1(X,Inlist1?,Outlist1?,Control).

vertex1(N,Inlist,Outlist,halt) ←
  infowrite(vertex(N),inlist,Inlist),
  infowrite(vertex(N),outlist,Outlist).

vertex1(N,Inlist,Outlist,Control) ←
  pushed(Amt,Inlist,Inlist1),
  returned(Amt1,Outlist,Outlist1) |
  Excess := Amt1 + Amt,
  push(N,Excess?,Outlist1?,Outlist2,Excess1),

```
        return(Excess1?,Inlist1?,Inlist2),
        vertex1(N,Inlist2?,Outlist2?,Control).
source(Initflow,Outlist,Control,Xs) ←
        saturate(Initflow,Outlist,Outlist1),
        source1(Outlist1?,Control,Xs).
source1(Outlist,halt,Xs) ←
        infowrite(source,outlist,Outlist).
source1(Outlist,Control,Backflow.Xs) ←
        returned(Backflow,Outlist,Outlist1) |
        send(∅,down,Outlist1,Outlist2),
        write(flow_returned(Backflow)),
        source1(Outlist2?,Control,Xs).

saturate(Q,c(Cap,Cap.Down,Up).List,c(∅,Down,Up).List1) ←
        saturate(Q1,List?,List1),
        Q := Cap + Q1.
saturate(∅,nil,nil).

target(Inlist,Control,Ys) ←
        send(∅,up,Inlist,Inlist1),
        target1(Inlist1?,Control,Ys).
target1(Inlist,halt,Ys) ←
        infowrite(target,inlist,Inlist).
target1(Inlist,Control,Outflow.Ys) ←
        pushed(Outflow,Inlist,Inlist1) |
        send(∅,up,Inlist1,Inlist2),
        write(target_received(Outflow)),
        target1(Inlist2?,Control,Ys).

monitor(∅,_,_,halt).
monitor(Goal,X.Xs,Y.Ys,Control) ←
        Goal > ∅ |
        Goal1 := Goal − X − Y,
        monitor(Goal1?,Xs?,Ys?,Control).

wait_list(X.Xs,X.List) ←
        wait(X) |
        wait_list(Xs?,List).
wait_list(nil,nil).
infowrite(N,Listtype,List) ←
        wait_list(List,X) |
        write(N),
        write(Listtype),
```

call(writechlist(X)),
call(newline).

Appendix 9.3: The Implementation of Algorithm 2

vertex(Name,Inlist,Outlist,Control) ←
    buildtree(Inlist,Intree), .
    buildtree(Outlist,Outree),
    send(∅,up,Intree?,Intree1),
    send(∅,down,Outree?,Outree1),
    vertex1(Name,Intree1?,Outree1?,Control).

buildtree(List,Newlist) ←
    buildtree(Val,List,Newlist).
buildtree(Val,L.List,c(Val?,X?,Y?)) ←
    firstel(List?,N),
    N ≠ nil |
    split(L.List,A,B),
    buildtree(Val1,A?,X),
    buildtree(Val2,B?,Y),
    Val := Val1 + Val2.
buildtree(Q,c(Q,Down,Up).List,c(Q,strm(Down),strm(Up))) ←
    firstel(List?,nil) | true.

split(X.Y.List,X.A,Y.B) ←
    split(List?,A,B).
split(X.nil,X.nil,c(∅,nil,nil).nil).
split(nil,nil,nil).

pushed(Amt,c(Flow,c(A,B,C),Y),c(Newflow?,W?,Z?)) ←
    pushed(Amt1,c(A,B,C),W),
    pushed(Amt2,Y?,Z),
    Amt := Amt1 + Amt2,
    Newflow := Flow + Amt.
pushed(X,c(Flow,strm(X.Xs),Y),c(Newflow?,strm(Xs?),Y)) ←
    Newflow := Flow + X.
pushed(∅,c(∅,strm(nil),strm(nil)),c(∅,strm(nil),strm(nil))).

returned(Amt,Outree,Outree1) ←
    returned1(Amt,Dec,Outree,Outree1).
returned1(Amt,Dec,c(Val,X,c(A,B,C)),c(Newval,W?,Z?)) ←
    returned1(Amt1,Dec1,X?,W),

```
    returned1(Amt2,Dec2,c(A,B,C),Z),
    Amt := Amt1 + Amt2,
    Dec := Dec1 + Dec2,
    Newval := Val - Dec.
returned1(∅,Val,c(Val,Xs,strm(block,Ys)),c(∅,Xs,strm(Ys?))).
returned1(Y,Val,c(Val,Xs,strm(Y.Ys)),c(∅,Xs,strm(Ys?))) ←
    Y ≠ ∅,
    Y ≠ block | true.
returned1(∅,∅,c(Val,Xs,strm(∅,Ys)),c(Val,Xs,strm(Ys?))).
returned1(∅,∅,c(∅,strm(nil),strm(nil)),c(∅,strm(nil),strm(nil))).

push(Qin,c(Cap,X,Y),Newtree,Excess) ←
    Qout := min(Qin,Cap),
    Excess := Qin - Qout,
    push1(Qout?,c(Cap,X,Y),Newtree).
push1(Q,c(Cap,c(Cap1,W,X),c(Cap2,Y,Z)),c(Newcap?,M?,N?)) ←
    Newcap := Cap - Q,
    Q1 := min(Q,Cap1),
    push1(Q1?,c(Cap1,W,X),M),
    Q2 := Q - Q1,
    push1(Q2?,c(Cap2,Y,Z),N).
push1(Q,c(Cap,strm(Q.Out),strm(In)),c(Newcap?,strm(Out),strm(In))) ←
    Newcap := Cap - Q.
push1(∅,c(∅,strm(nil),strm(nil)),c(∅,strm(nil),strm(nil))).

return(Q,Oldtree,Newtree) ←
    Q ≠ ∅ |
    return1(Q,Oldtree,Newtree).
return(∅,Oldtree,Newtree) ←
    send(∅,up,Oldtree,Newtree).
return1(Q,c(Flow,c(Flow1,W,X),c(Flow2,Y,Z)),c(Newflow?,M?,N?)) ←
    Newflow := Flow - Q,
    Q1 := min(Q,Flow1),
    return1(Q1?,c(Flow1,W,X),M),
    Q2 := Q - Q1,
    return1(Q2?,c(Flow2,Y,Z),N).
return1(Q,c(Flow,strm(In),strm(Q.Out)),c(Newflow?,strm(In),strm(Out))) ←
    Q ≠ ∅ |
    Newflow := Flow - Q.
return1(∅,c(Flow,strm(In),strm(block.Out),c(Flow,strm(In),strm(Out))).
return1(∅,c(∅,strm(nil),strm(nil)),c(∅,strm(nil),strm(nil))).
```

vertex1(N,Intree,Outree,halt) ←
    write(vertex(N)),
    write(intree(Intree)),
    write(outree(Outree)).
vertex1(N,Intree,Outree,Control) ←
    pushed(Q,Intree,In1),
    returned(Q1,Outree,Out1),
    Excess := Q + Q1,
    push(Excess?,Out1?,Out2,Excess1),
    return(Excess1?,In1?,In2) |
    vertex1(N,In2?,Out2?,Control).

source(Cap,Outlist,Control,Xs) ←
    buildtree(Outlist,c(Cap,A,B)),
    push(Cap?,c(Cap?,A?,B?),Outree1,Excess),
    source1(Outree1?,Control,Xs).
source1(Outree,halt,Xs) ←
    write(source),
    write(outree(Outree)).
source1(Outree,Control,Backflow.Xs) ←
    returned(Backflow,Outree,Outree1),
    wait_write(Backflow,flow_returned(Backflow)),
    send(∅,down,Outree1?,Outree2) |
    source1(Outree2?,Control,Xs).

target(Inlist,Control,Xs) ←
    buildtree(Inlist,Intree),
    send(∅,up,Intree?,Intree1),
    target1(Intree1?,Control,Xs).
target1(Intree,halt,Xs) ←
    write(target),
    write(intree(Intree)).
target1(Intree,Control,Outflow.Xs) ←
    pushed(Outflow,Intree,Intree1),
    wait_write(Outflow,target_received(Outflow)),
    send(∅,up,Intree1?,Intree2) |
    target1(Intree2?,Control,Xs).

monitor(∅,_,_,halt).
monitor(Goal,X.Xs,Y.Ys,Control) ←
    Goal > ∅ |
    Goal1 := Goal – X – Y,
    monitor(Goal1?,Xs?,Ys?,Control).

send(Msg,Dir,c(Q,c(A,B,C),Y),c(Q,M?,N?)) ←
    send(Msg,Dir,c(A,B?,C),M),
    send(Msg,Dir,Y?,N).
send(Msg,down,c(Q,strm(Msg.X),Y),c(Q,strm(X),Y)).
send(Msg,up,c(Q,X,strm(Msg.Y)),c(Q,X,strm(Y))).
send(Msg,Dir,c(∅,strm(nil)),strm(nil),c(∅,strm(nil),strm(nil))).

firstel(N.List,N).
firstel(nil,nil).

Appendix 9.4: The Implementation of Algorithm 3

vertex(N,Inlist,Outlist,Control) ←
    call(length(Inlist,Inedges)),
    build_stacktree(1,Inedges?,Stacktree),
    build_intree(1,Inlist,Intree),
    build_outree(Outlist,Outree),
    send(∅,up,Intree?,Intree1),
    send(∅,down,Outree?,Outree1),
    vertex1(N,1,1,Inedges?,Stacktree?,Intree1?,Outree1?,Control).
vertex1(N,Pulse,Pulses,Inedges,Stacktree,Intree,Outree,halt).
vertex1(N,Pulse,Pulses,Edges,Stacktree,Intree,Outree,Control) ←
    pushed(Amt1,Pulse,Pulses,Edges,Stacktree,Intree,Pulses1,Stacktree1,
        Intree1),
    returned(Amt2,Outree,Outree1) |
    write(vertex(N,Pulse)),
    Excess := Amt1 + Amt2,
    push(Excess?,Outree1,Outree2,Excess1),
    return(Excess1?,Stacktree1,Intree1,Stacktree2,Intree2),
    Pulse1 :– Pulse + 1,
    vertex(N,Pulse1?,Pulses1?,Edges,Stacktree2?,Intree2?,Outree2?,Control).

pushed(Amt,Pulse,Pulses,Edges,Stacktree,Intree,Pulses1,Stacktree1,Intree1) ←
    findpulse(stacktree,Stacktree,Pulse,Pulses,Edges,Edgetree,Stacktre1,
        Pulses1,Amt?,Edgetree1?),
    pushed1(Amt,Pulse,Pulses,Edgetree?,Intree,Edgetree1,Intree1).
pushed1(Amt,Pulse,Pulses,c(∅,Edgeleft,Edgeright),c(Inval, Inleft,Inright),
      c(Amt?,Edgeleft1?,Edgeright1?),c(Inval,Inleft1?,Inright1?)) ←
    pushed1(Amt1,Pulse,Pulses,Edgeleft,Inleft,Edgeleft1,Inleft1),
    pushed1(Amt2,Pulse,Pulses,Edgeright,Inright,Edgeright1,Inright1),
    Amt := Amt1 + Amt2.

pushed1(X,Pulse,Pulses,c(∅,nil),c(Inval,strm(X.Xs),strm(Ys), Subtree),
    c(X,strm1(Z)),c(Inval1?,strm(Xs?),strm(Ys),Subtree1?)) ←
  Inval1 := Inval + X,
  findpulse(intree,Subtree,Pulse,Pulses,_,Leaf,Subtree1,_,∅,strm1(Z?)).
pushed1(∅,Pulse,Pulses,c(∅,nil),c(Inval,strm(nil),strm(nil),Subtree),
    c(∅,nil),c(Inval,strm(nil),strm(nil),Subtree)).

findpulse(Type,Tree,Pulse,Pulses,Edges,Leaf,Tree1,Pulses,Val,Leaf1) ←
  Pulse ≤ Pulses |
  P1 := Pulses / 2,
  findpulse(Tree,Pulse,P1?,P1?,Leaf,Tree1,Val,Leaf1).
findpulse(Type,Tree,Pulse,Pulses,Edges,Leaf,Tree2,Pulses1,Val,Leaf1) ←
  Pulses < Pulse |
  Pulses1 := Pulses * 2,
  build_pulses(Type,Pulses,Edges,New_halftree),
  join(Tree,New_halftree?,Tree1),
  findpulse(Tree1?,Pulse,Pulses,Leaf,Tree2,Val,Leaf1).

findpulse(c(V,Left,Right),Pulse,Midpt,Partsize,Leaf,c(V1?,Left,Right1?),
    Val,Leaf1) ←
  Midpt < Pulse |
  V1 := V + Val,
  Partsize1 := Partsize /2,
  Midpt1 := Midpt + Partsize1,
  findpulse(Right,Pulse,Midpt1?,Partsize1?,Leaf,Right1,Val,Leaf1).
findpulse(c(V,Left,Right),Pulse,Midpt,Partsize,Leaf,c(V1?,Left1?,Right),
    Val,Leaf1) ←
  Pulse ≤ Midpt,
  Partsize ≠ ∅ |
  V1 := V + Val,
  Partsize1 := Partsize / 2,
  Midpt1 := Midpt – Partsize1,
  findpulse(Left,Pulse,Midpt1?,Partsize1?,Leaf,Left1,Val,Leaf1).
findpulse(c(X,Y),Pulse,Midpt,∅,Y,c(X1?,New),Val,New) ←
  X1 := X + Val.

build_stacktree(Pulses,Edges,Stacktree) ←
  build_pulses(stacktree,Pulses,Edges,Stacktree).

build_intree(Pulses,Inlist,Intree) ←
  build_edgetree(intree,Pulses,Inlist,Intree).

build_outree(Outlist,Outree) ←
  build_edgetree(outree,_,Outlist,Outree).

build_pulses(Type,Pulses,X,c(∅,Left?,Right?)) ←
    Pulses ≠ 1 |
    Pulses1 := Pulses / 2,
    build_pulses(Type,Pulses1?,X,Left),
    build_pulses(Type,Pulses1?,X,Right).
build_pulses(stacktree,1,N,c(∅,Edgetree?)) ←
    build_empty_edgetree(N,Edgetree).
build_pulses(intree,1,_,c(∅,nil)).

build_edgetree(Type,Pulses,List,Edgetree) ←
    build_edgetree(Val,Type,Pulses,List,Edgetree).
build_edgetree(Val,Type,Pulses,L.List,c(Val?,X?,Y?)) ←
    firstel(List?,N),
    N? ≠ nil |
    split(L.List,A,B),
    build_edgetree(Val1,Type,Pulses,A?,X),
    build_edgetree(Val2,Type,Pulses,B?,Y),
    Val := Val1 + Val2.
build_edgetree(Q,outree,Pulses,c(Q,Down,Up).List,c(Q,strm(Down),strm(Up))) ←
    firstel(List?,nil) | true.
build_edgetree(∅,intree,Pulses,c(Q,Down,Up).List,c(Q,strm(Down),strm(Up),
        Subtree?)) ←
    firstel(List?,nil) |
    build_pulses(intree,Pulses,_,Subtree).

split(X.Y.List,X.Xs,Y.Ys) ←
    split(List?,Xs,Ys).
split(X.nil,X.nil,c(∅,nil,nil).nil).
split(nil,nil,nil).

build_empty_edgetree(N,c(∅,X?,Y?)) ←
    N ≠ 1 |
    ceiling_div(N,2,N1),
    build_empty_edgetree(N1?,X),
    build_empty_edgetree(N1?,Y).
build_empty_edgetree(1,c(∅,nil)).

firstel(N.List,N).
firstel(nil,nil).

push(Qin,c(Cap,X,Y),Newtree,Excess) ←
    Qout := min(Qin,Cap),
    Excess := Qin – Qout,
    push1(Qout?,c(Cap,X,Y),Newtree).

push1(Q,c(Cap,c(Cap1,W,X),c(Cap2,Y,Z)),c(Newcap?,M?,N?)) ←
    Newcap := Cap – Q,
    Q1 := min(Q,Cap1),
    push1(Q1?,c(Cap1,W,X),M),
    Q2 := Q – Q1,
    push1(Q2?,c(Cap2,Y,Z),N).
push1(Q,c(Cap,strm(Q.Down),strm(Up)),c(Newcap?,strm(Down),strm(Up))) ←
    Newcap := Cap – Q.
push1(∅,strm(nil),strm(nil)),c(∅,strm(nil),strm(nil))).

returned(Amt,Outree,Outree1) ←
    returned1(Amt,Dec,Outree,Outree1).
returned1(Amt,Dec,c(Val,X,c(A,B,C)),c(Newval?,W?,Z?)) ←
    returned1(Amt1,Dec1,X?,W),
    returned1(Amt2,Dec2,c(A,B,C),Z),
    Amt := Amt1 + Amt2,
    Dec := Dec1 + Dec2,
    Newval := Val – Dec.
returned1(∅,Val,c(Val,Xs,strm(block.Ys)),c(∅,Xs,strm(Ys?))).
returned1(Y,Val,c(Val,Xs,strm(Y.Ys)),c(∅,Xs,strm(Ys?))) ←
    Y ≠ ∅,
    Y ≠ block | true.
returned1(∅,∅,c(Val,Xs,strm(∅.Ys)),c(Val,Xs,strm(Ys?))).
returned1(∅,∅,c(∅,strm(nil),strm(nil)),c(∅,strm(nil),strm(nil))).

return(∅,Stacktree,Intree,Stacktree,Intree1) ←
    send(∅,up,Intree,Intree1).
return(Q,Stacktree,Intree,Stacktree1,Intree1) ←
    Q ≠ ∅ |
    pop_stack(Q,Stacktree,Stacktree1),
    collect_return(Amt,Intree,Intree1).

pop_stack(Q,c(Val,Left,Right),c(Val1?,Left1?,Right1?)) ←
    Val1 := Val – Q,
    val(Right,V2),
    Q1 := min(Q,V2),
    pop_stack(Q1?,Right,Right1),
    Q2 := Q – Q1,
    pop_stack(Q2?,Left,Left1).
pop_stack(Q,c(Val,Subtree),c(Val1?,X1?)) ←
    subtree(Subtree) |
    Val1 := Val – Q,
    pop_stack(Q,Subtree,X1).

pop_stack(Q,c(Val,strm1(Q.Xs)),c(Val1?,strm1(Xs))) ←
    Val1 := Val – Q.
pop_stack(∅,c(∅,nil),c(∅,nil)).

collect_return(Amt,c(Val,Left,Right),c(Val,Left1?,Right1?)) ←
    collect_return(Amt1,Left,Left1),
    collect_return(Amt2,Right,Right1),
    Amt := Amt1 + Amt2.
collect_return(Q,c(Val,strm(Xs),strm(Q1?.Ys),Subtree),
        c(Val1?,strm(Xs),strm(Ys),Subtree1)) ←
    collect(Q,Subtree,Subtree1),
    what_to_send(Q?,Q1),
    Val1 := Val – Q.

collect(Q,c(V,Left,Right),c(V,Left1?,Right1?)) ←
    collect(Q1,Left,Left1),
    collect(Q2,Right,Right1),
    Q := Q1 + Q2.
collect(Q,c(V,strm1(Q.Zs)),c(V,strm1(Zs?))).
collect(∅,c(V,nil),c(V,nil)).

ceiling_div(X,Y,Z) ←
    Z := X / Y,
    M := Z * Y,
    M? = X | true.
ceiling_div(X,Y,Z1) ←
    Z := X / Y,
    M := Z * Y,
    M? ≠ X |
    Z1 := Z + 1.

join(Tree,New_half,c(Val?,Tree,New_half)) ←
    val(Tree,Val).

send(Msg,Dir,c(Q,Left,Right),c(Q,Left1?,Right1?)) ←
    subtree(Left) |
    send(Msg,Dir,Left,Left1),
    send(Msg,Dir,Right,Right1).

send(Msg,down,c(Q,strm(Msg.X),Y),c(Q,strm(X),Y)).
send(Msg,up,c(Q,X,strm(Msg.Y),Subtree),c(Q,X,strm(Y),Subtree)).
send(Msg,Dir,c(∅,strm(nil),strm(nil),S),c(∅,strm(nil),strm(nil),S)).
send(Msg,Dir,c(∅,strm(nil),strm(nil)),c(∅,strm(nil),strm(nil))).

source(Cap,Outlist,Control,Xs) ←

    build_outree(Outlist,c(Cap,L,R)),
    push(Cap?,c(Cap?,L?,R?),Outree1,Excess),
    source1(Outree1?,Control,Xs).
source1(Outree,halt,Xs).
source1(Outree,Control,Backflow.Xs) ←
    returned(Backflow,Outree,Outree1) |
    wait_write(Backflow,flow_returned(Backflow)),
    send(∅,down,Outree1?,Outree2),
    source1(Outree2,Control,Xs).

target(Inlist,Control,Ys) ←
    call(length(Inlist,Inedges)),
    build_stacktree(1,Inedges?,Stacktree),
    build_intree(1,Inlist,Intree),
    send(∅,up,Intree?,Intree1),
    target1(1,1,Inedges?,Stacktree?,Intree1?,Control,Ys).
target1(Pulse,Pulses,Edges,Stacktree,Intree,halt,Ys).
target1(Pulse,Pulses,Edges,Stacktree,Intree,Control,Outflow.Ys) ←
    pushed(Outflow,Pulse,Pulses,Edges,Stacktree,Intree,Pulses1,Stacktree1,
        Intree1) |
    wait_write(Outflow,target_received(Outflow)),
    send(∅,up,Intree1?,Intree2),
    Pulse1 := Pulse + 1,
    target1(Pulse1?,Pulses1,Edges,Stacktree1,Intree2,Control,Ys).

monitor(∅,_,_,halt).
monitor(Goal,X.Xs,Y.Ys,Control) ←
    Goal > ∅ |
    Goal1 := Goal − X − Y,
    monitor(Goal?,Xs?,Ys?,Control).

what_to_send(Q,Q) ←
    Q ≠ ∅ | true.
what_to_send(∅,block).
val(c(Val,X,Y),Val).
val(c(Val,X),Val).

subtree(c(Val,X,Y,Z)).
subtree(c(Val,X,Y)).
subtree(c(Val,X)).

Chapter 10

A Concurrent Prolog Based Region Finding Algorithm

Lisa Hellerstein

University of California at Berkeley

Abstract

This paper presents a parallel algorithm for finding regions in a self intersecting polygon. It also presents a Concurrent Prolog implementation of the algorithm, as well as an analysis of the computational complexity of the implementation. The algorithm was designed with the intention of implementing it in Concurrent Prolog. This contrasts with the approach in (Hellerstein and Shapiro, Chapter 9), in which an algorithm designed for a parallel Von Neumann based architecture was adapted so that it could be implemented in Concurrent Prolog. The region finding algorithm was easy to implement in Concurrent Prolog, and the implementation was computationally efficient. The algorithm and its implementation together form an example of Concurrent Prolog based algorithm design, and support the claim that Concurrent Prolog is a usable algorithmic programming language.

10.1 Introduction

One standard technique in evaluating a new or unusual programming language is to compare that language to conventional languages, with conventional languages as a standard. This technique can be useful in the early stages of a new language. First, it can give the language credibility. Second, it can reveal many of the capabilities of the language. However, the technique of comparison can also be harmful. It can obscure the fact that it is frequently necessary to judge a language on its own merits. There is no such thing as a perfect all-purpose language. To fully evaluate a language, one must use it in ways that will reveal its strengths.

The comparative technique has been used in evaluating Concurrent Prolog as an implementation language for efficient parallel algorithms. In Hellerstein and Shapiro (Chapter 9), it was shown that Concurrent Prolog could be used to efficiently implement an intricate parallel algorithm designed for a von Neumann language. In developing the Concurrent Prolog implementation, many of the language's capabilities were revealed. Nevertheless, to perform a complete evaluation of Concurrent Prolog as an algorithmic language, it is still necessary to create algorithms that are specifically designed for implementation in Concurrent Prolog. In this paper we present one such algorithm, an algorithm that finds regions in a self-intersecting polygon. The algorithm can also be easily adapted to more general region finding problems.

The region-finding algorithm presented in this paper is rooted in Concurrent Prolog. Because it was designed for the language, it was relatively easy to implement. Moreover, one final step in the algorithm was directly inspired by the use of the language. It is highly doubtful that this step would have appeared in the algorithm if the algorithm had been designed for another language.

The problem of region-finding in a self-intersecting polygon is adapted from a paper by Nievergelt and Preparata (1982). Nievergelt and Preparata present both a statement of the problem and a sequential algorithm that solves it. Their sequential algorithm uses a plane sweep technique that traverses the plane from left to right. It makes heavy use of data structures to discover and record the regions. We approached the problem of region-finding in a totally different manner. As concurrent programmers, we did not view the graph sequentially from left to right, but as a network of concurrent communicating vertex processes. We sought to find regions in the graph by sending messages along communication channels.

One of our concerns in designing the algorithm was to make sure that the Concurrent Prolog implementation would be efficient. Our complexity calculations are based on a shared memory model in which uncontested memory accesses and basic arithmetic operations take constant time. To evaluate the complexity of unifications, we follow the basic principles of the unification algorithm found in Taylor et al. (Chapter 39). Let n be the number of vertices defining the self intersecting polygon. Let s be the number of intersection points of edges of the self intersecting polygon. In the shared memory model, we were able to obtain a bound of $O(n+s)$ on the algorithm. Nievergelt and Preparata's sequential algorithm runs in time $O(n \log n+s)$. Our implementation uses $O(n+s)$ processors.

We begin the discussion of our algorithm with a formal description of the region-finding problem. Following the description, we present an informal specification of the algorithm. We continue with a formal description of the algorithm and its implementation, and with an analysis of the complexity of the implementation.

10.2 The Problem

The algorithm presented in this paper solves the problem of finding the regions of a self-intersecting polygon. An internal region is identified by a list of the vertices that determine its outer boundary. An external, unbounded region, is identified by a list of the vertices that determine its inner boundary.

Our algorithm is not based on the plane figure in question being a self intersecting polygon. The algorithm can therefore be easily adapted to handle the more general case of arbitrary plane figures formed from line segments. In the general case, single, non-convex regions may be represented by more than one list. These extra lists define the outer boundaries of smaller regions contained in the non-convex region.

The following problem definition describes the problem of region finding in a self-intersecting polygon. The definition is taken from Nievergelt and Preparata (1982).

> Given a sequence of n points $V_i = (X_i, Y_i)$, $i = 1, 2, \ldots, n$, in the plane, a polygon with vertices V is the sequence of line segments $\overline{V_1 V_2}$, $\overline{V_2 V_3}$, $\ldots, \overline{V_n V_1}$. These n line segments in general define intersection points $W_j = (X_j, Y_j)$, $j = 1, 2, \ldots, s$. When $s = 0$, the polygon is called simple and divides the plane into two regions, an internal bounded region R_1 and an external unbounded region R_0. In general, $s = O(n^2)$ and the polygon divides the plane into $r + 1 \geq 2$ disjoint regions, namely, the external unbounded region R_0 and r simply connected internal regions $R_1, \ldots, R_r$ (when the polygon is non-degenerate, $r = s + 1$). Each region is itself a simple polygon that has as its vertices some subset of $\{ V_1, \ldots, V_n, W_1, \ldots, W_n \}$. The desired result is a list of all regions, where each region is given by a cyclic list of its vertices ... the external region in clockwise order, the internal regions in counterclockwise order.

Example. Input sequence is

(0,0),(2,2),(0,2),(2,0),(0,0) [Figure 10.1].

The self intersecting polygon defined by this list has two internal regions and one external region. The internal regions are defined by the lists

(0,2),(1,1),(2,2),(0,2)

and

(0,0),(2,0),(1,1),(0,0).

The external region is defined by the list

(0,0),(1,1),(0,2),(2,2),(1,1),(2,0),(0,0).

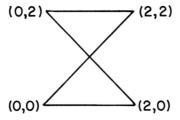

Figure 10.1: A self interesting polygon.

10.3 An Informal Specification of the Algorithm

Imagine that we are tracing the boundaries of an internal region R by walking clockwise along the inside of the edges bounding that region [Figure 10.2].

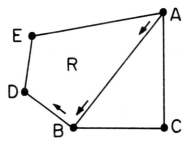

Figure 10.2: Tracing the boundary of an interior region R

We start at a vertex A, travel along the inside of an edge, and then arrive at another vertex B (A and B are either original vertices of the polygon, or vertices formed by intersecting edges). B may have many edges emanating from it. Nevertheless, in order to stay within our region, we must continue our trip along only one of these edges. The edge we must choose is the one adjacent to $\overline{AB}$ in a counterclockwise direction. Or, stated differently, it is the edge forming the smallest angle with $\overline{AB}$, provided that we measure our angle beginning at $\overline{AB}$ and move in a counterclockwise direction [Figure 10.3]. This is true in all cases

Figure 10.3: Choosing the counterclockwise adjacent angle. Our trip will continue in a similar fashion to all the vertices of R until we return again to A.

in the self-intersecting polygon and indeed in any case where we trace the outer boundary of an interior region.

Our trip will continue in a similar fashion to all the vertices of R until we return again to A.

Of course, R is an arbitrary internal region, and thus we may trace all the internal regions of a self-intersecting polygon in the same way. Suppose that in tracing the regions, we leave two arrows at every vertex we visit. One arrow will point towards the vertex and will be positioned inside the region, along the edge that led us to the vertex. The other arrow will point away from the vertex and indicate the path taken in leaving the vertex. We call the resulting picture an *arrow diagram* [Figure 10.4].

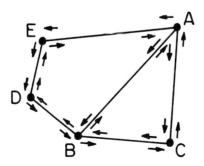

Figure 10.4: Completed arrow diagram for a self intersecting polygon

Let us now trace the inner boundary of the unbounded region of the polygon. As we move along this boundary in a counterclockwise direction, we arrive at a vertex V along edge E. As we leave V, we follow the edge which is counterclockwise adjacent to E. We will choose the counterclockwise adjacent edge at any vertex. It is possible to verify this fact by positioning angles in different positions on the plane, and by considering either the obtuse or the acute side of the angle to determine the outside of a region. This argument also applies to the case of the internal regions.

We may now add to our previous arrow diagram by tracing and marking the outer region of the graph in counterclockwise direction. The result will be a figure with the following three properties:

(1) Each angle in the graph will be delineated by arrows, because each angle bounds either one inner or one outer region.

(2) The arrows will all be arranged so that the outgoing arrow is counterclockwise adjacent to the incoming arrow. That is, if we consider all arrows and edges adjacent to a vertex to be actually emanating from that vertex, each incoming arrow will be counterclockwise adjacent to its corresponding outgoing arrow.

(3) By joining all the incoming and outgoing arrows that lie along the same side of an edge, we can form continuous rings of arrows which outline the boundaries of all of the regions.

10.4 The Algorithm

Our algorithm finds the regions of a self-intersecting polygon by first finding all vertices in the graph, including intersections, and then forming a realization of the arrow diagram. The "arrows" are actually communication channels between vertices. An incoming arrow is the receiving end of a communication channel. An outgoing arrow is the sending end. Moreover, the outgoing and incoming arrows lined up along the same side of an edge are represented by the same communication channel.

At the end of the program a process is initiated for every angle in the graph. A vertex at the point of many angles will be represented by many processes. Each "vertex" process has access to its receiving and sending channels. The vertex processes try to run in parallel. Each one contributes to the calculation of the regions.

In the following discussion, we will include many code fragments from the implementation. The full code can be found in Appendix 10.1.

For reference, we present the top level clause of the program here.

```
find_regions( CircularList ) ←
```

```
make_edgetuples( CircularList, EdgeList ),
gen_intsc( EdgeList?, IntscList ),
sort_intersections( IntscList?, IntscList1 ),
make_vertlist( IntscList1?, Vlist ),
make_vertices( Vlist?, IntscList1? ).
```

In order to make our presentation of the Concurrent Prolog code clearer, we will include specifications of the domains of some of the predicates. The domains will be written using BNF notation, with some added predicates when necessary. Words starting with capital letters are non-terminal symbols. Terminal symbols include left parentheses, right parentheses, commas, and words beginning with a lower case letter[*].

Some initial definitions:

Vertex ::= v(Integer, Integer)

ListofVertex ::= [Vertex|ListofVertex] | [ ]

Edge ::= e(Vertex, Vertex)

CircularList ::= [Vertex|ListofVertex]

such that *firstvertex*(CircularList) = *lastvertex*(CircularList).

If the domains for the main arguments of a process are unclear, we include a sample call to the process.

We begin by taking the list of vertices defining the polygon and transforming that list into a list of corresponding "edgetuples". An edgetuple consists of a term identifying the endpoints of the edge and a temporarily uninstantiated list of all points of intersection along that edge.

```
make_edgetuples( [V1,V2|List], [t( e(V1,V2), Is )|List1]) ←
    make_edgetuples( [V2|List?], List1 ).
```

make_edgetuples([V1], [ ]).

We then calculate the intersections of the edges in parallel, using pipelining.

IntersectionList ::= ListofVertex

Intsctns ::= ListofIntersectionList

Edgetuple ::= t(Edge, IntersectionList)

ListofEdgetuples ::= [Edgetuple|ListofEdgetuples] | [ ]

Edgelist ::= ListofEdgetuples

---

[*] Domain definitions and their format suggested by Jan Komorowski, personal communication.

Outlist ::= Edgelist

gen_intsc([EdgeTuple | EdgeList]) ←
    gen_intsc1(EdgeTuple, EdgeList?, Outlist),
    gen_intsc(Outlist?).

gen_intsc([ ]).

gen_intsc1(t(E1, [I | Is]),
    [t(E2, [I | Js]) | List],
    [t(E2, Js) | List1]) ←
        intersect(E1, E2, I) |
        gen_intsc1(t(E1, Is), List?, List1).

gen_intsc1(t(E1, Is),
    [t(E2, Js) | List],
    [t(E2, Js) | List1]) ←
        no_intersect(E1, E2) |
        gen_intsc1(t(E1, Is), List?, List1).

gen_intsc1(t(E, [ ]), [ ], [ ]).

At this stage, for every edge of the polygon we have a list of the points of intersection of that edge with other edges of the polygon. In the example we gave above, the edge joining $(0,0)$ and $(2,2)$ intersected other edges at the points $(2,2)$, $(0,0)$, and $(1,1)$. Note that the endpoints of the edge are included among the intersection points. This is because the endpoints are also points at which the edge intersects other edges. (To be consistent with Nievergelt and Preparata's definition, we do not count endpoints as intersecting points when we do our complexity analysis.)

We now want to sort the intersection points on each edge, so that we can detect adjacent intersection points on the edge. This will enable us to break the edge into subedges and to form a new graph with a vertex at every intersection point.

To sort the points on the line, we use a parallel quicksort adapted from Shapiro's (Chapter 2) quicksort program. Because we are dealing with points in the plane, we can basically use an "up and to the right" criterion in ordering the vertices. We then eliminate any repeated intersection points occurring in the sorted list. Repeated points occur when two or more edges intersect a third in a common point.

In our example, the intersection points along the edge joining $(0,0)$ and $(2,2)$ appear in sorted order as $(0,0)$, $(1,1)$, $(2,2)$. This breaks the edge into two subedges, one joining $(0,0)$ and $(1,1)$, and the other joining $(1,1)$ and $(2,2)$.

IntscList ::= [ListofVertex|IntscList] | [ ]

In ::= [Vertex|In]   { Read only channel }

Out ::= [Vertex|Out]   { Write only channel }

Channel ::= c(In, Out).

Path ::= p(Vertex, Channel) |

ListofPath ::= [Path|ListofPath] | [ ]

ListofListofPath ::= [ListofPath | ListofListofPath] | [ ]

IntscList1 ::= ListofListofPath

Call:
?– sort_intersections(IntscList?, IntscList1).

sort_intersections([Is | List], [NewIs2? | List1]) ←
    quicksort(line, Is?, NewIs),
    eliminate_dupls(NewIs?, NewIs1),
    make_channels(NewIs1?, NewIs2),
    sort_intersections(List?, List1).

sort_intersections([ ], [ ]).

With each intersection point I, we associate a bi-directional communication channel. This channel will belong to the subedge, if any, which joins I to the next intersection point along the edge. By "next", we mean next in the sorted list of intersection points. The channel will have the form $c(In, Out)$, where In is the receiving channel at the point, and Out is the sending channel.

I ::= Vertex

Is ::= ListofVertex

NewIs ::= ListofVertex

NewIs1 ::= ListofPath

Call:
?– make_channels(NewIs?, NewIs1).

make_channels([I | Is], [p(I, c(In, Out)) | NewIs]) ←
    make_channels(Is?, NewIs).

make_channels([ ], [ ]).

Using the lists of intersection points along each edge, we generate a composite list of all points of intersection in the graph (eliminating duplicates). These points of intersection will be the vertices that define the regions of the self intersecting polygon. In our example the vertex list consists of the points $(0,0)$, $(1,1)$, $(2,2)$, $(2,0)$, and $(0,2)$.

Edges ::= ListofListofPath

VertList ::= ListofVertices

Vlist ::= ListofVertices

List1 ::= ListofVertices

Nlist ::= ListofVertices

make_vertlist(Edges, VertList) ←
    one_list(Edges, List),
    make_vlist(List?, VertList).

one_list([[p(V, X) | Xs]|List], [V|List1]) ←
    one_list([Xs?|List], List1).

one_list([[ ]|List], List1) ←
    one_list(List?, List1).

one_list([ ], [ ]).

make_vlist([I | Is], [I | Vlist]) ←
    make_vlist1(I, Is?, List1),
    make_vlist(List1?, Vlist).

make_vlist([ ], [ ]).

make_vlist1(I, [I | Is], Nlist) ←
    make_vlist1(I, Is?, Nlist).

make_vlist1(I, [J | Is], [J | Nlist]) ←
    vert_neq(I, J) |
    make_vlist1(I, Is?, Nlist).

make_vlist1(I, [ ], [ ]).

The list of points of intersection is used to generate vertex processes. Each vertex process belongs to a region adjacent to the vertex. The vertex processes also contain the communication channels that will be used in tracing the regions.

make_vertices([V|Vs], Edges) ←
    adjacencies(V, Edges, Adjs),
    break_up(V, Adjs?),
    make_vertices(Vs?, Edges).

The first step in forming the vertex processes is to take the vertex list and to form lists of the edges adjacent to each vertex V. At the same time, we want to bring along the bi-directional communication channel associated with each adjacent edge. We want the channel to have the form $c(In, Out)$, where In is the channel leading to V. This may involve rearranging the order of the two channels as they appear in the lists of intersections.

The adjacency list is formed by having each vertex (in the composite list of intersection points) "examine" the sorted lists of intersection points along each edge. In our example, vertex *(1,1)* "examines" the sorted intersections points along the four edges of the polygon. It is determined to be adjacent to the four edges which join it to *(0,0)*, *(2,2)*, *(2,0)*, and *(0,2)*. Each of these edges has an associated bi-directional communication channel.

> V ::= Vertex
>
> V1 ::= Vertex
>
> Path ::= p(Vertex, Channel).
>
> Edges ::= ListofListofPath
>
> Adjs ::= ListofPath
>
> Call:
>
> ?– adjacencies(V, Edges, Adjs).
>
> adjacencies(V, [[p(V,X),p(V1,Y)|Is]|List], [p(V1,X)|Js]) ←
>   adjacencies(V, [[p(V1,Y) | Is] | List], Js).
>
> adjacencies(V, [[I, p(V,X) | Is] | List], [I1 | Js]) ←
>   switch_chans(I, I1),
>   adjacencies(V, [[p(V,X) | Is] | List], Js).
>
> adjacencies(V, [[p(M,X), p(N,Y) | Is] | List], Js) ←
>   vert_neq(V, M),
>   vert_neq(V, N) |
>   adjacencies(V, [[p(N,Y) | Is] | List], Js).
>
> adjacencies(V, [[X] | List], Js) ←
>   adjacencies(V, List?, Js).
>
> adjacencies(V, [ ], [ ]).

Once the edges adjacent to a given vertex are determined, the next step is to find the pairs of those edges which are counterclockwise adjacent to each other. First, we sort the edges in counterclockwise order using a parallel quicksort. This can be done with a little calculation involving the angles formed by pairs of edges. Then, we extract the pairs of counterclockwise adjacent edges and form a vertex process for each pair. Each pair of edges determines an angle. Each edge brings with it an associated bi-directional communication channel.

In our example when the edges adjacent to *(1,1)* are sorted, the pairs of counterclockwise adjacent edges yield the four angles defined by the triples of vertices

$(2,0),(1,1),(2,2)$
$(2,2),(1,1),(2,0)$
$(2,0),(1,1),(0,0)$

and

$(0,0),(1,1),(2,0).$

Vertex (*1,1*) therefore generates four vertex processes, one for each of these angles.

```
break_up( V, Adjs ) ←
    quicksort( circle( V ), Adjs, Adjs1 ),
    first_el( Adjs1?, A ),
    break_up1( V, A?, Adjs1? ).

break_up1( V, A, [A1, A2 | Adjs] ) ←
    make_process( V, A1, A2 ),
    break_up1( V, A, [A2 | Adjs?] ).

break_up1( V, A, [A1] ) ←
    make_process( V, A1, A).

first_el( [A|B], A ).
```

The vertex process has three arguments. The first consists of the coordinates of the vertex joining the edges. The second and third arguments are communication channels. These channels correspond to arrows in the arrow diagram. Specifically, the first channel corresponds to the incoming arrow associated with the angle determined by the edge pair. The second channel corresponds to the outgoing arrow at the angle. To extract the proper channels, we need only look at the two edges in sorted order. We take the in-channel of the first edge (leading to the vertex), and the out-channel of the second edge.

In our example, the four vertex processes generated by the vertex (*1,1*) utilize the channels represented in Figure 10.5.

```
Adjacency ::= Path

V ::= Vertex

A1 ::= Adjacency

A2 := Adjacency

Call:
?- make_process( V, A1, A2 ).

make_process( V, p(V1, c(In1,Out1)), p(V2, c(In2,Out2)) ) ←
    vertex( V, In1?, Out2 ).
```

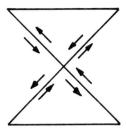

Figure 10.5: Vertex process

The vertex processes, when executed, form infinite circular lists delineating the boundaries of the associated regions. For each vertex process, a list is formed which has the coordinates of the vertex as the head and the in-channel associated with the vertex as the tail. In this way, a vertex process sends its own coordinates along to the next vertex and also "forwards" all messages on its receiving channel. Since the vertex processes in a region consist of a circular chain of communication channels, the communication channels are thus concatenated together into an infinite list containing the coordinates of all the vertices in the region. Each vertex process then takes the list which was its out-channel and, if the vertex has the smallest x-coordinate of any vertex in the region (use y-coordinate to break a tie), the process prints the list.

> vertex(V, In, [V | In]) ← print_cycle(V, In).

The list consists of messages received, starting with the message sent from the previous vertex, working backward. The list is therefore printed out in the order opposite to the direction in which the messages were sent. A clockwise list is printed out to represent the outer region. The inner regions are all defined by counterclockwise lists, as desired.

The region defined by the list *(0,2)*, *(1,1)*, *(2,1)*, *(0,2)*, in our example is generated by the conjunction of the goals

> vertex(v(0,2), X1?, X2),
> vertex(v(2,2), X2?, X3),
> vertex(v(1,1), X3?, X1). [Figure 10.6]

The following are sample runs of the program.

> | ?– listing(test1).

> test1 ←
>   find_regions([v(0,0),v(2,2),v(0,2),v(2,0),v(0,0)]).

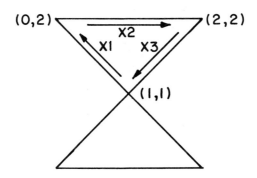

Figure 10.6

yes
| ?– cp(test1).
[v(0,2),v(1,1),v(2,2),v(0,2)]
[v(0,0),v(2,0),v(1,1),v(0,0)]
[v(0,0),v(1,1),v(0,2),v(2,2),v(1,1),v(2,0),v(0,0)]
∗ ∗ ∗ cycles: 35

yes
| ?– listing(test2).

test2 ←
    find_regions([v(0,0),v(2,2),v(2,0),v(0,2),v(3,5),v(8,0),v(0,0)]).

yes
| ?– cp(test2).
[v(1,1),v(2,0),v(2,2),v(1,1)]
[v(0,0),v(2,0),v(1,1),v(0,0)]
[v(0,2),v(1,1),v(2,2),v(2,0),v(8,0),v(3,5),v(0,2)]
[v(0,0),v(1,1),v(0,2),v(3,5),v(8,0),v(2,0),v(0,0)]
∗ ∗ ∗ cycles: 47

yes

The idea of having a vertex "send" its receiving channel was conceived while thinking about the Concurrent Prolog implementation of an earlier version of the algorithm.

Our implementation of the region-finding algorithm was not wholly correct, because it was written using only the arithmetic functions available in Concurrent Prolog. All calculations were thus done in integer arithmetic, which caused errors in any instances generating fractional vertex coordinates. It is possible to incorporate a rational number package into the program, to avoid such problems.

10.5 Complexity Issues

Our complexity calculations are based on a shared memory model of execution. Uncontested memory accesses and basic arithmetic operations are considered to take constant time. In speaking of the complexity of our algorithm, we are actually referring to the depth complexity. The depth complexity is the time from the execution of the first step of the algorithm, to the time the last processor stops working.

In many Concurrent Prolog programs, the complexity analysis is relatively straightforward. The sequence of unifications is completely determined by which processes spawn which other processes and by read-only variables which block the execution of one process until another is completed (basically a "send message/receive message" relation). In these programs one can look at the complexity of individual unifications independently of any other unifications, take the sequencing into account, and come up with a complexity analysis. The MAXFLOW program in Hellerstein and Shapiro (Chapter 9) is such a program.

In other programs the sequencing of unifications is more subtle. A program may have two goals whose execution sequence is not determined either by a spawning relation or by a "send message/receive message" relation. One might think that these two goals could be executed simultaneously and independently. However, the two goals may share common variables. Simultaneous execution of these goals could lead to a situation in which more than one process attempts to write to the same memory location at the same time. The existence of programs with multiple writers requires that a locking mechanism be present in a system running such programs. The locking mechanism insures the atomicity of the unifications. There are locking mechanisms which require only constant overhead in the case of single writers. It is therefore possible to incorporate a locking mechanism into a system without significantly affecting the complexity of programs with no multiple writers. In the case of multiple writers, though, the action of the locking mechanism may add to the complexity of the program. It is important to realize that in programs with multiple writers, unifications which look concurrent may actually be implicitly sequential because they must be handled by a locking mechanism. The details of one relevant locking mechanism was given by Taylor et al. (Chapter 39).

The only clause in the region-finding program which could conceivably cause a multiple writers situation is the clause with the head

vertex(V,In,[V|In]).

Consider the conjunction of vertex processes associated with a triangular region.

    vertex(v(0,0), X1?, X2),
    vertex(v(1,1), X2?, X3),
    vertex(v(2,0), X3?, X1).

The variables $X1$, $X2$, and $X3$ each appear in two goals. If we were to unify these three goals sequentially, we could successfully do it in any order. The result would be that $X1$, $X2$, and $X3$ would all be instantiated to circular lists. There is therefore no explicit sequence of execution associated with these three goals. If we ran the goals concurrently, it seems at first glance that the multiple occurrences of the variables would cause a multiple writers situation. Fortunately for the simplicity of our complexity analysis, this is not the case. Using the principles of the unification algorithm found in (Taylor et al., Chapter 39), we see that unification can proceed as follows. Consider unification of the goal *vertex(* $v(0,0)$, *X1?, X2*). The variable $X2$ will be bound to a list with $v(0,0)$ as its head, *X1?* as its tail. The unification of *X1?* with *In* has no purpose except to establish *X1?* as the tail of the list bound to *X2*. Thus the unification of *X1?* with *In* is treated in terms of global memory as a no-op. The goal *vertex(* $v(0,0)$, *X1?, X2*) does not write on *X1* at all. In fact, even if *X1* were not write protected, the unification of *X1* could still be executed as a no-op. We see from this that none of the vertex processes write on the variable which is their second argument, and that therefore there is no problem of multiple writers.

Because the vertex processes form a circular data structure, the program will only run on systems which do not perform the occur check.

The rest of the complexity analysis is fairly straightforward. Most of the tasks involved in generating the vertex processes (such as finding the intersection points, and setting up the communication channels), are pipelined constant time operations on lists with $O(n)$ or $O(n+s)$ elements. Sorting the intersection points along an edge, and sorting the adjacent edges to a vertex, are linear operations with the parallel quicksort, and the input lists to these quicksorts are of size $O(n+s)$. These tasks can therefore be accomplished with $O(n+s)$ processors. We just saw that the vertex processes take constant time to perform the unifications that instantiate the circular lists of vertices bounding a region. Once this unification takes place, the output can be printed. The depth complexity of the algorithm is therefore $O(n+s)$.

The planar graph formed at the end of the algorithm has $n+s$ vertices. It follows from Euler's formula that the graph has at most $3(n+s)-6$ edges (Liu, 1968). The number of vertex processes generated for the graph is equal to the sum over all the regions in the graph of the number of vertices in the polygon bounding the region. But the number of vertices in the polygon bounding the region is equal to the number of edges bounding the region. Since each edge borders exactly two regions, the number of vertex processes is exactly twice the number of edges in the graph. The total number of vertex processes is therefore $O(n+s)$, and the program uses $O(n+s)$ processors.

10.6 Conclusion

The parallel region-finding algorithm presented in this paper provides one example of Concurrent Prolog based algorithm design. The algorithm and its implementation support the claim that Concurrent Prolog is a usable algorithmic language. It is important now to try and develop efficient Concurrent Prolog based algorithms for a wide range of problems.

Research in related areas will be important to this effort. One major area of research is the development of efficient implementations of the Concurrent Prolog language – on sequential machines, on multiprocessors, and on truly parallel machines. Another related area of research is the complexity of Sequential and Concurrent Prolog unification. There are still important open questions in this area which could have ramifications both on the complexity analysis of Concurrent Prolog programs and on the implementations of the language.

Acknowledgements

Thanks to Ehud Shapiro and Jan Komorowski for their encouragement and advice and to Fernando Pereira for suggesting I look at the region finding algorithm. Eyal Yardeni assisted in editing this paper.

Appendix 10.1

```
% Given a circular list of cartesian coordinates which define a self-intersecting
% polygon, print out lists of vertices which define the regions formed by this
% polygon.

find_regions( CircularList ) ←
    make_edgetuples( CircularList, EdgeList ),
    gen_intsc( EdgeList?, IntscList ),
    sort_intersections( IntscList?, IntscList1 ),
    make_vertlist( IntscList1?, Vlist ),
    make_vertices( Vlist?, IntscList1? ).
make_edgetuples( [V1,V2|List], [t( e(V1,V2), Is )|List1]) ←
```

make_edgetuples([V2|List?], List1).

make_edgetuples([V1], [ ]).

% *gen_intsc*'s argument is a list of edge tuples. Each edge tuple is of the form
% *t(E,Is)*. *E* contains the coordinates of the endpoints of the edge.
% *I* is an uninstantiated list which will contain the coordinates of all points of
% intersection between that edge and other edges in the graph.

gen_intsc(EdgeTuples, Intsctns) ←
    intsc_list(EdgeTuples, Intsctns),
    gen_intsc(EdgeTuples).

gen_intsc([EdgeTuple|EdgeList]) ←
    gen_intsc1(EdgeTuple, EdgeList?, Outlist),
    gen_intsc(Outlist?).

gen_intsc([ ]).

gen_intsc1(t(E1, [I|Is]), [t(E2, [I|Js]) | List], [t(E2, Js)|List1]) ←
    intersect(E1, E2, I) |
    gen_intsc1(t(E1, Is), List?, List1).

gen_intsc1(t(E1, Is), [t(E2, Js)|List], [t(E2, Js)|List1]) ←
    no_intersect(E1, E2) |
    gen_intsc1(t(E1, Is), List?, List1).

gen_intsc1(t(E, [ ]), [ ], [ ]).

intsc_list([t(E, IList) | List], [IList | ILists]) ←
    intsc_list(List?, ILists).

intsc_list([ ], [ ]).

% Take each edge tuple and sort the list of intersection points along the edge.
% The sorted points will break the edge into sub-edges.

sort_intersections([Is | List], [NewIs2?|List1]) ←
    quicksort(line, Is?, NewIs),
    eliminate_dupls(NewIs?, NewIs1),
    make_channels(NewIs1?, NewIs2),
    sort_intersections(List?, List1).

sort_intersections([ ], [ ]).

% From the lists of edge intersections, generate a new list of all unique intersec-
% tion points in the graph (eliminating duplicates). These will be the vertices
% that define regions.

make_vertlist(Edges, VertList) ←

```
    one_list( Edges, List ),
    make_vlist( List?, VertList ).

one_list( [ [p(V, X) | Xs]|List], [V|List1] ) ←
    one_list( [Xs?|List], List1 ).

one_list( [ [ ]|List], List1 ) ←
    one_list( List?, List1 ).

one_list( [ ], [ ] ).

make_vlist( [I|Is], [I|Vlist] ) ←
    make_vlist( I, Is?, List1 ),
    make_vlist( List1?, Vlist ).

make_vlist( [ ], [ ] ).

make_vlist1( I, [I|Is], Nlist ) ←
    make_vlist1( I, Is?, Nlist ).

make_vlist1( I, [J|Is], [J|Nlist] ) ←
    vert_neq( I, J ) |
    make_vlist1( I, Is?, Nlist ).

make_vlist1( I, [ ], [ ] ).
```

% Taking a list of intersections, make a new list which associates a communi-
% cation channel with each intersection.

```
make_channels( [I | Is], [p( I, c( In, Out ) )|IList] ) ←
    make_channels( Is?, Ilist ).

make_channels( [ ], [ ] ).
```

% Eliminate duplicates from sorted list of vertices.

```
eliminate_dupls( [I1, I2|Is], [I1 | List] ) ←
    vert_neq( I1, I2 ) |
    eliminate_dupls( [I2 | Is?], List ).

eliminate_dupls( [I1, I1 | Is], [I1 | List] ) ←
    eliminate_dupls( I1, [I1 | Is?], List ).

eliminate_dupls( I, [I, J | Is], List ) ←
    eliminate_dupls( I, [J | Is?], List ).

eliminate_dupls( I, [I1, J | Is], List ) ←
    vert_neq( I, I1 ) |
    eliminate_dupls( [I1, J | Is], List ).

eliminate_dupls( I, [I], [ ] ).
```

eliminate_dupls(I, [X], [X]) ←
    vert_neq(I, X) |
    true.

eliminate_dupls([X], [X]).

% Make independent vertex processes by finding the [*sub-*]edges adjacent to
% each vertex and then forming one process for each region to which the
% vertex belongs.

make_vertices([V | Vs], Edges) ←
    adjacencies(V, Edges, Adjs),
    break_up(V, Adjs?),
    make_vertices(Vs?, Edges).

make_vertices([ ], Edges).

% Make list of endpoints of all edges adjacent to *V*, together with the two-way
% communication channels along that edge.

adjacencies(V, [[p(V, X), p(V1, Y)]|Is]|List] , [p(V1, X)|Js]) ←
    adjacencies(V, [[p(V1, Y)]|Is?]|List], Js).

adjacencies(V, [[I, p(V, X)]|Is]|List], [I1?|Js]) ←
    switch_chans(I, I1),
    adjacencies(V, [[p(V, X)]|Is?]|List], Js).

adjacencies(V, [[p(M, X), p(N, Y)]|Is]|List], Js) ←
    vert_neq(V, M),
    vert_neq(V, N) |
    adjacencies(V, [[p(N, Y)]|Is?]|List], Js).

adjacencies(V, [[X] | List], Js) ←
    adjacencies(V, List?, Js).

adjacencies(V, [ ], [ ]).

switch_chans(p(V, c(In, Out)), p(V, c(Out, In))).

break_up(V, Adjs) ←
    quicksort(circle(V), Adjs, Adjs1),
    first_el(Adjs1?, A),
    break_up1(V, A?, Adjs1?).

break_up1(V, A, [A1, A2 | Adjs]) ←
    make_process(V, A1, A2),
    break_up1(V, A, [A2 | Adjs?]).

break_up1(V, A, [A1]) ←

make_process(V, A1, A).

make_process(V, p(V1,c(In1,Out1)), p(V2, c(In2,Out2))) ←
    vertex(V, In1?, Out2).

first_el([A | B], A).

% Form an infinite circular list tracing the boundaries of the region by making
% each vertex attach its input stream to its output stream.

vertex(V, In, [V | In]) ← print_cycle(V, In).

% One vertex from each region will print out the boundary.

print_cycle(V, [V1 | Vs]) ←
    print_cycle1(V, e(V, V1), [V1|Vs], Printlist) |
    write_list([V | Printlist]).

print_cycle(V, List) ←
    no_print(V, List) | true.

print_cycle1(V, e(V, V2), [V3, V4|Vs], [V3|Prlist]) ←
    vert_leq(V, V3),
    or_neq(V, V3, V2, V4) |
    print_cycle(V, e(V, V2), [V4 | Vs?], Prlist).

print_cycle1(V, e(V, V1), [V, V1 | Vs], [V]).

no_print(V, [V3 | Vs]) ←
    vert_leq(V, V3) |
    no_print(V, Vs?).

no_print(V, [V3 | Vs]) ←
    vert_gtr(V, V3) | true.

or_neq(V1, V3, V2, V4) ←
    vert_neq(V1, V3) | true.

or_neq(V1, V3, V2, V4) ←
    vert_neq(V2, V4) | true.

% Intersection routines.

intersection(L1,L2,I) ←
    not_parallel(L1,L2) |
    intersection1(L1,L2,I).

intersection1(L1,L2,I) ←
    vertical(L1,X) |
    vertic_int(X,L2,I).

vertic_int(X,L2,v(X,Y)) ←
    slope(L2,M),
    y_intercept(L2,B),
    Y := M * X + B.

intersection1(L1,L2,I) ←
    vertical(L2,X) |
    vertic_int(X,L1,I).

non_vert_int(L1,L2,I) ←
    slope(L1,M1),
    slope(L2,M2),
    y_intercept(L1,B1),
    y_intercept(L2,B2),
    calc_int(M1?,M2?,B1?,B2?,I).

calc_int(M1,M2,B1,B2,v(X,Y)) ←
    X := (B2 − B1)/(M1 − M2),
    Y := M1 * X + B1.

vertical(e(v(X,Y1),v(X,Y2)),X).

not_vertical(e(v(X1,Y1),v(X2,Y2))) ←
    X1 ≠ X2.

intersection1(L1,L2,I) ←
    not_vertical(L1),
    not_vertical(L2) |
    non_vert_int(L1,L2,I).

parallel(L1,L2) ←
    not_vertical(L1),
    not_vertical(L2) |
    slope(L1,M1),
    slope(L2,M2),
    M1 =:= M2.

parallel(L1,L2) ←
    vertical(L1,X1),
    vertical(L2,X2) |
    true.

not_parallel(L1,L2) ←
    not_vertical(L1),
    not_vertical(l2) |
    slope(L1,M1),

```
    slope(L2,M2),
    M1 ≠ M2.
not_parallel(L1,L2) ←
    vertical(L1,X),
    not_vertical(L2) |
    true.

not_parallel(L1,L2) ←
    vertical(L2,X),
    not_vertical(L1) |
    true.

intersect(E1,E2,I) ←
    intersection(E1,E2,I),
    on_edge(I?,E1),
    on_edge(I?,E2).

no_intersect(E1,E2) ←
    intersection(E1,E2,I),
    off_edge(I?,E2) |
    true.

no_intersect(E1,E2) ←
    intersection(E1,E2,I),
    off_edge(I?,E1) |
    true.

no_intersect(E1,E2) ←
    parallel(E1,E2) | true.

on_edge(v(X,Y),e(v(X1,Y1),v(X2,Y2))) ←
    between(X,X1,X2),
    between(Y,Y1,Y2).

between(X,X1,X2) ←
    in_order(X1,X2,X3,X4),
    X ≥ X3, X4 ≥ X.

off_edge(v(X,Y),e(v(X1,Y1),v(X2,Y2))) ←
    not_between(X,X1,X2) | true.

off_edge(v(X,Y),e(v(X1,Y1),v(X2,Y2))) ←
    not_between(Y,Y1,Y2) | true.

not_between(X,X1,X2) ←
    in_order(X1,X2,X3,X4),
```

$\qquad$ X < X3 | true.

not_between(X,X1,X2) ←
$\qquad$ in_order(X1,X2,X3,X4),
$\qquad$ X > X4 | true.

in_order(X1,X2,X1,X2) ←
$\qquad$ X2 ≥ X1 | true.

in_order(X1,X2,X2,X1) ←
$\qquad$ X2 < X1 | true.

slope(e(v(X1,Y1),v(X2,Y2)),M) ←
$\qquad$ M := (Y2 − Y1) / (X2 − X1).

y_intercept(e(v(X1,Y1),v(X2,Y2)),B) ←
$\qquad$ B := Y1 − ((Y2 − Y1) ∗ X1) / (X2 − X1).

% This program is adapted from the quicksort program appearing in Ehud
% Shapiro (Chapter 2).

quicksort(Criteria, Unsorted, Sorted) ←
$\qquad$ qsort(Criteria, Unsorted, Sorted, [ ]).

qsort(Criteria, [X | Unsorted], Sorted, Rest) ←
$\qquad$ partition(Criteria, Unsorted?, X, Smaller, Larger),
$\qquad$ qsort(Criteria, Smaller?, Sorted, [X | Sorted1]),
$\qquad$ qsort(Criteria, Larger?, Sorted1, Rest).

qsort(Criteria, [ ], Rest, Rest).

partition(Criteria, [X | Xs], A, Smaller, [X | Larger]) ←
$\qquad$ leq(Criteria, A, X) |
$\qquad$ partition(Criteria, Xs?, A, Smaller, Larger).

partition(Criteria, [X | Xs], A, [X | Smaller], Larger) ←
$\qquad$ gtr(Criteria, A, X) |
$\qquad$ partition(Criteria, Xs?, A, Smaller, Larger).

partition(Criteria, [ ], _, [ ], [ ]).

% Various comparisons, sorting criteria.

leq(line, V1, V2) ←
$\qquad$ vert_leq(V1, V2) |
$\qquad$ true.

gtr(line, V1, V2) ←
$\qquad$ vert_gtr(V1, V2) |
$\qquad$ true.

leq(circle(Center), p(V1, X), p(V2, Y)) ←
    circle_leq(Center, V1, V2) |
    true.

gtr(circle(Center), p(V1, X), p(V2, Y)) ←
    circle_gtr(Center, V1, V2) |
    true.

% Sorting criteria for vertices on a line.

vert_leq(v(X1, Y1), v(X2, Y2)) ←
    $X1 < X2$ | true.

vert_leq(v(X1, Y1), v(X2, Y2)) ←
    $X1 = X2$,
    $Y1 \leq Y2$ |
    true.

vert_gtr(V1, V2) ←
    vert_leq(V2, V1),
    vert_neq(V1, V2) |
    true.

vert_neq(v(X1, Y1), v(X2, Y2)) ←
    $X1 \neq X2$ | true.

vert_neq(v(X1, Y1), v(X2, Y2)) ←
    $Y1 \neq Y2$ | true.

% Sorting criteria for vertices around a central vertex. Each outer vertex defines
% an edge emanating from the center, and the edges are sorted in counterclock-
% wise order. *Note*: These clauses could be simplified immensely with a decent
% arithmetic/trigonometry package.

circle_leq(Center, V1, V2) ←
    same_hemisph(Center, V1, V2) |
    hemisph_leq(Center, V1, V2).

circle_leq(Center, V1, V2) ←
    hemisphere(Center, V1, upper),
    hemisphere(Center, V2, lower) |
    true.

circle_gtr(Center, V1, V2) ←
    circle_leq(Center, V2, V1),
    circle_neq(Center, V1, V2) |
    true.

circle_neq(Center, V1, V2) ←
    same_hemisph(Center, V1, V2) |
    hemisph_neq(Center, V1, V2).

circle_neq(Center, V1, V2) ←
    hemisphere (Center, V1, Hemisph),
    hemisphere(Center, V2, Hemisph1),
    Hemisph ≠ Hemisph1 |
    true.

same_hemisph(Center, V1, V2) ←
    hemisphere(Center, V1, Hemisph),
    hemisphere(Center, V2, Hemisph),
    true.

hemisphere(v(X, Y), v(X1, Y1), upper) ←
    Y1 > Y | true.

hemisphere(v(X, Y), v(X1, Y1), upper) ←
    Y = Y1, X < X1 | true.

hemisphere(v(X, Y), v(X1, Y1), lower) ←
    Y1 < Y | true.

hemisphere(v(X, Y), v(X1, Y1), lower) ←
    Y = Y1, X1 < X | true.

hemisph_leq(Center, V1, V2) ←
    orientation(Center, V1, horiz) |
    true.

hemisph_leq(Center, V1, V2) ←
    arctan(Center, V1, A),
    arctan(Center, V2, A1) |
    A1 ≤ A.

hemisph_neq(Center, V1, V2) ←
    orientation(Center, V1, O),
    orientation(Center, V2, O1),
    O ≠ O1 |
    true.

hemisph_neq(Center, V1, V2) ←
    arctan(Center, V1, A),
    arctan(Center, V2, A1),
    A ≠ A1 |
    true.

orientation(v(X, Y), v(X1, Y), horiz).

orientation(v(X, Y), v(X1, Y1), not_horiz) ←
    Y ≠ Y1 | true.

arctan(v(X, Y), v(X1, Y1), Arctan) ←
    orientation(v(X, Y), v(X1, Y1), not_horiz) |
    Arctan := (X1 – X) / (Y1 – Y).

% Output utility.

write_list(List) ←
    wait_list(List) |
    prolog((write(List), nl)).

wait_list([A | B]) ←
    wait(A) |
    wait_list(B).

Chapter 11

Distributed Programming in Concurrent Prolog

Avner Shafrir and Ehud Shapiro

The Weizmann Institute of Science

Abstract

Implementing distributed systems and algorithms is a notoriously difficult task. This paper reports on the implementation of two distributed algorithms in Concurrent Prolog. The first algorithm, for extrema finding in a unidirectional circle of processes, is simple, and so is its implementation, whose clauses exhibit a one-to-one correspondence with the English description of the process behavior rules. The second algorithm, for finding connected components in a graph, is one of the more complex distributed algorithms we know of. Its implementation exposed the strengths and weaknesses of Concurrent Prolog as a distributed programming language.

11.1 Introduction

This paper is a part of a research programme to explore the expressiveness and the applicability of the programming language Concurrent Prolog (Shapiro, Chapter 2). We set out to investigate the suitability of the language for the implementation of distributed algorithms. We picked out two algorithms. The first algorithm, the "Lord of the Ring" algorithm, is for extrema finding in a unidirectional circle. It uses at most $O(N \log N)$ messages (Dolev et al., 1982). The algorithm is simple, and so is its Concurrent Prolog implementation, which is six clauses long. The implementation exhibits a one-to-one correspondence between the rules of process behavior in the original description of the algorithm, and the Concurrent Prolog clauses. We use the implementation as a tutorial example for the design and implementation of a network of communicating processes and their associated algorithms in Concurrent Prolog.

The second algorithm, "A distributed algorithm for minimum weight spanning trees" (Gallager et al., 1979), is one of the more complex distributed algorithms we have encountered in the literature. Its complexity stems from the desire to minimize the number of messages sent in constructing the spanning tree. The algorithm uses six types of messages. Each process maintains bidirectional communication channels with all adjacent processes, three queues, one mailbox, and a local state consisting of nine elements. The original English description of the algorithm is seven pages long. The algorithm took several weeks to implement. The resulting program is 64 clauses long (320 lines of uncommented code). Its message complexity can be easily shown to be identical to that of the original algorithm.

The rest of the paper is organized as follows. Section 11.1 presents the "Lord of the Ring" algorithm, and Section 11.2 its implementation. Section 11.3 presents the main concepts of the minimum spanning tree (MST) algorithm. The reader is referred to the original reference (Gallager et al., 1979) for its full description. Section 11.4 described the implementation strategy, with an emphasis on the communication mechanism, and the queues and mailbox management. Section 11.5 analyses our experience in thinking, writing, and debugging in Concurrent Prolog. Appendix 11.1 presents the full code of the MST algorithm.

11.2 A Distributed Algorithm for Extrema Finding in a Circle

Consider a circular arrangement of N asynchronous communicating processes in which communication occurs only between neighbors around the circle. All processes have the same program, and differ only by having distinct numbers, say $M_1, M_2, \ldots, M_n$ (known only to the owners). The objective is to obtain an efficient algorithm which finds the maximum of these numbers. The basic idea is based on the fact that, since order of communication is preserved, the effect of the algorithm is as though the activities of the system could be separated into synchronous phases. Initially, at phase 0, all processes are sleeping. In one phase all processes become active and participate in this search. During each phase an active process creates and sends two messages (of two different types), and receives enough information to determine the local maximum out of its current number, and the numbers of the two active processes to its left. If the local maximum is the number of the active processor to its left, it assumes the local maximum as its number and continues as an active process to the next phase. Otherwise, it becomes passive. It is easy to prove that the number of active processes in phase

P+1 is at most half the number of active processes in phase *P*. Therefore, since a passive process acts only as a communication relay (it does not create messages, only forwards them), the total number of messages which are created during the algorithm is reduced approximately by half in each phase.

A process has the following structure:

proc(N,ST,M,L,S,R).

N – The name of the process.

ST – The state of the process (asleep, active, passive)

M – The number of the process, starting as the original process number and while the process remains active, becoming the local maximum

L – Used by an active process to store the number of the active process to its left.

S – Output channel to its right.

R – Input channel from the left.

The algorithm uses messages of two types:

1) *msg(1,i)*
2) *msg(2,i)*

We present the algorithm below exactly as it appears in the original reference (Dolev et al., 1982), combined with the Concurrent Prolog code.
Doing so demonstrates two important properties of Concurrent Prolog:

(1) There is almost a one-to-one correspondence between the english rules describing the behavior of process and its code in Concurrent Prolog.

(2) The code is naturally written in such a way that a process performs one reduction per message. Hence the complexity of the algorithm in terms of the number of messages sent is the same order as the complexity of the code itself.

As a result, when single stepping through the process, we usually have at least one interesting event per process step.

11.2.1 The algorithm and its code

A1) A sleeping process wakes up and sends *msg(1,M)*

```
P1)  proc(N,asleep,M,L,S,R) ←
        send(msg(1,M),S,S1),
        proc(N,active,M,L,S1,R).
```

A2) If a message $msg(1,i)$ arrives do as follows:

   A21) If $I \neq M$ then send $msg(2,I)$ and assign I to L

   A22) Otherwise, global maximum is M, halt.

   P21) proc(N,active,M,L,S,R) ←
          receive(msg(1,I),R,R1)
          M ≠ I |
          send(msg(2,I),S,S1),
          proc(N,active,I,I,S1,R1).

   P22) proc(N,active,M,L,S,R) ←
          receive(msg(1,M),R,R1) |
          halt.

A3) If a message $msg(2,J)$ arrives do as follows

   A31) If L is greater than both J and M
          then assign L to M and send $msg(1,M)$.

   A32) Otherwise, become passive.

   P31) proc(N,active,M,L,S,R) ←
          receive(msg(2,J),R,R1),
          L > J, L > M |
          send(msg(1,L),S,S1),
          proc(N,active,L,L,S1,R1).

   P32) proc(N,active,M,L,S,R) ←
          receive(msg(2,J),R,R1),
          L ≤ max(M, J) |
          proc(N,passive,−,−,S,R1).

A4) Passive processes pass on unchanged messages.

   P4) proc(N,passive,−,−,S,R)←
          receive(Msg,R,R1) |
          send(Msg,S,S1),
          proc(N,passive,−,−,S1,R1).

Send, receive, and halt are defined as follows:

   send(M,[M|X?],X).
   receive(M,[M|X],X?).
   halt.

11.3 A Distributed Algorithm for Minimum Weight Spaning Trees

The complexity of the algorithm prevents us from providing a full description of it. Rather, we try to convey its essential concepts only. The interested reader is referred to the original reference (Gallager et al., 1979).

In the distributed algorithm for minimum weight spanning tree we consider a connected undirected graph with N nodes and E edges, with a distinct finite weight assigned to each edge. The goal of the algorithm is to determine the minimal weight spanning tree (MST) of the graph. Initially each node (or process) knows the weight of each adjacent edge.

Each node performs the same algorithm, which consists of sending messages over adjoining links, waiting for incoming messages, and processing. Messages can be transmitted independently in both directions on an edge. After each node completes its local algorithm, it knows which adjoining edges are in the tree and also knows which edge leads to a particular edge designated as the *core* of the tree, a key concept of the algorithm explained below.

11.3.1 The algorithm

Nodes on the graph are initially asleep. One or more of the nodes then wake up in any order and start their local algorithm. A sleeping node wakes up upon receiving a message from an awakened neighbor, and proceeds with its local algorithm. During the algorithm, fragments of the MST are created all over the graph. The goal of each fragment is to grow, by connecting to other fragments. Based on this fact the algorithm has two major parts:

(A) The nodes of a fragment must cooperatively find the minimum weight outgoing edge (MOE) from the fragment.

(B) Two fragments combine into a higher level fragment at the appropriate time, depending on their levels.

Each fragment (other than a single node, fragment of level 0) has a name known to all the nodes of the fragment. This identity is in fact the weight of a particular edge in the fragment called *the core*. The nodes adjacent to the core-edge are the core-nodes. Each node of the fragment knows the direction (a weight of an outgoing edge) to the core in the fragment. This edge is called the *in-branch*. The core itself is the in-branch of its two adjacent nodes.

When a fragment tries to combine with another fragment, it sends a *connect* message to that fragment. Three cases may occur:

(1) Both fragments are at the same level.

(2) A low level fragment applies to connect to a high level fragment.

(3) A high level fragment applies to connect to a low level fragment.

A new fragment, at some level i, is formed when two fragments of level $i-1$ combine, both having the same MOE. That MOE becomes the core of the new fragment. Its former core-nodes broadcast an *initiate* message to the other nodes of their former fragments. This message is sent outward on the branches (each core-node to its side) and is relayed outward by the intermediate nodes on the tree. The initiate message carries the new fragment level and the identity of that fragment (the weight of the core-edge), providing all nodes of the fragment with this information.

The second case is when a low level fragment A is trying to connect to a high level fragment B. In that case B immediately broadcasts an initiate message to A. This initiate message causes A to become a part of B, where the core and level of the combined fragment are the same as the original core and level of B.

The third case is when a fragment of a higher level A is trying to connect to a fragment of a lower level B. In this case B will not initiate A. If it had done so, $A+B$ would have become an unbalanced fragment. Rather, B places A's request in its queue.

Upon receiving an initiate message, a node starts to search for its MOE. The goal of the search is to find a node with minimal weight that leads to another fragment. This is done by the node classifying each of its adjacent edges into one of three states:

> *Branch*, if the edge is a branch in the current fragment.
>
> *Rejected*, if the node on the other side of this edge has the same fragment name.
>
> *Basic*, if the edge is neither a branch nor rejected.

In order to find its MOE, a node picks the minimum weight edge in basic state and sends a *test* message on it. The test message carries the fragment identity and level as arguments. The node receiving a test message sends back *accept* if its own fragment identity differs from that in the message. Else the edge is put into rejected state and the node sends back *reject* message. When a node receives a reject message, it puts the edge in rejected state and tests the next best basic edge, continuing until it finds the MOE, which is accepted, or until basic edges are exhausted.

We have described how each node in a fragment eventually finds its MOE, if any. Each node must now cooperate by sending a report about its MOE to its core-node, to enable the core-nodes to determine which edge is the MOE in the entire fragment. If all nodes report that no MOE was found, the algorithm is completed. The report message is *report*(W) where W is a weight of a MOE or is infinite if none was found. In particular, a leaf node of the fragment sends a message *report*(W) towards the core; W is the weight of the MOE that the leaf node found out of its basic edges (if none was found, W is infinite). Any other (non-leaf) node collects all the report messages which arrive from its sons (from all the branch edges other then the in-branch edge) and together with the weight of its own MOE (if any) it picks the smallest of these weights, say W, and sends a *report*(W) towards the core.

After the two core-nodes have collected the reports from their sons, they exchange report messages to determine the MOE of the entire fragment. The core node that finds that the MOE is on its side then broadcasts a *change-root message*. This message traces the path to that MOE. (When a node reports to the core about the MOE of its sub-fragment, it stores the direction from which it received that MOE. This what makes it possible to trace this path.) The change-root message changes the In-Branch of the nodes in this path. The in-branch now is the direction to the MOE, since this MOE is going to be the new core. Note that other nodes of the fragment which are not on that path should not be changed.

When a node adjacent to the fragment's MOE receives a change-root message, it tries to connect over this edge with the fragment on the other side. The response to the connect message was explained above.

When a node receives a connect, test or report message, it checks if it can respond to the message, according to the rules of the algorithm. If it cannot do so, it places the message on a queue. Messages on the queue are served normally, when the appropriate conditions are fulfilled.

11.3.2 The implementation

Most of the algorithm was given by Gallager et al. (1979) in an Algol-like format. In this section we explain the mapping of the graph into a communication network, the handling of incoming messages, and the maintenance of the queues.

Mapping the graph into a communication network

Each node has a list of its adjacent edges. An element in the list can be regarded as a record which represents one edge and has the following structure:

(1) Incoming channel for receiving messages from the edge.

(2) Outgoing channel for transmitting messages over the edge.

(3) The weight of the edge.

(4) The state of the edge.

The weight of the edge is unique and can be regarded as its name.

Example. Given a connected graph of 3 nodes and 3 edges, each node (process) in the algorithm holds a list.

> node 1 holds the list:
> [x(A12,A21?,5,basic),x(B13,B31?,6,basic)].
> node 2 holds the list:
> [x(B31,B13?,6,basic),x(C32,C23?,10,basic)].
> node 3 holds the list:
> [x(A21,A12?,5,basic),x(C23,C32?,10,basic)].

For example, when a node wants to communicates over a given edge, i.e., a given weight, it should sequentially search the record of that edge and retrieve from that record the outgoing channel of the edge.

The mechanism for handling incoming messages

Each node has a mailbox, which is a list of messages. The message on the top of the mailbox is the message that the node is currently handling. When a node finishes handling of that message, it removes the message from the mailbox and handles the next one.

Example.

> proc(Name,Adjacency_list,...,[msg(initiate(...))|Mail_box]) ←
> handling the message initiate(X,Y) from edge J,
> proc(Name,Adjacency_list,...,Mail_box).

When the mailbox is empty, the node examines its input channels. The first message that arrives is put in the mailbox; other messages remain on the channels until the mailbox is empty again.

The code for receiving a message from a channel

> proc(Name,Adjacency_list,...,[ ]) ←
> get_msg(Adjacency_list,New_adjacency_list,Msg) |
> proc(Name,New_adjacency_list,...,[Msg|nil]).

Where *get-msg* is defined as follows:

> get_msg(x([Ie,Oe,We,Se]|Gn],[x([Ie1,Oe,We,Se)|Gn],msg(M,We))←
> receive(M,Ie,Ie1) | true.

> get_msg([C|Gn],[C|Gn1],Msg) ←
> get_msg(Gn,Gn1,Msg) | true.

> receive(M,[M|X],X?).

A node P with K edges maintains an adjacency list of K records, When the mailbox of P unifies with nil, P creates a guard *get_msg* which recursively creates at most K guards as follows:

> receive(M,I1,NI1)
> receive(M,I2,NI2)
> ⋮
> receive(M,Ik,NIk)

where Ij is the incoming channel of the edge of weight J in the adjacency list. When a message arrives, say on edge J, *get_msg* then succeeds, providing the node with the message $msg(Msg,J)$ on the top of the mailbox, and with a new adjacency list, the same as before, where the record of the edge of weight J has been changed from $x(Ij,Oj,J,Sj)$ to $x(NIj,Oj,J,Sj)$

> where $Ij = [Msg|NIj?]$

Serving the queue

    The algorithm defines one queue, but the Algol-like code does not imply when and how messages should be dequeued. To implement the algorithm we had to sort this problem out. We chose to use three queues: one for connect messages, a queue for test messages, and a queue for report messages. These queues are served differently, as specified below.

The code: The structure of a process is:

> proc(N,S,G,Q,L,F,...,M)

> 1) N Name
> 2) S State
> 3) G Adjacent list
> 4) Q Three queues, represented as difference-lists:
>   A queue of connect messages.
>   A queue of test messages.
>   A queue of report messages.
> 5) L Level number
>   ⋮
> 12) M Mailbox.

A process is initiated as follows:

> proc(N,sleep,G,q(X\X,Y\Y,Z\Z),0,...,nil).

Example. Let a message *connect(Lr)* be sent from process R on edge J to process P. Let the level Lp of P be smaller than Lr, P enqueue the message *connect(Lr)* together with J.

     proc(N,S,G,Q,Lp,...,[msg(connect(Lr),J)|M]) ←
     Lr ≥ Lp,
     ...
     enqueue(msg(connect(Lr),J),Q,Q1) |
     proc(N,S,G,Q1,Lp,...,M).

enqueue, places the connect message in its queue. Messages are dequeued from those queues at different times: connect queue upon receiving initiate message; test queue after a node changes its level; report queue after a node changes its state.

Example of dequeueing.

     state(Old_state,New_state,Old_queues,New_queues,Old_mail,New_mail).

is defined as follows:

     state(find,found,q(Q1,Q2,R_queue),q(Q1,Q2,X\X),Mail,Mail1)←
     appmail(R_queue,Mail,Mail1).

Where appending the messages to the mail is defined by the clause:

     appmail(H\T,T,H).

Which means: If state was changed from *find* to *found*, empty the queue of the report messages and append the messages on the end of the mailbox, where the messages will be served again. For example:

     proc(N,S,G,Q,L,...,msg(initiate(L,F,S),J).M) ←
     ...
     a process which may change states from S to S1,
     ...
     state(S,S1,Q,Q1,M,M1) |
     proc(N,S1,G,Q1,L,...,M1).

We have demonstrated some solutions for the main problems of the algorithm. After we had established these solutions, the rest was just mapping each rule of the algorithm into one clause in Concurrent Prolog. The resulting program is included as Appendix 11.1.

11.4 Conclusions

We have shown that Concurrent Prolog is a natural specification and implementation language for distributed algorithms. Concurrent Prolog clauses seem to be of the right granularity for specifying one process action, and the preconditions for such an action to take place. Often there are cases in which there is a one-to-one correspondence between the natural language description of the algorithm and Concurrent Prolog clauses. In the first algorithm, the transformation of the process behavior rules to executable Concurrent Prolog clauses was a rather mechanical operation.

The language supports modular programming, since there is no interdependence between clauses, and each clause can be written and debugged independently. Hence algorithms can be developed piecewise, and an incomplete implementation of an algorithm is often runable, and hence debugable. The uniformity of Concurrent Prolog aids in designing complex communication networks. There is no distinction between local variables and channel variables, or between streams, lists, and other data-structures.

On the other hand, the detailed case analysis — making sure that each combination of process state and incoming message has a clause that handles it — cannot be avoided, and doing it manually is a painful and error-prone activity. An automatic programming aid for the detection of untreated cases, cases which are treated by more than one clause, and other inconsistencies in the case analysis would be of great value.

One source of our programming difficulties might be attributed to the behavioral, rather then declarative, approach we have taken towards distributed programming in Concurrent Prolog. Thinking declaratively about distributed Concurrent Prolog programs means thinking about process histories, rather than about process actions. Each process can be viewed as computing a relation over message streams, and clauses as defining recurrence relations over these streams, i.e., defining legal histories of process actions inductively.

The general scheme of a clause for handling a specific type of message is:

> process(State1,...) ←
>   receive a message Message and other conditions |
>   transform State1 into State2, and send Responses,
>   process(State2,...).

State1 and the incoming message *M* are all that we need to determine the next operation, and no global information is needed.

For example consider the clause:

> process(State,Input,Output) ←
>   receive(Message,Input,NewInput) |
>   respond(State,Message,NewState,Response),
>   send(Response,Output,NewOutput),
>   process(NewState,NewInput,NewOutput).

It can be read, behaviorally: "if a process in state *State* receives *Message* on its input stream, then it sends *Response* on its output stream and enters *New-State*". Declaratively, it says: "if the following holds: *NewInput* and *NewOutput* constitute a legal I/O behavior for a process in initial state *NewState*; a process in state *State* can respond to *Message* with *Response* and enter state *NewState*; *Input=[Message|NewInput]*; and *Output=[Response|NewOutput]*, then *Input* and *Output* are legal I/O behaviors for a process in initial state *State*".

We believe that sophisticated programming tools, such as debuggers, can exploit the declarative reading by examining and analyzing process histories, possibly using concepts of Algorithmic Debugging (Shapiro, 1982; Takeuchi, Chapter 26). As long as such tools are not available, we do not find the declarative reading superior to the behavioral one, in spite of what the "ideology" of logic programming suggests.

The ability to treat each case in a separate clause also contributes to the modularity of Concurrent Prolog programs, and supports easy debugging and tracing, since all the information necessary to understand a process operation is given in a reduction.

Another implication of the granularity of Concurrent Prolog is the strong correspondence between high-level algorithm steps (e.g., messages sent) and Concurrent Prolog process reductions. Hence it is not difficult to ensure that the implementation achieves the complexity bounds claimed for the algorithm.

Concurrent Prolog might be too powerful, as is, to be a programming language for geographically distributed systems. The main problem is the ability of processes to share all kinds of data-structures, not only streams, and to send incomplete messages (i.e., messages that contain variables). Nevertheless, it is possible to conceive of a subset of Concurrent Prolog that is suitable as a simulation language for such systems, and, eventually, also as a programming language for them. The Concurrent Prolog programs in this paper would belong to this subset.

Acknowledgements

This research was supported by IBM Poughkeepsie, Data Systems Division. William Silverman assisted in editing this paper.

Appendix 11.1: A Concurrent Prolog implementation of the Distributed Minimum Weight Spanning Trees algorithm

This program was developed using a Concurrent Prolog interpreter written in Waterloo Prolog. The syntactic conventions of the underlying Prolog were observed. In particular, '.' is the list constructor, '*' is an anonymous variable, and '&' is the conjunction operator.

Data structure

Tree = t(Signal,Graph).t(Signal1,Graph1)...nil

    Signal = Start signal (0-start, 1-sleep)
    Graph = x(Ie,Oe,We,Se).x(Ie1,Oe1,We1,Se1)...nil
      Ie = incoming edge.
      Oe = outgoing edge.
      We = weight of an edge.
      Se = state of an edge.

proc (Nn,Sn,Gn,Qn,Ln,Fn,Be,Wt,Te,Ib,En,Mn).
    1) Nn = Name of a process (debugging aid).
    2) Sn = State of the proc(sleep,find,found).
    3) Gn = Graph. (Communication channels, weight & state of an edge)
    4) Qn = 3 queues. init: (Empty difference lists)
    5) Ln = Phase number. init: 0
    6) Fn = Fragment name.
    7) Be = Best edge.
    8) Wt = Best Wt
    9) Te = Test edge
  10) Ib   = In branch
  11) En = List. init: nil.
  12) Mn = Mail list. init: nil or start.nil

Spreading the tree

/* *t(I,Gn)* represents a node. If *I* is 0 the node is initiated with a 'start' message
in its mailbox; otherwise the mailbox will be empty, i.e initiated with nil. *Gn*
is the adjacency list of the node. It includes the communication channels, the
weight and the state of each edge of the node. */

mst(t(0,Gn).Xs,N) ←
    N1 := N + 1 |
    mst(Xs,N1) &
    proc(N1,sleep,Gn,q(C\C,T\T,R\R),0,*,*,*,*,*,nil,start.nil).

mst(t(1,Gn).Xs,N) ←
    N1 := N + 1 |
    mst(Xs,N1) &
    proc(N1,sleep,Gn,q(C\C,T\T,R\R),0,*,*,*,*,*,nil,nil).

mst(nil,*).

Get_msg procedure, Executed when mailbox is empty (nil)

proc(Nn,Sn,Gn,Qn,Ln,Fn,Be,Wt,Te,Ib,En,nil) ←
    get_msg(Gn,Gn1,Msg) |
    proc(Nn,Sn,Gn1,Qn,Ln,Fn,Be,Wt,Te,Ib,En,Msg.nil).

get_msg(x(Ie,Oe,We,Se).Gn,x(Ie1,Oe,We,Se).Gn,msg(M,We)) ←
    receive(M,Ie?,Ie1) | true.
get_msg(X.Gn,X.Gn1,Msg) ←
    get_msg(Gn,Gn1,Msg) | true.

receive(M,M.X,X?).
send(M,M.X,X).

Select edge record

/* Given a weight W or edge state Se, Select finds in the adjacency list of the
node, the communication record of that edge. Select may replace that record
with a new record. */

select(x(I,O,W,S),x(I,O,W,S).Gn,New,New.Gn).

select(x(I,O,W,S),x(Ie,Oe,We,Se).Gn,New,x(Ie,Oe,We,Se).Gn1) ←
    or(We ≠ W,S ≠ Se) |
    select(x(I,O,W,S),Gn,New,Gn1).

select(x(*,*,0,*),nil,*,nil).

Procedure WAKEUP

proc(Nn,sleep,Gn,Qn,Ln,Fn,Be,Wt,Te,Ib,En,start.nil) ←
    select(x(Ie,Oe,We,basic),Gn,x(Ie,Oe1,We,branch),Gn1) |
    send(connect(Ln),Oe,Oe1) &
    proc(Nn,found,Gn1,Qn,Ln,We,Be,Wt,Te,Ib,En,nil).

Response to Connect

proc(Nn,sleep,Gn,Qn,Ln,Fn,Be,Wt,Te,Ib,En,msg(connect(L),W).Mn) ←
    select(x(Ie,Oe,We,basic),Gn,x(Ie,Oe1,We,branch),Gn1) |
    send(connect(Ln),Oe,Oe1) &
    proc(Nn,found,Gn1,Qn,Ln,We,Be,Wt,Te,Ib,En,msg(connect(L),W).Mn).

proc(Nn,Sn,Gn,Qn,Ln,Fn,Be,Wt,Te,Ib,En,msg(connect(L),W).Mn) ←
    L < Ln &
    Sn =?= found &
    select(x(Ie,Oe,W,Se),Gn,x(Ie,Oe1,W,branch),Gn1) |
    send(initiate(Ln,Fn,Sn),Oe,Oe1) &

proc(Nn,Sn,Gn1,Qn,Ln,Fn,Be,Wt,Te,Ib,En,Mn).

proc(Nn,Sn,Gn,Qn,Ln,Fn,Be,Wt,Te,Ib,En,msg(connect(L),W).Mn) ←
    L < Ln &
    Sn =?= find &
    select(x(Ie,Oe,W,Se),Gn,x(Ie,Oe1,W,branch),Gn1) &
    add(W,En,En1) |
    send(initiate(Ln,Fn,Sn),Oe,Oe1) &
    proc(Nn,Sn,Gn1,Qn,Ln,Fn,Be,Wt,Te,Ib,W.En,Mn).

proc(Nn,Sn,Gn,Qn,Ln,Fn,Be,Wt,Te,Ib,En,msg(connect(L),W).Mn) ←
    L ≥ Ln &
    Sn ≠ sleep &
    select(x(Ie,Oe,W,basic),Gn,*,*) &
    enqueue(msg(connect(L),W),Qn,Qn1) |
    proc(Nn,Sn,Gn,Qn1,Ln,Fn,Be,Wt,Te,Ib,En,Mn).

proc(Nn,Sn,Gn,Qn,Ln,Fn,Be,Wt,Te,Ib,En,msg(connect(L),W).Mn) ←
    L ≥ Ln &
    Sn ≠ sleep &
    select(x(Ie,Oe,W,Se),Gn,x(Ie,Oe1,W,Se),Gn1) &
    Se ≠ basic &
    NL := Ln + 1 |
    send(initiate(NL,W,find),Oe,Oe1) &
    proc(Nn,Sn,Gn1,Qn,Ln,Fn,Be,Wt,Te,Ib,En,Mn).

Response to Initiate

proc(Nn,Sn,Gn,q(C,T,R),Ln,Fn,Be,Wt,Te,Ib,En,msg(initiate(L,F,S),J).Mn) ←
    sub_queue(msg(connect(X),J),C,C1) |
    proc(Nn,Sn,Gn,q(C1,T,R),Ln,Fn,Be,Wt,Te,Ib,En,msg(connect(X),J)
    .msg(initiate(L,F,S),J).Mn).

proc(Nn,Sn,Gn,Qn,Ln,Fn,Be,Wt,Te,Ib,En,msg(initiate(L,F,S),J).Mn) ←
    S =?= find &
    init_fragment(initiate(L,F,S),J,Gn,Gn1,En,En1) &
    exec_test(test(L,F),Gn1?,Gn2,Te1,En1?,S,Sn1,100,J) &
    phase(L,Ln,Qn,Qn1,Mn,Mn1) &
    state(S,Sn1,Qn1,Qn2,Mn1,Mn2) |
    proc(Nn,Sn1,Gn2,Qn2,L,F,0,100,Te1,J,En1,Mn2).

proc(Nn,Sn,Gn,Qn,Ln,Fn,Be,Wt,Te,Ib,En,msg(initiate(L,F,S),J).Mn) ←
    S ≠ find &
    init_fragment(initiate(L,F,S),J,Gn,Gn1,En,En1) &
    phase(L,Ln,Qn,Qn1,Mn,Mn1) &

```
    state(Sn,S,Qn1,Qn2,Mn1,Mn2) |
    proc(Nn,S,Gn1,Qn2,L,F,0,100,Te,J,En,Mn2).
```

Initiate fragment

```
init_fragment(Msg,J,x(Ie,Oe,We,Se).Gn,x(Ie,Oe1,We,Se).Gn1,En,We.En1) ←
    not_member(We,En) &
    Se =?= branch &
    We ≠ J &
    send(Msg,Oe,Oe1) |
    init_fragment(Msg,J,Gn,Gn1,En,En1).

init_fragment(Msg,J,x(Ie,Oe,We,Se).Gn,x(Ie,Oe1,We,Se).Gn1,En,En1) ←
    member(We,En) &
    Se =?= branch &
    We ≠ J &
    send(Msg,Oe,Oe1) |
    init_fragment(Msg,J,Gn,Gn1,En,En1).

init_fragment(Msg,J,x(Ie,Oe,We,Se).Gn,x(Ie,Oe,We,Se).Gn1,En,En1) ←
    or(We =?= J, Se ≠ branch ) |
    init_fragment(Msg,J,Gn,Gn1,En,En1).

init_fragment(*,*,nil,nil,En,En).
```

Response to Test

```
proc(Nn,sleep,Gn,Qn,Ln,Fn,Be,Wt,Te,Ib,En,msg(test(L,F),J).Mn) ←
    select(x(Ie,Oe,We,basic),Gn,x(Ie,Oe1,We,branch),Gn1) |
    send(connect(Ln),Oe,Oe1) &
    proc(Nn,found,Gn1,Qn,Ln,We,Be,Wt,Te,Ib,En,msg(test(L,F),J).Mn).

proc(Nn,Sn,Gn,Qn,Ln,Fn,Be,Wt,Te,Ib,En,msg(test(L,F),J).Mn) ←
    Sn ≠ sleep &
    L > Ln &
    enqueue(msg(test(L,F),J),Qn,Qn1) |
    proc(Nn,Sn,Gn,Qn1,Ln,Fn,Be,Wt,Te,Ib,En,Mn).

proc(Nn,Sn,Gn,Qn,Ln,Fn,Be,Wt,Te,Ib,En,msg(test(L,F),J).Mn) ←
    Sn ≠ sleep &
    L ≤ Ln &
    F ≠ Fn &
    select(x(Ie,Oe,J,Se),Gn,x(Ie,Oe1,J,Se),Gn1) |
    send(accept,Oe,Oe1) &
    proc(Nn,Sn,Gn1,Qn,Ln,Fn,Be,Wt,Te,Ib,En,Mn).
```

proc(Nn,Sn,Gn,Qn,Ln,Fn,Be,Wt,Te,Ib,En,msg(test(L,F),J).Mn) ←
    Sn ≠ sleep &
    Fn =?= F &
    L ≤ Ln &
    Te ≠ J &
    select(x(Ie,Oe,J,Se),Gn,x(Ie,Oe1,J,Se1),Gn1) &
    change_state(Se,Se1) |
    send(reject,Oe,Oe1) &
    proc(Nn,Sn,Gn1,Qn,Ln,Fn,Be,Wt,Te,Ib,En,Mn).

proc(Nn,Sn,Gn,Qn,Ln,Fn,Be,Wt,Te,Ib,En,msg(test(L,F),J).Mn) ←
    Sn ≠ sleep &
    Fn =?= F &
    Te =?= J &
    L ≤ Ln &
    select(x(Ie,Oe,J,Se),Gn,x(Ie,Oe,J,Se1),Gn1) &
    change_state(Se,Se1) &
    exec_test(test(Ln,Fn),Gn1,Gn2,Te1,En,Sn,Sn1,Wt,Ib) &
    state(Sn,Sn1,Qn,Qn1,Mn,Mn1) |
    proc(Nn,Sn1,Gn2,Qn1,Ln,Fn,Be,Wt,Te1,Ib,En,Mn1).

Procedure test and report

exec_test(Msg,Gn,Gn1,We,*,Sn,Sn,*,*) ←
    select(x(Ie,Oe,We,basic),Gn,x(Ie,Oe1,We,basic),Gn1) &
    We ≠ 0 |
    send(Msg,Oe,Oe1).

exec_test(Msg,Gn,Gn1,0,En,Sn,Sn1,Wt,Ib) ←
    select(x(Ie,We,W,basic),Gn,*,*) &
    W =?= 0 &
    report(0,En,Wt,Ib,Gn,Gn1,Sn,Sn1) |
    true.

report(0,nil,Wt,Ib,Gn,Gn1,Sn,found) ←
    select(x(Ie,Oe,Ib,Se),Gn,x(Ie,Oe1,Ib,Se),Gn1) |
    send(report(Wt),Oe,Oe1).

report(Te,En,Wt,Ib,Gn,Gn,Sn,Sn) ← Te ≠ 0 | true.

report(Te,X.Xs,Wt,Ib,Gn,Gn,Sn,Sn).

Response to Accept

proc(Nn,Sn,Gn,Qn,Ln,Fn,Be,Wt,Te,Ib,En,msg(accept,J).Mn) ←

J < Wt &
report(0,En,J,Ib,Gn,Gn1,Sn,Sn1) &
state(Sn,Sn1,Qn,Qn1,Mn,Mn1) |
proc(Nn,Sn1,Gn1,Qn1,Ln,Fn,J,J,0,Ib,En,Mn1).

proc(Nn,Sn,Gn,Qn,Ln,Fn,Be,Wt,Te,Ib,En,msg(accept,J).Mn) ←
J ≥ Wt &
report(0,En,Wt,Ib,Gn,Gn1,Sn,Sn1) &
state(Sn,Sn1,Qn,Qn1,Mn,Mn1) |
proc(Nn,Sn1,Gn1,Qn1,Ln,Fn,Be,Wt,0,Ib,En,Mn1).

Response to Reject

proc(Nn,Sn,Gn,Qn,Ln,Fn,Be,Wt,Te,Ib,En,msg(reject,J).Mn) ←
select(x(Ie,Oe,J,Se),Gn,x(Ie,Oe,J,Se1),Gn1) &
change_state(Se,Se1) &
exec_test(test(Ln,Fn),Gn1,Gn2,Te1,En,Sn,Sn1,Wt,Ib) &
state(Sn,Sn1,Qn,Qn1,Mn,Mn1) |
proc(Nn,Sn1,Gn2,Qn1,Ln,Fn,Be,Wt,Te1,Ib,En,Mn1).

Response to Report

proc(Nn,Sn,Gn,Qn,Ln,Fn,Be,Wt,Te,Ib,En,msg(report(W),J).Mn) ←
J ≠ Ib &
sub(J,En,En1) &
W ≥ Wt &
report(Te,En1?,Wt,Ib,Gn,Gn1,Sn,Sn1) &
state(Sn,Sn1,Qn,Qn1,Mn,Mn1) |
proc(Nn,Sn1,Gn1,Qn1,Ln,Fn,Be,Wt,Te,Ib,En1,Mn1).

proc(Nn,Sn,Gn,Qn,Ln,Fn,Be,Wt,Te,Ib,En,msg(report(W),J).Mn) ←
J ≠ Ib &
sub(J,En,En1) &
W < Wt &
report(Te,En1?,W,Ib,Gn,Gn1,Sn,Sn1) &
state(Sn,Sn1,Qn,Qn1,Mn,Mn1) |
proc(Nn,Sn1,Gn1,Qn1,Ln,Fn,J,W,Te,Ib,En1,Mn1).

proc(Nn,Sn,Gn,Qn,Ln,Fn,Be,Wt,Te,Ib,En,msg(report(W),J).Mn) ←
J =?= Ib & Sn =?= find &
enqueue(msg(report(W),J),Qn,Qn1) |
proc(Nn,Sn,Gn,Qn1,Ln,Fn,Be,Wt,Te,Ib,En,Mn).

proc(Nn,Sn,Gn,Qn,Ln,Fn,Be,Wt,Te,Ib,En,msg(report(W),J).Mn) ←
J =?= Ib & Sn ≠ find &

W > Wt |
  proc(Nn,Sn,Gn,Qn,Ln,Fn,Be,Wt,Te,Be,En,msg(change,*).Mn).

proc(Nn,Sn,Gn,Qn,Ln,Fn,Be,Wt,Te,Ib,En,msg(report(W),J).Mn) ←
  J =?= Ib & Sn $\overline{\text{find}}$ &
  W =?= 100 & Wt =?= 100 |
  proc(Nn,Sn,Gn,Qn,Ln,Fn,Be,Wt,Te,Ib,En,msg(halt,*).Mn).

proc(Nn,Sn,Gn,Qn,Ln,Fn,Be,Wt,Te,Ib,En,msg(report(W),J).Mn) ←
  J =?= Ib & Sn ≠ find &
  W ≤ Wt & or(W ≠ 100 , Wt ≠ 100) |
  proc(Nn,Sn,Gn,Qn,Ln,Fn,Be,Wt,Te,Ib,En,Mn).

Change_root procedure

/* If the change msg is inside sub-tree just change directions */

rroc(Nn,Sn,Gn,Qn,Ln,Fn,Be,Wt,Te,Ib,En,msg(change,J).Mn) ←
  select(x(Ie,Oe,Be,Se),Gn,x(Ie,Oe1,Be,Se),Gn1) &
  Se =?= branch |
  send(change,Oe,Oe1) &
  proc(Nn,Sn,Gn1,Qn,Ln,Fn,Be,Wt,Te,Be,En,Mn).

/* If the change msg is a leaf of sub-tree then to connect   */

proc(Nn,Sn,Gn,Qn,Ln,Fn,Be,Wt,Te,Ib,En,msg(change,J).Mn) ←
  select(x(Ie,Oe,Be,Se),Gn,x(Ie,Oe1,Be,branch),Gn1) &
  Se =?= basic |
  send(connect(Ln),Oe,Oe1) &
  proc(Nn,Sn,Gn1,Qn,Ln,Fn,Be,Wt,Te,Be,En,Mn).

/* Halt */

proc(Nn,Sn,Gn,Qn,Ln,Fn,Be,Wt,Te,Ib,En,msg(halt,*).Mn) ←
  send_halt(Nn,Gn).

send_halt(Nn,x(Ie,Oe,We,branch).Gn) ←
  send(halt,Oe,Oe1) &
  write(proc(Nn,We)) |
  send_halt(Nn,Gn).

send_halt(Nn,x(Ie,Oe,We,Se).Gn) ←
  Se ≠ branch |
  send_halt(Nn,Gn).

send_halt(Nn,nil).

Utilities

add(X,X.Xs,X.Xs).
add(X,Y.Xs,Y.Zs) ← X ≠ Y | add(X,Xs,Zs).
add(X,nil,X.nil).

sub(X,X.Xs,Xs).
sub(X,Y.Xs,Y.Ys) ← X ≠ Y | sub(X,Xs,Ys).
sub(X,nil,nil).

member(X,X.Xs).
member(X,Y.Xs) ← X ≠ Y | member(X,Xs).

not_member(X,Y.Xs) ← X ≠ Y | not_member(X,Xs).
not_member(X,nil).

or(X,Y) ← X | true.
or(X,Y) ← Y | true.

change_state(X,rejected) ← X =?= basic | true.
change_state(X,X) ← X ≠ basic | true.

enq(X,H-X.T,H-T).
deq(X,X.H-T,H-T).

appmail(H\T,T,H).

sub_queue(M,H\T,H1\T) ←
    s(H,T,M,H1).

s(nil,*,*,*) ← 1 = 0.
s(M.H,T,M,H).
s(M1.H,T,M,H1) ← M1 ≠ M | s(H,T,M,H1).

enqueue(msg(connect(X),Y),q(C,*1,*2),q(C1,*1,*2)) ←
    enq(msg(connect(X),Y),C,C1).

cnqueue(msg(test(X,Y),Z),q(*1,T,*2),q(*1,T1,*2)) ←
    enq(msg(test(X,Y),Z),T,T1).

enqueue(msg(report(X),Y),q(*1,*2,R),q(*1,*2,R1)) ←
    enq(msg(report(X),Y),R,R1).

dequeue(report,q(*1,*2,R),q(*1,*2,X\X),Mn,Mn1) ←
    appmail(R,Mn,Mn1).

dequeue(test,q(*1,T,*2),q(*1,X\X,*2),Mn,Mn1) ←
    appmail(T,Mn,Mn1).

dequeue(connect,q(C,*1,*2),q(X-X,*1,*2),Mn,Mn1) ←

appmail(C,Mn,Mn1).

phase(L,Ln,Qn,Qn2,Mn,Mn2) ←
    L > Ln |
    dequeue(test,Qn,Qn1,Mn,Mn1) &
    dequeue(connect,Qn1?,Qn2,Mn1?,Mn2).

phase(L,Ln,Qn,Qn,Mn,Mn) ←
    L ≤ Ln |
    true.

state(Sn,Sn1,Qn,Qn1,Mn,Mn1) ←
    Sn =?= find &
    Sn1 =?= found |
    dequeue(report,Qn,Qn1,Mn,Mn1).

state(Sn,Sn1,Qn,Qn,Mn,Mn) ←
    or(Sn1 ≠ found , Sn =?= found) | true.

Chapter 12

Image Processing with Concurrent Prolog

Shimon Edelman and Ehud Shapiro

The Weizmann Institute of Science

Abstract

The conventional parallel languages for image processing, such as Pascal enhanced with parallel-do instructions, are usually limited to cellular architectures in which simple arithmetical operations are carried out on the neighborhood of each pixel of the image simultaneously. In contrast with that, Concurrent Prolog is the first step towards a more expressive parallel language, better suited for symbolic image processing and computer vision. In this chapter we present the Concurrent Prolog implementations of several algorithms related to quadtrees, an important data structure for image processing. These implementations served as a test-bed for the development of message-passing techniques peculiar to this field of application. The experience thus gained was crucial to the formulation of a new fast curve tracing algorithm, described in Section 12.4. The availability of a Concurrent Prolog interpreter permitted actual implementation and testing of the quadtree and curve tracing algorithms.

12.1 Introduction

This paper describes a Concurrent Prolog implementation of quadtrees and quad pyramids, two related hierarchical data structures extensively used in image processing and computer vision. We show how to construct recursively an active quadtree or pyramid: a network in which there is a process corresponding to every tree or pyramid vertex, and a communication channel to every edge. We then outline several application algorithms which run on these process networks.

Previously published active quadtree algorithms (Dyer and Rosenfeld, 1981) were not concerned with the details of the underlying execution mechanism. As a counterpoint to this "abstract" approach to algorithm specification, our algorithms have been designed with Concurrent Prolog (Shapiro, Chapter 2) as the target implementation language, and the two-dimensional processing surface (Shapiro, 1983a) as the associated hardware model. Moreover, the curve tracing algorithm of Section 12.4 has a natural interpretation in terms of a spread of activation in a network of communicating processes (Edelman, 1987). Its design would have been much harder without a clear, working computation model for such a network.

The paper organization is as follows. The rest of this section is an overview of quadtrees and their use in image processing. Section 12.2 presents and analyzes several quadtree-building algorithms. The implementation of an optimal algorithm is discussed in detail. Section 12.3 contains two examples of computations that use a quadtree process-structure, one straightforward and the other more complicated. Section 12.4 outlines pyramid-related algorithms. Finally, Section 12.5 summarizes the experience gained in the design and the implementation of the algorithms. Sample runs and the full code of the programs were given by Edelman and Shapiro (1985).

12.1.1 Quadtrees in image processing

Quadtrees, trees of out-degree four, are a convenient way of region representation in binary images. This representation may be seen as the division of the picture into maximal square blocks such that each block has a constant value. For a $2^k \times 2^k$ image array, the root of the tree corresponds to the entire image. If the array does not consist only of 1's or 0's, then it is subdivided into four $2^{k-1} \times 2^{k-1}$ quadrants represented by the four children in the tree (Figure 12.1). This process is repeated for each of the quadrants until blocks consisting entirely of 1's or 0's are obtained. These leaf nodes are called *black* and *white*, respectively. Nonleaf nodes represent mixed regions and are said to be *gray*. The tree is usually unbalanced and has height of at most k. A recent complete survey of quadtrees and related topics was given by Samet (1984).

12.1.2 Active quadtrees

An active quadtree may be built by assigning a process to each node and connecting the processes according to the tree structure. The active quadtree represents the image. Its number of processes is generally smaller than the number needed for a cellular network representing the same region as a binary array (raster).

Dubitzki et al. (1981) outline several region property computation algorithms

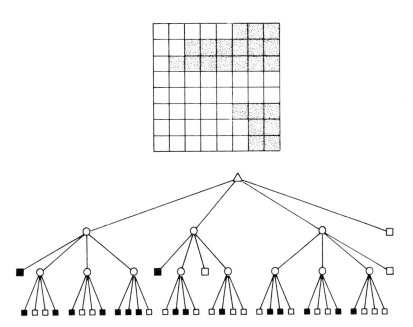

Figure 12.1: A binary array and its quadtree representation

for active quadtrees. The Euler number (genus), perimeter, area, distance transform and centroid can be computed in $O(\text{tree height}) = O(\log(\text{image diameter}))$ time.

12.2 Parallel Algorithms for Quadtree-Building

There are two types of parallel quadtree-building algorithms — top-down and bottom-up. We will consider two of each, noticing first that for a $2^k \times 2^k$ planar grid of processors with links only between the immediate neighbors, an optimal quadtree-building algorithm will take $O(2^k)$ time to determine the tree structure. Indeed, this is the minimal time (in terms of the number of messages passed) it takes the farthest node in the grid to communicate its value to the would-be root, no matter where the latter may be situated.

Consider first the following version of the top-down approach.

Algorithm TD-1:

(1) Build a pyramidal structure, starting from the root and passing down the image data.

If the image is not already represented in a quadtree form, then additional action is needed:

(2) Merge the leaves until maximal blocks are obtained.   ■

TD-1 may be implemented in Concurrent Prolog in a way resembling the H-tree implementation (Shapiro, 1983a). This algorithm requires either a preprocessing stage or a lot of unnecessary building, since the whole pyramid contains

$$2^{2k} + 2^{2(k-1)} + \ldots + 4 + 1 = (2^{2k+2} - 1)/3$$

nodes, the majority of which will be merged. In addition, being top-down, TD-1 cannot utilize parallel image input, which is crucial in applying parallel image-processing techniques to real-life problems.

Another kind of top-down algorithm, which can exploit the possibility of parallel image input, is shown below.

Algorithm TD-2 (Dubitzki et al., 1981):

(1) On a surface of processors spread a square array, representing the binary image.

(2) Construct a breadth-first spanning tree of the array.

(3) The leaves of the tree send their values up. A node relays a "different" signal up if the values of its children differ from each other; otherwise, the common color is relayed upwards.

(4) After $O(2^k)$ time, the distinguished node of the array, which is the spanning tree root, receives either a "different" signal, or a value. In the latter case, the quadtree has only one node, the root. In the former case, the array is subdivided into four quadrants and steps 2–4 are repeated for each of them.   ■

This algorithm has the following advantages:

-- The maximum number of active processes needed to support it is less by one third than the maximum of TD-1, and equals 2^{2k};

-- The running time, $O(2^k)$, is optimal. Indeed, at each stage the time required to check a block for uniformity and to subdivide it if necessary is O(block diameter). The successive block diameters are $2^k, 2^{k-1}, 2^{k-2}, \ldots, 1$, hence the total time is $O(2^k)$.

The main disadvantages of TD-2 are these:

–   The uniformity check is made in a redundant way, i.e., small blocks repeat the same check many times (with the same results);

–   Finding the distinguished node at successive stages is not as simple as might be (they must be sought out by a precalculated sequence of turns and advances).

Both these disadvantages stem from the top-down approach, which runs counter to Concurrent Prolog's "local" orientation. The result is unaesthetic code having less than optimal efficiency when executed on a distributed machine.

A better performance may be achieved by switching to a bottom-up approach, as follows.

Algorithm BU-1 (Dyer and Rosenfeld, 1981):

(1)   Start with the same processor array as TD-2.

(2)   Each node sends its value to its would-be parent (see Figure 12.2).

(3)   The parents check uniformity and decide whether to perform a merge.

(4)   This procedure is repeated on successively larger scales until the whole quadtree is grown.   ■

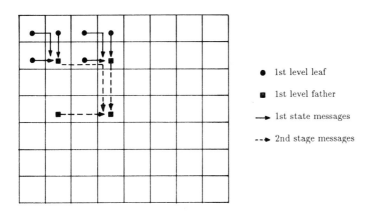

Figure 12.2: Algorithm BU-1: message-passing on the first two levels

BU-1 has all the advantages of TD-2 and none of its shortcomings. However, when trying to implement it, one realizes that each currently active node has to compute the direction and distance to its parent. ·This complication is unnecessary, as we shall see shortly.

12.2.1 An optimal parallel quadtree-building algorithm

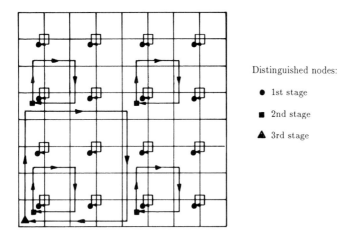

Figure 12.3: Algorithm BU-2: message-passing and the distinguished nodes

Algorithm BU-2 differs from BU-1 only in the pattern of message-passing. A single kind of message is used throughout the building process. Each message is issued by a distinguished node of the current stage and traverses a closed circuit (see Figure 12.3); note that at each stage there are several distinguished nodes and the messages propagate in parallel. The message structure is uniform at all stages and contains five variables:

M – travel distance,
S – current stage number,
NS – next stage number,
C – color,
Ls – list of contributions.

The node processes have the following structure:

$$\text{node(Synch,Ins,IJ,C,F,L,R,B,T,Q,S)},$$

where the parameters are:

$Synch$ – synchronization variable (for simulation only),
Ins – input stream,
IJ – coordinates,
C – color,

F – image frame size,
L – left channel,
R – right channel,
B – bottom channel,
T – top channel,
Q – local stack,
S – state.

Messages are sent by the distinguished nodes on their T ("Top") links. The nodes that have been distinguished during the previous stage save their contributions for the current stage on a local stack and wait till the messages arrive that will collect them. Each node traversal decreases M by 1. When M becomes equal to 1, a distinguished node from the previous stage has been reached. The code for the node process is shown in Program 12.1; the utility predicates (*get, put, push, pop*) are defined in Appendix 12.1.

Several actions are performed at this place:

(1)   The node compares the color stored from the previous stage with the color carried by the message. This comparison decides the color of the outgoing message.

(2)   The second stored value is contributed to the list (consed with Ls). This value is a parent-link (a variable) if a non-leaf was formed at the previous stage by this node; if a leaf was formed, then the value is the color of that leaf.

(3)   The node restores M to its initial value for the current stage and sends the new message to its right (see Figure 12.3).

The messages continue advancing (and turning, each time when M becomes equal to 1), collecting the current stage contributions, until each one gets back to its originating node (the code for the rest of the journey — three more "legs" — is not shown.

The first time M is equal to 1 and the message arrives from the right, the loop is completed and the message returns to the originating node. A decision is then made whether this node will be distinguished in the coming stage also. If not, it stores the information brought by the message about the quadrant it was responsible for and waits until another message arrives to collect this information. If the node is again distinguished, it starts a new cycle.

If the incoming message carries *gray* color, then the nodes it represents will not be able to participate in any future merges, so that a quadtree portion may be spawned for these nodes. If the message is *black* or *white*, the decision whether to spawn is delayed until the next stage is done. The spawning is done as shown in Program 12.2.

node(Synch,Ins,IJ,C,F,L,R,B,T,Q,start) ←
    distinguished(IJ,2) |
    put(m(1,1,2,C,[C]),T,T1),
    node(Synch,Ins,IJ,C,F,L,R,B,T1?,Q,work).
node(Synch,Ins,IJ,C,F,L,R,B,T,Q,start) ←
    nondistinguished(IJ,2) |
    push(q(C,C),Q,Q1),
    node(Synch,Ins,IJ,C,F,L,R,B,T,Q1?,work).
node(Synch,Ins,IJ,C,F,L,R,B,T,Q,work) ←
    get(m(M,S,NS,C1,Ls),B,B1),
    M > 1 |
    M1 := M – 1,
    put(m(M1?,S,NS,C1,Ls),T,T1),
    node(Synch,Ins,IJ,C,F,L,R,B1,T1?,Q,work).
node(Synch,Ins,IJ,C,F,L,R,B,T,Q,work) ←
    get(m(1,S,NS,C1,Ls),B,B1),
    pop(q(C2,What),Q,Q1) |
    color(C1,C2,C3),
    put(m(S,S,NS,C3?,[What|Ls]),R,R1),
    node(Synch,Ins,IJ,C,F,L,R1?,B1,T,Q1,work).
node(Synch,Ins,IJ,C,F,L,R,B,T,Q,work) ←
    get(m(1,S,NS,C1,Ls),R,R1),
    C1 = gray,
    NS ≠ F,
    NNS := 2 ∗ NS,
    nondistinguished(IJ,NNS) |
    spawn(S,NS,Ls,Parent),
    push(q(gray,Parent?),Q,Q1),
    node(Synch,Ins,IJ,C,F,L,R1,B,T,Q1?,work).
node(Synch,Ins,IJ,C,F,L,R,B,T,Q,work) ←
    get(m(1,S,NS,C1,_),R,R1),
    C1 ≠ gray,
    NS ≠ F,
    NNS := 2 ∗ NS,
    nondistinguished(IJ,NNS) |
    push(q(C1,C1),Q,Q1),
    node(Synch,Ins,IJ,C,F,L,R1,B,T,Q1?,work).

Program 12.1: A node process in BU-2 (partial)

```
node(Synch,Ins,IJ,C,F,L,R,B,T,Q,work) ←
    get(m(1,S,NS,C1,Ls),R,R1),
    C1 = gray,
    NS ≠ F,
    NNS := 2 * NS,
    distinguished(IJ,NNS) |
    spawn(S,NS,Ls,Parent),
    put(m(NS,NS,NNS,gray,[Parent?]),T,T1),
    node(Synch,Ins,IJ,C,F,L,R1,B,T1?,Q,work).
node(Synch,Ins,IJ,C,F,L,R,B,T,Q,work) ←
    get(m(1,S,NS,C1,_),R,R1),
    C1 ≠ gray,
    NS ≠ F,
    NNS := 2 * NS,
    distinguished(IJ,NNS) |
    put(m(NS,NS,NNS,C1,[C1]),T,T1),
    node(Synch,Ins,IJ,C,F,L,R1,B,T1?,Q,work).
```

Program 12.1: (Continued)

```
spawn(S,NS,Ls,F) ←
    spawn(S,NS,Ls,[ ],F).
spawn(S,NS,[c(Up,Down)|Ls],Ms,F) ←
    spawn(S,NS,Ls?,[c(Up,Down)|Ms],F).
spawn(S,NS,[L|Ls],Ms,F) ←
    L ≠ c(_,_) |
    qleaf(S,L,Ch?,Eq,S_b,E_b),
    create_X_channels(Ch,Ch1),
    spawn(S,NS,Ls?,[Ch1?|Ms],F).
spawn(S,NS,[ ],[D1,D2,D3,D4],Ch?) ←
    create_X_channels(Ch,Ch1),
    qnode(D4,D3,D2,D1,Ch1?,NS).
```

Program 12.2: Spawning a quadtree in BU-2

12.2.2 Correctness of Algorithm BU-2

Since the quadtree construction proceeds from the leaves upwards, it suffices to show that any *gray* node has maximal uniform-color blocks as its leaf-children. The whole tree structure will then be correct by an inductive argument. As mentioned above, the actual spawning of a node is done only when its children would not be able to take part in further merges (as indicated by a *gray* message color), hence the required maximality.

The algorithms described in this paper are designed for a distributed asynchronous machine. We must therefore define the meaning of their "running time". Our unit is the period of time it takes a processor to communicate a message to its immediate neighbor. We call *running time* the minimum number of such message-passings that must take place before the result appears at the output node. The resulting time presupposes that every processor in the machine communicates the answer for whichever computation it performs as soon as it is available, not an improbable assumption for a dedicated image-processing machine.

The running time of Algorithm BU-2 (the number of message-passings until the quadtree structure is determined) is

$$4 \times 2^{k-1} + 4 \times 2^{k-2} + \ldots + 4 = 4 \times (2^k - 1).$$

It is $O(2^k)$, and therefore optimal, since the shortest possible time in which the farthest node can communicate its color to the would-be quadtree root is of the order of the image array side (which is 2^k). Besides the advantages of the bottom-up approach (i.e., the ability to couple efficiently to an array of sensors), BU-2 scores on the following points: (1) each node in the original array is asked its value only once; (2) a standard message structure is used throughout the building process; and (3) communications are specified in local terms only (between the immediate neighbors), which makes the resulting code clear and concise.

It should be noted that BU-2 may cause a maximal load on certain processors that is of the order of $k = \log(\text{image diameter})$. These processors are the ones that serve as distinguished nodes on more than one level. Actually, only one processor may have a load of exactly k processes (the one corresponding to the tree root); four processors — a load of k–1 processes and so on. This worst-case congestion happens *only* if the input pattern results in a balanced quadtree and the number of leaves is equal to the number of pixels. The average case (depending on the image) is much better and does not justify introducing a complex spawning pattern.

The above considerations are valid also for the assessment of communication links congestion (logarithmic in the worst case). The links are more numerous in the left lower corners of the quadrants, as may be seen in Figure 12.4.

12.3 Computations by Active Quadtrees

Various image properties can be computed using an active quadtree representation. They may be divided into two general classes, according to whether the algorithm that computes the property is synchronous or asynchronous (Kung, 1979b). The implications of this dichotomy for a Concurrent Prolog programmer

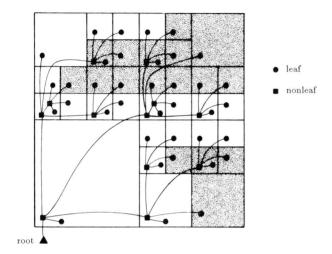

leaf

nonleaf

root

Figure 12.4: Algorithm BU-2: processor load and communications pattern

are clarified in the next two subsections, which describe algorithms for centroid coordinates computation and for connected components labeling.

12.3.1 Centroid computation

This parallel centroid algorithm for an active quadtree was shown by Dubitzki et al. (1981). It works as follows. The root starts the computation by passing its coordinates $(0,0)$ down to its children. A gray node at level i below the root computes its coordinates by adding or subtracting 2^{k-2-i} from its parent's coordinates. A black leaf computes its moment by multiplying its coordinates by the area and passes the results up. The moments are summed at the gray nodes on their way up to the root. Upon getting the final sums the root divides them by the total black area to yield the centroid coordinates.

Since each gray node must wait for data from all of its children to arrive before it can compute and pass up its own result, a natural synchronization is imposed by the flow of data from the leaves upwards. This enables each node to decide when to act next, and the root — to decide whether the whole process is finished. Such an algorithm is easy to implement on a truly distributed machine, since no centralized action is needed to supervise the timing of various processes. We call this kind of algorithm *naturally synchronous*. Its running time is easy to estimate: it is equal to $2\times$(maximal tree height), which is $O(k)$.

Program 12.3 includes the code for centroid computation. The structure of

```
qleaf(S,b,U,Eq,S_b,E_b) ←
    get(a(c(X,Y)),U,U1) |
    Area := S * S,
    Mx := X * Area,
    My := Y * Area,
    put(a(Area,Mx,My),U1,U2),
    qleaf(S,b,U2?,Eq,S_b,E_b).
qleaf(S,w,U,Eq,S_b,E_b) ←
    get(a(_),U,U1) |
    put(a(0,0,0),U1,U2),
    qleaf(S,w,U2?,Eq,S_b,E_b).

qnode(Ds,U,S) ←
    get_four(a(A1,Mx1,My1), a(A2,Mx2,My2),
    a(A3,Mx3,My3), a(A4,Mx4,My4),Ds,Ds1) |
    Mx := (Mx1+Mx2+Mx3+Mx4),
    My := (My1+My2+My3+My4),
    A := (A1+A2+A3+A4),
    put(a(A,Mx,My),U,U1),
    qnode(Ds1,U1?,S).
qnode(Ds,U,S) ←
    get(a(C),U,U1) |
    sw(C,C1,S), nw(C,C2,S),
    ne(C,C3,S), se(C,C4,S),
    put_four(a(C1?),a(C2?),a(C3?),a(C4?),Ds,Ds1),
    qnode(Ds1?,U1,S).

sw(c(X,Y),c(X1,Y1),S) ←
    S1 := S / 4, X1 := X – S1, Y1 := Y – S1.
nw(c(X,Y),c(X1,Y1),S) ←
    S1 := S / 4, X1 := X – S1, Y1 := Y + S1.
ne(c(X,Y),c(X1,Y1),S) ←
    S1 := S / 4, X1 := X + S1, Y1 := Y + S1.
se(c(X,Y),c(X1,Y1),S) ←
    S1 := S / 4, X1 := X + S1, Y1 := Y – S1.
```

Program 12.3: Centroid computation

the quadtree leaf and gray node processes is, respectively, $qleaf(S,C,U,N,S\_b,E\_b)$ and $qnode(Ds,U,S)$. The parameters of $qleaf$ are:

S – size,

C – color,
U – the link "up" to the parent,
N – name (the path from the root),
S_b – southern border flag,
E_b – eastern border flag.

The parameters of *qnode* are the list of child-links (Ds), the parent link (U), and size (S).

12.3.2 Connected component labeling

The sequential predecessor of this algorithm was shown by Samet (1981). The algorithm has three phases, the first and structurally the most interesting of these being the generation of the list of neighbor pairs of black leaves. The list is afterwards processed to find the equivalence classes, and the final labels are communicated to the leaves. The implementation of the first phase only is described below. In order to find all the pairs of neighboring black leaves (those with a common side), a parallel computation is executed, in which every black leaf looks for a possible neighbor to the south and to the east. This process is inherently *asynchronous*, because no gray node knows in advance how many of its children will report equivalence to the root. If the nodes pass the results up as soon as they arrive, then the root will ultimately face the problem of deciding when to stop waiting for more messages.

One way to solve the termination problem is to pose a time limit after which no more results can possibly arrive. This approach is taken (for a convexity algorithm in a pyramidal computer) by Miller and Stout (1984), where the algorithm is stopped if it "tries running longer" than a certain amount of time.

Instead of using a central clock, we have chosen to complicate the algorithm and keep it truly distributed. A general method of detecting distributed termination of a system of processes is presented and proved by Viner (1984). In our case the system is highly structured (there is a hierarchy of processes from the root down), and only a single kind of communications has to be monitored in order to detect termination (the communications between bottom-level processes). These features of the algorithm allow the use of the following technique, which is simpler than that of Viner (1984).

We keep one process (the root) informed about all the "important" events in the system. These events are message sending, message receival and a special kind of message relay, in which the message is split into two (which means an increase in the number of the currently travelling messages). In the initialization phase the root calculates the number of adjacency reports it will receive from the total number of black leaves (with the fact that the border leaves have less neighbors taken into account). The number is decremented each time a result is received and incremented each time a message split is reported. Because of the hierarchical process structure, the adjustment of the count at the root always precedes the arrival of the message that caused it (a message may be split only on its way down), therefore this distributed termination detection technique is correct.

Termination detection can be implemented in a logic programming language like Concurrent Prolog in a much cleaner way, without explicit message counting. The *short-circuit* technique, due to Takeuchi (1983), is described elsewhere in this book (e.g., Chapter 5). Its functional equivalence to the message-counting technique was realized only after the latter had been implemented.

We proceed to describe the connected components algorithm. The computation is started by the root sending down a *report_in* message. This message is relayed down by each gray node to all its children. By the time *report_in* reaches a leaf, it carries as its first argument a list describing the way to that leaf from the root. This list is unique and serves as the name of the leaf. The other two arguments are flags that designate whether the leaf is on the southern or eastern borders of the image, respectively. At the root both of these flags are true, and the southern (eastern) flag remains true at a given node iff every leg of the path to that node is in either south-eastern or south-western (north-eastern or south-eastern) direction. Upon receiving *report_in*, a black leaf sends up *report_in(N)*, where N is equal to 2 minus the number of its border-adjacent sides. White leaves respond by *report_in(0)*. The numbers are summed on their way up at the gray nodes, and the number that arrives at the root is stored there. This number is decremented each time an adjacency result reaches the root. When it becomes 0, the root knows that all the possible adjacencies have been reported, and the algorithm is terminated.

Program 12.4 implements this algorithm. It first computes the number of expected answers, using clauses 1–7.

The root then starts the next phase by sending down *start_conn*. This message is relayed to all the leaves (clause 8). The black leaves respond to it by sending up *conn_up* messages, one for each southern and eastern side that is not on the border. These messages ascend the tree until the lowest common ancestor of the source and the destination (neighbor) leaves is encountered. This condition is tested for at each gray node by comparing the neighbor direction carried by the message (south or east) with the direction from which the message arrived at the node (Samet, 1981). For example, if an eastern neighbor is looked for, then the first node to which *conn_up* arrives from the south-west or the north-west is the lowest common ancestor.

At this stage *conn_down* is sent down (clauses 14–17, 22, 23), using the moves that are mirror images of those made by *conn_up* on its way up (pushed by it on a local stack, see clauses 18–21). Reaching the bottom of the stack before arriving

```
qnode(Ds,U,S) ←                                          % 1
    get(report_in(Path,South_b,East_b),U,U1) |
    put_four(report_in([sw|Path],South_b,no),
    report_in([nw|Path],no,no),
    report_in([ne|Path],no,East_b),
    report_in([se|Path],South_b,East_b),Ds,Ds1),
    qnode(Ds1?,U1,S).
qleaf(S,w,U,_,_,_) ←                                     % 2
    get(report_in(Name,S_b,E_b),U,U1) |
    put(report_in(0),U1,U2),
    qleaf(S,w,U2?,Name,S_b,E_b).
qleaf(S,b,U,E,_,_) ←                                     % 3
    get(report_in(Name,no,no),U,U1) |
    put(report_in(2),U1,U2),
    qleaf(S,b,U2?,Name,no,no).
qleaf(S,b,U,E,_,_) ←                                     % 4
    get(report_in(Name,no,yes),U,U1) |
    put(report_in(1),U1,U2),
    qleaf(S,b,U2?,Name,no,yes).
qleaf(S,b,U,E,_,_) ←                                     % 5
    get(report_in(Name,yes,no),U,U1) |
    put(report_in(1),U1,U2),
    qleaf(S,b,U2?,Name,yes,no).
qleaf(S,b,U,E,_,_) ←                                     % 6
    get(report_in(Name,yes,yes),U,U1) |
    put(report_in(0),U1,U2),
    qleaf(S,b,U2?,Name,yes,yes).
qnode(Ds,U,S) ←                                          % 7
    get_four(report_in(One),report_in(Two),
    report_in(Thr),report_in(Fou),Ds,Ds1) |
    N_blacks := One + Two + Thr + Fou,
    put(report_in(N_blacks?),U,U1),
    qnode(Ds1?,U1?,S).
```

The nodes look for the neighbors:

```
qnode(Ds,U,S) ←                                          % 8
    get(start_conn,U,U1) |
    put_all(start_conn,Ds,Ds1),
    qnode(Ds1?,U1,S).
```

Program 12.4: Connected components

```
qleaf(S,w,U,Name,S_b,E_b) ←                          % 9
    get(start_conn,U,U1) |
    qleaf(S,w,U1?,Name,S_b,E_b).
qleaf(S,b,U,Name,no,no) ←                            % 10
    get(start_conn,U,U1) |
    put(conn_up(Name,s,[ ]),U1,U2),
    put(conn_up(Name,e,[ ]),U2?,U3),
    qleaf(S,b,U3?,Name,no,no).
qleaf(S,b,U,Name,no,yes) ←                           % 11
    get(start_conn,U,U1) |
    put(conn_up(Name,s,[ ]),U1,U2),
    qleaf(S,b,U2?,Name,no,yes).
qleaf(S,b,U,Name,yes,no) ←                           % 12
    get(start_conn,U,U1) |
    put(conn_up(Name,e,[ ]),U1,U2),
    qleaf(S,b,U2?,Name,yes,no).
qleaf(S,b,U,Name,yes,yes) ←                          % 13
    get(start_conn,U,U1) |
    qleaf(S,b,U1,Name,yes,yes).
```

Lowest common ancestor (east) is found:

```
qnode(Ds,U,S) ←                                      % 14
    get4(1,conn_up(Name,e,Path),Ds,Ds1) |
    put4(4,conn_down(Name,e,Path),Ds1,Ds2),
    qnode(Ds2?,U,S).
qnode(Ds,U,S) ←                                      % 15
    get4(2,conn_up(Name,e,Path),Ds,Ds1) |
    put4(3,conn_down(Name,e,Path),Ds1,Ds2),
    qnode(Ds2?,U,S).
```

Lowest common ancestor (south) found:

```
qnode(Ds,U,S) ←                                      % 16
    get4(2,conn_up(Name,s,Path),Ds,Ds1) |
    put4(1,conn_down(Name,s,Path),Ds1,Ds2),
    qnode(Ds2?,U,S).
qnode(Ds,U,S) ←                                      % 17
    get4(3,conn_up(Name,s,Path),Ds,Ds1) |
    put4(4,conn_down(Name,s,Path),Ds1,Ds2),
    qnode(Ds2?,U,S).
```

Program 12.4: (Continued)

Relay conn_up, recording the turns:

```
qnode(Ds,U,S) ←                                              % 18
    get4(3,conn_up(N,e,Path),Ds,Ds1) |
    push(ne,Path,Path1),
    put(conn_up(N,e,Path1?),U,U1),
    qnode(Ds1,S).
qnode(Ds,U,S) ←                                              % 19
    get4(4,conn_up(N,e,Path),Ds,Ds1) |
    push(se,Path,Path1),
    put(conn_up(N,e,Path1?),U,U1),
    qnode(Ds1,U1?,S).
qnode(Ds,U,S) ←                                              % 20
    get4(1,conn_up(N,s,Path),Ds,Ds1) |
    push(sw,Path,Path1),
    put(conn_up(N,s,Path1?),U,U1),
    qnode(Ds1,U1?,S).
qnode(Ds,U,S) ←                                              % 21
    get4(4,conn_up(N,s,Path),Ds,Ds1) |
    push(se,Path,Path1),
    put(conn_up(N,s,Path1?),U,U1),
    qnode(Ds1,U1?,S).
```

Relay conn_down:

```
qnode(Ds,U,S) ←                                              % 22
    get(conn_down(N,Sense,Ms),U,U1),
    pop(Move,Ms?,Ms1) |
    reflect(Sense,Move,Mirr),
    steer(conn_down(N,Sense,Ms1),Mirr?,Ds,Ds1),
    qnode(Ds1?,U1,S).
qnode(Ds,U,S) ←                                              % 23
    get(conn_down(N,Sense,[ ]),U,U1) |
    reflect_two(Sense,Mv1,Mv2),
    steer(conn_down(N,Sense,[ ]),Mv1?,Ds,Ds1),
    steer(conn_down(N,Sense,[ ]),Mv2?,Ds1?,Ds2),
    put(report_eq_pair(add1),U1,U2),
    qnode(Ds2?,U2?,S).
```

Program 12.4: (Continued)

Relay up report_eq_pair:

```
    qleaf(S,w,U,Eq,S_b,E_b) ←                          % 24
        get(conn_down(_,_,_),U,U1) |
        put(report_eq_pair(no),U1,U2),
        qleaf(S,w,U2?,Eq,S_b,E_b).
    qleaf(S,b,U,Eq,S_b,E_b) ←                          % 25
        get(conn_down(N,K,P),U,U1) |
        put(report_eq_pair(eq(N,Eq)),U1,U2),
        qleaf(S,b,U2?,Eq,S_b,E_b).
    qnode(Ds,U,S) ←                                    % 26
        get_any(report_eq_pair(What),Ds,Ds1) |
        put(report_eq_pair(What),U,U1),
        qnode(Ds1,U1?,S).
```

Program 12.4: (Continued)

at a leaf signifies that the target leaf is smaller than the source one. In this case *conn_down* is "split" into two, and the twin messages are sent to the south-west and north-west, if an eastern neighbor is being sought, or to the north-west and north-east, otherwise. Also, the root is notified that one more answer should be expected, and the number stored there is incremented by one. Now, a black leaf getting *conn_down* sends to the root a *report_eq_pair* carrying the newly found equivalence pair, while a white leaf sends a "don't-care" message (clauses 24–26). The root waits for all the results to arrive and then goes on to another computation.

Various tradeoffs are possible in this algorithm implementation between the time complexity and the amount of memory required at each node. For example, the leaves could start looking for neighbors without waiting for the root's permission, which is issued after it receives the number of expected results. This would require adding at each gray node a queue to hold the pending messages it cannot process right away (e.g., the *conn_up* messages that arrive before all four *report_in* messages do). As it is in our implementation, the requirement of complete decentralization doubles the running time of the algorithm due to the communications delay between the root and the leaves. It is equal to $4 \times$(maximal tree height)$=O(k)$. Another contribution to the running time comes from the serial way in which the root processes the *report_eq_pair* messages. This contribution is equal to the number of neighbor pairs (both black-black and black-white) which, by Theorem 1 of Samet (1981) is $O(B)$, where B is the number of black leaves. The equivalence list processing phase (not implemented) may be performed by the root locally (i.e., in constant time according to the distributed processing model in which we charge for communications only). The last phase, that of informing the leaves of their component leader identity, should take $O(L)$ time, where $L \leq B$ is the number of final labels. The total running time is therefore $O(k+B)$.

Note that it is impossible to save time by making the gray nodes wait for the results instead of the root, because it is not known in advance via which node a *report_eq_pair* will ascend (the only certain thing is that it will get to the root, eventually). This result may be improved, however, provided we do not require the output to be via the root, thus removing the serial bottleneck there. It may be done by "roping" the equivalent black leaves by bidirectional communications channels and making a distinguished leaf (say, the one closest to the root) wait for all the leaves that are connected to it to report in. The distinguished leaf then labels them all by its own name and reports to the root. In such a way a two-level "connectivity tree" is built at the root, whose first level consists of the distinguished leaves. Each of these corresponds to a connected component of the image and has direct links to every member (leaf) of that component. This approach does not need a separate equivalence list processing and label distribution and results in $O(k+L)$ running time.

12.4 Curve Tracing Using a Pyramid Network of Processes

This section describes a distributed algorithm that solves the following version of the connectivity problem: given a binary image with one or more thin black curves and two black pixels, determine whether the pixels lie on the same curve (i.e., are connected). The problem may be solved by tracing the curve starting from one of the given points: the answer is positive if the second point is encountered. An algorithm using this approach would be linear in the curve length. Edelman (1987) developed a better than linear algorithm which used a pyramidal process structure to enable fast communications between any two points in the image. A detailed description of this algorithm, the proof of its correctness and termination, and a discussion of the relevant results from human vision was given by Edelman (1987). We outline here the implementation aspects of the algorithm.

12.4.1 Building a pyramid of processes

Here is an extension of the recursive technique used to build the quadtrees to a more complex structure: a pyramid in which every "inside" node has direct links to a parent, four same-level neighbors and four children.

The recursive call of *pyramid* is represented pictorially in Figure 12.5 and implemented in Program 12.5. It may be seen as a decomposition of the pyramid into its base layer of processes (*surface*) and a smaller pyramid (clause 1). The

```
pyramid(Height,As,Root) ←                                          % 1
    Height > 0 |
    surface(Height,As,Bs),
    Height1 := Height − 1,
    pyramid(Height1,Bs?,Root).
pyramid(0,Root,Root).                                              % 2

surface(H,Bottom,Top) ←                                            % 3
    D := 2**(H − 1),
    surface1(H,D?,D?,Bottom,South,North,Top),
    tie_streams(South?),
    tie_streams(North?).

surface1(H,X,Y,[B1,B2|Bs],South,North,[T|Ts]) ←                   % 4
    Y > 0 |
    row(H,X,Y,B1,B2,South,South1,T),
    Y1 := Y − 1,
    surface1(H,X,Y1,Bs?,South1?,North,Ts).
surface1(_,_,0,[ ],North,North,[ ]).                              % 5

row(H,X,Y,B1,B2,South,North,Top) ←                                % 6
    row1(H,X,Y,B1,B2,East,West,South,North,Top),
    tie_stream(East),
    tie_stream(West).

row1(H,X,Y,[A1,A2|As],[B1,B2|Bs],                                 % 7
    East,West1,[South|Ss],[North|Ns],[Top|Ts]) ←
    X > 0 |
    cell(H,X,Y,A1,A2,B1,B2,East,West,South,North,Top),
    X1 := X − 1,
    row1(H,X1,Y1,As,Bs,West,West1,Ss,Ns,Ts).
row1(_,0,_,[ ],[ ],West,West,[ ],[ ],[ ]).                        % 8

cell(H,X,Y,A1,A2,A3,A4,East,West,South,North,Top) ←              % 9
    depends on the application.

tie_streams([X|Xs]) ←                                             % 10
    tie_stream(X),
    tie_streams(Xs?).
tie_streams([ ]).                                                 % 11

tie_stream(X) ←                                                   % 12
    depends on the channel representation.
```

Program 12.5: Spawning a pyramid

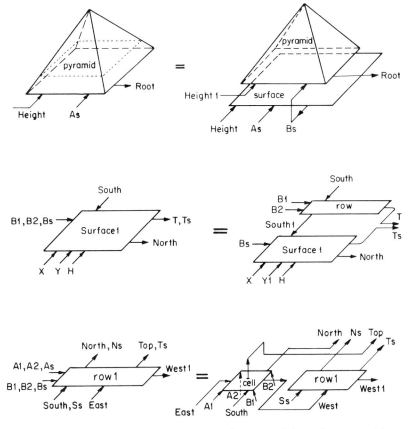

Figure 12.5: Recursive decomposition of a pyramid

recursion eventually "bottoms out" at the pyramid apex (*root*) (clause 2).

The *surface* process in its turn spawns two adjacent *row*s and recurses with a smaller Y-dimension (clause 4, see Figure 12.5).

The *row* process (which actually represents two adjacent rows) spawns an individual cell process and recurses with a smaller X-dimension (clause 7).

12.4.2 Algorithm outline

The algorithm to be described next uses a simpler pyramid (without lateral links in the intermediate layers). In its base layer each process corresponds to a single input pixel. It has bidirectional communication links to each of its four

immediate neighbors and to its parent in the second layer. A process in a higher
layer is linked to four children in the lower layer and to a parent in the higher
one. In such a way, a pyramid based on a $N \times N$ array has log N layers and a
total number of $\frac{4}{3}(N^2 - 1) + 1$ processes.

Algorithm CT (for Curve Tracing) performs an activation spread starting
from a given point. If the activation reaches a second given point, the two points
are connected. In a way, this may be seen as *coloring* the curve on which the
first point is situated and checking whether the second point gets the paint. The
algorithm consists of two phases which may partially overlap in time. In the first
phase each intermediate *node* in the pyramid is assigned status as a result of a
bottom-up computation. The status is *OK* if the coloring of the entire base of
the sub-pyramid whose apex is the node would not change the connectivity of
the image (by spreading the color to a curve not previously connected to the first
point). Otherwise the status is *bad*.

Edelman (1987) proved that the status assignment can be done according
to the following rules. The status is *OK* on two conditions: first, all four of the
node's children must be *OK*; second, the basis of the sub-pyramid that has the
node as its apex must contain at most one connected component. If the conditions
are not fulfilled, the status is *bad*. The status of any black process in the bottom
layer is always *OK*.

The test for one connected component (*OK*-check) is carried out by counting
the number of terminators, junctions and *I-points* (defined as the intersections
between the image curves and the two straight segments connecting the midpoints
of the region's opposite sides). Counting the *I*-points serves to detect cycles in
the figure. Effectively, it permits using the genus of the figure as the basis for the
OK-check.

Note that the *OK*-check involves only local operations, for which communications between immediate neighbors suffice. A process in the base of the pyramid
can find out whether its corresponding pixel is a terminator or a junction simply
by querying its neighbors for the color of their pixels. For algorithms involving
only local communications, the implementation in Concurrent Prolog is particularly easy and readable.

As soon as a process has computed its status, it is ready to participate in the
second phase of CT. In this phase the marked pixel at the bottom initiates the
activation by sending a message upwards. The message continues to ascend while
the status of the nodes it encounters is *OK*. At the first *bad* one it turns back
down and descends one level, returning to the last (highest) node that is *OK*. All
the pixels in the base of that node's subpyramid are then colored. On the borders
of the colored region new black pixels are activated by their neighbors and the
activation spreads concurrently from each of them.

The termination of Algorithm CT is determined using a variant of the message counting technique of Algorithm CC. In this case it is particularly effective: the overhead in terms of the number of messages dedicated to termination detection is $O(1)$ (Edelman, 1987).

The detailed description of Algorithm CT uses the following naming conventions: a process is called a *node* if it is in the bottom layer of the pyramid and a *pnode* otherwise. The pyramid's apex is linked to a special process, the *root*. The algorithm uses three kinds of messages (*compute_status*, *white*, *pt*) for the *OK*-check, and two more kinds (*request_to_color*, *color*) for the activation. In addition, special message-passing is done for termination detection, similarly to Algorithm CC. Some of the messages (e.g., *pt*) serve as "envelopes" with several slots. The clauses of Algorithm CT in the following description are grouped by the logical order of the activation process, rather than by process name (which would probably look more formal, at the expense of presentation clarity).

Algorithm CT (Edelman, 1987):

(1) The root of the pyramid commands the bottom nodes to start the status computation by sending down a *compute_status* message. This message is replicated at each pnode and relayed down, until a copy of it reaches every node.

(2) Once a black node gets *compute_status*, it computes the number of its black neighbors (by performing a neighbor poll) and sends up a *pt* message, carrying that number and the node's coordinates. White nodes respond to *compute_status* by sending up a *white* message.

(3) The pnodes wait until responses are available on all four "down" links, then compute their status. These are the three criteria by which the status is determined:

A pnode is *OK iff*

(1) All its children are *OK*.

(2) The genus of the image in the base of the sub-pyramid (computed from the number of terminators and junctions — see Edelman, 1987, for details) whose root is the pnode in question must be equal to 0 or 1.

(3) The number of I-points in the sub-pyramid base must be less than or equal to 1.

(4) As soon as the marked node replies to *compute_status* (this event signifies the end of its role in the first phase), it starts the activation by sending up a *request_to_color*. The color spreads therefore concurrently with the status computation, lagging behind it by at least one step; this guarantees that the two phases are spatially disjoint and that any pnode that will receive the

request_to_color, will have completed its status computation.

(5) The *request_to_color* ascends until it arrives at a *bad* pnode. There it is returned one level down, finding thus the highest pnode on its path that is *OK*. That pnode then responds by telling all its subordinate *nodes* to color themselves (by sending down the *color* message, which is replicated and relayed down at each level, until it reaches the base).

(6) The root keeps track of the activation progress in order to detect its termination. When it decides to terminate the run, the root broadcasts down a message to that effect.

(7) When a node gets *color*, it colors itself and informs its neighbors. Each one of the neighbors that hasn't been colored yet initiates its own activation as if it is the first marked node, by sending up a *request_to_color* (refer to step 5 above to follow the progress of the new *request_to_color*).

(8) Any pnode or node that receives the termination command relayed from the root goes to sleep. If one is interested in processing another image, then the termination command should clear the pnodes' status and make each node input a new pixel.

12.4.3 CT program highlights

We proceed to describe the Concurrent Prolog program for Algorithm CT (Program 12.6) in more detail. Following is the description of the instance variables of each of the three kinds of processes that together form the pyramid, *node*, *pnode* and *root*. The bottom layer of the pyramid contains only node processes:

> node(IJ,Color,Dimensions,Parent,Neighbors,Memory,Status)

The meaning of a node's variables is as follows:

> | *IJ* | – process (pixel) coordinates, |
> |---|---|
> | *Color* | – corresponding pixel color, |
> | *Dimensions* | – pyramid base dimensions, |
> | *Parent* | – parent pnode ("up") link, |
> | *Neighbors* | – 4 neighbor links, kept in a list structure, |
> | *Memory* | – local process memory, |
> | *Status* | – process status. |

The intermediate layers of the pyramid are formed by the pnode processes:

> pnode(Ds,U,S,Stage,Status)

The instance variables of pnode are:

> | *Ds* | – four children ("down") links, in a list structure, |
> |---|---|

```
root(Root,0) ←                                              % 1
    put(compute_status,Root,Root1),
    root(Root1?,1).

pnode(Ds,U,S,idle,[ ]) ←                                    % 2
    get(compute_status,U,U1) |
    put_all(compute_status,Ds,Ds1),
    pnode(Ds1?,U1,S,wait_for_count,[ ]).

node(IJ,w,D,F,Ls,Q,0) ←                                     % 3
    get(compute_status,F,F1) |
    put(white,F1,F2),
    node(IJ,w,D,F2?,Ls,Q,0).
node(IJ,b,D,F,Ls,Q,0) ←                                     % 4
    get(compute_status,F,F1) |
    put_all(rep_req_from(IJ),Ls,Ls1),
    node(IJ,b,D,F1,Ls1?,Q,0).
node(IJ,C,D,F,Ls,Q,0) ←                                     % 5
    get4(rep_req_from(IJ),Ls,Ls1,N) |
    put4(rep(w),Ls1,Ls2,N),
    node(IJ,C,D,F,Ls2?,Q,0).
node(IJ,C,D,F,Ls,Q,0) ←                                     % 6
    get4(rep_req_from(XY),Ls,Ls1,N),
    XY ≠ IJ |
    put4(rep(C),Ls1,Ls2,N),
    node(IJ,C,D,F,Ls2?,Q,0).
node(IJ,b,D,F,Ls,Q,0) ←                                     % 7
    get_four(rep(M1),rep(M2),rep(M3),rep(M4),Ls,Ls1),
    count_neigh([M1?,M2?,M3?,M4?],N) |
    put(blacks([pt(IJ,N,0),pt(IJ,N,0)]),F,F1),
    node(IJ,b,D,F1?,Ls1,N,color_from_mark).

pnode(Ds,U,S,wait_for_count,[ ]) ←                          % 8
    get_four(R1,R2,R3,R4,Ds,Ds1),
    wait(R1?,R11),
    wait(R2?,R22),
    wait(R3?,R33),
    wait(R4?,R44) |
    pnode(Ds1,U,S,waiting,[R11,R22,R33,R44]).
pnode(Ds,U,S,waiting,[R1,R2,R3,R4]) ←                       % 9
    call(comp_cnt([R1,R2,R3,R4],Next_Message,Status)) |
    write(pnode(num(S),sent,Next_Message,Status)),
    put(Next_Message,U,U1),
    pnode(Ds,U1?,S,idle,Status).
```

Program 12.6: Curve tracing

```
node(IJ,b,D,F,Ls,Q,color_from_mark) ←          % 10
    call(marked(IJ)) |
    put(color_req,F,F1),
    node(IJ,b,D,F1?,Ls,Q,0).
node(IJ,b,D,F,Ls,Q,color_from_mark) ←          % 11
    call(not(marked(IJ))) |
    node(IJ,b,D,F,Ls,Q,0).

pnode(Ds,U,S,idle,ok(N)) ←                     % 12
    get_from_any(color_req,Ds,Ds1) |
    put(color_req,U,U1),
    pnode(Ds1,U1?,S,idle,ok(N)).
pnode(Ds,U,S,idle,bad) ←                       % 13
    get4(color_req,Ds,Ds1,N) |
    put4(rejected,Ds1,Ds2,N),
    pnode(Ds2?,U,S,idle,bad).
pnode(Ds,U,S,colored,Stat) ←                   % 14
    get4(color_req,Ds,Ds1,N) |
    Mo := 0 - 1,
    put(notify_root(Mo?),U,U1),
    pnode(Ds1,U1?,S,colored,Stat).
pnode(Ds,U,S,idle,ok(N)) ←                     % 15
    get(rejected,U,U1),
    N ≠ 0 |
    put(notify_root(N),U1,U2),
    put_all(color,Ds,Ds1),
    pnode(Ds1?,U2?,S,colored,ok(N)).
pnode(Ds,U,S,idle,ok(N)) ←                     % 16
    get(rejected,U,U1),
    N = 0 |
    put_all(color,Ds,Ds1),
    pnode(Ds1?,U1,S,colored,ok(N)).
pnode(Ds,U,S,idle,ok(N)) ←                     % 17
    get(color,U,U1) |
    put_all(color,Ds,Ds1),
    pnode(Ds1?,U1,S,idle,ok(N)).
node(IJ,b,D,F,Ls,Q,0) ←                        % 18
    get(color,F,F1) |
    write('GOT_COLORED'(IJ)),
    put_all(color_neighbor(IJ),Ls,Ls1),
    node(IJ,c_b,D,F1,Ls1?,Q,0).
```

Program 12.6: (Continued)

```
node(IJ,b,D,F,Ls,Q,0) ←                              % 19
    Q ≠ 2,
    get(rejected,F,F1) |
    N := Q – 2,
    put(notify_root(N?),F1,F2),
    write('GOT_COLORED'(IJ)),
    put_all(color_neighbor(IJ),Ls,Ls1),
    node(IJ,c_b,D,F2?,Ls1?,Q,0).
node(IJ,b,D,F,Ls,Q,0) ←                              % 20
    Q = 2,
    get(rejected,F,F1) |
    write('GOT_COLORED'(IJ)),
    put_all(color_neighbor(IJ),Ls,Ls1),
    node(IJ,c_b,D,F1,Ls1?,Q,0).
node(IJ,w,D,F,Ls,Q,0) ←                              % 21
    get(color,F,F1) |
    write('GOT_COLORED'(IJ)),
    node(IJ,c_w,D,F1,Ls,Q,0).
node(IJ,w,D,F,Ls,Q,0) ←                              % 22
    get(rejected,F,F1) |
    write('GOT_COLORED'(IJ)),
    node(IJ,c_w,D,F1,Ls,Q,0).
node(IJ,C,D,F,Ls,Q,0) ←                              % 23
    get_from_any(color_neighbor(XY),Ls,Ls1),
    XY = IJ |
    node(IJ,C,D,F,Ls1,Q,0).
node(IJ,b,D,F,Ls,Q,0) ←                              % 24
    get_from_any(color_neighbor(XY),Ls,Ls1),
    XY ≠ IJ |
    put(color_req,F,F1),
    node(IJ,b,D,F1?,Ls1,Q,0).
node(IJ,C,D,F,Ls,Q,0) ←                              % 25
    C ≠ b,
    get_from_any(color_neighbor(XY),Ls,Ls1),
    node(IJ,C,D,F,Ls1,Q,0).

pnode(Ds,U,S,What,Stat) ←                            % 26
    get_from_any(notify_root(Note),Ds,Ds1) |
    put(notify_root(Note),U,U1),
    pnode(Ds1,U1?,S,What,Stat).
```

Program 12.6: (Continued)

U – parent ("up") link,
S – height of the pnode in the pyramid,
Stage – computation stage reached by the algorithm,
Status – the local process status.

The four components of the *Ds* list are the *Parent* variables of the pnode's children if these are nodes, or the U variables of the subordinate pnodes otherwise. This link arrangement achieves the desired pyramidal process communication structure.

There is only one root process in the pyramid. It has a link to the highest pnode and several private variables, whose number changes according to the computation stage. These will be described in detail below.

The execution is started when the pyramid root sends a *compute_status* message down and enters an idle state (clause 1).

This message is relayed by every intermediate pyramid node (*pnode*) to its descendants, after which the pnode enters a *wait_for_count* state. It may exit this state only when its status is determined as a result of the bottom-up computation started by the *compute_status* message (clause 2).

When a white node at the pyramid bottom gets a *compute_status* message, it just reports up its own color (clause 3).

A black node first queries its neighbors in order to determine its valency (number of black neighbors). The query is performed by sending them a message to that effect, carrying the sender's coordinates. This complication is a result of some of the border nodes' neighbor links being self-loops. In case a message arrives that carries the same name as the recipient node's one, the reply is always *white* (i.e., the nonexistent pixels beyond the borders are considered always white).

If the node gets a message from itself, *white* is the reply. In the case the neighbor is real, it is sent the node's color, wrapped into a *rep* message (clauses 4–6).

When all four replies are received at the requesting node, it computes its valency by calling *count_neigh* and sends up to its pyramid parent a *blacks* message. This message indicates to the parent that black pixels are present in the base of its sub-pyramid. The message structure permit information integration at the pnodes in a strictly bottom-up fashion. It is a variable-length list, consisting of one or more *pt* envelopes, or a *bad* symbol. Each *pt* envelope has four slots. The first of these carries the coordinates of the node at the bottom of the pyramid that initiated that particular message. Its role is to enable the detection of neighborhood relation between two or more *pt*'s as a step for the status computation at a pnode. The second slot accumulates the path information as the message ascends the pyramid. The third slot holds the real valency of the point in question, as computed at the pyramid bottom nodes. The last slot is cleared each time the message gets to a new pnode. It is then assigned the value of its *pt*'s valency as computed by the current pnode by examining the various *pts'* first slots to find neighbors among the points. Note that node here enters the *color_from_mark* state which permits the marked pixel to start the activation-spreading process, concurrently with the rest of the computation (clause 7).

Once a pnode which is waiting for count gets four messages from its inferiors, it calls a local procedure (*comp_cnt*) that knows how to compute the status and the next message, to be sent upwards (clauses 8, 9). The *comp_cnt* subroutine does not involve inter-node communications and its description will be omitted here.

As noted above, the node that is marked and has received already the root's permission to start coloring, sends up its request to color. The *color_req* message ascends, following the *pt* message sent immediately before (clauses 10, 11). If the receiving pnode is *OK* and has not yet been colored, it relays *color_req* up.

The request to color is rejected when the first *bad* pnode is reached. If the pnode is already colored, it simply ignores the request. The root is notified in this case to adjust its termination detection bookkeeping accordingly (clauses 12–14).

The pnode that receives a reject message from its superior, knows that it is the highest one that is *OK* in its subpyramid. It adjusts its status and grants its inferior nodes permission to color themselves. The root is notified how many new points to expect from this pnode. The value carried by the *notify_root* message increments a local register at the root, so that there is no need to send a message at all if that value is 0 (clauses 15, 16).

The permission to color is relayed down by the pnodes to all their descendants. The nodes obtaining the permission color themselves and broadcast to all their neighbors a message that spreads the color to the adjacent regions (clauses 17, 18). As it may be seen in clause 24, a black node receiving the *color_neighbor* message behaves exactly like the original marked one. If a node is rejected, it is the highest one that is *OK*, so it should notify the root like a pnode does (i.e., if the number to be sent is different from 0).

Clauses 23–25 describe the response of a node to a *color_neighbor* message. If its origin is from the node itself, it is ignored (this happens at the frame borders). Otherwise, the new blacks start the coloring process again, while the others ignore the *color_neighbor* message. Also, the root is notified accordingly.

Finally, any pnode that receives a notification for the root, relays it upwards (clause 26). This concludes the description of the main control structure of Algorithm CT.

12.5 Conclusions

This paper described Concurrent Prolog implementations of several distributed algorithms for active quadtrees and pyramids. The algorithms performed various image-processing tasks in parallel, by using multiple communicating processes. The main burden of computation for these algorithms resided in the interprocess communications. Concurrent Prolog played a crucial role in the design of the algorithms (especially CT) by providing a legible and, more importantly, working implementation medium.

Once the communication pattern has been devised, the actual code writing was easy. Therefore, we identify formulating the problem in terms of neighborhoods and communications as the first and most important step in algorithm design for Concurrent Prolog.

Another lesson regards the distinction between synchronous and asynchronous parallel algorithms. It is always good to be able to actually implement a parallel algorithm (a thing until now quite difficult and rarely done), no matter which kind. However, since there are tradeoffs and differences in performance between synchronous and asynchronous versions, they should be pointed out when the algorithm is described and analyzed. The termination problem for asynchronous distributed algorithms is one example. It has been solved for algorithms CC and CT by keeping the root node (via which the result was communicated) informed about the number of messages it had yet to receive before termination might be declared. We find this technique useful in many similar cases of termination decision problems in distributed systems.

Ideally, the maximal advantage of Concurrent Prolog techniques in image processing may be realized in low-level applications such as edge extraction, relaxation, thinning, bounded activation, and synchronous cellular algorithms. However, even if the efficiency of existing or anticipated implementations of Concurrent Prolog prevents it from being a useful low-level implementation language in the short term, it still is a powerful tool for the design and debugging of such algorithms, which may be implemented subsequently in lower-level languages.

Acknowledgements

Shimon Ullman supervised Shimon Edelman in the research that led to the formulation of Algorithm CT.

Eyal Yardeni assisted in editing this paper.

Appendix 12.1: Utility Predicates

```
get(Message,c([Message|In],Out),c(In?,Out)).
get_four(M1,M2,M3,M4,[A,B,C,D],[A1?,B1?,C1?,D1?]) ←
    get(M1,A,A1),
    get(M2,B,B1),
    get(M3,C,C1),
    get(M4,D,D1).
get4(M,[A,B,C,D],[A1?,B,C,D],1) ←
    get(M,A,A1).
get4(M,[A,B,C,D],[A,B1?,C,D],2) ←
    get(M,B,B1).
get4(M,[A,B,C,D],[A,B,C1?,D],3) ←
    get(M,C,C1).
get4(M,[A,B,C,D],[A,B,C,D1?],4) ←
    get(M,D,D1).
get_from_any(M,[A,B,C,D],[A1?,B,C,D]) ←
    get(M,A,A1).
get_from_any(M,[A,B,C,D],[A,B1?,C,D]) ←
    get(M,B,B1).
get_from_any(M,[A,B,C,D],[A,B,C1?,D]) ←
    get(M,C,C1).
get_from_any(M,[A,B,C,D],[A,B,C,D1?]) ←
    get(M,D,D1).
put(Message,c(In,[Message|Out]),c(In,Out)).
put4(M,[A,B,C,D],[A1?,B,C,D],1) ←
    put(M,A,A1).
put4(M,[A,B,C,D],[A,B1?,C,D],2) ←
    put(M,B,B1).
put4(M,[A,B,C,D],[A,B,C1?,D],3) ←
    put(M,C,C1).
put4(M,[A,B,C,D],[A,B,C,D1?],4) ←
    put(M,D,D1).
put_all(M,[A,B,C,D],[A1?,B1?,C1?,D1?]) ←
    put(M,A,A1),
    put(M,B,B1),
    put(M,C,C1),
    put(M,D,D1).
push(X,Q,[X|Q]).
pop(X,[X|Q],Q?).
```

Chapter 13

A Test for the Adequacy of a Language for an Architecture

Ehud Shapiro

The Weizmann Institute of Science

Abstract

The development of novel programming languages and novel computer architectures raises the question of the suitability of one for the other. The paper proposes a test for evaluating the adequacy of a programming language L for a machine M: Implement a simulator for M in L and establish that L can be implemented on M so that the simulator executes efficiently. A language L that passes this test can be used as a general-purpose programming language for M, in the sense that any algorithm that can be implemented on M can be implemented on it efficiently in L, and any other programming language L' for M can be implemented on M efficiently by embedding it in L.

The test is applied to Flat Concurrent Prolog and two machine models: a RAM and a network of RAMs.

13.1 Introduction

The computation model underlying conventional programming languages and the computation model of conventional machines are quite similar. Hence the question of whether such a language can be implemented efficiently on such a machine, and whether it can be used to express all interesting behaviors of the machine, has a straightforward affirmative answer. The answer to such a question becomes less straightforward when the computation model underlying the programming language and the machine architecture become further and further apart. This seems to be happening presently, as high-level programming languages and parallel machine architectures become the focus of attention.

Programming languages can be studied in the abstract, and machine architectures can be studied without regard to their programmability. However, it seems that any serious proposal in one of these fields cannot claim viability without looking into the matching solutions of the other. In other words, a proposal for a novel programming language should consider a target machine architecture and establish that the language can execute efficiently on that machine. A proposal for a machine architecture should consider what would be a usable programming language for it. Such a language should have all the standard machine-independent requirements of a useable programming language — simplicity, conciseness, ease-of-use, readability, modifiability, and maintainability, to name a few. In addition, its efficiency and expressiveness with respect to the target machine should be established.

In this paper we propose a simple test for evaluating the adequacy of a programming language for a computer architecture. First, an objective notion of expressiveness is proposed. Second, a notion of efficiency of a programming language with its associated compiler[1] for a given machine is defined. This notion can be used to evaluate, from a theoretical point of view, the efficiency of programming a given machine with the language.

Informally, a language L is said to be *M-expressive* with respect to a machine M if L can specify all possible behaviors of M. This notion is more refined then the Turing-computability notion of expressiveness, as it relates not only to the global function computed by a program running on M, but also to the intermediate steps in the computation. This difference is important especially when concurrent programming languages and parallel and distributed computer architectures are under investigation. A language L with an associated compiler for a machine M is said to be *M-adequate* if it can implement any algorithm on M with a small overhead.

Even under these loose definitions it should be clear that the machine language of M is M-expressive and with the associated identity-compiler is also M-adequate.

The advantage of a high-level language over a machine-language lies usually in dimensions other then efficiency and (objective) expressiveness, e.g., conciseness, readability, and maintainability. The proposed test can be used to evaluate the cost of using a high-level language, in terms of the notions of expressiveness and adequacy defined, compared with other languages, including the machine language

---

[1] Here and in the rest of the paper we use the term *compiler* as a generic term, to mean an implementation of a language on a machine. The discussion holds for other implementation techniques as well, e.g., interpreters.

itself.

In the following discussion we assume that a computation of a machine can be identified with a sequence of states. The same assumption is made for programs, where the states are the states of the abstract machine defining the operational semantics of the programming language. The time of a computation is the number of state transitions in the computation. We also assume a space complexity function from the set of states to the natural numbers, that reflects the space used in each state of the machine. The space required by a computation is the maximal value the space complexity function takes over the states of the computation.

Definition. Let $s=s_1,s_2,\ldots$ be a possibly infinite sequence of elements, possibly containing the undefined element $\perp$. The *defined subsequence* of s is the sequence obtained by deleting all the $\perp$ elements from s. A sequence s' is a *closed subsequence* of s if it is a subsequence of s which contains the first element of s and is infinite if s is infinite, or contains the last element of s if it is finite. ■

Definition. A program S is said to be a *detailed behavioral simulation* of a machine M (or behavioral simulation, for short) if there is a mapping f from states of execution of S to states of $M \cup \{\perp\}$ such that:

(1) For every execution $s_1,s_2,\ldots$ of S, the defined subsequence of $f(s_1),f(s_2),\ldots$ is equal to some execution of M.

(2) For every execution $m=m_1,m_2,\ldots$ of M there is an execution $s_1,s_2,\ldots$ of S for which the defined subsequence of $f(s_1),f(s_2),\ldots$ is equal to m.

A program S is said to be an *abstract behavioral simulation* of M if conditions 1 and 2 above hold with the phrase *equal to* replaced by the phrase *a closed subsequence of*. ■

Our notion of detailed behavioral simulation is similar to the notion of bisimulation of Milner (1984). The difference is that we allow the simulating program S to be in intermediate states, which do not correspond to states of the simulated machine M.

Note that the most abstract simulation of a finite computation starts from a state corresponding to the the initial state of M and ends with a state corresponding to the final state of M, with no meaningful states in between.

Definition. Let ML be the machine language of M, and L be a high-level language, with an associated compiler C on M (i.e., a compiler from L to ML). We say that L is *M-expressive* if there is a program S in L which is a detailed behavioral simulation of M. We say that the pair $\langle L,C \rangle$ is *M-adequate* if there is a detailed behavioral simulator S for M in L, and a constant c, such that for every ML program P, the time and space required for M to execute S simulating P, where S is compiled using C, are at most c times more then the time and space, respectively, required for M to execute P directly. ∎

If L is M-expressive, it is easy to see that any behavior of M can be realized by L, which implies that any algorithm that can be implemented on M at all can be implemented on it using L. If, in addition, L has a compiler C on M for which $\langle L, C \rangle$ are M-adequate, then the overhead of implementing an algorithm in L, rather then in M's machine language, can be bound by a multiplicative constant, both in time and space.

There is one obvious way of generating a compiler C for an M-expressive language L, such that the pair $\langle L, C \rangle$ is M-adequate. All the compiler has to do is to have a special case for recognizing some behavioral simulator S for M, and generate special code for executing it. Presumably this code would translate S's argument (the program P to be simulated) into a machine language program and then "branch" to execute it. When evaluating the adequacy of a language for a machine, we would like to exclude such "dishonest" compilers from the discussion.

Given the above definitions, we propose the following test for evaluating the adequacy of a language L for a machine M. First, implement in L a detailed behavioral simulator for M. This will establish that L is M-expressive. Sometimes it might be easier to implement an abstract behavioral simulator instead and argue that it can be made into a detailed behavioral simulator, if desired. Second, show an implementation technique of L on M, for which S will execute on M with overhead bounded by a multiplicative constant. This would establish that L can have a compiler with which it would be M-adequate.

We propose this as a standard test for evaluating the adequacy of a programming language for a machine architecture.

We demonstrate the method by applying it to the programming language Flat Concurrent Prolog (Shapiro, Chapter 5) and two machine models: a sequential Random Access Machine (RAM) and a parallel computer, composed of a network of RAMs (also called Direct Connection Machine). The network of RAMs model includes, among others, tree, mesh, hypercube, and cross-bar connected computers, as well as systolic arrays of various topologies. It is not obvious *a-priori* that a language like Flat Concurrent Prolog can either express a simulator for such a model, or be implemented on such a machine in a way that executing this simulator would incur only a constant overhead.

We show below that Flat Concurrent Prolog is adequate for these machine models, if augmented with a constant time multiway stream merger and stream distributor (Shapiro and Safra, Chapter 15; Ueda and Chikayama, 1984), and a process-to-processor mapping notation (Shapiro, Chapter 7).

The claim is demonstrated via working Flat Concurrent Prolog simulators of a RAM and a network of RAMs. The correctness of the simulators is argued informally and their complexity analyzed with respect to known compilation and parallel implementation techniques (Houri and Shapiro, Chapter 38; Taylor et al., Chapter 39). A formal proof of correctness is pending formalization of the semantics of the language.

The significance of this result, besides being an example of applying the proposed method, is threefold. First, Flat Concurrent Prolog is a cumbersome language for implementing von Neumann algorithms and exhibits its strength mostly when used to implement parallel algorithms, defined in terms of dynamic networks of asynchronous communicating processes. This result shows that even if such parallel algorithms are not known at present for a certain problem, and one must resort to an existing von Neumann algorithm, then Flat Concurrent Prolog can still be used efficiently.

Second, this result answers questions concerning the expressiveness of Flat Concurrent Prolog compared with other concurrent programming languages, such as CSP (Hoare, 1985), CCS (Milner, 1980), Occam (INMOS, 1984b), Multilisp (Halstead, 1984), and Ada. It shows, indirectly, that Flat Concurrent Prolog is as expressive and as efficient as any of these languages on any practical sequential or parallel computer, in the sense that it can simulate efficiently programs in these languages on these computers. (A more direct proof with respect to CSP and Occam is shown by Safra, 1986.)

Third, achieving the result required using a process-to-processor mapping notation. This provides some circumstantial evidence and a justification for introducing a mapping notation into high-level languages for parallel computers, as proposed by Shapiro (Chapter 7). Alternatively, it puts the burden of proof on those who deny the need for such a notation. In its absence, one should argue that the compiler or the runtime system of a given language would be able to map the simulator of a network of RAMs onto a physical network of RAMs in a way that preserves the performance of the underlying machine. Apparently, this requires that processes simulating a RAM be mapped to physical RAMs and simulated links be mapped to physical links in a way isomorphic to the underlying RAM network. Although theoretically possible, automatic construction of such a mapping seems to be way beyond the scope of present compilation or automatic mapping techniques.

We conjecture that this result holds also for other concurrent programming languages mentioned, provided they are augmented with a mapping notation, implying that all these languages are equivalent in this respect. However, the higher-level the language is, the larger the gap between it and the machine language, and the more difficult it is to establish its adequacy. Since Flat Concurrent Prolog's abstract computation model seems to be the furthest from that of a RAM or a network of RAMs amongst the languages mentioned, its membership in this class is the most surprising.

It should be mentioned that the same technique used here can be applied to other concurrent logic languages, such as PARLOG (Clark and Gregory, Chapter

3) and GHC (Ueda, Chapter 4), to obtain a similar result. The results shown hold also for Concurrent Prolog, provided the implementation techniques applied to its flat subset carry over to the full language.

It would be desirable to provide a natural example of a language and a machine for which the language is not adequate. Intuitively, it should seem clear that any conventional sequential language is not adequate for a parallel computer. Proving such a result is beyond the scope of this paper.

13.2 Simulating a Random Access Machine in Flat Concurrent Prolog

The RAM we chose to simulate is inspired by INMOS's Transputer (INMOS, 1984a). It has three registers, which operate like a stack, and one- and zero-argument instructions. Zero-argument instructions take their arguments from the registers. A simplified instruction set is shown in Figure 13.1.

loadc(Constant)
load(Address)
store(Address)
add
sub
jump(Address)
jumpgt(Address)
halt

Figure 13.1: A reduced RAM instruction set

The Flat Concurrent Prolog simulator is composed of two main processes, *cpu* and *memory*, which communicate via incomplete messages. Incomplete-messages are a Concurrent Prolog programming technique used to simplify communication protocols. The sender of a message that requires a response sends a message that contains an uninstantiated variable, called the *response variable*, and waits for this variable to be instantiated. The receiver of the message replies to it by instantiating the response variable to the actual response.

The cpu and memory communicate via two messages, *read(Address,Contents)* and *write(Address,Contents)*. The cpu sends the *read* messages to memory with *Address* instantiated and the response variable *Contents* uninstantiated, and memory responds by instantiating *Contents*. A *write* message is sent with both arguments instantiated.

The cpu process has five arguments: the program-counter, three registers A, B, and C, and a stream to memory. It has two additional arguments, used in the

```
cpu(ToMemory) ←
    cpu_fetch(0,0,0,0,ToMemory).
cpu_fetch(A,B,C,PC,[read(PC?,Instruction)|ToMemory]) ←
    decode(Instruction?,Opcode,Operand),
    PC1:=PC+1,
    cpu_execute(Opcode?,Operand?,A,B,C,PC1?,ToMemory).
cpu_execute(loadc,Constant,A,B,C,PC,ToMemory) ←
    cpu_fetch(Constant,A,B,PC,ToMemory).
cpu_execute(load,Address,A,B,C,PC,[read(Address,Contents)|ToMemory]) ←
    cpu_fetch(Contents?,A,B,PC,ToMemory).
cpu_execute(store,Address,A,B,C,PC,[write(Address,A)|ToMemory]) ←
    cpu_fetch(B,C,0,PC,ToMemory).
cpu_execute(add,_,A,B,C,PC,ToMemory) ←
    B1:=A+B,
    cpu_fetch(B1?,C,0,PC,ToMemory).
cpu_execute(sub,_,A,B,C,PC,ToMemory) ←
    B1:=A-B,
    cpu_fetch(B1?,C,0,PC,ToMemory).
cpu_execute(jump,Address,A,B,C,PC,ToMemory) ←
    cpu_fetch(A,B,C,Address,ToMemory).
cpu_execute(jumpgt,Address,A,B,C,PC,ToMemory) ←
    A>0 |
    cpu_fetch(B,C,0,Address,ToMemory).
cpu_execute(jumpgt,Address,A,B,C,PC,ToMemory) ←
    A≤0 |
    cpu_fetch(B,C,0,PC,ToMemory).
cpu_execute(halt,_,A,B,C,PC,[ ]).
```

Program 13.1: A simulator of a simple cpu

```
cell([read(Address,Contents)|In],Contents) ←
    cell(In?,Contents).
cell([write(Address,NewContents)|In],Contents) ←
    cell(In?,NewContents).
cell([ ],Contents).
```

Program 13.2: A memory cell process

execute cycle, which simulate the instruction register and the operand register. It has two procedures, *cpu_fetch* and *cpu_execute*, which correspond to the cpu's fetch and execute states. The code is shown in Program 13.1. As in Prolog, the term $[X \mid Xs]$ denotes a list or stream whose head (car) is X and tail (cdr) is Xs.

The memory is composed of memory cells. Each memory cell is simulated by a process that has two arguments: an input stream and a value. The code for a memory cell process is shown in Program 13.2.

The remaining question is how to interface the cpu to memory. One solution uses a tree of binary *distribute* processes. When a binary distribute process receives a read or write message on its input stream, it peels off the most significant bit of the address. If this bit is zero, it sends the message on the left stream, if one, on the right. Assuming that an address is represented as a list of bits when sent to memory, a binary distributor can be defined as in Program 13.3. The program also defines the process *distribute_tree(XXs, Ys)*, which, given a list of streams *XXs* to memory cells, spawns a balanced tree of binary *distribute* processes, whose root stream is *Ys*.

```
distribute(   [Request([0|Address],Contents)|In],
              [Request(Address,Contents)|Out1],
              Out2
) ←
      distribute(In?,Out1,Out2).
distribute(   [Request([1|Address],Contents)|In],
              Out1,
              [Request(Address,Contents)|Out2]
) ←
      distribute(In?,Out1,Out2).
distribute([ ],[ ],[ ]).

distribute_tree(XXs,Ys) ←
      XXs≠[_] |
      distribute_layer(XXs,YYs),
      distribute_tree(YYs?,Ys).
distribute_tree([Xs],Xs).

distribute_layer([Xs1,Xs2|XXs],[Ys|YYs?]) ←
      distribute(Xs1?,Xs2?,Ys),
      distribute_layer(XXs?,YYs).
distribute_layer([Xs],[Xs]).
distribute_layer([ ],[ ]).
```

Program 13.3: Spawning a balanced tree of binary stream distributors

Program 13.4 puts the different pieces together and constructs a simulator for a RAM with a given initial memory contents. Address translation (of words to lists of bits) is trivial and is not shown.

```
ram(InitialMemoryContent) ←
    cpu(ToMemory),
    address_translation(ToMemory?,ToMemory1),
    cells(InitialMemoryContent?,Cells),
    distribute_tree(Cells?,ToMemory1?).

cells([M|Ms],[C|Cs?]) ←
    cell(C?,M),
    cells(Ms?,Cs).
cells([ ],[ ]).
```

Program 13.4: A RAM simulator

We claim that when a cpu enters the nth fetch cycle, and its previous messages arrive at the memory cells, then the content of registers and memory of the processes defined by Program 13.4 correspond to the content of the registers and memory of the simulated RAM at the same fetch cycle, if its computation began with the same initial memory content.

To analyze the performance of this Flat Concurrent Prolog program on a RAM, one basic assumption must be made: that a process reduction takes a constant time. This constant may, of course, be program dependent. This assumption is behind the use of the term LIPS (Logical Inferences Per Second) for measuring the speed of implementations of logic programming languages. For Flat Concurrent Prolog, LIPS means process reductions per second. Although the folklore is that LIPS is a fairly stable measure, this assumption needs to be justified. Indeed, it is possible that a reduction would require to unify two arbitrarily large input terms and hence can take an unbounded amount of time. Fortunately, this is usually not the case in Prolog and Concurrent Prolog programs in general and does not happen in our simulator in particular, since no clause in the programs shown attempts to unify two input terms. The last claim can be verified by a mode analysis of the program. If general unification is not required, then the head of axioms in a procedure can be compiled into linear code, whose length is linear in the size of the source program (Warren, 1980). Hence we can assume that one process reduction takes a time bounded by some program-dependent constant.

It is easy to see that the cpu simulator performs at most five reductions and issues two memory requests per RAM instruction simulated, and that a memory cell simulator performs one reduction per request. Hence, excluding address translation and routing of memory requests, the simulator requires seven reductions per instruction simulated. Hence the simulation of one RAM instruction, excluding routing, takes a time bounded by a constant.

Considering space, note that on each reduction only a constant number of data-structures are created, and that the size of the active set of data in each fetch/execute simulation cycle, which cannot be garbage collected, is also constant as it contains just the memory requests for that cycle. The number of processes, excluding routing, is linear in the size of the memory of the simulated RAM. Hence the total amount of storage required, excluding routing, is a constant times the memory size of the simulated RAM. Using some real-time garbage collector (Baker, 1978a), the overhead of collecting the garbage is again a constant times the number of instructions simulated.

The distribution tree adds a logarithmic factor to the above analysis, both in time and in space. To reduce this factor, it can be substituted by a multiway stream distributor (Ueda and Chikayama, 1984). For any fixed n, a multiway distributor can be defined in Concurrent Prolog according to the scheme shown in Program 13.5. Note that this program does not require address translation.

```
distribute(  [Request(1,Contents)|In],
             [Request(1,Contents)|Out1],
             Out2,
             ...,
             Outn
) ←
     distribute(In?,Out1,Out2,...,Outn).
distribute(  [Request(2,Contents)|In],
             Out1,
             [Request(2,Contents)|Out2],
             ...,
             Outn
) ←
     distribute(In?,Out1,Out2,...,Outn).
...
distribute(  [Request(n,Contents)|In],
             Out1,
             Out2,
             ...,
             [Request(n,Contents)|Outn]
) ←
     distribute(In?,Out1,Out2,...,Outn).
```

Program 13.5: A multiway stream distributor

Although specifiable in Flat Concurrent Prolog, Program 13.5 is the wrong way to implement a stream distributor. It is bulky (the code size is n^2) and is inflexible (it needs a separate procedure for each n). Hence Ueda and Chikayama (1984) proposed to incorporate a general n-ary stream distributor as an extension ("system predicate") to Concurrent Prolog. It is straightforward to implement such a distributor on a RAM so that it would require a constant time to send a message and would occupy space linear in n.

Using such a multiway stream distributor, instead of the binary distribution tree, the RAM simulator would require constant time and space overhead.

13.3 Simulating a network of RAMs in Flat Concurrent Prolog

The model of a network of RAMs, we assume, is an abstraction of various existing and proposed architectures for parallel computers. A set of n RAMs is interconnected with bidirectional communication links, whose graph has a degree d. The degree can be a small constant (e.g., trees, rectangular and hexagonal meshes), or logarithmic in n (e.g., hypercubes, cube-connected cycles), or linear in n (e.g., a cross-bar switch).

The link architecture we chose is again influenced by the Transputer, though not identical to it. A link can be thought of as a processor, connected to the cpu, to memory, and to an adjacent link processor. It can receive requests from the cpu and acknowledge them. It can input messages from its adjacent link and output messages to it. It can also read from and write to memory.

A cpu can issue a *read(From, To)* or a *write(From, To)* request to a link. A link that receives a *write(From, To)* request from a cpu reads the *Contents* of address *From* from memory and outputs the message *write(To, Contents)* to its adjacent link. A link that receives a request *read(From, To)* from the cpu outputs it. A link that inputs a message *write(To, Contents)* from an adjacent link writes *Contents* at address *To* in memory. A link that inputs a message *read(From, To)* from its adjacent link reads the *Contents* of address *From* from memory and outputs the message *write(To, Contents)* back to its adjacent link.

We spell out a minimal set of assumptions about the cpu and links to be preserved by the simulator. A request from the cpu to a link to perform a read or a write is eventually served by the link. A message sent by a link is eventually received by the adjacent link. A message received by a link is eventually served. Link messages are served in the order in which they are issued, but no assumption is made on the time it takes to serve any individual message.

To prevent starvation, the sending and receiving of messages can be interleaved by the links. This technique is implemented in the lowest level of the communication protocol of the Transputer link, which interleaves data and acknowledgement packets. In addition, access to memory is timeshared between the cpu and the links.

To prevent the accumulation of unserved messages, some synchronization protocol between the cpu and links is necessary. The link acknowledges a cpu request upon completion of its service and acknowledges an input message upon receipt. Note that this synchronization has no relationship to the correctness of the execution, and its sole purpose is to eliminate the (possibly unbounded) hardware buffers needed in case less strict synchronization is used.

To simulate this machine, the RAM simulator shown above is extended with a set of link processes, one for each link simulated, and a merge/distribute network, shown in Figure 13.2, which distributes messages from the cpu to the links, and merges messages from the links and cpu to the memory. The cpu is extended with an output stream to the links. It definition is shown in Program 13.6.

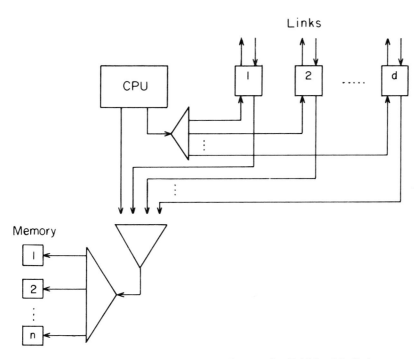

Figure 13.2: A simulator of a RAM with links

The instruction set is extended with two-argument link instructions, *read* and *write*, which take their arguments from the register stack. Both use the *A*

cpu(ToMemory,ToLinks) ←
    cpu_fetch(0,0,0,0,ToMemory,ToLinks).

cpu_fetch(A,B,C,PC,[read(PC?,Instruction)|ToMemory],ToLinks) ←
    decode(Instruction?,Opcode,Operand),
    PC1:=PC+1,
    cpu_execute(Opcode?,Operand?,A,B,C,PC1?,ToMemory,ToLinks).

cpu_execute(loadc,Constant,A,B,C,PC,ToMemory,ToLinks) ←
    cpu_fetch(Constant,A,B,PC,ToMemory,ToLinks).

... (similar to Program 13.1) ...

cpu_execute(read,_,LinkNo,From,To,PC,ToMemory,
    [read(LinkNo,From,To,Ack)|ToLinks]) ←
        cpu_wait(Ack?,0,0,0,PC,ToMemory,ToLinks).

cpu_execute(write,_,LinkNo,From,To,PC,ToMemory,
    [write(LinkNo,From,To,Ack)|ToLinks]) ←
        cpu_wait(Ack?,0,0,0,PC,ToMemory,ToLinks).

cpu_wait(true,A,B,C,PC,ToMemory,ToLinks) ←
    cpu_fetch(A,B,C,PC,ToMemory,ToLinks).

Program 13.6: A simulator of a cpu with links interface

register to specify the link number, the B register for the source memory address, and C for the destination address. Note that the link instructions can easily be extended to full block-transfer (DMA) instructions, as in the Transputer, e.g., by letting the instruction argument specify the length of the block to be read or written.

The cpu has one additional state, which it enters after issuing a link instruction, waiting for acknowledgement from the link. The link acknowledges the request after it completes serving it. The only reason to introduce this synchronization is to eliminate the need to buffer requests from cpu to the links. Clearly a more sophisticated processor architecture can be envisioned, in which the link instruction is executed asynchronously, notifying the cpu upon completion, as in the Transputer. The specification of such an architecture is beyond the purposes of this paper.

A link process that receives a read or write message from the adjacent link acknowledges it and responds by issuing the corresponding local read or write request. When it receives a read or write request from the cpu, it issues the local memory reads to fetch the necessary values and sends the request to the adjacent link.

The simulator shown here is not a detailed behavioral simulator, as it does not reflect all the intermediate states of the simulated network. However, it should be evident from the following discussion that the programming shortcuts taken are not essential and that a more pedestrian simulator, which mimics all the low-level communication protocols of the simulated machine, can be composed.

```
% link(FromCpu,FromLink,ToMemory,ToLink)

link(  [read(From,To,Ack)|FromCpu],
       FromLink,
       [write(To,Contents?)|ToMemory],
       [read(From,Contents,Ack)|ToLink]
) ←
       link(FromCpu?,FromLink?,ToMemory,ToLink).

link(  [write(From,To,Ack)|FromCpu],
       FromLink,
       [read(From,Contents)|ToMemory],
       [write(To,Content?,Ack)|ToLink]
) ←
       link(FromCpu?,FromLink?,ToMemory,ToLink).

link(  FromCpu
       [read(From,Contents,true)|FromLink],
       [read(From,Contents)|ToMemory],
       ToLink
) ←
       link(FromCpu?,FromLink?,ToMemory,ToLink).

link(  FromCpu
       [write(To,Contents,true)|FromLink],
       [write(To,Contents)|ToMemory],
       ToLink
) ←
       link(FromCpu?,FromLink?,ToMemory,ToLink).

link([ ],[ ],[ ],[ ]).
```

Program 13.7: A link simulator

For example, the link simulator, shown in Program 13.7, leaves many low-level details of the synchronization and acknowledgement protocols unspecified, in favor of higher-level programming techniques, including incomplete messages (Shapiro, Chapter 2). When receiving a read request *read(From,To,Ack)* from the cpu, where *Ack* is the uninstantiated response variable, the link issues the remote read request *read(From,Contents,Ack)*, with both *Contents* and *Ack* uninstantiated, on its output stream, and simultaneously issues the corresponding local write request *write(To,Contents)* to local memory. It does not wait for completion of the remote read, but instead forms a Concurrent Prolog channel (shared variable) named *Contents* between the two messages. When the remote read would be served, it would bind *Contents* to the appropriate value. Similarly, it does not wait for acknowledgement for the message, but rather forms a direct channel between the remote acknowledgement channel and the local acknowledgement channel to the cpu, called *Ack*. This frees the link to serve incoming messages, while ensuring that the cpu would not issue another link request before the current one completes.

The cpu, links, and memory are all hooked together as in Figure 13.2, using the code of Program 13.8.

```
ram_with_links(InitialMemoryContent,LinksIn,LinksOut) ←
    cpu(CpuToMemory,CpuToAllLinks),
    distributor(CpuToAllLinks?,CpuToLinks),
    links(LinksIn?,LinksOut?,CpuToLinks,LinksToMemory),
    cells(InitialMemoryContent?,ToCells),
    merger([CpuToMemory|LinksToMemory],ToMemory),
    distributor(ToMemory?,ToCells?).

links(  [FromLink|LinksIn],
        [ToLink|LinksOut],
        [FromCpu|CpuToLinks],
        [ToMemory|LinksToMemory]
    ) ←
        link(FromCpu?,FromLink?,ToMemory,ToLink),
        links(LinksIn?,LinksOut?,CpuToLinks,LinksToMemory).
links([ ],[ ],[ ],[ ]).

cpu(CpuToMemory,CpuToAllLinks) ← See Program 13.6

link(FromCpu?,FromLink?,ToMemory,ToLink) ← See Program 13.7

cells(Ms,Cs) ← See Program 13.4
```

Program 13.8: A simulator of a RAM with links

Arguing formally the correctness of the simulator would require defining a network of RAM's in some acceptable specification language for concurrent systems, and arguing the equivalence of the specification and the program. As said earlier, a precondition for such an endeavor is a formal semantics for concurrent Prolog. The author conjectures that a full formal specification of a network of

RAMs in any acceptable formalism would not necessarily be clearer or shorter than the Concurrent Prolog program shown.

Arguing about the simulator's performance requires an understanding of how Flat Concurrent Prolog can be implemented on a network of RAMs. One proposal was given by Tamaki (1985). A more general solution, which has been implemented on a hypercube-connected parallel computer, is given by Taylor et al. (Chapter 39). Here we outline only the necessary details. A logical variable is represented by a memory cell. A variable shared between processors has a home address, i.e., it resides in one of the processors' address space. Other occurrences of the variables are references to this address, which implies that a reference can be into another processor's address space. Reading the value of a remote logical variable can be achieved by sending to the remote processor a request to write the value of that variable on some local address. The remote processor responds by sending back the value of that variable, when available. This scheme has been incorporated in a parallel Flat Concurrent Prolog interpreter (Taylor et al., Chapter 39). That implementation also solves difficulties that arise when multiple processes on different processors attempt to write on the same logical variable. However, this condition does not arise in our simulator.

If we assume that adjacent link processes are actually mapped to adjacent processors, as discussed below, then it is possible to verify that sending a message that contains a remote logical variable, reading a remote logical variable, and writing on a remote logical variable can each be implemented using a constant amount of processing and communication.

The simulated read and write messages are incomplete messages of constant size, hence reading them and responding to them can be done using a constant number of underlying read and write link operations. In particular, receiving a simulated remote read or write request requires reading the message type and its *From* and *To* arguments and writing on the logical variable *Ack*. Sending it means serving the read messages for the simulator's message and type arguments, by sending the appropriate write messages and serving the write message that acknowledges the receipt. Hence both sending and receiving a simulated read or write message requires a constant number of underlying read and write messages.

The one component that was not specified or analyzed yet is the stream merger, that merges requests from the links and the cpu to memory. Using binary mergers (Shapiro and Safra, Chapter 15), a balanced binary merge tree can be constructed, whose delay per message is logarithmic in d, the number of links. Using a constant time multiway merger (Shapiro and Safra, Chapter 15; Ueda and Chikayama, 1984), the delay can be reduced to a constant, and the space occupied by the process structures to be linear in d.

Hence the entire RAM simulator simulates one instruction using a constant number of underlying RAM instructions and a remote read or write request using a constant number of underlying such requests.

The space required by the active set of data is not changed by the addition of links, since the links and the cpu are synchronized, and there can be at most one pending message from the cpu to the links. The links and memory are not synchronized, hence it is possible, under some malicious scheduling, that the stream to the memory will accumulate an unbounded number of unserved requests. This is easily rectified by adding an acknowledgement protocol between the memory and the links, but was omitted from the programs above for the sake of simplicity.

The space required by the process and data structures of the simulator is linear in $n+d$, but since $d \ll n$, we can conclude that it is linear in n.

The final aspect of the simulation is connecting the RAM simulators together and mapping them into the physical network of RAMs in a way isomorphic to this network. This can be achieved using the Turtle-programs mapping notation, proposed by Shapiro (Chapter 7).

We demonstrate the technique assuming the network is a rectangular mesh with toroidal end-connections, or a torus, for short. On a torus, the standard LOGO-like Turtle programs would suffice for mapping. The idea is simple: divide the plane between processors in the obvious way. View each process as a Turtle, having a position and a heading. A process executes on a processor with the same position. A new process P inherits the position and heading from its parent. It may have a Turtle-program T associated with it, as in $T@P$. In such a case it applies the Turtle program T to its inherited position and heading to compute its new position and heading. If the position has changed, it "goes" to the processor located in the new position in order to execute.

Program 13.9 shows the recursive construction of a torus-simulator and its mapping onto a torus of RAMs using Turtle programs. It is invoked with the initial memory contents of all processors, represented as a list of lists, and spawns a torus of RAM simulators, each with its own initial local memory.

Clause 1 in Program 13.9 unifies the bottom and top row links of the torus. Clause 2 spawns a *row* process, sets its heading to be 90 degrees to the right of the *torus* process, and iterates forward to the next processor. It also unifies the left and right end links of that row. Clause 4 does most of the work. It extracts the Left, Bottom and Top links for a RAM, and its Memory, and invokes it with these parameters, and a Right link. It iterates forward (remember it is heading orthogonally to the *torus* process) with the remaining Bottom and Top links, and the new Right link. Note that the recursive construction ensures that every two adjacent links agree which of the two link variables is input or output. For example, to the left the first argument is input and the second is output, and to the right the opposite convention is held.

The time to spawn the simulator process network is of course not included in the cost of simulation, as the time to bootstrap a machine is not included in

torus(TorusMemory) ←   % 1
    torus(TorusMemory,EndLinks,EndLinks).

torus([RowMemory|TorusMemory],BottomLinks,TopLinks) ←   % 2
    row(RowMemory,EndLink,EndLink,BottomLinks,NextLinks)@*right*,
    torus(TorusMemory?,NextLinks?,TopLinks)@*forward*.

torus([ ],EndLinks,EndLinks).   % 3

row([Memory|RowMemory],   % 4
      link(FromLeft,ToLeft),
      EndLink,
      [link(FromBottom,ToBottom)|BottomLinks],
      [link(ToTop,FromTop)|TopLinks]) ←
    ram_with_links(Memory?,
               [FromLeft?,FromRight?,FromBottom?,FromTop?],
               [ToLeft,ToRight,ToBottom,ToTop]
              ),
    row(RowMemory?,
        link(ToRight,FromRight),
        EndLink,
        BottomLinks?,
        TopLinks
)@*forward*.

row([ ],EndLink,EndLink,[ ],[ ]).   % 5

ram_with_links(Memory,LinksIn,LinksOut) ← See Program 13.8

Program 13.9: Spawning a torus of RAM simulators on a torus

the complexity analysis of algorithms it executes. However, two delicate points need to be addressed, to establish that the preconditions to the above complexity analysis hold. One condition is that each RAM simulator process resides in the appropriate RAM. This is easily verified for the current example. The other is that simulated links communicate via the appropriate physical links. This is more difficult to achieve, since the recursive construction of two adjacent rows is done independently, and in parallel. Hence it is not obvious how to ensure, for example, that the *FromBottom* variable of one link process is a direct reference to the *ToTop* variable of the adjacent link process just below it. Tamaki (1985) has proposed one technique to achieve this. However, even if his restrictions are relaxed a bit, the desired situation can be achieved if after initialization each link process would send one dummy message to the adjacent link that would contain a direct reference to the new link variable (Taylor et al., Chapter 39). This message would not necessarily be routed directly, but its cost can be apportioned to the initialization procedure.

13.4 Conclusion

We have shown simulators for a RAM and a network of RAMs in Flat Concurrent Prolog and argued that the language can be implemented in these machine models so that the simulators run with constant overhead on these machines. According to the criterion proposed, we have established the adequacy of the language for these machines.

Besides establishing the implications mentioned in the introduction, the paper was also an exercise in hardware specification. It seems that the distance from the simulator shown above to a functional specification of a network of microprocessors like the Transputer is not that far.

Acknowledgements

The ideas in this paper, as well as their presentation, were influenced by several discussions with Oded Shmueli and Alex Nicolau. Comments by Oded, Alex, David Harel, Marc Snir and Bernard Weinberg on earlier drafts are acknowledged.

Part III

Streams and Channels

Introduction

One-to-one and one-to-many communication is easily expressed in concurrent logic programming languages. A shared logical variable can either be unified with a single message, when a single communication is required, or with an incrementally-constructed message stream, for multiple communications. Many-to-one communication, however, requires the programming of an arbitration mechanism. Merging multiple message-streams into one is the common way to achieve this. It is investigated in the first three papers of this part.

Chapter 14, "Fair, Biased, and Self-Balancing Merge Operators: Their Specification and Implementation in Concurrent Prolog", by Shapiro and Mierowsky, explores efficient many-to-one communication in Concurrent Prolog, using the concept of merge-trees. It shows how biased merge-trees can merge a dynamically changing number of streams fairly. It argues that for efficiency merge-trees should be kept balanced, and shows a method for maintaining balanced merge-trees using the concept of two-three trees. Using this technique the delay (i.e., the number of operations per message) of a merge-tree can be logarithmic in the number of streams being merged.

Chapter 15, "Multiway Merge with Constant Delay in Concurrent Prolog", by Shapiro and Safra, improves further the performance of merge operators, using an abstract data-type called mutual-reference. This data-type can be viewed as a local optimization of a Concurrent Prolog program, specifying the merge operator using a multiple-writers stream. Such a merger is at the heart of the efficient RAM simulator described in Chapter 13.

Chapter 16, "Merging Many Streams Efficiently: The Importance of Atomic Commitment", by Saraswat, describes another technique for many-to-one communication, which performs well in case there are multiple input streams which are ready most of the time. This technique, implemented in his language FCP($\downarrow$), demonstrates the utility of atomic unification.

Chapter 17, "Channels: A Generalization of Streams", by Tribble, Miller, Kahn, Bobrow, Abbott, and Shapiro, describes a generalization of streams, called channels. In contrast to streams, which are totally ordered, channels are only partially ordered. Using channels reduces the necessary synchronization overhead required by multiple-writers streams, and increases the parallelism available when reading output produced by multiple writers.

The specification of a multiple-writers stream shown in this paper is the key component in the multiway merger shown in Chapter 15. The programming technique used in this specification, as well as in the specification of multiple-writers channels, exploits the atomicity of unification and properties of the read-only variable in a fundamental way. Hence neither multiple-writers streams nor channels seem to be easily specifiable in the other concurrent logic programming languages.

Chapter 18, "Bounded-Buffer Communication in Concurrent Prolog", by Takeuchi and Furukawa, addresses the problem of how to implement demand-driven communication and computation in a data-driven language. It shows that demand-driven bounded-buffer communication can be implemented on top of the synchronization mechanism of Concurrent Prolog. This programming technique justifies, in retrospect, the design decision not to include the bounded-buffer annotation of the Relational Language in Concurrent Prolog. It applies to any concurrent logic programming language that supports incomplete messages, i.e., all the languages reviewed except the Relational Language. In addition, the paper explores the specification of protected data using the read-only variable, as proposed by Hellerstein and Shapiro (Chapter 9), and its use in abstract stream operations.

Unlike Part II, the Concurrent Prolog and Flat Concurrent Prolog programs in Part III are not always translatable to GHC or PARLOG. Specifically, the mergers defined in Chapter 15 and Chapter 16, and the channel operations defined in Chapter 17, rely on atomic test unification. The technique for preserving message multiplicity used in Chapter 15 and Chapter 17 relies on properties of the read-only variable.

Chapter 14

Fair, Biased, and Self-Balancing Merge Operators: Their Specification and Implementation in Concurrent Prolog

Ehud Shapiro and Colin Mierowsky

The Weizmann Institute of Science

Abstract

The problem of allowing a dynamically changing set of processes fair access to a shared resource is considered, in the context of communication-stream based systems. It is argued that fair binary merge operators alone cannot solve this problem satisfactorily. Two solutions are proposed. One employs binary merge operators with a programmable bias; the other binary and ternary fair merge operators capable of self-balancing, using the concept of 2–3 trees. A Concurrent Prolog implementation of these operators is described. The implementation of the self-balancing merge operators illustrates the expressive power of incomplete messages, a programming technique that supports messages that contain communication channels as arguments. In the course of implementing the self-balancing merge operator, it was necessary to develop a distributed variant of the 2–3 tree deletion algorithm.

14.1 Introduction

Streams were proposed by Kahn and MacQueen (1977) as an elegant basis for process communication and synchronization. To support time-dependent applications such as the implementation of an operating system, stream-based languages were augmented by an indeterminate binary stream-merge operator (Arvind et al., 1977; Dennis, 1976). The operator is a process that accepts two streams of elements as input and produces an output stream that interleaves their elements.

The questions of what the desired properties of such a merge operator are, and how to specify them, were studied extensively (Brock and Ackerman, 1981; Park, 1980; Smyth, 1982).

We say that a merge operator ensures *n-bounded waiting* if, whenever a message M is ready as the first message in one of its input streams, then at most $n-1$ messages will be sent in the operator's output stream before M is sent.

We say that an n-ary merge operator is *strictly fair* (or *fair* for short) if it ensures $O(n)$-bounded waiting. Strict fairness is more restrictive and more realistic than the common definitions of fairness (Smyth, 1982), which relate to infinite computations.

Several programming languages incorporate a fair binary merge operator of some sort as a primitive (Arvind et al., 1977; Dennis, 1976). Concurrent Prolog, on the other hand, is expressive enough to define a variety of merge operators, including a fair binary merge operator, as shown below.

If more than two processes want to share a resource, then a tree of binary merge operators can be constructed. If the number of processes sharing the resource can be determined statically, then one can construct the merge tree to be balanced. We argue below that balanced merge trees composed of fair binary merge operators ensure linear bounded waiting, i.e., are fair.

However in some languages, including Concurrent Prolog, processes can be created dynamically in an order and at a rate that depends on the input-data, and hence cannot be determined *a priori*. To support access to a shared resource by a dynamically changing set of processes, one has to grow and shrink the merge tree dynamically. The naive solution to the problem is that every process with an access to the shared resource that forks adds a merge operator as a leaf to the tree, passes to it its output stream, and passes to the two newly created processes the two input streams of the merge operator. This can be specified in Concurrent Prolog with the clause:

$$p(X) \leftarrow p1(X1), p2(X2), merge(X1?,X2?,X).$$

in which p reduces itself to *p1*, *p2* and *merge*.

If the tree of merge processes can change only in this way, then child processes will always be ensured of only a fixed fraction of the access to the resource their parents had. In the example above, if p was ensured n-bounded-waiting, and *merge* is fair, then *p1* and *p2* will be ensured of *2n*-bounded waiting. It is shown below that an n-input merge tree that is dynamically constructed in this way may provide, in the worst case, bounded-waiting that is exponential in n.

It seems that there are applications in which a more flexible allocation of access to resources is required, in which the share of a process does not strictly depend on the way it was created. In the following we propose two strategies to overcome this problem, which enable the implementation of dynamic fair merge operators.

The rest of the paper is organized as follows. Section 14.2 shows how a fair binary merge can be implemented in Concurrent Prolog. Section 14.3 is a note on abstract data types, Section 14.4 introduces merge operators with a programmable bias, and Section 14.5 defines self-balancing merge operators. Section 14.6 examines other research, and Section 14.7 concludes the paper.

14.2 Fair Merge Operators

A logic-program implementation of a merge operator was suggested by Clark and Gregory (Chapter 1). To make this logic program into a runnable Concurrent Prolog program, it has to be augmented with read-only annotations, so that the *merge* process suspends if no messages are available in its input streams. One way to do so is the merge operator in Program 14.1a.

> merge([X | Xs],Ys,[X | Zs]) ← merge(Xs?,Ys,Zs).
> merge(Xs,[Y | Ys],[Y | Zs]) ← merge(Xs,Ys?,Zs).
> merge([ ],Ys,Ys).
> merge(Xs,[ ],Xs).

Program 14.1a: A binary merge operator

It works properly if, in the original invocation of the *merge* process, both input channels are annotated read-only, as in:

> merge(Xs?,Ys?,Zs).

In considering the fairness of the merge operator thus defined, we restrict our attention to a specific class of Concurrent Prolog machines, namely stable machines, introduced by Shapiro (Chapter 2). A *stable Concurrent Prolog machine* is a machine that, in attempting to reduce a process which has several clauses whose heads are unifiable with it and have empty guards, will pick the first such clause for reduction. A stable Concurrent Prolog machine executing Program 14.1a, will copy to the output stream only elements from the first input stream, if both are potentially infinite and are generated at least as fast as the *merge* consumes them. Hence this merge operator is not fair and certainly does not guarantee bounded-waiting. On the other hand, on a stable machine, the *merge* operator in Program 14.1b is fair.

It achieves fairness by alternating the priorities of the two streams, i.e., by switching the first and second streams on every reduction.

merge([X | Xs],Ys,[X | Zs]) ← merge(Ys,Xs?,Zs).
merge(Xs,[Y | Ys],[Y | Zs]) ← merge(Ys?,Xs,Zs).
merge([ ],Ys,Ys).
merge(Xs,[ ],Xs).

Program 14.1b: A fair binary merge operator

An *n-input merge tree* is a system of *merge* processes in which n input variables and one output variable occur only once, and all other variables occur exactly twice, once as input and once as output. A merge tree can easily be depicted as a tree, where processes correspond to nodes, and variables shared between processes correspond to edges. Hence we can talk about the size, height, root, and leaves of a merge tree, and the depth and weight of its nodes.

Definition. A merge tree is *balanced* if all its leaves are at depth h or $h + 1$, for some $h > 0$.

An example of a balanced merge tree is shown in Figure 14.1.

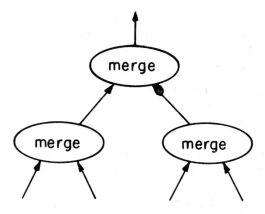

Figure 14.1: A balanced merge tree

Definition. A Concurrent Prolog scheduler is *fair* if, whenever a process P becomes ready for reduction, no other process becoming ready for reduction after P will be reduced before P is. This requirement can be weakened to give an upper bound, say k, on the number of process reductions before P is reduced. This we refer to as a k-fair scheduler.

Definition. A merge tree ensures *n-bounded-waiting* if, whenever a message M

is ready on one of its leaves' input streams, at most n messages not yet in the tree will exit the root of the tree before M does.

A class of merge trees ensures $f(n)$-*bounded-waiting* if every n-input merge tree in the class ensures $f(n)$-bounded-waiting.

Note: The fairness of the scheduler is assumed in all the boundedness results below. In the case of a k-fair scheduler, the results hold if an allowance is made for this k.

Another important aspect of a merge tree is its delay. The delay of a tree is a good measure for its communication overhead.

Definition. The *delay* of an input stream of a merge tree is the minimum number of process reductions required between the appearance of a message at the head of the stream and its exit at the root.

The *delay* of a merge tree is the maximum delay of the input streams which form its leaves. (Typically, this delay is proportional to the height of the tree plus *1*.)

A class of merge trees has a *delay of $f(n)$* if every n-input merge tree in the class has a delay of at most $f(n)$.

Claim. A balanced merge tree composed of fair binary merge operators ensures linear bounded waiting and has a logarithmic delay.

Proof. It can be shown by induction on the height of a tree that an n-inputs merge tree ensures $2n$-bounded-waiting and has a delay of $(\log n) + 1$. ∎

A balanced merge tree constructed out of fair binary merge operators seems to have satisfactory properties. However, if the number and topology of the communicating processes changes dynamically, and the tree is constructed as explained in the introduction by a user process splitting into a merge process and two other user processes, then awkward trees may be constructed. An example is the linear merge tree, as shown in Figure 14.2. A linear merge tree composed of n fair merge operators ensures the inputs to the merge process at depth n only 2^n-bounded-waiting. In other words, an exponential number of messages can be transmitted through the merge tree before a message that entered it on its deepest leaf will be output. In addition, the delay of messages entered at the deepest leaf is n. In other words, a linear merge tree has exponential bounded waiting and linear delay.

Our goal in the rest of the paper is to construct merge operators that compose dynamically into merge trees with linear bounded waiting and minimal delay. In Section 14.4 we define programmable biased merge operators, which compose into linear bounded-waiting merge trees with linear delay. In Section 14.5 we define self-balancing merge operators, which compose into linear bounded-waiting merge trees with logarithmic delay.

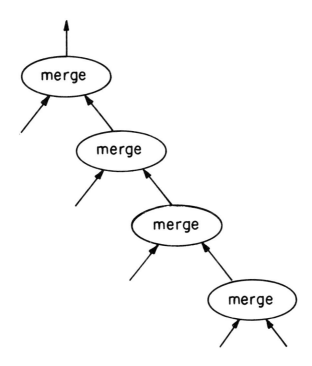

Figure 14.2: A linear merge tree

14.3 A Note on Abstract Data-Types

Another way to implement a *merge* operator uses "abstract-operations" on streams. If we define *send, receive, end_of_stream*, and *connect* as follows:

    send(X.[X | Xs],Xs).
    receive(X,[X | Xs],Xs?).
    end_of_stream([ ]).
    connect(Xs,Xs).

then the *merge* program can be rewritten as Program 14.2.

This definition of *merge* is slightly lengthier and less efficient, but it hides the internal representation of streams and is perhaps more readable. A preprocessor that performs straightforward partial-evaluation (Komorowski, 1982; Safra, 1986) can easily compact it back to the original definition in Program 14.1. Note that it is only in conjunction with a preprocessor which puts the tests for ready messages

merge(X,Y,Z) ←
    receive(M,X,X1) , send(M,Z,Z1) |
    merge(Y,X1,Z1).

merge(X,Y,Z) ←
    receive(M,Y,Y1) , send(M,Z,Z1) |
    merge(Y1,X,Z1).

merge(X,Y,Z) ←
    end_of_stream(X) | connect(Y,Z).

merge(X,Y,Z) ←
    end_of_stream(Y) | connect(X,Z).

Program 14.2: Merge implemented with abstract stream operations

back into the guard, that the stability of the machine will ensure fairness.

14.4 Merge Operators With a Programmable Bias

Our first strategy to obtain dynamic merge trees with linear bounded waiting employs biased merge operators. An *n:m-biased binary merge operator* ensures n-bounded-waiting to its first input stream and m-bounded-waiting to its second input stream. The pair *n:m* is called the *bias* of the operator. A *programmable biased binary merge operator* is a biased merge operator that can change its bias dynamically, according to special messages it receives.

Implementing dynamic merge trees with biased merge operators can be done as follows. Each merge operator maintains a bias that corresponds to the weight of its subtrees. When a subtree grows or shrinks, special messages are sent up the tree, which cause the bias of the operators on the path to the root to be updated. It is not difficult to see that such a strategy ensures linear bounded waiting.

More precisely, when a biased merge operator is created, it sends a *started* message on its output stream and initializes its bias to 1:1. If it receives a *started* message on an input stream, then it increments that stream's bias and forwards the message. If it receives a *halted* message in a stream, then it decrements its bias and forwards the message. If it reaches the end of an input stream, then it sends a *halted* message, connects (unifies) the other input stream to its output stream, and terminates. Other messages are forwarded, alternating priorities between the two streams according to the current bias. Program 14.3 implements this operator.

A programmable biased merge operator is invoked with the call *merge(X?, Y?,*

```
/* Initialization */
/* 1 */   merge(X,Y,Z) ←
               send(started,Z,Z1) |
               merge(1:1,1,X?,Y?,Z1).

/* Switch priorities */
/* 2 */   merge(Bx:By,0,X,Y,Z) ←
               merge(By:Bx,By,Y,X,Z).

/* Forward */
/* 3 */   merge(B,N,X,Y,Z) ←
               N > 0 ,
               forward(B,N,X,Y,Z,B1,N1,X1,Y1,Z1) |
               merge(B1,N1,X1,Y1,Z1).

/* End of stream */
/* 4 */   merge(_,_,X,Y,Z) ←
               end_of_stream(X) | send(halted,Z,Y).

/* 5 */   merge(_,_,X,Y,Z) ←
               end_of_stream(Y) | send(halted,Z,X).

/* 6 */   forward(Bx:By,N,[M | X],Y,[M | Z],Bx1:By,N1,X?,Y,Z) ←
               N1:=N–1 , update_bias(M,Bx,Bx1).

/* 7 */   forward(Bx:By,N,X,[M | Y],[M | Z],Bx:By1,N,X,Y?,Z) ←
               update_bias(M,By,By1).

/* 8 */   update_bias(started,B,B1) ← B1:=B+1.

/* 9 */   update_bias(halted,B,B1) ← B1:=B–1.

/* 10 */  update_bias(X,B,B) ← other(X) | true.

/* 11 */  other(X) ← X ≠ started, X ≠ halted.
```

Program 14.3: A programmable biased merge operator

Z). It then sends in Z the message *started*, and reduces itself to the process *merge(Bx:By,N,X?,Y?,Z)*, in which $(Bx:By) = (1:1)$ is the initial bias of the operator, and $N = 1$ is the number of messages to be forwarded from the first stream before priorities have to be switched. This is specified by Clause 1.

A counter N maintains the number of messages to be transmitted on the high-priority channel before the channels are switched. When this number reaches 0, the channels are switched by Clause 2.

Clause 3 forwards messages, using the *forward* procedure defined by Clauses

6 and 7. Clause 6 also decrements the counter N. The order of the clauses of *forward* guarantees, on a stable machine, that if a message is ready on the first stream then it will be picked before the message on the second stream.

If the message picked is *started*, then the bias of the stream from which the message arrived is incremented, as specified by Clause 8 of the *update_bias* procedure. If the message is *halted*, then that stream's bias is decremented, as specified by Clause 9.

Some delicate points are not addressed in Program 14.3. The root of the tree emits, in addition to the messages entered at the leaves, *halted* and *started* messages. A filter that absorbs these messages can be plugged in the tree's output stream. Also, nothing protects the tree from incoming fictitious *halted* or *started* messages. A user who wishes to abuse the system can send, for example, several *started* messages, thus modifying the bias in his favour. This can be prevented by plugging in the tree's input streams filters that wrap every message X with the tag $msg(X)$, so that inside the merge tree only three types of messages are sent: *halted*, *started*, and $msg(X)$. The filter on the output stream can unwrap the message. If this approach is taken, then user processes can no longer invoke *merge* processes themselves, but rather have to send messages to the input filters, requesting a new input channel to be opened. This technique is used by the self-balancing merge operators, as explained below.

Claim. A merge tree composed of programmable biased merge operators ensures linear bounded waiting and has a linear delay.

Proof. Let N be the counter that determines the number of messages served on the high-priority stream before the low priority stream is served. Messages arriving on the low priority stream have N bounded waiting. Since $N \leq$ the number of leaves the tree (input streams), the low priority stream has linear bounded waiting. On the high priority stream, there is no waiting. This argument holds for each level of the tree.

The height of the tree cannot exceed the number of input streams, so the delay is also linear.   ■

14.5 Self-Balancing Merge Operators

Self-balancing merge operators are introduced to reduce the linear delay of the biased merge operators. They achieve linear bounded waiting and logarithmic delay, using the concept of 2–3 trees (Aho et al., 1974).

A 2–3 merge tree is composed of binary and ternary fair merge operators. It grows according to the 2–3 tree insertion algorithm and shrinks using a concurrent variant of the 2–3 tree deletion algorithm. Growing the tree is much simpler than

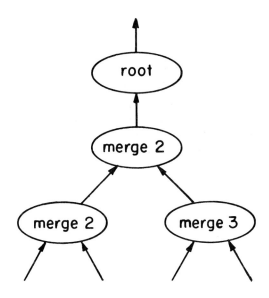

Figure 14.3: A 2–3 merge tree

send(M,c([M|Out?]),c(Out)).

receive(M,c([M|In]),c(In?)).

end_of_stream(c([ ])).

create_channel(c(X?),c(X)).

Program 14.4a: Uni-directional stream operations

shrinking it and hence will be explained first. The following description refers to Program 14.5.

14.5.1 Growing a 2–3 tree

We redefine the abstract operators needed to grow a 2–3 tree in Program 14.4a. This definition can be conveniently replaced for bi-directional channels needed in the sequel.

When a process connected to a leaf requests a new channel X (e.g., when forking) it sends the tree a request $start(X)$. The leaf that receives the request operates according to the 2–3 tree insertion algorithm, as follows.

If the leaf that receives the $start(W)$ message is a binary merge operator,

```
/* merge2 */
/* start a new stream */
/* 1 */   merge2(X,Y,Z) ←
              started2(W,X,Y,X1,Y1) |
              merge3(W,X1,Y1,Z).

          started2(W,X,Y,X1,Y) ←
              receive(start(W),X,X1) | true.
          started2(W,X,Y,X,Y1) ←
              receive(start(W),Y,Y1) | true.
/* forward a message */
/* 2 */   merge2(X,Y,Z) ←
              received2(M,X,Y,X1,Y1) |
              send(M,Z,Z1),
              merge2(Y1,X1,Z1?).

          received2(M,X,Y,X1,Y) ←
              receive(M,X,X1) , other(M) | true.
          received2(M,X,Y,X,Y1) ←
              receive(M,Y,Y1) , other(M) | true.
/* merge3 */
/* start a new stream */
/* 3 */   merge3(W,X,Y,Z) ←
              started3(U,W,X,Y,W1,X1,Y1) |
              create_channel(Vparent,Vchild),
              send(start(Vparent?),Z,Z1),
              merge2(U,W1,Vchild?),
              merge2(X1,Y1,Z1?).

          started3(U,W,X,Y,W1,X,Y) ←
              receive(start(U),W,W1) | true.
          started3(U,W,X,Y,W,X1,Y) ←
              receive(start(U),X,X1) | true.
          started3(U,W,X,Y,W,X,Y1) ←
              receive(start(U),Y,Y1) | true.
/* forward a message */
/* 4 */   merge3(W,X,Y,Z) ←
              received3(M,W,X,Y,W1,X1,Y1) |
              send(M,Z,Z1),
              merge3(X1,Y1,W1,Z1?).
```

Program 14.5: Growing a 2–3 merge tree

```
          received3(M,W,X,Y,W1,X,Y) ←
              receive(M,W,W1) , other(M) | true.
          received3(M,W,X,Y,W,X1,Y) ←
              receive(M,X,X1) , other(M) | true.
          received3(M,W,X,Y,W,X,Y1) ←
              receive(M,Y,Y1) , other(M) | true.
```

/* root */

/* start a new stream */
```
/* 5 */   root(Rin,Rout) ←
              receive(start(S),Rin,R1in) |
              create_channel(Rparent,Rchild),
              merge2(S,R1in,Rchild?),
              root(Rparent?,Rout).
```

/* forward a message */
```
/* 6 */   root(Rin,Rout) ←
              receive(M,Rin,R1in), other(M) |
              send(M,Rout,R1out),
              root(R1in,R1out).
```

```
          other(M)←M ≠ start(_), M ≠ alone(_).
```

Program 14.5: (Continued)

merge2(*X,Y,Z*), then it becomes a ternary merge operator *merge3*(*W,X,Y,Z*), as specified by Clause 1 in Program 14.5. If the leaf is a ternary merge operator *merge3*(*W,X,Y,Z*), then upon receiving a *start*(*U*) message in one of its input streams, it forks into two binary merge operators, *merge2*(*U,W,V*) and *merge2*(*X,Y,Z*), and sends a *start*(*V*) message on its output channel *Z* (Clause 3). When the root of the tree, *root*(*X,Y*), receives a *start*(*W*) message, it creates a *merge2*(*X,W,X1*) process and iterates with *X1* as its new input stream (Clause 5). This operation is the only one that increases the height of the tree.

Other messages are forwarded by the *merge2*, *merge3*, and root processes (Clauses 2, 4, and 6).

Program 14.5 deadlocks upon reaching the end of its streams, instead of shrinking the tree as streams end. A naive solution to handling the end of a stream is for a binary merge to connect its remaining input stream with its output stream, for a ternary merge to become a binary merge, and for the root to close its output stream and terminate. This is specified by Program 14.5a.

This solution destroys the property of the 2–3 tree for which it was intro-

merge2(X,Y,Z) ←
    end_of_stream(X) | connect(Y,Z).
merge2(X,Y,Z) ←
    end_of_stream(Y) | connect(X,Z).

merge3(W,X,Y,Z) ←
    ended3(W,X,Y,X1,Y1) | merge2(X1,Y1,Z).

ended3(W,X,Y,X,Y) ← end_of_stream(W) | true.
ended3(W,X,Y,W,Y) ← end_of_stream(X) | true.
ended3(W,X,Y,W,X) ← end_of_stream(Y) | true.

root(Rin,Rout) ←
    end_of_stream(Rin) | end_of_stream(Rout).

Program 14.5a: Shrinking a 2–3 merge tree naively

duced, the fact that it is always balanced, and in the worst case may result in a linear merge tree.

14.5.2 Bi-directional stream operations

The 2–3 tree deletion program requires messages to be sent both upwards and downwards, so we redefine the stream operations to operate on bi-directional streams as shown in Program 14.4b.

send(M,c(In,[M | Out]),c(In,Out)).

receive(M,c([M | In],Out),c(In?,Out)).

end_of_stream(c([ ],_)).

close_stream(c(_,[ ])).

create_channel(c(In?,Out),c(Out?,In)).

Program 14.4b: Bi-directional stream operations

The fact that we can change a program operating on unidirectional streams to one operating on bi-directional streams by changing the definition of the abstract operations, illustrates the flexibility inherent in their use.

14.5.3 Shrinking a 2–3 merge tree

Program 14.6, using the bi-directional stream operations of Program 14.4b, extends Program 14.5 to shrink the merge tree, maintaining its balance.

```
/* Shrink the tree */
/* 7 */   root(Rin,Rout) ←
              receive(alone(S),Rin,_) |
              root(S,Rout).

/* end of stream */
/* 8 */   merge2(X,Y,Z) ←
              ended2(X,Y,S) | send(S,Z,_).

          ended2(X,Y,alone(Y)) ←
              end_of_stream(X) | true.
          ended2(X,Y,alone(X)) ←
              end_of_stream(Y) | true.

/* receive an orphan from parent */
/* 9 */   merge2(X,Y,Z) ←
              receive(adopt(S,adopted),Z,Z1) |
              merge3(S,X,Y,Z1).

/* receive an orphan from child */
/* 10 */  merge2(X,Y,Z) ←
              single2(X,Y,S,X_or_Y) |
              send(adopt(S,A),X_or_Y,X1),
              merge2(waiting,A?,S,X1,Z).

          single2(X,Y,S,Y) ←
              receive(alone(S),X,_) | true.
          single2(X,Y,S,X) ←
              receive(alone(S),Y,_) | true.

/* waiting for adoption */
/* 11 */  merge2(waiting,adopted,_,X,Z) ←
              send(alone(X),Z,_).

/* 12 */  merge2(waiting,A,S,X,Z) ←
              remove_alone(X,X1) |
              create_channel(Nparent,Nchild),
              merge2(S?,X1?,Nchild),
              send(alone(Nparent),Z,_).

/* end of stream */
/* 13 */  merge3(W,X,Y,Z) ←
              ended3(W,X,Y,X1,Y1) |
              merge2(X1,Y1,Z).
```

Program 14.6: Shrinking a 2–3 merge tree

ended3(W,X,Y,X,Y) ←
    end_of_stream(W) | true.
ended3(W,X,Y,W,Y) ←
    end_of_stream(X) | true.
ended3(W,X,Y,W,X) ←
    end_of_stream(Y) | true.

/* receive an orphan from child */
/* 14 */   merge3(W,X,Y,Z) ←
               single3(W,X,Y,S,X1,Y1) |
               send(adopt(S,A),X1,X2),
               merge3(waiting,A?,S,X2?,Y1,Z).

           single3(W,X,Y,S,X,Y) ←
               receive(alone(S),W,_) | true.
           single3(W,X,Y,S,Y,W) ←
               receive(alone(S),X,_) | true.
           single3(W,X,Y,S,W,X) ←
               receive(alone(S),Y,_) | true.

/* waiting for adoption */
/* 15 */   merge3(waiting,adopted,_,X,Y,Z) ←
               merge2(X,Y,Z).

/* 16 */   merge3(waiting,A,S,X,Y,Z) ←
               remove_alone(X,X1) |
               create_channel(Nparent,Nchild),
               merge2(S?,X1?,Nchild?),
               merge2(Nparent?,Y,Z).

/* receive an orphan from parent */
/* 17 */   merge3(W,X,Y,Z) ←
               receive(adopt(S,adopted),Z,Z1) |
               create_channel(Vparent,Vchild),
               send(start(Vparent?),Z1,Z2),
               merge2(S,W,Vchild?),
               merge2(X,Y,Z2?).

/* 18 */   remove_alone(c([alone(X)|_],_),X).
           remove_alone(c([M|In],_),c([M|In1],Out)) ←
               not_alone(M) |
               remove_alone(c(In?,_),c(In1,Out)).

           not_alone(M) ← M ≠ alone(_).

Program 14.6: (Continued)

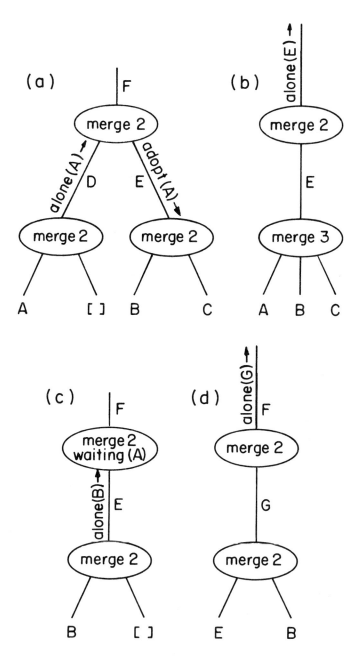

Figure 14.4: Termination of an input stream to a binary merge with a binary merge parent

When an input stream to a ternary merge terminates, the merge simply drops the ended stream and continues as a binary merge (Clause 13). A *merge2* process, on receiving an empty input stream, sends an *alone(S)* message upwards, where S is the other input stream, and terminates (Clause 8). The *alone(S)* message is a directive that S needs to be adopted by its uncle.

The root reacts to an *alone(S)* message by treating S as the new root input (Clause 7). This is the only operation that decreases the height of the tree.

A merge process, on receiving an *alone(S)* message from one of its children, sends an *adopt(S,A)* message to another of its children and waits for the acknowledgement of the adoption (the instantiation of A to *adopted*). (Clauses 10 & 14, Figures 14.4(a), 14.5(a)).

While the merge is waiting for this acknowledgement, the foster parent can also send an *alone(S1)* message upwards, due to one of its streams terminating, or its receiving of an *alone* from one of its children (Clauses 8, 11 & 12).

A *merge2* waiting for acknowledgement of adoption of S reacts to these two cases as follows. If the acknowledgement is received, it sends an *alone(X)* message upwards, where X is now the only child. This has the effect of propagating the delete operation upwards (Clause 11, Figure 14.4(b)). In the case of an *alone(S1)* being received before the adoption is acknowledged, $S1$ and S are merged, and their output is the argument of an *alone* sent upwards (Clause 12, Figure 14.4(c,d)). Note that the *alone(S1)* message need not be the first message received by the waiting *merge2* (although it is definitely the last), hence the need for the *remove_alone* process (Clause 18).

The action taken by a *merge3* process waiting for acknowledgement of adoption of S is similar though somewhat simpler. If the acknowledgement is received, it reduces itself to a *merge2* with its two remaining children as inputs (Clause 15, Figure 14.5(b)). If an *alone(S1)* message is received before the acknowledgement, then $S1$ and S are merged and their output merged with the third child (Clause 16, Figure 14.5(c,d)).

Adoptions are treated in a similar way to *start* messages, with the orphan as the new stream (Clauses 9 & 17) and cause instantiation of the acknowledge variable.

The introduction of bi-directional streams necessitates the use of a filter between the leaves of the tree and the output streams from the user process. Failing this, the user processes must ensure that they do in fact send bi-directional streams to the merge, albeit with only one direction used. Both approaches appear in Appendix 14.1.

Theorem. A 2–3 merge tree generated by Programs 14.4, 14.5 and 14.6 has linear bounded-waiting and logarithmic delay.

Proof. Since the tree is balanced, and the *merge2* and *merge3* operators are fair, a message arriving on any input stream will be preceded at the root by at most

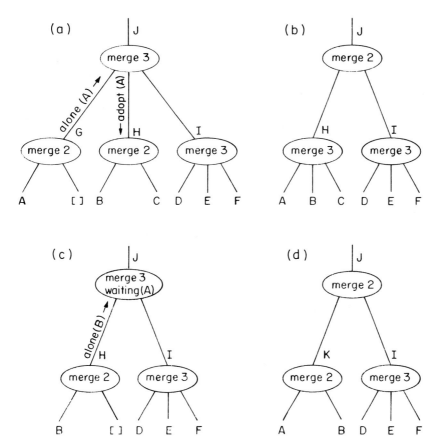

Figure 14.5: Termination of an input stream to a binary merge with a ternary merge parent

one message appearing on each other input stream after it. Hence the 2–3 merge tree has linear bounded waiting.

Aho et al. (1974) show that an n-leafed 2–3 tree has height k, where $2^k \leq n \leq 3^k$. Each message causes a constant number of process reductions, and the number of messages sent is proportional to the height of the tree, so a 2–3 merge tree has logarithmic delay. ∎

14.6 Another Approach

Kusalik (1984a) presents a different approach to the fair merge problem, which makes no assumption on the stability of the Concurrent Prolog machine.

This approach uses a meta-logical predicate analogous to Prolog's *var* to implement a block-on-input and busy-wait strategy. Binary and *n*-ary merges are described, and though no details are given as to how to increase the number of merge inputs dynamically, this can easily be added to the code. A far simpler and equally effective implementation of fair binary merge, also using *var*, is given in Program 14.7; the clauses simply reflect all the possibilities at any state of the merge process, viz.

(1)   There is a message ready on both streams (Clause 1).

(2)   There is a message ready on one stream but not the other (Clauses 2 & 3).

(3)   One stream has ended (Clauses 4 & 5).

```
/* 1 */   merge([M | X],[N | Y],[M,N |Z]) ←
              merge(X?,Y?,Z).

/* 2 */   merge([M | X],Y,[M | Z]) ←
              var(Y) |
              merge(X?,Y,Z).

/* 3 */   merge(X,[M | Y],[M | Z]) ←
              var(X) |
              merge(X,Y?,Z).

/* 4 */   merge([ ],Y,Y).

/* 5 */   merge(X,[ ],X).
```

Program 14.7: Binary merge using *var*

While this approach is interesting, it relies on a meta-logical predicate to achieve control, rather than on a control structure such as stability.

14.7 Conclusions

Concurrent Prolog introduces new questions not faced by more traditional programming languages. We find it satisfying that in solving these questions, concepts from mainstream computer science such as 2–3 trees are proven useful, thus transcending the von Neumann framework in which they were originally conceived.

The intricacy of the self-balancing merge tree could render it infeasible in practical applications, despite its desirable properties. In most applications, e.g., operating systems, the number of inputs to a merge will either be dynamic with low throughput, or static with a larger throughput. In the former case, the best strategy would probably be a simple binary merge tree with straightforward addition and deletion, while the latter is best solved by a balanced tree of binary merges, constructed either explicitly or implicitly, using a list of input streams as by Kusalik (1984a).

Acknowledgements

This research was supported by IBM Poughkeepsie, Data Systems Division. William Silverman assisted in editing this paper.

Appendix 14.1

The Input Filter

```
filter([ ],[ ]).
filter([start(X) | Xs],[start(c(X1?,[ ])) | Xs1]) ←
    filter(X?,X1),filter(Xs?,Xs1).
filter([X | Xs],[X | Xs1]) ←
    other(X) | filter(Xs?,Xs1).
```

Sample Test Cases

```
test(N) ←
    tree(N,[Ct | T]),msg(Ct,[ ],T,X),
    root(c(X?,[ ]),c(Y,[ ])),outstream(Y?).
msg(0,Cs,void,[ ]).
msg(0,Cs,t([Cl | L],[Cr | R]),[start(c(Ys?,[ ])) | Xs?]) ←
    msg(Cl,l(Cs),L,Xs),
    msg(Cr,r(Cs),R,Ys) | true.
msg(N,Cs,T,[(N,Cs) | Ns]) ←
    N1 := N – 1 , msg(N1,Cs,T,Ns) | true.
tree(1,[3,t([3,t([4,void],[1,void]]),[4,void]]).
tree(2,[3,t([3,void],[4,t([3,void],[2,void])])])
```

```
tree(3,[3,t([3,t([3,void],[3,void])],[3,t([3,void],[3,void])])
tree(c(M,N),[M,t(
    [M,t(
        [M,t(
            [M,t([N,void],[N,void])],
            [M,t([N,void],[N,void])])],
        [M,t(
            [M,t([N,void],[N,void])],
            [M,t([N,void],[N,void])])])],
    [M,t(
        [M,t(
            [M,t([N,void],[N,void])],
            [M,t([N,void],[N,void])])],
        [M,t(
            [M,t([N,void],[N,void])],
            [M,t([N,void],[N,void])])])])]).

tests(N) ← s(N,X),filter(X,X1),
    root(c(X1?,[ ]),c(Y,[ ])),outstream(Y?).

s(1,[a1,a2,start([
        b1,b2,start([
            c1,c2,c3,c4,start([
                d1,d2])
            ,c5]),start([
                e1,e2,start([
                    f1,f2])
                ])
        ]),start([
            g1,g2,start([
                h1,h2,start([
                    i1])
                ,g3,g4])
        ,a7,a8,start([
            j1,j2,j3,start([
                k1,start([
                    l1])
                ,k2,k3])
            ])
            b3])
        ,a9]).
s(2,[a1,a2,start([
```

```
b1,b2,start([
    c1,c2,start([
        d1,d2])
    ])
])
,a3,start([e1])
]).
```

Chapter 15

Multiway Merge with Constant Delay in Concurrent Prolog

Ehud Shapiro and Shmuel Safra

The Weizmann Institute of Science

Abstract

Multiway dynamic mergers with constant delay are an essential component of a parallel logic programming system. Previous attempts to define efficient mergers have required complex optimizing compilers and run-time support.

This paper proposes a simple technique to implement mergers efficiently. The technique requires an additional data type and the definition of an operation on it. The operation allows multiple processes to access a stream without incurring the cost of searching for the end of stream. It is specified in Concurrent Prolog and can be used to define multiple assignment variables using a monitor.

The technique forms the basis for stream merging in Logix, a practical programming environment written in Flat Concurrent Prolog.

15.1 Introduction

Communication in Concurrent Prolog is stream oriented; messages are passed on streams whose head is the message. When considering an operating system with monitors and shared resources, a many-to-one merge operation is needed. Since Concurrent Prolog is a single assignment language, the straightforward algorithm involving multiple assignment variables (Ahuja et al., 1986) cannot be used naively.

Efficient stream mergers in Concurrent Prolog were studied by Shapiro and Mierowsky (Chapter 14) and by Ueda and Chikayama (1984). The techniques for merging are evaluated by their *delay* which is the number of operations required for each message to be merged and by their *fairness*. Fairness implies that no input stream will be starved indefinitely.

The technique suggested by Shapiro and Mierowsky (Chapter 14) introduced a logarithmic delay using two-three trees. A technique which produces a constant delay was studied by Ueda and Chikayama (1984); it can be generated by applying an optimizing compiler to a specification written in Concurrent Prolog. The optimizing compiler needs to perform a global analysis of the program, and the size of the specification program is proportional to the number of streams to be merged. Hence, the technique is proposed as a system call which follows the specification but is implemented in the abstract machine. The technique requires the suspension mechanism to provide a process, which is woken up, with information about which clause to retry. In general this requires house keeping information to be stored and is complex to coordinate.

This paper proposes an alternative technique which produces a constant delay. The technique is first specified in Concurrent Prolog and then it is optimized without the need for global analysis of the program. The resulting program is fair, and the constant delay produced is small. The optimization proposed relies on an additional data type and an operation on it. Once these are added to the language, a technique specified in Concurrent Prolog can achieve constant delay by a legal optimization.

15.2 Specification

The multiway merge technique is specified in the Concurrent Prolog Program 15.1. The program produces a delay linear in the number of merged streams for each element added to the output stream. To reduce the delay, a new data type is introduced which allows a local optimization to be made. This optimization does not change the semantics of the program but improves its complexity.

```
merge([stream(Xs) | Streams], Output) ←        % new input
    copy(Xs?, Output),
    merge(Streams?, Output).
merge([ ], _).                                  % input ended

copy([X | Xs], Output) ←                        % an element
    stream_append(X, Output, New_Output) |
    copy(Xs?, New_Output).
copy([ ], _).                                   % stream ended
```

Program 15.1: A multiway merger

The program accepts as input a stream of streams; it produces a result stream which is the merge of all the input streams. A *copy* process is spawned for each input stream. It calls, for each element in its input stream, *stream_append*. This call advances along the output stream and upon detection of the unbound end of the stream, it assigns a list cell. The head of the cell is the input element and the tail is returned as the new unbound end of stream (*New_output*). The *copy* process continues recursively with the new unbound end of the stream.

The number of operations needed for *stream_append* is linear in the number of elements in the *Output*. Each *copy* process is required to perform one stream advance operation (*cdr*) for each element added to the output stream; thus, in general, the delay of adding one element to the output stream is linear in the number of input streams.

15.3 Optimization

To reduce the delay of the *merge* program, a new data type, *mutual reference*, is introduced. A mutual reference refers to a term but cannot unify with other mutual references. The only primitive that can access a term via a mutual reference is *stream_append*. It returns a mutual reference to the tail of the stream (*New_ref*). Since the semantics of *stream_append* states that it must advance to the end of the stream prior to binding it, an optimization can be made. Instead of each process advancing along the stream, *stream_append* may advance all pointers in unison. This is accomplished by destructively assigning the mutual reference as shown in Figure 15.1.

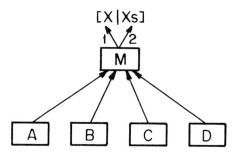

Figure 15.1

The processes *A*, *B*, *C* and *D* refer to the stream via the mutual reference *M*. The effect of the *stream_append* operation is to move the mutual reference from position 1 to position 2; this effectively gives all processes immediate access to the end of the output stream.

This simple optimization is local and does not require global analysis of the program by the compiler. It is justified by the semantics of *stream_append* and the fact that no other operations can access a term via a mutual reference.

All the *copy* processes may access the end of the stream in a constant number of operations. Thus the delay of the new program, for each element added to the stream, is constant.

```
merge(Xs, Output) ←                              % initialize
    allocate_mutual_reference(Ref, Output),      % allocate mutual ref
    merge1(Xs?, Ref).                            % call merge

merge1([stream(Xs) | Streams], Ref) ←           % a new stream
    copy(Xs?, Ref),
    merge1(Streams?, Ref).
merge1([ ], _).

copy([X | Xs], Ref) ←                            % an input element
    stream_append(X, Ref, New_ref) |
    copy(Xs?, New_ref).
copy([ ], _).
```

Program 15.2: A multiway merger using a mutual-reference

The mutual reference is initially allocated to refer to the output stream. Each *copy* process calls *stream_append* for each element of its input stream. The call assigns the unbound output stream to a list whose head is the added element. The mutual reference can be advanced to refer to the tail of the stream and is returned as *New_Ref*.

15.4 Termination Detection

When all the input streams are closed, the output stream should be closed. The above program does not close the output stream but rather leaves it unbound. The stream should be closed upon termination of all the *copy* processes; distributed termination needs to be detected.

A technique to detect distributed termination is presented by Takeuchi (1983) and is termed *short-circuit*. The best way to understand this technique is via an analogy.

Consider a blind slave-master who wants to detect whether his slaves have finished their work. He chains all the slaves in a row through their feet using iron chains. Each slave's right foot is connected to the left foot of another slave, except for the two ends of the chain; these are kept by the master. The master attaches one free end to power and the other, via a light-bulb, to ground.

Every slave combines his legs so that his two chains touch each other when he finishes working. If every slave obeys the rule (and no-one's body conducts electricity), the light-bulb will turn on when all slaves finish working. The remaining question, how does the blind master detect that the light is on, is left as an exercise to the reader.

An analogous technique can be used in Concurrent Prolog: subordinate processes represent slaves, and shared variables represent chains. The master process that creates the slave processes, chains them using shared variables. When a process terminates it unifies its two 'chain' variables. The master assigns one end of the chain (the 'power') to a constant and keeps the other end to itself. When it finishes spawning processes, it examines the other end of the chain (the 'ground') in read-only mode. If all processes have terminated the constant will appear at the free end of the chain.

The technique is used in Program 15.3, which is an enhancement of Program 15.2. The functionality added is that upon the detection of distributed termination, the merge process closes the output stream by *stream_close*.

```
merge(Xs, Output) ←                                    % initialise
    allocate_mutual_reference(Ref, Output),
    merge1(Xs?, Ref, done, Done),
    close_when_done(Done?, Ref).

merge1([stream(Xs) | Streams], Ref, Left, Right) ←     % a new stream
    copy(Xs?, Ref, Left, Middle),
    merge1(Streams?, Ref, Middle, Right).
merge1([[]], _, Chain, Chain).

copy([X | Xs], Ref, Left, Right) ←                     % an input element
    stream_append(X, Ref, New_Ref) |
    copy(Xs?, New_Ref).
copy([ ], _, Chain, Chain).

close_when_done(done, Ref) ←                            % close output
    stream_close(Ref) | true.
```

Program 15.3: A termination detecting multiway merger

The *stream_close* primitive advances to the unbound end of its stream and closes the stream by assigning empty list ([ ]) to it.

15.5 Variable Monitor

Using the above technique, a multiple assignment variable can be provided. A shared, updatable data-structure can be emulated by a monitor process that has a multiway merge as a front-end. Only a constant-time overhead is introduced over a direct use of conventional destructive shared variables.

An example of a *variable* monitor, which receives the messages *read(X)* and *write(X)*, is shown in Program 15.4. The initial streams from the processes sharing the variable are merged using the *merge* process.

```
variable(In) ←                    % initialise
    merge(In?, Out)
    variable(Out?, undefined).

variable([read(X) | In],X) ←      % read a value
    variable(In?, X).
variable([write(X) | In], _) ←    % write a value
    variable(In?, X).
variable([ ], _).                 % halt
```

Program 15.4: A variable monitor

Multiple assignment variables can also be implemented using the technique described above. An additional operation, which advances along a stream and returns the last message in it, can be used to read values from the stream.

15.6 Conclusion

Fast multiway dynamic merge is essential to the efficient realization of many applications in Concurrent Prolog. A simple technique has been specified which introduces a linear delay. The specification can be optimized using a mutual reference data type and an operation on it, *stream_append*. The resulting delay is constant. This performance improvement should not be so surprising, since this optimization effectively mimics the most straightforward way in which one would implement a shared stream in a conventional concurrent programming language (Gelernter, 1984).

All applications that may seem to require multiple assignment variables, to achieve the desired performance, can use a multiway merger instead with only a constant-time penalty. The one exception, mutable-arrays, can be implemented using the techniques proposed by Ueda and Chikayama (1984).

Acknowledgements

Early work on this research was carried out while the first author was visiting ICOT. He is grateful to Kazunori Ueda, for explaining his work on this subject and for stimulating discussions. We also wish to thank Steve Taylor for comments and discussions while reviewing this paper.

Chapter 16

Merging Many Streams Efficiently: The Importance of Atomic Commitment

Vijay A. Saraswat

Carnegie-Mellon University

Abstract

In this paper we discuss the problem of programming a *merge* operation on a dynamically varying number of streams in the concurrent logic programming (CLP) language FCP($\downarrow$) (Saraswat, 1987a). We present a simple model of computation for FCP($\downarrow$) and use it to define for a merge algorithm, the notions of *delay*, *overhead*, *weak-* and *strong-bounds* and *response-time*. We present the notion of a *merge ring*, which can merge n inputs with constant delay, linear weak-bound and an overhead that ranges from linear under low traffic conditions to constant under high traffic conditions. Next we combine merge rings to produce k-ary *trees* to reduce the worst-case overhead to $O(\log_k(n))$. These algorithms guarantee weak-bounded merge *without* using other extra-logical techniques such as *And-fairness*, stability, *otherwise* goals (Shapiro and Mierowsky, Chapter 14), 'destructive assignment' (Shapiro and Safra, Chapter 15), *varbl* (Kusalik, 1984a) or special implementation techniques (Ueda and Chikayama, 1984).

Languages such as FCP($\downarrow$) and Concurrent Prolog are *multiple-environment* languages: the unification of a goal and the head of a clause may produce bindings for variables in the goal. In all these algorithms we use this ability to obtain mutual exclusion between multiple processes competing for a shared resource. It would seem impossible to implement these techniques in a single environment language such as GHC, leading us to conjecture that a merge with the above properties may not be implementable in GHC.

16.1 Introduction

It is well-known that CLP languages are based on a notion of processes communicating with each other by means of single-assignment shared variables that may be thought of as channels or streams of communication. While streams are good for point-to-point communication (shared privately between two processes) or broadcasts (shared among n processes where each process has to accept *every* message), it often becomes necessary to program within the language a notion of merging the contents of n streams into one stream, preserving the order of messages in each input stream. The archetypal logical specification for a binary merge is the set of clauses:

merge([A | X], Y, [A | Z]) ← merge(X, Y, Z).
merge(X, [A | Y], [A | Z]) ← merge(X, Y, Z).
merge([ ], Y, Y).
merge(X, [ ], X).

The *bounded-merge* problem in CLP languages (Shapiro and Safra, Chapter 15; Ueda and Chikayama, 1984; Kusalik, 1984a) may informally be stated as follows. The problem is to design *efficient* algorithms for merging input from a dynamically varying number of streams such that no input stream is indefinitely ignored.

In what follows, we introduce the programming language FCP($\downarrow$), the model of computation, desirable properties of merge algorithms and the merge schemes proposed in the literature. We then present an efficient solution based on merge rings and trees of merge rings.

16.1.1 The programming language FCP($\downarrow$)

In this paper, we confine ourselves to using the programming language FCP($\downarrow$), one of the CP family of programming languages discussed extensively by Saraswat (1987).

Syntactically, programs in FCP($\downarrow$) are sets of definite clauses in a language whose non-logical symbols contain a special unary functor '$\downarrow$'. If t is a term in the language, whose functor is not '$\downarrow$' we say that $t\downarrow$ is an *annotated term*. Each clause in the program satisfies the syntactic restrictions:

(1) Annotated terms may occur only in the heads of clauses.

(2) Every super-term of an annotated term is annotated.

In what follows we *assume* that every super-term of an annotated term is annotated: hence only the innermost annotations are explicitly written.

The operational semantics of FCP($\downarrow$) programs is the same as the operational semantics of pure Horn clauses, except that in every step of the refutation process, the $mgu_\downarrow$ of two atoms is used, instead of the mgu (most general unifier). In detail, given a program P, we can derive in one step from the query (negative clause) N $\equiv \leftarrow a_1, \ldots, a_n$. $(n > 0)$ the query $N_1 \equiv \theta(a_1, \ldots, a_{i-1}, c_1, \ldots, c_k, a_{i+1}, \ldots a_n)$. if there exists a substitution θ which is an *annotated mgu* (denoted by $mgu_{\downarrow}$) of c and a_i (for some i, $1 \leq i \leq n$) where $c \leftarrow c_1, \ldots, c_k$. is a copy of a clause from P renamed apart from N. In case there does not exist an atom in the query and a head of a clause for which an $mgu_{\downarrow}$ exists, we can derive in one step the value $\bullet$, which stands for *abnormal termination*. Computation terminates *successfully* on the derivation of the empty query; in such cases, the *answer substitution* is the composition of the substitutions applied at each derivation step, restricted to the variables occurring in N.

Informally, computing the $mgu_{\downarrow}$ of two terms is just like computing the mgu of the two terms, with the additional rule that for the $mgu_{\downarrow}$ of a term t_1 and an annotated term $t_2 \downarrow$ to exist, the term t_1 must be a non-variable. (See Saraswat, 1986, 1987a for details, justification and formal definitions.)

If no equality theory is specified with the program, then the $mgu_{\downarrow}$ of two terms, when it exists, is unique, upto renaming. For this paper, however, we shall assume the presence of a special binary function symbol '$+/2$' which has been declared to be *associative* and *commutative*. Such a function symbol may be used to build up *bags* of terms, just as the function symbol '$./2$' in *Dec-10 Prolog* may be used to build up *lists* of terms.

Example. Given the clauses:

wait(X↓, Y, Y).
readonly(X↓,X).
in(X, elem(X)↓+Y).

the query $wait(A,B,C)$ succeeds iff A is a non-variable and B and C are unifiable. The query $readonly(A,B)$ succeeds iff A is a non-variable and A and B are unifiable. The query $in(A,B)$ succeeds iff A is *some* element in the bag B.

More precisely, the query succeeds iff B is a bag of the form $C+D$, and *either* C or D is either of the form $elem(A)$ or a structure (bag) built up from the function symbol $+$ such that $elem(A)$ is reachable from the root by traversing a path labelled entirely with the $+$ function symbol. Note that there may be finitely many such most general unifiers. (More details on AC-unification are given by Fages, 1984.)

Confluent FCP($\downarrow$) programs
___

In this paper we are concerned only with programs for which the derivation relation is *confluent* for admissible queries. For such programs, it is the case that for all admissible queries N, a successful (abnormal) derivation of N from P exists iff every derivation of N from P is successful (abnormal). (See Huet, 1980 for details.) Confluent programs may be executed safely by means of so-called *committed choice non-determinism*: the choice of the selected atom and clause may be made arbitrarily. No backtracking is necessary if at most one answer substitution is required, e.g., in the case of a *merge* where only *one* possible interleaving of the input streams is required.

For the purposes of the merge programs, an admissible query is a query of the form *?– ... merge(Out, In) ...* where the '...' represent atoms that will only consume (and never produce) bindings for the variable *Out*. This restriction is necessary because the merge program will produce *some* arbitrary interleaving for *Out*; if *Out* already has a binding then this may lead to failure or it may not, depending upon the particular choice of execution steps. Similar assumptions are (tacitly) made by other authors.

16.1.2 Model of computation

The importance of CLP languages lies in that programs in these languages may be executed in parallel. In this section we present, in a brief and simplified form, a *model of computation* that will enable us to define precisely cost metrics for analyzing the complexity of programs. More details are given by Saraswat (1987).

Our model of computation is based on the shared memory PRAM models of Shiloach and Vishkin (1981). Roughly, each goal in the current query is assigned a process; the bindings of the current query are maintained in shared memory. Computation proceeds in cycles. A cycle consists of a *read* and a *write* phase. In the read phase each process determines all the clause invocations with which its goal can '↓'-unify. If there is no such invocation, the process does not participate in the current cycle. After the read phase, all processes that can do so choose one clause invocation to commit. They then attempt to simultaneously *write* the bindings obtained in the first phase. Writing is done *atomically*: for each process, at the end of the write cycle it will have succeeded in writing either *all* its bindings, or *none*. (Note that the writing protocol may be implemented asynchronously: more than one process could attempt to bind a variable at the same time, possibly to different (ununifiable) values.) A process may be unable to write its bindings only in case some other process writes bindings that are incompatible (ununifiable) with it. If a process succeeds in writing its bindings, it also adds to the query the goals in the body of the committing clause. (We assume that finding new processors and allocating them to the new goals takes constant time.)

The write cycle also has the property that at its end there are no variable-variable chains longer than 1. To implement this would seem to require *dereference* phases interspersed with the write phase. For simplicity of analysis, we ignore the cost of this dereference phase. This simplification is not entirely satisfactory because it allows us to charge constant time for unifying $O(n)$ variables together in a single cycle (e.g., it allows us to assume that a short-circuit between n processes can be done in constant time); on the other hand variable-variable unification is isomorphic to graph-connectivity, which would seem to require $\log(n)$ time on shared-(updatable) memory PRAM (see Saraswat, 1987 for more details).

A process that fails to write bindings in a write cycle re-evaluates its remaining clause invocations in the next read cycle and may try again with a different clause invocation. The machine aborts in case no process can commit bindings at the end of the write cycle, and it terminates successfully in case there is no goal left.

The *width* of a cycle is the number of goals which reduce successfully in that cycle. The *depth* of computation is the number of cycles. The number of process reductions (an important metric for sequential implementations) is the sum, over all cycle, of the width of each cycle. The *cost* of each cycle is the sum of the cost of the read and the write phase. The cost of the read phase is the maximum, over each process, of the cost of unifying the goal with the heads of clauses.

We assume that unifying a variable with a term takes constant time. (As discussed above, this is a simplification.) In the algorithms discussed in this paper, we will not be unifying two large (i.e., $O(n)$) terms together; hence we will take the cost of unification of the head of a clause and a goal to be constant. This leads to the cost of a machine cycle being constant in the algorithms we discuss in this paper, though the number of processors active per cycle may be large.

16.1.3 Properties of merge algorithms

We can now provide more precise definitions for delay, overhead and bounds. In a query we identify some goals as part of the merge system and ignore other goals, e.g., the producers of the input streams. The only interaction of the merge system with its environment is that it receives input on its input channels and produces output on its output channels. We say that a message on an input channel is *accepted* by the merge system in the first cycle in which it appears either in the output or in some variable local to the merge system.

The *delay* of a merge is the minimum number of (machine) cycles before an input to the merge appears at the output. If binary merge processes as above are structured into a tree, with the output of a merge at depth k feeding into the input of a merge at depth $k-1$, and the input streams being the leaves of the tree, and the output stream being the output at the root, the delay will be $O(h)$, where h is the height of the tree. (Note that this definition is a generalization of the one given by Shapiro and Mierowsky, Chapter 14, where *reductions* instead of cycles are counted.)

The *overhead* of a merge is the average number of reductions made by the merge system for each output produced on the output stream. For a tree of merge processes as above, the overhead is $O(h)$.

The *weak-bound* for a merge algorithm is an upper bound on the number of output elements produced in the output stream in the (machine) cycles between the cycle in which an input was *accepted* at an input stream and the cycle in which the element is output on the output stream.

In the literature a stronger definition is used for boundedness: messages in the output stream are measured starting from the cycle in which the message *appears* in the input stream.

Bounded merging in the strong sense seems to be impossible without some cooperation between the merge system and the producers of the input streams. In this paper for the most part we consider weak-bounds; in Section 16.2.6 we return to show that with some cooperation between the merger and the producers, the weak-bound may be turned into a strong-bound. Henceforth in this paper, unless noted otherwise, by 'bound' we shall mean 'weak-bound'.

The binary merge tree construction does not guarantee bounded waiting because even after an input enters the tree from one leaf, it may consistently be ignored in favour of input streaming in from other leaves.

Finally some liveness properties are also important for a merge process. The *response-time* for a merge is the *maximum* number of cycles before an input accepted from an input stream appears at the output. As an example of a merge with an unbounded response time, consider a merge that polls each input in turn, waiting until it receives an input from a channel before proceeding to the next.

16.1.4 Some merge schemes

(1) Balanced merge trees

Shapiro and Mierowsky (Chapter 14) propose building up dynamically binary trees of *merge* processes, defined essentially by using the *merge* clauses above. To do this they introduce assumptions about the implementation, namely the notion of *stability* (clauses are evaluated in sequential order for a goal and the first one whose guard succeeds can commit) and of *And-fairness* (*'whenever a process p becomes ready for execution, any other process already being reduced will reduce only once more before p is reduced'*). This renders their results specific to those implementations (usually sequential) which obey these restrictive assumptions. In Section 16.2.10 we show that the 'merge ring tree' algorithm we present in this paper may, with a suitable choice of parameters, achieve comparable, even superior, performance *without* assuming either fairness or stability.

(2) Bounded merge using varbl

Kusalik (1984a) considers similar algorithms using another extra-logical notion *varbl* (which is a unary predicate that succeeds iff its argument is a variable), in place of stability. Such predicates are suspect because they may sanction unsound inferences: a call $p(X)$ may succeed with answer substitution the identity substitution while the call $p(a)$ may fail.

(3) Constant delay, constant overhead merges

(a) Using destructive assignment. In a later paper Shapiro and Safra (Chapter 15) propose a technique that takes a naive algorithm with linear delay and converts that into an algorithm with constant delay. To achieve this, they use destructive assignment, which is difficult to justify from a logic programming viewpoint. Moreover, they do not *guarantee bounded-waiting*. Their algorithm depends upon properties of their scheduler and *may not exist for an unfair scheduler*.

(b) Using special implementation techniques. Ueda and Chikayama (1984) propose to define for an *n*-ary merge *n* clauses of the form:

merge([X | Out], I1, ..., [X | Ii], ...,In) ←
    merge(Out, I1, ..., Ii, ..., In).

and then specify an implementation technique that will compile this code efficiently so that the resulting algorithm has $O(1)$ delay. This does not seem to be a satisfactory solution because of the large and unwieldy amount of code needed, special implementation support required, and unwieldy handling when *n* changes. Moreover, this scheme does not guarantee bounded merge.

(c) Using bags of channels. The merge of Ueda and Chikayama may be programmed simply by using bags. Instead of having different merges for every value of *n*, all the channels to be merged are bundled up into a bag. Any stream containing an input may be matched upon now in one unification, and the input removed. Addition and deletion of channels is straightforward. If an analysis of the program is done by an optimizing compiler, then it may be possible for it to detect that in one reduction at most one stream in the bag is affected; an 'incremental' matching algorithm may result in a reduction taking constant time.

merge(Out, In) ← bmerge(Out, stream(In)+end).

bmerge([X | Out], stream([message(X)↓ | In])+Others) ←
    bmerge(Out, stream(In)+Others).

bmerge(Out, stream([instream(I)↓ | In])+Others) ←
    bmerge(Out, stream(In)+stream(I)+Others).

bmerge(Out, stream([]↓)+Others) ←
    bmerge(Out, Others).

bmerge([ ], end).

In this paper, however, we are concerned with achieving efficient merges *without making any assumptions about the implementation* at all. The objective is to study the expressive power of the control structures in the language, rather than study the implementation techniques of a given compiler for the language.

16.2 The Concept of Merge Rings

16.2.1 Obtaining mutual exclusion using atomic commitment

We first consider the problem of guaranteeing mutually exclusive access to n processes sharing a common resource, R.

A standard way of achieving this in programming languages based on the notion of destructive assignment is through P and V operations on a semaphore. In languages such as CSP in which communication occurs through handshaking, a semaphore may be simulated rather simply by means of a perpetual process that keeps a local counter (Hoare, 1985). The process is always ready to accept a V message; after receipt it increments its local counter. It can accept a P message only if its counter is positive; after receipt it decreases the counter. In dataflow languages, in GHC and other such languages based on buffered communication, to *implement* mutual exclusion a merge operator seems essential.

We exhibit a simple technique for achieving mutual exclusion in FCP($\downarrow$), without employing a merge or an explicit central arbiter. This method depends on every process participating in the algorithm sharing a common channel, the *arbiter*, and having an identifier (Id) unique to it. The rules of behavior are:

process(Id, arb(Id, Res, Arb)$\downarrow$, State) ←
    consume(Res, State, NewRes, NewState, Arb),
    process(Id, Arb, NewState).

process(Id, arb(Id1$\downarrow$, Res, Arb), State) ←
    process(Id, Arb, State).

A process waits for the shared variable to be instantiated to a structure, which will contain a variable, the shared resource and another variable that will become the new shared variable after the current cycle of arbitration. It then tries to use the first rule to *capture* the shared resource by unifying its Id with the first variable. Even if all consumers attempt to do this simultaneously, atomic commitment ensures that some *one* process will succeed: it is the only one that enters its critical region. Such a process is called the *leader* for that arbitration cycle. (Any attempt by other consumers to commit using the first rule will fail because two distinct unique ids cannot unify with each other.) Once the process is done with the resource, it leaves the critical section by instantiating the new shared variable (*Arb*) to another arbiter structure *arbiter(AnId, NewRes, AnArb)*, where *AnId* and *AnArb* are new variables and *NewRes* is the new state of the shared resource.

A process can commit using the second clause only once some process enters its critical section, instantiating the first argument of the arbiter structure. Such a process (called the follower for the current arbitration cycle) then repeats its behaviors with the new shared variable obtained from the arbiter data structure.

Note that the above mutual exclusion protocol is not *fair*: it is possible for a process to repeatedly gain access to the shared resource locking out all other processes perpetually.

It would seem impossible to implement this technique in GHC: in GHC a process has to make a decision on which one of possibly many behaviors to follow based upon the current state of the environment. However, having made a decision it cannot *instantaneously* update the current state of the environment to reflect, it. Another competing process may make the same decision, thus destroying the desired mutual exclusion.

16.2.2 Obtaining single exclusion using atomic commitment

Mutual exclusion may be thought of as follows. Assume given n identical processes with two behaviors of interest, T_1 and T_2, possibly among others. A protocol is desired whereby at most one process may execute T_1; and once it does, all other processes cannot execute T_1 but must (eventually) execute T_2. *Single* exclusion is complementary in nature: upto $(n-1)$ processes may execute T_1, perhaps simultaneously; once they do, the remaining process cannot execute T_1 but must (eventually) execute T_2.

Termination detection is an example of a problem that may be solved simply by using single exclusion. Here T_1 is the behavior associated with normal process termination, and T_2 the behavior to be executed when a process discovers that all remaining processes have terminated.

The schematic solution for this is a variation of the usual short-circuit technique. Arrange the n processes in a chain, i.e., each process has two arguments *Left* and *Right* such that the *Left* argument of a process is identical to the *Right* argument of the process to its left. (The two arguments are also called the *terminals* on the chain.) Assume that the end points of the chain (the *Left* argument of the left-most process and the *Right* argument of the rightmost process) have been unified with two different constants, say *left* and *right* respectively. Now arrange that transition T_1 can be taken only if it is possible for the process to short (unify together) its two terminals. Arrange that transition T_2 can be taken only when the process discovers that its *Left* terminal is bound to *left* and its right terminal to *Right*. This implements the protocol. In detail:

$$\text{process}(\text{Args}, \text{X}\backslash\text{X}) \leftarrow \qquad \% \ T_1.$$
$$\text{process}(\text{Args}, \text{left}\downarrow\backslash\text{right}\downarrow) \leftarrow \qquad \% \ T_2.$$

In this paper we use an elaboration of the protocol for termination detection of the processes making up a merge ring (Chapter 16.2.5).

16.2.3 The duplex channel protocol using atomic commitment

One of the most fundamental operations in CLP languages is using a variable shared between two goals as a communication channel.

The operations of reading and writing to the channel may be defined by means of the rules:

$$\text{read}([\text{write}(\text{V})\downarrow \mid \text{L}], \text{V}, \text{L}).$$
$$\text{write}([\text{write}(\text{V}) \mid \text{L}], \text{V}, \text{L}).$$

Initially the reader and the writer share the same variable B. To write a value V on the channel, the writer invokes the call *write(B, V, NewB)* and recurs with the new value of the channel, *NewB*. To read a value from the channel, the reader invokes the call *read(B, V, NewB)* and recurs with the new value of the channel *NewB*. The call *read(B, V, NewB)* suspends until channel B has a message and then succeeds with V unified with the message and *NewB* with the new channel. Note that the length of the original shared variable between the reader and writer (which is proportional to the number of reductions each by the reader and the writer) is equal to the number of write operations performed on the channel.

Suppose now that we wish to design a *readlist/3* predicate such that the call *readlist(B, V, NewB)* succeeds with V being the (possibly empty) difference list of *all* the values written on the channel B till the instant the call succeeds, *NewB* being the channel that remains. It is now necessary for *read* to determine *whether there is no more input on the channel*. There is no more input on the channel just in case the channel is a variable. But it is impossible to write in FCP($\downarrow$) a program that determines whether a given term is a variable. However, a term is a variable just in case the term is known not to be some constant c, but can unify with the constant c. This is the basis of the following definitions:

$$\text{readlist}([\text{read} \mid \text{NewB}], \text{Tail}\backslash\text{Tail}, \text{NewB}).$$
$$\text{readlist}([\text{write}(\text{V}) \mid \text{B}]\downarrow, [\text{V}|\text{T}]\backslash\text{Tail}, \text{NewB}) \leftarrow \text{readlist}(\text{B}, \text{T}\backslash\text{Tail}, \text{NewB}).$$

$$\text{write}([\text{write}(\text{Item}) \mid \text{NewB}], \text{Item}, \text{NewB}).$$
$$\text{write}([\text{read}\downarrow \mid \text{B}], \text{Item}, \text{NewB}) \leftarrow \text{write}(\text{B}, \text{Item}, \text{NewB}).$$

A call *readlist(B, Hd\ Tl, NewB)* accumulates in the difference list $Hd\backslash Tl$ all the elements in the stream B that have been placed there by the writer, by repeatedly reducing via the first clause. As long as there is an item in the channel, the second clause is not applicable (*read* will not unify with *write*). When there are no more items in the channel, the channel is a variable. Now the second clause suspends (because of the wait annotation) but the first can commit. As a side-effect the read leaves an *endmarker* (*read*) each time it reads the channel. This characterizes the *duplex* protocol on channels: both the reader and the writer write on the same channel. (Note that this is different from the *bi-directional* channels of Shapiro and Mierowsky, Chapter 14.)

The clauses for *write* are straightforward: they merely skip over the read-markers placed by the reader.

Some consequences of these definitions:

(1) If the above protocol is used by the reader and writer of the shared variable B, then in a call *readlist*(B, L, *NewB*), the term B is either a variable or bound to a list of *write/1* terms terminating in a variable. (We ignore for the time being how to model termination of the writer process.) Symmetrically, in a call *write*(B, *Item*, *NewB*), the term B is either a variable or bound to a list of *read* terms terminating in a variable.

(2) Because of (1) above, it is possible for a reader to use *both* the routines *read* and *readlist* on the same input channel. The end-markers left by a call to *readlist* are never visible to a subsequent call to *read*.

(3) A call *readlist*(B, L, *NewB*) never suspends: if B is a variable, it returns L bound to the empty difference list and places a *read* endmarker on B.

(4) The length of the channel (which is the number of reductions performed each by the reader and writer) is now proportional to the number of reads and writes performed on the channel.

(5) Note that the reader and writer may both be asynchronously working on the same channel. If B is a variable, and a call *readlist*(B, L, *NewBr*) and a call *write*(B, *Item*, *NewBw*) both attempt to use their first clauses at the same time, then atomic commitment guarantees that some indeterminate one of them will succeed. The attempt by the other to use its first clause will fail (*read* will not unify with *write*(V), for any V); it will have to use its second clause.

This protocol would also seem impossible to implement in GHC for the same reason as above. If a *read* goal uses its first clause, it must record that information instantaneously so as to prevent a competing *write* goal from mistakenly choosing to use its first clause, and causing the whole system to fail. But the only way in GHC in which bindings can be produced for variables in the call is in the body of the clause. However, arbitrarily many events may happen between the commitment of a clause for a goal and the execution of goals in the body of that clause.

Later in this paper we will use this duplex protocol for reading and writing on channels to ensure a bounded merge.

16.2.4 Using mutual exclusion for merging many streams

The mutual exclusion algorithm (Section 16.2.1) can be used as the basis for a merging algorithm that treats the list being constructed as a shared data-object. The shared resource is the output list. A process competes for the resource when it has input on its input channel. If it captures the resource, it unifies it with a list whose head is the input and whose tail is the new shared resource.

$$\text{process(Id, arb(Id, [I|Rest], Arb)}\downarrow, \text{[I|In]} \leftarrow$$
$$\text{process(Id, Arb, In), Arb=arb(AnId, Rest, AnArb).}$$

$$\text{process(Id, arb(Id1}\downarrow, \text{R, Arb), In)} \leftarrow$$
$$\text{process(Id, Arb, In).}$$

The problem with this algorithm is that when an input stream places a value on the output stream, *every* input stream has to cycle past this value on the output stream, in order to compete for the *current* state of the resource. This causes an overhead of n process reductions per item placed on the output stream, even though it takes one cycle.

This overhead can be alleviated by two observations. First, each merging process need not request the bus each time it receives a message on its input: rather it could wait till it has accumulated a sufficiently large number of input messages, and then transfer them in one unification to the output stream. It can do that by keeping a local difference list into which it copies elements from its input stream. When the count in the difference list reaches a pre-determined threshold, it starts competing for the (arbiter) bus. The overhead for each transaction with the bus remains n process reductions, but now b messages may be transferred to the bus in one transaction, where b is the block size.

The second observation is that useful work could be done by *all* processes in the process reduction in which they move past the transaction made by the successful bidder for the bus. Namely, the pipelines for *all* the processes could be flushed in one step. In each transaction with the bus s messages may be communicated to the output instead of k, where $b \leq s \leq n \times b$ is the sum of *all* the messages on any pipeline.

This hinges on being able to combine n difference lists (some of which could possibly be empty) into *one* difference list in at most n process reductions. This may be done by maintaining a ring topology for the connectivity of the processes. Each process has two variables, a *Left* and a *Right* connection, such that the left variable for the process on its right is *Right* and the right variable for the process on its left is *Left*. In one step, each follower process unifies the head of its inner difference list with the head of its *Right* variable, and the tail with the head of its *Left* variable, recurring (for the next such cycle) with the tails of the *Right* and *Left* variables, respectively. After all but one of the processes is done executing this, for the remaining process the head of the *Left* variable is the head and the head of the *Right* variable the tail of a difference list which contains the contents of all the pipelines in the ring, concatenated together.

There remains the question of when the pipeline flushing phase is initiated and how to ensure that once the phase is initiated, every process in the ring will execute its *flush-pipeline* transition in a bounded number of steps. Our solution is straightforward. *Any* process whose pipeline gets filled up can initiate a *flush-pipeline* phase: if it succeeds, it is called the *leader* of the *flush* phase. It does this by trying to seize control of the arbiter bus (by instantiating its head with its own unique id in the *initiate-flush* transition). It is now the responsibility of the *leader* process to ensure that the pipelines get flushed in a bounded number of steps and that computation can restart after that for next fill and flush cycle.

Once a process has captured the bus, every other process will have the option of either continuing to use its *fill* transition (if its *pipeline-count* > *0*) or using the *flush* transition. But surely the *fill* transition can be executed only a bounded number of times, after which the only transition possible by the process is the *flush* transition.

It remains for the leader to detect when all the processes in the ring have executed their *flush-pipeline* transition. But this is easily achieved using the short-circuit technique.

The merge ring program

In detail, each process has five arguments: an Id, the arbiter bus, the ring, a pipe and the termination chain. The arbiter bus is an arbiter structure shared by all the processes in the ring. The ring is a binary structure with two components, the *left* and *right* connections. Usually these connections will be instantiated with a *message* structure that contains three components: the head (or tail) of the difference list being flushed, the short-circuit link, and the variable to be used for the next *message*. The pipe is a structure that contains the input stream, the local difference list, the current count and the maximum count.

Fill-pipeline transition. Usually processes loop and fill their pipeline:

```
process(Id, Arb↓, Ring,
        pipe([write(I)↓|In], Head, [write(I)|Tail], 1+Count, Max), TC
) ←
        process(Id, Arb, Ring, pipe(In, Head, Tail, Count, Max), TC).
```

Initiate-flush transition. When its pipeline is full (*Count = 1*), a process may try to capture the arbiter. Note that the messages in the pipeline of the process are immediately sent on the output channel of the merge; the messages, if any, obtained from the ring are concatenated to the end of the local pipeline (this is achieved by the two occurrences of *Tail* in the head of the clause). Note also that the output channel of the merge-ring for the next round (*NewHd*) is the same as the tail of the local difference list of the process to the right of the leader in the ring.

process(Id, arb(Id, Head, Arb)↓,
        ring(message(Tail, Done, Left),
           message(NewHd, done, Right)),
        pipe(In, Head, Tail, 1, Max), TC
) ←
        wait(Done, arb(AnId, NewHd, AnArb), Arb),
        process(Id, Arb, ring(Left, Right), pipe(In, New, New, Max, Max), TC).

wait(Done↓, Arb, Arb).

    Flush-pipeline transition. A process can flush its pipeline (note the two occurrences of *Head* and *Tail* in the head of the clause) when some other process obtains the bus. It initializes its count.

process(Id, arb(Id1↓, AHead, Arb),
        ring(message(Tail, Done, Left),
        message(Head, Done, Right)),
        pipe(In, Head, Tail, Count, Max), TC
) ←
        process(Id, Arb, ring(Left, Right), pipe(In, New, New, Max, Max), TC).

We now move on to consider various operations on this ring.

16.2.5 Creation of the ring, and changing the number of streams

    For simplicity we assume that the ring is spawned by a call *merge*(*O, I, B*) where *O* is the output stream, *I* the input stream and *B* the block size for the merge. Subsequently messages of the form *instream*(*S*) are interpreted by each process as a request to create a new process with input stream *S* and insert it in the ring.

        merge(Out, In, B) ←
           process(1, arb(AnId, Out, AnArb),
               ring(Left, Left), pipe(In, New, New, B, B), left\right).

A process may also accept a message asking it to change its block-size.

$$\text{process(Id, Arb}\downarrow, \text{Ring, pipe([size(M)}\downarrow \mid \text{In], Head, Tail,}$$
$$\text{Count+1, Max), TC}$$
$$) \leftarrow$$
$$\text{process(Id, Arb, Ring, pipe(In, Head, Tail, Count, M, TC).}$$

Termination of an input stream

A process can terminate when its input stream terminates. In order to achieve maximum parallelism, it is desirable not to force a process to capture and flush the ring upon termination. Rather, we allow a process to merely flush its local pipeline, short its *Done* terminals and the *Ring* terminals for the next round, and terminate. However, we must now ensure that all processes do not terminate simultaneously, lest no process flushes the ring and properly terminates the output stream. To that end we use the single exclusion protocol (Chapter 16.2.2). This yields the clauses:

process(Id, Arb↓, ring(message(Tail, Done, LR), message(Head, Done, LR)),
      pipe([ ]↓, Head, Tail, Count, Max), Term\Term).   % T_1
process(Id, arb(Id, Head, [ ])↓,
      ring(message(Tail, Done, [ ]), message([ ], Done, [ ])),
      pipe([ ]↓, Head, Tail, Count, Max), left↓\right↓).   % T_2

Adding an input stream

On receiving an *instream*(I) message, a process generates a unique identifier for the new process and splices it into the ring. To ensure that the identifier it generates is unique, the process doubles its *Id* and keeps it, and adds one and passes it to the new process. This scheme for 'distributed unique *Id* generation' is wasteful. More efficient schemes may be designed, but that is outside the scope of this paper.

$$\text{process(Id, Arb, ring(Left, Right),}$$
$$\text{pipe([stream(I)}\downarrow \mid \text{In], Head, Tail, Count1+Count2, Max), L\backslash R}$$
$$) \leftarrow$$
$$\text{process(Id+Id, Arb, ring(Left, Mid),}$$
$$\text{pipe(In, Head, Tail, Count1, Max), L\backslash M),}$$
$$\text{process(1+Id+Id, Arb, ring(Mid, Right),}$$
$$\text{pipe(I, New, New, Count2, Max), M\backslash R).}$$

This is the first time that an operation other than equality testing was needed on an *Id*. It would be straightforward to use an integer and to double it. Arithmetic evaluation is, however, cumbersome in CLP languages (e.g., what happens on integer overflow?); we choose here the conceptually simpler alternative of representing a number n in unary notation, as a bag of n *1*s. Note that if the new process is initialized with a *Max* count rather than *Count2*, a bounded merge may not be guaranteed. The new process may receive another request for spawning a new channel, *ad infinitum*. Instead we non-deterministically subtract some number *Count2* from the number of messages that the parent process can still accept.

16.2.6 On the need for unique Ids

In the above algorithm, unique Ids allowed all those processes whose local pipelines may have become full to compete for the shared resource. The process that is granted access to the resource is immediately able to transmit the contents of its pipeline to the output channel; it waits before all the other processes in the ring have executed their *flush-pipeline* transition before initiating the next cycle.

How crucial was the use of unique Ids in this scheme? If unique Ids are not used, then more than one process could execute its *initiate-flush* transition simultaneously. It cannot be the case, then, that as part of this transition each process unifies the current output stream with the contents of its local pipeline: to do so would force all the input streams to be identical! Each process would therefore have to flush its pipeline by unifying its right link with the head of its pipeline and the left with the tail. But now there must be *one special process* which is responsible for taking the contents of the ring after one phase and moving them to the output stream. Moreover, this process has to be pre-determined, and *it has to be the same process for each cycle*. The anti-clockwise distance from a process that initiates a flush to this special process determines the number of reductions necessary before the output of that process appears at the output stream.

16.2.7 Computational complexity

After some process decides to execute the *initiate-flush* transition, the system of processes can make at most $m+n$ transitions in $b+1$ cycles before $m+b$ messages are available as output on the merged stream, where $0 \leq m \leq (n\text{-}1) \times b$. This gives $O(n \times b)$-bounded merge, with a delay=b and response-time=b. Moreover, in b cycles up to $n \times b$, messages may be moved to the output stream: using difference list concatenation allows linear speedup.

We now argue that each cycle takes constant time. Clearly, moving input from the input stream into the local pipeline takes constant time. Choosing the leader takes one constant-time cycle; only one process is able to execute its *initiate-flush* transition in this cycle. All the processes can simultaneously output the contents of their local pipeline to the ring in constant time, if we assume that variable-variable unification takes constant time.

Bounds on waiting and And-fairness. Note that the program *allows* a merge process to accept input before flushing (if its pipeline is not full), but does not *force* it. Strongly bounded waiting, i.e., counting from the time that an input becomes *available* on an input stream, can be ensured if the producers of the inputs into the merge-system cooperate with the merge-system in using the duplex protocol on the channels. To cut down on the overhead of forcing the producer processes to cycle past the end-markers left by the merge processes, the *readlist* goal may be invoked by the merge process on the input channel only once every c cycles. This would then give an $O(c \times b \times n)$ (strongly-) bounded merge.

Efficient parallelizability. Note that in an actual implementation if n processors are available with one allocated to each merging process, then there is no need for the leader to force each process to suspend after it flushes its pipeline until *all* processes have flushed their pipeline. The synchronization is needed only if there are p ($1 \leq p < n$) processors available, and no assumption may be made about the scheduling algorithm.

Lastly, this scheme is easily modified to allow the *consumer* of the merged stream to decide when it wants to flush the pipeline. Simply place a dummy process with access to the arbiter bus and synchronization rings: the dummy process executes an *initiate-flush* transition whenever the producer wants some output. Note, however, that such a forced flush may yield no messages in the output stream, e.g., if all the pipelines are empty. More sophisticated control schemes in which a forced flush is initiated *only* if there is at least one message in *some* pipeline can be devised.

16.2.8 On combining merge rings with merge trees

The merge ring protocol discussed above suffers from the drawback that under low traffic conditions the overhead may be as high as $O(n)$, notwithstanding the constant delay.

We now investigate the combination of merge rings into merge trees, which are *B-trees* discussed by Knuth (1973) of order k. More specifically, a k:($2 \times k-1$) *merge tree* is a tree in which each node is a merge ring with between k and ($2 \times k-1$) processes, each process corresponding to a son of the node. Each node is connected to its parent node by the output channel of the merge ring at the node, which becomes the input channel of the process at the parent node it is connected to. Input flows in from the leaves of the tree, causes a ring-merge at a node and flows out from the node into the superior node, finally flowing out from the root of the tree. With this construction, the (worst-case) overhead per message is $O(k \times h)$, where h is the height of the tree; if the tree is kept balanced, and k is a constant, then the overhead decreases to $O(\log(n))$ where n is the number of streams being merged.

The price to be paid is twofold. First, the delay is now proportional to the height of the tree, and is unparallelizable. More importantly, because each merge ring operates independently of the other, output produced in one portion of the tree may be consistently ignored: the output may not be read by the merge process in the next higher ring. Note that in the merge-ring construction given in the previous section, the merge was bounded only with respect to inputs *accepted* by the merge system. In their presentation of balanced binary merge trees, Shapiro and Mierowsky (Chapter 14) side-stepped this problem by assuming their implementations were strictly And-fair and stable. We now show how to program boundedness within the language, without any implementation assumptions.

The scheme works as follows. Usually, the structure behaves like a merge tree, accepting input from the leaves and pumping it towards the root of the tree, with a ring merge being done at each node. However, once a leaf has pumped in a certain number p of values, where p is a function of k and n, it initiates a *freeze-dump* phase. In this phase, the leaf refuses to accept any more inputs and tries to make its ring frozen: when a ring freezes, it freezes all its inputs recursively, accepting only the input that is already in the system. Once all this input reaches the root, the root causes an unfreeze phase to propagate down to the leaves, and the usual merging operations resume. We choose to do this phase only when a sufficient number of inputs have entered the system since the last time this phase was done: doing so guarantees that the overhead is increased only by a constant factor.

In what follows, we make a minor change to the merge-rings discussed in the previous section. We assume that there are special processes at the root and leaves of the tree. The process at the root of the tree receives a stream of difference lists: the output of the whole merge system is the output of the root, and it is the list obtained by concatenating the difference lists in the stream input to the root. A leaf process receives input from its input stream, transfers it to a local pipeline (difference list), and passes on into the merge system a stream of difference lists. In the design of the merge rings, therefore, we need only be concerned with merge rings that accept a stream of difference lists in their inputs and produce a stream of difference lists in their output. Further, internally, the 'block-size' for the processes in a ring will be reduced to 1. This allows a much simpler presentation of the transition rules, without having an impact on performance.

16.2.9 Leader behaviors

A process receives and produces two kinds of messages: *write* and *freeze*. A write message contains two arguments, a difference list. A difference list $H \backslash T$ is *safe* (to consume) if H is a list which has T as an ultimate tail. Note that a difference list may be produced by concatenating a number of other difference lists: if all the pieces have not yet been unified, the difference list may not be safe, according to the definition above. The protocol ensures that the difference list is always safe. A *freeze* message also contains two arguments. The first argument is a difference list which represents (or will represent) *all* the inputs that have been received on the input channels contained in the merge tree rooted at the node in whose output the message appears. The protocol ensures that the difference list is always safe. The second argument (OK) is a variable that will be instantiated by the root of the whole merge system when the *freeze* phase has terminated. (By the time the root process can read the difference list in a *freeze* message it receives in its input, *all* the merge rings in the system will be suspended on OK. Instantiating OK will simultaneously unfreeze all of them.)

On receiving a write message in the input

Under usual circumstances, a process continually receives a *write* message on its input and attempts to capture the ring when the list in the message is safe. If it succeeds, it sends *write*($H \backslash T1$) on the output: the message contains a difference list $H \backslash T1$ which is the concatenation of the difference list $H \backslash T$ received in the input and the list ($T \backslash T1$) produced by flushing the ring. (Note that $H \backslash T1$ is safe when both $H \backslash T$ and $T \backslash T1$ are safe. The safety of $H \backslash T$ is a pre-condition for the transition below, and $T \backslash T1$ is safe when all the processes in the ring have made their transition for the current cycle, i.e., when *Done* is instantiated.)

As before, the next cycle for the merge ring is initiated only after all the processes in the ring have participated in the current cycle. This is ensured by the *wait* goal in the body of the clause.

```
process(Id, arb(Id, [write(Write) | Out], Arb)↓,
        ring(message(T, Done, Left), message(T1, done, Right)),
        [write((H\T)↓ | In], TC ←
    wait(Done, H\T1, Write),
    wait(Done, arb(AnId, Out, AnArb), Arb),
    process(Id, Arb, ring(Left, Right), In, TC).
```

It is important to note that a process cannot commit using this clause if the output of the merge ring has been sent a *freeze* message by the next higher merge ring. In that case the second argument of the *arb* structure in the process will be instantiated to a list whose first element is a *freeze* structure: hence the unification of the *arb* structures will fail. Recall the discussion of the duplex channel protocol, Chapter 16.2.2.

On receiving a freeze message in the input

When a process receives a *freeze* message on its input, it also attempts to capture the current cycle of the merge ring. If it succeeds, it sends a *freeze* message on its output. The difference list $H \backslash T1$ in the message is the concatenation of the list $H\backslash T$ received in the input and the list $T\backslash T1$ obtained by flushing the ring. (The ring is flushed in 'freeze mode': see below.)

process(Id, arb(Id, [freeze(Write, OK) | Out], Arb)↓,
            ring(message(T, Done, Left), message(T1, done, Right)),
            [freeze((H\T)↓, OK) | In], TC) ←
wait(Done, H\T1, Write),
wait(OK, arb(AnId, Out, AnArb), Arb),
process(Id, Arb, ring(Left, Right), In, TC).

Note the similarity between this and the previous transition. The only differences are that in one case a *write* message is received and propagated, and in the other a *freeze* message, and that in one case the next round of arbitration is not initiated until the current arbitration phase for the ring is complete, and in the other case it is not initiated until the current freeze phase for the tree of merge-rings is complete.

On receiving a freeze message in the output

We now turn to the rule governing the behavior of the leader process when the merge ring has received a *freeze(L, OK)* message from its superior ring. A merge ring must respond by unifying L with $H\backslash T$, where $H\backslash T$ is the (safe) difference list of all the messages (received from the leaf input streams) that are currently in the sub-tree rooted at the merge ring. Subsequently, the merge-ring must stay suspended on *OK*.

The list $H\backslash T$ may be obtained as follows. The current cycle is executed in 'freeze' mode. In this mode, the leader, and all the other (follower) processes in the ring execute the *freeze* operation on their input channels: $H\backslash T$ is the result of concatenating together the lists returned by this operation. As usual, the concatenation is done by the leader process by splicing its list in correctly with the difference list it can read off from both ends of the ring.

The freeze operation on an input channel

The freeze operation on an input channel returns a safe difference list $H\backslash T$, which is the concatenation of two lists $H\backslash T1$ and $T1\backslash T$. The list $H\backslash T1$ is the list obtained by concatenating together all the *write* messages already in the channel. The list $T1\backslash T$ is the list obtained from sending a *freeze(L1, OK)* message down the channel, and waiting for $L1$ to be instantiated to $T1\backslash T$. If, recursively, $L1$ is bound correctly, then the list $H\backslash T$ is indeed the list of all the messages received from the input streams to the merge system in the subtree rooted at the node whose output stream is the input stream of the leader process.

In the call *freeze(In, H\T, OK, NewIn, Term)*, *In* is the input stream on which the freeze operation is being executed, $H\backslash T$ is the list being returned, *OK* is the flag for the end of the freeze phase to be propagated down the tree, and *Term* is a difference list that is unified with the empty list when the *freeze* operation has terminated. The transitions are:

freeze([write((H\T1)↓ | In], H\T, OK, NewIn, Term) ←
    freeze(In, T1\T, OK, NewIn, Term).

freeze([freeze(Write, OK) | NewIn], H\T, OK, NewIn, Term) ←
    wait(Write, Write, H\T),
    wait(Write, Term, D\D).

read_only(X↓, X).

We can now return to define the transition rule for a leader process which discovers a *freeze* message on the output:

process(Id, arb(Id, [freeze(Write, OK)↓ | Out], Arb)↓,
    ring(message(T2, Done1, Left), message(T1, done, Right)),
    In, TC) ←
freeze(In, H\T2, OK, NewIn, Done\Done1),
wait(Done, H\T1, Write),
wait(OK, arb(AnId, Out, AnArb), Arb),
process(Id, Arb, ring(Left, Right), NewIn, TC).

The only difference between this transition and the *freeze* transition shown above is that in this transition, in addition, the leader does a *freeze* operation on its input channel. Note that *Done* will be instantiated (to *done*) only when both $H \backslash T2$ and $T2 \backslash T1$ are safe. The first *wait* goal in the body will then write out $H \backslash T1$ to the first argument of the *freeze* goal in the output stream. Note also that if the head of the input channel was already instantiated with a *freeze(write(H \ T2), OK)* message, the *freeze* operation would still work correctly because of the bi-directionality of unification: the list returned by the freeze operation would be $H \backslash T1$. Hence in case the leader process has a *freeze* message on its input and also detects a *freeze* message on the merge-ring's output, both the transition in this section and the transition shown before will work identically. This is crucial for the correctness of the protocol since simultaneously and asynchronously many freeze messages may be created in the merge system, and these messages must all interact correctly.

    As an aside, note that this transition implies that a process may compete for and win the current round, *even though it may have no messages on its input channel*. The appearance of a *freeze* message on the output is sufficient to force one of the processes in the merge ring to reduce and initiate a 'freeze-mode' cycle.

16.2.10 Follower behaviors

We now turn to the behavior of the *follower* processes. Recall that a follower process is one which could not capture the current arbitration cycle: hence in all these transitions the *Arbiter* structure is matched in the head with the pattern $arb(Id1\downarrow, \ldots)$.

If the current cycle is being executed in *write* mode (as indicated by the output stream of the merge ring containing a *write* message), then the process may pop a *write* message from its input when it is safe to do so. As discussed in the previous section, it must also be possible for a follower process to reduce (outputting the empty list) without suspending for input from its input channel. Hence the rules:

> process(Id, arb(Id1↓, [write(Awrite) | AnOut], Arb)↓,
>   ring(message(Tail, Done, Left), message(Head, Done, Right)),
>   [write((Head\Tail)↓) | In], TC) ←
>   process(Id, Arb, ring(Left, Right), In, TC.)

> process(Id, arb(Id1↓, [write(Awrite) | AnOut], Arb)↓,
>   ring(message(Empty, Done, Left), message(Empty, Done, Right)),
>   In, TC) ←
>   process(Id, Arb, ring(Left, Right), In, TC).

Finally, if the cycle is being done in freeze mode (output stream of merge ring contains a *freeze* message), a freeze message must be sent on the input. Note that the 'switch' *Done\AllDone* is shorted by the *freeze* goal in the body of the clause, which is done only after $H\setminus T$ is safe. Note also that the *OK* flag for the *freeze* goal is picked up from the message in the output stream.

> process(Id, arb(Id1↓, [freeze(_, OK) | AnOut], Arb)↓,
>   ring(message(T, Done, Left),
>   message(H, AllDone, Right)),
>   In, TC
>) ←
>   freeze(In, H\T, OK, NewIn, Done\Alldone),
>   process(Id, Arb, ring(Left, Right), NewIn, TC).

Root behaviors

The behavior of the root process is straightforward. It accepts *write* and *freeze* messages, and outputs them. It instantiates the *OK* flag when it outputs the list from a *freeze* message.

$$\text{merge(Out, [write((Out\backslash NewOut)\!\downarrow) \mid In])} \leftarrow$$
$$\text{merge(NewOut, In).}$$
$$\text{merge(Out, [freeze((Out\backslash NewOut)\!\downarrow, ok) \mid In])} \leftarrow$$
$$\text{merge(NewOut, In).}$$

Note that it is easy to arrange matters such that the root keeps a count of the number of elements output since the last freeze phase. When this count reaches a fixed number, the root may initiate a freeze phase. If the count is chosen appropriately, it may help lower the expected bound for the merge system.

Leaf behaviors

The leaf behaviors are straightforward and we omit the details. In brief, a leaf accepts messages on its input and places them in a local pipeline. When the pipeline count reaches a threshold, the pipeline is flushed and the count reset. The count of messages accepted from the input since the last freeze cycle is also kept. When this count reaches a bound p, a *freeze* message is sent on the output, together with the current contents of the pipeline. The leaf then suspends on the *OK* flag in the *freeze* message it sent out. When a leaf *receives* a *freeze* message on its *output* line, it behaves exactly as above: it flushes its pipeline (which may actually be empty if no messages were received since the last freeze cycle), and then suspends on the *OK* flag in the *freeze* message. (In both cases the pipeline count and the count of elements received since the last freeze cycle are rest.)

Note that if a strong bound is required, and the producers of the channels input into the merge-system observe the duplex protocol, then the leaf process will behave like an internal process. It will execute a freeze operation on its input line, and concatenate the list returned from this operation to the list in its local pipeline before unifying it with the difference list in the *freeze* message and suspending on the *OK* flag.

16.2.11 Operations on the merge tree

We omit the discussion on keeping the merge tree balanced when streams dynamically appear and disappear. The interested reader is referred to Shapiro and Mierowsky (Chapter 14) for a discussion on how to program the balancing of *2:3* trees in a CLP language. We note in passing that some more care is needed in the present situation because the trees are expected to be $k{:}(2 \times k{-}1)$, where k could be large. Further, the insertion technique discussed in that paper is actually sub-optimal because it could lead to trees as deep as $\log_k(n)$, where n is the number of leaves. It is better to split a node and send a new *instream* message to the parent *only when* no other siblings of the node at the same level can accept the new stream. This will help reduce the depth of the tree to $\log_{(2k-1)}(n)$ by keeping them more densely packed. This may be achieved by keeping all the children of a node in another ring, to enable them to communicate with each other directly, without going through their parent node.

16.2.12 Computational complexity

The performance of this merge system depends on various parameters, namely, the block-size b (which we assume to be *1* in the following analysis), the number of streams n, the branching factor in the tree k, and the frequency p at which the freeze cycle is initiated. Note that the *height* h of the tree will be $O(\log_{(2 \times k-1)}(n))$, if the tree is kept balanced as discussed above. This leads to a delay of $O(h)$ (note that delay measures the number of *cycles* and not reductions). The worst case overhead is $O(h \times k)$, because k reductions are needed at each node. The weak-bound is $O(p \times n)$, the maximum number of inputs that can enter between two freeze phases.

The number of reductions done in the freeze phase may be counted as follows. The tree has $O(n)$ internal channels: one *freeze* message per channel is processed. The number of reductions done in executing the freeze operation on a channel is the same as the number of messages in the channel: over all channels this total is bounded above by $n \times p$, the total number of messages which can enter the system between two freeze phases. Hence the number is $O(w + n)$, where w is bounded above by $n \times p$. To ensure that the freeze phase does not cause an increase in the average overhead per output element produced, it is enough to choose p such that $p \times k \times h$ (the number of reductions used in moving p messages from the input to the output) is the same as the cost of the freeze cycle. This gives $p = O(n/(k \times h))$.

We calculate the response time of the merge as follows. Once an input arrives on an input channel, it may be ignored only as long as there is input on the other channels coming into the same merge ring; hence after $O(n \times p)$ cycles it must have made its way out of the system. (Note that in each cycle every process that is enabled reduces.)

If k is reduced to a constant, then the merge-ring tree degenerates to the merge trees of Shapiro and Mierowsky, except that boundedness is being obtained without making any implementation assumptions, and in the best case overhead is constant instead of $\log_2(n)$. If $k=O(n^{1/\epsilon})$ for some constant $\epsilon > 1$ and $p=1$, then the merge-ring tree actually gives a better performance than the n-way merge ring discussed in the previous section, producing a delay of ϵ, an overhead of $O(\epsilon \times n^{(1/\epsilon)})$ and a linear bound.

Acknowledgement

This research was sponsored by the Defense Advanced Research Projects Agency (DOD), ARPA Order No. 4976, monitored by the Air Force Avionics Laboratory Under Contract F33615-84-K-1520.

This paper was inspired by an attempt to discover the limits on expressibility that the language rules of GHC introduce. Thanks to Kazunori Ueda for many discussions on GHC. I have also benefitted from comments by Ehud Shapiro on earlier versions of the paper. The work on a model of computation for FCP($\downarrow$) is being done in conjunction with Larry Rudolph. Thanks also to Lyle McGeoch for help at a critical moment.

Chapter 17

Channels: A Generalization of Streams

Eric Dean Tribble, Mark S. Miller, Kenneth Kahn,
Daniel G. Bobrow, Curtis Abbott

Xerox Palo Alto Research Center

Ehud Shapiro

The Weizmann Institute of Science

Abstract

Concurrent logic programming languages, as well as other computation models, support communication between multiple readers and multiple writers via streams. Streams unnecessarily limit concurrency by being totally ordered. We propose a generalization of streams called channels that allow elements to be partially ordered. We provide a mathematical and logic program definition of channels and describe their Concurrent Prolog implementation using a data-structure called multistream.

17.1 Introduction

Concurrent logic programming languages such as Concurrent Prolog can implement communication between multiple readers and writers using streams. We propose a communication mechanism, called channels, which abstracts and generalizes the essential properties of stream based communication between processes in concurrent logic programming languages.

17.1.1 Motivation

The channel abstraction evolved out of the analysis of communication between objects represented by processes in the Vulcan language (Kahn et al., Chapter 30). Vulcan is an object-oriented language designed as an extension to concurrent logic programming languages like Concurrent Prolog and GHC. It abstracts communication between objects, hides object deallocation, and supports object state encapsulation and change by providing a frame axiom for object state.

Since Vulcan objects are represented by recurrent processes, the abstraction for communication between objects applies equally well to communication between processes in general. The implementation of channels in Concurrent Prolog is based on and subsumes current stream communication techniques.

Since channels are partial orders, multiple writers need not synchronize their writing on a channel. Also, in many cases, readers can fork and serve independently written messages in parallel. Stateless servers are common examples of this.

17.2 Streams

Streams were introduced as a basic communication mechanism between concurrent processes by Kahn and MacQueen (1977). Single writer, multiple reader streams can be supported easily by all concurrent logic programming languages, including Concurrent Prolog, PARLOG, and GHC.

An extension to streams which allows multiple writers as well as multiple readers was suggested by Ahuja and Gelernter (1986) and is incorporated in Linda. We show below a mathematical and a logic program definition of the basic stream operations. Concurrent logic languages with atomic test unification such as the Concurrent Prolog family of languages can support multiple-writer streams as well, as shown below.

17.2.1 Abstract stream operations

Abstractly, a stream is a total and well ordered set of elements, each with an associated message. A stream S can be represented by a pair $\langle E, < \rangle$ where E is a set of elements and $<$ is a total ordering relation on the domain $E \times E$. We assume a global function, $\mathcal{M}$, such that for every element e, $\mathcal{M}(e)$ is the message associated with e. We define three abstract operations on streams by stating the constraints that they should satisfy: *read*, *write*, and *empty*. In the definitions below $\downarrow$ is the restriction operator, and $S_i = \langle E_i, <_i \rangle$.

> $read(M,S_1,S_2) \leftarrow$
> M labels the least element of S_1. S_2 is the remainder.

$\exists e \in E_1 [M = \mathcal{M}(e)$
$\quad \wedge\ E_2 = E_1 - \{e\}$
$\quad \wedge\ <_2\ =\ <_1 \downarrow E_2 \times E_2$
$\quad \wedge\ \forall e' \in E_2\ (e <_1 e')]$

$write(M, S_1, S_2) \leftarrow$
$\quad$ M labels an element of S_1 less than any element of S_2.
$\quad S_2$ is a subset of S_1.

$\exists e \in E_1 [M = \mathcal{M}(e)$
$\quad \wedge\ E_2 \cup \{e\} \subseteq E_1$
$\quad \wedge\ <_2\ =\ <_1 \downarrow E_2 \times E_2$
$\quad \wedge\ \forall e' \in E_2\ (e <_1 e')]$

$empty(S) \leftarrow$
$\quad$ The stream is empty.

$\quad S = \langle \phi, \phi \rangle.$

We define a three argument *write* operation to allow writers to impose order on their messages. With just a two argument *write*, the following operations, $write(a, S)$, $write(b, S)$, do not impose any ordering between a and b. With a three argument *write*, the programmer can ensure that b is after a in the stream *S1* with $write(a, S1, S2)$, $write(b, S2, S3)$. Note that the three argument *write* operation allows for multiple *write* operations on the same stream since it does not require the written element to be the first in the stream.

The semantics of a set of stream operations is defined as an assignment of minimal streams to the stream variables that satisfy the constraints imposed by the operations. Note that a set of *write* operations may have several minimal solutions. This reflects the nondeterminism of the operation. As will be discussed later, duplicated messages are allowed under certain circumstances.

17.2.2 Logic program specification of streams

The logic program specifying the above relations is shown in Program 17.1. The program uses list cells to represent the ordered elements, and logical terms for messages. The labeling function maps the list cell to the message in its head, so $\mathcal{M}([X|Xs]) = X$. The ordering relation is defined by the suffix relation on lists: $e < e'$ if $suffix(e', e)$, where *suffix* is defined by:

$\quad$ suffix(Xs, [X|Xs]).
$\quad$ suffix(Xs, [Y|Ys]) $\leftarrow$ suffix(Xs, Ys).

The logic program specification is slightly more restrictive than the mathematical one. For example, the two operations

$\quad$ write(a, S1, S2), write(b, S1, S2)

read(Message, [Message | Stream], Stream).

write(Message, [Message | Stream], Stream).
write(Message, [Ignored | Stream1], Stream2) ←
    Message ≠ Ignored,
    write(Message, Stream1, Stream2).

empty([ ]).

Program 17.1: A logic program for stream operations

have the solutions $S1=[a,b|S2]$ and $S1=[b,a|S2]$ under the mathematical definition, but no solution according to the logic program.

A stronger logic program specification can be obtained by removing the inequality test in the definition of *write*.

17.2.3 Flat Concurrent Prolog implementation of streams

An abstract interpreter of logic programs is a sound and complete theorem prover. The operational semantics of concurrent logic programming languages such as FCP define a sound, but incomplete, theorem prover, and provide additional synchronization and control to guide deductions. In the case of stream operations, the synchronization needed to ensure the success of the FCP program is trivial: nothing further is required for *read* and *empty*, while the implementation of *write* requires the addition of a commit operator.

    write(Message, [Message | Stream], Stream).
    write(Message, [Ignored | Stream1], Stream2) ←
        Message ≠ Ignored | write(Message, Stream1, Stream2).

Atomic unification

The correctness of this definition relies on the atomicity of unification and process reduction in (Flat) Concurrent Prolog. The necessity for atomicity is demonstrated by the following conjunction of processes:

    write(a, Stream1, Stream2),
    write(b, Stream2, Stream3),
    write(c, Stream1, Stream4),
    write(d, Stream4, Stream5).

The *write* processes will be referred to by the letter representing their message. The most obvious order of execution has process a execute before process b, and process c execute before process d. The simple race between the a and c processes, using atomic unification, test and set the message cell of the first available list cell atomically. When process b executes before process a, then *Stream2* instantiates to $[b \mid Stream3]$. If the d process completes similarly, then the contention between the a and c processes must mediate the second message of *Stream1* as well. Since unification is atomic, when process a commits, it will unify *Stream1* with $[a, b \mid Stream3]$ atomically. Process c is then forced to write its message on the third element of the stream, and d will be written fourth.

Without atomic unification, process c could have written in the second element of *Stream1*, causing failure when process b writes there. Unfortunately, the implementations for the abstract operations presented in this paper cannot be translated directly into GHC or PARLOG, since they lack the atomic unification property.

Preserving message multiplicity

The mathematical and logical definitions of *write* allow the conjunction $write(M,S_1,S_2)$, $write(M,S_1,S_3)$ to be equivalent to $write(M,S_1,S_2)$, $S_2=S_3$. Operationally, each use of *write* should introduce a new, unique element with which to associate the supplied message. This can be done by including a unique token in each message, which is quite tedious from a practical point of view. The following implementation achieves this effect without the need for unique identifiers:

> write(Message, [First? | Stream], Stream) ←
>   First = Message.
> write(Message, Stream1, Stream3) ←
>   Stream1? = [Ignored | Stream2] | write(Message, Stream2, Stream3).

This procedure iterates along the channel looking for an uninstantiated tail to unify with a new list cell containing *Message*. If the next list cell already contains a message, the first clause suspends unifying it with *First*. The second clause commits, however, because *Stream1* is already a list cell, and unification can proceed. The second clause spawns a write operation on the next list cell.

If a cell is uninstantiated, then the first clause commits, instantiating it to a list cell, and unifying the message variable of the new cell with *First?*. This unification locks the cell's message from interference by concurrent writers because they will suspend trying to unify their read-only variable with *First?*. This will force the writer to use the second clause and attempt to write one cell further down the list.

Note that atomic test unification without read-only variables is insufficient to implement the above procedure. If the first *write* clause instantiates the list cell to *Message* before it gets concurrently computed, then a concurrent writer could instantiate it to another message. With read-only variables, such an attempt would suspend because unification of two different read-only variables suspends. This FCP definition of *write* was required for the specification of the multiway merger of Shapiro and Safra (Chapter 15), but was not known at the time.

In contrast to the mathematical and logic program specifications, the above implementation of *write* is unidirectional. The directionality of these operations reduces the requirement for other synchronization (such as read-only annotation) since it is usually associated with process communication. For this practical reason, *read* and many of the later definitions should be unidirectional as well. Later sections assume that some definitions require read-only annotated inputs, but the operations can be implemented such that annotations are not required. One solution defines *read* by calling its real implementation with the correct read-only variables. The most efficient solution simply transforms the definition of *read* to use read-only variables internally. The translation of the current definition is:

read(Message, Channel1, Channel2) ←
    Channel1? = [Message | Channel2] | true.

Later definitions can be translated similarly.

Inefficiencies of streams

Given a naive implementation of the FCP program for write, n writes of distinct messages on the same stream require $O(n^2)$ operations. Using the mutual reference technique (Shapiro and Safra, Chapter 15), the number of operations can be reduced to $O(n)$. Nevertheless, both implementations require mutually exclusive access to the same shared location between n processes. Further, since the messages in a stream are totally serialized, messages must be read and processed from the stream sequentially, even though they may be completely independent. The channel abstraction described below avoids these bottlenecks.

17.3 The Channel Mechanism

The stream specification requires that all elements be totally ordered. Since independent processes write in an indeterminate order, the order introduced by streams is often superfluous. This mathematical inelegance of the specification directly results in the serial bottleneck of processes synchronizing on the tail of the stream. As partial orders, channels can represent both a lack of order between two messages, as well as an ordering imposed by the program.

17.3.1 Abstract channel operations

A channel is a partially ordered set of elements with associated messages. A channel is represented just like a stream, by a pair $\langle E, < \rangle$ except that its ordering relation, "$<$", is a partial order. The abstract operations on channels are defined by appropriately relaxing the constraints given above for streams:

$read(M,C1,C2) \leftarrow$
 M labels a minimal element of C_1. C_2 is the remainder.

$\exists e \in E_1 [M = \mathcal{M}(e)$
 $\wedge E_2 = E_1 - \{e\}$
 $\wedge <_2 \ = \ <_1 \downarrow E_2 \times E_2$
 $\wedge \forall e' \in E_2 \ \neg(e' <_1 e)]$

$write(M,C_1,C_2) \leftarrow$
 M is an element of C_1 less than any element of C_2. C_2 is a subset of C_1.

$\exists e \in E_1 [M = \mathcal{M}(e)$
 $\wedge E_2 \cup \{e\} \subseteq E_1$
 $\wedge <_2 \ = \ <_1 \downarrow E_2 \times E_2$
 $\wedge \forall e' \in E_2 \ (e <_1 e')]$

$empty(C) \leftarrow$
 The channel is empty.

$C = \langle \phi, \phi \rangle$

If a channel contains no minimum element, then *read* non-deterministically returns one of the minimal elements. Elements written on the same channel are unordered. Writing an ordered sequence of messages on a channel requires cascading of *write* operations, as shown above with streams. The following two operations will be discussed later:

$serialize(C_1, Stream_2) \leftarrow$
 $Stream_2$ is a totally ordered stream of the element of C_1.

$E_1 = E_2$
$<_1 \subseteq <_2$
$\forall e, e' \in E_2 \ e <_2 e' \oplus e' <_2 e$

$subset(C_1, C_2) \leftarrow$
 C_1 is a subset of C_2.

$E_1 \subseteq E_2$
 $\wedge <_1 \ = \ <_2 \downarrow E_1 \times E_1$

We define the semantics of a set of channel operations to be minimal partially-ordered sets of elements that satisfy the constraints associated with those operations.

17.3.2 Logic program specification of channel operations

A multistream is a representation of a channel that maintains the partial order constraints while minimizing extraneous ordering between elements. It is a polymorphic stream containing channel elements that may end with the special element $branch(C_1,C_2)$, where C_1 and C_2 are recursively multistreams. Elements on different branches have no order with respect to each other. The logic program specification for *read*, *write*, and *empty* in this representation is shown in Program 17.2.

read(Message, [Message | Channel], Channel).
read(Message, branch(LeftChannel1, RightChannel),
      branch(LeftChannel2, RightChannel)) ←
    read(Message, LeftChannel1, LeftChannel2).
read(Message, branch(LeftChannel, RightChannel1),
      branch(LeftChannel, RightChannel2)) ←
    read(Message, RightChannel1, RightChannel2).

write(Message, branch([Message | LeftChannel], RightChannel),
    LeftChannel).
write(Message, branch([Ignored | LeftChannel], RightChannel),
    Channel) ←
    Message ≠ Ignored,
    write(Message, RightChannel, Channel).

empty([ ]).
empty(branch(LeftChannel, RightChannel)) ←
    empty(LeftChannel),
    empty(RightChannel).

Program 17.2: A logic program for channel operations

Write creates a branch for each message written. The branch allows other elements to be written on the same stream with the same precedence. The asymmetry of branch traversal guarantees that *write* operations will not interfere with channels generated by other *write* operations for sequenced messages (returned in the third argument). The structure resulting from a sequence of *write* operations is shown in Figure 17.1, where each branch point is directly represented by a branch element.

Although correct, the implementation of channels in Program 17.2 is inefficient because it allocates superfluous logical variables. This allows the writing of unrelated messages on the same channel without imposing unnecessary ordering constraints. However, most channels have only a single writer. We show below an extension of the specification that optimizes operations on channels with a single writer at the expense of extra ordering constraints not implied by the abstract specification. Essentially, branches are only introduced when a writer discovers that another writer is using the channel. This results in a structure like that shown in Figure 17.2.

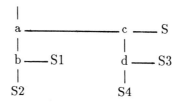

Figure 17.1: The multistream constructed by the sequence of operations:
write(a,S,S1), *write(b,S1,S2)*, *write(c,S,S3)*, *write(d,S3,S4)*

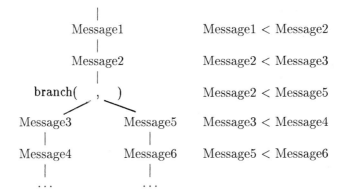

Figure 17.2: Partial ordering between elements in a multistream

Any message written on the above channel will have ordering added so that
its element is greater than either that of *Message4* or *Message6*. The optimized
definition of *write* is:

```
write(Message, [Message | Channel], Channel).
write(Message, branch(Ignored, RightChannel1), RightChannel2) ←
    write(Message, RightChannel1, RightChannel2).
write(Message, [Ignored | Channel1], Channel2) ←
    writeBranch(Channel1, [Message | Channel2])).

writeBranch(branch(LeftChannel, Ignored), LeftChannel).
writeBranch(branch(Ignored, RightChannel1), Channel2) ←
    writeBranch(RightChannel1, Channel2).
writeBranch([Ignored | Channel1], Channel2) ←
    writeBranch(Channel1, Channel2).
```

The *write* procedure writes directly on the channel or creates a branch in the channel, then writes on the left branch. Only when interference occurs must a writer search down the channel. The specification does not preclude arbitrarily many empty branches, but the implementation can.

17.3.3 Concurrent Prolog implementation

A Concurrent Prolog implementation of the channel operations is shown in Program 17.3. The Concurrent Prolog definition of *read* has very simple additional synchronization. At a branch in the multistream, each subchannel must be explored in the guard to nondeterministically choose between the minimal elements.

```
read(Message, [Message | Channel], Channel).
read(Message, branch(LeftChannel1, RightChannel),
        branch(LeftChannel2, RightChannel)) ←
    read(Message, LeftChannel1?, LeftChannel2) | true.
read(Message, branch(LeftChannel, RightChannel1),
        branch(LeftChannel, RightChannel2)) ←
    read(Message, RightChannel1?, RightChannel2) | true.

write(Message, Channel?, LeftChannel) ←
    Channel = branch([Message | LeftChannel], RightChannel) | true.
write(Message, ChannelIn, ChannelOut) ←
    ChannelIn? = branch(LeftChannel, RightChannel) |
    write(Message, RightChannel, ChannelOut).

empty([ ]).
empty(branch(Channel1, Channel2)) ←
    empty(Channel1?),
    empty(Channel2?) | true.

close([ ]).
close(branch(Channel1, Channel2)) ←
    close(Channel1),
    close(Channel2).
```

Program 17.3: A Concurrent Prolog implementation of channel operations

The definition of *write* given here uses read-only annotations to preserve the multiplicity of messages in channels. Removing the read-only annotations from the first clause results in a version that eliminates duplicate messages. This uses the same kind of mutual exclusion synchronization as the stream implementation.

write(Message, [First? | Channel], Channel) ←
    First=Message | true.
write(Message, ChannelIn, ChannelOut) ←
    ChannelIn? = branch(Ignored, RightChannel) |
    write(Message, RightChannel, ChannelOut).
write(Message, ChannelIn, ChannelOut) ←
    ChannelIn? = [Ignored | Channel2] |
    writeBranch(Channel2, [Message | ChannelOut]).

writeBranch(Channel1?, LeftChannel) ←
    Channel1 = branch(LeftChannel, Ignored) | true.
writeBranch(Channel1, Channel3) ←
    Channel1? = branch(Ignored, RightChannel) |
    writeBranch(RightChannel, Channel3).
writeBranch(Channel1, Channel3) ←
    Channel1? = [Ignored | Channel2] |
    writeBranch(Channel2, Channel3).

read(Message, [Message | Channel], Channel).
read(Message, branch(Branch1, Channel1),
        branch(Branch2,Channel2)) ←
    read(Message, Branch1, Branch2, Finished),
    read(Message, Channel1, Channel2, Finished).

read(Ignored, Channel, Channel, Finished) ←
    Finished? = true | true.
read(Message, Channel1, Channel2, Finished?) ←
    Channel1? = [Message | Channel2] |
    Finished = true.
read(Message, Branch, branch(Branch2,Channel2), Finished) ←
    unknown(Finished),
    Branch? = branch(Branch1, Channel1) |
    read(Message, Branch1?, Branch2, Finished),
    read(Message, Channel1?, Channel2, Finished).

Program 17.4: An FCP implementation of *read* and *write*
                optimized for a single-writer

The *empty* operation can be used to close a stream or to test whether it is closed. The stream implementation can be used to test by supplying the stream with a read-only annotation. The recursion in the channel definition does not allow this simplicity. Therefore we must define two procedures, *empty* and *close*, to test and set respectively. Like *read*, *empty* assumes a read-only annotated channel.

All the channel operations defined in Concurrent Prolog can be translated to Flat Concurrent Prolog (Codish and Shapiro, Chapter 32). Program 17.4 contains an FCP implementation of *read* and *write* optimized for a single-writer.

The FCP *read* algorithm spawns a process for each branch traversed. The shared variable representing the next message to be read is controlled through the *Finished* mutual exclusion variable.

Note that under certain scheduling conditions, a writer as defined in Program 17.4 can be starved and never reach the free tail of the stream.

17.3.4 Reading in parallel

Providing maximum potential concurrency is a primary motivation in the implementation of the abstract channel operations and in most significant concurrent logic programs. The channel abstraction increases potential concurrency by maintaining the partial order between messages: messages with the same precedence can be processed independently. Sequences of read operations on a channel lose the partial ordering information, though. We specify two new operations for manipulating channels and the partial ordering relations between messages, in order to allow applications to spawn concurrent readers for different parts of channels.

$min(M, C_1, C_2) \leftarrow$
    Read the minimum element, if one exists.

$\exists e_1 \in E_1 \; \forall e_2 \in E_2 \; (e_1 <_1 e_2)$
    $\wedge \; M = \mathcal{M}(e_1)$
    $\wedge \; read(M, C_{1'}, C_2)$

$branches(C_1, C_2, C_3) \leftarrow$
    C_2 and C_3 are disjoint subchannels of C_1.

$E_1 = E_2 \cup E_3$
    $\wedge \; <_1 \; = \; <_2 \cup <_3$
    $\wedge \; \forall e_2 \in E_2, e_3 \in E_3 \; (\neg(e_2 <_1 e_3) \wedge \neg(e_3 <_1 e_2))$

Min reads the minimum element if there is one. *Branches* splits the supplied channel into two distinct subchannels containing minimal elements of the same precedence. *Branches* can possibly return an empty subchannel, but the implementation will minimize those cases. As will be shown in the next few sections, these operations allow better exploitation of the available parallelism. The Concurrent Prolog multistream implementations are:

min(Message, [Message | Channel], Channel).

branches(branch(Channel1, Channel2), Channel1, Channel2).

Like the *read* operation, *min* and *branches* assume the input channel is read-only annotated.

Mutual exclusion between these two predicates is biased in favor of *branches*: *min* can fail even if a minimum element exists when it encounters an empty branch element. In practice, *min* is used to iterate through the messages, so the single branch containing the minimum element will be examined again. A simple example using these operations to process channel elements in parallel is:

compute(C) ←
    min(X,C?,C1) |
    process(X),
    compute(C1).
compute(C) ←
    branches(C?,C1,C2) |
    compute(C1),
    compute(C2).
compute(C) ←
    empty(C?) | true.

The real uses of these operations follow the above form.

17.3.5 Reading sequentially

The basic *read* operation is not very efficient for reading sequentially. It slows in the presence of many branches because every *read* reconstructs branch elements to make the new channel. On the other hand, reading channels without branches requires only comparisons because it can simply return the tail of the stream representing the channel. *Serialize* bridges this gap by making a totally ordered stream from the messages in a channel, while maintaining the partial ordering between messages. The total ordering of the stream maintains generality because consecutive read operations from a channel would likewise order the messages. In fact, a simple implementation of *serialize* could use *read*:

serialize(Channel1, [Message | Stream?]) ←
    read(Message, Channel1?, Channel2) |
    serialize(Channel2, Stream).
serialize(Channel, [ ]) ←
    empty(Channel?) | true.

Serialize is a unidirectional operation, just as the use of *read* implies. Conceptually, it copies the elements read from the supplied channel onto the stream. In an implementation, *serialize* can be faster because processes can be spawned for the branches to simultaneously traverse each side.

> serialize(Channel1, [Message | Stream?]) ←
>   min(Message, Channel1?, Channel2) |
>   serialize(Channel2, Stream).
> serialize(Channel, Stream) ←
>   branches(Channel?, Channel1, Channel2) |
>   serialize(Channel1, Stream1),
>   serialize(Channel2, Stream2),
>   merge(Stream1?, Stream2?, Stream).
> serialize(Channel, [ ]) ←
>   empty(Channel?) | true.

The *merge* operation makes *Stream* a nondeterministic merge of *Stream1* and *Stream2*. Though the above code has the same complexity as *read* (*merge* forms a binary tree of processes paralleling the *branch* hierarchy), a better algorithm could generate a balanced tree of *merge* processes (Shapiro and Mierowsky, Chapter 14). The multiway merge technique can also be used, reducing the overhead of the *merge* processes to constant time (Shapiro and Safra, Chapter 15).

Notice that *write* is an illegal operation on the stream produced by *serialize*. *Serialize* constructs the stream on an element by element basis. If any process writes on the stream, unification of the element written by that process and the element forced into that location in the stream will fail (*write* would create a *branch* element, where *serialize* could never produce one).

17.3.6 The subset operation

The *subset* operation allows programs to perform operations on a channel, then associate that channel with a larger one. A primary result of the minimality constraint for the semantics of subset is that the elements of the *subset* will be only the elements that were written on the subset; it will not include extraneous elements from the superset.

A server process can use the directionality of *subset* to provide multiple writers with private channels to it by providing each writer with a *subset* channel. Since no subset will have elements on it besides those written specifically on that subset, no writer can access another writer's messages. An implementation of *subset* using *min* and *branches* essentially copies the partial order in parallel from the subset channel onto the superset channel:

```
subset(Subset1, Superset1) ←
    min(Message, Subset1?, Subset2) |
    write(Message?, Superset1, Superset2),
    subset(Subset2, Superset2).
subset(Subset, Superset) ←
    branches(Subset?, Subset1, Subset2) |
    subset(Subset1, Superset),
    subset(Subset2, Superset).
subset(Subset, Superset) ←
    empty(Subset?) | true.
```

An implementation using the asymmetry of the multistream *write* operation is:

```
subset(Subset, Superset) ← writeBranch(Superset, Subset).
```

This takes full advantage of the optimizations in *serialize*.

When the writers on a channel are known, explicitly providing each writer with a subset of the channel being read minimizes synchronization between the writers. This is another use for the subset operation.

17.3.7 An example

This example developed out of an exploration of algorithms for massively parallel machines. While inefficient for machines with fewer processors, it demonstrates the extra concurrency provided by the channel abstraction. The table associates values with specific keys within some linear space of keys. The discussion assumes that the space is the number line. Each process spans a portion of the number line. Their lower bounds are the keys associated with their values. When a key gets looked up, only the process spanning the portion of the number line containing the key responds. If the key is its lower bound, then the key is within the database, and it returns associated value and *true*. If the key is somewhere else within the process's range, then it returns *false*. This simple procedure requires an extension to handle accesses outside the range of the lookup table.

Storing a value is done similarly. The process spanning the portion of the number line containing the new key spawns two processes, one spanning from the original lower bound to the new key, and one spanning from the new key to the original upper bound. The open-coded stream implementation shown in Program 17.5, and the channel based implementation shown in Program 17.6 are quite similar.

The differences are subtle. The open coded use of streams forces all readers to have the same serialization of messages. The definition using channels allows different readers to have different serializations. The benefit is the elimination of the synchronization necessary at the end of a single stream for multiple readers

```
table([lookup(Key,Value,true) | Self], Key, Value, HighKey).
    table(Self?, Key, Value, HighKey).
table([lookup(Key, Ignored, false) | Self], LowKey, Value, HighKey) ←
    LowKey < Key,
    Key < HighKey |
    table(Self?, Key, Value, HighKey).
table([store(Key,Value) | Self], LowKey, LowValue, HighKey) ←
    LowKey < Key,
    Key < HighKey |
    table(Self, LowKey, LowValue, Key),
    table(Self, Key, Value, HighKey).
table([store(LowKey,NewValue) | NewSelf],
        LowKey, Ignored, HighKey) ←
    table(NewSelf?, LowKey, NewValue?, HighKey).
```

Program 17.5: A parallel lookup table using streams

```
table(Self, LowKey, Value, HighKey) ←
    read(lookup(LowKey,Value,true), Self?, NewSelf) |
    table(NewSelf, LowKey, Value, HighKey).
table(Self, LowKey, Value, HighKey) ←
    read(lookup(Key, Ignored, false), Self?, NewSelf),
    LowKey < Key,
    Key < HighKey |
    table(NewSelf, Key, Value, HighKey).
table(Self, LowKey, Value, HighKey) ←
    read(store(Key,HighValue), Self?, NewSelf),
    LowKey < Key,
    Key < HighKey |
    table(NewSelf, LowKey, Value, Key),
    table(NewSelf, Key, HighValue, HighKey).
table(Self, LowKey, Ignored, HighKey) ←
    read(store(LowKey,NewValue), Self?, NewSelf) |
    table(NewSelf, LowKey, NewValue, HighKey).
```

Program 17.6: A parallel lookup table using channels

and writers. In addition, when the table is distributed across different machines, message propagation time will vary along different branches of the channel. The greater flexibility of serialization allows different table processes to respond immediately to whatever data is available to them. The implementation is still correct because any given point on the number line only sees one serialization — it shares the history of its spawning process.

17.3.8 Channel unification

True unification of channels is not supported by the implementations shown. The *branch* functor is logically associative and commutative, but plain unification does not support this. Associative-commutative unification is quite expensive to implement and use. Our implementation, however, supports the important special case of unifying a logical variable (uninstantiated channel) with an already existing channel.

17.3.9 Comparison with communication in Actors

Actor systems provide a different model of process communication at the foundational level (Clinger, 1981). One major difference is that actor communication does not provide any ordering. Sequentiality is accomplished by other means and the communication mechanism is not constrained to maintain any ordering between messages. Actors essentially trade the ease of expression resulting from the partial ordering of messages in channels for implementation freedom. The other major difference from actors is that the actor abstraction does not provide access to the communication structures. Each actor has a single unique message queue which is not program accessible. The channel abstraction is intended to provide objects with the flexibility of sharing channels, reading from multiple channels, and passing references to channels in messages. Actors can implement explicit, sharable channels, so the above difference is only between foundational concepts.

17.4 Future Directions

We have presented channels as an abstract data-type and have given operations on channels a mathematical semantics in terms of minimal solutions to constraints on labeled partial orders and a logical semantics using logic programs. We presented an efficient implementation in Concurrent Prolog. Channels are more general than the streams currently in use and avoid much of their unnecessary serialization.

We believe that the utility of channels in concurrent systems is not limited to concurrent logic programming languages but can be adapted for general concurrent systems.

Further investigation into the relation between the mathematical and logical specification of channel operations and their Concurrent Prolog implementation is required.

This research grew out of some difficulties in basing the Vulcan language upon Concurrent Prolog streams (Kahn et al., Chapter 30). We are planning to redesign and reimplement Vulcan based upon channels.

Acknowledgements

Comments by Michael Hirsch, William Silverman and Daniel Szoke are acknowledged.

Chapter 18

Bounded Buffer Communication
in Concurrent Prolog

Akikazu Takeuchi and Koichi Furukawa

Institute for New Generation Computer Technology

Abstract

In this paper we examine the expressive power of the communication mechanism of Concurrent Prolog and show that the language can express both unbounded buffer and bounded buffer stream communication only by using shared logical variables and the read-only annotation. We also present an abstraction technique which hides buffer control inside stream operations and makes it invisible to user programs.

18.1 Communication Via Shared Logical Variables

In this paper, we clarify the basic communication mechanism of Concurrent Prolog and present an important communication technique which realizes bounded buffer communication in a clear way. Bounded buffer communication using "protected data" (Hellerstein and Shapiro, Chapter 9) is also shown, and the general implication of the concept of "protected data" is discussed.

In Concurrent Prolog, interprocess communication is realized by logical variables shared among processes. A process can send a message to other processes by instantiating a variable shared among them to the message. Since a destructive assignment to a logical variable is not permitted, communication using one variable cannot be done more than once. However, in general, because there is no restriction on the number of processes sharing a variable, the message to which one of the processes instantiates the shared variable will be sent to the rest of the processes at the same time. Therefore, broadcasting of a message is realized without any additional mechanisms.

Shared variables are created when, for example, a process forks into subprocesses.

$$p(X) \leftarrow q(X,Y), r(Y?).$$

In the example above, the variable Y is shared between the processes q and r and may be used for communication between them.

However, as mentioned above, communication using one shared variable cannot be done more than once. Therefore in order to enable successive communications among processes, there must be some mechanism to create a new shared logical variable dynamically. The most general method for this is the technique of stream communication of Clark and Gregory (Chapter 1).

In stream communication, a shared variable is instantiated to a data structure which contains a message and a new uninstantiated variable. In the Relational Language, a list cell was used for such a structure.

$$[\langle message \rangle | \langle variable \rangle].$$

The variable contained in the structure is sent with the message from the sender to the receivers and becomes a new shared variable among processes that may be used for the next communication. Consequently, as long as a process sends a message in this way, every time a message is sent a new shared variable is created, so that a sequence of communications is established.

In general, a communication consists of two phases.

> Phase 1:   A shared variable is instantiated to a message.
> Phase 2:   A new shared variable is created.

In phase 1, the action most essential to communication is performed. In phase 2, an action that enables the next communication is performed. In the case of stream communication, both phases are performed at the same time by the same process, the sender. However there is no reason for the two phases to be performed by the same process, and there is no restriction on the order of execution of phase 1 and phase 2. By separating the two phases, we are able to realize sophisticated communication styles based only on shared logical variables and the read-only annotation. As an example, we present in this section the bounded buffer communication mechanism based on shared logical variables. Before that, we summarize the unbounded buffer stream communication method.

18.1.1 Unbounded buffer communication

In stream communication, both phases are performed at the same time by the sender of a message, which instantiates a shared variable to a pair of the message and a variable. Therefore every time a sender sends a message, it creates a new shared variable, so that it can send the next message as soon as it sends this message. In contrast, a receiver can read a message only after it is received, and the receiver has to wait when it tries to read a message and no message is received yet. This suspension mechanism is realized by making the occurrence of the shared variable read-only in the receiver. Because there is no mechanism which inhibits the sender from sending a message, this type of communication realizes unbounded buffer communication. Note that the essence of unbounded buffer communication is that both phases of communication are performed by the same process, the sender of the messages.

sq_num(N,Ss) ← integers(1,N,Is) , square(Is?,Ss).

integers(I,N,[I|Is]) ←
    I≤N | J := I+1 , integers(J,N,Is).
integers(I,N,[ ]) ←
    I>N | true.

square([I|Is],[I2|Ss]) ←
    I2 := I*I , square(Is?,Ss).
square([ ],[ ]).

Program 18.1: A stream of squares

As an example of unbounded buffer stream communication, see Program 18.1. *sq_num(N,Ss)* generates a list *Ss* of squares of numbers from *1* up to *N*. The program consists of two communicating processes which are invoked by *integers(1,N,Is)* and *square(Is?,Ss)* respectively. The former process creates a stream *Is* of integers from *1* up to *N*. The latter process receives the stream *Is* and creates a list *Ss*, each element of which is a square of each element in the stream *Is*.

Note that *square* suspends when its first argument is an uninstantiated variable, because it is read-only. The predicates $X > Y$ and $X \leq Y$ suspend when either X or Y is a variable and the predicate $X := Y$ evaluates the expression Y and unifies the result with X when Y is a ground term, otherwise it suspends. In the example above, message sending and receiving are described in the head parts. We can write a similar program more abstractly, as shown by Program 18.2.

The predicate *is_integer* suspends if its argument is an uninstantiated variable, otherwise it is true or false depending on the value of its argument. In both sq_num(N,Ss) ← integers(1,N,Is) , square(Is?,Ss).

integers(I,N,Is) ←
    I≤N | J := I+1 , send(I,Is,Iss) , integers(J,N,Iss).
integers(I,N,Is) ←
    I>N | close(Is).

square(Is,Ss) ←
    receive(I,Is?,Iss) , square2(I,Iss,Ss).
square2(I,Iss,[ ]) ← closed(I?) | true.
square2(I,Iss,[I2|Ss]) ← is_integer(I) | I2 := I*I,
    square(Iss,Ss).

send(Msg,[Msg|NStrm],NStrm).
receive(Msg,[Msg|NStrm],NStrm).

close([end_of_stream]).

closed(end_of_stream).

Program 18.2: Stream of squares with abstract operations

predicates *send* and *receive* the first argument is a message, the second argument a current communication variable and the third argument a new communication variable. The predicate *close* is used to close the communication channel and *closed* to detect the termination of the stream.

The advantages of using *send, receive, close* and *closed* are that they hide the internal structure to which the shared variable is instantiated and that they modularize programs. Shapiro and Mierowsky (Chapter 14) adopt the same abstract approach, when they introduce bi-directional streams in order to hide a complicated data structure. In fact, even if we use another data structure, say *stream(⟨message ⟩,⟨variable⟩)*, instead of the list cell [⟨*message*⟩|⟨*variable*⟩], the programs which have to be changed are only *send, receive, close* and *closed* and all other programs can be left unchanged. The new definitions are:

send(Msg,stream(Msg,NStrm),NStrm).
receive(Msg,stream(Msg,NStrm),NStrm).
close(stream(end_of_stream,nil)).
closed(end_of_stream).

Section 18.2 discusses an abstraction technique which hides whether the communication mechanism uses unbounded or bounded buffer control.

18.1.2 Bounded buffer communication

In bounded buffer communication, message sending is delayed when there are n unread messages in the buffer of the receiver, where n is the size of the buffer.

From the previous analysis of communication through shared variables, we can naturally find a mechanism to realize this kind of communication. The key idea is the separation of the places of execution of the two phases of communication. Now, phase 1 (instantiation) is performed by the sender at the moment it sends a message, and phase 2 (allocation) is performed by the receiver when and only when it reads a message from the buffer. Therefore the sender cannot send more messages than the size of the buffer if the receiver did not read any message, that is, it did not generate a new shared variable.

We explain the method when the buffer size is equal to two, using the previous example, modified as shown in Program 18.3.

> sq_num2(N,Ss) ← integers(1,N,[X,Y|Z]) , square([X,Y|Z]–Z,Ss).
>
> integers(I,N,Buf) ←
>   I≤N | J := I+1, send(I,Buf?,NBuf) , integers(J,N,NBuf).
> integers(I,N,Buf) ←
>   I>N | close(Buf?).
>
> square(Buf,Ss) ←
>   receive(I,Buf,NBuf) , square2(I,NBuf,Ss).
> square2(I,Buf,[ ]) ← closed(I?) | true.
> square2(I,Buf,[I2|Ss]) ← is_integer(I) |
>   I2 := I∗I , square(Buf,Ss).

Program 18.3: Buffered stream of squares

Note that the second argument of *send* is read-only annotated, while in Program 18.2, the second argument of *receive* is annotated as such. The new definitions of *send*, *receive*, *close* and *closed* for bounded buffer communication are:

> send(Msg,[Msg|NBuf],NBuf).
> receive(Msg,[Msg|NBuf]\[NSlot|NTail],NBuf\NTail).
> close([end_of_stream|Rest]).
> closed(end_of_stream).

Here again we use a list cell for implementing the stream. The second argument of *receive* corresponds to a buffer which is represented by a difference-list, $H \backslash T$, where H and T correspond to the head and tail of the difference-list respectively. The buffer consists of slots (variables) which are filled with messages by the sender. The buffer is extended by one slot when and only when the receiver picks up a message from the buffer by the *receive* predicate, so that the length of the difference-list (buffer) remains the same. Although the sender shares the buffer with the receiver, it cannot extend the buffer, because the *send* predicate has only read access to the buffer, and all it can do is to fill empty slots with messages, if there are any such slots. Note that, since the slot picked up by the receiver may not contain a message, the receiver process has to wait for the message if the slot does not contain a message. This suspension is achieved by both *closed* and *is_integer* predicates.

When the size of the buffer is equal to two, the buffer looks like:

[X,Y|Z] \ Z

From the sender's perspective, the buffer has one of the following forms:

(1) [X,Y|Z]
(2) [Y|Z]
(3) Z

where X, Y and Z are all uninstantiated variables. (1) corresponds to an empty buffer, that is, there are two empty slots and (2) corresponds to the case in which there is room for sending one message. (3) corresponds to a full buffer, that is, there is no room for sending a message. Because the second argument of *send* is treated as read-only, *send* suspends in case (3). Figure 18.1 illustrates the situation when the sender tries to send three messages, *ab*, *cd* and *ef* when the buffer is empty.

It is more convenient if we could parameterize the size of the buffer. In Program 18.4, *sq_num3(N,Ss,Size)* takes a third argument specifying the size of the buffer and invokes two processes that communicate through this buffer. *open* takes an argument specifying the size of a buffer and creates the buffer as a difference list, *Buf\Tail*.

sq_num3(N,Ss,Size) ←
    open(Size,Buf\Tail), integers(1,N,Buf) , square(Buf\Tail,Ss).

open(0,X\X).
open(N,[X|Y]\Z) ← N>0 | N1:=N−1, open(N1?,Y\Z).

Program 18.4: Opening a parameterized buffer

The programs presented so far work when the buffer size is larger than or equal to zero, because the receiver processes in these programs first extends the buffer and picks a slot, then checks whether the slot contains a message or not. It is possible to write a program in which a receiver extends the buffer only when the slot picked up contains a message. In this case, however, the program works only when the size of the buffer is larger than or equal to one.

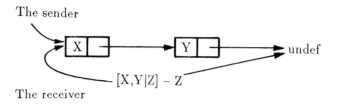

(a) The initial state

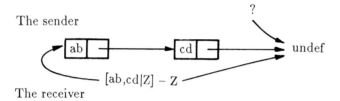

(b) After the sender sent two messages

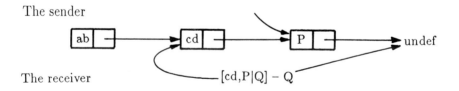

(c) After the receiver picked up one message

Figure 18.1: Trace of bounded buffer communication

The bounded buffer communication method is very useful when there are several processes, each of which produces or consumes data in different speed. Suppose that, in the example above, the speed of integer generation in *integers* is much faster than that of data consumption in *square*. In this case if we use unbounded buffer communication between the two processes, a huge number of unprocessed integers will be produced. Bounded buffer communication is a simple and efficient method to combine processes having different rates of data processing by controlling the rate of production of data according to its consumption.

As an example of the application of the bounded buffer communication method, we define a *2×2* communication switch which has two input ports and two output ports. It can receive inputs from two ports and sends them to the output port which has at least one empty slot. If both output ports are not available, the *switch2×2* suspends (see Figure 18.2 and Program 18.5).

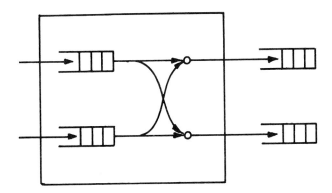

Figure 18.2: 2 × 2 communication switch

```
switch2×2(In1,In2,Out1,Out2) ←
    receive(M,In1,Ins1) , send(M,Out1,Outs1) |
    switch2×2(Ins1,In2,Outs1,Out2).
switch2×2(In1,In2,Out1,Out2) ←
    receive(M,In2,Ins2) , send(M,Out1,Outs1) |
    switch2×2(In1,Ins2,Outs1,Out2).
switch2×2(In1,In2,Out1,Out2) ←
    receive(M,In1,Ins1) , send(M,Out2,Outs2) |
    switch2×2(Ins1,In2,Out1,Outs2).
switch2×2(In1,In2,Out1,Out2) ←
    receive(M,In2,Ins2) , send(M,Out2,Outs2) |
    switch2×2(In1,Ins2,Out1,Outs2).
```

Program 18.5: A 2 × 2 communication switch

18.2 Abstract Stream Communication

Abstraction of a program is very important, since it hides internal data structures and low level control structures and makes the program more readable and maintainable. In this section, we consider an abstraction technique of stream operations which makes a program independent of specific communication control, such as unbounded or bounded buffer control. The technique is based on the so-called *protected data* concept of Concurrent Prolog, which was first suggested by Hellerstein and Shapiro (Chapter 9).

The concept of *protected data* gives an alternative view of communication in Concurrent Prolog. Usually, as in the programs above, read-only annotations are attached to variables in the arguments of consumer processes in order to prevent the consumer processes from instantiating communication variables to non-variable terms. However, the concept of *protected data* suggests another programming style, in which a variable, which is exported from a producer process to consumer processes together with a message in order to become a new shared variable, is annotated as read-only (see Program 18.6). This causes consumer processes not to be able to unify the new shared variable with a non-variable term until the producer instantiates it.

> sq_num2(N,Ss) ← integers(1,N,[X,Y|Z?]) , square([X,Y|Z]–Z,Ss).
>
> integers(I,N,Buf) ←
>   I≤N | J := I+1, send(I,Buf,NBuf) , integers(J,N,NBuf).
> integers(I,N,Buf) ←
>   I>N | close(Buf).
>
> square(Buf,Ss) ←
>   receive(I,Buf,NBuf) , square2(I,NBuf,Ss).
>
> square2(I,Buf,[ ]) ← closed(I) | true.
> square2(I,Buf,[I2|Ss]) ← is_integer(I) |
>   I2 := I*I , square(Buf,Ss).
>
> send(Msg,[Msg|NBuf],NBuf?).
>
> receive(Msg?,[Msg|NBuf]–[NSlot|NTail?],NBuf–NTail).
>
> close([end_of_stream|Rest]).
>
> closed(end_of_stream).

Program 18.6: Buffered stream of squares using protected data

Program 18.3 can be rewritten using this concept as follows. In Program 18.6, protected data is generated by *send* and *receive* predicates. The *send* predicate protects a new communication variable, *NBuf*, in order to prevent the next invocation of *send* from instantiating *NBuf*. The *receive* predicate protects a message, *Msg* and a new tail of the buffer, *NTail*, because *Msg* may still be a variable and *NTail* might be instantiated by the *integers* process. Using *protected*

integers(I,N,Is) ←
    I≤N | J := I+1 , send(I,Is,Iss) , integers(J,N,Iss).
integers(I,N,Is) ←
    I>N | close(Is).

square(Is,Ss) ←
    receive(I,Is,Iss) , square2(I,Iss,Ss).

square2(I,Iss,[ ]) ← closed(I) | true.
square2(I,Iss,[I2|Ss]) ← is_integer(I) |
    I2 := I*I , square(Iss,Ss).

send(Msg,[Msg|NStrm?],NStrm).

receive(Msg?,[Msg|NStrm],NStrm?).

close([end_of_stream]).

closed(end_of_stream).

Program 18.7: Unbuffered stream of squares using protected data

data, Program 18.2 can be also rewritten as Program 18.7.

It is interesting to compare Program 18.6 with Program 18.6. The two programs differs only in the definitions of four basic predicates which relate to communication, that is, *send*, *receive*, *close* and *closed*. The rest of the program, the definitions of *integers*, *square* and *square2*, are the same. From comparison of these two programs, we see that if we combine the concept of *protected data* with abstract operations on stream communication, not only can we hide the internal structure which realizes the stream, but we can also hide the control of communication used such as bounded or unbounded buffer communication. Therefore if we write a program with abstract operations on streams, it may be executed both as an unbounded communication program and as a bounded buffer program only by changing the definitions of *send*, *receive*, *close* and *closed*.

Since protected data is a data structure carrying a synchronization primitive, generally it is always possible to abstract access control to some data structures by making them protected data. This is a great advantage of the *protected data* concept from the point of view of the control abstraction of a program.

The concept of *protected data* is central to understanding the difference between Concurrent Prolog and other logic based parallel programming languages such as the Relational Language and PARLOG. In Concurrent Prolog, any process which requires access to the value of a variable annotated as read-only will be forced to suspend until the value becomes available. Therefore, it can be said that synchronization in Concurrent Prolog is controlled by data, especially by read-only variables. In contrast, in the Relational Language and PARLOG, every procedure has a mode declaration and a procedure suspends if arguments declared as input mode are uninstantiated when it is invoked. Therefore, synchronization in the Relational Language and PARLOG is controlled by procedures. Since procedures and data are basic complementary constructs in programming languages, the difference between Concurrent Prolog and other parallel logic programming languages is significant.

18.3 Concluding Remarks

The basic communication mechanism using shared logical variables is based on processes sharing a partially defined data structure, the producer process incrementally defining its structure and consumer processes reading it subsequently. The ability to handle a partially defined data structure is one of the basic features of languages based on unification including logic programming languages. Therefore, it is straightforward to realize communication sequences by shared data structures which are instantiated incrementally. The key idea of this communication style in logic programming languages was first proposed by van Emden and de Lucena (1982).

Communication based on shared variables is not a new method and has been implemented by sharing physical memory cells. The difference between the communication mechanism of Concurrent Prolog and that of conventional languages is the abstraction level of the shared object. In Concurrent Prolog, shared objects are logical variables which can be objects of the unification operation. Therefore it is possible to unify two communication channels.

Since several processes share a data structure, there must be some synchronization mechanism for accessing the data structure. Concurrent Prolog introduces the read-only annotation for this purpose, and the Relational Language and PARLOG introduce a mode declaration.

In this paper, we have shown that bounded buffer communication can be realized using the read-only annotation only. It is possible to realize bounded buffer communication based on the same idea presented here, using mode declarations. This is presented by Clark and Gregory (Chapter 3). We have also shown that if we adopt the read-only annotation for the realization of bounded buffer communication with the *protected data* concept, it is possible to abstract programs using stream communication so that they will be independent of any specific communication control mechanism.

Acknowledgement

We thank Ehud Shapiro and Kazunori Ueda for their many helpful insights and discussions. We would also like to thank Kazuhiro Fuchi, Director of ICOT Research Center, and all the other members of ICOT, both for help with this research and for providing a stimulating place in which to work.

Jacob Levy assisted in editing the paper.

References

Ackerman, W.B., Data flow languages, *IEEE Computer* **15**(2), pp. 15–25, 1982.

Adobe Systems Inc., *PostScript Language Manual*, Addison-Wesley, 1985.

Aho, A.V., Hopcroft, J.E., and Ullman, J.D., *The Design and Analysis of Computer Algorithms*, Addison-Wesley, 1974.

Ahuja, S., Carriero, N., and Gelernter, D., Linda and Friends, *IEEE Computer* **19**(8), pp. 26–34, August 1986.

Ali, K.A.M., Object-Oriented Storage Management and Garbage Collection in Distributed Processing Systems, Ph.D. Thesis, Royal Institute of Technology, Stockholm, 1984.

Ali, K.A.M., Or-parallel execution of Prolog on a multi-sequential machine, SICS Tech. Report, 1986a.

Ali, K.A.M., Or-parallel execution of Horn clause programs based on the WAM and shared control information, SICS Tech. Report, November 1986b.

Allen, J., *The Anatomy of Lisp*, McGraw-Hill, 1978.

Anderson, J.M., Coates, W.S., Davis A.L., Hon, R.W., Robinson, I.N., Robison, S.V. and Stevens, K.S., The architecture of FAIM1, *Computer* **20**(1), pp. 55–66, 1987.

Andrews, G.R., Synchronizing resources, *ACM Trans. on Programming Languages and Systems* **3**(4), pp. 405–430, 1981.

Andrews, G.R., The distributed programming language SR — mechanisms, design and implementation, *Software — Practice and Experience* **12**(8), pp. 719–754, 1982.

Andrews, G.R., and Olsson, R., The evolution of the SR programming language, Tech. Report 85-22, Department of Computer Science, Univ. of Arizona, 1985.

ANSI PL/I, ANS X3.53–1976, American National Standards Institute, 1976.

Apt, K.R., and van Emden, M.H., Contributions to the theory of logic programming, *J. ACM* **29**(3), pp. 841–863, 1982.

Arvind, K., and Brock, J.D., Streams and managers, in Maekawa, M., and Belady, L.A. (eds.), *Operating Systems Engineering*, *LNCS* **143**, pp. 452–465, Springer-Verlag, 1982.

Arvind, K., Gostelow, K.P., and Plouffe, W., Indeterminacy, monitors and dataflow, *Proc. 6th ACM Symposium on Operating Systems Principles, Operating Systems Reviews* **11**(5), pp. 159–169, 1977.

Arvind, K., Gostelow, K.P., and Plouffe, W., An asynchronous programming language and computing machine, Tech. Report TR114a, University of California at Irvine, 1978.

Arvind, K., and Thomas, R.E., I-structures: An efficient data type for functional languages, Tech. Mem. TM-178, Laboratory for Computer Science, MIT, Cambridge, Massachusetts, 1978.

Av-Ron, E., and Taylor, S., A distributed garbage collector for FCP, Department of Computer Science, The Weizmann Institute of Science, Rehovot, 1986.

Baker, H., Actor systems for real-time computation, Tech. Report TR-197, Laboratory for Computer Science, MIT, Cambridge, Massachusetts, 1978a.

Baker, H., Shallow binding in LISP 1.5, *Comm. ACM*, **21**(7), 1978b.

Baker, H., and Hewitt, C., The incremental garbage collection of processes, *ACM Conference on Artificial Intelligence and Programming Languages*, Rochester, *SIGPLAN Notices* **12**(8), pp. 55–59, New York, 1977.

Bar-on, U., A distributed implementation of Flat Concurrent Prolog, M.Sc. Thesis, Department of Computer Science, The Weizmann Institute of Science, Rehovot, 1986.

Bawden, A., Burke, G.S., and Hoffman, C.W., MacLISP extensions, Tech. Report TM-203, Laboratory for Computer Science, MIT, Cambridge, Massachusetts, 1981.

Beckman, L., Haraldson, A., Oskarsson, O., and Sandewall, E., A partial evaluator and its use as a programming tool, *Artificial Intelligence* **7**(4), pp. 319–357, 1976.

Berman, F., and Snyder, L., On mapping parallel algorithms into parallel architectures, *Proc. IEEE International Conference on Parallel Processing*, 1984.

Bloch, C., Source-to-source transformations of logic programs, Tech. Report

CS84-22, Department of Computer Science, The Weizmann Institute of Science, Rehovot, 1984.

Bobrow, D.G., What it takes to support AI programming paradigms or, if Prolog is the answer, what is the question?, *IEEE Trans. on Software Engineering*, **11**, pp. 1401–1408, 1985.

Bobrow, D.G., and Hayes, P.J., Artificial intelligence: Where are we? *Artificial Intelligence* **25**, pp. 375–415, 1985.

Bobrow, D.G., Kahn, K., Kiczles, G., Masinter, L., Stefik, M., and Zdybel, F., CommonLoops: Merging Common Lisp and object-oriented programming, *ACM Conference on Object-Oriented Programming Systems, Languages and Applications*, pp. 17–29, Portland, Oregon, 1986.

Bobrow D.G., and Stefik, M., *The LOOPS Manual* (Preliminary version), Memo KB-VLSI-81-13, Xerox Parc, 1983.

Bokhari, S.H., On the mapping problem, *IEEE Trans. on Computers*, **C-30**(3), pp. 207–214, 1981.

Borning, A., The programming language aspects of ThingLab, a constraint-oriented simulation laboratory, *ACM Trans. on Programming Languages and Systems* **3**(4), pp. 353–387, 1981.

Bowen, D.L., Byrd, L., Pereira, L.M., Pereira, F.C.N., and Warren, D.H.D., PRO-LOG on the DECSystem-10 User's Manual, Tech. Report, Department of Artificial Intelligence, University of Edinburgh, 1981.

Bowen, K.A., and Kowalski, R.A., Amalgamating language and metalanguage in logic programming, in Clark, K.L., and Tärnlund, S.-Å. (eds.), *Logic Programming*, pp. 153–172, Academic Press, London, 1982.

Brock, J.D., and Ackerman, W.B., Scenarios: A model of non-determinate computations, in Dias and Ramos (eds.), *Formalization of Programming Concepts*, *LNCS* **107**, pp. 252–259, Springer-Verlag, 1981.

Broda, K., and Gregory, S., PARLOG for discrete event simulation, Tärnlund, S.-Å. (ed.), *Proc. 2nd International Conference on Logic Programming*, pp. 301–312, Uppsala, 1984.

Bruynooghe, M., Adding redundancy to obtain more reliable and more readable Prolog programs, *Proc. 1st International Conference on Logic Programming*, pp. 129–134, ADDP-GIA, Faculte des Sciences de Luminy, Marseille, 1982.

Bryant, R.E., and Dennis, J.B., Concurrent programming, in Maekawa, M., and Blady, L.A. (eds.), *Operating Systems Engineering*, *LNCS* **143**, pp. 426–452, Springer-Verlag, 1982.

Buettner, K., and Bowen, K.A., FLIP — a functional language in Prolog, Tech. Report CIS-86-12, Syracuse University, 1986.

Bundy, A., and Silver, B., Homogenization: Preparing equations for change of unknown, *Proc. 7th International Joint Conference on Artificial Intelligence*, pp. 551–553, 1981.

Bundy, A., and Welham, B., Using meta-level inference for selective applicaiton of multiple rewrite rules in algebraic manipulation, *Artificial Intelligence* **16**, pp. 189–212, 1981.

Burke, G.S., Carrette, G.J., and Eliot, C.J., The NIL reference Manual, Tech. Report 311, Laboratory for Computer Science, MIT, Cambridge, Massachusetts, 1984.

Burkimsher, P.C., PRISM — A DSM multiprocessor reduction machine for the parallel implementation of applicative languages, *Proc. Declarative Programming Workshop*, pp. 189–202, London, 1983.

Ciepielewski, A., Towards a computer architecture for Or-parallel execution of logic programs, Ph.D. Thesis, TRITA-CS-8401, Department of Computer Systems, Royal Institute of Technology, Stockholm, 1984.

Clark, K.L., Negation as failure, in Gallaire, H., and Minker, J. (eds.), *Logic and Data Bases*, pp. 293–322, Plenum Publishing Co., New York, 1978.

Clark, K.L., Predicate logic as a computational formalism, Research Monograph 79/59 TOC, Department of Computing, Imperial College, London, 1979.

Clark, K.L., and Gregory, S., A relational language for parallel programming, *Proc. ACM Conference on Functional Languages and Computer Architecture*, pp. 171–178, 1981. Also Chapter 1, this volume.

Clark, K.L., and Gregory, S., Notes on systems programming in PARLOG, *Proc. International Conference on Fifth Generation Computer Systems*, pp. 299–306, Tokyo, 1984.

Clark, K.L., and Gregory, S., Notes on the implementation of PARLOG, Research Report DOC84/16, 1984. Also in *J. Logic Programming* **2**(1), pp. 17–42, 1985.

Clark, K.L., and Gregory, S., PARLOG: Parallel programming in logic, *ACM TOPLAS* **8**(1), pp. 1–49, 1986. Also Chapter 3, this volume.

Clark, K.L., and McCabe, F.G., *micro-PROLOG: Programming in Logic*, Prentice-Hall, New Jersey, 1984.

Clark, K.L., McCabe, F.G., and Gregory, S., IC-PROLOG — language features, in Clark, K.L., and Tärnlund, S.-Å. (eds.), *Logic Programming*, pp. 253–266,

Academic Press, London, 1982.

Clark, K.L., and S.-Å. Tärnlund, A first-order theory of data and programs, in Gilchrist, B. (ed.), *Information Processing* **77**, pp. 939–944, North-Holland, 1977.

Clinger, W., Foundations of actor semantics, Tech. Report TR-633, Artificial Intelligence Laboratory, MIT, Cambridge, Massachusetts, 1981.

Clocksin, W.R., and Alshawi, H., A method for efficiently executing Horn clause programs using multiple processors, Tech. Report, Department of Computer Science, Cambridge University, Cambridge, May 1986.

Clocksin, W.F., and Mellish, C.S., *Programming in Prolog*, 2nd Edition, Springer-Verlag, New York, 1984.

Codish, M., Compiling Or-parallelism into And-parallelism, M.Sc. Thesis, Department of Computer Science, The Weizmann Institute of Science, Rehovot, 1985.

Codish, M., and Shapiro, E., Compiling Or-parallelism into And-parallelism, *New Generation Computing* **5**(1), pp. 45–61, 1987. Also Chapter 32, this volume.

Coffman, E.G., and Denning, P.J., *Operating Systems Theory*, Prentice-Hall, New Jersey, 1973.

Cohen, S., Parallel computation, Ph.D. Thesis, The Hebrew University of Jerusalem, 1983.

Cohen, S., The APPLOG language, in DeGroot, D., and Lindstrom, G. (eds.), *Logic Programming — Functions, Relations and Equations*, pp. 239–276, Prentice-Hall, New Jersey, 1986.

Colmerauer, A., Kanui, H., and van Kanegham, M., Last steps towards an ultimate Prolog, *Proc. 7th International Joint Conference on Artificial Intelligence*, pp. 947–948, 1981.

Colmerauer, A. et al., *PROLOG II: Reference Manual and Theoretical Model*, Groupe d'Intelligence Artificielle, Faculte des Sciences de Luminy, Universite d'Aix-Marseille II, 1982.

Conery, J.S., The AND/OR process model for parallel interpretation of logic programs, Ph.D. Thesis, Tech. Report 204, Department of Information and Computer Science, University of California, Irvine, 1983.

Conery, J.S., and Kibler, D.F., Parallel interpretation of logic programs, *Proc. ACM Conference on Functional Programming Languages and Computer Architecture*, pp. 163–170, 1981.

Cousot, P., and Cousot, R., Abstract interpretation: A unified lattice model for static analysis of programs by construction or approximation of fixpoints, *Proc. ACM Symposium on Principles of Programming Languages*, pp. 238–252, 1977.

Crammond, J., A comparatie study of unification algorithms for Or-parallel execution of logic languages, *Proc. IEEE International Conference on Parallel Processing*, pp. 131–138, 1985.

Darlington, J., Field, A.J., and Pull, H., The unification of functional and logic languages, in DeGreeot, D., and Lindstrom, G. (eds.), *Logic Programming — Functions, Relations and Equations*, pp. 37–70, Prentice-Hall, New Jersey, 1986.

Darlington, J., and Reeve, M.J., ALICE: A multi-processor reduction machine, *Proc. ACM Conference on Functional Programming Languages and Computer Architecture*, pp. 65–75, Portsmouth, New Hampshire, 1981.

Dausmann, M., Persch, G., and Winterstein, G., Concurrent logic, *Proc. 4th Workshop on Artificial Intelligence*, Bad Honnef, 1979.

Davis, A.L., and Keller, R.M., Data flow graphs, *Computer* **15**(2), pp. 26–41, 1982.

DeGroot, D., Mapping Computation Structures onto SW-Banyan Networks, Ph.D. Thesis, University of Texas at Austin, 1981.

DeGroot, D., Restricted And-parallelism, *Proc. International Conference on Fifth Generation Computer Systems*, pp. 471–478, Tokyo, 1984.

DeGroot, D., and Lindstrom, G. (eds.), *Logic Programming — Functions, Relations and Equations*, Prentice-Hall, New Jersey, 1986.

Dennis, J.B., First version of a data flow procedure language, in Rodiner, B. (ed.), *Programming Symposium: Proceedings, Colloque sur la Programmation*, *LNCS* **19**, pp. 362–376, Springer Verlag, 1974.

Dennis, J.B., *A language design for structured concurrency*, Williams, J.H., and Fischer, D.A. (eds.), *LNCS* **54**, pp. 231–242, Springer-Verlag, 1976.

Dijkstra, E.W., Guarded commands, nondeterminacy and formal derivation of programs, *Comm. ACM* **18**(8), pp. 453–457, 1975.

Dijkstra, E.W., *A Discipline of Programming*, Prentice-Hall, New Jersey, 1976.

Dijkstra, E.W., Feijen, W.H., and van Gasteren, A.J.M., Derivation of a termination algorithm for distributed computation, *Inf. Proc. Lett.* **16**, pp. 217–219, 1983.

Dinic, E.A., Algorithm for solution of maximum flow in a network with power estimation, *Soviet Math. Dokl.* **II**, pp. 1277–1280, 1970.

Dolev, D., Klawe, M., and Rodeh, M., An $O(N \log N)$ unidirectional distributed algorithm for extrema finding in a circle, *J. of Algorithms* **3**, pp. 245–260, 1982.

Dubitzki, T., Wu, A., and Rosenfeld, A., Parallel region property computation by active quadtree networks, *IEEE Trans.*, **PAMI-3**, pp. 626–633, 1981.

Dyer, C., and Rosenfeld, A., Parallel image processing by memory-augmented cellular automata, *IEEE Trans.*, **PAMI-3**, pp. 29–41, 1981.

Foderaro, J.K., Sklower, K.L., and Layer, K., *The Franz Lisp Manual*, Unix Programmer's Manual, Supplementary Documents, 1983.

Edelman, S., Line connectivity algorithms for an asynchronous pyramid computer, *Computer Vision, Graphics and Image Processing*, 1987 (to appear).

Edelman, S., and Shapiro, E., Quadtrees in Concurrent Prolog, *Proc. IEEE International Conference on Parallel Processing*, pp. 544–551, 1985.

Edelman, S., and Shapiro, E., Image processing with Concurrent Prolog, Chapter 12, this volume.

Ellis, J.R., Mishkin, N., van Leunen, M., and Wood, S.R., Tools: An environment for timeshared computing and programming, Research Report 232, Department of Computer Science, Yale University, 1982.

van Emden, M.H., and Kowalski, R.A., The semantics of predicate logic as a programming language, *J. ACM* **23**(4), pp. 733–742, 1976.

van Emden, M.H., and de Lucena, G.J., Predicate logic as a language for parallel programming, in Clark, K.L., and Tärnlund, S.-Å. (eds.), *Logic Programming*, pp. 189–198, Academic Press, London, 1982.

Ershov, A., On the partial evaluation principle, *Inf. Proc. Lett.* **6**(2), pp. 38–41, 1977.

Even, S., *Graph Algorithms*, Computer Science Press, 1979.

Fages, F., Associative-commutative unification, *Proc. 7th Conference on Automated Deduction*, *LNCS* **170**, pp. 194–208, Springer-Verlag, 1984.

Fahlman, S.E., Hinton, G.E., and Sejnowski, T.J., Massively parallel architecture for AI — NETL, THISTLE and Boltzmann machines, *Proc. National Conference on Artificial Intelligence*, pp. 109–113, 1983.

Ferrand, G., Error diagnosis in logic programming: An adaptation of E.Y. Shapiro's method, Rapport de Recherche 375, INRIA, 1985.

Fiat, A., Shamir, A., and Shapiro, E., Polymorphic arrays: An architecture for a programmable systolic machine, *Proc. IEEE International Conference on Parallel Processing*, pp. 112–117, 1985.

Fisher, A.F., Kung, H.T., Monier, M., and Yasunori, D., Architecture of the PSC: A programmable systolic chip, *Proc. 10th IEEE Annual International Symposium on Computer Architecture*, pp. 48–58, 1983.

Fortune, S., and Wyllie, J., Parallelism in random access machines, *Proc. 10th ACM Annual Symposium on Theory of Computing*, pp. 114–118, 1978.

Foster, I., Gregory, S., and Ringwood, G.A., A sequential implementation of PARLOG, in Shapiro, E. (ed.), *Proc. 3rd International Conference on Logic Programming*, LNCS **225**, pp. 149–156, Springer-Verlag, 1986.

Foster, I., and Taylor, S., Flat PARLOG: A basis for comparison, Tech. Report, Department of Computer Science, The Weizmann Institute of Science, Rehovot, 1987.

Friedman, D.P., and Wise, D.S., The impact of applicative programming on multiprocessing, *Proc. IEEE International Conference on Parallel Processing*, pp. 263–272, 1976a.

Friedman, D.P., and Wise, D.S., CONS should not evaluate its arguments, in Michaelson, D., and Milner, R. (eds.), *Automata, Languages and Programming*, Edinburgh University Press, 1976b.

Friedman, D.P., and Wise, D.S., Aspects of applicative programming for parallel processing, *IEEE Trans. on Computers* **C-27**(4), pp. 289–296, 1978.

Friedman, D.P., and Wise, D.S., An approach to fair applicative multiprogramming, in Kahn, G. (ed.), *Semantics of Concurrent Computation*, LNCS **70**, pp. 203–226, Springer-Verlag, 1979.

Friedman, D.P., and Wise, D.S., An indeterminate constructor for applicative programming, *Conference Record 7th ACM Symposium on Principles of Programming Languages*, pp. 245–250, 1980.

Fuchi, K., Revisiting original philosophy of fifth generation computer systems project, *Proc. International Conference on Fifth Generation Computer Systems*, Tokyo, 1984.

Fuchi, K., Aiming for knowledge information processing systems, in van Canegham, M., and Warren, D.H.D. (eds.), *Logic Programming and its Applications*, pp. 279–305, Ablex Publishing Co., 1986.

Fuchi, K., and Furukawa, K., The role of logic programming in the Fifth Generation Computer Project, *New Generation Computing* **5**(1), pp. 3–28, 1987.

Furukawa, K., Kunifuji, S., Takeuchi, A., and Ueda, K., The conceptual specification of the Kernel Language version 1, ICOT Tech. Report TR-054, Institute for New Generation Computer Technology, Tokyo, 1984a.

Furukawa, K., Nakajima, R., and Yonezawa, A., Modularization and abstraction in logic programming, *New Generation Computing* **1**(2), pp. 169–177, 1983.

Furukawa, K., Takeuchi, A., Kunifuji, S., Yasukawa, H., Ohki, M., and Ueda, K., Mandala: A logic based knowledge programming system, *Proc. International Conference on Fifth Generation Computer Systems*, pp. 613–622, Tokyo, 1984b.

Futamura, Y., Partial evaluation of computation process — an approach to a compiler-compiler, *Systems, Computers, Controls* **2**(5), pp. 721–728, 1971.

Futo, I., and Szeredi, J., *T-Prolog: A Very High Level Simulation System*, Tech. Report, SZKI, Budapest, 1981.

Gallager, R.G., Humblet, P.A., and Spira, P.M., A distributed algorithm for minimum weight spanning trees, Tech. Report LIDS-P-906-A, MIT, Cambridge, Massachusetts, 1979.

Gallagher, J., An approach to the control of logic programs, Ph.D. Thesis, Department of Computer Science, Trinity College, Dublin, Ireland, 1983.

Gallagher, J., Transforming logic programs by specialising interpreters, *Proc. 7th European Conference on Artificial Intelligence*, pp. 109–122, Brighton, 1986.

Gelernter, D., A note on systems programming in Concurrent Prolog, *Proc. IEEE International Symposium on Logic Programming*, pp. 76–82, Atlantic City, New Jersey, 1984.

Gentleman, M., Some complexity results for matrix computations on parallel processors, *J. ACM* **25**, pp. 112–115, 1978.

German, S.M., and Lieberherr, K.J., Zeus: A language for expressing algorithms in hardware, *IEEE Computer*, **18**(2), pp. 55–65, 1985.

Gettys, J., Newman, R., and Della Fera T., Xlib — C language X interface protocol version 10, 1986.

Goguen, J.A., and Meseguer, J., Equality, types, modules and generics for logic programming, Tärnlund, S.-Å. (ed.), *Proc. 2nd International Conference on Logic Programming*, pp. 115–125, Uppsala, 1984. Also in *J. Logic Programming* **1**(2), pp. 179–210, 1984.

Gosling, J., SunDew, A Distributed and Extensible Window System, in Hopgood F.R.A., et al. (eds.), *Methodology of Window Management*, Springer-Verlag, 1986.

Gottlieb, A., Grishman, R., Kruskal, C.P., McAuliffe, K.P., Rudolph, L., and Snir, M., The NYU ultracomputer — designing an MIMD shared memory parallel computer, *IEEE Trans. on Computers* **C-32**(2), pp. 175–190, 1983.

Green, C.C., Theorem proving by resolution as a basis for question answering, in B. Meltzer and D. Michie (eds.), *Machine Intelligence* **4**, pp. 183–205, Edinburgh University, 1969.

Gregory, S., Implementing PARLOG on the Abstract PROLOG Machine, Research Report DOC 84/23, Department of Computing, Imperial College, London, 1984a.

Gregory, S., How to use PARLOG, Unpublished report, Department of Computing, Imperial College, London, 1984b.

Gregory, S., *Parallel Logic Programming in PARLOG*, Addison-Wesley, 1987.

Gregory, S., Foster, I.T., Burt, A.D., and Ringwood, G.A., An abstract machine for the implementation of PARLOG on uniprocessors, Research report, Department of Computing, Imperial College, London, 1987.

Gregory, S., Neely, R., and Ringwood, G.A., PARLOG for specification, verification and simulation, *Proc. 7th International Symposium on Computer Hardware Description Languages and their Applications*, pp. 139–148, Tokyo, 1985.

Gullichsen, E., BiggerTalk: Object-oriented Prolog, Tech. Report STP-125-85, MCC-STE, Austin, Texas, 1985.

Hagiya, M., On lazy unification and infinite trees, *Proc. Logic Programming Conference '83*, Institute for New Generation Computer Technology, Tokyo, 1983 (in Japanese).

Halstead, R.H., MultiLisp - A language for concurrent symbolic computation, *ACM Trans. on Programming Languages and Systems* **7**(4), pp. 501–538, 1985.

Halstead, R.H., and Loaiza, J.R., Exception handling in multilisp, *Proc. IEEE International Conference on Parallel Processing*, pp. 822–830, 1985.

Hansen, P.B., The programming language Concurrent Pascal, *IEEE Trans. on Software Engineering* **SE-1**(2), pp. 199–207, 1975.

Hansson, A., Haridi, S., and Tärnlund, S.-Å., Properties of a logic programming language, in Clark, K.L., and Tärnlund, S.-Å. (eds.), *Logic Programming*, pp. 267–280, Academic Press, London, 1982.

Harel, D., and Nehab, S., Concurrent And/Or programs: Recursion with communication, Tech. Report CS82-09, Department of Comptuer Science, The

Weizmann Institute of Science, Rehovot, 1982.

Harel, D., and Pnueli, A., On the development of reactive systems, Tech. Report CS85-02, Department of Computer Science, The Weizmann Institute of Science, Rehovot, 1985.

Harrison, W.L., Compiling Lisp for evaluation on a tightly coupled multi-processor, Ph.D. Thesis, University of Illinois at Urbana-Champain, 1986.

Havender, J.W., Avoiding deadlock in multitasking systems, *IBM Systems J.* **7**(2), pp. 74–84, 1968.

Hellerstein, L., A Concurrent Prolog based region finding algorithm, Honors Thesis, Computer Science Department, Harvard University, 1984. Also Chapter 10, this volume.

Hellerstein, L., and Shapiro, E., Implementing parallel algorithms in Concurrent Prolog: The MAXFLOW experience, *J. Logic Programming* **3**(2), pp. 157–184, 1984. Also Chapter 9, this volume.

Henderson, P., *Functional Programming — Application and Implementation*, Prentice-Hall, New Jersey, 1980.

Henderson, P., Purely functional operating systems, in Darlington, J., Henderson, P., and Turner, D. (eds.), *Functional Programming and Its Applications*, Cambridge University Press, 1982.

Henderson, P., and Morris, J.H., A lazy evaluator, *Proc. 3rd ACM Symposium on Principles of Programming Languages*, pp. 95–103, 1976.

Hewitt, C., Description and theoretical analysis (using schemata) of PLANNER: A language for proving theorems and manipulating models in a robot, Tech. Report TR-258, Artificial Intelligence Laboratory, MIT, Cambridge, Massachusetts, 1972.

Hewitt, C., A universal, modular Actor formalism for artificial intelligence, *Proc. International Joint Conference on Artificial Intelligence*, 1973.

Hewitt, C., Viewing control structures as patterns of passing messages, *Artificial Intelligence* **8**, pp. 323–363, 1977.

Hewitt, C., The Apiary network architecture for knowledgeable systems, *Proc. IEEE Conference on Lisp and Functional Programming*, pp. 107–117, 1980.

Hewitt, C., The challenge of open systems, *Byte Mag.*, pp. 223–242, April 1985.

Hewitt, C., Atardi, G., and Lieberman, H., Specifying and proving properties of guardians for distributed systems, in Kahn, G. (ed.), *Semantics of Concurrent Computations*, *LNCS* **70**, pp. 316–336, Springer-Verlag, 1979.

Hewitt, C., and Lieberman, H., Design issues in parallel architectures for artificial intelligence, *Proc. IEEE Computer Conference*, pp. 418–422, 1984.

Hirakawa, H., Chart parsing in Concurrent Prolog, ICOT Tech. Report TR-008, Institute for New Generation Computer Technology, Tokyo, 1983.

Hirakawa, H., Chikayama, T., and Furukawa, K., Eager and lazy enumerations in Concurrent Prolog, Tärnlund, S.Å. (ed.), *Proc. 2nd International Logic Programming Conference*, pp. 89–101, Uppsala, 1984.

Hirakawa, H., Onai, R., and Furukawa, K., Implementing an Or-Parallel Optimizing Prolog System (POPS) in Concurrent Prolog, ICOT Tech. Report TR-020, Institute for New Generation Computer Technology, Tokyo, 1983.

Hirata, M., Self-description of Oc and its applications, *Proc. 2nd National Conference of Japan Society on Software Science and Technology*, pp. 153–156, 1985 (in Japanese).

Hirsch, M., The Logix system, M.Sc. Thesis, Department of Computer Science, The Weizmann Institute of Science, 1987.

Hirsch, M., Silverman, W., and Shapiro, E., Layers of protection and control in the Logix system, Tech. Report CS86-19, Department of Computer Science, The Weizmann Institute of Science, Rehovot, 1986. Revised as Chapter 20, this volume.

Hoare, C.A.R., Monitors: An operating system structuring concept, *Comm. ACM* **17**(10), pp. 549–557, 1974.

Hoare, C.A.R., Communicating sequential processes, *Comm. ACM* **21**(8), pp. 666-677, 1978.

Hoare, C.A.R., *Communicating Sequential Processes*, Prentice-Hall, New Jersey, 1985.

Hogger, C.J., Concurrent logic programming, in Clark, K.L., and Tärnlund, S.-Å. (eds.), *Logic Programming*, pp. 199–211, Academic Press, London, 1982.

Hogger, C.J., *Introduction to Logic Programming*, Academic Press, London, 1984.

Holt, R.C., Graham, G.S., Lazowska, E.D., and Scott, M.A., *Structured Programming with Operating Systems Applications*, Addison Wesley, 1979.

Hopcroft, J.E., and Ullman, J.D., *Introduction to Automata Theory, Languages, and Computation*, Addison-Wesley, 1979.

Hopgood, F.R.A., Duce, D.A., Fielding, E.V.C., Robinson, K., and William, A.S., *Methodology of Window Management*, Springer-Verlag, 1986.

Houri, A., and Shapiro, E., A sequential abstract machine for Flat Concurrent

Prolog, Tech. Report CS86-20, Department of Computer Science, The Weizmann Institute of Science, Rehovot, 1986. Also Chapter 38, this volume.

Hudak, P., Functional programming on multiprocessor architectures, Research Report 447, Department of Computer Science, Yale University, 1985.

Hudak, P., and Smith, L., Para-functional programming — A paradigm for programming multiprocessor systems, Research Report 448, Department of Computer Science, Yale University, 1985.

Huet, G., Confluent reductions: Abstract properties and applications to term rewriting systems, *J. ACM*, **27**(4), pp. 797–821, 1980.

Hwang, K., and Briggs, F.A., *Computer Architecture and Parallel Processing*, McGraw-Hill, 1984.

Ingalls, D.H., The Smalltalk-76 programming system: Design and implementation, *Conference Record 5th Annual ACM Symposium on Principles of Programming Languages*, pp. 9–16, 1978.

INMOS Ltd., *IMS T424 Transputer Reference Manual*, INMOS, 1984a.

INMOS Ltd., *OCCAM Programming Manual*, Prentice-Hall, New Jersey, 1984b.

Jefferson, D., and Sowizral, H., Fast Concurrent simulation using the time warp mechanism, Part 1: Local control, N-1906-AS Rand Corporation, 1982.

Jensen, K., and Wirth, N., *Pascal User Manual and Report*, Springer-Verlag, Berlin, 1974.

Johnson, S.D., Circuits and systems: Implementing communications with streams, Tech. Report 116, Computer Science Department, Indiana University, 1981.

Jones, N.D., Sestoft, P., and Sondergaard, H., An experiment in partial evaluation: The generation of a compiler generator, DIKU Report 85/1, University of Copenhagen, 1985.

Kahn, G., and MacQueen, D., Coroutines and networks of parallel processes, in Gilchrist, B. (ed.), *Information Processing* **77**, *Proc. IFIP Congress*, pp. 993–998, North-Holland, 1977.

Kahn, K., Uniform — a language based upon unification which unifies (much of) Lisp, Prolog, and Act 1, *Proc. 7th International Joint Conference on Artificial Intelligence*, pp. 933–939, Vancouver, Canada, 1981.

Kahn, K., A partial evaluator of Lisp written in Prolog, *Proc. 1st International Conference on Logic Programming*, pp. 19–25, Marseille, 1982a.

Kahn, K., Intermission — Actors in Prolog, in Clark, K.L., and Tärnlund, S.-Å.

(eds.), *Logic Programming*, pp. 213–228, Academic Press, London, 1982b.

Kahn, K., The compilation of Prolog programs without the use of a Prolog compiler, *Proc. International Conference on Fifth Generation Computer Systems*, pp. 348–355, Tokyo, 1984a.

Kahn, K.M., A primitive for the control of logic programs, *Proc. IEEE International Symposium on Logic Programming*, pp. 242–251, Atlantic City, New Jersey, 1984b.

Kahn, K.M., and Carlsson, M., How to implement Prolog on a LISP machine, in Campbell, J.A. (ed.), *Implementations of Prolog*, pp. 117–134, Ellis Horwood, 1984.

Kahn, K., Tribble, E.D., Miller, M.S., and Bobrow, D.G., Objects in concurrent logic programming languages, *Proc. ACM Conference on Object Oriented Programming Systems, Languages, and Applications*, Portland, Oregon, *SIGPLAN Notices* **21**(11), pp. 242–257, 1986.

Kahn, K., Tribble, E.D., Miller, M., and Bobrow, D.G., Vulcan: Logical concurrent objects, in Shriver, B., and Wegner, P. (eds.), *Research Directions in Object-Oriented Programming*. Also Chapter 30, this volume.

Kasif, S., Kohli, M., and Minker, J., PRISM: A parallel inference system for problem solving, *Proc. Logic Programming Workshop '83*, pp. 123–152, Algarve, Portugal, 1983.

Katzenellenbogen, D., A distributed window system in Flat Concurrent Prolog, M.Sc. Thesis, Department of Computer Science, The Weizmann Institute of Science, Rehovot, 1987.

Katzenellenbogen, D., Cohen, S., and Shapiro, E., An architecture of a distributed window system and its FCP implementation, Tech. Report CS87-09, Department of Computer Science, The Weizmann Institute of Science, Rehovot, 1987. Also Chapter 23, this volume.

Keller, R.M., Data structuring in applicative multiprocessing systems, *Proc. IEEE Conference on Lisp and Functional Programming*, pp. 196–202, 1980a.

Keller, R.M., Some theoretical aspects of applicative multiprocessing, *Proc. Conference on Mathematical Foundations of Computer Science*, pp. 58–74, 1980b.

Keller, R.M., and Lindstrom, G., Applications of feedback in functional programming, *ACM Conference on Functional Languages and Computer Architecture*, pp. 123–130, 1981.

Keller, R.M. et al., Rediflow: A multiprocessing architecture combining reduction with data-flow, Unpublished Manuscript, Department of Computer Science,

University of Utah, 1983.

Kleene S., *Introduction to Metamathematics*, Van Nostrand, New York, 1952.

Kliger, S., Towards a native-code compiler for Flat Concurrent Prolog, M.Sc. Thesis, Department of Computer Science, The Weizmann Institute of Science, Rehovot, 1987.

Knuth, D.E., *The Art of Computer Programming*, Vol. 3: *Searching and Sorting*, Addison-Wesley, 1973.

Komorowski, H.J., Partial evaluation as a means for inferencing data-structures in an applicative language: A theory and implementation in the case of Prolog, *Conference Record 9th Annual ACM Symposium on Principles of Programming Languages*, pp. 255–268, 1982.

Kornfeld, W.A., The use of parallelism to implement a heuristic search, *Proc. International Joint Conference on Artificial Intelligence*, pp. 575–580, 1981.

Kornfeld, W.A., Equality for Prolog, *Proc. 7th International Joint Conference on Artificial Intelligence*, pp. 514–519, 1983.

Kornfeld, W.A., and Hewitt, C., The scientific community metaphor, *IEEE Trans. on Systems, Man, and Cybernetics* **SMC-11**, pp. 24–33, 1981.

Kowalski, R.A., Predicate logic as programming language, *Proc. IFIP Congress* **74**, pp. 569–574, North-Holland, Stockholm, 1974.

Kowalski, R.A., *Logic for Problem Solving*, Elsevier, North-Holland, 1979.

Kowalski, R.A., Logic programming, *Proc. IFIP Congress*, pp. 133–145, 1983.

Kung, H.T., Let's design algorithms for VLSI systems, *Proc. Conference on Very Large Scale Integration: Architecture, Design, Fabrication*, pp. 65–90, Caltech, 1979a.

Kung, H.T., The structure of parallel algorithms, Tech. Report 79-143, Carnegie-Mellon University, 1979b.

Kung, H.T., Why systolic architectures?, *IEEE Computer* **15**(1), pp. 37–46, 1982.

Kung, H.T., The warp processor: A versatile systolic array for very high speed signal processing, Tech. Report, Department of Computer Science, Carnegie-Mellon University, Pittsburgh, Pennsylvania, 1984.

Kung, H.T., Memory requirements for balanced computer architectures, Tech. Report CMU-CS-85-158, Department of Computer Science, Carnegie-Mellon University, Pittsburgh, Pennsylvania, 1985.

Kung, H.T., and Leiserson, C.E., Algorithms for VLSI processor arrays, in Mead,

C.A., and Conway, L. (eds.), *Introduction to VLSI Systems*, pp. 271–292, 1980.

Kusalik, A.J., Bounded-wait merge in Shapiro's Concurrent Prolog, *New Generation Computing* **1**(2), pp. 157–169, 1984a.

Kusalik, A.J., Serialization of process reduction in Concurrent Prolog, *New Generation Computing* **2**(3), pp. 289–298, 1984b.

Lam, M., and Gregory, S., PARLOG and ALICE: A marriage of convenience, Lassez, J.-L. (ed.), *Proc. 4th International Conference of Logic programming*, MIT Press, 1987.

Lamport, L., A recursive concurrent algorithm, 1982 (unpublished note).

Lampson, B.W., and Redell, D.D., Experience with processes and monitors in Mesa, *Comm. ACM* **23**(2), pp. 105–117, 1980.

Leiserson, C.E., *Area-Efficient VLSI Computation*, The MIT Press, 1983.

Lenat, D.B., The role of heuristics in learning by discovery: Three case studies, in Michalski, R.S., Carbonnel, J.G., and Mitchell, T.M. (eds.), *Machine Learning: An Artificial Intelligence Approach*, pp. 243–305, Tioga Publishing Company, Palo Alto, 1983.

Levi, G., Logic programming: The foundations, the approach and the role of occurrency, in de Bakker, J.W., de Roever, W.P., and Rozenberg, G. (eds.), *Current Trends in Concurrency, Overviews and Tutorials*, *LNCS* **224**, pp. 396–441, Springer-Verlag, 1986.

Levi, G., and Palamidessi, C., The declarative semantics of logical read-only variables, *IEEE Symposium on Logic Programming*, pp. 128–137, Boston, 1985.

Levy, J., A unification algorithm for Concurrent Prolog, Tärnlund, S.-Å. (ed.), *Proc. 2nd International Conference on Logic Programming*, pp. 333–341, Uppsala, 1984.

Levy, J., A GHC abstract machine and instruction set, in Shapiro E. (ed.), *Proc. 3rd International Conference on Logic Programming*, *LNCS* **225**, pp. 157–171, Springer-Verlag, 1986.

Levy, J., CFL — A concurrent functional language embedded in a concurrent logic programming environment, Tech. Report CS86-28, Department of Computer Science, The Weizmann Institute of Science, Rehovot, 1986. Revised as Chapter 35, this volume.

Levy, J., and Friedman, N., Concurrent Prolog implementations — two new schemes, Tech. Report CS86-13, Department of Computer Science, The Weizmann Institute of Science, Rehovot, 1986.

Levy, J., and Shapiro, E., Translation of Safe GHC and Safe Concurrent Prolog to FCP, Tech. Report CS87-08, Department of Computer Science, The Weizmann Institute of Science, Rehovot, 1987. Also Chapter 33, this volume.

Lichtenstein, Y., Codish, M., and Shapiro, E., Representation and enumeration of Flat Concurrent Prolog Computations, Chapter 27, this volume.

Lieberman, H., A preview of Act 1, Tech. Report AIM-625, Artificial Intelligence Laboratory, MIT, Cambridge, Massachusetts, 1981.

Lieberman, H., Using prototypical objects to implement shared behavior in object-oriented systems, *Proc. ACM Conference on Object Oriented Programming Systems, Languages, and Applications*, Portland, Oregon, *SIGPLAN Notices* **21**(11), pp. 214–223, 1986.

Lindstrom, G., Or-parallelism on applicative architectures, Tärnlund, S.-Å. (ed.), *Proc. 2ⁿᵈ International Conference on Logic Programming*, pp. 159–170, Uppsala, 1984.

Lint, B., and Agerwala, T., Communication issues in the design and analysis of parallel algorithms, *IEEE Trans. on Software Engineering*, **SE-7**(2), pp. 174–188, 1981.

Liskov, B., Atkinson, R., Bloom, D., Moss, E., Schaffert, J.C., Scheifler, R., and Snyder, A., *CLU Reference Manual*, *LNCS* **114**, Springer-Verlag, 1981.

Liu, C.L., *Introduction to Combinatorial Mathematics*, McGraw-Hill, 1968.

Lloyd, J.W., *Foundations of Logic Programming*, Springer-Verlag, 1984.

Lloyd, J.W., Declarative error diagnosis, Tech. Report 86/3, Department of Computer Science, University of Melbourne, 1986.

Lloyd, J.W., and Takeuchi, A., A framework for debugging GHC, ICOT Tech. Report TR-186, Institute for New Generation Computer Technology, Tokyo, 1986.

MacQueen, D.B., Models for distributed computing, Rapport de Recherche 351, INRIA, France, 1979.

Mago, G.A., A cellular computer architecture for functional programming, *Proc. IEEE Computer Conference*, pp. 179–187, 1984.

Martin, A.J., The Torus: An exercise in constructing a processing surface, *Proc. Conference on Very Large Scale Integration: Architecture, Design, Fabrication*, pp. 52–57, California Institute of Technology, 1979.

Matsumoto, Y., A parallel parsing system for natural language analysis, *New Generation Computing* **5**(1), pp. 63–78, 1987.

McCabe, F.G., Abstract PROLOG machine — a specification, Research Report DOC 83/12, Department of Computing, Imperial College, London, 1984.

McCabe, F.G., Lambda Prolog, Internal Report, Department of Computing, Imperial College, London, 1986.

McCarthy, J., A basis for a mathematical theory of computation, in Brafford P., and Hirchberg, D. (eds.), *Computer Programming and Formal Systems*, pp. 33–70, North-Holland, 1963.

McCarthy, J., Abrahams, P.W., Edwards, D.J., Hart, T.P., and Levin, M.I., *LISP 1.5 Programmer's Manual*, The MIT Press, 1965.

Mellish, C., and Hardy, S., Integrating Prolog in the POPLOG environment, in Campbell, J.A. (ed.), *Implementation of Prolog*, pp. 147–162, Ellis Horwood, 1984.

Mierowsky, C., Taylor, S., Shapiro, E., Levy J., and Safra, S., The design and implementation of Flat Concurrent Prolog, Tech. Report CS85-09, Department of Computer Science, The Weizmann Institute of Science, Rehovot, 1985.

Miller, M.S., Merge filters, 1987 (in preparation).

Miller, M.S., Bobrow D.G., Tribble, E.D., and Levy, J., Logical Secrets, Lassez, J.-L. (ed.), *Proc. 4th International Conference on Logic Programming*, pp. 704–728, MIT Press, 1987. Also Chapter 24, this volume.

Miller, R., and Stout, Q., Convexity algorithm for pyramid computers, *Proc. IEEE Conference on Parallel Processing*, pp. 177–184, 1984.

Milne, G., and Milner, R., Concurrent processes and their syntax, *J. ACM* **26**(2), pp. 302–321, 1979.

Milner, R., A theory of type polymorphism in programming, *J. Computer and System Sciences* **17**(3), pp. 348–375, 1978.

Milner, R., A Calculus of Communicating Systems, *LNCS* **92**, Springer-Verlag, 1980.

Milner, R., A complete inference system for a class of regular behaviours, *J. Computer and System Sciences*, **28**, pp. 439–466, 1984.

Minsky, M., *Society of Mind*, Simon and Schuster, 1986.

Mishra, P., Towards a theory of types in Prolog, *Proc. IEEE International Symposium on Logic Programming*, pp. 289–298, 1984.

Miyazaki, T., Takeuchi, A., and Chikayama, T., A sequential implementation of Concurrent Prolog based on the shallow binding scheme, *IEEE Symposium on Logic Programming*, pp. 110–118, 1985. Also Chapter 37, this volume.

Moens, E., and Yu, B., Implementation of PARLOG on the Warren machine, Tech. Report, Department of Computer Science, University of British Columbia, Vancouver, 1985.

Moon, D., MacLISP reference manual, revision 0, Artificial Intelligence Laboratory, MIT, Cambridge, Massachusetts, 1974.

Moss, C.D.S., Computing with sequences, *Proc. Logic Programming Workshop '83*, pp. 623–630, Algarve, Portugal, 1983.

Morris, J.H., et al., Andrew: A distributed personel computing environment, *Comm. ACM* **29**(3), pp. 184–201, 1986.

Moto-Oka, T., et al., Challenge for knowledge information processing systems (Preliminary Report on Fifth Generation Computer Systems), *Proc. International Conference on Fifth Generation Computer Systems*, pp. 1–85, Tokyo, 1981.

Moto-Oka, T., Tanaka, H., Aida, H., Hirata, K., and Maruyama, T., The architecture of a parallel inference engine – PIE, *Proc. International Conference on Fifth Generation Computer Systems*, pp. 479–488, Tokyo, 1984.

Mycroft, A., and O'Keefe, R., A polymorphic type system for Prolog, *Proc. Logic Programming Workshop '83*, pp. 107–121, Algarve, Portugal, 1983.

Naish, L., *MU-Prolog 3.1db Reference Manual*, Internal Memorandum, Department of Computer Science, University of Melbourne, 1984.

Nakashima, H., Tomura, S., and Ueda, K., What is a variable in Prolog?, *Proc. International Conference on Fifth Generation Computer Systems*, pp. 327–332, Tokyo, 1984.

Narain, S., A technique for doing lazy evaluation in logic, *J. Logic Programming* **3**(3), pp. 259–276, 1986.

Nelson, T.H., *Literary Machines*, Ted Nelson, Box 128, Swarthmore, Pennsylvania 19081, 1981.

Nievergelt, J., and Preparata, J.P., Plane sweep algorithms for intersecting geometric figures, *Comm. ACM* **25**, p. 10, 1982.

Nitta, K., On a Concurrent Prolog interpreter, Preprint of the 8th WGSF Meeting, Information Processing Society of Japan, 1984 (in Japanese).

Noda, Y., Kinoshita, T., Okumura, A., Hirano, T., and Hiruta, N., A parallel logic simulator based on Concurrent Prolog, *The Logic Programming Conference '85*, pp. 353–363, Tokyo, 1985 (in Japanese).

O'Donnel, J.T., Hardware description with recursion equations, *Proc. of CHDL-87*, pp. 363-382, Elsevier Science Publishing, 1987.

Panangaden, P., Abstract interpretation and indeterminacy, Seminar on Concurrency, Carnegie-Mellon University, Pittsburgh, Pennsylvania, *LNCS* **197**, pp. 497–511, Springer-Verlag, 1984.

Papert, S., *Mindstorms: Children, Computers, and Powerful Ideas*, Basic Books, New York, 1980.

Park, D., On the Semantics of fair parallelism, in Bjorner, D. (ed.), *LNCS* **86**, pp. 504–526, Springer-Verlag, 1980.

Pereira, F.C.N., *C-Prolog User's Manual*, EdCAAD, University of Edinburgh, 1983.

Pereira, L.M., Logic control with logic, *Proc. 1st International Conference on Logic Programming*, pp. 9–18, Marseille, 1982.

Pereira, L.M., Rational debugging in logic programming, in Shapiro, E. (ed.), *Proc. 3rd International Conference on Logic Programming*, *LNCS* **225**, pp. 203–210, Springer-Verlag, 1986.

Pereira, L.M., and Monteiro, L., The semantics of parallelism and coroutining in logic programming, *Proc. Colloquium on Mathematical Logic in Programming*, Salgotarjan, 1978.

Pereira, L.M., and Nasr, R., Delta-Prolog: A distributed logic programming language, *Proc. International Conference on Fifth Generation Computer Systems*, pp. 283–291, Tokyo, 1984.

Pike, R., Graphics in overlapping bitmap images, *ACM Trans. in Graphics* **2**(2), pp. 133–150, 1983.

Plotkin, G.D., A note on inductive generalization, in Melzer, B., and Michie, D. (eds.), *Machine Intelligence* **5**, pp. 153–164, 1969.

Plotkin, G.D., A further note on inductive generalization, in Melzer, B., and Michie, D. (eds.), *Machine Intelligence* **6**, pp. 101–124, 1970.

Plotkin, G.D., A powerdomain construction, *SIAM J. Computing* **5**(3), pp. 452-487, 1976.

Pnueli, A., Applications of temporal logic to the specification and verification of reactive systems: A survey of current trends, in de Bakker, J.W., de Roever, W.P., and Rozenberg, G. (eds.), *Current Trends in Concurrency, Overviews and Tutorials*, *LNCS* **224**, pp. 510–584, Springer-Verlag, 1986.

Pollard, G.H., Parallel execution of Horn clause programs, Ph.D. Thesis, Department of Computing, Imperial College, London, 1981.

Pratt, V.R., On the composition of processes, *Conference Record 9th ACM Symposium on Principles of Programming Languages*, pp. 213–223, 1982.

Quintus Prolog Reference Manual, Quintus Computer Systems Ltd., 1985.

Ramakrishnan, R., and Silberschatz, A., Annotations for Distributed Programming in Logic, *Conference Record 13^{en} ACM Symposium on Principles of Programming Languages*, pp. 255–262, 1986.

Reddy, U.S., On the relationship between logic and functional languages, in DeGroot, D., and Lindstrom, G. (eds.), *Logic Programming — Functions, Relations and Equations*, pp. 3–36, Prentice-Hall, New Jersay, 1986.

Rees, J.A., and Adams, IV, N.I., T: A dialect of Lisp or, Lambda: The ultimate software tool, *Proc. ACM Symposium on Lisp and Functional Programming*, pp. 114–122, 1982.

Reeve, M.J., A BNF description of the ALICE compiler target language, Department of Computing, Imperial College, London, 1985 (unpublished report).

Richie, D.M., and Thompson, K., The Unix time-sharing system, *Comm. ACM* **17**(7), pp. 365–375, 1974.

Rivest, R., Shamir, A., and Adleman, L., A method for obtaining digital signatures and public-key cryptosystems, *Comm. ACM* **21**(2), pp. 120–126, 1978.

Roberts, G., *The Waterloo Prolog Reference Manual, Version 1.3*, 1979.

Robinson, J.A., A machine oriented logic based on the resolution principle, *J. ACM* **12**(1), pp. 23–41, 1965.

Robinson, J.A., and Sibert, E.E., LOGLISP — motivation, design and implementation, in Clark, K.L., and Tärnlund, S.-Å. (eds.), *Logic Programming*, pp. 299–314, Academic Press, London, 1982.

Roussel, P., *Prolog: Manual de Reference et d'Utilisation*, Groupe d'Intelligence Artificielle, Marseille-Luminy, 1975.

Safra, S., Partial evaluation of Concurrent Prolog and its implications, Tech. Report CS86-24, Department of Computer Science, The Weizmann Institute of Science, Rehovot, 1986.

Safra, S., and Shapiro, E., Meta-interpreters for real, *Information Processing 86*, pp. 271–278, North-Holland, 1986. Also Chapter 25, this volume.

Samet H., Connected component labeling using quadtrees, *J. ACM* **28**(3), pp. 487–501, 1981.

Samet H., The quadtree and related hierarchical data structures, *ACM Computing surveys* **16**(2), pp. 187–260, 1984.

Sandewall, E., Programming in an interactive environment: The Lisp experimence, *ACM Computing Surveys*, pp. 35–72, 1978.

Saraswat, V.A., Partial Correctness Semantics for CP[↓,|,&], *Proc. 5th Conference on Foundations of Software Technology and Theoretical Computer Science*, *LNCS* **206**, pp. 347–368, New Delhi, 1985.

Saraswat, V.A., Problems with Concurrent Prolog, Tech. Report 86-100, Carnegie-Mellon University, 1986.

Saraswat, V.A., Merging many streams efficiently: The importance of atomic commitment, Chapter 16, this volume.

Saraswat, V.A., Concurrent Logic Programming Languages, Ph.D. Thesis, Carnegie-Mellon University, 1987 (in preparation).

Saraswat, V.A., The concurrent logic programming language CP: Definition and operational semantics, *Proc. ACM SIGACT-SIGPLAN Symposium on Principles of Programming Languages*, pp. 49–63, 1987a.

Saraswat, V.A., The language GHC: Operational semantics, problems and relationship with CP[↓,|], *Proc. IEEE Symposium on Logic Programming*, San Francisco, 1987b.

Sato, M., and Sakurai, T., Qute: A functional language based on unification, *Proc. International Conference on Fifth Generation Computer Systems*, pp. 157–165, Tokyo, 1984.

Sato, H., Ichiyoshi, N., Dasai, T., Miyazaki, T., and Takeuchi, A., A sequential implementation of Concurrent Prolog — based on deep binding scheme, *The 1st National Conference of Japan Society for Software Science and Technology*, pp. 299–302, 1984 (in Japanese).

Schlichting, R.D., and Purdin, T.D.M., Failure handling in distributed programming languages, Tech. Report 85-14, Department of Computer Science, University of Arizona, 1985.

Schwans, K., Tailoring software for multiple processor systems, Ph.D. Thesis, Tech. Report CMU-CS-82-137, Department of Computer Science, Carnegie-Mellon University, 1982.

Schwarz, J., Using annotations to make recursion equations behave, Research Report 43, Department of Artificial Intelligence, University of Edinburgh, 1977.

Sejnowiski, M.C., Upchurch, E.T., Kapur, R.N., Charlu, D.P.S., and Lipovski,

G.J., An overview of the Texas reconfigurable array computer, *Proc. AFIPS Conference*, pp. 631–641, 1980.

Sequin, C.H., Doubly twisted torus networks for VLSI processor arrays, *Proc. 8th IEEE International Conference on Computer Architecture*, pp. 471–480, 1981.

Shafrir, A., and Shapiro, E., Distributed programming in Concurrent Prolog, Tech. Report CS83-12, Department of Computer Science, The Weizmann Institute of Science, Rehovot, 1983. Also Chapter 11, this volume.

Shahdad, M., Lipsett, R., Marschner, E., Sheehan, K., Cohen, H., Waxman, R., Ackley, D., VHSIC hardware description language, *IEEE Computer* **18**, pp. 94–102, 1985.

Shamir, A., and Fiat, A., Polymorphic arrays: A novel VLSI layout for systolic computers, *J. Computer and System Sciences* **33**(1), pp. 47–65, 1986.

Shapiro, E., *Algorithmic Program Debugging*, The MIT Press, 1982.

Shapiro, E., A subset of Concurrent Prolog and its interpreter, ICOT Tech. Report TR-003, Institute for New Generation Computer Technology, Tokyo, 1983. Revised as Chapter 2, this volume.

Shapiro, E., Lecture notes on the Bagel: A systolic Concurrent Prolog machine, ICOT TM-0031, Institute for New Generation Computer Technology, Tokyo, 1983a.

Shapiro, E., Logic programs with uncertainties: A tool for implementing rule-base systems, *Proc. 8th International Joint Conference on Artificial Intelligence*, pp. 529–532, Kalsruhe, 1983b.

Shapiro, E., Notes on sequential implementation of Concurrent Prolog, Summary of Discussions in ICOT, 1983c (unpublished).

Shapiro, E., Systolic programming: A paradigm of parallel processing, *Proc. International Conference on Fifth Generation Computer Systems*, pp. 458–471, 1984. Revised as Chapter 7, this volume.

Shapiro, E., Alternation and the computational complexity of logic programs, *J. Logic Programming* **1**(1), pp. 19–33, 1984.

Shapiro, E., Systems programming in Concurrent Prolog, in van Canegham, M., and Warren, D.H.D. (eds.), *Logic Programming and its Applications*, pp. 50–74, Ablex Publishing Co., 1986. Also Chapter 19, this volume.

Shapiro, E., Concurrent Prolog: A progress report, *IEEE Computer*, **19**(8), pp. 44–58, August 1986. Also Chapter 5, this volume.

Shapiro, E., On evaluating the adequacy of a language for an architecture, Tech. Report CS86-01, Department of Computer Science, The Weizmann Institute of Science, Rehovot, 1986. Revised as Chapter 13, this volume.

Shapiro, E., An Or-parallel execution algorithm for Prolog and its FCP implementation, Lassez, J.-L. (ed.), *Proc. 4th International Conference of Logic programming*, pp. 311–337, MIT Press, 1987. Revised as Chapter 34, this volume.

Shapiro, E., and Mierowsky, C., Fair, biased, and self-balancing merge operators: Their specification and implementation in Concurrent Prolog, *New Generation Computing* **2**(3), pp. 221–240, 1984. Also Chapter 14, this volume.

Shapiro, E., and Safra, S., Multiway merge with constant delay in Concurrent Prolog, *New Generation Computing* **4**(2), pp. 211–216, 1986. Also Chapter 15, this volume.

Shapiro, E., and Takeuchi, A., Object-oriented programming in Concurrent Prolog, *New Generation Computing* **1**(1), pp. 25–49, 1983. Also Chapter 29, this volume.

Shiloach, Y., and Vishkin, U., Finding the maximum, merging and sorting in a parallel computation model, *J. Algorithms* **2**(1), pp. 88–102, 1981.

Shiloach, Y., and Vishkin, U., An $O(log\ n)$ parallel connectivity algorithm, *J. Algorithms* **3**, pp. 57–67, 1982a.

Shiloach, Y., and Vishkin, U., An $O(n^2 log\, n)$ parallel MAX-FLOW algorithm, *J. Algorithms* **3**, pp. 128–146, 1982b.

Silverman, W., Houri, A., Hirsch, M., and Shapiro, E., The Logix system user manual, Tech. Report CS86-21, Department of Computer Science, The Weizmann Institute of Science, Rehovot, 1986. Also Chapter 21, this volume.

Smith, B.C., Reflection and semantics in a procedural language, Ph.D. Dissertation, MIT, 1982.

Smyth, M.B., Finitary relations and their fair merge, Internal Report CSR-107-82, Department of Computer Science, University of Edinburgh, 1982.

Snyder, A., Encapsulation and inheritance in object-oriented programming, *ACM Conference on Object-Oriented Programming Systems, Languages and Applications*, pp. 38–45, Portland, Oregon, 1986.

Snyder, L., Parallel programming and the Poker programming environment, *IEEE Computer* **17**(7), pp. 55–62, 1984.

Steele, C.S., Placement of Communicating Processes on Multiprocessor Networks, Ph.D. Thesis, California Institute of Technology, 1985.

Steele, G.L., The definition and implementation of a computer programming language based on constraints, Tech. Report TR-595, Artificial Intelligence Laboratory, MIT, Cambridge, Massachusetts, 1980.

Steele, G.L., *Common Lisp: The Language*, Digital Press, 1984.

Steele, G.L., Jr., and Sussman, G.J., The revised report on scheme, a dialect of Lisp, AI Memo 379, Artificial Intelligence Laboratory, MIT, Cambridge, Massachusetts, 1978a.

Steele, G.L., Jr., and Sussman, G.J., The art of the interpreter or, the modularity, complex, Tech. Memorandum AIM-453, Artificial Intelligence Laboratory, MIT, Cambridge, Massachusetts, 1978b.

Stefik, M., The next knowledge medium, *AI Mag.* **7**(1), pp. 34–46, 1986.

Steinberg, S.A., The butterfly Lisp system, *Proc. National Conference on Artificial Intelligence*, pp. 730–742, 1986.

Sterling, L.S., Expert System = Knowledge + Meta-interpreter, Tech. Report CS84-17, Department of Computer Science, The Weizmann Institute of Science, Rehovot, 1984.

Sterling, L.S., Bundy, A., Byrd, L., O'Keefe, R., and Silver, B., Solving symbolic equations with PRESS, in *Computer Algebra*, *LNCS* **144**, pp. 109–116, Springer-Verlag, 1982.

Sterling, L.S., and Codish, M., PRESSing for parallelism: A Prolog program made concurrent, *J. Logic Programming* **3**(1), pp. 75–92, 1986. Also Chapter 31, this volume.

Sterling, L.S., and Shapiro, E., *The Art of Prolog*, The MIT Press, 1986.

Stone, H., Multiprocessor scheduling with the aid of network flow algorithms, *IEEE Trans. on Software Engineering* **SE-3**, pp. 85–93, 1977.

Stone, H., and Bokhari, S.H., Control of distributed processes, *Computer* **11**, pp. 97–106, July 1978.

Subrahmanyam, P.A., and You, J.H., FUNLOG = Functions + Logic: A computational model integrating functional and logic programming, *Proc. IEEE International Symposium on Logic Programming*, pp. 144–153, Atlantic City, New Jersey, 1984a.

Subrahmanyam, P.A., and You, J.H., Conceptual basis and evaluation strategies for integrating functional and logic programming, *Proc. IEEE International Symposium on Logic Programming*, Atlantic Ciry, New Jersey, 1984b.

Subramahnyam, P.A., and You, J.H., FUNLOG — a computational model integrating logic programming and functional programming, in DeGroot, D., and Lindstrom, G. (eds.), *Logic Programming — Functions, Relations and Equations*, pp. 157–198, Prentice-Hall, New Jersey, 1986.

Sun Microsystems Inc., *NeWS Preliminary Technical Overview*, 2550 Garcia Avenue, Mountain View, California 94043, October 1986.

Sun Microsystems Inc., *User's Manual for the SUN Unix System*, 2550 Garcia Avenue, Mountain View, California 94043.

Sussman, G.J., and Steele, G.L., Scheme — An interpreter for extended lambda calculus, AI Memo 349, Artificial Intelligence Laboratory, MIT, Cambridge, Massachusetts, 1975.

Sussman, G.J., and Steele, G.L., Constraints — A language for expressing almost-hierarchical descriptions, *Artificial Intelligence* **14**, p. 39, 1980.

Suzuki, N., Experience with specification and verification of complex computer using Concurrent Prolog, in Warren, D.H.D., and van Caneghem, M. (eds.), *Logic Programming and Its Applications*, pp. 188-209, Ablex Pub. Co., New Jersey, 1986.

Takahashi, N., and Ono, S., Strategic bug location method for functional programs, *Proc. 6th RIMS Symposium on Mathematical Methods in Software Science and Engineering*, RIMS, Kyoto University, 1985.

Takeuchi, A., How to solve it in Concurrent Prolog, 1983 (unpublished note).

Takeuchi, A., Algorithmic debugging of GHC programs and its implementation in GHC, ICOT Tech. Report TR-185, Institute for New Generation Computer Technology, Tokyo, 1986. Also Chapter 26, this volume.

Takeuchi, A., and Furukawa, K., Bounded-buffer communication in Concurrent Prolog, *New Generation Computing* **3**(2), pp. 145–155, 1985. Also Chapter 18, this volume.

Takeuchi, A., and Furukawa, K., Partial evaluation of Prolog programs and its application to meta-programming, ICOT Tech. Report TR-126, Institute for New Generation Computer Technology, Tokyo, 1985. Also in *Information Processing 86*, pp. 415–420, North-Holland, 1986.

Takeuchi, A., and Furukawa, K., Parallel logic programming languages, in Shapiro, E. (ed.), *Proc. 3rd International Conference on Logic Programming*, *LNCS* **225**, pp. 242–255, Springer-Verlag, 1986. Also Chapter 6, this volume.

Takeuchi, I., Okuno, H., and Osato, N., A list processing language TAO with multiple programming paradigms, *New Generation Computing* **4**, pp. 401–444, 1986.

Tamaki, H., A distributed unification scheme for systolic logic programs, *Proc.*

IEEE International Conference on Parallel Processing, pp. 552–559, 1985.

Tamaki, H., and Sato, T., A transformation system for logic programs which preserves equivalence, ICOT Tech. Report TR-018, Institute for New Generation Computer Technology, Tokyo, 1983.

Tanaka, J., Miyazaki, T., and Takeuchi, A., A sequential implementation of Concurrent Prolog — based on lazy copying scheme, *The 1ˢᵗ National Conference of Japan Society for Software Science and Technology*, pp. 303–306, 1984 (in Japanese).

Tarski, A., A lattice-theoretical fix-point theorem and its application, *Pacific J. Mathematics* **5**, pp. 285–309, 1955.

Taylor, S., and Shapiro, E., Compiling concurrent logic programs into decision graphs, Tech. Report, Department of Computer Science, The Weizmann Institute of Science, Rehovot, 1987.

Taylor, S., Av-Ron, E., and Shapiro, E., A layered method for process and code mapping, *J. New Generation Computing*, (in press). Also Chapter 22, this volume.

Taylor, S., Hellerstein, L., Safra, S., and Shapiro, E., Notes on the complexity of systolic programs, *J. Parallel and Distributed Computing*, (in press). Also Chapter 8, this volume.

Taylor, S., Safra, S., and Shapiro E., A parallel implementation of Flat Concurrent Prolog, *J. Parallel Programming* **15**(3), pp. 245–275, 1987. Also Chapter 39, this volume.

Thompson, C.D., and Kung, H.T., Sorting on a mesh-connected parallel computer, *Comm. ACM* **20**(4), 1977.

Treleaven, P.C., Brownbridge, D.R., and Hopkins, R.P., Data-driven and demand-driven computer architecture, *Computing Surveys* **14**(1), pp. 93–143, 1982.

Tribble, E.D., Miller, M.S., Kahn, K., Bobrow, D.G., and Abbott, C., Channels: A generalization of streams, Lassez, J.-L. (ed.), *Proc. 4ᵗʰ International Conference of Logic Programming*, pp. 839–857, MIT Press, 1987. Also Chapter 17, this volume.

Turchin, V., Semantics definitions in REFAL and the automatic production of compilers, in Jones, N.D. (ed.), *Semantics-Directed Compiler Generation*, *LNCS* **94**, pp. 441–474, Springer-Verlag, 1980.

Turner, D.A., A new implementation technique for applicative languages, *Software Practice and Experience* **9**, pp. 31–49, 1979.

Turner, D.A., The semantic elegance of applicative languages, *Proc. of the ACM*

Conference on Functional Programming Languages and Computer Architecture, pp. 85–92, Portsmouth, New Hampshire, 1981.

Uchida, S., Towards a new generation computer architecture: Research and development plan for computer architecture in the Fifth Generation Computer project, ICOT Tech. Report TR-001, Institute for New Generation Computer Technology, Tokyo, 1982.

Uchida, S., Inference machine: From sequential to parallel, *Proc. 10ᵗʰ Annual International Symposium on Computer Architecture*, pp. 410–416, Stockholm, 1983.

Ueda, K., Concurrent Prolog re-examined, ICOT Tech. Report TR-102, Institute for New Generation Computer Technology, Tokyo, 1985.

Ueda, K., Guarded Horn Clauses, ICOT Tech. Report TR-103, Institute for New Generation Computer Technology, Tokyo, 1985. Also in Wada, E. (ed.), *Logic Programming*, *LNCS* **221**, pp. 168–179, Springer-Verlag, 1986. Also Chapter 4, this volume.

Ueda, K., Guarded Horn Clauses — A parallel logic programming language with the concept of a guard, ICOT Tech. Report TR-208, Institute for New Generation Computer Technology, Tokyo, 1986a.

Ueda, K., Introduction to Guarded Horn Clauses, ICOT Tech. Report TR-209, Institute for New Generation Computer Technology, Tokyo, 1986b.

Ueda, K., Making exhaustive search programs deterministic, *New Generation Computing* **5**(1), pp. 29–44, 1987.

Ueda, K., and Chikayama, T., Efficient stream/array processing in logic programming languages, *Proc. International Conference on Fifth Generation Computer Systems*, pp. 317–326, Tokyo, 1984.

Ueda, K., and Chikayama, T., Concurrent Prolog compiler on top of Prolog, *Proc. IEEE Symposium on Logic Programming*, pp. 119–126, 1985.

Ullman, J.D., *Principles of Database Systems*, Computer Science Press, Maryland, 1982.

Vegdahl, S.R., A survey of proposed architectures for the execution of functional languages, *IEEE Trans. on Computers* **33**(12), pp. 1050–1071, 1984.

Viner, O., Distributed constraint propagation, Tech. Report CS84-24, Department of Computer Science, The Weizmann Institute of Science, Rehovot, 1984.

Wadge, W.W., An extensional treatment of dataflow deadlock, in Kahn, G. (ed.), *Semantics of Concurrent Computations*, *LNCS* **70**, pp. 283–299, Springer-Verlag, 1979.

Warren, D.H.D., Implementing Prolog — compiling predicate logic programs, Tech. Report DAI 39/40, Department of Artificial Intelligence, University of Edinburgh, 1977.

Warren, D.H.D., Logic programming and compiler writing, *Software-Practice and Experience* **10**, pp. 97–125, 1980.

Warren, D.H.D., MegaLIPS now!, 1982a (unpublished note).

Warren, D.H.D., Perpetual processes: An unexploited Prolog programming technique, *Proc. Prolog Programming Environments Workshop*, Datalogi, Linkoping, 1982b.

Warren, D.H.D., Higher order extensions to Prolog — are they needed?, *Machine Intelligence* **10**, pp. 441–454, 1982c.

Warren, D.H.D., An abstract Prolog instruction set, Tech. Report 309, Artificial Intelligence Center, SRI International, 1983.

Warren, D.H.D., Pereira, L.M., and Pereira, F.C.N., PROLOG — The language and its implementation compared with Lisp, *SIGPLAN Notices* **12**(8), pp. 109–115, 1977.

Warren, D.S., Efficient Prolog memory management for flexible control strategies, *New Generation Computing* **2**(4), pp. 361–369, 1984.

Weinbaum, D., and Shapiro, E., Hardware description and simulation using Concurrent Prolog, *Proc. CHDL '87*, pp. 9–27, Elsevier Science Publishing, 1987. Also Chapter 36, this volume.

Weinreb, D., and Moon, D., Flavors: Message passing in the Lisp machine, Memo 602, Artificial Intelligence Laboratory, MIT, Cambridge, Massachusetts, 1980.

Weinreb, D., and Moon, D., Lisp machine Lisp, Artificial Intelligence Laboratory, MIT, Cambridge, Massachusetts, 1983.

Weiser, U., and Davis, A.L., A wavefront notation tool for VLSI array design, in Kung, H.T., Sproull, R.F., and Steele, G.L., Jr. (eds.), *VLSI Systems and Computations*, pp. 226–364, Carnegie-Mellon University, Computer Science Press, 1981.

Weng, K.S., Stream-oriented computation in recursive data flow schemes, Tech. Report MTMM-68, MIT, Cambridge, Massachusetts, 1975.

White, J.L., NIL — A perspective, *Proc. Macsyma Users Conference*, 1979.

Wise, M.J., A parallel Prolog: The construction of a data driven model, *ACM Symposium on Lisp and Functional Programming*, pp. 56–67, 1982a.

Wise, M.J., Epilog = Prolog + data flow — arguments for combining Prolog with a data driven mechanism, *SIGPLAN Notices* **17**(12), pp. 80–86, 1982b.

The XEROX Learning Research Group, The Smalltalk-80 System, *BYTE* **6**(8), pp. 36–48, August 1981.

Yaghi, A.A.G., The compilation of a functional language into intensional logic, Theory of Computation Report 56, Department of Computer Science, University of Warwick, 1983.

Yardeni, E., A type system for logic programs, M.Sc. Thesis, Department of Computer Science, The Weizmann Institute of Science, Rehovot, 1987.

Yardeni, E., and Shapiro, E., A type system for logic programs, Chapter 28, this volume.

Yokota, M., Yamamoto, A., Taki, K., Nishikawa, H., Uchida, S., Nakajima, K., and Mitsui, M., A microprogrammed interpreter for the personal sequential inference machine, *Proc. International Conference on Fifth Generation Computer Systems*, pp. 410–418, Tokyo, 1984.

Index

Note: Page numbers in roman type refer to Volume 1; page numbers in italic type refer to Volume 2.

The MIT Press, with Peter Denning, general consulting editor, and Brian Randell, European consulting editor, publishes computer science books in the following series:

ACM Doctoral Dissertation Award and Distinguished Dissertation Series

Artificial Intelligence, Patrick Winston and Michael Brady, editors

Charles Babbage Institute Reprint Series for the History of Computing, Martin Campbell-Kelly, editor

Computer Systems, Herb Schwetman, editor

Exploring with Logo, E. Paul Goldenberg, editor

Foundations of Computing, Michael Garey, editor

History of Computing, I. Bernard Cohen and William Aspray, editors

Information Systems, Michael Lesk, editor

Logic Programming, Ehud Shapiro, editor; Fernando Pereira, Koichi Furukawa, and D. H. D. Warren, associate editors

The MIT Electrical Engineering and Computer Science Series

Scientific Computation, Dennis Gannon, editor